JUDICIAL SELECTION IN THE STATES

Using detailed case studies of the relevant US states, Herbert Kritzer provides an unprecedented examination of the process and politics of how states select and retain judges. The book is organized around the competing goals of politics and professionalism, namely whether the focus in choosing judges should be on the substance of future judicial decisions (court outputs) or on the court processes by which those decisions are reached. Or, in considering who should be a judge, whether the emphasis should be on political credentials or on professional credentials. One important finding is that political concerns have surpassed professionalism concerns since 2000. Another is that voters have been more supportive of professionalism in selecting appellate judges than in choosing trial judges. *Judicial Selection in the States* should be read by anyone seeking a deep understanding of the complex interplay between politics and the judiciary at the state level in the United States.

HERBERT M. KRITZER is the Marvin J. Sonosky Chair of Law and Public Policy at the University of Minnesota Law School. He is the author or coauthor of eight previous books, including *Justices on the Ballot* (Cambridge, 2015), and more than 100 articles or book chapters.

Judicial Selection in the States

POLITICS AND THE STRUGGLE FOR REFORM

HERBERT M. KRITZER
University of Minnesota Law School

CAMBRIDGE
UNIVERSITY PRESS

CAMBRIDGE
UNIVERSITY PRESS

University Printing House, Cambridge CB2 8BS, United Kingdom

One Liberty Plaza, 20th Floor, New York, NY 10006, USA

477 Williamstown Road, Port Melbourne, VIC 3207, Australia

314–321, 3rd Floor, Plot 3, Splendor Forum, Jasola District Centre, New Delhi – 110025, India

79 Anson Road, #06–04/06, Singapore 079906

Cambridge University Press is part of the University of Cambridge.

It furthers the University's mission by disseminating knowledge in the pursuit of education, learning, and research at the highest international levels of excellence.

www.cambridge.org
Information on this title: www.cambridge.org/9781108496339
DOI: 10.1017/9781108866941

First published 2020

A catalogue record for this publication is available from the British Library.

Library of Congress Cataloging-in-Publication Data
NAMES: Kritzer, Herbert M., 1947– author.
TITLE: Judicial selection in the states : politics and the struggle for reform / Herbert M. Kritzer, University of Minnesota School of Law.
DESCRIPTION: Cambridge, United Kingdom ; New York, NY, USA : Cambridge University Press, 2020. | Includes bibliographical references and index.
IDENTIFIERS: LCCN 2019050399 (print) | LCCN 2019050400 (ebook) | ISBN 9781108496339 (hardback) | ISBN 9781108791960 (paperback) | ISBN 9781108866941 (epub)
SUBJECTS: LCSH: Judges–Selection and appointment–United States–States.
CLASSIFICATION: LCC KF8776 .K75 2020 (print) | LCC KF8776 (ebook) | DDC 347.73/14–DC23
LC record available at https://lccn.loc.gov/2019050399
LC ebook record available at https://lccn.loc.gov/2019050400

ISBN 978-1-108-49633-9 Hardback
ISBN 978-1-108-79196-0 Paperback

To my wonderful grandchildren, that they may live in a world of justice and peace:

Molly Jean Burke

Kiera Margaret Burke

Benjamin Eli Kritzer

Daniel Aaron Kritzer

Contents

Figures

Tables

Preface

In the process of working on my previous Cambridge University Press book, *Justices on the Ballot*, I noted the large number of changes in how state supreme court justices were selected and retained in the post–World War II period. After the completion of that book, my focus shifted sharply in another direction, to research on lawyers' professional liability (legal malpractice). Once the book from that project was wrapped up, I decided to return to the judicial selection process and delve in depth into the politics of states' changing methods of judicial selection and retention, not limited to the state supreme court level.

As I thought about how I might approach the issue of change, I came back to a framework I had first learned about, now almost fifty years ago, from my dissertation advisor at the University of North Carolina at Chapel Hill, Richard ("Dick") J. Richardson. Dick and Kenneth N. Vines, his dissertation advisor from Tulane University, had published a book entitled *The Politics of Federal Courts* (1970) that introduced the ideas of the legal and democratic subcultures. I have always been fascinated by these concepts and frequently referred to them during the roughly thirty years I taught undergraduate courses on the American judicial system at the University of Wisconsin–Madison. These concepts seemed like the logical place to start and suggested some of the hypotheses that framed my research at the beginning. As the book makes clear, the politics underlying debates over changing judicial selection and retention are considerably more complex than the ideas reflected in my initial hypotheses.

This book could not have been written without the assistance of a large number of people, starting with three wonderful research assistants, Christopher Salvatore (JD 2019, University of Chicago), Robert Wilde (JD 2019, University of Minnesota), and Connor Shaull (JD 2020, University of Minnesota). In addition, I have received support from the wonderful reference staff at the University of Minnesota Law Library, particularly Connie Lenz, Scott Dewey, Michael Hannon, and Vicente Garces.

Over the course of my research I interacted with scholars and others in many of the states. Some of these interactions involved receiving comments on drafts of chapters or sections of chapters, some involved extended interviews, and some involved answering questions that I had about what had transpired in their state. These people, and the state each assisted me with, include:

Arkansas: Jay Barth (Hendrix College); Janine Parry (University of Arkansas)
Connecticut: Tim Fisher (University of Connecticut); Jim Wade
Florida: Roger Handberg (Florida Central University); Drew Lanier (Florida Central University)
Georgia: Judge Dorothy Beasley; Charles S. Bullock III (University of Georgia); Melvin Hill (University of Georgia); Thomas Walker (Emory University)
Kansas: Chuck Epp (University of Kansas)
Minnesota: Mark Cohen; State Senator Sandra Pappas
Mississippi: David Case (University of Mississippi); Reid Krell (University of Alabama)
Missouri: Peverill Squire (University of Missouri); Steven Puro (Saint Louis University)
Nevada: Michael Bowers (University of Nevada, Las Vegas)
New Hampshire: Lynn Mather (University at Buffalo, SUNY; formerly at Dartmouth College, 1972–2002)
North Carolina: J. Michael Bitzer (Catawba College); Todd Collins (Western Carolina University); James Drennan (University of North Carolina at Chapel Hill); Ruth Ann Strickland (formerly at Appalachian State University)
Ohio: Lawrence Baum (Ohio State University); Michael Solimine (University of Cincinnati)
Rhode Island: John Marion
South Carolina: David Wilkins; John Crangle; Kevin R. Eberle (Charleston Law School); Bob Bosch (University of South Carolina, Aiken)
South Dakota: Thomas Barnett
Tennessee: John Scheb II (University of Tennessee, Knoxville); Margaret Behm
Texas: Anthony M. Champagne (University of Texas at Dallas)
Utah: Roger Tew; Adam Brown (Brigham Young University); Tim Shea
West Virginia: Richard Brisbin (West Virginia University); John Kilwein (West Virginia University); Timothy J. Manchin; Barbara Fleischauer

Any misunderstandings or errors – I am sure that there must be some – regarding individual states remain solely my responsibility.

Margaret Brehm and Candi Henry kindly granted me permission to include a lengthy quote from their article "Judicial Selection in Tennessee: Deciding 'the

Decider,'" *Belmont Law Review* (vol. 1, 2014). Adam Bonica (Stanford University) provided some information regarding the database measuring political ideology based on campaign contributions that he and others created. Larry Aspin (Bradley University) provided me with some information from the database of retention elections that he has assembled over many years.

Table of Cases

1

Introduction

The Challenges of Judicial Selection and Retention in the States

How to select state judges has been a recurring issue since the founding of the United States. Between 1946 and 2018, 23 of the 38 states that were using some form of popular election for their state supreme courts made significant changes to their methods of selection and/or retention.[1] The most common change was a switch to a yes–no referendum for retention of judges, what is known as a "retention election." A total of 18 states switched to retention elections with 3 of those states continuing to use partisan elections for initial terms and the other 15 states relying on appointment for initial selection; 2 of the 15 had previously switched from partisan to nonpartisan elections.[2] Five additional states switched from partisan to nonpartisan elections. Overall, fifteen states entirely stopped using partisan elections for their supreme courts, six states abandoned nonpartisan elections, and one state abandoned any use of elections for its highest court between 1946 and 2018.[3] Many similar changes were made for lower level courts, although fewer states shifted away from partisan or nonpartisan elections. During this period, only two states that had stopped using partisan elections switched back:[4] Tennessee in 1974, from a system combining

[1] In my reference here and throughout the book to "state supreme courts," I include the New York Court of Appeals, which is the court of last resort in New York; I exclude what is called the "Supreme Court" in New York, which encompasses both the highest trial court and the intermediate Court of Appeals.

[2] The count of 15 excludes New Mexico even though the controlling law makes it appear that all judges are initially appointed. This is explained in Chapter 9. In a nonpartisan election, candidates are not selected by the parties and no party labels appear on the ballot.

[3] Two states, Florida and Utah, initially switched from partisan to nonpartisan elections, and then from nonpartisan to a system using retention elections (only for appellate courts in Florida).

[4] Prior to these two switches back to partisan elections, the last two to do so were Florida, which instituted partisan elections for Circuit Court judges who had, since Reconstruction, been appointed by the governor (see www.judicialselection.us/judicial_selection/reform_efforts/formal_changes_since_inception.cfm?state=FL, accessed September 2, 2017), and Pennsylvania, which in 1921 repealed a 1913 law making appellate elections nonpartisan and reverted to partisan elections for those elections (see www.judicialselection.us/judicial_selection/reform_efforts/formal_changes_since_inception.cfm?state=PA).

gubernatorial appointment with retention elections for its Supreme Court,[5] and North Carolina in 2016–2017 from nonpartisan elections.[6]

In 1971 the Democratic-controlled Tennessee legislature passed a slightly modified version of what was called the Missouri Plan, after the state first that adopted it. The basic Missouri Plan consists of three elements: nomination by a screening body, usually referred to as a nominating commission; selection from the list of nominees by the governor; and periodic retention elections. Proponents of this system have dubbed it "merit selection." Because that label has also been applied to nonelectoral systems that use a nominating commission to constrain the appointing authority, I will use the label Missouri Plan for systems incorporating the three core elements, including systems that include a requirement of some form of legislative confirmation of the governor's choice.[7]

In 1972, before any vacancies occurred on the Tennessee Supreme Court, a Republican, Winfield Dunn, was elected governor, and under the system adopted in 1971, he was to have the opportunity to appoint four justices prior to the 1974 election. This led the legislature, still controlled by the Democrats but without a veto-proof majority, to repeal the modified Missouri Plan as applied to the state's Supreme Court, leaving it in place for the other two appellate courts. Not surprisingly, Dunn vetoed the repeal. He had also vetoed legislation creating a second state medical school, which would compete for resources with the existing medical school located in the governor's hometown. The governor's vetoes of both measures were eventually overridden as a result of a vote swap agreed to between the Democratic House speaker and a Republican representative from the district where the new medical school would be built.[8] Elections for the Tennessee Supreme Court reverted to partisan elections, with nominations made at party conventions.[9] As is discussed in Chapter 5, a further-modified version of the Missouri Plan was to be readopted in 1992. In 2014 the nomination requirement was dropped in response to a drive by conservative interests to again reinstitute partisan elections.

5 See Chapter 4.

6 See Chapter 2.

7 The original Missouri Plan, referred to at the time of its adoption as the "Missouri Nonpartisan Court Plan," included specific provisions as to the selection of members of the nominating commission, how long a judge would serve prior to facing the electorate for retention, and the percentage of voters who had to support retention; for details, see Richard A. Watson and Rondal G. Downing. *The Politics of the Bench and Bar: Judicial Selection under the Missouri Nonpartisan Court Plan* (New York: John Wiley & Sons, 1969), 13–14.

8 See Alan Wilson, "Demos Deal Two Blows to Dunn," *Clarksville Leaf-Chronicle* (February 15, 1974), 2.

9 While nominations were formally made by the party conventions, in practice the party executive committees put forward a slate of candidates that was adopted by the convention; see Tom Humprhey, "'Choice' Deceptive Term in Partisan Judge Elections," *Memphis Commercial Appeal* (September 16, 2012), 1, http://infoweb.newsbank.com.ezp2.lib.umn.edu/resources/doc/nb/news/1415EC4867A4C9D8?p=AWNB, accessed September 2, 2017.

In the early 2000s, North Carolina changed judicial elections for most of its courts, including all appellate courts, from partisan to nonpartisan.[10] Then, in 2015, the North Carolina House of Representatives passed a bill that would have returned all judicial elections to the partisan format, complete with partisan primaries. However, the version passed by the state Senate and signed into law was more limited, applying only to elections for the Court of Appeals. Under the law that went into effect for the 2016 elections, candidates for that court were required "at the time of filing the notice of candidacy ... [to] indicate on the notice of candidacy the political party recognized under Article 9 of this Chapter with which that candidate is affiliated or any unaffiliated status."[11] The ballot for the Court of Appeals included the party affiliation information. If there were more than two candidates, a blanket primary (sometimes called a "jungle primary") would be held, with all candidates regardless of party running together,[12] with the top two candidates going on to the general election.[13] As is discussed in Chapter 2, this change was to be only the first of a series of changes made over the next two years that returned all judicial elections for North Carolina state judges to partisan ballots.

Why would North Carolina switch back to partisan elections when the national pattern since 1946 had been to move *away* from partisan elections, with many states abandoning the use of any form of contested election? An examination of the political situation, and the later changes that were proposed and then enacted, makes it clear that the goal was to advantage Republican candidates for judgeships. In 2013, for the first time in more than a century, Republicans had gained control of the two "political" branches of the North Carolina government, winning both chambers of the legislature and the governorship. Over the next four years, North Carolina Republicans sought to solidify their control of state government: passing restrictive voting laws that targeted likely Democratic voters, gerrymandering congressional and legislative districts, abolishing public funding of some elections, and changing judicial elections in ways that they hoped would advantage Republican candidates. Even with the election of a Democratic governor in 2016, Republicans retained a veto-proof majority in both houses of the legislature, which allowed them to continue those efforts.[14]

10 As is discussed in detail in Chapter 2, the same change had been made a few years earlier for one of the state's trial level courts.

11 House Bill 8, G.A. (N.C. 2015), accessed September 2, 2017.

12 The only other state using this system for at least some judicial elections is Louisiana, which adopted blanket primaries in 1977; see Herbert M. Kritzer, *Justices on the Ballot: Continuity and Change in State Supreme Court Elections* (New York: Cambridge University Press, 2015), 40, n.15.

13 See Mark Binker, "Bill Requires Court of Appeals Candidates to List Parties," WRAL (September 29, 2015), www.wral.com/bill-requires-court-of-appeals-candidates-to-list-parties/14935703/, accessed July 21, 2017.

14 See John Zengerle, "Is North Carolina the Future of American Politics?" *New York Times Magazine* (June 25, 2017), online version dated June 20, 2017, www.nytimes.com/2017/06/20/magazine/is-north-carolina-the-future-of-american-politics.html?_r=0, accessed July 24, 2017.

In contrast to developments in North Carolina and Tennessee, most of the changes to judicial selection in the post–World War II era seemingly had the goal of reducing the role of traditional politics, particularly partisan politics, in judicial selection and retention. One mechanism for this was the shift to nonpartisan elections. A more prominent mechanism was the adoption of constraints on who could be appointed to judicial positions by requiring potential appointees to be nominated by a screening body, the argument being that the focus of screening bodies would be on the candidates' professional qualifications. The nominating commission is one of the central elements of the basic Missouri Plan, versions of which were adopted in fifteen states for some or all courts. However, the requirement of nomination by a screening commission was also added to systems that did not include all three elements of the Missouri Plan. Five states that did not use any form of popular election added a nominating commission to systems of gubernatorial appointment, sometimes in addition to a requirement of legislative confirmation and sometimes replacing such a requirement. South Carolina, where judges are elected by the legislature, added a requirement that the candidates for legislative election be nominated by a judicial merit selection commission. Seven states that continued to use popular elections for some or all courts added the requirement that the filling of interim vacancies by gubernatorial appointment be from a list of candidates nominated by a screening commission.[15]

However, as becomes clear in several chapters of this book, changes that appear on their face to have the goal of reducing partisanship can be intended to preserve the power of one political party or group. For example, Georgia and Mississippi shifted to nonpartisan elections in the 1980s and the 1990s, and similar switches occurred in North Carolina and Arkansas during the first decade of the current century. These changes might have been intended to limit traditional political influences, or they might have been made to protect Democratic incumbents during the period when the one-party Democratic South was fading. As the various chapters show, this was clearly true in North Carolina and somewhat true in Arkansas, but not a major factor in Georgia or Mississippi.

One can also ask why changes did not occur in some states where they were proposed. For example, in 2007 the Quie Commission, reacting to the U.S. Supreme Court's 2002 decision in *Republican Party of Minnesota v. White*,[16] advanced proposals to change Minnesota's judicial selection system from one using nonpartisan elections to a Missouri Plan system.[17] Although the proposal received some positive attention in the Minnesota state legislature and strong support from several former governors, current and former members of the Minnesota Supreme Court, and

[15] This count includes New Mexico, which has its own unique system; see Chapter 9.

[16] 536 U.S. 765 (2002).

[17] Al Quie, chair, Citizens Committee for the Preservation of an Impartial Judiciary, Final Report and Recommendations (March 26, 2007), www.mnbar.org/docs/default-source/judiciary-committee/citizenscommfinalreport032607.pdf?sfvrsn=0, accessed October 29, 2017.

former vice-president Walter Mondale, it was not adopted.[18] As is discussed in Chapter 13, at least part of the reason for this result was a lack of interest, if not outright opposition, from Republicans in the state legislature.[19] This opposition came at a time when the Republican Party was beginning to endorse candidates in Minnesota judicial elections, and it would seem reasonable to infer that at least some in the Republican Party believed that party-endorsed candidates would have a significant chance of defeating incumbents appointed by Democratic governors.

OUTLINE OF THE BOOK

This book explores the broad question of the dynamics behind states changing how their judges are selected and retained. There are three primary subquestions:

(1) What are the goals of those seeking to alter how state judges are selected and retained?
(2) What explains the timing of changes that do occur?
(3) Why are some efforts successful and others unsuccessful?

To answer these questions, I examined all major changes in state judicial selection systems that occurred between 1980 and 2018, plus the unsuccessful efforts that got significant traction. The former include changes that occurred in 13 states and the latter include unsuccessful efforts in 11 states. Two states had both successful and unsuccessful efforts, which makes a total of 22 states that I considered.

In the balance of this first chapter, I explicate the theoretical framing that I began this study with, present a brief history of state judicial selection in the United States, and summarize the changes that were made and the changes that were proposed but failed to be enacted. The chapter concludes with a brief methodological note describing one measure that I use in many of the chapters and a brief discussion of sources.

The remainder of the book has three parts plus a concluding chapter. Part I consists of four chapters, each considering one of four states – North Carolina, Arkansas, West Virginia, and Tennessee – where the successful efforts to make major changes to judicial selection reflected clear partisan considerations. As some of those chapters show, the nature of the partisan interests was not always as straightforward as one might expect.

Part II consists of five chapters covering a total of seven states (Georgia, Mississippi, Utah, New Mexico, Connecticut, Rhode Island, and South Carolina)

[18] See Barbara L. Jones, "Minnesota Senate Broaches the Subject of Judicial Elections," *Minnesota Lawyer* (February 11, 2008). There was also opposition from a number of groups, including many trial judges who feared that they might face last-minute opposition such that they would not be in a position to mount a response.

[19] Michelle Lore, "Judicial Election Reform Proponents Move Forward: Undaunted by the Incoming GOP Majority," *Minnesota Lawyer* (November 29, 2010), https://minnlawyer.com/2010/11/24/judicial-election-reform-proponents-move-forward/, accessed November 27, 2019.

where the impetus for change came more from the legal subculture side of the divide. Sometimes the precipitating factor was scandal and at other times it was part of a broader effort aimed at modernizing the state's judicial system. Importantly, even if the primary factor was not partisan advantage, there were often elements of partisanship involved.

Part III looks at unsuccessful efforts at change in a total of eleven states.[20] In eight of these states – Florida, South Dakota, Nevada, Ohio, Minnesota, Pennsylvania, Texas, and New Hampshire – the motivation was largely one of good government, although the opposition in some was clearly more partisan in its motivation. In two of these states – Florida and South Dakota – voters had previously approved a Missouri Plan for appellate courts, but then rejected that system for trial courts. In another two of the seven – Nevada and Ohio – voters rejected Missouri Plan proposals for some or all courts, three times in Nevada. In the three remaining states – Missouri, Kansas, and Oklahoma – efforts for change were precipitated by state Supreme Court decisions that came under attack by conservatives; in all three, the effort was to eliminate the role of a nominating commission that constrained governor's choice of appellate judges. In Kansas, the legislature was able on its own to eliminate the nominating commission for the state's intermediate appellate court, but in none of the three states was the legislature able to get the constitutional amendment on the ballot as is required to make a similar change for the courts that are beyond the direct control of the legislature.

The concluding chapter returns to examine the usefulness of my original organizing framework. I find that although the distinction between the legal and democratic subcultures carries some weight in the analysis, the case studies make

[20] Absent from this list, and from the following chapters of this book, are Louisiana and Alabama. Louisiana is incorrectly listed as a state where voters (in 1989) rejected a proposal for a Missouri Plan system. In 1986, a group of African American lawyers filed suit, claiming that the districts used for judicial elections in Louisiana violated the 1965 Voting Rights Act. One of the ideas that came up during the litigation and in the legislature was to implement a variant of the Missouri Plan. A listing of unsuccessful proposals for "merit selection" published by the American Judicature Society (www.judicialselection.us/uploads/documents/Merit_selection_chronology_1C233B5DD2692.pdf, accessed June 8, 2019) seems to say that the proposal got to the voters and was "soundly defeated." However, the two proposals presented to the voters dealt only with districting, not with the method of selection. The suit was eventually resolved by creating several majority African American judicial electoral districts. A proposal that would create a system combining initial contested elections with retention elections for subsequent terms (similar to the system used in Illinois, New Mexico, and Pennsylvania), did pass at least one chamber of the state legislature. However, despite support from some quarters for a Missouri Plan system, the core issue throughout the litigation was not the method of selection but underrepresentation of African Americans on the bench.

In the 1990s there was a brief flurry of activity in Alabama, with proposals advanced both for a Missouri Plan system and for a shift from partisan to nonpartisan elections. Although there was some support for a change to nonpartisan elections in the legislature – proposals were approved by committees – there was never any floor action; see Glenn C. Noe, "Alabama Judicial Selection Reform: A Skunk in Tort Hell," *Cumberland Law Review* 28 (1998), 223–224.

clear that the politics of judicial selection/retention change are both more complex and subtler. The chapter also discusses two interesting phenomena that come out through the case studies. The first is that groups that were once inclined to be prime backers of systems limiting the role of the electorate and using nominating commissions to constrain whom governors (or legislators) could select for judgeships have switched positions and now tend to favor elections and disfavor the use of constraining nominating commissions. The second is the greater willingness of voters to support Missouri Plan systems for appellate courts than for trial courts. One could make the argument that it is the appellate judges, particularly state supreme court justices, who are the most involved in making policy and hence should be subject to accountability through elections; in contrast, most of the work of trial judges is highly routine and their decisions tend to be highly constrained by the law and are subject to at least one level of appellate review as a matter of right.

The last chapter ends with a report of the results of a brief survey asking respondents to rate the importance of fourteen characteristics, half related to political qualifications and half to professional qualifications, as considerations in who should be elected or selected to be state judges. Each respondent made separate ratings for trial court judges and justices of the state supreme court. The survey shows clearly that professional qualifications dominate over political qualifications – also this is less so for trial courts than for the state supreme court.

LEGAL AND DEMOCRATIC SUBCULTURES: THE EVER-PRESENT TENSION

In their 1970 book, Richard Richardson and Kenneth Vines distinguished between what they called the legal and democratic subcultures as important in understanding the courts. Their interest was in decision-making by the lower federal courts, and they sought to emphasize that "courts engage in some activities which are usually seen as legal and others which are commonly identified as political."[21] The legal and democratic subcultures are, according to Richardson and Vines, aspects of the larger American political culture and involve fundamental orientations toward aspects of the judiciary including:[22]

> (1) cognitive orientations that concern knowledge of the judicial process and provide theories and concepts for intellectual mastery of the objects and processes in judicial institutions; (2) affective orientations that deal with the attitudes and feelings held toward judicial actors, roles, and policies of the federal courts; and (3) evaluative orientations that refer to opinions and judgments concerning various aspects of the judiciary.

[21] Richard J. Richardson and Kenneth N. Vines, *The Politics of Federal Courts* (Boston: Little, Brown and Co., 1970), 7.

[22] *Id.*, 7–8.

Although Richardson and Vines were focused on the lower federal courts, these ideas apply with equal – and in some ways greater – force to the state courts at all levels.

In Richardson and Vines's conceptualization, the legal subculture focuses on norms that seek to insulate judges from political pressures, calling on them to rely on legal texts, precedent, and the like in arriving at their decisions. This is part of what Charles Gardner Geyh labels the "legal culture paradigm." In his words, "the legal community has a distinct culture," the norms of which are inculcated in law school, entrenched in practice, and perpetuated on the bench" and "take the role of law as a constraint on judicial behavior seriously."[23] The inculcation of these norms is a central part of American legal education. Law schools do not simply teach budding lawyers the content of the law, but rather to "think like a lawyer," which includes "an appreciation of the pervasive indeterminacy inherent in the nature of an adversarial system in which opposing lawyers offer competing perspectives on applicable facts and law."[24] Central to the legal subculture are the norms of judicial independence and judicial impartiality, but there is also a recognition that the personal values of a judge can influence the judge's decision in situations of ambiguity subject to the law's setting the "range of acceptable outcomes."[25] These norms are reinforced by interaction with professional peers and by the nature of day-to-day legal practice that for most judges precedes going on the bench. The values and norms of the legal subculture appear in codes of behavior for judges and are advanced by groups such as bar associations, law schools, and associations of judges. Thus the legal subculture is closely tied to the professional world in which judges work, reflecting training, norms of analysis, and respect from professional peers. In the chapters that follow, I refer to the goal of "professionalism" or "legal professionalism" as reflecting the norms of the legal subculture.

The democratic subculture reflects the democratic values of representation and accountability. It is epitomized by the idea that the decisions of those holding government positions should reflect the ideals, goals, and needs of the electorate. Elections are the primary mechanism for achieving this. Federal judges are substantially insulated from democratic pressures because of life tenure. Although democratic values have always played some role in the process of selecting federal judges, particularly Supreme Court justices, those values today suffuse the selection process for most, if not all, Article III judges.[26] Even with the changes that

[23] Charles Gardner Geyh, *Courting Peril: The Political Transformation of the American Judiciary* (New York: Oxford University Press, 2016), 8.

[24] *Id.*, 82–83.

[25] *Id.*, 91.

[26] Nancy Scherer, *Scoring Points: Politicians, Activists, and the Lower Federal Court Appointment Process* (Stanford, CA: Stanford University Press, 2005); Sarah A. Binder and Forrest Maltzman, *Advice and Dissent: The Struggle to Shape the Federal Judiciary* (Washington, DC: Brookings Institution Press, 2009); Amy Steigerwalt, *Battle over the Bench: Senators, Interest Groups, and Lower Court Confirmations* (Charlottesville: University of Virginia Press, 2010).

have occurred in federal judicial selection, most states employ systems of selection and/or retention in which the democratic subculture plays a larger role than it does in the federal system.

Central to the democratic subculture is that judges should reflect the politics and policy preferences of the community in which they serve. By "politics," I mean the partisan preferences of the community; that is, in constituencies that are strongly oriented toward one political party, the judges serving that constituency should generally come from that party, perhaps having served in other elective offices as members of that party even where judges are not selected through partisan elections. By "policy," I mean views on specific policy issues, and that judges' own views on those issues should generally accord with the majority view of their constituency. Thus, judges where there is strong support for the death penalty should themselves be supporters of the death penalty; judges in communities that support environmental concerns over property development should be supportive of environmental concerns. Although "politics" and "policy" are distinct, in early twenty-first-century United States, they are closely related. Thus, in the chapters that follow, I often equate the concerns of the democratic subculture with what I label "politics/policy."

Clearly, the ideas of the legal and democratic subcultures have some similarities to the frequently discussed tension between the goals of independence versus accountability. This tension can be overstated because there are mechanisms of accountability beyond the traditional tools of reelection and reappointment. First and most obvious is the appellate process. Except for the U.S. Supreme Court and state supreme courts dealing with questions that are purely matters of state law, decisions of judges are subject to review on appeal.[27] A decision that departs from the law can be appealed and, if appealed, has a significant chance of being overturned. Even factual determination by trial judges has the potential of being overturned if the appellate court finds that the trial judge abused his or her discretion in finding the facts.[28] Except for decisions on the law based on the U.S. Constitution or on a state constitution, the legislature can change the law, both statutory and common law, as found by a court, although the change will generally not apply to parties in previously decided cases. Research shows that this is not infrequent at the federal level.[29] Modifying the law as determined on a constitutional basis is more difficult, although it does not always require a constitutional

[27] Geyh, *Courting Peril*, *supra* note 23, 106.

[28] See www.justia.com/trials-litigation/appeals/, accessed January 30, 2019. Although it is very difficult for an appellate court to overturn facts determined by a jury, it is not uncommon for a trial judge to do so by rendering a judgment notwithstanding the verdict (JNOV) if the judge finds that the jury's finding was unreasonable.

[29] See, for example, William N. Eskridge. "Overriding Supreme Court Statutory Interpretation Decisions," *Yale Law Journal* 101 (1991), 331–456; Jeb Barnes, *Overruled? Legislative Overrides, Pluralism, and Contemporary Court-Congress Relations* (Stanford, CA: Stanford University Press, 2004).

change; the legislature can revise or rewrite the offending law so that it passes constitutional muster.[30] For decisions based on state constitutions, changes to those constitutions are generally easier than those for the federal constitution, and in nineteen states may be initiated by citizen petitions.[31]

A second form of accountability arises through judges' concerns about their reputations among what Lawrence Baum refers to as their audiences.[32] One such audience is their colleagues on the bench.[33] A particularly important subgroup of colleagues in trial courts may be those with administrative responsibilities that include assignment to courthouses and courtrooms, calendar allocations (i.e., the type or types of cases a judge handles), and the distribution of support personnel.[34] A second is the broader legal profession, including practicing lawyers, legal academics, and judges of other courts.[35] A third is the broader public, regardless of whether a judge is concerned about reelection or reappointment.[36] Judges are no different than other people in their desire for respect and esteem, and this desire serves as a form of accountability outside the processes through which political or democratic accountability function.

A third, but more marginal mechanism of accountability, consists of the various procedures for judicial discipline.[37] In all states except Hawaii and Oregon,[38] the legislature has one or more mechanisms through which it can remove a judge from office. These mechanisms are not confined to impeachment, which typically requires the legislature finding that the offending judge has engaged in something akin to "high crimes and misdemeanors." There are also procedures that allow the removal of a judge without legislative action, typically through a disciplinary body, often with a final decision by the state supreme court.[39] A prominent example of the

30 See J. Mitchell Pickerill, *Constitutional Deliberation in Congress: The Impact of Judicial Review in a Separated System* (Durham, NC: Duke University Press, 2004), 31–61; James Meernik and Joseph Ignagni, "Judicial Review and Coordinate Construction of the Constitution," *American Journal of Political Science* 41 (1997), 447–467; see also Keith E. Whittington, *Repugnant Laws: Judicial Review of Acts of Congress from the Founding to the Present* (Lawrence: University Press of Kansas, 2019).

31 See "Initiative and Referendum States," www.ncsl.org/research/elections-and-campaigns/chart-of-the-initiative-states.aspx, accessed January 28, 2019.

32 Lawrence Baum, *Judges and Their Audiences: A Perspective on Judicial Behavior* (Princeton, NJ: Princeton University Press, 2006), 89–90.

33 *Id.*, 50–60.

34 Roy B. Flemming, Peter F. Nardulli, and James Eisenstein, *The Craft of Justice: Politics and Work in Criminal Court Communities* (Philadelphia: University of Pennsylvania Press, 1992), 79–80.

35 Baum, *Judges and Their Audiences*, *supra* note 32, 97–104.

36 *Id.*, 118–123.

37 Geyh, *Courting Peril*, *supra* note 23, 108–114.

38 See www.judicialselection.com/judicial_selection/methods/removal_of_judges.cfm?state, accessed January 28, 2019.

39 *Id.* Some states also have procedures for voters to recall a judge, although that gets into the realm of the democratic subculture; a recent example is Aaron Persky, a California judge who was recalled after imposing a sentence of only three months on a college athlete convicted of

latter was the removal or suspension of Alabama Chief Justice Roy Moore twice, once in 2003 over his refusal to remove a Ten Commandments monument and again in 2016 after he ordered the state's probate judges to disregard the U.S. Supreme Court's decision in *Obergefell v. Hodges*[40] and to refuse to issue marriage licenses to same-sex couples.[41] Disciplinary processes can also lead to reprimands, either private or public, or short-term suspensions, all of which would be embarrassing to most judges. The result is that judges almost always seek to keep their behavior within the bounds of the state's judicial code of conduct.

Although the goals of independence and accountability are subsumed by the two subcultures, the subcultures go beyond the independence-versus-accountability dichotomy to include a range of elements. These include the nature of qualifications judges should bring to their work, the nature of the values they should bring, and the appropriate role for various players in the judicial selection and retention process. As one example, what role, if any, should be played by judicial evaluation commissions in decisions concerning judicial retention and what qualifications should members of those commissions have? The legal subculture would expect such commissions to play an important role and expect that the members of the commission should largely be persons acculturated into the norms of the legal subculture. In contrast, the democratic subculture would see little role for such commissions, and if there were such commissions, would believe that the membership should be dominated by elected officials or their surrogates.

In a 2017 review essay of studies of state supreme court elections, Baum adopted the terms "values" and "interests" to refer to concepts very similar to what Richardson and Vines labeled the "legal" and "democratic" subcultures. Baum refers to values and interests as two distinct sets of motivations. In his words, the values motivation "is an effort to improve the performance of the courts, primarily by fostering what advocates view as desirable forms and degrees of accountability." In contrast, the interests motivation "is an effort to advance the political and policy goals of the participants."[42] I will use the subculture labels or the terms "political/policy" and "professionalism" rather than Baum's two labels for what he calls "motivations."

As suggested above, the tension between the legal and democratic subcultures is greater for state-level judiciaries than for the federal judiciary, due to the differences in the systems of selection and tenure in office. Federal Article III judges are never

sexual assault; see Maggie Astor, "California Voters Remove Judge Aaron Persky, Who Gave a 6-Month Sentence for Sexual Assault," *New York Times* (June 6, 2018), www.nytimes.com/2018/06/06/us/politics/judge-persky-brock-turner-recall.html, accessed January 28, 2019.

40 Obergefell v. Hodges, 135 S. Ct. 2071 (2015).

41 Jess Bidgood, Richard Fausset, and Campbell Robertson, "Moore Defiance Is New Chapter in Long History," *New York Times* (November 18, 2017), A1.

42 Lawrence Baum, "Supreme Court Elections: How Much They Have Changed, Why They Changed, and What Difference It Makes," *Law and Social Inquiry* 47, No. 3 (Summer 2017), 902.

subject to reappointment or reelection. The only state whose judges have life tenure is Rhode Island; in New Hampshire and Massachusetts, judges serve without reappointment or reelection until reaching the mandatory retirement age of 70, and in New Jersey after an initial reappointment, judges serve until mandatory retirement at age 70. In the other forty-six states, judges are subject to a retention process involving either reappointment or some form of election.

In some states, the precise nature of selection and retention processes varies depending on the level of court involved, and in a small number of states the nature of these processes for trial-level courts varies geographically within the state. The length of terms judges serve varies between 4 and 14 years, and in states with both long terms and mandatory retirement, such as the 14 years for judges of New York's highest court (called the Court of Appeals) with mandatory retirement at age 70, many judges may be selected but may never actually face a retention process. Many judges in states with mandatory retirement who were previously retained do not face future retention if their current term expires after they reach the mandatory retirement age.[43]

The nature of the selection and retention process varies greatly among the 50 states.[44] Some form of popular election is the method used to select and/or retain some or all judges in 39 of the 50 states. In 15 of these states, judges of some or all courts are always initially appointed, most after being nominated by a screening commission. However, even if the state constitution specifies election as the means of selecting (as distinct from retaining) judges, interim vacancies are filled by appointment, almost always by the governor; in all but two states (Arkansas and Louisiana), those appointed to fill a vacancy can then run in the subsequent election to keep their positions. In nine states, the executive makes initial appointments of the judges of some or all courts, with reappointment in those states either by the governor or by some other body. In two states, Virginia, and South Carolina, the legislature selects and reappoints (retains) judges, which essentially means the members of the legislature elect the judges. The previous paragraphs only capture the broad methods of selection and retention; there are many variations, including whether some type of legislative confirmation is required for gubernatorial appointees; the process for retention in states without elections; the type of contested election (partisan, nonpartisan, or "hybrid"[45]); timing of elections; geographic scope of elections for appellate judges; plurality, majority, or supermajority requirement for election or retention;

43 See www.judicialselection.us/, accessed July 25, 2017, for information on selection, retention, and mandatory retirement of state judges.

44 This discussion does not include minor local courts or specialized courts such as tax courts and the like.

45 Two states currently use a hybrid method in which nominations are formally made by the parties, by party primaries in Ohio and by party convention (only for the Supreme Court) in Michigan, with no party labels on the general election ballot. Arizona used a hybrid system until switching to the Missouri Plan with retention elections starting in 1976.

partisan or blanket primaries in states using partisan general elections; term length; single or multiple seat elections;[46] presence of a straight-ticket option in partisan elections; and whether incumbency is indicated on the ballot.[47]

In his review essay of studies of judicial elections, Baum asserts that "although values typically dominate public discourse about alternative selection systems, on the whole interests play a more powerful part in determining the outcomes of debates over these systems."[48] Although it is true that "all the competing systems in the states give central roles in the selection process to people in the political sector (the chief executive, legislators, and the general public) as distinguished from the legal sector (lawyers and judges),"[49] this does not mean that all systems place equal weight on the two sectors or that the political sector, with its interests and motivations, always plays a more powerful role when selection systems are modified. One way to view the central question addressed in this book is whether Baum is correct: Has "interests"/the democratic subculture been dominant over the "values"/the legal subculture in debates over the methods of judicial selection and retention? As I discuss in the concluding chapter, over the period from 1980 through 2018, there has been a shift, with the legal subculture dominating through 1999 and the democratic subculture dominating between 2000 and 2018. A closely related question is: When does one motivation or subculture succeed and the other fail in efforts to change or block changes to selection/retention systems? These questions are explored throughout the chapters in this book.

A BRIEF HISTORY OF JUDICIAL SELECTION IN THE UNITED STATES[50]

The history of judicial selection in the United States has been told many times.[51] In this section I provide a short version of that history to set the context for later chapters.

46 "Multiple-seat elections" refers here to systems in which two or more seats, N, on a court are up for election, candidates for all of the seats are listed together, and the top N vote-getters win the seats.

47 For more detail on these variations, see Kritzer, *Justices on the Ballot, supra* note 12, 43–50.

48 Baum, "Supreme Court Elections," *supra* note 42, 902.

49 *Id.*, 901.

50 Much of this section is taken verbatim from Kritzer, *Justices on the Ballot, supra* note 12, 31–39.

51 See, for example, Jed H. Shugerman, *The People's Courts: Pursuing Judicial Independence in America* (Cambridge, MA: Harvard University Press, 2012); Charles Gardner Geyh, *Who Is to Judge? The Perennial Debate over Whether to Elect or Appoint America's Judges* (New York: Oxford University Press, 2019), 24–43; Kermit L. Hall, "Progressive Reform and the Decline of Democratic Accountability: The Popular Election of State Supreme Court Judges, 1850–1920," *American Bar Foundation Research Journal* 1984 (Spring 1984), 345–369; G. Alan Tarr, *Without Fear or Favor: Judicial Independence and Accountability in the States.* (Stanford, CA: Stanford University Press, 2012); Greg Goelzhauser, *Choosing State Supreme Court Justices: Merit Selection and the Consequences of Institutional Reform* (Philadelphia, PA: Temple University Press, 2016), 15–34.

Selecting State Judges in the Earliest Years of the Republic

In the early years of the United States' independence from England, almost all judges were either appointed by the executive or elected by the legislature. The one exception was Vermont, which under its 1777 constitution called for the "freemen in each county" to choose judges for many of the nascent state's lower courts;[52] however, Vermont abandoned popular elections nine years later in favor of legislative elections.[53] Some states adopted life tenure ("on good behavior") for judges, with others limiting the tenure to fixed terms as short as one year.[54] Retention in the absence of life tenure was either by reappointment or reelection by the legislature.

The Move to Judicial Elections

Judicial elections began to reappear early in the nineteenth century. Georgia provided for the popular election of some judges in 1812, followed by Indiana in 1816.[55] However, the popular election of state judges was largely a development of the middle third of the nineteenth century.[56] Mississippi adopted elections in 1832,[57] and elections were adopted for some trial courts in Georgia in 1835 and in Michigan in 1836.[58] However, it would be another ten years before any other states made this move. In fact, between 1834 and 1845, nine states held state constitutional conventions, but failed to change to elections for the selection and retention of judges. Over a 14-year period starting in 1846, 17 states, led by New York, held constitutional conventions, and all but 2 of those states adopted judicial elections. Another 8 states amended their constitutions to allow for judicial elections for some or all courts.[59] Overall, 12 states switched to elections for all judges, with another 5 adopting elections for at least some judges. By 1860, elections were being used to select some or all judges in 23 of the then 31 states.[60]

52 Lawrence M. Friedman, *A History of American Law* (New York: Simon & Schuster, 1973), 111; see also Shugerman, *The People's Courts*, *supra* note 51, 58; he notes (p. 20) that Connecticut retained judicial elections that it had adopted during the colonial period, but abandoned elections by 1784. Shugerman (p. 28) also points out that in some states there was not a strict separation of powers and there were elected officials who exercised judicial functions.

53 See www.judicialselection.us/judicial_selection/reform_efforts/formal_changes_since_inception.cfm?state=VT, accessed July 25, 2017. This source says that as of 1777 all judges were appointed by the governor with the consent of the council; however, in *The People's Courts*, *supra* note 51, 58–59, Shugerman reports that under the 1777 Vermont Constitution, the voters were empowered "to elect some of their judges" including "the judges of inferior court of common pleas, sheriff, justices of the peace, and judges of probates."

54 Shugerman, *The People's Courts*, *supra* note 51, 20.

55 *Id.*, 58–62.

56 Tarr, *Without Favor or Fear*, *supra* note 51, 41–46.

57 Shugerman, *The People's Courts*, *supra* note 51, 66–77.

58 *Id.*, 276–77.

59 *Id.*

60 *Id.*, 105.

Because judicial elections began to be adopted during the period associated with Jacksonian democracy, some historians have suggested that the move to elections was intended to increase the accountability of judges. The shift to elections was, in the words of Willard Hurst, "one phase of the general swing toward broadened suffrage and broader popular control of public office which Jacksonian Democracy built on the foundations laid by Jefferson."[61] In this view, a central goal in moving from appointment to elections was to increase judges' accountability to the electorate.

Selecting judges through election puts front and center the tension between judicial independence and judicial accountability,[62] or, in the terms used above, the tension between the legal and democratic subcultures. It seems logical to view the goal of the shift to elections, coming in the wake of the height of Jacksonian democracy, to be to shift the balance in the direction of accountability and the democratic subculture.[63] However, Shugerman and others argue that the move to elections reflected a goal of *increasing* judicial independence, although the independence that was sought was from politicians rather than from voters.[64] In these authors' view, it was discontent over judges essentially doing the bidding of the elected officials who appointed them that led to the adoption of elections. The reformers believed that elections would separate judges from the other elected officials because the judges would have their own constituencies, and those constituencies would reward judges for acting independently.

Because of the need to keep the courts operating, it was not possible to eliminate appointments completely. Under the system of electing judges, it became common for an elected official, usually the governor, to be empowered to fill judicial vacancies, with the appointee holding office at least until the next election. Not surprisingly, judges appointed to fill vacancies usually would then run for the office they had been appointed to fill on a temporary basis. Regardless of whether an election involved a previously elected incumbent, an incumbent appointed to fill a vacancy that had occurred since the previous election, or an open seat, the candidates were generally highly dependent on the party leaders who played a central role in mid-nineteenth-century elections.

Until the last two decades of the nineteenth century, the mechanics of elections looked very different than what contemporary voters have come to expect. Voting machines did not exist and there were no "official" ballots listing officially

[61] James Willard Hurst, *The Growth of American Law: The Law Makers* (Boston, MA: Little, Brown, 1950), 140.

[62] See Charles G. Geyh, "The Endless Judicial Selection Debate and Its Implications for the Future of an Independent Judiciary," *Georgetown Journal of Legal Ethics* 21 (2008), 1259–1281.

[63] Susan B. Carbon and Larry C. Berkson. "Judicial Retention Elections in the United States" (Chicago, IL: American Judicature Society, 1980), 1.

[64] Shugerman, *The People's Courts, supra* note 51; Tarr, *Without Fear or Favor, supra* note 51, 46–51; Kermit L. Hall, "The Judiciary on Trial: State Constitutional Reform and the Rise of an Elected Judiciary, 1846–1860," *The Historian* 45, no. 3 (1983), 337–354.

nominated candidates. Voters indicated their choices on plain pieces of paper and placed those ballots into a ballot box sitting out in public. Because of the number of offices to be filled, voters often did not know much about the candidates for many of the offices on the ballot and the absence of official ballots meant that there were no cues, such as party labels, for voters. A common practice was for party leaders to prepare preprinted ballots listing the party's chosen candidates for party workers to distribute to party supporters, who could deposit the preprinted ballots it in the ballot box. If there were judicial offices to be filled, the party's candidates for those offices would be included on the preprinted ballot. Political machines often went one step further, printing their ballots on a distinct color of paper so that party officials monitoring the polling place could observe the color of the ballot those believed to be their supporters had deposited in the ballot box. Some party bosses would bring their supporters to the polls in groups, distribute the preprinted ballots, and march their voters to the ballot box while the voters held the colored ballots aloft.[65] With this device, the bosses knew whom to reward for party loyalty and whom to punish for defection. Significantly, this was also before the development of party primaries, which meant that party leaders substantially controlled the nomination of candidates made at party conventions. The result was that party leaders, who were often also the elected officials who would choose whom to appoint as interim judges or who would have appointed judges prior to the shift to elections, had substantial control of who was a candidate for judicial office, thus undercutting the goal of increasing judges' independence from other politicians.

Most judicial elections then and now are conducted simultaneously with elections for other offices. Some states tried to reduce the influence of political parties by scheduling judicial elections at times apart from other elections.[66] At least some of those efforts were short-lived due to cost and lack of participation. One state that has done this throughout its existence is Wisconsin; that separation was required under the state's first constitution. Wisconsin's judicial elections initially occurred in September but subsequently moved to April, which is when they take place today, along with elections for other nonpartisan state and local offices.[67]

The nature of elections changed after 1884 with the introduction of the Australian ballot, the preprinted, official ballot marked in private that is standard today. The adoption of the Australian ballot was very rapid, with 39 of 45 states using them by 1896.[68] The use of such ballots reduced the control of party leaders. With the official, preprinted ballot it became easy for voters to split their votes among

65 Ian Ayres, "Disclosure versus Anonymity," in Ian Shapiro and Stephen Macedo, eds., *Designing Democratic Institutions* (New York: Oxford University Press, 2000), 49.

66 Tarr, *Without Fear or Favor*, *supra* note 51, 51.

67 Kritzer, *Justices on the Ballot*, *supra* note 12, 12; in presidential election years, the spring primary would coincide with the presidential primary.

68 See Jill Lepore, "Rock, Paper, Scissors: How We Used to Vote," *The New Yorker* (October 13, 2008), www.newyorker.com/magazine/2008/10/13/rock-paper-scissors, accessed July 25, 2017.

candidates of different parties, or alternatively to choose not to vote for some offices on the ballot. This was to some extent encouraged in states using the Australian format of the preprinted ballot, today referred to as the "office block" format; this type of ballot is organized so that all candidates for a specific office are listed in a single block in one column.[69] Many states opted instead for the "party-column" format, which lists candidates for all offices from a particular party in a single column. This latter format makes it easy to provide a single circle or box at the top of the column, which a voter can mark to indicate a "straight-ticket" vote – a vote for all the candidates of the indicated party.[70] Regardless of which form a state chose to use, there was no easy way for party leaders to monitor the action of individual voters as had possible prior to the adoption of preprinted, official ballots. However, the process of making official nominations to put candidates on the ballot meant that parties continued to play a central role in the election process.

The Development of Nonpartisan Elections

The ability to have a system of formally nonpartisan elections was one of the major impacts of the Australian ballot. With the official ballot, the option was now available to make elections formally nonpartisan by listing candidates on the official ballot without party designations. This did not necessarily eliminate the parties' role as nominators or as active participants in the election campaign. It did, however, generally dampen partisan patterns in voting. In the early years of the twentieth century, states began adopting nonpartisan elections for a range of offices.

Some of the earliest offices for which nonpartisan ballots were adopted were judgeships.[71] The first state to do so was Washington in 1907,[72] with eight others following by 1920.[73] By 1945, fifteen states, all in the Midwest and West, had adopted nonpartisan elections for the members of their state supreme courts.[74] The goal of

[69] See https://ivn.us/2013/11/18/history-straight-ticket-voting-movement-abolish/, accessed July 25, 2017.

[70] This format, also called the Belgian ballot, has existed in the United States since at least the 1890s; see *id.* According to one early twentieth-century source, the Belgian ballot format was the format "in general use in the United States," Robert Ellsworth Fast and Hu Maxwell, *The History and Government of West Virginia* (Morgantown, WV: Acme Publishing Co., 1901), 325.

[71] Even with the adoption of official ballots, judicial candidates in Wisconsin chose not to list a party affiliation; see Kritzer, *Justices on the Ballot*, *supra* note 12, 12–13.

[72] Tarr, *Without Fear or Favor*, *supra* note 51, 64.

[73] In addition, two states adopted nonpartisan ballots for the general election but left it to the parties to make nominations: Michigan in 1939 (party conventions only for the Supreme Court), and Ohio in 1911, and Arizona effectively adopted this system when it became a state in 1912.

[74] The other states making the change in roughly the first third of the twentieth century were Idaho in 1934, Maryland in 1944, Minnesota in 1912, Montana in 1935 (an earlier attempted change in 1909 was struck down by the Montana Supreme Court in State v. O'Leary, 11 P. 204 [Mont. 1911]), Nebraska in 1909, Nevada in 1915, North Dakota in 1909, Oregon in 1931, South Dakota in 1921, Utah in 1951, Wisconsin in 1911 (only formalizing actual practice by statute),

adopting nonpartisan judicial elections was to increase the independence of judges by preventing capture by "ideology and special interests."[75] Although the use of nonpartisan elections did dampen partisanship, it quickly became evident that the proponents of nonpartisan elections held overly optimistic views of the electorate, which had lost its single most important voting cue: a candidate's political party.

The absence of party labels on the ballot led many voters to rely on cues based on the candidates' names. This was clearly evident in the quirky nature of some election results in which voters relied on mistaken name recognition. A clear example of this occurred in Washington in 1990 when Chief Justice Keith Callow ran for reelection to the Washington Supreme Court. An unknown local lawyer, believing that no election should go uncontested, entered the contest. Much to the challenger's surprise, to say nothing of the incumbent's shock and the surprise of the legal establishment in Washington, the challenger won.[76] The unknown lawyer who defeated Justice Callow was named Charles W. Johnson. There were at the time three relatively well-known Charles Johnsons in the state: a Tacoma television news anchor, a superior court judge, and a former sergeant-at-arms in the state senate. Presumably, many voters mistook Charles W. Johnson for one of these other Charles Johnsons.[77]

Ohio is an interesting state to look at regarding the role of name recognition in the absence of partisan labels on the ballot. In Ohio candidates for the state Supreme Court seek nominations through party primaries, but no party labels appear on the general election ballot. Moreover, in Ohio, there are some family names that have, or at one time had, strong partisan linkages. The most prominent such name is "Taft";[78] one might almost say that t-a-f-t is an alternate spelling for "Republican" in Ohio. Even in the absence of party labels, a Taft running for the

and Wyoming in 1915. Three (Ohio in 1911, Michigan in 1939, and Arizona from when it became a state in 1912) of those fourteen states had hybrid systems in which parties retained a formal role in the nominating process, either through primaries or conventions, but no party labels appeared on the general election ballot. In addition, Pennsylvania shifted from partisan to nonpartisan elections in 1913, but reverted back to partisan elections eight years later; see Shira J. Goodman and Lynn A. Marks, "A View from the Ground: A Reform Group's Perspective on the Ongoing Effort to Achieve Merit Selection of Judges," *Fordham Urban Law Journal* 34, no. 1 (2007), 428n.16.

75 See Shugerman, *The People's Courts*, *supra* note 51, 167.

76 See Robb London, "For Want of Recognition, Chief Justice Is Ousted," *New York Times* (September 28 1990), www.nytimes.com/1990/09/28/us/law-for-want-of-recognition-chief-justice-is-ousted.html?pagewanted=1, accessed July 26, 2017.

77 One possible element here is that Washington had, until 2013, a system whereby there is a primary even if there were only two candidates, and if a candidate in the primary won a majority (which will always be true with only two candidates unless there is a tie), that winner was elected and there was no contest at the general election. In 1990, Charles Johnson won at the primary.

78 Robert A. Taft was the dominant Republican figure in Ohio in the 1940s and 1950s and was often referred to as "Mr. Republican." He unsuccessfully sought the Republican presidential nomination in 1948 and 1952.

Ohio Supreme Court produces a strong partisan voting pattern. There is at least one example in Ohio of how name recognition without party labels on the ballot can cause serious confusion. A second name that at one time had a strong association with the Republican Party was "Brown."[79] In 1970, *Democrat* Allen Brown ran against *Republican* J. J. P. Corrigan; "Corrigan" was a name moderately associated with the Democratic Party, in part because of its Irish origins. The voting pattern in this election had counties that leaned Republican voting more strongly for Brown and counties that leaned Democratic voting more strongly for Corrigan than would normally be expected.

The search for alternate cues and the resulting name confusion was not the only result that can be associated with the adoption of nonpartisan elections. Voter participation declined,[80] fewer incumbents were turned out of office, and independence did increase, but not necessarily in the way reformers had hoped. However, as incumbents became more secure, an increasing number of judges initially obtained their offices by appointment, because of the power of governors in most states to fill midterm vacancies. Not surprisingly, governors regularly used these positions as a source of patronage, filling vacancies with supporters who were likely to reflect the policy preferences of the governors who appointed them.

Although adoption of nonpartisan ballots in southern and border states did not start until the 1970s,[81] judicial elections in most southern states were effectively nonpartisan. Nine of the eleven states that were part of the Confederacy employed formally partisan elections prior to the first switch in 1971.[82] As described by V. O. Key in his classic work, *Southern Politics*,[83] for the most part the Democratic Party was the only game in town for state politics, and for most local politics as well. The result was that the Democratic Party primary decided most elections, including judicial elections. This meant that nonpartisan elections for state and local offices, including judgeships, effectively existed in most areas of the South and in many border states because the Democratic primary, sometimes with a runoff, determined the election outcome. Kermit Hall argued that the effect of the southern one-party

79 Clarence J. Brown, father and son, were longtime Republican members of the U.S. House of Representatives from a district in central Ohio; together they served from 1939 to 1983. Clarence Brown Sr. had previously served as both lieutenant-governor and secretary of state.

80 Tarr, *Without Fear or Favor, supra* note 51, 64.

81 In 1971 Florida became the first southern state to adopt (by statute) nonpartisan elections for its courts, followed in 1975 by Kentucky with approval of a constitutional amendment reforming the court system that included shifting to nonpartisan elections. Over the next forty years, five additional southern and border states made the change: Georgia followed in 1983, Mississippi in 1994, Arkansas in 2000, North Carolina in 2002, and West Virginia in 2015.

82 The two exceptions were Virginia and South Carolina. In addition, several border states – Oklahoma, Kentucky, Maryland (until 1944, after which it shifted to nonpartisan elections), and West Virginia – used partisan elections, although they are best described as having a one-party tendency rather than being thoroughly dominated by the Democratic Party.

83 V. O. Key Jr., *Southern Politics* (New York: Knopf, 1949).

system was to increase the independence of the appellate judiciary in the South, consequently decreasing its accountability to the electorate.[84]

The Development and Adoption of the Missouri Plan

Even with the elimination of political parties as formal players in judicial elections, elements of what could be labeled the "legal subculture" sought to end direct elections as methods of selecting and/or retaining judges or, failing that, to further limit the role of elections in the judicial selection and retention process. The ideal solution for many proponents of further change was to move to a "short ballot" system whereby only a small number of offices would be filled by election; most of the offices subject to elections, including judgeships, would then be filled by appointment. However, popular sentiment favored elections, as is the case still today.[85]

To solve the problem of retaining a role for the electorate, Northwestern University law professor Albert Kales devised a plan that included what we today call "retention elections." Under Kales's 1914 plan,[86] the state's chief justice would be the only judge directly elected by the voters. Nominations for other judgeships would be made by a judicial council consisting of presiding judges, with the elected chief justice then making appointments from among the persons nominated by the judicial council; neither the governor nor the legislature would have any role in judicial selection. After a probationary period of two or three years, the judge would stand in a noncompetitive election in the form of a yes–no referendum on whether the judge should retain his office (all judges at this time were male). If retained in office, the judge would serve a full term and then could stand for retention for another term. This would continue until the judge chose not to run, reached mandatory retirement age, resigned for other reasons, was removed from office through some disciplinary procedure, or died.[87] The retention election was included to mollify the electorate and to create at least an appearance of

[84] Kermit L. Hall, "The 'Route to Hell' Retraced: The Impact of Popular Election on the Southern Appellate Judiciary, 1832–1920," in David J. Bodenhamer and James W. Ely Jr., eds., *Ambivalent Legacy: A Legal History of the South*, (Jackson: University Press of Mississippi, 1984), 229–255, 251.

[85] The range of state and local offices subject to election in the United States is striking, from sewage district to library board and, in at least one location, the legendary dogcatcher, although now called "animal control officer." See Doug Ireland, "Danville Animal Control Officer Race Heats Up," *Danville Eagle Tribune* (February 5, 2013), www.eagletribune.com/news/local_news/danville-animal-control-officer-race-heats-up/article_e9430566-1bb2-56c6-84c3-f1637d86b7d6.html, accessed July 27, 2017.

[86] See Albert Kales, *Unpopular Government in the United States* (Chicago: University of Chicago Press, 1914), 51. Kales also served as director of research at the nascent American Judicature Society, which became a primary supporter of the plan.

[87] Carbon and Berkson, *Judicial Retention Elections in the United States*, *supra* note 63, 2–3.

accountability.[88] The expectation of Kales and others who advocated for a system along these lines was that the accountability was to be a matter of competence and not related to the judges' decisional propensities.

Although several variants of Kales's plan were advanced,[89] it was not until 1934 that any state adopted a system with some of the innovations Kales had proposed. That year, California adopted a system for its appellate courts, still in use, under which the governor nominates a candidate for a vacant or soon-to-be-vacated judgeship. If the judgeship is then vacant, the nominee is presented to the Commission on Judicial Appointments (consisting of the chief justice, the attorney general, and a presiding judge from the Court of Appeals) for approval, and if approved the nominee assumes office; the judge or justice then stands for retention the next time judicial elections are held. If the current incumbent for the judgeship is still in office but has decided not to run for another term, the nominee is placed on the ballot at the next election and, if successful, takes office upon the expiration of the incumbent's term. In either situation, the candidate runs without opposition, and the electorate is asked to vote yes or no on the question, "For [office—e.g., Associate Justice of the Supreme Court] shall XXXX be elected to the office for term provided by law?" If the judge currently holds the office, the judge's title is included with his name (e.g., "... shall Associate Justice XXXX be elected ... ?").[90] Unlike Kales's plan or methods used in most states that subsequently adopted plans derived from what Kales proposed, the California system does not limit the governor's choice by restricting that choice to a candidate nominated by a required screening commission.

In 1940, Missouri adopted the second system derived from Kales's model.[91] Under Missouri's Nonpartisan Court Plan, or the "Missouri Plan" as it came to be called, a nominating commission consisting of a mix of lawyers selected by the bar, lay persons selected by the governor, and one judge screens potential nominees. The commission then forwards three names to the governor, who has sixty days to make a selection from that list; if the governor fails to act, the nominating commission then

[88] Glenn R. Winters, "The Merit Plan for Judicial Selection and Tenure–Its Historical Development," *Duquesne Law Review* 7 (1968), 75.

[89] Carbon and Berkson, *Judicial Retention Elections in the United States*, *supra* note 63, 7.

[90] For a history of judicial selection and judicial elections in California, see Gerald F. Uelmen, "Supreme Court Retention Elections in California," *Santa Clara Law Review* 28, no. 2 (1988), 333–355. Only once has a gubernatorial selection for the California Supreme Court been rejected by what is now called the Commission on Judicial Appointments, and that was in 1940 when the governor nominated law professor Max Radin; after Radin's rejection, the governor nominated law professor Roger Traynor, who went on to have an illustrious career on the California Supreme Court; see Malcolm Smith, "The California Method of Selecting Judges," *Stanford Law Review* 3 (1951), 591–594.

[91] See Jack W. Peltason, "The Missouri Plan for the Selection of Judges," *University of Missouri Studies* 20, no. 2 (1945). A similar plan had been rejected by the voters in Ohio two years earlier; see Shugerman, *The People's Courts*, *supra* note 51, 193–194.

makes a selection.[92] The selected person serves for one year and then stands for election on the question, "Shall Judge XXX be retained in office?" At the end of each subsequent term, the judge stands again for retention.[93] The next state to adopt a Missouri Plan type system was Kansas in the late 1950s; the system applied only to positions on the Kansas Supreme Court.[94] Subsequently fourteen states have adopted some version of the Missouri Plan involving nominating commissions, gubernatorial appointment, and retention elections for some or all of their courts; no state has adopted or extended the use of this system since 1994 when Tennessee extended it to justices of its Supreme Court,[95] although there has been at least one local adoption of a Missouri Plan system where a local option exists.[96]

In the late 1950s, proponents of the Missouri Plan dubbed it "merit selection."[97] The argument of the proponents is that the screening by a nominating commission improves the quality of those appointed to the bench. It is likely that labeling the system "merit selection" contributed to its adoption in many of the states that switched to that system. However, the extensive academic literature comparing the judges under different selection systems dating back 50 years[98] has found little or no

92 See www.courts.mo.gov/page.jsp?id=297, last visited September 24, 2012.

93 Watson and Downing, *The Politics of the Bench and Bar, supra* note 7, 13–14.

94 At the time, Kansas did not have an intermediate appellate court. When an intermediate appellate court was created in 1977, its judges were subject to a similar system of selection and retention. In 1972, an amendment to the Kansas constitution provided a local (district-based) option to shift to a Missouri Plan type system for trial judges; initially 23 of 29 districts changed, but some changed back to partisan elections. As 2018, 17 of 31 districts employed a Missouri Plan system; see https://ballotpedia.org/Judicial_selection_in_Kansas, accessed January 30, 2019.

95 See Roy A. Schotland, "New Challenges to States' Judicial Selection," *Georgetown Law Journal* 95, no. 4 (2007), 1085; Schotland includes California in his list, but I omit it because it does not have a required nominating commission. As discussed earlier, Tennessee established a Missouri Plan type system, which it called the Tennessee Plan, for its intermediate courts of appeals in 1971. The other states that adopted a Missouri Plan system are Alaska (1959, when the state was established), Arizona (1974), Colorado (1966), Florida (1976 for appellate courts, 1998 created local option for trial courts but was not adopted by any local districts), Indiana (1970, appellate courts plus a rarely used local option), Iowa (1962), Maryland (1976, appellate courts only), Nebraska (1962 for Supreme Court and district court; 1974 for county court), Oklahoma (1967 for two courts of last resort; 1987 for intermediate civil appeals court), South Dakota (1980 for Supreme Court, rejected for trial courts by voters in 2004), Utah (1985), Wyoming (1972 for Supreme Court and district court; 1977 for county court).

96 Greene County, Missouri adopted it in 2008; see https://ballotpedia.org/Judicial_selection_in_Missouri, accessed January 30, 2019.

97 Shugerman, *The People's Courts, supra* note 51, 175. The association of "merit" with the Missouri Plan system appears to have first appeared in Nebraska in 1953 with the leading organizational proponent of the plan, the American Judicature Society adopting the phrase "merit selection" by 1963; see Goelzhauser, *Choosing State Supreme Court Justices, supra* note 51, 69.

98 Nicholas O. Alozie, "Distribution of Women and Minority Judges: The Effects of Judicial Selection Methods," *Social Science Quarterly* 71, no. 2 (June 1990), 315–325; Bradley C. Canon, "The Impact of Formal Selection Processes on the Characteristics of Judges – Reconsidered," *Law & Society Review* 6, no. 4 (May 1972), 579–593; Philip L. Dubois, "The Influence of Selection System and Region on the Characteristics of a Trial Court Bench," *Justice System*

systematic evidence that judges selected using a nominating commission are better than those either appointed without the use of such a commission or directly elected by the voters,[99] although there is good evidence that the system of retention can influence directly or indirectly the decisions judges make.[100]

Although retention elections are generally associated with the Missouri Plan, that need not be the case, as was true with the first adoption of retention elections by California in the 1930s. In additional to California, there are three other variants in how retention elections are used without a Missouri Plan type nominating commission. First, two states using nonpartisan elections adopted a provision whereby if an incumbent was unopposed for election, the election reverted to a retention format. Montana adopted this practice in 1973, and Utah had it starting in 1967, lasting until it switched to a complete Missouri Plan system in 1985.[101] The second variant combines a partisan election for an initial term with retention elections for subsequent terms; this system has been adopted in Illinois (1964), New Mexico (1988), and Pennsylvania (1968). Third, Kansas in 2013 and Tennessee in 2016 adopted

Journal 8, no. 1 (1983), 59–87; Kevin M. Esterling and Seth S. Andersen, "Diversity and the Judicial Merit Selection Process: A Statistical Report," *Research on Judicial Selection 1999* (2000), 1–39; Victor E. Flango and Craig R. Ducat, "What Difference Does Method of Judicial Selection Make? Selection Procedures in State Courts of Last Resort," *Justice System Journal* 5 no. 1 (1979), 25–44; Henry R. Glick and Craig F. Emmert, "Selection Systems and Judicial Characteristics: The Recruitment of State Supreme Court Judges," *Judicature* 70, no. 3 (December–January 1987), 228–235; Barbara Luck Graham, "Do Judicial Selection Systems Matter? A Study of Black Representation on State Courts," *American Politics Quarterly* 18, no. 3 (July 1990), 316–336; Herbert Jacob, "The Effect of Institutional Differences in the Recruitment Process, Case of State Judges," *Journal of Public Law* 13, no. 1 (1964), 104–119.

99 A central problem in assessing whether one system or another produces "better" judges is defining what one means by a "better" judge in any kind of truly neutral fashion. Reddick looked at whether the incidence of judicial discipline in 9 states where some judges were selected using "merit" screening panel with others using either partisan or nonpartisan elections, and found evidence that in 6 of those states "merit-selected judges are disciplined less often than elected judges"; see Melia Reddick, "Judging the Quality of Judicial Selection Methods: Merit Selection, Elections, and Judicial Discipline," American Judicature Society White Paper (2010), available at SSRN: https://ssrn.com/abstract=2731018, accessed September 5, 2017. See also Schotland, "New Challenges to States' Judicial Selection," *supra* note 95, 1087–1088; and Penny J. White and Malia Reddick, "A Response to Professor Fitzpatrick: The Rest of the Story," *Tennessee Law Review* 75, no. 3 (2008), 538. Another study looked at whether the nature of the conduct subject to discipline varied depending on method of selection, and found some statistically significant differences, but concluded that "none of [the] differences could be considered substantively strong or overwhelming"; see Jona Goldschmidt, David Olson, and Margaret Eikman, "The Relationship between Method for Judicial Selection and Judicial Misconduct," *WIbidener Law Journal* 18, no. 2 (2009), 477.

100 For a review of the literature on the impact of retention methods on decisions, see Herbert M. Kritzer, "Impact of Judicial Elections on Judicial Decisions," *Annual Review of Law and Social Science* 12 (2016), 353–371.

101 In addition, one state, Nevada (since 1976), provides the option of voting for "none of the above" in judicial and other elections; this makes an uncontested election equivalent to a retention election.

systems for some courts that combined retention elections with gubernatorial appointment without a merit-based nominating commission but with legislative confirmation.[102] To avoid confusion I use the label "retention elections" to refer to any system using yes–no referenda to retain (or in California to sometimes confirm) judges. I reserve the term "Missouri Plan" for systems with the three elements of (1) a mandatory nominating commission, (2) gubernatorial appointment from among those nominated by the commission, and (3) retention elections; I include under this label states that also require legislative confirmation of the governor's selection from the nominating commission. I prefer "Missouri Plan" to the alternative "merit selection," because the latter has also been applied to systems without retention elections in which a nominating commission must be used to identify candidates.[103] I refer to the systems in states using a nominating commission without the use of retention elections as using a system of "constrained appointment"; I include here South Carolina where judges are "elected" by the legislature from a list of candidates provided by a nominating commission.

Patterns of Change in Judicial Selection: A Summary

Over time there has been a pattern to the changes in state judicial selection. In the mid-nineteenth century the shift was from appointment to elections, with new states also adopting judicial elections. Over about a thirty-year period, from 1907 through the late 1930s, several western and midwestern states switched from partisan elections to nonpartisan elections. From the late 1950s through about 1980, changes again came in several western and Midwestern states in the form of shifts from contested elections to Missouri Plan systems. And starting in the 1970s, six southern and border states shifted from partisan elections to nonpartisan elections; three southern states adopted Missouri Plan systems for their appellate

[102] Three states – Maryland, Montana, and Utah – use a modified Missouri Plan that requires legislative confirmation of the governor's selection from among the nominees put forward by the body charged with making the nominations; see www.judicialselection.us/judicial_selection/methods/selection_of_judges.cfm?state=, accessed June 29, 2019.

[103] States with laws requiring the use of a nominating commission without retention elections are Connecticut (1986), Hawaii (1978), New York (1977, appellate courts only), Rhode Island (1994), South Carolina (1996) and Vermont (1967); governors in Delaware (1977) have chosen to use a similar procedure. Nominating commissions are also used in some states with partisan or nonpartisan elections to fill midterm vacancies: by law in Florida (1972, all courts), Kentucky (1975), Nevada (1976), North Dakota (1976), South Dakota (1980 for trial courts), and Utah prior to adopting the Missouri Plan (1967); and by custom by at least some governors in Maryland (1970), Minnesota (for Court of Appeals, and for the Supreme Court since 1983 and by statute for lower courts since 1990), New York (trial judges, since mid-1970s), Pennsylvania (1964), and Wisconsin (1983). In Hawaii, Rhode Island, and Vermont, the governor's selection from the list of nominees is subject to confirmation by the state senate; see www.judicialselection.us/judicial_selection/methods/selection_of_judges.cfm?state=, accessed June 29, 2019.

courts starting in the late 1960s. Clearly, the types of changes that have occurred have tended to come in clusters.

CHANGING METHODS OF JUDICIAL SELECTION, 1980–2017

Between 1980 and 2017 thirteen states made major changes in their processes for selecting and retaining some or all of their judges. Most states made changes similar to what had been done by other states in earlier years. The most common change, seen in five states, was a shift from partisan to nonpartisan elections:

- Arkansas, 2000, by constitutional amendment.
- Georgia, 1983, by constitutional amendment.
- Mississippi, 1994, by statute.[104]
- North Carolina, 1996 for superior court judges, 2001 for district court judges, and 2002 for appellate court judges, all by statute.
- West Virginia, 2015, by statute.

Three states shifted to Missouri Plan systems for some or all judges:

- South Dakota, 1980 for Supreme Court, by constitutional amendment, from nonpartisan elections.
- Tennessee, 1994 for Supreme Court, by statute, from partisan elections.[105]
- Utah, 1985, by constitutional amendment, from nonpartisan elections.

One state combined appointment from a nominating commission list with a system of partisan elections for initial terms and retention elections for subsequent terms:[106] New Mexico, 1988, by constitutional amendment. All these changes followed broad patterns of earlier changes to nonpartisan elections, Missouri Plan type systems, or the combination of partisan elections followed by retention elections. Most recently, there have been changes deviating from these earlier patterns.

Three of the states not using popular elections also made changes that were in some ways consistent with the pattern of moving away from highly partisan systems. In Rhode Island, for example, Supreme Court justices had previously been elected by the two chambers of the state legislature sitting together as a "grand committee," with lower court judges appointed by the governor subject to legislative confirmation. In 1994, the legislative election of Supreme Court justices was ended in favor of having all judges appointed by the governor from a list of nominees provided by a nominating commission, with confirmation by the Senate. In

[104] Mississippi initially retained partisan elections for Justice Courts (more commonly called justice of the peace courts) but switched to nonpartisan elections for those courts in 2008.

[105] As discussed earlier in this chapter, Tennessee adopted a Missouri Plan system for all appellate judges in 1971, but then repealed it for the Supreme Court in 1974.

[106] In the 1960s two states, Illinois and Pennsylvania, had adopted similar systems omitting the appointment aspect.

Connecticut, where judges had been appointed by the governor subject only to legislative approval,[107] the system was modified to limit the governor's selection to a standing list of persons who had been found to be qualified by the Judicial Selection Commission. In South Carolina, where judges are elected by the legislature, a nominating commission was added to the process; only persons on lists provided by the nominating commission can be chosen by the legislature.

As discussed earlier, North Carolina shifted back toward partisan elections for its Court of Appeals in 2015. In 2016, the North Carolina legislature passed a bill, signed into law by the governor, that changed selection/retention for its Supreme Court to a system that was similar to what existed in Illinois, New Mexico, and Pennsylvania: a contested election for the initial terms followed by retention elections for subsequent terms; the contested election was to remain in the nonpartisan format. However, as is discussed in detail in Chapter 2, that change was struck down by a state court as violating the state constitution. In 2017, the North Carolina legislature passed legislation that was signed into law, reverting to partisan elections for all levels of courts. Kansas passed legislation that was signed into law, eliminating the role of the nominating commission element of the Missouri Plan – the first state to do so[108] – for its Court of Appeals in 2013; with this change, governors are no longer limited in their choices to persons nominated by a nominating commission. Under the new system, which is modeled on the process for appointing federal judges, the governor is empowered to appoint any person with the qualifications required by law, subject to confirmation by a majority vote of the state Senate;[109] retention elections continue to be used for subsequent terms. In 2014, Tennessee voters passed a state constitutional amendment adopting a plan for the state's appellate courts similar to that adopted the prior year for the Kansas Court of Appeals; Tennessee governors can now appoint any person with the required legal qualifications, subject to confirmation by both chambers of the state legislature, with the judges standing in retention elections for subsequent terms.[110]

107 The formal language was that judges were "nominated" by the governor and then "elected" by legislature.

108 Technically speaking, one might argue that Tennessee was the first to abandon the merit element when it repealed the Missouri Plan system for its Supreme Court, which had been adopted in 1971 for all appellate courts. However, as noted previously, that plan was never actually used in Tennessee for the Supreme Court; the first retention election for the Supreme Court did not occur until after the plan was reinstated.

109 If the Kansas Senate fails to act within 60 days, the nomination is deemed confirmed. The statute authorizes the chief justice to make the appointment, subject to senate confirmation, should the governor fail to make the appointment within 60 days of the vacancy occurring.

110 If either chamber of the legislature fails to act within 60 days, the nomination is deemed confirmed unless two-thirds or more of the membership of one chamber has voted to reject, in which case the nominee is rejected; see Richard Locker, "Tennessee Senate OKs Judicial Confirmation Process," *Memphis Commercial Appeal* (January 27, 2016), www.commercialappeal.com/story/news/government/state/2016/01/27/tennessee-senate-oks-judicial-confirmation-process/90386360/, accessed September 3, 2017.

In addition to these major changes, states made a range of minor, but still important, changes to various procedures. For example, Washington (2013) ended the practice of judicial elections being decided at the primary election when there were only two candidates. West Virginia (2013) instituted a requirement that when a vacancy occurs for a position of magistrate judge, the person appointed to fill the position must be of the same party as the departing judge. Texas passed legislation in 2017, effective with the 2020 election, eliminating the straight-ticket option on ballots that had included all levels of courts and often had a significant effect on results in trial court elections in some of the large urban counties. Several states established systems for judicial performance evaluations, and various changes were instituted in the membership and/or processes used by nominating commissions or performance evaluation commissions.

The changes that were made are only a small fraction of the proposals that received at least some legislative action between 1980 and 2018. I was able to identify almost 100 unsuccessful proposals for changes coming from thirty-one different states that received at least some serious legislation attention. There were many more proposals introduced that failed to receive any legislative action. From 2008 through 2018, the Gavel-to-Gavel[111] website lists almost 1,700 proposals for change to judicial selection systems or procedures, although many of those listings represented minor variations on other listings, concerned relatively minor matters of selection/election administration, or had been carried over from the previous legislative session. Nonetheless, there were probably between 800 and 1,000 distinct proposals for changes to state judicial selection with only 2 or 3 percent becoming law.

CONTEMPORARY POLITICS OF JUDICIAL SELECTION REFORM

The chapters that follow examine the politics of judicial selection reform since 1980, covering both successful and unsuccessful efforts to make changes. What will become evident through these chapters is that there has been a shift in the dynamics of judicial selection change. From the 1950s through the 1980s, change was largely in the direction of reducing the *explicit* role of partisan and interest politics by shifting to constrained appointment or some version of the Missouri Plan, which in the words of a pair of advocates for the system, "minimize[s] the role of politics in judicial selection [which means that] judicial aspirants in merit plan states are not required to raise money, seek party support, or campaign for office as are judicial candidates in elective states."[112] However, by the 1990s one begins to see efforts to make changes that, although possibly labeled as reducing partisanship, have clear partisan or interest-group motivations and were intended to maintain or

[111] See http://gaveltogavel.us/.

[112] White and Reddick, "A Response to Professor Fitzpatrick," *supra* note 99, 541.

shift which side of the political spectrum would be advantaged in the selection and retention process.

The latter shift is evident in two phenomena. First, there has been a growing effort to end or effectively alter the role of the nominating bodies that were claimed to make the Missouri Plan a system of merit selection. At least some advocates tie this to the dominant role of lawyers, many of whom were selected in some way by their professional colleagues, on most of the nominating bodies. The ending of the requirement regarding some courts in Tennessee and Kansas that the governor select appointees from lists prepared by an independent nominating commission was mentioned previously. When the Tennessee statute requiring the use of a nominating commission was renewed for two years in 2009, the composition of the commission was changed so that all members were appointed by legislative leaders and required that at least one and no more than seven of the members be nonlawyers.[113] Previously, 14 of 17 members had to be lawyers, and although the legislative leaders made the appointments, 12 of the 14 lawyer members had to come from names submitted by four specific lawyer organizations.[114] The move to limit or end the role of independent nominating commissions was motivated in part by the perception, or at least the assertion, that the domination of the commissions by members of the legal profession resulted in nominees who were too liberal because the legal profession leaned to the Democratic, and hence liberal, side of the political spectrum.[115]

The second development is seen in changes in North Carolina, which is discussed in detail in Chapter 2. First came a change under Democratic control from partisan to nonpartisan elections for judicial offices when it became clear that Republicans were winning an increasing number of those elections. Then, after Republicans gained control of the "political" branches of state government, there was a change back to partisan elections, arguably because Democrats had continued to have significant success in the nonpartisan Supreme Court elections. Another example can be seen in West Virginia. After Republicans gained control of the state legislature, they shifted to nonpartisan elections, probably because Democrats were having continued success in those elections; interestingly, the legislation making the change was not vigorously opposed by Democrats and was signed by the Democratic governor.

Why was there a shift in the direction of the successful change efforts after the 1980s? One explanation is that much of the change was happening in formerly

[113] See Monica Mercer, "Locals Apply to Panel to Nominate State Judges," *Chattanooga Times Free Press* (August 3, 2009), 11, http://infoweb.newsbank.com.ezp1.lib.umn.edu/resources/doc/nb/news/13DD86F9112BDBD8?p=AWNB, accessed September 4, 2017.

[114] Brian T. Fitzpatrick, "Election as Appointment: The Tennessee Plan Reconsidered," *Tennessee Law Review* 75, no. 3 (2008), 483.

[115] See Brian T. Fitzpatrick, "The Politics of Merit Selection," *Missouri Law Review* 74, no. 3 (Summer 2009), 679–681, 690–691; Stephen J. Ware, "The Missouri Plan in National Perspective," *Missouri Law Review* 74 (2009), 758–766.

one-party Democratic states in the South. The timing of this shift coincided with the breakdown of Democratic dominance in the state politics of southern states and led to efforts by Democrats to slow down Republicans gaining control of the appellate courts or efforts by Republicans to seize or consolidate control. The second explanation relates to the success of efforts in 1986 by business interests to remove three California Supreme Court justices seen as unsympathetic to those interests. Prior to this time, business interests tended to view the election of judges as threatening their interests because candidates would need to appeal to voters who would not be sympathetic with big business. The 1986 experience in California taught conservatives and other business interests that they could use the public's fear of crime as a vehicle to attack incumbent judges they wanted to get off the bench or to oppose candidates for open seats they feared would be unsympathetic to business interests.

A METHODOLOGICAL NOTE AND A COMMENT ON SOURCES

In several of the chapters I use a measure of partisanship in statewide judicial elections that I label the "partisan correlation." This measure, which I used extensively in my book on state supreme court elections,[116] was pioneered by Kathleen Barber, David Adamany, and Philip Dubois.[117] The partisan correlation uses county level election results for judicial elections and gubernatorial elections. For partisan judicial elections and formally nonpartisan judicial elections in which candidates are formally nominated by the political parties, the measure is the correlation between the percent in each county voting for the Democratic gubernatorial candidate and for the Democratic judicial candidate. When there is no contemporaneous gubernatorial election, the average percent in each county across the gubernatorial elections most immediately preceding and following the judicial election is used to compute the correlation.[118] In theory, this correlation can be either positive or negative, and has occasionally been negative in the two states where parties nominate judicial candidates, but the general election is formally nonpartisan because no party label appears on the general election ballot. In the case of the other nonpartisan elections, those without formal party nominations, no attempt was made to identify the party affiliations of the judicial candidates, and the absolute value of the correlation is used. For retention elections, the correlation is

[116] See Kritzer, *Justices on the Ballot, supra* note 12.

[117] See Kathleen L. Barber, "Ohio Judicial Elections – Non Partisan Premises with Partisan Results," *Ohio State Law Journal* 32 (Fall 1971), 762–789; David Adamany and Philip Dubois, "Electing State Judges," *Wisconsin Law Review* 1976, no. 3 (1976), 731–779; and Philip L. Dubois, *From Bench to Ballot: Judicial Elections and the Quest for Accountability* (Austin: University of Texas Press, 1980).

[118] A weighted average of the gubernatorial election results is used when those elections are not equidistant in time from the judicial election.

between the percent voting in favor of retention and the percent voting for the Democratic gubernatorial candidate; this correlation can be negative if counties voting more heavily Republican also voted more heavily in favor of retention.

The research for the chapters that follow relied upon a wide range of sources, including reports, scholarly articles, articles in bar journals, voting records in legislative journals, interviews or correspondence with key actors or knowledgeable academics, online sources such as Ballotpedia.com and Wikipedia.com,[119] and newspaper reports. The newspaper sources were what was available in digitized form. Some of these were in the form of online publications of individual newspapers or broadcast media. Much more came from two digitized collections of newspapers, newspapers.com and newsbank.com; where possible, when articles found on one of these sources include the original page number in the printed version, I have included that information in the relevant footnote. I also draw on data on state supreme court elections, either those specifically reported in my book on those elections,[120] or those that I have archived on Dataverse.[121]

[119] Wikipedia was particularly useful for quick access to historical information on party strength in the states studied, although I did discover occasional inaccuracies in the Wikipedia information.

[120] Kritzer, *Justices on the Ballot*, *supra* note 12.

[121] https://dataverse.harvard.edu/dataset.xhtml?persistentId=doi:10.7910/DVN/1P1JFG.

PART I

Change as an Exercise in Partisan Politics

2

North Carolina

Partisanship in the Extreme

During the first two-thirds of the twentieth century, the North Carolina court system consisted of two levels of state courts plus large numbers of local courts of various sorts. The state courts were the appellate Supreme Court and the trial-level superior courts. Judges for both these courts were formally selected by statewide partisan elections, although in practice most judges were initially appointed by the governor to fill vacancies. The method of selection of local judges varied. The superior court had jurisdiction over felonies and major civil cases plus appeals from the local courts; the local courts handled misdemeanors and smaller civil matters. In the 1960s, the North Carolina legislature consolidated the local courts into a district court division consisting of the district court and the magistrates' court.[1] Judges of the district courts are elected in the local district; magistrates are nominated by the clerks of the superior courts and appointed by the senior resident superior court judge.[2] In 1967, the legislature created the Court of Appeals to ease the appellate burden on the Supreme Court.[3] Judges of these new courts, the Court of Appeals and the district courts, were subject to partisan elections, and this continued to be the case for judges of the superior court and the Supreme Court.

Between 1996 and 2017, North Carolina made substantial changes to judicial selection and retention. Over that period, the state legislature changed all judicial elections from partisan to nonpartisan, changed the Court of Appeals to include partisan designations on the ballot with blanket primaries if there were more than

1 See "Creation of the District Courts in North Carolina: A Brief Overview," http://celebrate.nccourts.org/sites/default/files/CelebrateNC-Brief_Overview_DistrictCourts.pdf, accessed September 1, 2017. In 1962 the voters of North Carolina approved a constitutional amendment that gave the state legislature the authority to restructure the state's system to trial courts.

2 "The North Carolina Judicial System, 2008 Edition," www.lwvhcnc.org/PDFs/NCCourtSystem_Overview.pdf, accessed November 20, 2019.

3 *Id.*, 2. A constitutional amendment authorizing the creation of the Court of Appeals was approved by the voters in 1965; see "Creation of the District Courts in North Carolina: A Brief Overview," *supra* note 1.

two candidates, passed legislation to change from nonpartisan to retention elections for Supreme Court justices who had been previously elected, changed all judicial elections back to partisan elections with traditional party primaries, and then suspended the primary elections for appellate courts for 2018. Although, as suggested in Chapter 1, it is easy to see the political motivations in some of these changes, in this chapter I will show that all – or virtually all[4] – of the changes were motivated by the goal of partisan advantage, even the changes that have traditionally been seen as reducing the role of traditional partisan politics. Moreover, the timing of the changes reflected clear political calculations by the political parties.

JUDICIAL ELECTIONS IN NORTH CAROLINA: HISTORICAL PERSPECTIVES

A Primer on North Carolina Politics

The Democratic Party dominated the politics of North Carolina, as was true in the other states that formed the Confederacy. However, politics in North Carolina were not entirely typical of the South. V. O. Key, in his classic work, *Southern Politics*, labeled North Carolina a "progressive plutocracy" and described it as being seen by many as "a closer approximation to national norms or national expectations of performance, than [found] elsewhere in the South."[5] Key showed that there were areas of Republican strength in North Carolina, particularly in the western part of the state, and that Republican gubernatorial candidates won over 40 percent of the statewide vote in two elections between 1920 and 1948.[6] He argued that the strength of the Republican Party in North Carolina served to increase the cohesion of the state's Democratic Party.[7]

The first Republican to win the governorship in North Carolina in the twentieth century was James Holshouser in 1972, the year of the Nixon landslide against George McGovern.[8] That year also saw the election of Jesse Helms as the first Republican US senator from North Carolina in the twentieth century. Under the then existing constitutional limit allowing only a single term, Holshouser could not run for reelection in 1976 and was succeeded by Democrat Jim Hunt, who served

4 The caveat reflects my inability to find good information on the change to nonpartisan elections for the district courts that occurred in 2002.

5 V. O. Key Jr. , *Southern Politics in State and Nation* (New York: Alfred Knopf, 1949), 205.

6 *Id.*, 218–223. The Republican candidate for president, Herbert Hoover, carried the state in 1928, but that was probably due to anti-Catholic sentiment vis-à-vis the Democratic candidate, Al Smith.

7 *Id.*, 223–228.

8 For an overview of North Carolina state politics starting in the last third of the twentieth century, see J. Michael Bitzer and Charles Prysby, "North Carolina," in Charles S. Bullock III and Mark J. Rozell, eds., *The New Politics of the Old South: An Introduction to Southern Politics*, 6th ed. (Lanham, MD: Rowman & Littlefield, 2018), 186–213.

two terms.[9] Hunt was succeeded by another Democrat, who served only one term, being defeated by Republican Jim Martin in 1984; Martin served two terms, ending in January 1993. It would be twenty years before the Republicans again captured the governor's office in North Carolina. Republicans had more success in holding North Carolina's two US Senate seats between 1973 and 2017. In that 44-year period, they held one of those seats for all but one 6-year term and held the other for 24 of those years.[10] Republicans finally secured a majority of North Carolina's US House seats in the 1994 election and then won a majority of the seats in eight of the twelve elections that followed.[11]

Judicial Appointments and Elections, 1973–1996

The occupation of the governorship by Republicans created an opportunity for Republicans to be appointed to judicial positions that became vacant. As fate would have it, James Holshouser was not presented with any opportunities to fill vacancies on the North Carolina Supreme Court, but he did make two appointments to the Court of Appeals; however, neither of his appointees ran to retain his seat on the Court of Appeals in the subsequent election in 1974.[12] Although it is certain that Holshouser also appointed some Republicans as trial court judges, none of his appointees to the superior courts were able to win the statewide election to retain their seats.[13]

The next Republican governor, Jim Martin, was more fortunate regarding Supreme Court vacancies. Martin made four appointments during his tenure; however, all of those appointees lost when they stood for election, three in 1986 and one in 1992. One of those appointments was for the chief justiceship. Martin chose to break from the tradition of appointing the senior associate justice, James Exum, and appointed another justice, Rhoda Billings, whom he had appointed to a vacancy on the court a year earlier. Exum resigned his associate justice position and defeated Billings in the subsequent hotly contested election,[14] despite advertising attacking

9 The limit to a single term as governor that had long existed in North Carolina was removed by a constitutional amendment that was ratified in 1977; see Jack D. Fleer, *North Carolina Government & Politics* (Lincoln: University of Nebraska Press, 1994), 56.

10 See https://en.wikipedia.org/wiki/List_of_United_States_Senators_from_North_Carolina, accessed August 9, 2017.

11 Bitzer and Prysby, "North Carolina," *supra* note 8, 189.

12 One ran unsuccessfully as the Republican nominee for a seat on the North Carolina Supreme Court and the other ran unsuccessfully as the Republican nominee for attorney general; see "A History of the North Carolina Court of Appeals, 1968–2008," 12, http://celebrate.nccourts.org/sites/default/files/NCCOA1968_2008.pdf, accessed August 31, 2017.

13 I say this because it was not until 1988 that a Republican won a statewide judicial election in the twentieth century; see Mary Miller and Beth Velliquette, "Campaigns Boil Right Up to Election Day; Final Push in Orange, N.C. Contests," *Raleigh News Observer* (November 8, 1994), A1.

14 James Drennan, "Judicial Reform in North Carolina," in Anthony Champagne and Judith Haydel, eds., *Judicial Reform in the States* (Lanham, MD: University Press of America), 27–28.

him for decisions on death penalty cases.[15] Martin also made five appointments to the Court of Appeals. Three of those appointees subsequently lost their bids to retain their seats and one chose not to run. The fifth, Robert Orr, was appointed by Martin to fill a vacancy on September 3, 1986, but then lost in the November 4, 1986 election. Orr was reappointed by Martin on November 26, 1986 to fill another vacancy and then won the election to retain his seat in 1988.[16] Orr was the first Republican in North Carolina to win a statewide judicial race in the twentieth century; he was reelected in 1992.[17]

The first Republican success in elections for the North Carolina Supreme Court came in 1994, when Republicans won both seats up for election. One election was for an open seat and was won by Robert Orr, who received 56.5 percent of the vote. For the other seat, I. Beverly Lake Jr. defeated incumbent associate justice Sarah Parker, winning 55 percent of the vote. Lake switched from the Democratic Party to Republican Party in 1980 and ran that year as the Republican candidate for governor, losing to incumbent Jim Hunt. In 1990, Lake ran unsuccessfully for the North Carolina Supreme Court, losing to the incumbent by less than 2,000 votes. He was then, in 1992, one of those appointed to the Court by Republican Jim Martin, but, as noted previously, he lost the seat in the 1992 election for the remainder of the term. In the 1992 Supreme Court election, Lake got 46.7 percent of the vote, running against Sarah Parker, whom he defeated in a rematch two years later.

One can identify several periods of competition in North Carolina Supreme Court elections between 1946 and 1992. Between 1946 and 1954 there were Republican candidates in 7 of 16 elections, with another 7 elections uncontested and 2 involving contests only in the Democratic primary. Between 1956 and 1970, Republicans contested only 4 of 22 elections, with 17 of the remaining 18 elections uncontested. Republican candidates began to appear with regularity again in 1972, contesting half of the 28 elections that occurred through 1992; 10 of the other elections were uncontested. The average vote won by the Republicans went from 29.4 percent in the first period, to 40.5 and 40.1 during the second and third periods, respectively. The 1994 election marked the beginning of a new era for Republicans running for the North Carolina Supreme Court. Republicans contested all 10 elections between 1994 and 2002, winning seven and averaging 51.6 percent of the vote.

[15] The attacks on his record on death penalty cases were sponsored by an organization called Citizens for a Conservative Court; see Maura Dolan and Don Irwin, "Anti-Bird Drive Inspires Moves in Other States," *Los Angeles Times* (October 25, 1986), http://articles.latimes.com/1986-10-25/news/mn-7395_1_death-penalty, accessed August 10, 2017.

[16] See "A History of the North Carolina Court of Appeals, 1968–2008," 19–22, http://celebrate.nccourts.org/sites/default/files/NCCOA1968_2008.pdf, accessed August 31, 2017.

[17] Miller and Velliquette, "Campaigns Boil Right Up to Election Day," *supra* note 13, A1.

ENDING PARTISAN JUDICIAL ELECTIONS

Missouri Plan Proposals

Although there were some discussions of changing to a Missouri Plan type system as early as the late 1950s, the winds of change in how judges in North Carolina should be selected really began to blow in the 1970s after a Courts Commission established in the 1960s recommended adoption of a Missouri Plan system.[18] Bills were introduced for various changes – nonpartisan elections, gubernatorial appointment, and Missouri Plan – in most legislative sessions between 1971 and 2002, and on several occasions made some progress in the legislature.[19] In 1974 and 1977, bills calling for a Missouri Plan system made it to the House floor before failing. The 1977 measure had been endorsed by the chief justice and the North Carolina Bar Association. In 1989, the North Carolina Senate passed a bill creating a Missouri Plan system for appellate judges; it was backed by the state bar and many appellate judges but opposed by some sectors of the bar and died in the House. Similar bills, some with the addition of legislative confirmation of appointees and/or omission of a nominating commission, were passed by the Senate in 1991, 1995, and 1999, but all failed in the House.

The support for these proposals came heavily from the bench and some segments of the legal profession and reflected a desire to have an impartial judiciary that could not be bought by campaign dollars. An editorial writer in the *Charlotte Observer* quoted one judge who had ruled against a plaintiff, "There is one less vote and one less contribution for next time."[20] Drawing on interviews with eighteen candidates for judgeships in the 1986 election, the writer described concerns about the need for fundraising and the conflicts that need created, along with concerns about whether campaigning for elective office impugned the dignity of the judicial office that was being sought. However, there was little support for change among Democrats, who still had firm control of the legislature, even though some observers in the state believed that the 1986 election would be the "best chance for Republicans to win a seat in the appellate level courts in decades."[21] North Carolina voters were still strongly tied to the Democratic Party for state-level offices, and judicial offices were still included as part of the straight-ticket voting option, from which the presidential contest had been excluded. In fact, as noted previously, the three Republican

[18] Drennan, "Judicial Reform in North Carolina," *supra* note 14, 22–24.

[19] See www.judicialselection.us/judicial_selection/reform_efforts/failed_reform_efforts.cfm?state=NC, accessed August 10, 2017.

[20] Jerry Shinn, "There Must Be a Better Way," *Charlotte Observer* (October 13, 1986); see also Martin H. Brinkley, "Judicial Selection in North Carolina, 1776–2016 (February 16, 2016), slide 34, https://nccalj.org/wp-content/uploads/2016/02/Judicial-Selection-in-N.C.pdf, accessed August 13, 2017.

[21] Pam Kelly, "GOP's Shot at Judgeships May Be Best in Decades," *Charlotte Observer* (October, 26, 1986), 1B.

incumbents on the Supreme Court, all of whom had been appointed to vacancies and were facing the electorate for the first time as justices, were defeated in 1986.

In the wake of the 1986 election, there were renewed calls for adoption of a Missouri Plan system.[22] In 1987, the legislature created a Judicial Selection Study Commission, with members appointed by various elected officials.[23] The Study Commission proposed a system of gubernatorial appointment from a list prepared by a nominating commission with those appointments subject to confirmation by both chambers of the state legislature for an initial term of four years; judges so appointed would be subject to review by a nonpartisan commission and reconfirmation by the legislature of additional terms of eight years.[24] A bill to implement such a system for appellate courts passed the North Carolina Senate in 1989, but languished in the House.[25] The inclusion of the confirmation provision is suggestive of political concerns. Although the governor was at this time still a Republican, he was barred from running for reelection in 1992. Democrats had strong expectations of regaining control of the executive branch because the popular former governor, Jim Hunt, was again running.[26] If Hunt or another Democrat won in 1992, the retention model would reduce the risk of defeat of the Democratic appointees and of the current elected incumbents, all of whom were Democrats, given that incumbents were rarely defeated in retention elections. The requirement for legislative confirmation of future appointments would allow the Democratic-controlled legislature to block a Republican governor from making appointments that Democrats saw as too conservative.

It is noteworthy that two Republicans had won statewide judicial contests in 1988, the first two to do so during the twentieth century. Both had been appointed to their positions by the Republican governor, as discussed previously. Robert Orr won the election to retain his seat on the Court of Appeals. In addition, Howard Manning successfully retained his position on the trial-level superior court.[27] As already noted, the first Republican victory in a Supreme Court election would come in 1994, when Republicans won two seats, one by Judge Orr. In 2002, the last election prior to the first nonpartisan judicial elections in 2004, Republicans won both Supreme Court

22 See Jerry Shinn, "Let's Stop Electing Judges," *Charlotte Observer* (April 6, 1987), page ED.

23 Drennan, "Judicial Reform in North Carolina," *supra* note 14, 32.

24 See Report of the Judicial Selection Study Commission (February 15, 1989), https://ncleg.net/Library/studies/1989/st10579.pdf, accessed November 28, 2018. There was apparently no interest in a Missouri Plan system in the Commission, nor was there any significant interest in switching to a system of nonpartisan elections (see page 17).

25 John Drescher, "Appointment of Judges a Veto Rider," *Charlotte Observer* (June 22, 1990), 3D.

26 North Carolina governors are limited to two *consecutive* terms, not to two terms in total.

27 Foon Rhee, "GOP Gets Foothold in High Courts," *Charlotte Observer* (November 9, 1994), 13A. Actually, Orr had been appointed twice by Republican governor Martin. Orr was first appointed in early September 1986 to fill a vacancy on the court, but then lost to a Democrat in the November election; he was almost immediately appointed again in late November to fill another vacancy. See "Judge Reappointed to N.C. Court of Appeals," *Charlotte Observer* (November 26, 1986), 4B.

contests and four of five Court of Appeals elections, defeating incumbents in three of those elections and only losing a close election by 15,000 votes out of 2.1 million cast for one of the two open seats. While it would take a few more years to come to fruition, by 1990 the prospect that future voting trends might favor Republican judicial candidates was becoming increasingly evident.[28]

In a 1990 debate between candidates for chief justice of the North Carolina Supreme Court, both candidates advocated changing the method of judicial selection and retention. The incumbent, Democrat James Exum, expressed support for a Missouri Plan type system. Exum's Republican opponent, Wake County Superior Court judge Howard Manning, called for a change to nonpartisan elections. Interestingly, the Republican governor favored the system backed by Democrat Exum rather than nonpartisan elections. The governor also expressed the view that it would take statewide victories by Republican judicial candidates to convince the legislature to change the system of judicial selection and retention.[29] On this point, he would be proven prescient. The early 1990s saw continued efforts to put a constitutional amendment on the ballot to create a Missouri Plan system. In the 1991–1992 legislature, the Senate again passed the necessary legislation, but as before that legislation died in the House despite signs of support for such a change by some House Democrats.

One interesting development during this time was an effort by the Republican governor to, in essence, extend the term of his appointees. Under North Carolina law, judicial appointees are required to run for the office in the next even-numbered-year general election. By custom, the winner of that election served the remainder of the term of the person who had left the court. After Robert Orr won the 1988 Court of Appeals election, the Secretary of State issued a certificate of election providing that the election was for the unexpired term of office, meaning that Orr would have to stand again in 1992. However, in September 1991, the governor issued a commission to Orr stating that he was to serve a full eight years so that he would not have to stand again until 1996. When the State Board of Elections decided there would be no election for Orr's seat in 1992 and consequently refused to accept a notice of candidacy from a potential Democratic challenger, that challenger, Superior Court Judge Anthony Brannon, filed suit against the Board of Elections, demanding injunctive relief to force the Board to accept his notice of candidacy and schedule an election. Brannon's position was supported by statutory language that an appointment was only until the end of the original term.[30] The Board, joined by Orr and three other Court of Appeals judges, defended its position based on language in the state constitution

[28] Drennan, "Judicial Reform in North Carolina," *supra* note 14, 38–40.

[29] Greg Trevor, "N.C. Chief Justice Candidates Agree and Disagree," *Charlotte Observer* (October 24, 1990), 1B.

[30] North Carolina General Statutes, § 163–69.

that stated that judges "shall be elected . . . and shall hold office for terms of eight years,"[31] and argued that this provision meant that the statute was invalid. The trial court ruled in Brannon's favor, and the Board appealed to the North Carolina Supreme Court. The Supreme Court, in a decision written by Chief Justice Exum, upheld the trial court.[32] The result was that Brannon did contest the 1992 election against Orr, but Orr went on to win that election by less than 5,000 votes.[33]

In 1994, Chief Justice Exum appointed a commission to consider a range of issues concerning the North Carolina judicial system, including selection and retention. The Commission for the Future of North Carolina Courts, also known as the Medlin Commission after its chairman, was continued by Chief Justice Burley Mitchell, who succeeded Exum after the latter retired on January 1, 1996. The Commission's report, issued in December 1996, called for a Missouri Plan type system for judicial selection and retention for all major courts. State or circuit judicial councils, minus court official members of those councils, would serve as the nominating commission charged with submitting three names to the governor. These same bodies would make recommendations regarding retention, based on regular evaluations conducted for each judge.[34]

Something of a turning point was probably reached in 1994. Although Democrats had won every statewide election in 1992 except for the Court of Appeals seat held by Judge Orr, in 1994 Republicans took control of the lower chamber of the state legislature, winning 67 of the 120 seats (a gain of 25 seats compared to 1992) and won all four appellate-level judicial races. Republicans did not take control of the upper chamber, but came close with a gain of 13 seats, which left the chamber closely divided with 26 Democrats and 24 Republicans. Although the strong swing in North Carolina was probably part of the general Republican trend in 1994, the year that Republicans took control of the US Congress for the first time since 1952, it clearly foreshadowed what was to come. In 1996, Democrats held on to the governorship, won both Supreme Court elections and the one Court of Appeals election that year; Republicans maintained control of the lower chamber of the legislature.

Although Democrats would go on to regain control of the lower chambers in 1998 and hold both chambers and the governorship through 2010, the pattern was very different in statewide judicial elections. From 1998 through 2002, Republicans won all 6 Supreme Court elections and 6 of 14 Court of Appeals election. Also, in 1997, in a case that would pre-shadow *Republican Party of Minnesota v. White*,[35]

[31] North Carolina Constitution, Article IV, § 16.
[32] Brannon v. N.C. State Board of Elections, 331 N.C. 335, 416 S.E.2d 390 (N.C. 1992).
[33] "Judge Orr's Election Victory Certified," *Charlotte Observer* (November 25, 1992), 2C.
[34] "Without Favor, Denial or Delay: A Court System for the 21st Century," http://ncleg.net/Library/studies/1996/st12134.pdf, accessed August 13, 2017.
[35] 536 U.S. 765 (2002).

Federal District Judge Frank Bullock struck down North Carolina's limits on what judicial candidates could say during their campaigns.[36] Thus, although the Democrats continued to control the legislative and executive branches, it looked as though it might be time to find a way to undercut the Republican success in judicial elections.

The push from before 1980 through the latter part of the 1990s had been for a Missouri Plan system, or something similar, under which all judges would be appointed and then subject to periodic retention elections. Support came heavily from the legal profession, the bench, and editorial writers. Once a Republican won the governorship, there was support from Republican legislators, because retention elections would eliminate the risk of Democratic candidates defeating Republican appointees. With the growing success of Republicans in winning judicial elections, however, the landscape had changed. Republican legislators no longer saw gubernatorial appointment combined with retention elections as a means of protecting Republican appointees; if anything, that was now a system that would protect Democratic incumbents, and with the election of a Democrat to the governorship in 1996, elections, particularly partisan elections, were the mechanism for increasing the number of Republican judges.[37] Although some Democratic representatives had come to support a Missouri Plan type system, their support was still weak, possibly out of a concern that their constituents were not ready to give up competitive elections and/or that the current Democratic governor might be replaced by a Republican in the 2000 election.

ADOPTING NONPARTISAN ELECTIONS

Trial Courts

As discussed previously, there are two levels of trial courts in North Carolina, the superior court and the district court. The superior court handles all felony cases and civil cases exceeding a dollar threshold, currently $25,000. It also hears appeals of misdemeanor cases adjudicated in the district court. The district court hears family cases including divorce, child custody, and child support matters, and other civil cases involving less than the threshold for the superior court. Criminal matters less than felonies (misdemeanors and "infractions") go to the district court, at least initially; there are no juries in criminal cases in the district court but a defendant who is found guilty by the judge can appeal to the superior court and obtain a jury trial.

36 "Choosing Judges," *Charlotte Observer* (July 31, 1997), 10A.

37 See Jack Betts, "Going Nowhere Slowly – General Assembly Sidetracks the Court Reform Express," *Charlotte Observer* (June 2, 1997), 8A.

The political dynamics behind the shift to nonpartisan elections were very clear for the superior court but less clear for the district court. Consequently, I consider each separately starting with the superior court.[38]

Superior Court

Into the 1990s, superior court judges were nominated by primaries held in individual districts where the candidates were required to live, but then they were elected on statewide ballots.[39] Given the regional variation in North Carolina politics, this largely blocked Republicans from that court, because even if they lived in an area that tended to vote Republican, they were extremely unlikely to win statewide elections prior to 1990; as of 1992, only one Republican had been elected to the superior court during the twentieth century. Some aspects of the structure for staffing the superior courts were challenged in the mid-1980s in a lawsuit brought by the North Carolina Association of Black Lawyers , who alleged that the system of electing superior court judges violated the Voting Rights Act;[40] specifically, the system of voting was designed to dilute nonwhite voting strength and effectively served to accomplish that goal.[41] That case was resolved by a consent decree after the General Assembly adopted various changes that presumably mitigated the problems alleged in the suit;[42] however, the system of district nomination with statewide ballots was retained.

Because the legislature failed to end statewide ballots in the 1987 legislation, the Republican Party of North Carolina, represented by a prominent law firm, described by some as a "Republican law firm,"[43] brought a federal lawsuit challenging the use of statewide elections after district-based nominations through party primaries.[44] The suit alleged that the current "method of nomination and election [of superior court judges] contravenes the Fourteenth Amendment by diluting the votes of those who vote for Republican candidates and violates the First Amendment by restricting the rights of Republican voters to free speech and political association."[45] In response to a motion brought by the defendants, the Federal District Court dismissed the case,

38 The Missouri Plan proposals in the late 1980s and early 1990s originally included the trial courts. That proposal brought strong opposition from the Academy of Trial Lawyers (composed primarily of attorneys who represented criminal defendants and civil plaintiffs). Appointment of trial judges was also opposed by the Association of Black Attorneys, as well as the Association of Women's Attorneys. Trial court judges were dropped from the proposal. See Drennan, "Judicial Reform in North Carolina," *supra* note 14, 34–36.

39 This system had been in place since the 1870s; see Tracia Vance, "Superior Court Judges to Be Elected by District," *Wilmington Star-News* (November 4, 1994), 1A, 4A.

40 Drennan, "Judicial Reform in North Carolina," *supra* note 14, 29–31.

41 See Alexander v. Martin, No. 86–1048–CIV–5 (E.D.N.C. Nov. 25, 1987).

42 See State *ex rel.* Martin v. Preston, 325 N.C. 438, 385 S.E.2d 473 (1989).

43 Jeri Roe, "Election of Judges Remains Uncertain," *Greensboro News & Record* (July 27, 1996), B1.

44 Republican Party of North Carolina v. Martin, 980 F.2d 943 (4th Cir. 1992).

45 *Id.*, 949.

concluding that the complaint raised a nonjusticiable political issue. The Republican Party appealed the dismissal, and in 1992 the Fourth Circuit Court of Appeals reversed, ruling that the Republican Party's claim of political gerrymandering was justiciable.[46]

Two years later, a few days before the 1994 election, the Federal District Court for Eastern North Carolina issued a ruling ordering that superior court judges be elected based on the vote in their districts rather than statewide.[47] In the election the following week, Republicans won 5 of 8 contested superior court judgeships based on district-level results, as ordered by the federal court. Ironically, if the outcomes had been determined based on the statewide vote, Republicans would have won all 8 contests.[48]

The state went on to appeal the court decision ordering district-based elections for the superior court. Despite calls for legislation to implement the court order from both the Democratic governor and the Democratic chief justice, enough Democrats in the state assembly refused to go along to block passage. The suit dragged on and the plaintiff's legal fees, which under federal statutes would be payable by the defendants unless the defendants ultimately prevailed, continued to accumulate.[49] The lawsuit was finally resolved in 1996 when the Democrats who controlled the Senate agreed to a compromise with the Republicans who controlled the House, and both chambers passed S.B. 41 with a unanimous vote in the Senate and only two dissenters in the House.[50] Starting with the 1996 election, superior court elections would be district-based. However, in a move that probably was thought to protect Democratic incumbents, effective in 1998, party labels would be removed from the ballot.

District Court

Five years later, in 2001, the General Assembly changed district court elections from partisan to nonpartisan ballots, effective with the 2002 election. A bill to make this change was introduced in 1999 (S.B. 119) and passed the Senate only to be bottled up in the House. In the Senate, the final vote was 38–11. That vote was not on strict party lines but had strong party overtones with all but 2 of 34 Democrats voting in favor and a majority – 9 of 15 – Republicans voting against. Two years later the proposal to change to district court elections to a nonpartisan format passed on

[46] *Id.*, 961. The appeals court upheld the dismissal of the claim based on the First Amendment.
[47] Vance, "Superior Court Judges to Be Elected by District," *supra* note 39.
[48] Kathleen McClain, "Superior Court Adds 5 Republicans," *Charlotte Observer* (November 10, 1994), 8A.
[49] "It's Past Time to End Million Dollar Court Case," *Greensboro News & Record* (August 22, 1995), A8.
[50] Vote information is from the *Journal of the 1995 General Assembly of the State of North Carolina, Second Extra Session* 1996, p. 109 of the House journal and page 95 of the Senate journal, http://digital.ncdcr.gov/cdm/search/searchterm/North%20Carolina%20Digital%20State%20Documents!journals%20of%20the%20house%20and%20senate/field/relatig!relatig/mode/exact!exact/conn/and!and/order/date/page/11, both accessed August 16, 2017.

strongly partisan votes in both chambers. The final vote in the Senate was 32 to 12 with only 1 Democrat voting against and only 3 Republicans voting in favor. In the House, the vote was closer, given the closer division in party membership: 54 to 52; only 4 Democrats voted against and only 4 Republicans voted in favor.

I could find little that helped explain the politics behind the change to nonpartisan elections for the district courts at that time. One simple explanation is that many legislators might have felt that elections for the two levels of trial courts should have the same format. That is, if the superior court elections had to be nonpartisan, then the district court elections should also be nonpartisan. A more likely and more political explanation, endorsed by a person long active in North Carolina politics,[51] is the increasing success of Republican candidates in district court elections; switching to nonpartisan elections would protect Democratic incumbents by dampening Republican success in future elections. Information on district court elections is not readily available for years prior to 1996. For the three election years (1996, 1998, and 2000) immediately prior to the passage of the bill switching the district court elections to nonpartisan ballots, a large proportion of those elections were uncontested. The numbers contested were 36, 26, and 27 for the three years, respectively,[52] and Republicans won about the same percentage each year (41.7 percent, 43.5 percent, and 44.1 percent). Perhaps of most concern to Democrats in the legislature was that Republicans defeated Democrats in four or five of the district court elections each year while Democrats defeated Republicans in only one election each year.

Appellate Courts

One way Democrats sought to undercut Republican success in judicial elections at the turn of the millennium was to increase the number of Court of Appeals judgeships from 12 to 15. Although Democrats argued that the new positions were needed to deal with the appellate caseload, the judiciary had not asked for additional judges. Appropriate legislation was passed during the legislative session that ended in July 2000, with the new judges to take office after the first of the year. This was after the party primaries, which made it impossible for the three positions to be filled by election in November. As a result, in December 2000, Governor Hunt, who was to be succeeded by another Democrat, filled the positions by appointment. Under the legislation creating the positions, the new judges were to serve four years before having to stand for election. A Republican legislator filed suit, challenging both the creation of the positions and the length of the initial terms.[53] The North Carolina

51 Email from Gerry Cohen, November 27, 2018.

52 The number of elections in each of those years were 104, 87, and 118 respectively.

53 "Not So Fast, Supreme Court: Legislators Can't Bypass Constitution," *Charlotte Observer* (December 21, 2001), 18A.

Supreme Court, now dominated by Republicans, upheld the creation of the new positions, but ruled that the new judges would have to stand for election in 2002 rather than 2004.[54] The Court used the same logic as in *Brannon v. N.C. State Board of Elections,* when Democrats successfully challenged the term-length issue created by a Republican governor.

The election of another Democrat as governor made a system with gubernatorial appointment and retention elections attractive to Democratic legislators. In April 2001, the Senate approved a proposed constitutional amendment that would have appellate judges appointed by the governor, confirmed by the general assembly, and subject to retention elections. The vote on the bill proposing the amendment, which required a supermajority of 60 percent for passage, was 31–17, with 31 of 33 Democrats present in favor and all Republicans opposed. The proposed constitutional amendment failed to make it out of committee in the House, almost certainly because the bill could not garner the necessary 60 percent if it came to a vote of the full House.[55] Although Democrats had an overwhelming majority in the Senate (35 Democrats to 15 Republicans), the House was closely divided, with 62 Democrats to 58 Republicans.[56] This meant that to move the amendment to the ballot, at least 10 Republicans would have needed to vote in favor, an unlikely prospect.

Perhaps in anticipation of inaction by the House on the proposed constitutional amendment, the day after the Senate approved the amendment, a bill was introduced that was called the Judicial Campaign Reform Act (JCRA). When eventually signed into law eighteen months later, the JCRA provided for nonpartisan elections of appellate judges and made available public funding for judicial elections. Importantly, the change to nonpartisan elections did not require a constitutional amendment, because the state constitution only specified that all judges should be "elected by the qualified voters."[57] Consequently, the bill could be passed with the simple majorities held by Democrats in both chambers of the legislature. In 2002 the JCRA passed overwhelmingly in the Senate, 34–12,[58] with all Democrats voting in favor joined by two Republicans. The vote in the House was closer, 57 to 54, again with all Democrats in favor joined by a single Republican.

54 Pope v. Easley, 556 S.E.2d 265 (N.C. 2001).

55 The 60 percent (three-fifths) requirement was based not on those present and voting, but on the total membership; thus, support was needed from 30 members of the 50-member Senate and 72 members of 120-member House. See Drennan, "Judicial Reform in North Carolina," *supra* note 14, 37–38.

56 See "N.C. General Assembly Party Affiliations," www.ncleg.net/library/Documents/GAPartyAffiliations.pdf, accessed August 13, 2017.

57 North Carolina Constitution, Article IV, §16.

58 See www.ncleg.net/gascripts/BillLookUp/BillLookUp.pl?Session=2001&BillID=S1054&votesToView=all, accessed August 13, 2017. This was the final vote, concurring with the version passed by the House. The vote on the version sent to the House was 27–16 with all Republicans against joined by two Democrats.

The partisan motivations underlying JCRA seem clear. First, Democrats had been greatly outspending Republicans but still losing elections. The switch to public funding might mitigate this as well as assuaging public concerns about the influence of campaign contributions on judicial decisions. Given the growing success of Republicans in running for the appellate courts, getting the party label off the ballot could help Democratic candidates, and in fact the change did help, particularly in Supreme Court elections. Between 1994 and 2002, Democrats won only two of ten Supreme Court elections; between 2004 and 2014, the candidates aligned with the Democratic Party won 7 of 13 elections.[59] In Court of Appeals elections, Republicans won 9 of 18 elections between 1994 and 2002; between 2004 and 2014, there were 20 elections for the Court of Appeals. Two of these were uncontested and one involved a vacancy arising after the primary; the latter saw nineteen candidates compete in a plurality election. Of the other 17 elections, all but 2 showed moderate to strong partisan patterns and 13 reflected a Democratic-oriented pattern; only 2 reflected a Republican-oriented pattern. One of the two elections with no clear partisan pattern involved two candidates with Democratic credentials; in the other, the winner was the candidate with clear Republican credentials. Clearly, the switch to nonpartisan elections aided the candidates that the voters tended to associate in some way with the Democratic side of the partisan divide.

RETURNING TO PARTISAN JUDICIAL ELECTIONS

The political landscape changed when Republicans obtained control of all three branches of North Carolina's government in 2013. Republicans moved to consolidate their control and to handicap Democrats in future elections. With regard to the courts, the first step was taken in 2013. On August 6, the Republican governor signed a bill (S.B. 340) ending the public financing of judicial elections that had been established by JCRA.[60] The bill, which included many changes and clarifications regarding North Carolina elections, passed the House on a near party-line vote, all Republicans voting in favor and 43 of 53 Democrats voting against; Republicans in the Senate were also unanimously in favor and 11 of 13 Democrats voted against.[61]

As discussed previously, although party labels disappeared from North Carolina's judicial election ballots starting in 2004, partisanship never quite disappeared, at least in the voting patterns for the Supreme Court. As I showed in *Justices on the Ballot*, the partisan correlation (defined in our Chapter 1) did drop starting 2004.[62]

59 I determined which party a judge aligned with based on the partisan correlation (defined in Chapter 1).

60 The elimination of public funding applied to all elections, not just judicial elections.

61 See www.ncleg.net/gascripts/BillLookUp/BillLookUp.pl?Session=2013&BillID=S403&votesToView=all, accessed August 16, 2017.

62 Herbert M. Kritzer, *Justices on the Ballot: Continuity and Change in State Supreme Court Elections* (New York: Cambridge University Press, 2015), 184.

However, that drop was relatively modest; the average went from .947 prior to 2004 to .718 for the period 2004–2014.[63] Data were not available to compute partisan correlations for most years prior to 2004 for the Court of Appeals, but with the partisan ballot, it was certainly similar to that for the Supreme Court; in the 2004–2014 period, that correlation averaged .638. In many elections, it continued to be quite strong, exceeding .8 in seven of thirteen elections and dropping below .5 in only two elections. There were elections for four Supreme Court seats in 2014, which were the first elections after Republicans gained control of both the legislative and executive branch of state government. Democrats won three of those contests. The one Republican victory was for chief justice. The Republican candidate for chief justice, Mark Martin, who had been an associate justice on the Court since 1999, had been appointed chief justice only about three months before the November election. One of the Democratic victories was the defeat of the incumbent who had been appointed in August to fill the associate justice vacancy when Justice Martin was advanced to the chief justice's seat. The partisan correlations for the four 2014 elections were .676, .813, .919, and .942, with the lowest coming in the election won by the Republican. There were four Court of Appeals elections in 2014, one of which was uncontested by an incumbent with Republican leanings; another was the election to fill a last-minute vacancy and involved nineteen candidates. The other two were won by the Democratic-oriented candidate, with partisan correlations of .953 and .796.

The results of the 2014 North Carolina Supreme Court elections provided strong motivations for the Republican legislators and Republican governor to do something to protect the slim 4 to 3 majority that Republicans held on the Supreme Court. The lack of success in Court of Appeals elections was another motivation to do something to enhance the chances of Republicans in those elections. As the 2016 election approached, the Republican-controlled legislature sought to make some changes. Two bills dealing specifically with the Court of Appeals were passed by the legislature and signed into law by Republican governor Pat McCrory. A third bill that became law dealt specifically with the North Carolina Supreme Court.

The first bill, H.B. 8, was passed in 2015 and dealt specifically with just the Court of Appeals. As passed by the House of Representatives, H.B. 8 would have made all elections for judgeships partisan and would have brought back party primaries. However, the version passed by the Senate and signed into law after concurrence by the House was limited to the Court of Appeals, perhaps because there were four Court of Appeals seats up for election in 2016. The new law required that candidates for the Court of Appeals "at the time of filing the notice of candidacy . . . indicate on

[63] In the 35 elections between 1946 and 2002 with both Democratic and Republican candidates, the lowest partisan correlation was .854, and only 5 elections had a partisan correlation of less than .9.

the notice of candidacy the political party recognized under Article 9 of this Chapter with which that candidate is affiliated or any unaffiliated status."[64] The ballot for the Court of Appeals would then include this party affiliation information. If there were more than two candidates, a blanket primary – sometimes called a "jungle primary" – would be held in which all candidates regardless of party would run together;[65] with the top two candidates going on to the general election.[66]

The second bill concerning the Court of Appeals, S.B. 667, was passed at the end of June 2016 on a strict party-line vote.[67] Most of S.B. 667 dealt with various housekeeping functions, but Section 3 changed how the order of listing on the ballot was determined. Previously, the order in which candidates were listed on the ballot was decided randomly.[68] Section 3 specified:[69]

> Candidates registered with political parties that reflect at least five percent of statewide voter registration, according to the most recent statistical report published by the state board of elections, [be listed] in alphabetical order by party beginning with the party whose nominee for governor received the most votes in the most recent gubernatorial election and in alphabetical order within the party.

This change would favor candidates affiliated with the political party of the incumbent governor, who was a Republican at the time the bill was passed. Being listed first could increase a candidate's vote in a low-profile election such as those for most judgeships.[70] More specifically, the change favored a particular candidate running for an open seat. Administrative law judge Philip E. Berger Jr. (a Republican) was running against incumbent judge Linda Stephens (a Democrat). Prior to the bill's passage, election officials had done a random drawing with the result that Stephens would have appeared first; that changed with the new law so that Berger would appear first. Although it was Philip Berger *Junior* running for the Court of Appeals, Philip Berger *Senior* was the Republican leader in the North Carolina Senate, and

64 North Carolina House Bill 8, G.A. (N.C. 2015).

65 The only other state using this system for at least some judicial elections is Louisiana which adopted blanket primaries in 1977; see Kritzer, *Justices on the Ballot*, *supra* note 62, 40n.15.

66 See Mark Binker, "Bill Requires Court of Appeals Candidates to List Parties," WRAL (September 29, 2015), www.wral.com/bill-requires-court-of-appeals-candidates-to-list-parties/14935703/, accessed July 21, 2017.

67 North Carolina Senate Bill 667, G.A. (N.C. 2016); NCGA, *Roll Call for SB 667*, NCGA (June 2016), www.ncleg.net/gascripts/voteHistory/RollCallVoteTranscript.pl?sSession=2015&sChamber=H&RCS=1423, accessed July 21, 2017.

68 Michael Gordon, "Court Observer – Partisan Name Change Could Decide Court Race," *Charlotte Observer* (July, 2016), 5A.

69 Text of the bill is at www.ncleg.net/Sessions/2015/Bills/Senate/PDF/S667v4.pdf, accessed July 21, 2017.

70 Jonathan G. S. Koppell and Jennifer A. Steen, "The Effects of Ballot Position on Election Outcomes," *Journal of Politics* 66, no. 1 (2004), 267–281; David Brockington, "A Low Information Theory of Ballot Position Effect," *Political Behavior* 25, no. 1 (2003), 1–27; or Marc Meredith and Yuval Salant, "On the Causes and Consequences of Ballot Order Effects," *Political Behavior* 35, no. 1 (2013), 175–197.

was described by some as "North Carolina's most powerful politician."[71] Berger Jr. won what turned out to be a close election, with a margin of about 22,000 votes out of close to 4.5 million cast.[72] However, as discussed later in the chapter, the change in ballot order for the Court of Appeals, combined with the listing of party affiliations in the four Court of Appeals contests, may have led to unexpected effects in the election for the North Carolina Supreme Court.

The two changes to the Court of Appeals elections were clearly intended to benefit Republican candidates. That is arguably also true for an attempted change in the nature of elections for retention of North Carolina Supreme Court justices. Going into the 2016 election, the North Carolina Supreme Court was closely divided, with four Republican-oriented justices and three Democratic-oriented justices. Given the Republican control of the legislature and governorship, and the expected continued Republican control, it was important to the Republican-dominated branches of North Carolina's government to maintain Republican control of the Supreme Court. To accomplish this, the Republicans in the legislature opted to switch from nonpartisan elections to a retention election format in which an elected incumbent would not face any opponent; the voters would be given the option of voting yes or no on the question of whether the incumbent should be retained in office, and nonpartisan elections were to be continued for open seats.[73] The change was signed into law on June 11 by Governor McCrory, which was four days after the nonpartisan primary on June 7.

Only one justice, Robert Edmunds, was up for reelection in 2016. Edmunds had run for the Court in 2000, when the elections still used a partisan ballot, as a Republican. In that election, he defeated a Democratic incumbent who had been appointed to fill a vacancy in August 1999. Edmunds had been reelected in 2008, but the election was close; he received just 51 percent of the vote. Although Edmunds had solid credentials as a Republican, it is likely that the closeness of the 2008 election was worrisome to Republican leaders, and a retention-type election would all but guarantee his continuance in office. However, the shift to the retention format brought a legal challenge asserting that the change violated the state's constitution. The defendant in the suit was the State Board of Elections.[74]

71 Emily Cadei, "North Carolina's Most Powerful Politician Paints the State Red," *The Daily Dose* (May 13, 2015), www.ozy.com/provocateurs/north-carolinas most-powerful-politician-paints-the-state-red/40942, accessed July 21, 2017; Michael Gordon, "GOP Headed Toward 5-Seat Sweep in State Appeal Court Races," *Raleigh News & Observer* (November 8, 2016), www.newsobserver.com/news/politics-government/election/article113431613.html, accessed July 24, 2017.

72 See https://ballotpedia.org/Phil_Berger_Jr., accessed July 21, 2017.

73 North Carolina House Bill 222, G.A. (2015); under the bill appointed incumbents would initially stand in nonpartisan elections, with subsequent terms won through retention elections.

74 Faires v. State Board of Elections, 2016 WL 865472 (N.C. Super., March 4, 2016).

The North Carolina Constitution specifies:[75]

> Justices of the Supreme Court, Judges of the Court of Appeals, and regular Judges of the Superior Court *shall be elected* by the qualified voters and shall hold office for terms of eight years and until their successors are elected and qualified. Justices of the Supreme Court and Judges of the Court of Appeals *shall be elected* by the qualified voters of the State. Regular Judges of the Superior Court *may be elected* by the qualified voters of the State or by the voters of their respective districts, as the General Assembly may prescribe [emphases added].

The key question presented in the challenge was whether the proposed retention format constituted an "election" in the sense used in the constitutional provision. A second question was whether the statute created a qualification beyond that which was in the constitution ("authorized to practice law" in North Carolina, qualified to vote, age 21, and not otherwise disqualified from holding office);[76] to wit, a candidate had to be an incumbent. The Board of Elections sought to have the case dismissed on the grounds that the plaintiff lacked standing. The Board also asserted that if an incumbent judge were to lose the retention election, there would follow an open election in which the candidates would not be sitting judges.[77]

Under North Carolina law, constitutional challenges are heard by a three-judge superior court panel. Two of the three judges who heard the case were appointed by the then current Republican governor. The third member of the panel had been elected to the North Carolina district court as a Republican prior to being elected to the superior court on a nonpartisan ballot and had previously served as United States Attorney for the Middle District of North Carolina during President George W. Bush's administration. Thus, the challenge to the Republican-desired legislation was heard by three judges with Republican credentials.

The three-judge panel unanimously granted the plaintiff's motion for summary judgment, effectively striking down the legislature's attempt to switch to retention elections. The Board of Elections appealed to the North Carolina Supreme Court. Because of the obvious conflict of interest, Justice Edmunds recused himself from the appeal. The result was a 3–3 vote, along party lines, leaving the superior court's decision in place.[78] That meant that the 2016 North Carolina Supreme Court election would be on a nonpartisan basis.

75 North Carolina Constitution, Article IV, §16 (emphasis added).

76 North Carolina Constitution, Articles IV, § 22 and VI, §§ 6 and 8.

77 Sharon McCloskey, "Challenge to Supreme Court Retention Elections Set for Argument Tuesday (UPDATED)," NC policywatch (February 16, 2016), www.ncpolicywatch.com/2016/02/16/challenge-to-supreme-court-retention-elections-set-for-argument-tuesday/

78 As is discussed in Chapter 5, this contrasts with what happened in the 1970s in Tennessee after the legislature adopted a Missouri Plan for its appellate courts. The Tennessee Supreme Court upheld the constitutionality of the change even though the language of the state constitution calls for all state judges to be "elected by the qualified voters;" see State *ex rel.* Higgins v. Dunn, 496 S.W.2d 480 (Tenn. 1973)). It was upheld a second time after the legislature reinstated the plan for the Tennessee Supreme Court; see State *ex rel.* Hooker v. Thompson, 249 S.W.3d 331

Justice Edmunds was opposed in the November 2016 election by Superior Court Judge Michael Morgan, who had come in second in the four-candidate June 7 primary that had occurred before legislature had passed the law changing the format for Supreme Court elections. Morgan, an African American, had previously won elections to the district court as a Democrat. Although Edmunds had easily come in first in the primary, winning 48.0 percent of the vote to 34.4 percent for Morgan, Morgan won the general election, garnering 54.5 percent of the vote.

An interesting question is why Morgan did so well. Donald Trump won North Carolina by 3.6 percentage points (49.8 percent to 46.2 percent for Hillary Clinton) and Democrat Roy Cooper's defeat of Pat McCrory in the gubernatorial election was by a hair's breadth, less than 10,000 votes (49.0 percent to 48.8 percent). A likely explanation for Morgan's victory relates back to the legislation that changed the ballot order for candidates to the Court of Appeals and added party affiliation to the ballot for those candidates who were required to declare party affiliations. Because of those changes, in the five statewide Court of Appeals elections, the Republican candidates were listed first with the candidates' party affiliations indicated on the ballot. The random draw for the Supreme Court election put Morgan's name first.[79] This might have produced confusion at the polls with voters thinking that first-listed Morgan was the Republican candidate on the Supreme Court ballot; the order also gave him any advantage that comes with being listed first on ballots for obscure offices.

With the defeat of both Governor McCrory and Justice Edmunds, Republicans in the legislature were concerned about future decisions of the North Carolina Supreme Court. One possibility was to increase the size of the court to nine justices before the new Democratic governor took office, in order that outgoing Governor McCrory could fill those new positions and thus change the 4 to 3 advantage of Democrats to a 5 to 4 advantage for Republicans. Even discussion of such a plan produced a backlash, with Common Cause spending about $200,000 airing a television ad opposing the Republican's "court-packing" plan,[80] along with threats of lawsuits if such a plan were passed.[81] However, although the Supreme Court was to stay at seven members, the lame-duck legislature and governor did enact

(Tenn. 1996). For a discussion of litigation over what was referred to as the Tennessee Plan, see Brian T. Fitzpatrick, "Election as Appointment: The Tennessee Plan Reconsidered," *Tennessee Law Review* 75, no. 3 (2008), 486–490.

79 See John Hood, "Spotlight Now Turns to State Courts," *Roxboro Courier-Times* (December 31, 2016).

80 See Craig Jarvis, "Common Cause Ad Opposes 'Court Packing,'" *Charlotte Observer* (December 12, 2016), www.charlotteobserver.com/news/politics-government/article120370743.html, accessed July 14, 2017.

81 Colin Campbell, "NAACP Will Sue If Republicans Pursue 'Court Packing' of Supreme Court, Barber Says," *Raleigh News & Observer* (November 18, 2016), www.newsobserver.com/news/politics-government/politics-columns-blogs/under-the-dome/article115717423.html, accessed July 24, 2017.

legislation that changed both Court of Appeals and Supreme Court elections to partisan ballots, starting in 2018.

The 2016 election also produced the narrow defeat of the Republican incumbent governor, Pat McCrory. However, Republicans maintained a veto-proof majority in both chambers of the state legislature. Using this power, in 2017 the Republican legislature passed a bill that made elections for both levels of trial courts partisan contests with party primaries. The bill passed on near party-line votes, but was then vetoed by the Democratic governor Roy Cooper, which forced the legislature to override the veto, again on near party-line votes.

Although the Republicans backed off from the idea of increasing the size of the Supreme Court to allow the outgoing Republican governor to appoint two justices, the Republican-dominated legislature did approve a change to the Court of Appeals that had something of that effect for that court. H.B. 239, enacted over the governor's veto, reduced the number of judges on the statewide Court of Appeals from 15 to 12. The change was justified on the grounds of a decreasing caseload. Filings had in fact dropped by about 13 percent in 2013–2016, compared to 2006–2012,[82] but not enough to justify reducing the court size by 20 percent. The effect of this change was to prevent the new Democratic governor from appointing anyone to the Court of Appeals until four judges had departed the court. As the legislation was being considered, it was anticipated that one judge, Douglas McCullough, who was a registered Republican, would have to step down in May when he reached the mandatory retirement age, and the legislation would block the governor from filling that position. However, in the interregnum between the governor's veto of H.B. 239 and the legislature's override of that veto, Judge McCullough resigned, allowing the governor to immediately appoint a successor, John Arrowood. Arrowood, a registered Democrat and openly gay, had previously served as a trial judge and a Court of Appeals judge.[83] McCullough explained his decision to step down: "I did not want my legacy to be the elimination of a seat and the impairment of a court that I have served on."[84]

[82] See Chart of Court of Appeals caseload from 2006–2017, found at NC Policy watch, Melissa Boughton, "An In-Depth Look at N.C. Lawmakers' Attempt to Shrink the Court of Appeals," NC Policy Watch (March 16, 2017). www.ncpolicywatch.com/2017/03/16/depth-look-n-c-lawmakers-attempt-shrink-court-appeals/

[83] Melissa Boughton, "Court of Appeals Judge Resigns in Reaction to Bill Shrinking Bench; Cooper Appoints New Judge in Wake of Veto," NC Policy Watch (April 24, 2017), pulse.ncpolicywatch.org/2017/04/24/court-appeals-judge-resigns-reaction-bill-shrinking-bench-cooper-appoints-new-judge-wake-veto/#sthash.yJGoF6vz.qoEL8gHT.dpbs. Arrowood had been appointed to a vacancy on the Court of Appeals in 2007 by Democratic governor Mike Easley but was then defeated when he stood for election by a Republican in 2008.

[84] Anne Blythe and Mark Binker, "Cooper Appoints Democrat to Fill NC Appeals Court Seat after GOP Judge Makes Surprise Early Retirement," *Raleigh News & Observer* (April 24, 2017), www.newsobserver.com/news/politics-government/politics-columns-blogs/under-the-dome/article146378394.html, accessed August 8, 2017.

A third bill that had been introduced but not passed by the time of the veto of H.B. 239 would have blocked the governor from appointing John Arrowood to the McCullough vacancy. Governor Cooper could make that appointment because under North Carolina law, the governor is free to appoint any person with the required qualifications to fill a judicial vacancy at the trial or appellate level. H.B. 335 would limit whom the governor could appoint to such vacancies by requiring that any vacancy must be filled by a person sharing the party affiliation of the outgoing judge or justice. H.B. 335 passed the House in April 2017 with all Republicans but only one Democrat voting in favor of the bill, but it was not acted upon by the Senate.[85]

The Republican-controlled legislature did make one other change in 2017. Given that a Democrat had most recently won the gubernatorial election, the provision calling for candidates of the governor's party being listed first on the ballot would mean that the Democrats would come first and enjoy whatever advantage there might be from being toward the top of the ballot. To remedy this problem, legislation was passed calling for candidates to be listed in alphabetical order, with the starting letter determined by a random draw conducted by the State Board of Elections and Ethics Enforcement; this meant that if the letter k was drawn, the ordering would be k to z, followed then by a to j. Separate drawings were to be held for the primary and general elections.

As the 2017 legislative session was winding down, Mark Martin, the Republican chief justice of the North Carolina Supreme Court, told the attendees at the annual meeting of the North Carolina Bar Association that the state should "step away from ordinary politics and let the people decide whether our judges should be chosen through a merit selection process rather than partisan elections." He called for the General Assembly to place a constitutional amendment on the ballot that would allow the voters to decide whether to adopt a Missouri Plan system. After his speech, Martin told reporters, "When it comes to the courts, we need to say, 'Let's keep the politics over in the executive and legislative branches and let's get our judges focused on the constitution and the law.'"[86] Nothing was to come from Martin's advocacy.

In anticipation of the 2018 Supreme Court election, the legislature canceled any primary for that election and for the three elections for the Court of Appeals.[87] This meant that there could be more than one candidate for a party on the ballots for those elections and the winners would be the candidates in each contest who

[85] This was part of efforts to diminish the governor's power to appoint judges; those efforts came under attack from the five living ex-governors, two of whom were Republicans. See David Zucchino and Richard Fausset, "Federal Court Declared a Congressional Map Unfair," *New York Times* (August 29, 2018), A13.

[86] Mark Barrett, "Chief Justice Pushes Merit Selection of NC Judges in Asheville," *Ashville Citizen Times* (June 24, 2017), www.citizen-times.com/story/news/local/2017/06/24/chief-justice-pushes-merit-selection-nc-judges-here/426174001/, accessed April 24, 2019.

[87] Zucchino and Fausset, "Federal Court Declared a Congressional Map Unfair," *supra* note 85.

received the most votes. This was intended to help the Republican incumbent in the one Supreme Court election. The probable thinking was that there would be multiple Democrats challenging that Republican incumbent and this would split the Democratic vote across the multiple Democrats running to the incumbent's advantage. As things would have it, in June it looked as though there would be only a Democratic challenger, Anita Earls, running against Republican incumbent Barbara Jackson for the Supreme Court. When the drawing was done in February to determine which letter would be first for setting the order of listing on the ballot, the letter that came up was f. Under the existing legislation, a second drawing would be done prior to the general election. However, in mid-June the Republicans in the legislature pushed through a provision that eliminated the second drawing, which meant that candidates whose names started with e would be listed last on the ballot. This result was that Republican Jackson would be listed first and the Democrat Earls would be last.[88]

Then, on the last filing day, a third candidate entered the race. Chris Anglin filed to run as a Republican. Anglin had changed his party registration from Democrat to Republican in early June that year.[89] Republicans were not happy, and the legislature responded by passing a bill that would allow listing of a candidate's party affiliation on the ballot only if the "candidates' party affiliation or unaffiliated status is the same as on their voter registration at the time they filed to run for office and 90 days prior to that filing."[90] This provision applied only to candidates for judicial office. In early August, a trial court judge ordered that no ballots be printed, pending the outcome of a challenge to the law brought by Anglin;[91] the challenge was successful,[92] and the election went forward with two Republicans and one Democrat on the ballot.[93] Democrat Earls won the Supreme Court election, receiving just under 50 percent of the vote. In addition, Democrats won all three Court of Appeals elections: one involved a Democratic incumbent against a single Republican

[88] "How a Small Change in the Law Could Have a Big Impact on NC's Supreme Court Race," WBTV.com (July 6, 2018), www.wbtv.com/story/38588010/how-a-small-change-in-the-law-could-have-a-big-impact-on-ncs-supreme-court-race, accessed August 7, 2018.

[89] "Late Candidacy Could Help Democrats Win N.C. Supreme Court Race," *Winston-Salem Journal* (July 5, 2018), www.journalnow.com/news/elections/state/late-candidacy-could-help-democrats-win-n-c-supreme-court/article_458f25af-7304-5210-b5d3-1fa3db655a8c.html, accessed August 7, 2018.

[90] Will Doran and Colin Campbell, "Why Don't Republicans Want Voters to Know This Supreme Court Candidate Is a Republican?" *Raleigh News & Observer* (July 24, 2018), www.newsobserver.com/news/politics-government/article215443760.html, accessed August 7, 2018.

[91] Will Doran, "Judge Hands NC Legislators a Temporary Loss in Lawsuits over Political Labels," *Raleigh News & Observer* (August 6, 2018), www.newsobserver.com/news/politics-government/article216187915.html, accessed August 7, 2018.

[92] Anglin v. Burger, 18-CVS-9748 (Wake County, NC Superior Court, August 13, 2018), http://ballot-access.org/wp-content/uploads/2018/08/18CVS9748-Christopher-J.-Anglin_Order-on-PI.pdf, accessed July 19, 2019.

[93] WFAE, "Democrats Pick Up Seats on NC Supreme Court, Appeals Court," www.wfae.org/post/democrats-pick-seats-nc-supreme-court-appeals-court#stream/0, accessed November 8, 2018.

challenger, one involved an open seat contested by one Democrat and two Republicans, and one involved an open seat with a Democrat, a Republican, and a Libertarian.[94]

Finally, unhappy with not being able to block Democratic governor Roy Cooper's judicial appointments, the legislature in June 2018 voted to submit a constitutional amendment giving the "legislators more say over who can fill judicial vacancies,"[95] by creating a pseudo-merit selection system. The proposed selection commission would forward its evaluation of all candidates for a judicial vacancy to the General Assembly. The General Assembly would then send to the governor two or more of the nominees deemed qualified by the commission. The governor would have ten days to make an appointment from the forwarded nominees, and if no appointment was made, the General Assembly would choose the nominee to fill the position, specifically requiring Senate confirmation of "all officers whose appointments are not otherwise provided for" in the state constitution.[96] This would include appointments to fill judicial vacancies.[97] If the amendment passed, the General Assembly would effectively control judicial appointments.[98] The Democratic governor sued unsuccessfully in an effort to keep the amendment off the ballot.[99] He was joined by the five living former governors, both Republicans and Democrats. A political action committee, Stop Deceptive Amendments, spent $7.7 million in opposing that amendment and several others.[100] Opposition also came from the Koch-backed group Americans for Prosperity, which labeled the amendment a "backdoor effort that would lead to manipulation and cronyism in an institution that must remain fair, independent and impartial."[101] Voters rejected the amendment 2 to 1.[102]

[94] Will Doran, "Democrat Anita Earls Claims Victory in NC Supreme Court Race, *Raleigh News & Observer* (November 7, 2018), www.newsobserver.com/news/politics-government/article221037190.htm, accessed November 9, 2018.

[95] "Late Candidacy Could Help Democrats Win N.C. Supreme Court Race," *Winston-Salem Journal* (July 5, 2018).

[96] See www.ncleg.net/Sessions/2017/Bills/House/PDF/H913v4.pdf, accessed August 7, 2018.

[97] See www.ncleg.net/EnactedLegislation/SessionLaws/HTML/2017-2018/SL2018-118.html, accessed November 9, 2018.

[98] "Judicial Vacancy Amendment Heading to North Carolina Voters," Associated Press Wire (June 28, 2018).

[99] Cooper v. Burger, 18 CVS 9805 (Wake County, NC Superior Court, August 21, 2018); see also, "Cooper Loses at Supreme Court; Amendments on Ballot," *Bladen Journal* (September 5, 2018).

[100] Lynn Bonner, "NC Voters Reject Constitutional Amendments Limiting Governor's Power; 4 Others Pass," *Ralley News & Observer* (November 7, 2018), www.newsobserver.com/news/politics-government/article221039145.html, accessed November 9, 2018.

[101] Craig Jarvis, "A Koch-Backed Group Comes Out Against a GOP-Written Constitutional Amendment," *Raleigh News & Observer* (October 15, 2018), www.newsobserver.com/news/politics-government/article220022910.html, accessed November 9, 2018.

[102] See https://er.ncsbe.gov/?election_dt=11/06/2018&county_id=0&office=REF&contest=0, accessed November 9, 2018.

CONCLUSION

In North Carolina, both Democrats and Republicans have manipulated the system of judicial selection and retention for their party's advantage. Although one can come up with justifications other than partisan advantage for the changes attempted and made during the early 2000s and between 2015 and 2017, the substance, timing, and patterns of voting by legislators make clear that the goal was one of political advantage. Democrats controlling the state government in the first of these two periods saw Republicans starting to win statewide judicial elections as well as elections within districts where the Republican Party was strong. Democrats saw the presence of the label "Republican" on the ballot as assisting Republican candidates in both winning open-seat judicial elections and defeating Democratic incumbents. Eliminating party labels would protect some Democratic incumbents and thereby slow down gains by Republican judicial candidates. Once Republicans secured control of the two nonjudicial branches of North Carolina state government about a decade later, they sought to advance Republican control of the state judiciary by reverting to partisan judicial ballots, thus undoing the Democratic strategy of protecting Democratic judges through nonpartisan elections.

This is not to say that the other justifications for partisan ballots advanced by Republicans are nonsensical. For example, Republicans argued that the switch to partisan elections would help voters and increase participation by providing partisan information on the ballot. Evidence is clear that participation, as measured by what is called roll-off, is higher in partisan judicial elections. "Roll-off" refers to the pattern whereby voters cast votes for offices at the top of the ballot, such as president, governor, and/or Congress, but do not bother to vote in "down-ballot" elections;[103] some of that decreased roll-off can result from the presence of a straight-ticket voting option that encompasses partisan judicial elections.[104] There is also evidence that the influence of interest groups and the impact of negative advertising is less when a partisan ballot is used.[105] And I have argued elsewhere that for these and other reasons, if elections are going to be used to select and/or retain judges, it is better to provide voters with information that they are going to use, which is what a partisan

[103] See Matthew J. Streb, Brian Frederick, and Casey LaFrance, "Voter Rolloff in a Low-Information Context: Evidence from Intermediate Appellate Court Elections," *American Politics Research* 37, no. 4 (July 1, 2009), 644–669; Christopher Shortell, "Voting in Trial Court Elections: Ballot Roll-Off in Partisan, Nonpartisan, and Retention Elections in High-Population Counties," *Justice System Journal* 34, no. 2 (2013), 153–170.

[104] Herbert M. Kritzer, "Roll-Off in State Court Elections: The Impact of the Straight-Ticket Voting Option," *Journal of Law and Courts* 4, no. 2 (2016), 409–435; Chris W. Bonneau and Eric Loepp, "Getting Things Straight: The Effects of Ballot Design and Electoral Structure on Voter Participation," *Electoral Studies* 34 (2014), 119–130.

[105] See Melinda Gann Hall, *Attacking Judges: How Campaign Advertising Influences State Supreme Court Elections* (Stanford, CA: Stanford University Press, 2014), 110–113.

ballot provides.[106] However, even with these arguments, one would have to be naïve to believe that Republicans sought to change the format of judicial elections in North Carolina during this period for reasons other than political advantage.

Although the goal of both parties was one of political advantage, the results of elections after the changes show that the manipulations did not always achieve that goal. At best, Democrats may have slowed down the increase in Republican judges. As evidenced by North Carolina Supreme Court elections in 2016 and 2018, the various manipulations by the Republican legislature backfired, producing a Democratic majority on the court.

[106] Kritzer, *Justices on the Ballot*, *supra* note 62, 261–264.

3

Arkansas

Third Time Was the Charm

Arkansas switched from partisan to nonpartisan elections starting in 2002, the same year North Carolina began using nonpartisan elections for its lower trial courts and two years before it made the change for its appellate courts. Given the similar timing and that both North Carolina and Arkansas are in the group of states that Bullock and Rozell labels the "rim South states,"[1] one might expect the dynamics of the changes in the two states to have been similar. Although partisan politics played a role in both states, the political factors themselves were quite different. This reflects both some differences in the political structures in the two states and differences in when the two states' Republican parties began to have substantial influence in state politics, which included achieving significant success in judicial elections.

For a period of 125 years, the structure of the Arkansas court system was governed largely by a constitution that came into effect in 1874. Various amendments affecting the courts were adopted over the years, including one increasing the size of the Arkansas Supreme Court (Amendment 9, passed in 1924) and one authorizing the Arkansas General Assembly to create an intermediate Court of Appeals (Amendment 58, adopted in 1978).[2] By the middle of the twentieth century, Arkansas had a complex system of courts. At the trial level, there were still separate courts of equity and courts of law, although in some counties the same judge covered both courts.[3] Moreover, there were "six distinct types of minor courts, each of which was presided over by various city and county officials,"[4] most of whom

[1] Charles S. Bullock III and Mark J. Rozell, eds., *The New Politics of the Old South: An Introduction to Southern Politics*, 6th ed. (Lanham, MD: Rowman & Littlefield, 2018).

[2] William D. Schreckhise and Janine Alisa Parry, "Arkansas," in Herbert M. Kritzer, ed., *Legal Systems of the World: A Political, Social, and Cultural Encyclopedia*, vol. 1 (Santa Barbara, CA: ABC-CLIO, 2002), 75.

[3] Diane D. Blair and Jay Barth, *Arkansas Politics and Government*, 2nd ed. (Lincoln: University of Nebraska Press, 2005), 228.

[4] *Id.*, 74.

were not trained in law. These minor courts handled, among other things, juvenile cases, disputed paternity cases, and other types of minor civil cases. By the 1960s, it was clear to state leaders that the judicial system, and the constitution in its entirety, was ripe for a major overhaul.

In 1970 and again in 1980, proposals for a revised constitution were submitted to the electorate.[5] Both proposals were defeated, 57–43 in 1970 and 63–37 in 1980. These proposed constitutions would have made substantial changes to the courts, including – most important for our purposes here – changes in how judges would be selected and retained. Specifically, these proposals would have ended partisan elections that had been in use since the adoption of the 1874 constitution.[6] That constitution simply stated that judges "shall be elected by the qualified electors."[7] Although that language did not specifically state that elections should be partisan, that became the norm, and it was effectively institutionalized when Arkansas adopted the Australian (preprinted, official) ballot in 1891.[8]

JUDICIAL ELECTIONS IN ARKANSAS: HISTORICAL PERSPECTIVES

A Primer on Arkansas Politics

V. O. Key's capsule summary of Arkansas politics in the first half of the twentieth century was that it was "pure one-party politics."[9] This is traceable to election changes made in the 1890s: the adoption of the secret ballot and the poll tax.[10] By 1900, Republicans virtually disappeared from state offices in Arkansas. Between 1900 and 1978, there were never more than 5 Republicans in the 100-member Arkansas House of Representatives and never more than one in the 35-member

5 For a general discussion of the chronology of changes to judicial election methods in Arkansas dating back to 1836, see Mark Nabors and J. R. Baxter, "The Evolution of Judicial Selection in Arkansas: External and Internal Explanations of Change and Potential Future Directions," *Midsouth Political Science Review* 17 (2016), 83–113, http://uca.edu/politicalscience/files/2016/11/MPSR-Vol-17-2016-Nabors-and-Baxter.pdf, accessed May 23, 2018.

6 Prior to 1874, Arkansas had used a range of methods for selecting judges: legislative elections, "election by the people," and, for the chief justice, gubernatorial appointment. See www.judicialselection.us/judicial_selection/reform_efforts/formal_changes_since_inception.cfm?state=AR, accessed May 8, 2018.

7 Arkansas Constitution of 1874, Article 7, §§6, 17, 29, and 38.

8 See "Election Law of 1891," *Encyclopedia of Arkansas History & Culture*, www.encyclopediaofarkansas.net/encyclopedia/entry-detail.aspx?entryID=4033, accessed May 8, 2018. Arguably, the adoption of the Australian ballot served to facilitate the Democratic Party's white primary rule, which was adopted in Arkansas in 1906; see "African Americans," *Encyclopedia of Arkansas History & Culture*, www.encyclopediaofarkansas.net/encyclopedia/entry-detail.aspx?entryID=407, accessed May 8, 2018.

9 V. O. Key Jr., *Southern Politics in State and Nation* (New York: Alfred Knopf, 1949), 183. See Blair and Barth, *Arkansas Politics and Government, supra* note 3, 35–115, for an extensive treatment of Arkansas politics in the second half of the twentieth century.

10 See Chris M. Branam, "Another Look at Disfranchisement in Arkansas, 1888–1894, *Arkansas Historical Quarterly* 69, no. 3 (Autumn 2010), 253.

Arkansas Senate. Once during this period, a Republican did win the gubernatorial election – Winthrop Rockefeller – in 1966. Republicans began winning more seats in the General Assembly in the 1980s, but through the first decade of the current century they continued to be a distinct minority, holding roughly a quarter of the seats in the Assembly.[11] During this time, Republicans running for statewide office had more success. In 1980, Republican Frank White defeated incumbent governor Bill Clinton, but then lost to Clinton in the 1982 rematch. Republican Mike Huckabee won a close (51–49) special election for lieutenant governor in 1993 after the position became vacant when the incumbent lieutenant governor,[12] Jim Guy Tucker, succeeded Bill Clinton as governor after Clinton became president; Tucker won reelection in 1994 with almost 60 percent of the vote. In 1996, Huckabee succeeded to the governorship when Tucker had to resign after being convicted of mail fraud; he won election to the office in November of that year and reelection in 1998 and 2002. In 1996, Tim Hutchinson won one of Arkansas's seats in the US Senate in 1996 to become the first Republican from Arkansas to serve in the Senate since the 1870s.[13]

Prior to 1950, the politics of the Democratic Party was marked by the absence of strong continuing factions, clear sets of issues motivating such factions, or "dominating personalities."[14] Politics in the state was largely a matter of local interests and winning the support of local party leaders, who in some locales controlled party machines. Arguably, this changed in the 1950s with the Supreme Court's decision in *Brown v. Board of Education of Topeka*. This led to the desegregation crisis in Little Rock when the then governor Orval Faubus called out the Arkansas National Guard to block African American students from entering Little Rock High School under a desegregation plan that had been ordered by the Federal District Court. This led to President Dwight Eisenhower federalizing the National Guard and then dispatching 1,000 members of the 101st Airborne Division to maintain order.[15] Faubus was ultimately elected to six two-year terms and served from January 1955 until January 1967.

The election of Republican Winthrop Rockefeller in 1966 marked a change in Democratic politics in Arkansas. Rockefeller, although a Republican, was a

[11] Much of the success during the last decades of the twentieth century had a regional basis; Republicans had success in the Ozark region in northwest Arkansas. This was an area with strong in-migration, both of retirees and of persons coming to work at the large corporate headquarters of Walmart and Tyson Foods. See Blair and Barth, *Arkansas Politics and Government*, *supra* note 3, 82–84.

[12] Huckabee had run against incumbent senator Dale Bumpers in 1992, but garnered only 40 percent of the vote.

[13] See "Political Party Strength in Arkansas," https://en.wikipedia.org/wiki/Political_party_strength_in_Arkansas, accessed May 9, 2018.

[14] Key, *Southern Politics*, *supra* note 9, 195.

[15] Anthony Lewis, "President Sends Troops to Little Rock, Federalizes Arkansas National Guard; Tells Nation He Acted to Avoid an Anarchy," *New York Times* (September 25, 1957), 1.

progressive in the context of Arkansas politics. The Democratic governors who succeeded Rockefeller brought a more progressive style than had Faubus. Actually, Faubus himself shifted slightly in a progressive direction, and, as discussed later in the chapter, played a role in trying to initiate the modernization of the Arkansas court system. It was also about this time that the percentage of Arkansans identifying with the Republican Party began to increase, and this continued through the remainder of the twentieth century. In 1966, less than 10 percent called themselves Republicans and 58 percent called themselves Democrats. By the turn of the century, about a third of Arkansans said they were Republicans and the percentage identifying as Democrats had dropped to 43 percent.[16] This shift reflected a combination of substantial in-migration of persons who viewed themselves as Republicans,[17] generational turnover, and individual conversion.[18]

Even with an increasing proportion of the electorate identifying as Republican, the Republican Party of Arkansas faced significant difficulties in its operation. Until 1995, party primaries in Arkansas were the responsibility of the parties, not the state. This meant that the parties had to organize the primaries and cover all the expenses of running them. This extended to the requirement that the parties locate and, if necessary, rent space for the primaries. To cover these costs, the parties, rather than the state, collected filing fees from the candidates; The parties themselves set the amount of the fee for a given office. The Republican Party had neither the financial nor staff resources to effectively run primaries; for example, in one rural county, there were thirty-two polling places for Democratic primaries but only one polling place for Republican primaries.[19] As late as 1978, the official Arkansas election returns did not show a single contested Republican primary for a state-level office.[20] The official 1980 election returns show a contested Republican primary for governor, but a total of only 8,177 votes cast,[21] although part of the reason for the scanty participation was likely that many Republicans chose to vote in the Democratic primary, because they knew that was where the election would be decided.[22]

Judicial Elections in Arkansas prior to the Change to the Nonpartisan Format

An important aspect of judicial selection in Arkansas is a constitutional provision barring persons appointed to the bench from running for the position in which they

16 Blair and Barth, *Arkansas Politics and Government*, *supra* note 3, 98.
17 In the 1990s, over 70 percent of the population growth in Arkansas came from in-migration, and Arkansas was one of the fastest-growing states during that decade; see *id.*, 82.
18 *Id.*, 95–98.
19 *Id.*, 65.
20 See www.sos.arkansas.gov/uploads/elections/1978%20Election%20Results.pdf, accessed May 14, 2018.
21 See www.sos.arkansas.gov/uploads/elections/1980%20Election%20Results.pdf, p. 43, accessed May 14, 2018. In the 1978 Democratic primary for governor, 445,406 votes were cast; *id.*, p. 38.
22 Blair and Barth, *Arkansas Politics and Government*, *supra* note 3, 104.

are serving.[23] The only other state with a similar restriction is Louisiana.[24] This means that Arkansas has a judiciary that is largely elected, meaning that most sitting judges initially obtained their current positions by standing in an election.[25] This results in a large proportion of judicial elections in Arkansas being for open seats, although some of those open-seat elections are uncontested.[26] Between 1970 and 2000, there were 31 elections for the Arkansas Supreme Court; 15 of those were for open seats. Only 3 of the 16 elections involving incumbents were contested: one in the 1976 Democratic primary and 2 in general elections, one each in 1990 and 2000; the incumbent won all three. In contrast, only 4 of the open seats were uncontested; 4 were contested in the general election without a Democratic primary contest and 7 in the Democratic primary. The first general election contest going back to 1946 was for an open seat in 1984.[27]

One challenge in examining judicial elections in Arkansas is that most of the published election results omit uncontested races. This makes it difficult to assess the frequency of competition.[28] Two brief studies that combined cover the period 1976 through 1990 show that incumbents stood in 179 appellate and major trial court elections; they faced opposition in only 32 of those elections, but only 6 of those incumbents, all trial court judges, lost.[29] In the election results available on the Arkansas Secretary of State website,[30] the first Republican candidates in contested elections appear in 1978. The first contested election won by a Republican occurred in 1984; a second came two years later. The first Republican primaries for judicial positions appeared in 1990, and in that year Republicans contested eight general elections for trial court judgeships, winning only one but also taking at least one

23 This provision, Amendment 29, is not specific to judicial positions. Section 1 reads, "Vacancies in the office of United States Senator, and in all elective state, district, circuit, county, and township offices except those of Lieutenant Governor, Member of the General Assembly and Representative in the Congress of the United States, shall be filled by appointment by the Governor." Section 2 of the Amendment ends with the following sentence, "No person appointed under Section 1 shall be eligible for appointment or election to succeed himself."

24 See www.judicialselection.us/judicial_selection/methods/selection_of_judges.cfm?state=LA, accessed May 9, 2018.

25 Blair and Barth, *Arkansas Politics and Government, supra* note 3, 236.

26 A survey of trial judges in the mid-1980s found that almost half of the respondents were first elected without opposition; see *id.*, 237.

27 Between 1946 and 1968 there were 26 elections. Ten were for open seats with all but one contested; 6 of the 10 elections with incumbents were contested, and incumbents won 5. All contests during this period were in the Democratic primary, often with a runoff.

28 The information regarding Arkansas Supreme Court elections was assembled for my book on state supreme court elections, *Justices on the Ballot: Stability and Change in State Supreme Court Elections* (New York: Cambridge University Press, 2015).

29 See James D. Gingerich, "Campaign Finance in Judicial Elections," *Arkansas Lawyer* 23 (April 1989), 69; James D. Gingerich and Warren Readnour, "The 1990 Arkansas Judicial Elections: Much Ado About Nothing," *Arkansas Lawyer* 26 (July 1992), 39.

30 See www.sos.arkansas.gov/elections/research/election-results, accessed May 9, 2018; the posted results start with 1976. My examination of the earlier years seems to suggest that they may not always be complete. Also, some of the files seemed to be corrupted.

other seat in which there was a Republican primary but no Democratic opposition in the general election. There may have been other trial court elections in which a Republican faced no opposition in either the primary or the general election. In 1998 Republicans contested 11 trial court elections, winning 3. More generally, during the last decade of the twentieth century, about two-thirds of the contests in judicial elections were still occurring in the Democratic primary; during that decade there were only 29 contested trial court elections with Republican candidates, compared to 68 contested Democratic primaries.[31]

The first contested general election for the Court of Appeals that involved both Democratic and Republican candidates did not occur until 2000. In the five Supreme Court elections contested by Republicans prior to the General Assembly voting in 1999 to put a revised judicial article on the ballot, the Republican candidate never succeeded in winning more than 41 percent of the vote, and that was in the 1984 election. In three of the other elections, Republicans won between 31 and 33 percent of the vote, and in the fifth, 40 percent. Overall, by 1998, Republicans were contesting a meaningful fraction of judicial elections, but their success in those contested elections was limited to a relatively small number of trial court positions. This stands in contrast to North Carolina, discussed in Chapter 2, where by 2000 Republicans were having substantial success in Supreme Court elections, having won almost half of the contested elections between 1990 and 2000.

FAILED EFFORTS TO REFORM JUDICIAL SELECTION

An important issue in ending partisan elections in Arkansas relates to filing fees paid by candidates who wanted to stand in party primary elections. As noted previously, in Arkansas, those filing fees were set by the political parties and paid to the parties themselves rather than to the state treasury. This made sense when the parties had the responsibility for conducting and paying for the primaries. However, this practice ended after a 1995 federal court ruling that it was unconstitutional;[32] the state then took over responsibility for the party primaries.[33] Nonetheless, the parties have continued to set and collect the filing fees, and by the time the General Assembly voted in 1999 to submit the new judicial article to the voters that would end partisan judicial elections, the Democratic Party was generating over $100,000 in filing fees from judicial candidates, constituting about 10 percent of the party's annual budget. Given the small number of Republican

[31] See Jay Barth, "Post-Amendment 80 Judicial Politics in Arkansas: Have the Changes Undermined the Argument for Selection by Appointment?" *University of Arkansas at Little Rock Law Journal* 30 (2008), 759.

[32] See Republican Party v. Faulkner County, Arkansas, 49 F.3d 1289 (8th Cir. 1995).

[33] Jay Barth, "Arkansas: More Signs of Momentum for Republicanism in Post-'Big Three' Arkansas," *American Review of Politics* 2, No. 4 (2003), 115.

candidates, the take for the Republican Party was only about $20,000, constituting only about 3 percent of its budget.[34]

The Arkansas Judiciary Commission Proposals, 1965

In his 1963 inaugural address, Governor Orval Faubus proposed that the legislature create a body to study the current issues facing the Arkansas judiciary. The legislature took up this proposal and created the Arkansas Judiciary Commission.[35] The Commission submitted its report to the legislature in early 1965, and among its recommendations was that the state shift from partisan judicial elections to a Missouri Plan system of gubernatorial appointment of judges from a slate of nominees selected by a screening commission, with appointees subject to periodic retention elections. Although several of the Commission's recommendations were enacted by the legislature (increasing judicial salaries, improvements in judicial pensions, and creating a state office of court administration headed by the chief justice), changing the method of judicial selection would require an amendment to the state constitution, and there was no legislative action to submit such a change to the voters.

The Proposed Constitution of 1970

In February 1968, Governor Winthrop Rockefeller called a special session of the General Assembly to consider a range of issues, including whether to submit to the voters at the coming fall election the question of whether to call a state constitutional convention to revise the now almost 100-year-old document, which with 53 amendments had grown from 21,500 words to approximately 46,000 words.[36] The voters narrowly approved the call for a constitutional convention (only 51.5 percent voted in favor, with more than a third of the voters who came to the polls not voting). The Seventh Arkansas Constitutional Convention convened in early January 1969 and completed its work about thirteen months later.[37]

The proposed new constitution, a much sparser document (totaling 13,573 words in the main body), would have made significant changes to a wide range of elements of state government. The judicial branch would be streamlined by unifying major courts into a single set of "district courts" and unifying the disparate

[34] See "History of Reform Efforts: Arkansas," www.judicialselection.us/judicial_selection/reform_efforts/formal_changes_since_inception.cfm?state=AR, accessed May 10, 2018.

[35] "Judicial Setup in Arkansas Dates Back of [sic] Days of Monroe," *El Dorado Times* (January 18, 1965), 1.

[36] Robert W. Meriwether, "The Proposed Arkansas Constitution of 1970," *Nebraska Law Review* 50, No. 4 (1971), 601. In comparison, the U.S. Constitution, including its 27 amendments, contains 7,591 words.

[37] *Id.*, 604, 617.

minor courts into county courts. The new constitution authorized the creation of an intermediate Court of Appeals by the joint action of the Supreme Court and the General Assembly. Most important, it would change judicial elections from partisan to nonpartisan. According to one analysis, the "most spirited and learned debate at the convention" concerned whether to adopt a Missouri Plan type system as had been recommended in the 1965 report of the Arkansas Judiciary Commission.[38] The choice of nonpartisan elections rather than a Missouri Plan system reflected a concern that it "would be almost impossible to sell [such a plan] to the voters."[39]

The proposed constitution was submitted to the voters in November 1970. It was resoundingly rejected, with only 42.6 percent voting in favor.[40] One observer suggested that the provisions of the new judicial article "were the most damaging to the fate of the proposed constitution."[41] A central part of the opposition came from holders of judicial office. In fact, the main opposition was headed by a former member of the Arkansas Supreme Court, who had also served on the Arkansas Judiciary Commission. He attacked the proposal as "the first step toward a Fascist state," and argued that it would "destroy the finest state court system in the country."[42] Strong opposition also came from county and judicial office holders, who lobbied their friends and neighbors to vote no.[43] It does not seem that the proposed shift to nonpartisan elections was what created this judicial opposition; rather, it was the reorganization of the courts and the creation of a centralized administrative structure.

If You Don't Succeed, Try, Try Again: The Proposed Constitution of 1980

And that is exactly what Arkansas tried to do. In the decade following the defeat of the 1970 proposed constitution, five additional amendments to the 1874 constitution were approved by the voters, including Amendment 58, allowing the creation of a Court of Appeals. In 1975, the General Assembly, in response to a proposal from newly elected Governor David Pryor, agreed to another constitutional convention. The legislation calling for the convention was struck down by the Arkansas Supreme Court because it placed some parts of the 1874 constitution outside the convention's purview. The following year, the Assembly submitted the question of whether to convene another convention on the November ballot, and voters approved it 54–46. Delegates were elected to the convention on a nonpartisan ballot in 1978, with 400 candidates running for the 100 positions. The delegates convened the following

38 *Id.*, 611.
39 *Id.*, 611–612.
40 *Id.*, 620.
41 *Id.*, 610.
42 Quoted in *id.*, 619.
43 *Id.*, 620.

year, and spent May and June preparing the draft constitution to be submitted to the voters in 1980.[44]

Changes proposed for the judicial branch were similar to those in the 1970 proposed constitution. These included strengthening the administrative structure, consolidating the limited jurisdiction courts into county courts, and changing to nonpartisan elections for judges. Unlike the 1970 proposal, the major trial courts were not to be consolidated. One might speculate that this was done to avoid the kind of opposition from judges that occurred in 1970. Also, by this time an intermediate Court of Appeals had been authorized by a specific amendment passed in 1978.

According to one analysis, "the selection of judges was a major source of controversy within the convention."[45] The controversy does not appear to have been over whether to retain partisan elections. There was agreement that trial judges should be subject to nonpartisan election, but there was no agreement regarding appellate court judges as to whether a Missouri Plan should apply or they too should be chosen and retained in nonpartisan elections. The delegates decided to ask the voters to choose between two alternatives for the appellate courts.[46] This choice would only be relevant if the voters approved the new constitution. Hence, there were two questions on the ballot in 1980: whether to adopt the new constitution and which method should be used to select and retain appellate judges.[47]

I did not find any suggestion that judges or legal professionals opposed the new constitution, although there might have been opposition from persons then serving as judges on limited jurisdiction courts. Some opposition did arise due to the estimated cost of implementing the new constitution, much of which would be attributable to the creation of the new county courts. There was opposition related to other issues, including usury provisions and the mention of gender in a "declaration of rights" section, with the former probably producing the most opposition. The 1980 proposed constitution fared considerably worse with the voters than had the 1970 constitution, garnering only 37.3 percent of votes in favor. Given the choice between nonpartisan elections for all judges and a mixed system with a Missouri Plan for appellate and nonpartisan elections for trial judges, 55.8 percent of voters preferred the former compared to 44.2 percent for the latter. However, the defeat of the 1980 constitution made the vote on how to select and retain judges moot.[48]

[44] Arthur English and John J. Carroll, "Constitutional Reform in Arkansas: The 1979–1980 Convention," *National Civic Review* 71, No. 5 (May 1982), 241–243.

[45] *Id.*, 242.

[46] The text on the ballot referred specifically to the Supreme Court justices and the Appellate Court judges; see *Referenda and Primary Election Materials; Part 24: Referenda Elections for Arkansas* (Ann Arbor, MI: Inter-university Consortium for Political and Social Research, 2002), 20, www.icpsr.umich.edu/cgi-bin/file?comp=none&study=6&ds=24&file_id=654734&path=, accessed May 11, 2018.

[47] *Id.*, 245–246.

[48] *Id.*, 250.

If You Don't Succeed, Try, Try, Try Again: The 1990s

The defeat of two proposed constitutions in ten years meant that it would be another fifteen years before the voters were again asked to call a constitutional convention. In 1995 Democratic governor Jim Guy Tucker convened a Task Force for a New Constitution. The Governor's Task Force developed a plan that called for revising several articles, including the judicial article. The proposed judicial article would have changed to nonpartisan elections and authorized the General Assembly to ask the voters to decide whether appellate judge selection/retention should be based on the Missouri Plan.[49] However, at a special election held in December 1995, only 20 percent of those voting supported holding a convention.[50]

There were two alternatives open to the General Assembly for modifying the method of judicial selection, short of an overall constitutional rewrite. First, in order to adopt the Missouri Plan or some variant of that plan involving appointment and retention elections, it would be necessary to submit a constitutional amendment to the voters. This had been done successfully regarding one element of the defeated 1970 constitution: obtaining authorization for the General Assembly to create an intermediate Court of Appeals; Amendment 58 was overwhelmingly approved by the voters in 1978 with 67 percent voting in favor. A constitutional amendment that would adopt the Missouri Plan for appellate judges and switch to nonpartisan elections for trial judges came very close to being submitted to the electorate. This amendment had the backing of the Arkansas Bar Association's judicial article task force and the Arkansas Judicial Council. The Arkansas Senate approved putting the proposal on the ballot; however, by a single vote, the proposal failed to pass the House.[51]

The second option for changing the method of judicial selection would take advantage of the language in the 1874 constitution that specified only that judges should be elected. Given this language, the Assembly could by statute change to nonpartisan elections for some or all courts. In 1995 the Arkansas Senate passed a bill on a near unanimous vote switching both appellate and trial judge elections to nonpartisan ballots, but the bill failed in the House due to the opposition of the Democrats. In the wake of the defeat of the bill changing to nonpartisan judicial elections, the chairman of the Arkansas Democratic Party, Bynum Gibson, advanced a proposal for a Missouri Plan system, with the addition of Senate confirmation, for appellate judges; his proposal did not include a change from

[49] Meredith Oakley, "Nonpartisan Election of Judges," *Arkansas Democrat-Gazette* (September 13, 1995), 11B.

[50] "Governor Tucker," *Jim Guy Tucker Papers*, https://ualrexhibits.org/tucker/virtual-exhibit/political-career/governor-tucker/, accessed May 10, 2018.

[51] "History of Reform Efforts: Arkansas," www.judicialselection.us/judicial_selection/reform_efforts/failed_reform_efforts.cfm?state=AR, accessed May 10, 2018.

partisan elections for trial court judges.[52] This was a clever plan. First, retaining partisan elections for trial court judges would have a minimal effect on party revenue because the overwhelming majority of judicial candidates ran for trial court positions. Second, the requirement of Senate confirmation would allow the Democratic majority, which was expected to be maintained for the foreseeable future, to block nominees of a Republican governor whom Democrats found objectionable. The Arkansas House failed to act, and the proposal died.

In January 1997, the Senate rejected, 14–19, a bill (S.B. 14) changing to nonpartisan judicial elections that was sponsored by the Republican minority leader and had the backing of Republican governor Mike Huckabee.[53] In March of that year, the Republican minority leader reintroduced the proposal (now S.B. 661), and this time it passed the Senate but died in the House.[54] The switch probably reflects that the Senate Majority Leader Wayne Dowd opposed the proposal in January, but "later reversed course and said he leaned toward nonpartisan judicial races."[55] It is unclear why Dowd changed his position in the two months between the first and second votes. Also, nothing suggests that the opposition to the proposed change reflected a concern that a nonpartisan ballot would disadvantage Democratic candidates. Rather, the opposition focused on the loss of the filing fees from Democratic judicial candidates.[56] Republicans would also lose filing fees, but Democrats would lose much more, and arguably Republicans believed that the larger loss to the Democratic Party was worth giving up the small contribution that filing fees made to the Republican Party treasury. Democrats also argued that voters needed the information provided by party labels to make good choices at the polls.[57]

SUCCESS AT LAST: AMENDMENT 80

Perseverance can pay off. In 1999 the General Assembly approved a broad rewrite of the judicial article for consideration by the voters at the 2000 general election. The proposed article would reorganize the courts, create a statewide administrative structure, and change all judicial elections by removing party labels from the ballot. Unlike the full constitution rewrites of 1970 and 1980, the voters approved what became Amendment 80, with 57 percent in favor. The proposed amendment was approved overwhelmingly in 1999 by the Arkansas Senate with only a single dissenting vote. The amendment faced significant opposition in the Arkansas House, with

52 Rachel O'Neal, "Gibson Charts Election Reform," *Arkansas Democrat-Gazette* (June 14, 1995), 13A.
53 Rick McFarland, "A Partisan Vote on Nonpartisan Judges? Amid GOP Grumbles," *Arkansas Democrat-Gazette* (January 29, 1997), 1A.
54 "History of Reform Efforts: Arkansas," *supra* note 51.
55 Chris Oasher, "Huckabee, Beebe Back Court Changes," *Arkansas Democrat-Gazette* (June 17, 2000), B1.
56 McFarland, "Partisan Vote," *supra* note 53.
57 "Partisan Justice," *Arkansas Democrat-Gazette* (February 2, 1997), 4J.

that opposition coming from the Democratic members. Final passage came on a 55–33 vote. All 24 Republican members of the House voted in favor; the vote among Democrats who voted (12 Representatives abstained, all Democrats) was 33–31 against. This vote came after unsuccessful efforts by some Democratic representatives to strike "nonpartisan" from the proposed amendment.[58] Almost certainly the negative votes reflected the opposition from Democratic Party officials who were concerned about losing the revenue from candidate filing fees. Again, there was no hint of concerns about advantage or disadvantage on the ballot, although Democrats did argue that the party labels would help voters.[59]

The proposed amendment came at a time when the governor of Arkansas was a Republican. Although the Democrats had secure control of the state legislature and at the time probably did not anticipate losing that control, they must have recognized that the governor's office was not secure. Given the advantage of incumbency, particularly in the absence of party labels, in most states one might have expected opposition to nonpartisan elections from Democrats out of a concern that appointees of Republican governors would be advantaged when they initially stood for election. However, this would not be a problem in Arkansas, given the constitutional provision barring appointees to judicial office from running in the subsequent election for the office the appointee occupied.[60]

The proposed amendment, or at least some version of what became the proposed amendment, was drafted by the combined efforts of representatives of the Arkansas Bar Association (ArBA) and the Arkansas Judicial Council (AJC).[61] One important difference between the ArBA/AJC draft and what the General Assembly eventually passed and put on the 2000 ballot was the inclusion of a Missouri Plan system for the appointment and retention of appellate judges,[62] something that had been long sought by representatives of the legal profession in Arkansas.[63] The adoption of the Missouri Plan for appellate courts was not in the amendment that emerged from the General Assembly. Exactly why is unclear, although it is likely that there was some concern that other provisions of the amendment – reorganizing the courts and creating a modern administrative structure – were more important and that including such a provision would increase opposition, decreasing the chances of passage.

58 "History of Reform Efforts: Arkansas," *supra* note 51.

59 Seth Blomley, "Public Undecided on Proposed Amendment to Revamp State's Courts," *Arkansas Democrat-Gazette* (October 10, 2000), B1.

60 Interim appointees are permitted to challenge an incumbent holding the equivalent position, or to run for a different open seat for an equivalent position.

61 The Arkansas Judicial Council is the official body representing the Arkansas judiciary; https://courts.arkansas.gov/administration/arkansas-judicial-council, accessed May 11, 2018.

62 Dave Hughes, "Proposed Court Changes to Be Discussed in LR [Little Rock] Consensus Could Be Put Before Voters in 1982," *Arkansas Democrat-Gazette* (March 13, 1998), B1.

63 See "Arkansas Legislature Enacts Judiciary Commission Recommendations," *Journal of the American Judicature Society* 49 (1965), 72.

Constitutional amendments changing from partisan or quasi-partisan systems to Missouri Plan systems had been rejected during the 1980s by voters in Ohio, New Mexico, and Nevada;[64] the last successful popular vote to adopt the Missouri Plan came in Utah in 1985,[65] and that was a change from a nonpartisan system. Other considerations might have included the preference of sitting judges for nonpartisan elections; in the words of a member of the Arkansas Supreme Court, "On two occasions in recent years, the Arkansas Judicial Council ... has voted overwhelmingly to convert to nonpartisan elections."[66] Also, as discussed previously, when Arkansas voters in 1980 had been given the choice between nonpartisan elections and the Missouri Plan for selecting and retaining appellate judges, the majority preferred nonpartisan elections.

Although the proposed amendment did not call for a Missouri Plan selection/retention system, it did not ignore such a system entirely. The amendment includes a provision that allows the General Assembly to call for a referendum on whether to adopt a "merit selection system" for appellate judges. The provision says little about the structure of such a system, beyond stating that if the voters approve, the General Assembly would then be required to "enact laws to create a judicial nominating commission for purposes of nominating candidates for merit selection to the Supreme Court and Court of Appeals."[67]

As noted previously, the proposed amendment restructuring the courts and switching to nonpartisan elections was approved by the voters, 57–43. Supporters of the amendment undertook a significant campaign, spending $206,207, with 75 percent coming from the Arkansas Bar Association and another 13 percent from individual lawyers and law firms. The Arkansas Republican Party also supported the campaign to approve the amendment, contributing $15,000.[68] Opposition did come from at least some elements of the Democratic Party, presumably reflecting a concern about losing revenue from filing fees, but there is no readily available information on how much, if anything, was spent in opposition. Moreover, other elements of the Democratic Party supported the amendment.[69]

64 See Chapters 9 and 12 for discussions of reform efforts in these three states.

65 As discussed in Chapter 8, by 1985 Utah had already adopted most elements of the Missouri Plan; the actual change was less dramatic than it would have been in Arkansas. The last state where voters approved a switch from partisan elections to the Missouri Plan was Indiana in 1970, and this was limited to appellate courts.

66 See Robert L. Brown, "Judges Without Parties," *Arkansas Lawyer* 30, no. 1 (Winter 1966), 16; it is unclear whether the Missouri Plan was offered as an option. However, in another article, Justice Brown makes clear his own preference for nonpartisan elections over the Missouri Plan; see Robert L. Brown, "From Whence Cometh Our State Appellate Judges: Popular Election Versus the Missouri Plan," *University of Arkansas at Little Rock Law Journal* 20 (1998), 20.

67 Arkansas Constitution, Amendment 80, §18(A).

68 See "History of Reform Efforts: Arkansas," *supra* note 51.

69 See Seth Blomley, "Public Undecided on Proposed Amendment to Revamp State's Courts," *Arkansas Democrat-Gazette* (October 10, 2000), B1.

Aftermath of Amendment 80's Passage

The passage of Amendment 80 left much to be decided by the General Assembly as to the amendment's implementation. Some of these issues concerned the nonpartisan elections that would start in 2002. There are several ways that states have implemented nonpartisan elections. The most common system is to hold a nonpartisan primary if there are more than two candidates, with the top two candidates running in the general election. Several states have, or used to have, provisions that if a candidate wins a majority at the primary, the candidate is declared elected, and there is no contest at the time of the general election. In these states, there is a primary election even if there are only two candidates. In this setup, the November general election effectively serves as a runoff if no candidate secures a majority. Georgia has fluctuated between this system and one in which there is no primary, with a runoff in December if the November election fails to produce a majority for one candidate. West Virginia was the most recent state to adopt nonpartisan elections; in that state the judicial election occurs at the time of the spring primary, with no majority required; the candidate with the most votes wins the seat even if that candidate receives less than 50 percent of the votes.[70] In states where one party is strongly dominant, as the Democratic Party in Arkansas still was circa 2000, having nonpartisan elections at the time of the primary with a runoff in November tends to favor the dominant party, because it is more likely to have contested primaries that produce turnout among party supporters.[71] Among these various options, the Arkansas General Assembly adopted a system with the initial elections for judicial positions in the spring and a runoff in November if no candidate secures a majority.[72] In the early 2000s, there were many more contested Democratic primaries than Republican primaries, and thus many more Democrats voting at the time of the primary. In 2006, for example, 277,220 votes were cast in the Democratic primary for lieutenant governor, compared to only 62,868 in the Republic primary.[73] It is not clear whether this logic was part of the thinking in the General Assembly, in which Democrats held about three-quarters of the seats in 2001, when the implementation legislation was passed.

There is one other element of the implementation legislation suggesting that the dominant Democrats were thinking about potential ways of gaining an advantage in the nonpartisan elections. Section 4 of the draft of the implementation legislation (S.B. 789) prohibited candidates from seeking the endorsements from

[70] See Chapter 4.

[71] See Barth, "Post-Amendment 80 Judicial Politics in Arkansas," *supra* note 31, 759–760.

[72] Arkansas Senate Bill (S.B.) 789 (2001).

[73] See Barth, "Post-Amendment 80 Judicial Politics in Arkansas," *supra* note 31, 759–760. By 2014, the turnout for the two parties' gubernatorial primaries was roughly equal; 153,343 in the Democratic primary and 179,225 in the Republican primary; http://results.enr.clarityelections.com/AR/51266/133405/en/summary.html, accessed May 11, 2018.

political parties or claiming to have such endorsements.[74] Although such restrictions might have been problematic after the U.S. Supreme Court's decision in *Republican Party of Minnesota v. White*,[75] that case was not decided until 2002. The Democratic-controlled Senate deleted the prohibitions related to party endorsements, leaving judicial candidates free to seek such endorsements and to publicize any party endorsements they received. Presumably, as long as Arkansas voters tended to favor Democratic candidates for local office, endorsements from the Democratic Party would work to the advantage of candidates running for judicial offices. When the bill came up for approval in the House of Representatives, not a single Republican voted in favor; the Republican nays were joined by just six from Democrats. This partisan pattern seems to confirm that the decisions on how to structure the primaries were designed to help candidates likely to be preferred by Democratic voters.

ARKANSAS JUDICIAL ELECTIONS AFTER 2000

Recall that in Arkansas's last decade of partisan judicial elections, 1990 to 2000, there were only 29 contested general jurisdiction trial elections involving Republicans, in contrast to 68 contested Democratic primaries.[76] In the final set of partisan judicial elections in 2000, there were 21 appellate and general jurisdiction judgeships on the ballot. Only 9 of those positions were contested with Republicans appearing in 5 of those contests; 3 of those 5 Republican candidates had been appointed to appellate judgeships by Republican governor Huckabee and were running for different judgeships because Arkansas law barred them from running for the seat to which Huckabee had appointed them.[77] A sixth Republican ran unopposed for the Court of Appeals. In the eight election cycles prior to the change to nonpartisan elections, there were 18 elections for the Arkansas Supreme Court; 8 of elections were contested, 6 in the general election without primaries for either party, plus 2 just in the Democratic primary. The voting pattern in the elections contested by Republicans was, not surprisingly, partisan but not as partisan as was typical in partisan state supreme court elections. As with North Carolina, I measure the

74 "No candidate for a nonpartisan judicial office shall seek the endorsement of a political party, nor shall the candidate hold himself or herself out as having been endorsed by a political party," www.arkleg.state.ar.us/assembly/2001/R/Amendments/SB789-S1.pdf, accessed May 11, 2018.

75 Republican Party of Minnesota v. White, 536 U.S. 765 (2002); see also Chris W. Bonneau, Melinda Gann Hall, and Matthew J. Streb, "White Noise: The Unrealized Effects of *Republican Party of Minnesota vs. White* on Judicial Elections," *Justice System Journal* 32, no. 3 (2011), 247–268.

76 See Barth, "Post-Amendment 80 Judicial Politics in Arkansas," *supra* note 31, 759.

77 *Id.*, 758. Barth reports that there were only 5 races with Republican candidates, but I count 6, including one in which the Republican ran unopposed by a Democrat. Barth also points out that 3 of the elections with Republican candidates involved Republicans appointed by Republican governor Huckabee.

partisanship of Supreme Court using the partisan correlation, which I defined in Chapter 1. In states using partisan elections, this correlation averages something over .85, and in some decades averaged over .90.[78] The partisan correlation for the six partisan elections in Arkansas between 1984 and 2000 ranged between .63 and .79, with an average of .72.

How did judicial elections change in the nine election cycles since the switch to nonpartisan elections? First, regarding the Arkansas Supreme Court, there were 18 elections between 2002 and 2018. Of those elections, 11 (61 percent) were contested with 9 of those decided at the time of the spring primary. Although this is an increase from the 44 percent contested in the last eight election cycles of partisan elections, the change is not great enough to allow a conclusion that it was anything more than chance.[79] However, the switch to nonpartisan elections did dampen partisanship; the partisan correlation ranged between .07 and .51, with a mean of .31. The decrease in the partisan correlation cannot be attributed to chance.[80]

Partial information on courts below the Supreme Court is available for the eight election cycles with nonpartisan elections. It is partial in the sense that the available reports vary as to whether there is information on uncontested elections provided in the official reports for the last four election cycles. Table 3.1 shows the number of elections for each cycle. Roughly one-quarter of the elections were contested between 2002 and 2010. Because of the absence of information on uncontested elections in any of the pre-2002 reports of election results, it is difficult to draw good comparisons. However, as noted earlier, studies covering 1976 to 1990 found that only about one-sixth of seats up for election were contested. If this figure applied through 2000, when the last partisan elections occurred, the shift to nonpartisan elections has clearly increased the likelihood of elections for judicial office being contested.

In the 2014 election, Republicans secured control of both the Arkansas legislature and the governor's office for the first time since 1873. As of 2019, they hold about three-quarters of the seats in both chambers of the state legislature, about the same percentage held by Democrats in 2000. One might wonder whether there is any regret among Republicans that the change to nonpartisan elections was made and that it is embedded in the state constitution. The only state to switch back to partisan elections from nonpartisan is North Carolina, and that was possible because the state constitution only requires that judges be elected; there is no requirement for nonpartisan elections, as now exists in the Arkansas constitution.

78 See Herbert M. Kritzer, "Judicial Elections in the 2010s," *DePaul Law Review* (67, no. 2 (Winter 2018), 413.

79 A Fisher's exact test shows that the probability is .51 that if there was no effect we would observe this pattern of change.

80 $t = 7.634$, $p < .001$. The two highest correlations occurred in 2016; without those two, the mean is .26.

TABLE 3.1 *Contestation in Arkansas court of appeals and circuit court elections, 2002–2016*

Year	Contested	Uncontested
2002	24	76
2004	6	14
2006	5	7
2008	24	81
2010	5	16
2012	14	
2014	29	
2016	26	
2018	3	

This potential regret might be both from a policy perspective and from a party financial perspective. If there were still partisan elections, judicial candidates carrying the Republican label would be highly advantaged statewide and in most local areas. Although in 2000 the action was still largely in the Democratic primaries, as of 2019 it is largely in the Republican primaries. The parties still set and collect filing fees from persons wanting to run in their primaries. For the legislature, Democrats charge candidates $2,250 for either the Senate or the House; Republicans charge Senate candidates $7,500 and House candidates $3,000. There is no way to know what fees would be charged if the judicial elections were still partisan, but in 2019 it would be the Republicans with the financial advantage.

4

West Virginia

Change and Chaos

As this was written in 2019, West Virginia was the most recent state to switch from partisan to nonpartisan judicial elections. When the legislature approved the switch in 2015, it had been over a decade since another state had made such a change. In fact, in the years since 2002 when legislation changing to nonpartisan elections for the elections for North Carolina Supreme Court had been passed (effective with the 2004 election), the movement on judicial selection had been more in the direction of reintroducing partisanship, either by adding party labels back on the ballot, as was done in 2015 for North Carolina Court of Appeals elections, or by lifting constraints on whom a governor could appoint as happened in Tennessee for its appellate courts in 2014[1] and in Kansas for its Court of Appeals in 2013.[2]

Three developments led to the change in West Virginia. Two of those were controversial elections for the West Virginia Supreme Court of Appeals (WVSCA), one in 1988 and another in 2004. The final development was the capture of control of the legislature by the Republican Party in the 2014 election, the first time Republicans had controlled even one chamber since 1932, and the first time they had controlled both chambers since 1930. The first two developments brought the debate over judicial selection reform squarely to the political agenda, and the third development provided the political motivation and ability to make the change.

The specific electoral structure that was chosen, plurality elections held at the time of the spring primary (i.e., the judicial election itself has no primary), raised some issues when the first election for the WVSCA in 2016 produced a winner who obtained less than 40 percent of the vote. This led to proposals for further modifications, but as this was written in 2019, those proposals had produced little legislative action. For reasons discussed in detail in the concluding sections of this chapter, two special elections took place in November 2018, both attracting ten candidates

[1] This is discussed in detail in the next chapter.
[2] See Chapter 14.

including the two persons appointed to fill vacancies created by resignations, both of whom were the plurality winners of their respective elections.

JUDICIAL ELECTIONS IN WEST VIRGINIA: HISTORICAL PERSPECTIVES

A Primer on West Virginia Politics

West Virginia became a state in 1863 after it split off from secessionist Virginia.[3] Surprisingly, the Democratic Party dominated, starting in 1870 through the last few years of the nineteenth century, after which the Republican Party dominated for about thirty-five years. The Depression brought Democrats back into dominance. Between 1933 and 2014, Democrats controlled both chambers of the state legislature. Between 1932 and 2004, there were 139 elections to statewide offices; Republicans managed to win only 10 of those elections.[4] When Republicans did manage to win a gubernatorial election,[5] the Republican governor faced a legislature in which Democrats usually held a veto-proof majority. Democrats held such a majority as late as 2010, when they held 76 percent of House seats and 71 percent of Senate seats. Republicans gained control of the legislature in the 2014 election. The Democratic gubernatorial candidate won all of the gubernatorial elections between 2000 and 2016. However, the Democratic candidate in 2016, Jim Justice, had been a Republican but switched to the Democratic Party in 2015. He defeated two rivals in the Democratic primary, won the 2016 election with 49 percent of the vote, compared to the Republican candidate's 42 percent, and then switched back to the Republican Party in August 2016.

The strength of the Democratic Party was tied to the role of labor unions, particularly the United Mine Workers of America (UMWA). Between 1933 and 1937, UMWA membership grew from 16,000 to 107,000.[6] The UMWA and other traditional labor unions began to weaken in the 1960s; the number of coal miners dropped from 120,000 in 1948 to 28,100 in 2007,[7] and then to 11,600 in 2016.[8] However, the decrease in membership in the UMWA and other private-sector

[3] For a brief discussion of the breakaway of West Virginia from Virginia, see Richard A. Brisbin Jr., Robert Jay Dilger, Allan S. Hammock, and L. Christopher Plein, *West Virginia Politics and Government*, 2nd ed. (Lincoln: University of Nebraska Press, 2008), 21–22, 107.

[4] *Id.*, 49.

[5] Republicans controlled the governorship from 1957–1961 (Cecil H. Underwood); 1969–1977 (Arch Moore); 1985–1989 (Moore Jr.); and 1997–2001 (Underwood), https://en.wikipedia.org/wiki/Political_party_strength_in_West_Virginia, accessed March 5, 2019.

[6] Michael K. Wilson, "History of Law and West Virginia Politics," *West Virginia Historical Society Quarterly* 22, no. 2 (April 2008), 3; www.wvculture.org/history/wvhs/wvhs2202.pdf, accessed July 18, 2018.

[7] Brisbin et al., *West Virginia Politics and Government*, *supra* note 3, 25.

[8] See "Coal-Mining Employment in West Virginia from 2009 to 2016, by Mine Type," www.statista.com/statistics/215786/coal-mining-employment-in-west-virginia/, accessed July 21, 2018.

unions was partially offset by increased membership in unions representing public-sector workers.[9] The decline in coal mining in West Virginia led to a population shift linked to partisan loyalties because population declined in areas where the Democratic Party had been particularly strong. At the same time population increased in the eastern panhandle of West Virginia, fueled in significant part by migrants from the Washington, DC, metropolitan area seeking to avoid high local taxes. Based on surveys conducted by the West Virginia Institute for Public Affairs, in 1992 the party split among voters was 47.6 percent Democrat versus 26.5 percent Republican, with 21.1 percent calling themselves Independent (including those who said they were closer to one or the other major parties). Thirteen years later, in 2005, the division was much less pronounced: 42.6 percent Democrat versus 38.3 percent Republican, with 11.4 Independent.[10] A 2018 survey of registered voters found that the shift had continued in the Republican direction, with 39 percent of voters identifying as Republican, 29 percent as Democrat, and 32 percent as Independent. However, the party registration of voters still leaned Democratic, with 44 percent registered as Democrats and 36 percent as Republicans.[11]

Although labor was a key part of the Democratic Party's support in West Virginia, that party was also marked by divisions. According to one analysis, there have been three distinct factions. One is the liberal–labor faction, which evolved to include organized labor, trial lawyers, advocates for women's rights, and environmentalists. The second is a conservative faction that at one time was described as the "Bourbon" faction because of its affinity for the South; however, by the early part of the twenty-first century it was composed of economic and social conservatives, including various business leaders who had not yet switched to the Republican Party. The third faction consists of those whose primary concern is winning and holding office, and thus being able to distribute patronage; it has generally been nonideological.[12]

Political corruption has been a long-standing feature of West Virginia politics.[13] During the 1980s and into the early 1990s, almost 100 people, government officials and those benefiting from the actions of those officials, were convicted on corruption charges.[14] The history of corruption in West Virginia was detailed in a 2006 book by future West Virginia Supreme Court of Appeals Justice Allen

[9] Wilson, "History of Law and West Virginia Politics," *supra* note 6, 7–8.

[10] Brisbin et. al., *West Virginia Politics and Government, supra* note 3, 44. These figures are based on two surveys conducted by the West Virginia Institute of Public Affairs.

[11] "West Virginia: Dems Doing Well in Senate, CD03," Monmouth University Poll (June 20, 2018), 9, www.monmouth.edu/polling-institute/documents/monmouthpoll_wv_062018.pdf/, accessed August 30, 2018.

[12] See Brisbin et al., *West Virginia Politics and Government*, supra note 3, 49–50; this description is based in part on an analysis by John H. Fenton, *Politics of the Border States* (New Orleans, LA: Hauser Press, 1957).

[13] See Brisbin et al., *West Virginia Politics and Government, supra* note 3, 30–31.

[14] *Id.*, 30.

Loughry.[15] Loughry's 623-page tome details corruption from the birth of West Virginia to contemporary times. He details corruption in elections such as vote tampering, bribery in the executive branch (focusing on, among others, governors Arch Moore and William Barron, both of whom served time in federal prison in connection with various felony charges), campaign contributions to politicians including US senators, questionable behavior by judges of both trial and appellate courts, and much more.[16] Loughry was subsequently elected to the West Virginia Supreme Court of Appeals in 2012. Ironically, as is discussed in more detail later in this chapter, Loughry himself ended up in federal prison after being convicted on charges of corruption in 2018.

Judicial Elections in West Virginia

At the time of statehood in 1863, two courts of record were created: the Supreme Court of Appeals and the circuit court. Judges were to be elected by the people, with terms of 12 years for the WVSCA and 6 years for the circuit court; terms for the latter were increased to 8 years in 1872 when the present state constitution was ratified. In addition to the two courts of record, justices of the peace handled minor matters. Between 1872 and 1974, a range of other trial level courts was created to serve specific locales; these included courts of common pleas, criminal courts, juvenile courts, and something called the intermediate court.[17] In 1974, voters approved a constitutional amendment to create a unified court system that did away with the various trial courts other than the circuit courts, and replaced the justices of the peace with a system of magistrates; the amendment also gave the legislature the authority to create an intermediate appellate court, but as of 2018, no such court had been created. The elimination of the justice of the peace (JP) court came in the wake of rulings by the WVSCA that the system of payment for justices of the peace, fees assessed against the losing party in civil cases and against defendants in criminal

[15] Allen Loughry, *Don't Buy Another Vote. I Won't Pay for a Landslide. The Sordid and Continuing History of Political Corruption in West Virginia* (Parsons, WV: McClain Printing Company, 2006); this was originally written as Loughry's dissertation for an SJD (Doctor of Juridical Science) degree, which he received from American University's Washington School of Law.

Of course, corruption is not unique to West Virginia. One need only think about Maryland and Spiro Agnew, who had to resign the vice-presidency when he was indicted on corruption charges related to his time as governor (with some payments continuing after he became vice-president); see Richard M. Cohen, *A Heartbeat Away: The Investigation & Resignation of Vice-President Spiro T. Agnew* (New York: Viking, 1974). In Illinois, 4 of 8 governors who served between 1961 and 2009 ended up in prison on corruption charges.

[16] It is not clear from Loughry's discussion that there was widespread *systemic* corruption of the type commonly described in the political corruption literature.

[17] These are courts I found listed in the judicial election results between 1950 and 1972. See also https://en.wikipedia.org/wiki/West_Virginia_Circuit_Courts, accessed July 21, 2018.

cases, was unconstitutional.[18] Magistrates, who are elected to four-year terms, are not required to be lawyers; a survey of magistrates conducted in 2005 found that only 2.6 percent reported having a law degree.[19] The municipal courts are the lowest level courts in West Virginia; these are locally created and administered, and handle only violations of local ordinances;[20] judges of these courts, who are not required to be lawyers, are "selected to varying terms in a variety of manners depending on the municipality they serve in."[21] In 2000, a third state trial court was created, the family court; this court became operational in 2002 with judges who are elected and serve eight-year terms.[22]

One feature of elections for the circuit court and family court judges is that the terms of all judges run concurrently. Judges who are appointed to vacancies run in the next even-year election for any years remaining of the unexpired term. In contrast, the terms of the five justices of the WVSCA are staggered. As with the trial court judges, appointees to vacancies on the WVSCA run in the next even-year election for any remaining years of the unexpired term. For courts in which multiple seats were up simultaneously, West Virginia commonly used what some have called the "cattle call" method.[23] In this system, voters cast X votes, with X being the number of seats to be filled; the winners are the top X vote-getters. This system was in place for the circuit courts until 1990,[24] and for the WVSCA prior to 2016.[25]

The last partisan election for the WVSCA occurred in 2012. Between 1946 and 2012, there were 40 elections for that Court. Only one of the 40 elections was uncontested, although 5 were contested only in the Democratic primary. Of the 34 elections contested by both Democratic and Republican candidates, the Democratic candidate won 31. Charles Haden, who had been appointed by Republican governor Archie Moore in 1972, won election that year to serve the remainder of his predecessor's term, but then stepped down before that term expired. Brent Benjamin won a controversial election, discussed later in the chapter, in 2004. The third Republican to win election to the Court between 1946 and 2012 was Allen Loughry,

[18] H. John Rogers, "Justices of the Peace," *West Virginia Encyclopedia*, www.wvencyclopedia.org/articles/1084, accessed July 18, 2018.

[19] Brisbin et al., *West Virginia Politics and Government*, *supra* note 3, 105; 10.5 percent had held other elected office and 44.7 percent had had careers as civil servants.

[20] Commission on the Future of the West Virginia Judicial System, *Final Report* (1998), B-3, www.courtswv.gov/court-administration/ReportAll.pdf, accessed July 19, 2018.

[21] See https://ballotpedia.org/Judicial_selection_in_West_Virginia, accessed July 19, 2018.

[22] Initially the term was for 6 years, but it was changed to 8 years starting with those elected in 2008; see Brisbin et al., *West Virginia Politics and Government*, *supra* note 3, 194.

[23] See Hoppy Kercheval, "West Virginia Moving toward Non-Partisan Judicial Elections," *MetroNews* (February 19, 2015), http://wvmetronews.com/2015/02/19/west-virginia-moving-toward-non-partisan-judicial-elections/, accessed July 19, 2018.

[24] Under H.B. 2305, passed by the legislature in 1990, multijudge circuits were split into numbered divisions, one judge per division; effective since 1992, judges run separately by division.

[25] This same system applied to magistrate elections, at least prior to 2016; see *Id.*

TABLE 4.1 *Patterns in West Virginia trial court elections, 1952–2014*

Cycle	Number of elections	% two-party contested	% of contested won by Republican	% any contest	% uncontested	% held by Republicans
1952–1958	51	66.7	14.7	72.5	27.5	21.6
1960–1966	53	56.6	36.7	56.6	43.4	28.3
1968–1974	48	56.3	29.6	68.8	31.3	27.1
1976–1982	56	42.9	37.5	44.6	55.4	23.2
1984–1990	72	45.8	27.3	69.4	30.6	16.7
1992–1998	79	17.7	42.9	34.2	65.8	13.9
2000–2006	100	15.0	60.0	35.0	65.0	21.0
2008–2014	71	19.7	50.0	39.4	60.6	25.4

who won a full 12-year term in an open-seat election in 2012.[26] Several other Republicans were appointed to the Court, but either chose not to run for election or were defeated when they did run.

I assembled information on trial court elections for the period 1952 through 2014.[27] Because the terms of all trial judges run concurrently, three out of every four years have only a small number of trial court elections, all involving partial terms.[28] For this reason, I collapsed the information for the three elections following the year of the concurrent elections with the information for the concurrent election. The first concurrent election for which I have information is 1952; I combined the information for that election with the information for the 1954, 1956, and 1958 elections. The last cycle prior to the change to nonpartisan elections covers 2008, 2010, 2012, and 2014. Table 4.1 summarizes information for these elections.

There are several noteworthy patterns in Table 4.1. First, Republicans have had a presence in trial court elections throughout the period, although the nature of this presence has changed over time. Republicans were considerably more likely to contest elections in the 1950s and 1960s, with between 56 and 67 percent of elections involving candidates from both parties. The percentage of elections featuring two-party contests then dropped to 43 and 46 percent in the 1970s and 1980s, falling further to under 20 percent starting in the 1990s. The percentage of contested elections won by Republicans varied over time, from a low of 15 percent in the

[26] As noted earlier, Loughry had authored a book on corruption in West Virginia politics, but as is discussed in the final sections of this chapter, Loughry himself became embroiled in corruption charges leading to federal charges, resulting in his conviction and resignation from the Court.

[27] This information was accessed at the website of the West Virginia Secretary of State, https://sos.wv.gov/elections/electionreturns/Pages/default.aspx. The website includes results for the 1950 election, which I did collect, but for reasons discussed earlier, I did not include in the analysis.

[28] An exception is 2002, when the judges for the newly created family court were first elected.

earliest cycle to a high of 60 percent in the 2000–2006 cycle; however, the pattern of variation is inconsistent. Although it does appear to have risen in the last three cycles, those are the cycles when Republicans contested less than 20 percent of elections. Throughout the period covered in Table 4.1, there were some elections in which Republican candidates were not opposed by Democrats,[29] and they account for much of the proportion of elections "won" by Republicans. Except for the two cycles covering 1984 through 1998, Republicans were elected to between 21 and 28 percent of the trial court seats.

From a partisan political perspective, the most important questions concern those statistics just discussed: How often do the two parties contest an election? How often does each party's candidate win a contested election? What proportion of elections, whether contested or not, is "won" by each party? However, there are two other questions that could be asked: How likely is an election to be contested, including in a party primary? What role does incumbency play in candidate success? Unfortunately, the published West Virginia election results do not include any indication of incumbency, and there is no easy way to determine this for every election; consequently, I cannot address the role of incumbency in West Virginia trial court elections. As for the second question, Table 4.1 does show the percentage of elections in each period in which there is either a contested primary or a contested general election. In the five cycles between 1952 and 1990, the percentage of elections contested varies substantially, ranging from 44.6 percent to 72.5 percent; for three of these five periods, at least 69 percent of elections saw some form of contest.[30] However, starting with the 1992–1996 cycle, the percentage contested dropped to under 40 percent. During the last three cycles, about half of all contested elections were contested only in either the Democratic or Republican primary, usually the Democratic primary.

THE CHANGE TO NONPARTISAN JUDICIAL ELECTIONS

There were three key elements that arguably set the conditions for the West Virginia legislature passing and the governor signing the legislation in 2015 that changed judicial elections in the state to the nonpartisan format. The first was a very nasty Democratic primary for seats on the WVSCA, which occurred in 1988. The second was the controversy surrounding the 2004 WVSCA election and the litigation and U.S. Supreme Court decision that followed.[31] These elections made it clear that

[29] Many, if not most, of these elections occurred in counties in northern and west-central West Virginia, where a majority of voters identified as Republican.

[30] These figures omit elections in which a small number of write-in votes were cast.

[31] Brad McElhinny, "Ugly Race May Fuel Changes in Judicial Selection," *Charleston Gazette & Daily Mail* (November 5, 2004), 1A, wrote, "The push for changes in judicial election rules appeared to gain support after last year's contentious Supreme Court race"; Associated Press, *Charleston Gazette & Daily Mail* (February 15, 2005), 5A.

there were problems with the way judicial elections in West Virginia were being conducted and led to increasing support among both the public and the judiciary for making changes to judicial selection. The final piece was the Republican Party's winning control of both chambers of the West Virginia legislature in the 2014 election for the first time since 1928; the Republican Party had long sought a change to nonpartisan judicial elections.[32]

Judicial Selection Reform Efforts prior to 2004

Early Discussions of Reform

The West Virginia State Bar Association (WVSBA) had long sought to move the state away from partisan judicial elections. In 1950, the WVSBA prepared a bill for a constitutional amendment that would have instituted a modified Missouri Plan system. It was submitted to the legislature, with the backing of the West Virginia Judicial Association (the organization representing trial and appellate judges in the state),[33] but it "did not receive serious consideration by the Legislature."[34] In 1968 the *West Virginia State Bar News* carried a brief report of a "Conference on Judicial Improvement" that was held the prior year in Charleston; that conference, which was cosponsored by the WVSBA,[35] brought together more than 110 lay participants. According to the brief report, among a range of proposals, the conference participants called for the adoption of a Missouri Plan system.[36] This led to an organization called the Citizens Conference on the Administration of Justice (CCAJ). Over the next several years, the CCAJ worked to prepare a proposal for a constitutional amendment that would overhaul the West Virginia court system. In 1972, the CCAJ submitted such a proposal, one part of which was a switch to a

[32] Jim Wallace, "GOP Asks Justices to be Non-Partisan. Lawmakers Make Annual Push for Supreme Court," *Charleston Gazette & Daily Mail* (February 14, 2002), 12A, wrote, "Republican lawmakers are making another push for one of their perennial issues: the nonpartisan election of state Supreme Court justices;" see also Tom Searle, "GOP Wants Parties Out of Judicial Races," *Charleston Gazette & Daily Mail* (February 25, 2004), 6A; Alison Knezevich, "GOP Delegates Lay out Agenda; Priorities: Tax Cuts, Marriage Amendment," *Charleston Gazette & Daily Mail* (February 11, 2009), 3A. The first line of the Knezevich article lists three priorities: "tax cuts, nonpartisan judicial elections and a constitutional amendment defining marriage."

[33] Rupert A. Sinsel, "The President's Annual Address," *West Virginia State Bar News* 2, no. 6 (November–December 1960), 44.

[34] Oshel C. Parsons, "Report of Secretary-Treasurer to Fifth Annual Meeting," *West Virginia State Bar News* 1, no. 18 (September 1952), 158. It appears that, although the proposal was prepared by a group from the WVSBA, it had not actually been approved by the bar membership. ("The State Bar never approved any specific plan for the selection of judges and no such plan has been considered by any State Bar committee.")

[35] "Laymen to Discuss Judicial System," *Charleston Daily Mail* (November 9, 1967), 3.

[36] "Consensus Report of Citizens Conference on the Administration of Justice in West Virginia," *West Virginia State Bar News* no. 41 (October 1968), 363.

Missouri Plan selection and retention system.[37] However, when, in 1974, the legislature approved a proposed amendment for submission to the voters, it had stripped out the proposed change to the selection/retention system, leaving the system unchanged.[38]

During the two or three years after the adoption of the judicial reform amendment, there were continuing discussions of moving away from partisan elections, with support often coming from the judges and the judicial candidates themselves.[39] The focus was on nonpartisan elections, probably because that could be accomplished by statute – the state constitution only required that judges be "elected by the people" – without submitting another constitutional amendment for voter approval. Legislation was introduced in 1977 to make the change to nonpartisan elections,[40] but there was no action on the bill, and the discussion of nonpartisan judicial elections seemed to disappear for about a decade.[41]

The 1988 Supreme Court Primary and Its Aftermath

The idea of changing judicial selection mechanisms reemerged in the late 1980s in the wake of a nasty Democratic primary in the 1988 election for WVSCA. In that election, Circuit Judge Margaret Workman, a challenger, sharply criticized her two incumbent opponents in the primary.[42] Workman won one of the two Democratic slots on the November ballot, defeating Darrell McGraw, who had defeated a Republican appointee in 1976;[43] she went on to win a seat in the November

[37] Robert C. Welling, "Judicial Reform Measure November Vote Doubtful: Opposition from JP Courts," *Charleston Daily Mail* (January 25, 1972), 1.

[38] A review of news coverage available through newspapers.com showed no reference to the inclusion of provisions modifying the selection system in the judicial amendment that was ultimately approved by the legislature and ratified the voters in November 1974; the key controversy regarding the amendment was the abolition of the JP courts and their replacement with a new system of magistrates.

[39] See, for example, Martin Vogel, "Nonpartisan Elections Favored by Aspirants," *Charleston Daily Mail* (October 27, 1976), 14; however, there was also a preference to retain partisan elections among at least some sitting judges; see C. Berkeley Lilly, "Nonpartisan Election of Judges: The Argument Against," *Beckley Post-Herald – Raleigh Register* (March 27, 1977), 7.

[40] "Judge It Well," *Beckley Post-Herald – Raleigh Register* (March 27, 1977), 6.

[41] A search on newspapers.com found no stories between 1978 and 1988, but that may reflect the coverage in that database. However, the state bar publication, which was available for electronic searching, was silent on judicial selection/retention reform.

[42] See "Workman Blasts McGraw," *Beckley Register-Herald* (January 21, 1988), 6A; or Jack Deulich, "Workman Running High-Wire Campaign in Gale-Force Winds," *Beckley Register-Herald* (April 21, 1988), B1.

[43] Darrell McGraw should not be confused with Warren McGraw, who lost to Benjamin in the controversial 2004 election; the two McGraws are brothers. Darrell McGraw went on to win and serve four terms as West Virginia attorney general before narrowly losing to a Republican in 2012. In 2016, he ran unsuccessfully for WVSCA in the first nonpartisan election for that Court; he came in second in a five-candidate field, garnering 23 percent of the vote, compared to almost 40 percent for the winner, Beth Walker.

election.[44] The election involved a noticeable ideological division among candidates, particularly on issues of interest to business such as tort law; the decisions of the Court in tort and workers' comp cases had shifted to noticeably pro-plaintiff in the years 1977–1985.[45] The election campaign for the court seats also saw significant spending by interest groups.[46] A column by the state bar president in the bar's journal commented that the 1988 election for the WVSCA "cried out for changes in the way we pick our judges."[47] Discussions of change coming from the state bar continued into the 1990s, with the president of the state bar calling for merit selection in the *West Virginia Lawyer* in 1991.[48] A survey of bar members conducted in 1994 found that 57 percent felt that the system of judicial selection should be changed, compared to 36 percent who did not want change; 72 percent of those desiring change favored a system of merit selection.[49]

Discussion of change continued in the latter part of the 1990s. In 1997, the WVSCA appointed a 38-member Commission on the Future of the West Virginia Judicial System. Commissioners included attorneys, business leaders, labor leaders, legislators, judges, and persons from the executive branch. One issue the Commission considered was whether to recommend changes to judicial selection. In the end, the majority of the Commission voted down a proposal to recommend a Missouri Plan system of selection and retention. The Commission Report did include a lengthy minority report arguing for such a change.[50]

Around this time, bills to switch to nonpartisan elections were introduced into the legislature, with expressions of support coming from at least some judges.[51] In 1998, a proposal to make judicial elections nonpartisan was offered as an amendment to a proposed constitutional amendment, the main purpose of which was to give the

44 Workman resigned from the Court in 1999 and returned to private practice. Then, in 2008 she ran again for the WVSCA. There were four candidates in the 2008 Democratic primary; Workman came in first, with the one incumbent running, Chief Justice Elliot Maynard, coming in third; see "Vacation Photos Doom W. Va. Top Judge in Primary," *Huntington Herald-Dispatch* (May 14, 2008), www.herald-dispatch.com/news/vacation-photos-doom-w-va-top-judge-in-primary/article_95651bf6-441f-5236-b8b0-d463517bd7be.html, accessed August 30, 2018. Workman came in second in the general election, ahead of the one Republican candidate running, Beth Walker, who was elected to the Court in 2016, defeating Benjamin and several other candidates in a nonpartisan plurality election.

45 See John Patrick Hagan, "Policy Activism in the West Virginia Supreme Court of Appeals, 1930–1985," *West Virginia Law Review* 89 (1986), 162; between 1977 and 1985, 73 percent of the Court's decisions in torts and workers' comp had been pro-plaintiff/claimant, compared to around 40 percent during the preceding 25 years.

46 Communication from Professor Richard Brisbin, August 2, 2018.

47 R. Kemp Morton, "Professionalism and the Bar," *West Virginia Lawyer* 1, no. 3 (April 1988), 5.

48 Charles F. Bagley III, "President's Page," *West Virginia Lawyer* 5, no. 5 (December 1991), 4.

49 Thomas R. Tinder, "Tinder Box: 'Important Issues,'" *West Virginia Lawyer* (April 2000), 36.

50 Commission on the Future of the West Virginia Judicial System, "Final Report," 58–63, https://web.archive.org/web/20110105061849/http://www.state.wv.us/wvsca/future/report/contents.htm, accessed July 22, 2018.

51 Stacey Ruckle, "Bill Deals with Election of Judges; Delegate Says Supreme Court Races Should Be Nonpartisan," *Charleston Gazette & Daily Mail* (March 24, 1997), 6A.

legislature flexibility to establish specialized courts;[52] the change to nonpartisan elections was voted down in the House of Delegates, 32–65 with 25 of the votes in favor coming from the 26 Republican members.[53] Support for change to nonpartisan judicial elections also came from the Republican governor, Cecil Underwood.[54] A public opinion poll conducted around this same time found the electorate closely divided between partisan and nonpartisan elections, with 38 percent preferring the former and 35 percent the latter; 19 percent preferred gubernatorial appointment.[55] A poll of the members of the bar found them largely unchanged from their preferences of five years earlier: 59 percent thought change was needed, and 70 percent of those wanting change preferred a merit selection system.[56] Republicans continued their push for nonpartisan elections into the early 2000s, but the legislation was blocked in committee by the Democratic majority.[57]

Prior to the early 2000s, most of the attention on judicial selection reform in West Virginia was on the WVSCA. Starting in 2003, the West Virginia Chamber of Commerce published a series of reports criticizing trial court outcomes and decisions as harmful to the state's economy and business climate.[58] In 2006, the American Tort Reform Association had West Virginia at the top of its annual list of judicial hellholes.[59] With these developments, the selection/retention of judges at all levels became part of the reform discussion.

The 2004 Supreme Court Election and Subsequent Litigation

The 2004 election of Brent Benjamin to the WVSCA brought judicial selection in West Virginia to national attention. In August 2002, a West Virginia jury returned a verdict in favor of Hugh Caperton, awarding him $50 million. Caperton had sued the Massey Coal Company, claiming that Massey had effectively put Caperton's

52 The voters ultimately rejected the proposed amendment, but two years later approved a more limited amendment authorizing the creation of a family court.

53 Fanny Seiler, "Nonpartisan Judgeships Voted Down," *Charleston Gazette & Daily Mail* (March 6, 1998), 1A; it is unclear whether the remaining one Republican voted against the change or was one of the three delegates not voting.

54 Karin Fischer, "Underwood Backing Judicial Reform; Governor Says Elections Should Be Nonpartisan," *Charleston Gazette & Mail* (September 10, 1999), 1C.

55 "System of Picking Judges Divides Voters, Poll Shows," *Charleston Gazette & Daily Mail* (January 27, 1998), 5A.

56 Tinder, "Tinder Box: 'Important Issues,'" *supra* note 49, 36.

57 See Jim Wallace, "GOP Asks Justices to Be Non-partisan; Lawmakers Make Annual Push for Supreme Court," *Charleston Gazette & Daily Mail* (February 14, 2002), 12A; Tom Searle, "GOP Wants Parties Out of Judicial Races," *Charleston Gazette & Daily Mail* (February 25, 2004), 6A.

58 See West Virginia Chamber of Commerce, "The Cost of the Law," *Court Watch* (July 2003); West Virginia Chamber of Commerce, "Property and Casualty Insurance Crisis Costing Consumers Millions," *Court Watch* (February 2004); West Virginia Chamber of Commerce, "W. Va. Supreme Court Decisions Hindering Job Growth, Creation," *Court Watch* (August 2004); West Virginia Chamber of Commerce, *Comprehensive Civil Justice Reforms* (2006).

59 See www.judicialhellholes.org/archive-2006/, accessed August 31, 2018; the full report is at www.judicialhellholes.org/wp-content/uploads/2010/12/JH2006.pdf.

coal company out of business by canceling a supply contract with the company. The 2004 election became controversial when the CEO of Massey, Don Blankenship, spent $3 million in an effort to defeat incumbent Justice Warren McGraw. McGraw, a Democrat, had been elected in 1998 to complete an unexpired term, defeating the Republican incumbent who had been appointed at the beginning of 1998 by the then Republican governor to fill a vacancy. McGraw had a reputation as being pro-plaintiff, and Blankenship wanted to see a justice elected who would be more inclined to support Massey in an appeal.

Under West Virginia law, Blankenship could contribute a maximum of $1,000 to Benjamin's campaign. To get around this limit, Blankenship arranged for ads to be run by various groups, to which he contributed a total of $3 million. These ads attacked McGraw along a range of issues, including his decisions in criminal cases involving sexual abuse. One of the organizations Blankenship created and funded, And for the Sake of Kids, received the largest share of Blankenship's money. It was reported to have run a television ad attacking McGraw for a decision refusing to revoke the probation of a young man who had been convicted of sexually abusing his half-brother, the opening of which was phrased in a way that someone hearing it might think McGraw himself was the abuser.[60] Benjamin won the election with 53 percent of the vote.

When the *Caperton* appeal came to the WVSCA in 2007, Caperton asked that Benjamin recuse himself because of the election support he had received from Blankenship. Benjamin refused to do so, and the Court overturned the $50 million verdict on a vote of 3–2. Caperton petitioned for a rehearing after photos came out showing one of the other justices in the majority, Elliot "Spike" Maynard, vacationing with Massey;[61] as part of the petition, Caperton asked that both Benjamin and Maynard recuse themselves. Massey asked that a third judge, Larry Starcher, who had been one of the dissenters, recuse himself. Maynard did recuse, as eventually did Starcher, but Benjamin declined to recuse, and served as acting chief justice for the rehearing. In that role, Benjamin selected two trial court judges to replace the recused justices. The decision was again 3–2, overturning the jury award.[62]

Caperton sought review by the U.S. Supreme Court on the grounds of a violation of due process. The Supreme Court granted review and reversed the WVSCA on a vote of 5–4, with the four "liberal" justices (Stevens, Souter, Breyer, and Ginsburg) and Justice Kennedy in the majority. In his majority opinion, Justice Kennedy found that the magnitude of Blankenship's donations were such that recusal was required because "there is a serious risk of actual bias – based on objective and reasonable

[60] "He sexually molested multiple West Virginia children. Liberal Judge Warren McGraw cast the deciding vote to set up this reprehensible criminal free"; see Stephanie Mencimer, *Blocking the Courthouse Door: How the Republican Party and Its Corporate Allies Are Taking Away Your Right to Sue* (New York: Simon & Schuster, 2006), 72.

[61] Adam Liptak, "Motion Ties W. Virginia Justice to Coal Executive," *New York Times* (January 15, 2008), www.nytimes.com/2008/01/15/us/15court.html, accessed August 30, 2018.

[62] Caperton v. A. T. Massey Coal Co., 690 S.E.2d 322 (W.V. 2009).

perceptions – when a person with a personal stake in a particular case had a significant and disproportionate influence in placing the judge on the case by raising funds or directing the judge's election campaign when the case was pending or imminent."[63] When the case got back to the WVSCA, the bench that heard the case included several acting justices and only one of the original justices. Again, the Court overturned the $50 million award, ruling on a 4 to 1 vote that the case should have been filed in Virginia rather than in West Virginia, because of a clause in the contract at issue.[64]

Because of the issues raised by the McGraw-Benjamin election, and the subsequent litigation over whether Benjamin should have recused himself, the events and the litigation received extensive attention, including in the general news media and the legal press.[65] The controversy surrounding the 2004 election put the issue of judicial selection reform in West Virginia squarely on the political agenda. However, actual change did not come until the third piece, Republican control of the West Virginia legislature, was in place.[66]

Adoption of Nonpartisan Elections

Perhaps anticipating the controversy that would follow the 2004 election, legal interests renewed their call for a system of merit selection in the months prior to the election.[67] The board of governors of the state bar narrowly approved a study of the issue that summer,[68] and in July the president of the state bar appointed a

63 Caperton v. A. T. Massey Coal Co., 556 U.S. 868, 884 (2009).

64 Caperton v. A. T. Massey Coal Co., Inc., 690 S.E.2d 322, 340–41 (W.Va. 2009).

65 For detailed background on the case, see Laurence Leamer, *The Price of Justice: A True Story of Greed and Corruption* (New York: Times Books/Henry Holt, 2013). The case also served as the inspiration for John Grisham's 2008 novel, *The Appeal.*

66 Controversy continued to follow Don Blankenship. In the wake of a major disaster at one of Massey's mines in 2010, which resulted in the deaths of 29 miners, in 2016 Blankenship was convicted of conspiring to violate federal mine safety standards and was sentenced to a year in prison; see Alan Binder, "Donald Blankenship Sentenced to a Year in Prison in Mine Safety Case," *New York Times* (April 6, 2016), A12. In 2018, he ran unsuccessfully in the Republican primary for the United States Senate, attracting support of only 20 percent of Republican primary voters; despite losing the primary, he stayed in the Senate race as the candidate of the West Virginia Constitution Party – see Blair Guild, "Don Blankenship to File as Third-Party Candidate in West Virginia Senate Race," CBS News (July 24, 2018), www.cbsnews.com/news/don-blankenship-to-file-as-third-party-candidate-in-west-virginia-senate-race/, accessed August 30, 2018. Also noteworthy, and discussed later in this chapter, is that when Benjamin stood for reelection in 2016, in what was then a nonpartisan election, he came in a dismal third.

67 Larry R. Rowe, "Merit-Based Proposal: Voters Should Remain in Control of Judicial Selection," *Charleston Gazette & Daily Mail* (January 30, 2004), 5A.

68 "Planned State Bar Study Not a New Idea; Talk of End to Partisan Judicial Elections First Came Up in 1996; Panel to Look at Issue Again," *Charleston Gazette & Daily Mail* (August 2, 2004), 4B; see also, Chris Wetterich, "Battle Heats Up over Elected Judges; State Bar Might Study Issue; Justice Wants Review Quashed," *Charleston Gazette & Daily Mail* (July 21, 2004), 1C.

Judicial Selection Committee (JSC), but the JSC did not immediately convene. In the days immediately following the election, the JSC chairperson announced that it would have its first meeting in December, and he expressed the hope that a recommendation would be ready sometime in the spring.[69] However, the JSC was not able to release its report and recommendations until September 2005. By an 8–7 vote, the overall JSC approved the report of the subcommittee recommending a merit selection system. However, the JSC also recognized that enacting such a system would be problematic, presumably because of a combination of potential opposition, a concern that a change to a Missouri Plan system would constrain the governor's choice, and the requirement that doing away with contested elections and instituting retention elections would necessitate approval of a constitutional amendment by the electorate.[70] As an alternative, the JSC recommended, by a vote of 9–6, that the legislature adopt nonpartisan elections for the WVSCA and for any intermediate Court of Appeals that might be created.[71] Unsurprisingly, given the 2004 election, bills were introduced to end partisan ballots, at least for the Supreme Court of Appeals, when the legislature convened in 2005, well before any report or recommendations from the JSC. Critics of the proposals observed that nonpartisan elections would not end the problem of big money in Supreme Court campaigns; one critic called it a "sham solution."[72]

Change did not come immediately. Nothing emerged from the legislature in 2005. Bills to make some or all judicial elections nonpartisan, or to shift to an appointive system, were introduced every year between 2006 and 2015.[73] Activity seemed to accelerate starting in 2008. That year, the legislature created a joint interim subcommittee to examine the issues associated with various selection/retention alternatives. The subcommittee heard a variety of views from experts and others.[74] In mid-2008, the state bar created another study group to look at, among other things, possible changes to judicial selection. At the end of 2008, there was a news report that Democratic governor Joe Manchin was supportive of ending

69 Lawrence Messina, "State Bar to Review Judicial Elections; Messy Matchup between Benjamin and McGraw Cited," *Charles Gazette & Mail* (November 4, 2004), 1A.

70 The report itself does not explain why the JSC thought adopting a "merit plan" would be problematic; these are my speculations.

71 See the Judicial Selection Committee report, http://web.archive.org/web/20091114041547/http://www.judicialreform.wv.gov/reports/Documents/Bar%20Report.pdf, accessed July 25, 2018.

72 "Bill Requires High Court Ballots to Be Printed Minus Party Affiliation," *Charleston Gazette & Daily Mail* (February 15, 2005), 5A.

73 This is mostly from the Gavel to Gavel database of proposed legislation concerning the courts introduced between 2008 and 2015, http://gaveltogavel.us/database/, accessed July 24, 2018. The database does not extend prior to 2008, but I was able to locate proposed legislation or constitutional amendments on the legislature's bill-stats website www.wvlegislature.gov/Bill_Status/Bills_all_bills.cfm, accessed August 30, 2018.

74 Lawrence Messina, "W. Va. Lawmakers Eye New Ways to Pick Judges," *Charleston Gazette & Daily Mail* (September 9, 2008).

partisan judicial elections, and that he had approached the West Virginia Judicial Association to get its support for the proposal.[75] In his February 2009 State of the State Address, Manchin announced he would appoint a committee to look at modernizing the court system, including "determining the best system for selecting judges among partisan election, nonpartisan election, and merit selection systems."[76] He subsequently created a nine-member Independent Commission on Judicial Reform (ICJR), with a request that it report by the end of the year, both on judicial selection and on other issues such as whether to create an intermediate Court of Appeals.[77] The legislative session ended in April without any action on judicial selection. Then, in June 2009, the U.S. Supreme Court handed down its decision in *Caperton*,[78] ruling that that the magnitude of Blankenship's donations to Benjamin's 2004 campaign were such that Benjamin's refusal to recuse himself from the WVSCA consideration of the appeal in *Caperton v. Massey* violated Caperton's due process rights.

In November 2009 the ICJR issued its final report.[79] The report did not recommend a change to nonpartisan elections. While noting the arguments in favor of nonpartisan elections, it went on to observe that opponents "insist that nonpartisan elections deprive voters of valuable information and frequently result in decreased voter participation in judicial elections."[80] Regarding merit selection, the report suggested that a significant portion of circuit judges were already selected through a merit-like system, 45 percent of the then active judges had been appointed to fill vacancies, and that Governor Manchin and his immediate predecessors used advisory committees to make recommendations of candidates to fill such vacancies.[81]

Although presumably the governors had generally followed the recommendations they received from their advisory committees, the ICJR's report failed to explicitly point out that the governor was not legally bound by the committees' recommendations. That is, unlike the Missouri Plan or other "merit" selection systems, the governor was free to appoint anyone having the legal qualifications for a judicial position; this was because the state constitution granted the governor broad powers in filling midterm vacancies on the courts listed in the judicial article of the constitution. The ICJR did suggest that the legislature "enhance and codify the

75 Lawrence Messina, "Nonpartisan Judiciary Possible; Manchin Sees Benefits to End of Electing Judges on Partisan Lines," *Charles Gazette & Daily Mail* (December 1, 2008).

76 Phil Kahler, "'The Hard Work Is Not Over': W. Va. Will Face Recession without Fear, Manchin Says," *Charleston Gazette & Daily Mail* (February 12, 2009).

77 Lawrence Messina, "Research on State Courts Nears End; Study of System Will End with Recommended Changes," *Charleston Gazette & Daily Mail* (September 28, 2009), 5A.

78 Caperton v. A. T. Massey Coal Co., 556 U.S. 868 (2009).

79 See www.scribd.com/document/22604435/West-Virginia-Independent-Commission-on-Judicial-Reform-Final-Report, accessed July 24, 2018.

80 *Id.*, 23.

81 *Id.*, 21.

advisory committee process utilized to fill midterm interim judicial vacancies."[82] It went on to recommend that if the legislature created an intermediate Court of Appeals, as the ICJR recommended it should,[83] the initial selection of judges should be through a merit process. The language in the report appears to suggest that because this would be a legislatively created court rather than one listed in the state constitution, the legislature could bind the governor to appoint judges from among those recommended by a screening committee.[84] The report left open the question of how judges of the new court should be retained; it did not even mention retention elections, but presumably, given constitutional silence on the issue of retention and selection of an intermediate appellate court, there would be the option of retention elections. Thus, the IJCR saw a new, legislatively created intermediate appellate court as an opportunity to experiment with an alternative method of judicial selection and retention.

Despite support for nonpartisan elections from the Democratic governor, proposed legislation from 2009 to 2014 to make the change never made it out of committee in the Democratic-controlled legislature. Then, in 2014, for the first time since 1928, Republicans won a majority in both chambers of the legislature (18–16 in the Senate and 64–36 in the House).[85]

Legislation to change all judicial elections to use nonpartisan ballots moved rapidly through the now Republican-controlled legislature after it convened in January 2015.[86] In early February, the House of Delegates passed H.B. 2010 on a vote of 90–9, with all nine negative votes coming from Democrats.[87] There were two other noteworthy provisions: future judicial elections would occur in the spring, coinciding with the party primaries in May, and candidates for the WVSCA would run for individual seats, ending the "cattle call" format that had been done away with for the circuit courts in 1990.

There were several potential explanations for the decision to hold the judicial elections in the spring. Among the stated reasons were:

[82] *Id.*, 24.

[83] Lawrence Messina, "Judicial Reform in W. Va.: 2nd Appeals Court Needed," *Charleston Gazette & Daily Mail* (November 17, 2009) 5A.

[84] The language of Section 1 of Article VIII authorizes the creation of an intermediate appellate court, but no language in the Constitution specifies how judges of such a court would be selected or retained; www.wvlegislature.gov/WVCODE/WV_CON.cfm#articleVIII, accessed July 24, 2018.

[85] See https://en.wikipedia.org/wiki/Political_party_strength_in_West_Virginia, accessed July 25, 2018.

[86] Interestingly, the association of West Virginia judges neither supported nor opposed the change; Whitney Burdette, "Panel Rejects Changes to Election Bill," *Charleston Gazette & Mail* (January 29, 2015), 2A.

[87] "Judicial Measure Passes House," *Huntington Herald-Dispatch* (February 5, 2015), www.herald-dispatch.com/news/judicial-measure-passes-house/article_0140e6c3-ccc8-50f4-8b7a-68fb7cca8a54.html, accessed January 20, 2019.

- May elections would mean a shorter campaign season resulting in candidates not having to raise as much money.[88]
- May elections would encourage more lawyers to run for judgeships.[89]
- May elections would allow lawyers newly elected to the bench time to close their legal practices.[90]
- May elections would allow time for training of new judges.[91]

An unstated reason for the May elections was what some saw as advantaging candidates with Republican leanings,[92] presumably because Republicans are more likely to turn out for the May primary, particularly given the increasing success of Republican candidates and the consequential likelihood of contested Republican primaries. A proposal to change the legislation so that judicial elections would continue to be in November was overwhelmingly defeated.[93] No one seems to have considered the implications of omitting any provision for a runoff, should no candidate garner a majority of the vote;[94] this means that in an election with three or more candidates, all that is needed to win is a plurality. This happened in the first WVSCA election in 2016 and then in the two elections in 2018, when the winning candidates received less than 40 percent of the vote.

The vote on H.B. 2010 in the House of Delegates had strong partisan overtones: all the Republicans voted in favor, with Democrats splitting and nine voting against the bill. It is noteworthy that the loudest voice against the change to nonpartisan elections came from the West Virginia Association for Justice, the organization of personal injury plaintiffs' lawyers;[95] given that the plaintiffs' bar has generally supported Democratic candidates, it is unsurprising that there were some negative votes by Democrats. Opponents cited at least three reasons for their opposition:

88 Whitney Burdette, "House Oks Elections Change; Judicial Reform Bill Would End Use of Party Affiliation in Voting for Judges," *Charleston Gazette & Daily Mail* (February 5, 2015), 2A.

89 Eric Eyrem, "House Oks Nonpartisan Judge Elections," *Charleston Gazette & Daily Mail* (February 5, 2015), 1C.

90 Phil Kabler, "Senate Signs Amendment to Hold Nonpartisan Judge Elections in May," *Charleston Gazette & Daily Mail* (February 20, 2015), 1C.

91 *Id.*

92 Telephone interview with Stephen Skinner, April 3, 2018. Mr. Skinner is a former Democratic member of the House of Delegates.

93 Whitney Burdette, "House Advances Judicial Bill; Legislation Making Elections for Judges Nonpartisan Moves to Floor Vote Today," *Charleston Gazette & Daily Mail* (February 4, 2015), 2A.

94 I was told by Stephen Skinner that allowing judicial elections to be determined by a plurality rather than requiring a majority (and, hence, needing to provide for a runoff) was unintentional.

95 Whitney Burdette, "House Bill Changes Election of Judges," *Charleston Gazette & Daily Mail* (January 27, 2015), 1A; Whitney Burdette, "Judicial Elections Bill Incites Disputes; Measure Aims to Remove Partisan Politics State's Court Races," *Charleston Gazette & Daily Mail* (April 8, 2015), 1A; Eric Eyre, "House OKs Nonpartisan Judge Elections."

- Voters rely on the information provided by the party labels in deciding for whom to vote.[96]
- Holding elections at the time of the primary advantages conservative – i.e., Republican – candidates.[97]
- The bill did not go far enough because campaign contributions continue to be unlimited.[98]

The Senate passed a slightly different version of the bill on a vote of 33–1. The two chambers quickly resolved the differences and sent the measure on to Governor Manchin. Manchin found several minor technical defects in the legislation and vetoed the bill. The House and Senate rectified the defects and sent the bill back to the governor, who signed the legislation in late March of 2015.

THE 2016 JUDICIAL ELECTIONS AND BEYOND

Given West Virginia's system of running terms for all trial judges concurrently, there has been only a single round of elections for judges of the circuit and family courts as this was written in 2019. In 2016, there were elections for 69 trial court positions; 42, or 60.9 percent, were contested.[99] Between 1992 and 2014, there were 250 trial court elections, only 36.0 percent of which were contested, including elections that were contested only in the primary. This pattern is interesting because it runs counter to research showing a lower rate of contestation in nonpartisan trial court elections than in partisan trial court elections.[100] Perhaps proponents of spring elections were correct in their argument that having judicial elections at that time would increase lawyers' interest in running for judgeships.

There was an election for the WVSCA in 2016 as well. In that election Justice Brent Benjamin, who won the controversial 2004 election, sought to retain his seat on the Court. He faced four opponents. Benjamin had won the 2004 election running as a Republican. Two of his opponents in 2016 had solid Democratic credentials. One was Darrell McGraw, who previously had been elected to the WVSCA as a Democrat in 1976 but came in third in the nasty 1988 Democratic

96 Whitney Burdette, "House Bill Changes Election of Judges"; Whitney Burdette, "House Oks Election Changes; Judicial Reform Bill Would End Use of Party Affiliation in Voting for Judges," *Charleston Gazette & Daily Mail* (February 5, 2015), 2A.

97 This was implicit in the observation of Democrat Marcum Mingo that conservative states with nonpartisan elections hold them in the primary season; see Burdette, "House Advances Judicial Bill," *supra* note 93. In fact, Mingo was incorrect. States with primary-time judicial elections include Wisconsin, Oregon, Arkansas, Idaho and, prior to 2016, Washington.

98 "Judicial Measure Passes House," *supra* note 87; Burdette, "House OKs Election Changes," *supra* note 96.

99 An additional 6 trial court elections were contested in 2018; it is unclear if there were also some uncontested elections for the trial court.

100 Michael J. Nelson, "Uncontested and Unaccountable? Rates of Contestation in Trial Court Elections," *Judicature* 94, no. 5 (March–April 2011), 216.

primary described previously; he then served four terms as the Democratic attorney general of West Virginia, taking office in 1997; he was defeated for reelection in 2012. The other candidate with Democratic credentials was Bill Wooton, who had served in the state legislature, in both the House of Delegates and the Senate, for a total of twenty-two nonconsecutive years. The two other candidates were lawyers in private practice, Beth Walker and Wayne King, neither of whom had run for office previously. Although Benjamin had attracted support from business groups in addition to that from Don Blankenship in the 2004 election, the conservative and probusiness political action committees backed Walker, spending more than $3 million in supporting her and in attacking the two candidates with Democratic credentials.[101] Walker won with 39.6 percent of the vote. Incumbent Benjamin got a measly 12.5 percent; the two Democrats, McGraw and Wooton, got 23.1 percent and 20.7 percent respectively. The partisan correlation (defined in Chapter 1) was .681; this compares to an average correlation of for the period 1980 to 2014 between the county-level percent for the Democratic candidates for WVSCA and governor of .760. Thus, the voting pattern in the 2016 election for WVSCA was almost as partisan as the partisan elections of the previous thirty-five years.

THE ENSUING CHAOS OF 2018

Although no election for the WVSCA was anticipated to occur in 2018, the justices of that Court, including the recently elected Beth Walker, were impeached, which resulted in the resignation of two justices in time for special elections to be scheduled to take place in November along with the other legislative and congressional elections.

In June 2018, Justice Allen Loughry, the author of the lengthy book on corruption in West Virginia politics and government and the first Republican to be elected (in 2012) to a full twelve-year term in at least fifty years, was charged by the West Virginia Judicial Investigation Commission (JIC) with thirty-two violations of the Code of Judicial Conduct.[102] The charging document quoted from Loughry's book:[103]

> Part of the driving force behind my decision to write this book is the fact that I am so outraged with my state's political corruption. The countless disgusting examples of politicians violating the people's trust are not just embarrassing and disheartening but have completely shattered my confidence in my state's government.[104]

[101] Phil Kabler, "Benjamin Ousted from High Court by Beth Walker," *Charleston Gazette & Daily Mail* (May 11, 2016), 1A.

[102] Brad McElhinny, "Justice Loughry Named in 32-Count Judicial Complaint Saying He Lied Over and Over," *MetroNews* (June 6, 2016), https://s3.amazonaws.com/wvmetro-uploads-prod/2018/06/Loughry-JIC.pdf?x43308, accessed July 18, 2018.

[103] The charging document can be found at https://s3.amazonaws.com/wvmetro-uploads-prod/2018/06/Loughry-JIC.pdf?x43308, accessed July 18, 2018.

[104] Loughry, *Don't Buy Another Vote*, *supra* note 15, xxvii.

Ironically, in his book, Loughry made it clear that corruption was a particularly bad problem if it involved the judiciary:

> Of all the criminal politicians in West Virginia, the group that shatters the confidence of the people the most is a corrupt judiciary. It is essential that people have the absolute confidence in the integrity and impartiality of our system of justice.[105]

A couple of weeks after the initiation of disciplinary charges, Loughry was indicted by a federal grand jury on charges of fraud and swindle, fraud by wire, making false statements, and witness tampering;[106] a charge of obstruction of justice was added later.[107] He was subsequently convicted on 11 of 22 charges, including wire fraud, mail fraud, making false statements to federal investigators, and witness tampering; the jury acquitted him on ten other charges and deadlocked on one.[108] He was sentenced to twenty-four months in federal prison and fined $10,000.[109]

In July 2018, soon after Loughry was indicted, former justice Menis Ketchum abruptly retired with two years remaining on his term. A report to the legislature earlier in the year by legislative auditors found that Ketchum had used state-owned vehicles for personal matters – personal commuting and pleasure trips – when they were only supposed to be used for business purposes. Ketchum had reimbursed the state for at least some of that use as well as for a state-owned grandfather clock that he had taken to his home.[110] Subsequently, Ketchum agreed to plead guilty a federal charge of defrauding taxpayers by his personal use of the state car;[111]

[105] *Id.*, 294.

[106] Lacie Pierson, "WV Supreme Court Justice Loughry Indicted on Fraud, Other Charges," *Charleston Gazette-Mail* (June 20, 2018), www.wvgazettemail.com/news/cops_and_courts/wv-supreme-court-justice-loughry-indicted-on-fraud-other-charges/article_7f6bc8cb-663b-5b5d-bf94-7cee270acbfc.html, accessed July 19, 2018.

[107] "'Very, Very Serious Charge' Added to Those Against Suspended Supreme Court Justice Ahead of This Week's Impeachment Hearing," *Metro News* (July 18, 2018), http://wvmetronews.com/2018/07/18/very-very-serious-charge-added-to-those-against-suspended-supreme-court-justice-ahead-of-this-weeks-impeachment-hearings/, accessed July 19, 2018.

[108] Lacie Pierson, "WV Supreme Court Justice Guilty on 11 of 22 Federal Charges," *West Virginia Gazette and Mail* (October 12, 2018), www.wvgazettemail.com/news/cops_and_courts/wv-supreme-court-justice-loughry-guilty-on-of-federal-charges/article_dd705b7d-dc3b-5cfb-9edd-a2257d584deb.html, accessed October 18, 2018.

[109] Phil Kabler, "Former Supreme Court Justice Loughry Sentenced to 24 Months in Federal Prison," *Charleston Gazette-Mail* (February 13, 2019), www.wvgazettemail.com/news/cops_and_courts/former-supreme-court-justice-loughry-sentenced-to-months-in-federal/article_bb22ed30-e4f1-5e28-9ef1-b95f48efb635.html, accessed March 4, 2019.

[110] Lori Kersey and Lacie Pierson, "On Eve of Impeachment Meetings, Ketchum Quits WV Supreme Court," *Charleston Gazette-Mail* (July 11, 2018), www.wvgazettemail.com/news/politics/on-eve-of-impeachment-meetings-ketchum-quits-wv-supreme-court/article_0bb52c20-b886-53c9-b221-b3f3991554ce.html, accessed July 19, 2018.

[111] Lacie Pierson, "Ketchum Agrees to Plead Guilty to Fraud," *Huntington Herald-Dispatch* (August 1, 2018), www.herald-dispatch.com/news/ketchum-agrees-to-plead-guilty-to-fraud/article_4be30714-4f8c-5f68-99fe-c85f2dba537b.html, accessed August 8, 2018.

he was sentenced to three years' probation, fined $20,000, and ordered to pay $749 in restitution.[112]

In the wake of the charges against Justice Loughry, the West Virginia legislature initiated an investigation as to whether to seek the impeachment of Loughry and other members of the WVSCA, including Beth Walker, who had been on the Court for less than two years, having taken office in 2017 after winning the first nonpartisan election for the Court in 2016.[113] The potential impeachment of Loughry would deal with both the federal criminal charges and related allegations of using state cars and other state resources for personal purposes. There were also reports of inappropriate use of state resources by the other justices. At the same time that the legislature was considering impeachment of Loughry and other justices, the JIC was investigating whether ethics complaints should be brought against the three other justices (Margaret Workman, Robin Davis, and Beth Walker); the JIC closed the investigation without bringing any charges.[114] Despite the JIC decision, on August 7 the legislative committee considering impeachment approved fourteen articles of impeachment covering all four remaining justices, and sent the question of impeachment on to the full House of Delegates. The charges included "maladministration, corruption, incompetency, neglect of duty and certain high crimes." Each justice was "charged with 'unnecessary and lavish' spending of state taxpayer dollars to renovate their offices in the East Wing of the Capitol" and "failing to develop and maintain court policies regarding the use of state resources, including cars, computers and funds in general."[115]

On August 13, the West Virginia House of Delegates voted to impeach all four remaining justices. The House approved 11 of 14 proposed articles of impeachment. The various charges included lavish spending on office furniture (e.g., a $32,000 office sofa purchased by Loughry), wasteful spending on office renovations, making personal use of state-owned property, overpaying retired judges filling in to hear cases, and failing to create policies to rein in each other's wasteful spending.[116]

112 "Ex-W. Va. Justice Sentenced in Corruption Scandal," *Washington Post* (March 6, 2019), www.washingtonpost.com/national/the-latest-ex-wva-justice-sentenced-in-corruption-scandal/2019/03/06/4f8e4126-4044-11e9-85ad-779ef05fd9d8_story.html?utm_term=.a50f522b4e2e, accessed March 11, 2019.

113 Lacie Pierson, "Investigation into WV Supreme Court Impeachment Begins in House," *Charleston Gazette-Mail* (July 12, 2018), www.wvgazettemail.com/news/politics/investigation-into-wv-supreme-court-impeachment-begins-in-house/article_455952e5-9b8c-5b9d-b430-0ffeb7067e04.html, accessed July 19, 2018.

114 "JIC Clears Workman, Davis, Walker in Ethics Complaint," *Metro News* (July 23, 2018), http://wvmetronews.com/2018/07/23/jic-clears-workman-davis-walker-in-ethics-complaint/, accessed July 24, 2018.

115 Lacie Pierson, "WV House Committee Approves 14 Articles of Impeachment against Justices," *Charleston Gazette-Mail* (August 7, 2018), www.wvgazettemail.com/news/politics/wv-house-committee-approves-articles-of-impeachment-against-justices/article_f4795b83-ba20-5ac8-a267-aeb4b10060fa.html.

116 Campbell Robertson, "West Virginia House of Delegates Votes to Impeach Entire State Supreme Court," *New York Times* (August 14, 2018), www.nytimes.com/2018/08/14/us/west-virginia-impeach-supreme-court.html, accessed September 1, 2018.

Four articles were approved with little or no dissent. Votes on four other articles were roughly 2 to 1 in favor (64–33, 62–34, 61–35, and 61–33). The votes approving the other three articles were more divided (56–41, 51–45, and 51–44).[117]

Strong support for impeachment came from Republican delegates, who held 64 of the 100 seats in the House of Delegates. In the votes in which 61 to 63 delegates voted in favor, all or almost all of those votes came from Republicans, with only one Republican voting against. In the closer votes approving an article of impeachment (i.e., 51 to 56 delegates voting in favor), Democrats voted strongly against, with only between 1 and 4 voting in favor; Republicans were more divided, with between 7 and 15 voting against the article. With this pattern it is not surprising that some Democratic delegates complained, in the words of one of them, that what happened was a "coup" that would allow the complete takeover of the WVSCA by the Republicans, because replacements would be named by the Republican governor for any justices who resigned or were removed from office by conviction on impeachment by the Senate.[118] However, that complaint ignores the fact that Democrats voted unanimously in favor of four articles covering three of the four justices, one of whom had been elected as a Democrat.

The day after the House of Delegates voted to impeach the four justices, Justice Robin Davis, one of the three Democrats on the Court, announced her immediate resignation. Davis made her resignation effective the previous day so that there would have to be a special election in November to fill her seat for the remainder of her term.[119] After resigning, Davis filed a federal lawsuit naming as defendants the governor and several legislators, claiming the action of legislators voting in favor of impeachment was motivated by gender bias, and that she would not have been impeached "had she not been a woman." She asked that the pending impeachment trial against her be halted.[120]

[117] "West Virginia Supreme Court Articles of Impeachment: A Closer Look," *Wheeling News-Register* (August 15, 2018), www.theintelligencer.net/news/top-headlines/2018/08/west-virginia-supreme-court-articles-of-impeachment-a-closer-look/, accessed September 1, 2018. Details on the roll-call votes can be found on the legislature's website at www.wvlegislature.gov/legisdocs/2018/2X/votes/house/00604.pdf through www.wvlegislature.gov/legisdocs/2018/2X/votes/house/00619.pdf, accessed September 1, 2018; if there was a roll-call vote on Article XI, it was missing from the website.

[118] Campbell Robertson, "A Coup or a Couch? What's Behind the Impeachment of West Virginia's Supreme Court," *New York Times* (August 14, 2018), www.nytimes.com/2018/08/14/us/west-virginia-impeachment-supreme-court.html, accessed September 1, 2018.

[119] Jake Zuckerman, "WV Supreme Court Justice Davis Resigns, Says People, Not Politicians, Should Choose Successor," *Charleston Gazette-Mail* (August 14, 2018), www.wvgazettemail.com/news/cops_and_couts/wv-supreme-court-justice-davis-resigns-says-people-not-politicians/article_91a8f5ae-0030-5c98-b6e2-639827e46929.html, accessed September 3, 2018.

[120] John Raby, "Ex-West Virginia Justice Blames Impeachment on Gender Bias" (September 26, 2018), www.whsv.com/content/news/Ex-West-Virginia-justice-blames-impeachment-on-gender-bias-494437551.html, accessed October 18, 2018.

With Davis's resignation, there were now two vacancies on the five-member court (the other was the position previously occupied by Menis Ketchum), both to be filled by special elections. About ten days after Davis's resignation, Republican governor Jim Justice appointed two well-known conservative Republicans to replace the two justices who had resigned, both of whom had been elected as Democrats;[121] the new appointees would face the electorate in a special election in November. As one might expect, the appointments were praised by Republican leaders and sharply criticized by Democrats. The appointees successfully retained their positions in the November election. Both faced nine opponents, and both received much less than a majority of the votes: 36 percent for one and 26 percent for the other.[122]

The first impeachment trial, of Beth Walker, took place at the beginning of October. The West Virginia Senate rejected impeachment, 32–1, but then proceeded to unanimously censure her on a voice vote.[123] About a week later, shortly before the impeachment trial of Chief Justice Margaret Workman was scheduled to start, the West Virginia Supreme Court of Appeals, consisting of five acting justices, effectively blocked the trial from proceeding by issuing an order prohibiting the justice who was to preside at the trial from doing so.[124] The Court found several defects in the impeachment articles, including issues related to separation of powers – the impeachment articles were based on the Code of Judicial Conduct, which the court found could only be enforced by the Supreme Court itself – and the absence of any findings of fact. Part of the problem related back to the text of the impeachment provision in the West Virginia State Constitution: "Any officer of the state may be impeached for maladministration, corruption, incompetency, gross immorality, neglect of duty, or any high crime or misdemeanor ... The Senate shall have the sole power to try impeachments ... and the senators shall be on oath or affirmation to do justice according to law and evidence."[125] In its ruling, the Supreme Court found that the legislature "was not doing justice 'according to law and evidence.'"[126]

[121] Dave Mistich, "Gov. Justice Appoints Armstead, Jenkins to West Virginia Supreme Court," West Virginia Public Broadcasting (August 25, 2018), www.wvpublic.org/post/gov-justice-appoints-armstead-jenkins-west-virginia-supreme-court#stream/0, accessed August 26, 2018.

[122] These percentages are based on unofficial returns, at electionresults.wvmetronews.com/countybycounty.cfm, accessed November 9, 2018.

[123] "W. Va. Senate Rejects Impeachment, Approves Censure of State Supreme Court Justice Beth Walker" (October 2, 2018), www.wvnews.com/news/wvnews/w-va-senate-rejects-impeachment-approves-censure-of-state-supreme/article_dd036743-341d-5907-b810-0035bbd8290e.html, accessed October 15, 2018.

[124] State *ex rel.* Workman v. Carmichael, 819 S.E.2d 251 (W. Va. 2018).

[125] West Virginia Constitution, Article IV, §9.

[126] State *ex rel.* Workman v. Carmichael, 264; see also, Meagan Flynn, "West Virginia Botches Impeachment of Chief Justice; Faces Constitutional Crisis; Stay Tuned," *Washington Post* (October 15, 2018), www.washingtonpost.com/news/morning-mix/wp/2018/10/15/west-virginia-botches-impeachment-of-chief-justice-faces-constitutional-crisis-stay-tuned/?utm_term=.591e42eacff7, accessed October 18, 2018.

About three weeks after the Court ruling blocking the impeachment trials, the governor issued a proclamation calling the legislature into special session to consider impeachment of Allen Loughry in light of his conviction on federal criminal charges. Presumably the thought was that impeachment charges against Loughry could be based on his criminal behavior rather than on the Code of Judicial Conduct. Loughry, who had been suspended from the Court after his federal indictment, resigned from the Court the day after the governor's proclamation.[127]

With Loughry's resignation, the governor had the opportunity to make a third appointment to the Supreme Court of Appeals. His choice was John Hutchinson, a long-time trial judge who is also a long-time personal friend of the governor.[128] Hutchinson had been appointed to his trial court position in 1995 by Democratic governor Gaston Caperton. There will be a special election in May 2020 in which Hutchinson will presumably be a candidate to retain the Court seat.[129]

[127] Jeff Jenkins, "Loughry Resigns from the Supreme Court," *MetroNews* (November 10, 2016), http://wvmetronews.com/2018/11/10/loughry-resigns-from-supreme-court/, accessed November 12, 2018.

[128] Jeff Jenkins, "Hutchison to Take Seat on State Supreme Court," *MetroNews* (December 12, 2018), http://wvmetronews.com/2018/12/12/hutchison-to-take-seat-on-state-supreme-court/, accessed March 5, 2019.

[129] Wendy Holdren, "Raleigh Judge John Hutchison Appointed to State Supreme Court," *Beckley Register-Herald* (December 12, 2018), www.register-herald.com/news/raleigh-judge-john-hutchison-appointed-to-state-supreme-court/article_64d279de-9ec6-5a16-a52a-fa777e653714.html, accessed January 6, 2019.

5

Tennessee

Unconstraining the Governor's Choice of Appellate Judges

Tennessee has witnessed a long-running battle over the process of selection and retention of the state's appellate judges. Prior to 1971, partisan election was the method of selection and retention for all judges. Since then, there have been a series of changes to the process for choosing appellate judges. Most trial judges continue to be elected in partisan elections,[1] although large counties (over 825,000 as of the 2010 census) can switch to nonpartisan elections if two-thirds of the county legislators vote in favor of such a change;[2] at least one county, Shelby (Memphis), now uses nonpartisan elections for trial judges. Between 1971 and 2018, Tennessee made five distinct changes to the selection/retention of appellate judges:

1. Instituting a slightly modified Missouri Plan system[3] for appellate courts through statute rather than by constitutional amendment (1971)
2. Reinstituting partisan elections for Supreme Court justices (1974)
3. Adding additional modifications to the Missouri Plan, relabeled the "Tennessee Plan" and reinstituting it for Supreme Court justices (1994)
4. Allowing the nominating commission to cease operation under the sunset provisions of the Tennessee Governmental Entity Review Law,[4]

[1] William Lyons, John M. Scheb II, Billy Stairand and Joseph G. Jarret, *Government and Politics in Tennessee*, 2nd ed. (Knoxville: University of Tennessee Press, 2017), 160.

[2] Tennessee Code §2-13-203(e). Another provision, Tennessee Code §16-15-202(b), would switch all county court elections in a county to nonpartisan if the state legislature added one or more judges to the court, with the specification that those new judges should be elected on nonpartisan ballots. As is discussed in this chapter, an unsuccessful attempt to amend the state constitution in 1996–1997 would have changed judicial selection for all judges to a system modeled on the Missouri Plan.

[3] The only difference between what was adopted in Tennessee and the Missouri Plan was the length of time between appointment and initially standing in a retention election.

[4] Tennessee Code §4-29; see also William Lyons and Patricia K. Freeman, "Sunset Legislation and the Legislative Process in Tennessee," *Legislative Studies Quarterly* 9, no. 1 (February 1984), 151–159. Under the sunset law, agencies such as the nominating commission are

and then reconstituting the nominating commission with a different name and different membership (2009)

5. Ending the constraint that required the governor to appoint appellate judges from a list of nominees forwarded by a nominating commission, and adding legislative confirmation for appellate court appointments (2014).

This chapter traces and analyzes these changes, some of which were unique to Tennessee.

BACKGROUND

Tennessee Politics

As was true of the other southern states that were part of the Confederacy, Tennessee was dominated by the Democratic Party through much of the twentieth century. However, it was not quite a one-party state to the degree that was true in most other southern states. This reflected the state's regional character. V. O. Key described Tennessee as having "not one one-party system but rather two one-party systems."[5] Democrats controlled middle and western Tennessee, and Republicans controlled eastern Tennessee, usually electing two Republicans to the U.S. House of Representatives. The Republicanism of east Tennessee reflected, in Key's analysis, the history of that region's opposition to secession and its support for the Union during the Civil War with concomitant repression from the supporters of secession, who had overall dominance in the state.[6] After the Civil War, the voters of eastern Tennessee remained loyal to the Republican Party, and this continued into and through the twentieth century.

Despite the strong Republican base in eastern Tennessee, Democrats dominated state-level politics through the end of the twentieth century. Republicans managed to win three gubernatorial elections in the early 1900s, and then alternated with Democrats starting with the 1970 election. However, control of the legislature stayed almost entirely in Democratic hands until 2005. The exceptions occurred in the Tennessee House of Representatives for two sessions (1969 and 1970), when the two parties had equal numbers of representatives joined by one independent, and for one session in the Tennessee Senate (1996) when two senators elected as Democrats switched parties, giving the Republicans control.[7] Between 2004 and 2010, the

reviewed every 6 years and must be reauthorized by the legislature; presumably this happened with regularity at least until around 2008 or 2009.

5 V. O. Key, *Southern Politics in State and Nation* (New York: Alfred Knopf, 1949), 75.

6 *Id.*, 75–76.

7 See https://en.wikipedia.org/wiki/Political_party_strength_in_Tennessee, accessed August 10, 2018.

divisions between Democrats and Republicans in the two chambers of the state legislature remained small, but the division increased after the 2010 election, with Republicans increasingly dominant; between 2013 and 2018, Republicans held over 70 percent of the seats in both chambers, with a Republican as governor.

Appellate Court Elections prior to the Tennessee Plan

The Tennessee constitution lists only a single court, the Tennessee Supreme Court. It authorizes the legislature to create lesser courts,[8] and the legislature has used that authority to create two intermediate appellate courts: a Court of Appeals in 1925 and a Court of Criminal Appeals in 1967; the latter was created because of the increasing number of criminal appeals.[9] One noteworthy aspect is the state constitution's explicit recognition of the states' regionalism, referred to as the "grand divisions." It specifies that the membership of the Supreme Court must be drawn from the three state regions: "The Supreme Court shall consist of five judges, of whom not more than two shall reside in any one of the grand divisions of the state."[10] The two appellate courts are similarly organized around the three grand divisions; as of 2019 each court consists of twelve judges,[11] four from each of the divisions. Despite the divisions, all appellate judges were elected on a statewide basis. Judicial elections took place in the first week of August, the same time as party primaries. Even when the statewide judicial elections were partisan, there were no primaries because candidates were selected by the party executive committees.[12]

Partisan elections for the Tennessee Supreme Court continued through 1990.[13] Between 1946 and 1990, there were 40 Supreme Court elections. Only 8 elections were contested by Republicans; another 2 were contested by independents or third-party candidates. Democrats won all 10 contested elections. The only incumbent to lose an election was George Brown, who had been appointed by Republican governor Lamar Alexander about six weeks before the election. Although no other incumbent lost an election, in 1990 two Democratic incumbents were denied renomination by the Democratic Party Executive Committee. One interesting

8 Tennessee Constitution, Article VI, Section 1: "The judicial power of the State shall be vested in One Supreme Court and such Circuit, Chancery and other inferior Courts as the Legislature shall from time to time, ordain and establish."

9 See www.tncourts.gov/sites/default/files/docs/introduction_to_the_tn_judicial_system_ _all_handouts.pdf, page 5, accessed August 10, 2018.

10 Tennessee Constitution, Article VI, Section 2. The three grand divisions (East Middle, and West) are defined by statute, Tennessee Code §4-1-2.

11 For part of the period for which I discuss election patterns, each court had only 9 judges; the number was increased for the Court of Criminal Appeals before a similar increase was made for the Court of Appeals.

12 Email to Herbert Kritzer from Lyle Reid, March 16, 2008.

13 For a discussion of judicial selection through the nineteenth century and into the twentieth, see N. Houston Parks, "Judicial Selection – The Tennessee Experience," *Memphis State University Law Review* (1977), 621–632.

aspect of the two-party contests was that in many of the elections, the pattern of voting, measured in terms of the partisan correlation,[14] was substantially less partisan than for other states using partisan elections during the period 1946 to 1990; the average for Tennessee was .678 compared to .865 for those other states.[15]

Republican governors made one other appointment to the Tennessee Supreme Court between 1946 and 1992. During Republican governor Winfield's tenure and for the first time during the brief period in the 1970s when the modified Missouri Plan applied to the Supreme Court, a vacancy occurred on the Court on June 19, 1972 with the death of one of the justices. Dunn asked the newly created nominating commission for a set of names, and on July 18 he received three names from the newly created nominating commission;[16] three days later Dunn selected Thomas F. Turley Jr., U.S. Attorney for the Western District of Tennessee, who was the only Republican on the list. Per Turley's request, the appointment was to take effect September 1.[17]

The appointment created issues, both with the language of Article VI of the Tennessee Constitution and with the provisions of the recently enacted modified Missouri Plan. The constitution specified that justices and other judges be elected by the qualified voters of the state or district[18] and that elections for judicial officers take place on the first week in August in even-numbered years with the term of office starting the following September 1. Article VI then goes on to provide:

> No special election shall be held to fill a vacancy in the office of judge or district attorney, but at the time herein fixed for the biennial election of civil officers; and such vacancy shall be filled at the next biennial election occurring *more than thirty days after the vacancy occurs.*[19]

Under the modified Missouri Plan, vacancies on the appellate courts were to be filled by gubernatorial appointment from a list of three candidates screened and forwarded by the nominating commission, with a retention election to take place the August following the date of the vacancy, provided that the election was scheduled at least thirty days after the occurrence of the vacancy. Assuming an incumbent, either recently appointed or having previously stood in a retention election, filed a declaration of candidacy within the time limits set in the statute, "only the names of

[14] See Chapter 1 for the definition of "partisan correlation."

[15] Two-sample difference of means *t*-test: $t = 6.026$, $p < .001$.

[16] "State Justice Named Today?" *Clarksville Leaf-Chronicle* (July 19, 1972), 8.

[17] "Turley to Get Court Post?" *Kingsport Times* (July 21, 1972), 2; "Bulletin," *Murfreesboro Daily News-Journal* (July 21, 1972), 1.

[18] Tennessee Constitution, Article VI, Sections 3 and 4.

[19] Tennessee Constitution, Article VII, Section 5 (time of election of civil officers; terms; temporary appointments); emphasis added. Although the constitution (Article III, Section 14) did provide for the governor to fill interim vacancies in positions for which "the right of ... appointment is ... vested in the General Assembly," there was no constitutional provision providing a procedure to fill a judicial vacancy between its occurrence and the next election. This was covered by statute.

[the incumbent] without party designation will be submitted to the electorate" using a retention ballot.

The circumstances surrounding the appointment of Turley created a range of conflicts with these various provisions. The vacancy occurred more than thirty days before the election on August 3, 1972. Although Turley had been named to the position before the election, his appointment was not to take effect until September 1; thus, there was no incumbent to stand in the retention election. The language of the statute, combined with the constitutional requirement of an election if the vacancy occurs more than thirty days prior to the election, could be interpreted as requiring a contested (partisan) election if a vacancy had occurred more than thirty days earlier and there was no incumbent. Although there was no space on the ballot for a Supreme Court election, Robert Taylor, a former judge of the state appeals court, mounted a write-in campaign for the position. Less than 2,000 votes were cast, with Taylor receiving several times more votes than Turley. Two weeks after the election, the Secretary of State issued a Certificate of Election to Taylor, but in the following days, Governor Dunn issued a commission appointing Turley as a justice of the Supreme Court from September 1.[20]

The mess ended up in the courts. The litigation dealt with both who should get the Court seat and the broader question of the validity of the modified Missouri Plan, given the language of the constitution stating that judges should be elected by the qualified voters. It took until March 1974 for the Tennessee Supreme Court to make its judgment.[21] The Court denied the seat to both contestants, ordering a do-over in the appointment process. More importantly, the Court upheld the modified Missouri Plan, with the exception of one element concerning the composition of the nominating commission, which I discuss later in this chapter.[22] In the wake of the Court's decision, the governor went back to the nominating commission. Just before the commission named three nominees, Thomas Turley withdraw – "dramatically and bitterly" – from consideration,[23] and just three days before this, the state legislature passed a bill removing the Supreme Court from the modified Missouri Plan.[24] The nominating commission forwarded to the governor the names of three sitting judges, two sitting on the Courts of Appeals and one trial judge, William Fones. Both of the appellate judges had been named to their positions by Democratic governors and had run unopposed as Democrats in the elections following their appointments. Fones, who was described as an "independent," had

20 Margaret Behm and Candi Henry, "Judicial Selection in Tennessee: Deciding 'the Decider,'" *Belmont Law Review* 1 (2014), 153.

21 The case was first heard in a chancery court before being appealed to the Tennessee Supreme Court.

22 State *ex rel.* Higgins v. Dunn, 496 S.W.2d 480 (Tenn. 1973); see also Kenneth Jost, "Taylor, Turley Denied; Missouri Plan Upheld," *Nashville Tennessean* (March 20, 1973), 1.

23 Kenneth Jost, "Dunn Gets Court Nominees as Turley Quits, Hits Dispute," *Nashville Tennessean* (May 6, 1973), 1.

24 "Judge Election Bill Passes," *Kingsport Times* (May 2, 1973), 3.

been appointed to a circuit court position by Dunn three years earlier. Within a few days, Governor Dunn both vetoed the bill returning to partisan elections for the Supreme Court and named Judge Fones to the vacant seat on that Court. By the time that Fones came up for election in 1974, Dunn's veto of the return to partisan elections had been overturned. Fones then secured the nomination of the Democratic Party and ran unopposed in the subsequent election.[25]

Turning to the two intermediate courts, by my count from newspaper coverage,[26] there were a total of forty-two elections for the Court of Appeals between 1946 and 1970, after which retention elections were used for that court. Not a single election was contested by a Republican candidate between 1946 and 1970. In 1970 there were an additional four elections for the recently created Court of Criminal Appeals. All four were contested by candidates from both parties; the Democratic candidates won all four; one incumbent, a Republican who had been appointed to the Court of Criminal Appeals by Democratic governor Buford Ellington,[27] was defeated.[28] As for the retention elections between 1972 and 1992, seventy-two judges stood for retention and all were retained, even though bar polls branded an appellate judge as "unqualified" on at least one occasion.[29]

Reform Efforts in the 1970s

Adoption of the Modified Missouri Plan, 1971

Change to judicial selection and retention in Tennessee did not appear to have come on the political agenda in Tennessee until the 1960s, when several states were considering – and often adopting – systems based on the Missouri Plan. There were a couple of brief references to the Missouri Plan as a possibility for Tennessee in the press in the late 1940s, one reporting an address by the dean of the University of Tennessee College of Law[30] and a second in an address by U.S. Court of Appeals Judge John J. Parker.[31] It is also possible that there was some discussion of change

[25] Carl A. Pierce, "The Tennessee Supreme Court and the Struggle for Independence, Accountability, and Modernization, 1974–1998," in *A History of the Tennessee Supreme Court*, James W. Ely Jr., ed. (Knoxville: University of Tennessee Press, 2002), 273.

[26] The results of elections prior to 1990 do not appear to have been published by the Tennessee Secretary of State's office.

[27] "Candidates for State, Metro Bench," *Nashville Tennessean* (July 5, 1970), 3B.

[28] Hugh Lafollette, "Judge Mitchell Retains Court of Appeals Seat," *Nashville Tennessean* (August 9, 1970), 14A.

[29] Phil Williams, "Lawyers' Poll Brands Two Judges as Unqualified," *Nashville Tennessean* (July 12, 1990), 4B.

[30] "U.T. Law School Dean Would Abolish Court of Appeals and Increase Size of Supreme Court," *Jackson Sun* (November 29, 1946), 1946.

[31] "Jurist Urges Adoption of 'Missouri Plan,'" *Murfreesboro Daily News-Journal* (December 6, 1948), 4.

within bar circles during the 1950s, but if so, it was unreported.[32] In the early 1960s, the bar began serious discussions, including a debate, at the bar's 1961 annual convention.[33] That same year, a bar committee called for a "serious study" of adopting a Missouri Plan system for appellate judges.[34] In the mid-1960s the broader issue of court modernization became a topic of discussion, and changing judicial selection was one of the issues that was under consideration.[35] There were calls to hold a state constitutional convention to consider rewriting the judicial article (Article VI), including the provisions regarding judicial selection.[36] One such call came in a report to the legislature in 1967 or 1968 from the Tennessee Law Revision Commission, in which the Commission highlighted judicial selection as needing attention:[37]

> The existing system of judicial selection, partially by popular election, but largely by appointment of the governor in filling vacancies, is not adequate. A more adequate procedure for judicial selection should therefore be developed with more emphasis on merit and less emphasis on purely political considerations, but with the right to remove retained in the people, in addition to other procedures for removal.

In 1968, the legislature voted to put on the ballot five issues that would be considered in a limited constitutional convention to be held in 1971, if the voters agreed. The first item on the list was to be a rewriting of the judicial article.[38] Only one of the five issues was approved, and that was tax reform; the proposal for the convention to examine the judicial article attracted the support of only 46 percent of the voters.[39]

Pressure from the bar did not end with the defeat of the constitutional convention proposal. In 1969, a poll of judges and attorneys found that 63 percent were dissatisfied with the system in operation for filling court vacancies, with 69 percent of attorneys favoring a shift to an appointment-based system of selection based on the

32 The *Tennessee Bar Journal* did not begin publication until 1965.

33 Pat Anderson, "Bar to Debate Lifetime Terms for State Judges," *Nashville Tennessean* (June 8, 1961), 1.

34 "Group Asks Appellate Judge Study for State, *Nashville Tennessean* (February 12, 1961), 14-A.

35 See "Overlapping of Courts Hit," *Nashville Tennessean* (June 11, 1966), 7; Frank N. Bratton, "Report on Tennessee Citizens' Conference to Improve the Administration of Justice," *Tennessee Bar Journal* 3 (May 1977), 15; Ellis Binkley, "Methods of Selecting Judges," *Kingsport Times* (November 14, 1967), 15.

36 John Parish, "Cold Water Is Thrown on Efforts of Court Reform Committee," *Jackson Sun* (January 29, 1967), 7.

37 Special Report of [Tennessee] Law Revision Commission to the Eighty-fifth General Assembly Concerning a Bill to Submit to the People the Question of Calling a Limited Constitutional Convention to Consider the Revision of Article VI of the Constitution Relating to the Judicial Department, Including All Aspects of the Judicial System and the Administration of Justice (undated), 12.

38 Larry Daughtrey, "Constitutional Call: Help or Hurt?" *Nashville Tennessean* (September 29, 1968), B1.

39 "Voters Approve '71 Convention," *Clarksville Leaf-Chronicle* (November 6, 1968), 1.

Missouri Plan.[40] Two years later, a coalition of three groups – the Tennessee Bar Association, the Tennessee Judicial Council, and the Citizens for Court Modernization – presented a proposal for statutory changes to improve the courts, including the adoption of a Missouri Plan system of selection and retention for appellate judges.[41] The proposal to adopt a "modified Missouri Plan" system for appellate judges drew broad support that year, the General Assembly passed the needed legislation during its 1971 session,[42] and Governor Dunn signed it into law.

Tennessee's modified Missouri Plan system included several noteworthy provisions:

- Judges would stand in retention in the first even-numbered-year August election occurring thirty days or more after the position became vacant.
- The nominating commission was required by the legislation to submit three names to the governor, but the governor could request an additional three names, and could keep asking for another three until a person who was satisfactory to the governor was nominated.
- The nominating commission was required to submit a list within thirty days; if it failed to meet that deadline, the governor was free to appoint any qualified licensed attorney.
- The nominating commission was to consist of nine members: three to be appointed by the governor (no more than one could be a licensed attorney), one from each of the state's grand divisions; three licensed attorneys, one to be elected by the bar of each grand division; and three members of the General Assembly, one from each of the grand divisions and at least one each from the House of Representatives and from the Senate.[43]

Later in 1971, there was discussion of extending the modified plan to the trial courts,[44] but nothing came of those discussions until several years later.

As discussed previously, the messy situation that arose with the first selection under this system led to litigation. The key question in that litigation, aside from

40 Joe Hatcher, "Appointment of Judges Unsatisfactory," *Nashville Tennessean* (October 1, 1969), 1, 16.

41 Ellis Binkley, "Lawmakers May Help Courts," *Kingsport Times* (November 18, 1970), 18; Larry Daughtrey, "Court Reform Bills Readied for Assembly," *Nashville Tennessean* (January 9, 1971), 6.

42 Jerry Thompson, "House Clears Bill Letting Incumbent Appeals Judges to Run on Record," *Nashville Tennessean* (May 7, 1971), 2.

43 See Chapter 198, *Tennessee Public Acts*, 1971.

44 Larry Daughtrey, "Court Reorganization Urged," *Nashville Tennessean* (October 28, 1971), 10; John Mott, "Court Modernization Everybody's Job, Says Former Justice Clark," *Nashville Tennessean* (November 17, 1971), 17. Earlier, there had been at least some expression of concern over the failure of the proposal passed earlier that year to include the trial courts in the new selection system; see "[Editorial] Bar Proposal Has Merit, but Doesn't Go Far Enough," *Nashville Tennessean* (April 11, 1971), 16.

which of the two claimants was entitled to the Supreme Court seat, was the validity of the system, both whether the retention election was sufficient to meet the constitutional requirement that judges be elected by the qualified voters and whether any specific details of the plan violated other provisions of the constitution. The Court upheld that general plan, but struck down the provision for legislators serving on the nominating commission as violating Article II, Section 10 of the state constitution, which provided that: "No senator or representative shall, during the time for which he was elected, be eligible to any office or place of trust, the appointment to which is vested in the executive or the General Assembly,"[45] The legislature quickly responded, increasing the size of the Appellate Court Nominating Commission to 11 and modifying its composition so that in addition to the 3 elected by the bar, 4 were now appointed by the governor with no more than 2 being attorneys, and 3 each appointed by the Speakers of the House and Senate, with the stipulation that no more than 1 of each pair could be from the same political party; none of the members of the commission could be state or federal employees or hold offices in political parties or organizations.[46]

Repeal of the Modified Missouri Plan as Applied to the Supreme Court

As noted previously, terms of appellate judges all run concurrently. This meant that 1974 would be the year in which all members of the Supreme Court would stand for retention under the modified Missouri Plan. Any justice who chose not to seek another term would be replaced by the governor from a list provided by the nominating commission. In 1973, as the litigation arising from the Turley appointment and the new system more generally progressed through the courts, several incumbents announced their intention not to seek to continue on the Court. Governor Dunn would name their successors, who would then stand in retention elections without opposition. Democrats, who controlled the legislature, did not like the prospect of the Supreme Court under the control of justices appointed by a Republican governor; they wanted to be able to have Democrats run against any Republican appointees. As the 1973 session drew to a close, the legislature passed a bill returning selection/retention of Supreme Court justices to the system existing prior to 1972. The vote in the House was 50–26, the exact number needed for passage;[47] in the Senate the vote was 19–11; Republicans split almost evenly (4–6) with Democrats strongly in favor (14–5).[48]

Not surprisingly, the governor vetoed the legislation – too late for an override vote that session, but in Tennessee the legislature could seek to override the veto

45 Higgins v. Dunn, 496 S.W.2d 490 (1973).
46 Tennessee Public Acts, 1973, Chapter 265.
47 "Judge Election Bill Passes," *Kingsport Times* (May 2, 1973), 3.
48 *Senate Journal of the 88th General Assembly of the State of Tennessee* (1973), 707; the nineteenth vote in favor was from a senator aligned with something labeled "the American Party."

when it met in 1974, and in the 1974 session the veto was overridden. This came as it was clear that without action, Dunn would be able to name three new justices.[49] The vote to override in the Senate was 17–11,[50] on straight party lines;[51] the House vote was 53–42, with four Republicans from eastern Tennessee in the House joining the Democrats.[52] There were some suggestions that the Republican support was part of a deal that would allow a second medical school to be built in the eastern part of the state.[53] As things were to develop, the only incumbent seeking to stay on the Court was Governor Dunn's one appointee, William Fones, who obtained nomination by the Democratic Party. The elections for the other four seats were open, with the four Democratic candidates defeating all their Republican opponents.

The 1977 Limited Constitutional Convention: Voters' Defeat of Judicial Reform

In 1968 the voters rejected a proposal that would have had a limited constitutional convention rewrite the judicial article. In 1976 the legislature tried again, this time structuring the proposal for a limited constitutional convention as a single ballot question at the August 1976 election, but including a list of the areas to be considered at the convention; one of the areas was the judiciary.[54] Major backing came from bankers, who wanted an amendment to remove a constitutional ceiling on interest rates. There was opposition to the proposed convention from some quarters, including the Democratic governor, whose opposition reflected that the proposed matters to be considered did not include the provisions that would allow a state income tax, something that would require a constitutional change.[55] Voters backed the call for a convention, with 54 percent voting in favor.[56]

The convention produced a set of thirteen proposed constitutional changes, including substantial changes to the judicial article. Those changes included creating a uniform system of trial courts (eliminating separate chancery, probate, and criminal courts), restricting the legislature's power to create new courts, creating a Missouri Plan for the selection and retention of *all* judges, requiring that court rules be submitted to the legislature for approval, reducing the length of terms of elected

49 "Bill Promised to Take Sting Out of Veto Vote," *Clarksville Leaf-Chronicle* (February 8, 1974), 14.

50 *Id.*

51 *Senate Journal of the 88th General Assembly of the State of Tennessee* (1974), 2046.

52 Alan Wilson, "Demos Deal Two Blows to Dunn," *Clarksville Leaf-Chronicle* (February 15, 1974), 1.

53 *Id.*, 2.

54 See John Parish, "Side Concerns Cloud Convention Passage," *Jackson Sun* (August 1, 1976), 6A.

55 Kenneth Jost, "TBA Eyes Major Role During Call," *Nashville Tennessean* (August 8, 1976), 6.

56 *Id.*

district attorneys, requiring the legislature to create a statewide public defender system, omitting an existing provision prohibiting the lowering (or raising) of sitting judges' salaries, and authorizing the legislature to eliminate or combine the popularly elected circuit court clerks. The combination of these changes, along with some changes that were not included (e.g., continuing the practice of having the Supreme Court appoint the state attorney general rather than making it an elective office as preferred by most of the Republican leadership), produced some vocal opposition, including from at least one member of the Supreme Court.[57]

The thirteen proposals were submitted to the voters at a special election in March 1978. The usual time to consider ballot questions such as constitutional amendments was the August election, but a special election was chosen with the expectation that it would reduce turnout and increase the prospects of passage. Registered voters stayed home in droves, with only 17 percent casting ballots and all but one of the thirteen proposals passed. The one that lost, 54–46 against, was the overhaul of the judicial amendment.[58]

REFORM EFFORTS, 1980–2009

Revising the Modified Missouri Plan and Reinstituting It for the Supreme Court

Whether to extend the modified Missouri Plan to again include the Tennessee Supreme Court remained a point of discussion through the 1980s. Bills to make that change were introduced in at least several legislative sessions between 1980 and 1989, and some of those bills made it out of one of the legislative judiciary committees.[59] The Tennessee Bar Association continued to push for restoration of the plan for Supreme Court justices,[60] as did the justices themselves.[61] There was opposition to such a change as well, including the Tennessee Trial Lawyers Association.[62] There was also some support for abandoning the modified Missouri Plan for the Court of Appeals,[63] and even for ending the governor's power to fill

[57] Lewis L. Laska, *The Tennessee State Constitution: A Reference Guide* (New York: Greenwood Press, 1990), 23–27.

[58] *Id.*, 25–26.

[59] James Pratt, "Senate Panel Votes to Appoint, Rather Than Elect, Justices," *Nashville Tennessean* (April 6, 1988), B1.

[60] Kirk Logan, "Bar Board Backs Change in Court Justices' Selection," *Nashville Tennessean* (March 7, 1984), 4B; Lee Smith, "Politics Mire Justices," *Jackson Sun* (December 16, 1987), 10A.

[61] Jeff Wilson, "Senators Hint at Swapping Judge Selection for Remap Plan," *Jackson Sun* (February 19, 1982), 1.

[62] Lee Smith, "Legal Eagles Fuming over Judge Post," *Murfreesboro Daily News-Journal* (March 2, 1989), 4.

[63] "Appeals Court Mischief," *Jackson Sun* (April 3, 1988), 2E.

vacancies – an idea raised by Democrats in 1981, two years into Republican Lamar Alexander's tenure as governor.[64]

In Tennessee bills die only at the end of a legislature, not at the end of each session, and in 1990 there was a proposal pending that added a new wrinkle to the discussion. Specifically, the proposal included a provision to create a judicial evaluation commission to assess incumbents' performance in advance of their standing for retention.[65] There was no action in 1990, but the proposals came to fruition when the legislature met in 1994. This was in part because of a push from the Democratic Speaker of the Senate, John Wilder, who wanted a modified Missouri Plan to apply to both appellate and trial courts.[66] However, there was pushback from trial judges, who wanted to retain the current system of partisan election for their positions.[67] Wilder eventually came around to the position that the plan should be extended only to the Supreme Court, but with the caveat that if that was not done, the modified Missouri Plan should be abandoned for the Court of Appeals and contested elections be reinstated.[68] The proposal would also revamp the nominating commission; one element of that change was presumably targeted to win over the trial lawyers by specifying that 3 of the 15 members of the nominating commission would be chosen by legislative leaders from a list of nominees provided by the Tennessee Trial Lawyers Association.[69]

Toward the end of the 1994 session, the legislature easily approved a substantially revised version of the modified Missouri Plan. Votes were 64–34 in the House[70] and 27–4 in the Senate;[71] the division in the House was not on clear party lines, with significant numbers from each party on both sides. What was now to be called the Tennessee Plan would be used in appointing judges of the two intermediate appellate courts and justices of the Supreme Court. Under the Tennessee Plan, the new Tennessee Judicial Selection Commission (TJSC) would also screen and nominate candidates for appointment by the governor to fill interim vacancies in the

64 "Bill Would Take Judge Appointments from Governor," *Jackson Sun* (February 4, 1981), 3A; but see Marsha Vandeberg, "Modified Missouri Plan for Supreme Court Sets Stage for a Partisan Legislative Battle," *Nashville Tennessean* (November 22, 1981), 2B.

65 Phil Williams, "Hicks, the Man Who 'Wasn't There,' Puts Election of Judges Plan on Hold," *Nashville Tennessean* (May 16, 1989), 3B.

66 John Wright, "Committee Votes to Add State Supreme Court to Modified 'Missouri Plan,'" *Jackson Sun* (April 6, 1988), 4B; M. Lee Smith, "Legislature's Hands Full with Elections on Horizon," *Murfreesboro Daily News-Journal* (January 12, 1994), A4.

67 Kirk Loggins, "Most Trial Judges Want Popular Vote," *Nashville Tennessean* (January 23, 1994), 2B.

68 Karen Miller, "Wilder Calls for Vote on His Modified Missouri Plan," *Jackson Sun* (April 4, 1994), 6A.

69 *Id.* Nominees for other positions on the commission would come from other lawyer groups, including district attorneys, the criminal defense bar, the civil defense bar, and the Tennessee Bar Association; see Behm and Henry, "Judicial Selection in Tennessee," *supra* note 20, 157.

70 Tennessee House of Representatives, *98th General Assembly Journals*, accessed August 13, 2018, 4156.

71 "Final Onslaught of Bills Bogs Legislators," *Jackson Sun* (April 21, 1994), 5.

trial courts; however, trial court judges would continue to stand in contested elections, and if a trial judge decided to stand down at the end of his or her term, a contested open election would be held. The membership of the TJSC would include representation of various lawyer groups plus three nonlawyers, all selected by the Speaker of the House or the Speaker of the Senate.[72] In total there would be 12 lawyers and 3 nonlawyers on the TSJC. The overwhelming dominance of lawyers reflected the plan's position that "lawyers are the best judges of judges."[73] The two Speakers making the appointments were also charged with insuring diversity in terms of race and gender.[74] Also, under the new Tennessee Plan, the governor could make only one request for an additional three nominees; previously, there was no limit on the number of lists the governor could request.

A key addition to the plan was the creation of the Tennessee Judicial Performance Evaluation Commission (TJEC), to be composed of 12 members, 4 of whom would be nonlawyers. The TJEC was charged with conducting and publishing evaluations of appellate justices, including a recommendation regarding retention.[75] An important provision of the evaluation element was that if the TJEC did not recommend retention for a judge or justice, the subsequent election would revert to a contested partisan election with the parties making nominations. However, during the time that the TJEC operated, it recommended retention for every judge and justice it reviewed, and the provision to revert to a contested election never came into play.

The Penny White Controversy

In December 1994, Democratic governor Ned McWherter appointed Court of Criminal Appeals Judge Penny White to a vacancy on the Tennessee Supreme Court. She was the first appointee to that Court after the Tennessee Plan's reinstatement for the Supreme Court and the first member of the Court to have been through a formal screening process; she was also the first woman to serve on that Court.[76] Under Tennessee law, she was required to stand for retention for the balance of her predecessor's term in the 1996 election; she would be joined on the retention ballot by three appointees to the intermediate appellate court. One noteworthy fact about White's appointment is that it came in the waning days of

[72] Each of the relevant groups was to submit three names for each of their designated positions that was open.

[73] Behm and Henry, "Judicial Selection in Tennessee," *supra* note 20, 164.

[74] In 2001, legislation was passed that added two additional lawyers, not designated by any of the groups, to the TJSC, one to be appointed by each of the Speakers; *Id.*, 157 n.72.

[75] The language of the statute appears to limit evaluation to appellate judges standing for a full term in the August election; however, in 1996 a court found that the evaluation requirement applied to all judges standing for retention; see Behm and Henry, "Judicial Selection in Tennessee," *supra* note 20, 160.

[76] "A New Female Justice," *Nashville Tennessean* (December 18, 1984), 4D; see also Larry Daughtrey, "3 Judges Named Finalists for Supreme Court Seat," *Nashville Tennessean* (December 7, 1994), 2B.

Democratic governor McWherter's tenure; he was to be succeeded about a month after he appointed White by Republican Don Sundquist. Behm and Henry describe the chaos that ensued.[77]

> Justice White's appointment was subject to retention election on August 1, 1996. However, she was not reviewed by the Judicial Evaluation Commission prior to being placed on the ballot for election. This was apparently due to the belief on behalf of the State and the Judicial Evaluation Commission that subsequent to its creation by July 1, 1995, it was not required to conduct judicial evaluations until judicial candidates were standing for complete terms, which would not occur until August 1998. Indeed, this belief likely came from the language of the statute itself: "The judicial evaluation program, including the public report and the ballot information, shall apply to each appellate court judge who seeks to serve a complete term after September 1, 1994." However, others took the position that the overall construction of the Tennessee Plan provided that no appointed judge could have his or her name placed on a retention ballot without having first been evaluated by the Commission [TJEC], and, indeed, at least one appellate judge in the State who was slated to stand for election after having been appointed to an unexpired term repeatedly and unsuccessfully requested evaluation by the commission.
>
> Operating on the argument that no judge could appear on a retention ballot without having first been evaluated, attorneys Lewis Laska and John J. Hooker each sought to declare their candidacy for the statewide election in early 1996. The State Coordinator of Elections declined to provide them with nominating positions, noting that Justice White would be running unopposed on the ballot in a retention election. Both sued, and their suits were eventually consolidated for review by a Special Supreme Court since the sitting Justices recused themselves on a matter regarding their own election.
>
> The Special Supreme Court agreed that the Tennessee Plan required Justice White to be evaluated by the Commission prior to standing for election by retention ballot. In the absence of such an evaluation, the Special Supreme Court essentially held that a statewide contested election was required but that no candidates had validly qualified for election prior to the deadline. The Special Supreme Court gave Justice White dispensation to file belatedly for candidacy and ordered that Hooker could not be placed upon the ballot because he failed to meet the necessary requirement, as his law license had lapsed. The Court also eventually ordered that Mr. Laska's name could not be placed on the ballot under state law because Justice White was appointed to fill the unexpired term of Justice O'Brien, and his vacancy must be filled by a resident of the same Grand Division as he. While Justice White met the residency requirement, Mr. Laska did not. The Court allowed John King, the putative Republican candidate for the office held by Justice White, to file an amicus curiae brief. He was ultimately granted an extension of the qualifying

77 Behm and Henry, "Judicial Selection in Tennessee," *supra* note 20, 159–161, internal citations omitted. Quoted with the permission of the authors.

deadline so that he would have the opportunity for his name to be placed on the ballot, should the matter have ultimately proceeded to a contested election.

In its final opinion on the matter, the Special Supreme Court concluded "that the yes/no retention vote provided for in the Tennessee Plan is in compliance with the Article VI, Section 3 mandate of the Tennessee Constitution that Judges of the Supreme Court be 'elected by the qualified voters,'" adding that "[n]o authority was cited by any party to these proceedings, nor has any been found by this Court, that would dictate a different result under the United States Constitution."[78] The Special Court further found that neither Article I, Section 5 of the Tennessee Constitution, requiring elections to be "free and equal," nor Article II, Section 1 of the Tennessee Constitution, providing for the separation of powers among the three branches, were in conflict with the terms of the Tennessee Plan.

Meanwhile, two federal court cases addressing the August 1996 judicial elections were filed and consolidated. Several appellate judges, including Justice White, asserted a property right to a retention election as bestowed by the Tennessee Plan's statutes and by the assurances of State officials made to her regarding the official status of her candidacy. Hooker countered that the Special Supreme Court's ruling required a contested election. Ultimately, the federal district court determined that Justice White was entitled to appear on a retention ballot. Thus, the retention elections were ordered to proceed. The federal court left undisturbed the Special Supreme Court's ruling that the General Assembly was empowered to dictate the manner of judicial elections in the State.

Better known than the litigation around the 1996 election are the political attacks mounted by conservative groups against Justice White. This came after she joined her four colleagues on the Supreme Court in ordering the resentencing of a man who had been sentenced to death in connection with the rape and stabbing of an elderly woman.[79] White was defeated in the retention election, and her replacement was named by the Republican governor. Two years later, conservative groups unsuccessfully sought to unseat another member of the Supreme Court.[80]

The year before the Tennessee Plan was adopted, the Tennessee Supreme Court created and appointed the Commission on the Future of the Tennessee Judicial System to conduct a comprehensive assessment of the system.[81] The 34-member commission was made up of lawyers, laypersons, and judges. In 1996 the commission issued a 92-page report recommending a complete overhaul of the Tennessee judiciary including the consolidation of all trial courts and a reduction in the

[78] See State *ex rel.* Hooker v. Thompson, 249 S.W.3d 331 (Tenn. 1996), and Hooker v. Burson, 960 F. Supp. 1283 (M.D. Tenn. 1996).

[79] State v. Odom, 928 S.W.2d 18 (Tenn. 1996); For descriptions of the campaign waged against Penny White, see Traciel V. Reid, "The Politicization of Retention Elections: Lessons from the Defeat of Justices Lanphier and White," *Judicature* 83 (1999), 68–77; and Behm and Henry, "Judicial Selection in Tennessee," *supra* note 20, 161–162.

[80] Reid, "The Politicization of Retention Elections," *supra* note 79, 73–74.

[81] Larry Daughtrey, "State Court System to Undergo Check," *Nashville Tennessean* (September 7, 1993), B1.

number of judicial districts.[82] The Commission also endorsed staggered terms for Supreme Court justices and the need for "merit selection" at all levels of the Tennessee judiciary. Nothing came of these recommendations.

Changing the Nominating Commission

In the fall of 2006, controversy again erupted over the selection process for appellate judges. The TJSC provided lists of three nominees for each of two positions on the Tennessee Supreme Court, one of which was being vacated by the only African American then on the court. Democratic governor Phil Bredesen made a selection to fill one of the positions, but when the only African American on the second list withdrew, he requested a new list for that position from TJSC, specifically asking that it include "qualified minority candidates."[83] When the TJSC provided a new list, it included one African American, but one of the two white males on the list had also been on the prior list that the governor had rejected. The governor filed suit against the TJSC, asserting that it was improper to relist a candidate who had been on a previously rejected list. His position was upheld by the trial court,[84] and the TJSC announced it would not appeal.[85]

However, the trial court's decision did not end the immediate controversy. The two white males on the original list sought to intervene by asking the Tennessee Supreme Court stay the trial court's ruling, claiming that they were discriminated against because of their race.[86] In February 2007, the Tennessee Supreme Court upheld the trial court's decision and rejected the two disappointed nominees' claims of discrimination.[87] However, in April, just before the TJSC was to meet to select nominees for the other vacant Supreme Court seat, the head of a conservative think tank filed suit in federal court requesting the Court to halt the selection process, claiming that the voters should decide who gets judgeships, rather than the governor and the TJSC.[88] The federal court quickly denied that request, and the nomination

[82] Report from The Commission on the Future of the Tennessee Judicial System, www.tncourts.gov/sites/default/files/docs/report_of_future_of_tn_judicial_system.pdf, accessed August 13, 2018.

[83] Behm and Henry, "Judicial Selection in Tennessee," *supra* note 20, 163.

[84] "Judge Upholds Bredesen's Rejection of Repeat Supreme Court Candidates," *Murfreesboro Daily News-Journal* (December 15, 2006), A10.

[85] Sheila Burke, "Group Moves Forward with Justice Picks," *Nashville Tennessean* (December 20, 2006), 2B.

[86] Lucas Johnson II, "Unfairly Treated Say White Hopefuls; Rejected as Candidates for Seat on High Court," *Nashville Tennessean* (December 14, 2006), 6B; Sheila Burke, "2 Passed Over for Bench Take Case to Justices; Bredesen Rejected Nominees to State Supreme Court," *Nashville Tennessean* (December 28, 2006), B1.

[87] Bredesen v. Tenn. Judicial Selection Commission, 214 S.W.3d 419 (Tenn. 2007); see also "Governor Wins in Fight over Supreme Court," *Murfreesboro Daily News-Journal* (February 22, 2007), 8.

[88] "Effort to Appoint High Court Justice Stalled," *Nashville Tennessean* (April 8, 2007), B2.

process proceeded.[89] The TJSC sent a new list to the governor, and although the governor expressed dissatisfaction with the list, he had no alternative but to select one of the three candidates.[90] He complained that the TJSC was thwarting his efforts to insure diversity on the appellate courts.[91]

As this controversy was raging, there were important political developments in Tennessee. Although Democrat Bredesen would serve for eight years, from January 2003 until January 2011, Republicans gained control of the Senate in 2005 and the House in 2009. A Republican, Ron Ramsey, was elected as Speaker of the Senate, replacing Democrat John Wilder, who had served in that position for thirty-six years. Ramsey pledged to make appointments to the TJSC with an eye to there being nominees with a conservative slant.[92] Moreover, under Tennessee's sunset law, the TJSC expired on June 30, 2008 and would cease to operate twelve months later unless renewed by the legislature. If the TJSC was not renewed, the selection system for appellate justices and judges would revert to the partisan elections, with the governor unconstrained in filling interim vacancies (including in the trial courts) with anyone having the legal qualifications. During the legislature's 2008 session, Ramsey used this prospect, along with the possibility of holding hostage other agencies due to close down, as a way of pushing a proposal to limit the role of lawyers' groups in making nominations for persons to serve on the TJSC,[93] a major goal of some critics who opposed such groups having a large role.[94] At the same time, the former Speaker, who was retiring at the end of the 2008 session, pushed to renew the existing TJSC. Neither the Democratic proposal to renew the TJSC in its then current form nor the Republican proposal to revise the process for selecting the members of the TJSC was passed, with the former blocked in the Republican-controlled Senate and the latter blocked in the Democratic-controlled House.[95] Absent action by the legislature during its 2009 session, the sunset law dictated that the TJSC would cease operating at the end of

89 "Panel Again Evaluates Supreme Court Applicants: Federal Judge Upholds Selection Process," *Murfreesboro Daily News-Journal* (April 14, 2007), B4. The court found that the plaintiffs lacked standing; see Johnson v. Bredesen, No. 307-0372, 2007 WL 1387330 (M.D. Tenn. May 8, 2007). The Court of Appeals affirmed the trial court's decision; see Johnson v. Bredesen, 356 F. App'x 781 (6th Cir. 2009).

90 "Bredesen Unhappy with Candidates for Supreme Court," *Murfreesboro Daily News-Journal* (April 19, 2007), 3.

91 Erik Schelzig, "Judicial Panel Blocks Diversity, Governor Says," *Nashville Tennessean* (August 7, 2007), B2.

92 "Ramsey: Judicial Nominees Will Have Conservative Slant," *Murfreesboro Daily News-Journal* (January 25, 2007), A8.

93 Theo Emery, "Agency Closures Threatened; Judicial Debate Entangles Renewal of Health, Safety Departments," *Nashville Tennessean* (May 7, 2008), 1B, 4B.

94 Theo Emery, "Lawmakers Delay Decision on Judicial Selection Process," *Nashville Tennessean* (September 10, 2008), B1.

95 "Pair of Retiring Lawmakers Decry Partisan Politics," *Nashville Tennessean* (May 25, 2008, B1, B2; "GOP's Judicial Selection Proposal Stalls," *Murfreesboro Daily News-Journal* (May 10, 2008), 3.

June 2009. Also, during this time, there was substantial editorial and op-ed commentary, much advocating keeping the existing system but some arguing for a return to a system of electing appellate judges.[96]

With the 2008 election Republicans had nominal control of both chambers of the state legislature. In the House, the split was 50–49, but there was some controversy when Republican Kent Williams cut a deal with the 49 Democrats to be elected Speaker over the choice of the Republican caucus,[97] and was subsequently stripped of his membership in the Republican Party. Williams continued to call himself a Republican and expressed no intention of joining the Democratic Party.[98] Nonetheless, Republicans were now in a better position to push changes to judicial selection. Two major proposals were considered toward the end of the 2009 session. One would continue the TJSC while reducing the number of seats reserved for lawyers and removing the formal role various lawyers' groups currently had in making nominations for appointment to the TJSC. The second would have the governor select judges without the constraint of a nominating commission; judges of the two intermediate appellate courts would continue to stand in retention elections, but Supreme Court justices could be challenged in contested elections.[99] There was also some discussion of all this being an interim arrangement with the idea of bringing a constitutional amendment to the voters in 2014 that would erase any questions regarding the use of retention elections.[100]

The legislation that passed (S.B. 1573) allowed the existing TJSC to go out of business as of June 30, 2009 and created a new Tennessee Judicial Nominating Commission (TJNC) that was to sunset in four years. The legislation passed the Senate on a 27 to 5 vote, with all the nays coming from Republicans. The senators rejected an amendment that would have eliminated the nominating commission; that was on a 9 to 22 vote; all but one of the ayes coming from Republicans, with 10 Republicans and 12 Democrats voting no.[101] In the House, the vote was 57 to 39, with all but three of the nays coming from Republicans; 36 of the 51 Republicans voting on the measure voted nay.[102] The new commission had 17 members, again appointed by the Speakers of the Senate and House. At least 10 of the members had to be licensed attorneys; however, there was no formal role for groups such as the

96 In searching for "judicial nominating commission" during the period 2006–2008 on newspapers.com, I found many pieces. A good example is R. Culver Schmid, "Judicial Selection Should Be Done by State's Voters," *Nashville Tennessean* (December 7, 2008), A23.

97 Theo Emery, "Speaker Vote Blindsides GOP," *Nashville Tennessean* (January 14, 2009), A1.

98 Lucas Johnson, II, "Tenn. GOP Ousts House Speaker from Party," *Jackson Sun* (February 10, 2009), 5.

99 Erik Schelzig, "Rival Judge-Choice Bills Advance in Legislature," *Nashville Tennessean* (April 30, 2009), B3.

100 "Judicial Selection Bill Advances," *Nashville Tennessean* (May 27, 2009), B2; Erik Schelzig, "Speaker Seeks Deal on Judicial Selections," *Nashville Tennessean* (May 1, 2009) B2.

101 *Senate Journal of the 106th Tennessee General Assembly* (2009), 1500–1501.

102 *House Journal of the 106th Tennessee General Assembly* (2009), 1722.

Tennessee Bar Association or the Tennessee Trial Lawyers Association. The new legislation did not take any position regarding lawyers being the best judges of judges. The governor retained the right to request a second list of nominees, but now could appoint from either of the two lists.[103] Otherwise, the procedures remained largely the same as for the TJSC.

The 2009 law made two other noteworthy changes. First, although the system of evaluating judges prior to their standing for retention was continued, the composition of the commission charged with conducting the evaluations changed. Its size was reduced from 12 to 9, and the various lawyers' organizations no longer were guaranteed a presence on the commission. The judges on the revised commission were to be appointed by the Speakers of the House and Senate, rather than by the Tennessee Judicial Council, which the legislature allowed to cease operation on June 30, 2009, under the state's sunset law.[104] The other change was to the format of the ballot. Previously, voters were asked to vote yes or no on the question of whether a judge or justice shall be "elected and retained in the office." Under the new law, voters were to be asked whether a judge "shall be retained or replaced in office," with the two choices labeled "retain" and "replace."[105]

2014: UNCONSTRAINING THE GOVERNOR

For reasons described here, the 2009 legislation can be seen as a temporary adjustment that largely maintained the status quo for appellate court selection and retention. Despite two decisions by the Tennessee Supreme Court upholding the system, critics of the Tennessee Plan continued to argue that it was inconsistent with the state constitution's provision requiring that Supreme Court justices "shall be elected by the qualified voters of the state." However, as one commentator pointed out, the state constitution "uses the term 'election' to refer to both yes/no referendums and popular elections."[106] The 2009 changes did nothing to end the debate over the validity of the Tennessee Plan. Legislative leaders seemed to realize that what was really needed was either a return to contested elections for Tennessee's appellate courts or a constitutional amendment making clear the validity of appointment combined with retention elections.

Under the Tennessee Constitution,[107] the adoption of a constitutional amendment requires two-thirds approval from each chamber of the legislature, and the

[103] Behm and Henry, "Judicial Selection in Tennessee," *supra* note 20, 164–165. Also noteworthy is that although the prior legislation included language to make court appointments "nonpolitical," the new statute simply sought "to make the courts less political."

[104] *Id.*, 166.

[105] *Tennessee Public Acts 2009* (2009), Chapter 517, page 8; for an example, see "Sample Ballot," *Nashville Tennessean* (July 16, 2010), W9.

[106] Robert J. Mendes, "Foes Cast a Smoke Screen to Change Judicial Selection," *Nashville Tennessean* (April 20, 2011), A10.

[107] See Tennessee Constitution, Article XI, Section 3.

approval must be done twice by two separate legislatures; this means that there must be a legislative election between the two times the legislature votes on the amendment. After the legislature's action, the amendment goes to the voters at the same time as a gubernatorial election. Thus, amendments can only be presented to voters every fourth year.[108] For the amendment to be approved, it must receive favorable votes equal to at least half the number of voters casting ballots for governor. This latter provision has the potential of rejecting the amendment even if a majority votes in favor if many voters fail to cast a vote on the amendment; there is also the potential of approving an amendment with less than a majority in favor if for some reason large numbers of voters skip the gubernatorial ballot but vote on the amendment. Given these constitutional requirements, action in 2009 could not get an amendment before the voters until at least 2014.

To get a constitutional amendment on the ballot in 2014, the legislature would need to approve it in 2011–2012 and again in 2013–2014. This meant that there was little need to put judicial selection on the legislative agenda in 2010. Serious discussions got underway in 2011. By this time, the legislature was in solid Republican control: 20 to 13 Republicans to Democrats in the Senate and 64 to 34 with one independent in the House.[109] Given the two-thirds requirement, Republicans almost, but not quite, had the votes to do whatever they wanted. Moreover, GOP leaders did not immediately agree on what to do. The governor wanted to keep an appointive system with retention elections, something the Speaker of the Senate would agree to only if a constitutional amendment could be passed.[110] In the absence of a constitutional amendment the Speaker favored returning to partisan elections that would not require a constitutional amendment, and he backed a bill to do that.[111] Although the Republican-controlled legislature could have overridden a gubernatorial veto and there was substantial support for a return to (partisan) contested elections among Republican legislators, it probably would have raised political issues, given that the governor was also a Republican, and he was strongly in favor of keeping the Tennessee Plan.[112] In the end, there was no action during the 2011 legislative session.[113] To get a constitutional amendment on the ballot in 2014, there would have to be action by the legislature during its 2012 session.

In the fall of 2011, as that next legislative session approached, the push intensified to either return to contested elections or put to the voters a constitutional amendment that would settle the 40-plus-year debate over selection and retention.

[108] At the time the procedure was adopted, gubernatorial elections were every other year.

[109] See https://en.wikipedia.org/wiki/Political_party_strength_in_Tennessee, accessed August 16, 2018.

[110] Erik Schelzig, "GOP Leaders Disagree on Judges," *Nashville Tennessean* (March 31, 2011), B2.

[111] Chas Sisk, "Ramsey Backs Judicial Vote Bill," *Nashville Tennessean* (April 1, 2011), B1.

[112] "Haslam Defends System for Picking Judges," *Nashville Tennessean* (September 18, 2011), B4.

[113] See Lucas L. Johnson II, "Sen. Speaker: Pleased with GOP Leaders," *Murfreesboro Daily News-Journal* (May 30, 2011), 4.

One state senator advanced a proposal modeled on the federal system with gubernatorial appointment and Senate confirmation. It differed from the federal system of life tenure for judges by setting term length of eight years with the possibility of reappointment.[114] The proposal attracted both support and skepticism; some of the skeptics, including some judges, preferred the existing system, with others preferring a return to contested elections.[115] As the legislative term got underway in January, the governor and Speakers of both chambers, all Republicans, came out in support of a system combining gubernatorial appointment and retention elections.[116] One question was whether to keep the system that constrained the governor's selection to those on a list provided by some type of nominating commission. Others in the legislature strongly preferred returning to contested elections, and bills to accomplish this progressed through the legislative process alongside joint resolutions for a constitutional amendment.[117]

In mid-April, a proposal for a constitutional amendment specifically requiring the popular elections of Supreme Court and intermediate appellate judges, with the latter running in districts rather than statewide, died in a Senate committee. A few days later, the Senate approved on a 21–9 vote a joint resolution calling for a popular vote on an amendment that would give the legislature the clear authority to adopt a Missouri Plan system; in the absence of the legislature adopting such a system, contested elections would be held for all judges.[118] The vote was highly partisan: 18–1 in favor by the Republicans and 8–3 against by the Democrats.[119] Presumably, this satisfied both factions of Republicans, because although it cleared the way for a Missouri Plan system, such a system would have to gain a majority in both chambers of the legislature. However, that plan was not what went forward to the voters.

A few days later, an alternate plan was approved by the Senate on a 23–8 vote. This plan was a hybrid of the federal system and the Missouri Plan for the three appellate courts. The nominating commission would be eliminated for both appellate and trial courts, allowing the governor to appoint any qualified person to an open judgeship, but with proposed appointees to the appellate courts subject to confirmation by the General Assembly.[120] The proposed system was similar to what had

[114] Brandon Gee,"New Way to Pick Judges Proposed; Plan Call for 8-Year Terms," *Nashville Tennessean* (October 19, 2011), B1.

[115] Branden Gee, "Nomination Plan Draws Skepticism among Judges," *Nashville Tennessean* (October 21, 2011), B4; Erik Schelzig, "Judge Measure Awaiting Action," *Clarksville Leaf-Chronicle* (April 2, 2012), 1.

[116] Lucas L. Johnson II and Erik Schelzig, "Haslam, Speakers Want to Keep Judge Appointments," *Jackson Sun* (January 26, 2012), B2.

[117] See Erik Schelzig, "Judge Measure Awaiting Action," *Clarksville Leaf-Chronicle* (April 2, 2012), 1.

[118] "Judicial Vote Advances," *Nashville Tennessean* (April 17, 2012), B5.

[119] *Senate Journal of the 107th Tennessee General Assembly* (2012), 3761.

[120] Chas Sisk, "Embryo Bill Passes Senate," *Nashville Tennessean* (April 24, 2012), B1, B2.

been used in California since the 1930s for appellate judges,[121] with the added feature of legislative confirmation. On this version, the partisan division was virtually identical to the vote a few days earlier: 19–1 in favor for the Republicans and 8–3 against for the Democrats.[122] It was this version that the House went on to approve on a 70 to 28 vote, with majorities of both Republicans and Democrats voting in favor.[123] Before going to the voters, the proposed amendment needed passage with two-thirds in favor again in the legislature elected in November 2012. In March 2013, the two chambers again passed the proposal, 29–2 in the Senate and 78–14 in the House.[124] During the 2013 session, the legislature did nothing to extend either the Tennessee Judicial Nominating Commission or the Judicial Performance Evaluation Commission; the former expired on June 30, 2013[125] and the latter on June 30, 2014.[126] The state attorney general issued an opinion that this allowed the governor to appoint any qualified person because a clause in the 2009 statute authorized such action if the Judicial Nominating Commission failed to act within sixty days of being notified of a vacancy.[127]

This change reflects a shift in conservative preferences regarding judicial selection and retention. As is discussed in the concluding chapter, conservatives historically had tended to oppose contested judicial elections, preferring models based on the Missouri Plan. However, sometime in the first decade of this century, they had become less enamored with that plan, preferring popular elections instead.[128] As I discuss in detail in the concluding chapter, there are probably two reasons for this.

121 See Herbert M. Kritzer, *Justices on the Ballot: Continuity and Change in State Supreme Court Elections* (New York: Cambridge University Press, 2015), 38–39; in California, proposed appointees are subject to confirmation by the Commission on Judicial Appointments, or in rare cases, by the voters in a retention-type ballot.

122 *Senate Journal of the 107th Tennessee General Assembly* (2012), 3890–3891.

123 *House Journal of the 107th Tennessee General Assembly* (2012), 5315. The split among Democrats was fairly close, 17–13, compared to 53–11 for Republicans.

124 There was no clear partisan pattern in the House vote; see *House Journal of the 108th Tennessee General Assembly* (2013), 609–610. In the Senate, both of the no votes came from Republicans; see *Senate Journal of the 108th Tennessee General Assembly* (2013), 357.

125 Sheila Burke, "Legislature Leaves Open Question about Judges," *Clarkesville Leaf-Chronicle* (May 2, 2013), A6.

126 See www.tncourts.gov/boards-commissions/boards-commissions/judicial-performance-evaluation-commission, accessed August 16, 2018.

127 See Richard Locker, "Tennessee Attorney General: Governor Can Appoint Judges in Absence of Nominating Commission," *Memphis Commercial-Appeal* (October 2013), www.marknorris.org/blog1/2013/10/09/tennessee-attorney-general-governor-can-appoint-judges-in-absence-of-nominating-commission/, accessed August 16, 2018.

128 One vocal critic in of the Tennessee Plan was Brian Fitzpatrick, a law professor at Vanderbilt University and a member of the conservative Federalist Society; see Brian T. Fitzpatrick, "Election as Appointment: The Tennessee Plan Reconsidered," *Tennessee Law Review* 75, no. 3 (2008), 473–500; Brian T. Fitzpatrick, "The Politics of Merit Selection," *Missouri Law Review* 74, no. 3 (Summer 2009), 690–703. "Elections as Appointment" was based heavily on a report the Federalist Society commissioned Fitzpatrick to write, "A Report on Reauthorization of the Tennessee Plan," https://fedsoc.org/commentary/publications/a-report-on-reauthorization-of-the-tennessee-plan, accessed August 16, 2018.

First, conservative business interests had been having substantial success in using contested judicial elections to oust Supreme Court justices who made decisions seen as antithetical to business.[129] Second, lawyers have been strong proponents of Missouri Plan systems,[130] and conservatives have become skeptical about the dominant role of lawyers in nominating commissions, because they perceived lawyers as a group as being too liberal. There is some evidence that lawyers tend to be more liberal than the population as a whole.[131] This conservative take on lawyers has led at least some conservatives to oppose a system in which a governor's choice is limited to persons on a list prepared by a nominating commission. In the words of one of those opponents, "Merit systems select judiciaries with ideological preferences to the left of those that would have been selected by the public or its elected representatives ... merit systems may simply move the politics of judicial selection into closer alignment with the ideological preferences of the bar."[132]

The amendment that was going to the voters in 2014 replaced the constraints of a lawyer-dominated nominating commission with a legislative confirmation provision, keeping the retention election format for subsequent terms. One might ask why that was the end result of the legislative process. Perhaps the best explanation is that Republicans may have been confident that they would control the General Assembly for the foreseeable future. As long as a Republican governor was filling vacancies, conservatives would be happy with the persons going onto the appellate bench. The pattern in Tennessee over the prior 100 years was that, although the minority party occasionally won the gubernatorial election, the legislature was much more stable in terms of party control. With this in mind, Republicans could have felt that they would be in the position to block potential appointments of a Democratic governor if persons selected were too far to the left. Moreover, if the initial appointees were satisfactory, the retention format would, absent some mobilizing issue, avoid challengers that might get them defeated.

The proposed amendment was presented to the voters for approval in November 2014, along with three unrelated constitutional amendments. For the amendment to be approved, the percentage voting in favor had to exceed 50 percent of the number of persons casting ballots in the gubernatorial election. The supporters of the amendment, including the then current Republican governor and a former Democratic governor, built support of passage of the amendment in the spring of 2014 in

[129] See Fitzpatrick, "Election as Appointment," *supra* note 128. For a response to Fitzpatrick's article, see Penny J. White and Malia Reddick, "A Response to Professor Fitzpatrick: The Rest of the Story," *Tennessee Law Review* 75, no. 3 (2008), 501–544.

[130] See F. Andrew Hanssen, "On the Politics of Judicial Selection: Lawyers and State Campaigns for the Merit Plan," *Public Choice* 110, no. 1 (2002), 79–97.

[131] See Adam Bonica, Adam S. Chilton, and Maya Sen, "Political Ideologies of American Lawyers," *Journal of Legal Analysis* 8, no. 2 (Winter 2016), 277–335; see also, Fitzpatrick, "The Politics of Merit Selection," *supra* note 128.

[132] Chris W. Bonneau, "True 'Merit' in Judicial Selections?" *Philadelphia Inquirer* (April 8, 2012), quoting Vanderbilt law professor Brian Fitzpatrick.

anticipation of the November popular vote on whether it should be adopted.[133] The campaign in support brought together a range of groups, from the Farm Bureau to the Business Chamber of Commerce and Industry.[134] The campaign was described as "well-financed and well-organized."[135] The amendment had the support of all sitting justices and all sitting appellate judges.[136] One group not happy about the proposed system was the Tennessee Bar Association; its position was that a system including a nominating commission that was charged with recommending candidates solely on merit was preferable.[137] Opposition also came from the state Democratic Party.[138] Democratic leaders were especially concerned that Democratic voters might stay home because the Democratic gubernatorial candidate was a political novice who made no significant effort to campaign, and thus had no chance of winning. Alternatively, Democratic voters who came to the polls might be inclined to skip voting in the gubernatorial election. Democratic voters staying at home would reduce the number of voters who would, hopefully, vote no on the amendment. Also, if large numbers of voters who did come to the polls skipped the gubernatorial part of the ballot, the number of yes votes needed for ratification would be reduced, such that an amendment could be passed with less than half of those voting on the amendment voting in favor of its adoption.

On November 4, 2014, the amendment was approved by the voters with 729,163 votes in favor (52.6 percent) and 657,192 against. The number voting in favor as a percentage of the number of ballots cast in the gubernatorial election (1,353,728) was 53.9 percent, but under the constitution's provisions, if the same total number of votes had been cast on the amendment, it would have passed if only 678,965 (48.8 percent) votes had been in favor. The approval of the amendment ended the long-running debate over judicial selection in Tennessee, at least through the time this chapter was written in 2019.

CONCLUSION

The years-long battle over judicial selection in Tennessee arose because of the unique decision of the Tennessee General Assembly to create a Missouri Plan type system through legislation rather than through a constitutional amendment that

[133] Chas Sisk, "Bredesen to Speak Out on Judicial Selection Fight," *Nashville Tennessean* (April 27, 2014), A4.
[134] Chas Sisk, "Judicial Amendment Campaign Begins; Haslam, Others Ask Voters to Approve Selection Revision," *Nashville Tennessean* (April 30, 2014), A5.
[135] Tom Humphrey, "Battle Lines Drawn on Judicial Selection," *Nashville Tennessean* (September 29, 2014), A1.
[136] *Id.*, A7.
[137] Eric Schelzig, "Haslam Unsure of Reason for Few Court Applicants," *Clarksville Leaf-Chronicle* (December 14, 2013), A1.
[138] Michael Cass, "Democrats Urged Not to Skip Ballot for Governor; Party Leaders Fear Low Turnout Will Help Pass the Amendment," *Nashville Tennessean* (August 13, 2014), A1.

either directly imposed such a system or explicitly authorized the legislature to do so. Every other state that has shifted to a Missouri Plan system did so through an amendment to the state constitution, or applied it to courts not covered by the state constitution's provisions concerning judicial selection.[139]

Tennessee was the first state to abandon a system modeled on the Missouri Plan, and it did so twice. In 1974 the Democratic-controlled General Assembly passed legislation over the Republican governor's veto that returned selection and retention for the Supreme Court to contested (partisan) elections. This was done for straight political reasons: without the change, the Republican governor was going to be able to appoint most of the justices, who would not have faced opponents in subsequent elections. In 1994, the legislature modified the plan still in use for the Courts of Appeals and returned the selection and retention of Supreme Court justices to the same modified Missouri Plan system. Then, in 2012 and 2013, the legislature finally passed a constitutional amendment specifying a system of appointment and retention elections for appellate judges, but without the constraint that the governor appoint from a list screened by a nominating commission; the voters approved the amendment in 2014. As this was written in 2019, the only other state that had abandoned a Missouri Plan system for some or all of its courts was Kansas, where the legislature removed the legislatively created Court of Appeals from that plan in 2013; the Kansas experience is discussed in detail in Chapter 14.

Importantly, although the 2014 amendment freed the governor of Tennessee to appoint any qualified candidate, three days after the 2014 election, Republican governor Bill Haslam issued an executive order establishing a new Governor's Council for Judicial Appointments (GCJA), which was charged with vetting applicants and forwarding a set of three finalists to him; a key difference between the new CGJA and the previous commissions is that the governor, not legislative leaders, selects all members for the CGJA.[140] The CGJA was continued by Haslam's successor Bill Lee; however, future governors are free to structure similar bodies as they please, or do without any kind of formal body to screen potential court appointments.

[139] The latter situation can occur when the legislature creates a court not listed in the constitution and the constitutional provisions regarding judicial selection are in the context of the courts enumerated by the constitutional text. One such example, discussed in Chapter 14, is the intermediate appellate court in Kansas.

[140] "Lawmakers Prep for Judge Selection Change," *Nashville Tennessean* (November 7, 2014), A5. The executive order may be found at www.tncourts.gov/sites/default/files/docs/executive_order_54_1.pdf, accessed August 16, 2018.

PART II

Change as Court Modernization or Good Government

6

Georgia

Nonpartisan Elections as Part of Court Modernization

Georgia has a complex system of courts. Statewide, there is the Georgia Supreme Court, the Georgia Court of Appeals (created in 1906), and the trial-level superior court organized in circuits, all of which are courts of general jurisdiction. In addition, there is a hodgepodge of limited jurisdiction local courts including probate courts, municipal courts, county recorder's courts, magistrates' courts, juvenile courts, "civil" courts, and "state" courts.[1] This in fact represents a simplification of the system that existed prior to the adoption of a new judicial article (Article VI) for the Georgia Constitution in 1983.[2] It was the adoption of the new judicial article that changed the method of selection of judges for the three general jurisdiction courts and one limited jurisdiction court, from partisan to nonpartisan elections. That change is the focus of this chapter, although there was a significant change that occurred in 1966 regarding superior court elections, which I note later in the chapter.

In sharp contrast to what transpired in North Carolina, there is little evidence that partisan advantage was a motivating factor in the change to nonpartisan judicial elections. Rather it appears to be part of a broad effort to modernize a complex and overly decentralized system during the period when there was a national movement toward "court modernization,"[3] a major theme of which was unification of trial

1 See www.courtstatistics.org/Other-Pages/State_Court_Structure_Charts/Georgia.aspx, accessed January 26, 2018.

2 As of 1980 one also found county courts, justice of the peace courts, small claims courts, recorder's courts, mayor's courts, criminal courts, city council courts, and police courts. At that time there were almost 2,600 distinct courts in Georgia; see Bureau of Justice Statistics, *State Court Organization* (Washington, DC: U.S. Department of Justice, 1982), 200. Today most of Georgia's trial courts (superior, juvenile, magistrate, and probate) are organized by county, with one court in each county; in addition there are 365 municipal courts, 2 "civil" courts, and 71 "state" courts (see http://data.ncsc.org/QvAJAXZfc/opendoc.htm?document=Public%20App/SCO.qvw&host=QVS@qlikviewisa&anonymous=true&bookmark=Document\BM136, accessed January 26, 2018).

3 See, for example, Victor E. Flango, "Court Administration and Judicial Modernization," *Public Administration Review* 35 (1975), 619–625.

courts.[4] There is evidence of partisanship in one vote that occurred in the Georgia House of Representatives, but the context differed substantially from what transpired in North Carolina and other states that showed politically motivated change.

JUDICIAL ELECTIONS IN GEORGIA: HISTORICAL PERSPECTIVES

A Brief Primer on Georgia Politics

The complex nature of the Georgia court system prior to 1982 reflected the emphasis on localism in Georgia politics. Georgia has 159 counties, a number exceeded only by Texas with 254 counties. More importantly, prior to the 1964 U.S. Supreme Court decision mandating state legislative chambers be based on roughly equal population districts,[5] the individual counties had disproportionate influence not only in legislative elections, but also in statewide elections through what was called the "county unit system."[6] Under this system, each county had a minimum of two "unit votes" regardless of population, and no county had more than six unit votes. Although technically this applied only to primary elections, given the one-party structure of southern politics into the 1960s, this meant that rural counties controlled all aspects of state politics. V. O. Key reported that as of 1940, the 8 most populous counties (each with 6 unit votes) had about a third of the state's population and voters, but less than 12 percent of the unit votes; the 30 next most populous counties (each with 4 unit votes) had about a quarter of the state population and voters, and 29 percent of the unit votes; the remaining 121 counties (each with 2 unit votes), with around 40 percent of the population and voters, had 59 percent of the total unit votes.[7] By 1960, the 121 counties with 2 unit votes were down to 32 percent of the state population but still controlled 59 percent of the unit votes.[8] One effect of this system was to make candidates for statewide office beholden to local leaders, who

4 See Larry C. Berkson and Susan B. Carbon, *Court Unification: History, Politics and Implementation* (Washington, DC: U.S. Government Printing Office, 1978); Thomas A. Henderson, *The Significance of Judicial Structure: The Effect of Unification on Trial Court Operations* (Washington, DC: U.S. Department of Justice, National Institute of Justice, 1984); Victor E. Flango, "Court Unification and Quality of State Courts," *Justice System Journal* 16 (1994), 33–55.

5 Reynolds v. Sims, 377 U.S. 533 (1964).

6 The system was created by the Neill Primary Act of 1917 but had operated informally in Democratic primaries since 1898; see Scott E. Buchanan, "County Unit System," *New Georgia Encyclopedia*, www.georgiaencyclopedia.org/articles/counties-cities-neighborhoods/county-unit-system, accessed March 1, 2018. Technically, the Neill Act would have applied to Republican as well as Democratic primaries, but no statewide Republican primaries occurred during the period the Act was in place.

7 V. O. Key, *Southern Politics in State and Nation* (New York: Alfred A. Knopf, 1949), 119; Key points out (p. 120) that in 1946, there were 14,092 popular votes per unit vote in the most populous county (Fulton, which includes Atlanta) compared to 132 popular votes per unit vote in the least populous county (Chattahoochee).

8 See Buchanan, "County Unit System," *supra* note 6.

had effective control of the unit votes of their counties. The result of this was what Key labeled, in titling his chapter on Georgia, "Rule of the Rustics."

The dominance of rural interests ended with the U.S. Supreme Court's decision in *Gray v. Sanders*,[9] which found that the system operating in Georgia violated the Fourteenth Amendment's Equal Protection Clause.[10] However, the end of rural dominance did not produce a shift in the partisan character of Georgia *state* politics even though Georgia did tend to swing to the Republican side in presidential elections starting with the 1964 election, when Barry Goldwater won 54 percent of the state's vote. Since that time, Democrats have carried the state in only three presidential elections, and in two of those elections, the Democratic candidate was Georgia's own Jimmy Carter.[11]

At the state level, Republican gubernatorial candidate Howard ("Bo") Callaway won a plurality of the general election vote, with the Democratic and segregationist candidate Lester Maddow only 3,000 votes behind.[12] There was no majority because Democrat Ellis Arnall,[13] who had won a plurality in the 1964 Democratic primary but then lost to Maddox in a runoff, waged a write-in campaign, and secured almost 53,000 votes. Under Georgia law at the time, if no candidate in an election received a majority in the general election, it fell to the legislature to determine the winner from the top two candidates, and the Democratic dominated legislature chose Lester Maddox.[14] A Republican candidate for governor would not win in Georgia for another twenty-six years,[15] and it would be the 1990s before Republicans began to gain significant strength in the state legislature. In 1980, Republicans held roughly 10 percent of the seats in the Georgia legislature's two chambers, with many if not most of those Republicans coming from two suburban counties around Atlanta,

9 372 U.S. 368 (1963).

10 After a three-judge federal district court struck down the unit-vote system in 1962, the 1962 statewide Democratic primaries were conducted on a popular-vote basis.

11 In 1968, third-party candidate George Wallace carried the state with 43 percent of the vote; the Democratic candidate, Hubert Humphrey, came in third with 27 percent.

12 Calloway had been a Democrat before switching parties and running successfully as a "Goldwater Republican" for the U.S. House of Representatives in 1964.

13 Arnall was a relatively liberal Democrat who had won the Georgia governorship in 1942 by defeating the sitting governor, Eugene Talmadge, in the Democratic primary; see Charles S. Bullock III and M. V. Hood, "The Damnedest Mess: An Empirical Evaluation of the 1966 Georgia Gubernatorial Election," *Social Science Quarterly* 96, no. 1 (March 2015), 104–118.

14 A three-judge federal court initially struck down the constitutional provision providing for legislative selection in the absence of a majority, but the U.S. Supreme Court overruled that court, allowing the legislature to choose Maddox; Fortson v. Morris, 385 U.S. 231 (1966).

15 A Republican did win a statewide election in 1980 when Matt Mattingly defeated incumbent U.S. Senator Herman Talmadge; however, that victory was interpreted more as a "denunciation of Talmadge [rather than] a Republican triumph or Republican over Democratic sentiments;" see Henry Eason, "2-Party System Not Yet Reality in Georgia," *Atlanta Constitution* (November 10, 1980), 1C. The only Georgia Republican elected to the U.S. House of Representatives that year was one-term incumbent Newt Gingrich.

DeKalb and Cobb.[16] By the start of the 1990s, Republican strength in the legislature was up to roughly 20 percent, and by the end of that decade Republicans held about 40 percent of the seats; that changed little in the 2000 election.[17]

Republican control of the executive and legislative branches of Georgia's state government began in 2002, with Republican Sonny Perdue's surprise victory, he narrowly defeated the Democratic incumbent 51 percent to 46 percent.[18] That same year, Republicans secured a majority in the Georgia Senate for the first time since Reconstruction,[19] and then two years later won a majority in the House of Representatives for the first time ever.[20] Republicans have controlled both the legislature and the governorship since 2005.

Judicial Selection and Judicial Elections in the Postwar Period

I focus here exclusively on elections for three general jurisdiction courts, because they were all affected by the shift to nonpartisan elections in the 1980s.[21] Between 1946 and 1982, no Republicans appeared in the contests for election to either the Georgia Supreme Court or the Georgia Court of Appeals, and there were very few contests in the Democratic primaries for these courts. During this period, only 7 Supreme Court seats were contested,[22] and 3 of those contests occurred in 1982, 2 involving incumbents; of the 4 such contests prior to 1982, 3 were for open seats. Incumbents won all four elections in which they faced opposition in the Democratic primary. During that same period, there were 62 elections for the Court of

[16] David K. Secrest, "Do Republicans Own Cobb Politically? After Last Week, Looks Like They Might," *Atlanta Constitution* (November 13, 1980), G8.

[17] See Charles S. Bullock IIII, "Georgia: Republicans Still Dominate," in Charles S. Bullock III and Mark J. Rozell, eds., *The New Politics of the Old South: An Introduction to Southern Politics*, 6th ed. (Lanham, MD: Rowman and Littlefield, 2018), 70.

[18] The outcome of the gubernatorial election was a surprise, given that the last poll before the election showed the incumbent with an 11-percentage-point lead and he outspent Perdue 6 to 1; see Danny Hayes and Seth C. McKee, "Booting Barnes: Explaining the Historic Upset in the 2002 Georgia Gubernatorial Election," *Politics & Policy* 32, no. 4 (December 2004), 708–738.

[19] Democrats held a majority of seats, 29 to 27, as a result of the election, but the Friday after the election three Democratic incumbents switched parties, giving the Republicans a 30 to 26 majority; see David M. Halbfinger, "The 2002 Election: Georgia; Bush's Push, Eager Volunteers and Big Turnout Led to Georgia Sweep," *New York Times* (November 10, 2002), www.nytimes.com/2002/11/10/us/2002-election-georgia-bush-s-push-eager-volunteers-big-turnout-led-georgia-sweep.html

[20] See https://en.wikipedia.org/wiki/Political_party_strength_in_Georgia_(U.S._state), accessed January 26, 2018.

[21] The change also applied to the limited jurisdiction state courts. Those courts may be created by special local acts of the legislature to serve counties with populations exceeding a threshold. In 1980, state courts existed in 60 counties; see *State Court Organization 1980* (Washington, DC: U.S. Department of Justice, 1982), 56.

[22] In 1982, there were two elections for the same seat with same candidates; one for the short remaining term and one for the full term that followed. I have not counted the election for the short remaining term.

Appeals, with only 7 of those elections contested in the Democratic primary. The reality was that most appellate judges came to their positions through appointment by the governor to fill vacancies, and those appointees seldom faced any opposition in retaining their seats on the courts.

Although there were some pockets of Republican success in state legislative elections by the mid-1960s, there were no Republicans serving as judges on the superior courts. This was due to the election system for those courts. As was true in North Carolina during this time, superior court judges were nominated in circuit-based primary elections, but were then elected in a statewide ballot in the general election. This meant that even if a Republican ran in a circuit with Republican strength, the Democratic nominee would carry the statewide vote in the general election. This was made even more certain by the presence of a straight-ticket voting option in Georgia during this period.[23] Thus, the meaningful elections for superior court judges occurred in the Democratic primary. Between 1946 and 1966 there were approximately 270 primary elections for the superior court, with about one-third of those elections contested.[24]

As part of an unsuccessful state constitutional revision in 1964, a proposal was advanced to limit the electors (i.e., qualified voters) for the general election of superior court judges to the electors residing in the circuit where the judge would serve. However, that proposal was rejected in order "to 'protect' judges from being replaced by Republicans."[25] Later that year, a Republican candidate for solicitor

[23] Georgia abolished the straight-ticket option in 1994; see www.ncsl.org/research/elections-and-campaigns/straight-ticket-voting.aspx, accessed January 26, 2018. It had previously (H.B. 1053, passed early in 1968) taken the presidential race off the straight-ticket option, perhaps reflecting a concern that the anticipated candidate, Lyndon Johnson, would be a drag on other Democratic candidates; see Bruce Galphin, "The Coattail Ride," *Atlanta Constitution* (November 4, 1968), 4. Professor Charles Bullock III (University of Georgia), provided an alternative explanation for the abolition: "The decision to separate the presidential election from the remainder of the ticket was a result of the defeat of Rep. Jim Mackey in 1966. Mackey attributes his 360-vote loss to a number of voters who used the straight ticket punch for the GOP but then also punched for his name. (I know that DeKalb which constituted the bulk of Jim's district was using punch cards; I don't know about Rockdale or Fulton although I suspect Fulton also had punch cards at that point.) 1966 was the first time in a century that the GOP had a gubernatorial candidate and so many GA voters were not used to having a partisan choice in November. Mackey's defeat alerted Democrats to what could happen in a presidential election although 1968 would probably not have been a problem since GA voted solidly for Wallace that year. Of course, when the legislature was meeting in January–March of 1968 they would not have known that Wallace would mount a third-party effort" – email from Charles Bullock III to Herbert Kritzer, March 20, 2018.

[24] I derived these figures from various volumes of the *Georgia Official and Statistical Register*. I say "approximately" because the format in which the election results are shown does not always make clear how many positions were being filled or whether when several candidates are shown there was a contested election.

[25] Achsay Posey, "Revisers Keep Statewide Vote for Judges, Fearing GOP Gains," *Atlanta Constitution* (May 14, 1964), 12. While the draft constitution of 1964 was approved by the legislature, it was never submitted to the electorate, because of concerns about malapportionment of the legislature; see LaVerne W. Hill and Melvin B. Hill, "Georgia Constitution," *New Georgia*

general, a local office that was elected in the same way as superior court judges, filed suit in federal court, challenging as unconstitutional the use of statewide ballots for both superior court judges and solicitor general.[26] A three-judge federal court held oral argument about a month after the suit was filed,[27] and less than two weeks later issued a decision rejecting the plaintiff's contention that the statewide elections violated the Equal Protection Clause.[28] Although a notice of appeal was filed,[29] there is no evidence that an actual appeal to the U.S. Supreme Court was ever filed.[30]

The use of statewide general elections for the superior court ended in 1968 after Georgia voters in 1966 overwhelmingly approved a constitutional amendment changing the general elections for the superior court so only persons residing in the circuit where the judge served were eligible to vote in the election.[31] From 1968 through 1982, when partisan elections for superior court judges ended, the number of positions on the superior court increased substantially such that there were about 400 elections for superior court judges. The most interesting change was the appearance of an occasional Republican running for a seat on the superior court. The first such candidate was in 1968 in Stone Mountain Circuit, which is composed largely of Atlanta suburbs in DeKalb County; in that election, the Republican defeated the Democratic incumbent. In the words on one longtime observer of Georgia politics who was in the DeKalb County courthouse the night of the 1968 election, "Everyone was stunned, especially Judge Jones [the incumbent]. His friends were commiserating just as if his nearest and dearest had died."[32] Between 1970 and 1982, Republicans contested a very small fraction of superior court elections, a total of fourteen in all. Those elections occurred in only four circuits: Stone Mountain and Cobb (which are comprised of Atlanta suburbs), Atlanta, and Chattahoochee;[33] Republicans won 5 of the 14. Even as an occasional Republican challenged Democratic candidates in superior court elections, the

Encyclopedia, www.georgiaencyclopedia.org/articles/government-politics/georgia-constitution, accessed January 30, 2018.

26 "GOP Sues to Ban Vote for Judges: Candidate Seeks Circuit Elections," *Atlanta Constitution* (August 12, 1964), 12.

27 Achsah Posey, "U.S. Court Considers GOP Suit," *Atlanta Constitution* (September 17, 1964), 1.

28 Stokes v. Fortis, 234 F. Supp. 575 (N.D. Georgia, 1964).

29 "Statewide Voting on Judges to Be Put to Supreme Court," *Atlanta Constitution* (November 20, 1964), 5.

30 Under the law as it existed in 1964, the plaintiff would have an appeal as of right to the Supreme Court, and if such an appeal had been filed, some disposition would appear in the reports of the Supreme Court.

31 See https://ballotpedia.org/Georgia_Election_of_Judges,_Amendment_18_(1966), accessed January 26, 2018.

32 Email to Herbert Kritzer, from Professor Charles Bullock III (University of Georgia), January 25, 2018.

33 The Chattahoochee Circuit is in southwest Georgia around Columbus, a city dominated by Fort Benning.

likelihood of Democratic candidates facing a contested primary election decreased. While about one-third of such primaries were contested between 1946 and 1968, only about one-sixth of such primaries were contested after the electorates were confined to the circuit where the judge would sit for the general election.

THE 1983 JUDICIAL ARTICLE: NONPARTISAN ELECTIONS

In 1976 Georgia voters approved a "new" state constitution. In fact, it was not new in terms of content but "rather was a reorganization and editorial revision of the Constitution of 1945."[34] In turn, the 1945 constitution had been taken largely from the post-Reconstruction constitution in effect since 1877; although there were some significant changes in the 1945 constitution, such as creating the office of lieutenant governor and several new constitutional officers, "approximately 90 percent of the provisions were taken from the Constitution of 1877."[35]

For much of the twentieth century, until the adoption of a new constitution in 1982, the Georgia constitution was a long, complex document, and included a large number of amendments, a majority of which dealt with matters that would be handled by ordinary legislation in most states. Moreover, many of the amendments were applicable to only a single political jurisdiction within the state. Even though these "local constitutional amendments" applied to single jurisdiction, they appeared on the statewide ballot, because under the 1945 (and 1976) constitutions they required the approval of the electors in the affected jurisdiction and also approval statewide.[36] Combining local and "general amendments," it was not unusual to have over 100 amendments on what came to be referred to as the "bedsheet ballot."[37] According to one study, between 1946 and 1966, 717 proposed amendments had appeared on the Georgia ballot, 549 of which had been approved by the voters; only 113 of the 717 proposed amendments applied statewide, 83 of which were approved.[38] The 1976 constitution did not solve the problem of local amendments; 87 local amendments appeared on the ballot in 1978 and 121 in 1980.

A year after the 1976 constitution was ratified, the state legislature created a Select Committee on Constitutional Revision. This committee was chaired by the governor and composed of top elected officials from all three branches of government.

[34] George D. Busbee, "An Overview of the New Georgia Constitution," *Mercer Law Review* 35, No. 1 (1983), 3.

[35] Hill and Hill, "Georgia Constitution," *supra* note 25; other notable changes included the creation of a board of corrections and a department of veterans' services, increasing the size of the Georgia Supreme Court to 7 members, and authorizing jury service for women.

[36] Melvin B. Hill Jr., *The Georgia State Constitution* (New York: Oxford University Press, 2011), 26.

[37] *Id.*, 24, 27.

[38] Albert B. Saye, "Proposals for Constitutional Revision," *Georgia State Bar Journal* 3 (February 1987), 287–288.

The committee's goal was to produce a new document that was characterized by "brevity, clarity, and flexibility."[39] Thus, it set out to totally revise the constitution in a way that would avoid the need for frequent amendments generally, and local amendments entirely. As the committee and its article-focused subcommittees worked, they were attentive to best practices employed in states around the country; in the words of one observer, the process was driven by "a goal of good government rather than by interest groups."[40]

One major focus was on revising the judicial article, Article VI.[41] According to Melvin Hill, who served as staff director for the overall committee, in 1978, "the judicial system in Georgia was in terrible disarray… many referred to this as the judicial 'nonsystem,'"[42] even though both the 1945 and 1976 constitutions contained the statement, carried over to the 1983 constitution, "All courts of the state shall comprise a unified judicial system."[43] One observer described the judicial system as a "many *splintered* thing." That observer listed a range of failings of the then current system:[44]

- No supervisory power vested in our highest court
- No court administrator to assist in supervising the operation
- No program or standards for the recruitment, promotion, or compensation of court personnel
- No uniform procedures for the preparation and analysis of the budgets of the courts
- No uniform procedures for the purchase of supplies for the operation of the courts
- No statistical system to provide statistical facts.

There is evidence of at least some interest among the members of the bar in changing methods of judicial selection as far back as 1949, when the president of the Georgia Bar Association called for the adoption of the Missouri Plan and reported that the Bar Association would sponsor legislation to that effect.[45] Bills proposing some version of the Missouri Plan were introduced in 1956, 1964,

39 Hill., *The Georgia State Constitution*, *supra* note 36, 24.

40 Telephone interview with Professor Thomas G. Walker (Emory University), July 14, 2017.

41 The initial focus included two other articles – Article II on the elective franchise and Article X on retirement systems and educational scholarships. The groups working on these two amendments submitted drafts to the legislature in 1978; they were approved and put on the November ballot and then rejected by the voters.

42 Hill., *The Georgia State Constitution*, *supra* note 36, 137. In a telephone interview (February 5, 2018), Mr. Hill reported that the "judicial article took the longest time to resolve," and, in fact, the deliberations of the Judicial Article Committee stretched over four years, 1977 to 1981.

43 *Id.*, 140.

44 Robert H. Hall, "The Facts about Georgia Courts and Judges Today," *Georgia State Bar Journal* 2 (May 1966), 392.

45 "Bar Asks Ban on Politics in Courts," *Atlanta Constitution* (January 15, 1949), 2.

and 1968.[46] In 1966, the state bar journal published an article by the president of the Missouri Bar Association describing Missouri's experience with its system of selection and retention over the roughly twenty-five years it had been in place;[47] the article was based on an address presented at the "Citizens' Conference on Georgia's Judicial System," which was held in April 1966.[48]

To develop the new Article VI, a Committee to Revise the Judicial Article (CRJA) was created, headed by Representative Wayne Snow, who was the chair of the Georgia House of Representatives Judiciary Committee. The membership of CRJA included the chief justice of Georgia, the chair of the Georgia Senate Judiciary Committee, the chief judge of the Court of Appeals, a judge of the superior court, one or more judges from limited jurisdiction courts, the attorney general, law school deans, several district attorneys, representatives of the Georgia Bar Association, and representatives of several groups such as business, labor, and the League of Women Voters. After meetings and hearings spanning a three-year period, CJRA proposed, "All judges shall be elected on a nonpartisan basis for a term of six years . . . provided that judges of limited jurisdiction may by law be elected or may be appointed from nominees certified as qualified by a judicial nominating commission."[49] Based on the transcripts of the committee meetings and of the hearings held by the committee, it seems that the decision to adopt nonpartisan elections was noncontroversial. Much more controversial was the reorganization of the court system, particularly the abolition of the justice of the peace courts.

At the second meeting of the committee, August 5, 1977, the possibility of adopting a system based on the Missouri Plan came up,[50] along with the possibility of nonpartisan elections.[51] This Missouri Plan was briefly raised again at the next meeting a month later, initially in reference to how the attorney general might be selected and retained.[52] In the course of this discussion, both the chief justice and a judge representing of the chief judge of the Court of Appeals made clear their

[46] "Judiciary Reforms Can Serve Justice," *Atlanta Constitution* (January 18, 1956), 4; "Special Session to Consider Reorganizing of Courts Setup," *Atlanta Constitution* (March 19, 1964), 1; "Bill Would Curb Governor's Power to Fill Court Seats," *Atlanta Constitution* (January 11, 1968), 27.

[47] Loyd E. Roberts, "Twenty-Five Years Under the Missouri Plan," *Georgia State Bar Journal* 2 (November 1966), 185–195.

[48] In 1967, a judge of the Georgia Court of Appeals called on the participants at the annual meeting of the Grand Jurors Association to "push for implementation in Georgia of the Missouri Plan of merit selection;" see "Merit System Asked for State Judiciary," *Atlanta Constitution* (January 20, 1967), 12.

[49] Draft dated October 27, 1980; Select Committee on Constitutional Revision 1977–1981, Transcripts of Meetings, Committee to Revise Article VI, vol. 3, 944, http://dlg.galileo.usg.edu/ggpd/docs/1981/ga/c675_pc6/m1/1981/t7/v_p9.con/1.pdf, accessed February 2, 2018. Note that all page numbers cited for these transcripts are the sequential numbers in the PDF, rather than any page number appearing on the actual page.

[50] *Id.*, vol. 1, 94–99.

[51] *Id.*, vol. 1, 103–104.

[52] *Id.*, vol. 1, 253–254.

opposition. In the words of the chief justice, "I'm against the Missouri Plan per se. I'm for non-partisan elections and ballots. I don't believe in running against yourself." A representative of the Court of Appeals judge concurred, "We're against it per se, too."[53] Additional discussion of the Missouri Plan option centered around the opposition it might provoke, particularly in the legislature. The "compromise" was to go with nonpartisan elections, which was thought to be more likely to get through the larger process.[54] In the words of one member of the committee, "It was clear to me that there was no way we were getting away from elections, [but we could] improve elections by making them nonpartisan."[55] That member went on to explain that a change to nonpartisan elections was seen as likely to change the characteristics of the elections by deemphasizing money and campaign contributions.[56]

There was at least some perception that there were elements of the Missouri Plan in the proposed system,[57] by which was meant the provision in the draft article provided that vacancies were to be filled from a list of nominees prepared by "an impartial nominating commission."[58] At the time, the use of such a commission was a matter of practice, initiated by Jimmy Carter when he was governor, rather than a matter of law. The proposal to require in the text of the new Article VI that judicial elections be conducted on a nonpartisan basis produced relatively little discussion, although at one of the final meetings of the committee in 1980, a member made a motion to delete the word "nonpartisan," which would have given the legislature the discretion to choose between partisan and nonpartisan elections; that motion died for lack of a second.[59]

From the CRJA, the draft of a new Article VI went to the Legislative Overview Committee (LOC). The LOC made one significant change related to judicial selection when it considered Article VI in August 1981.[60] Specifically, it eliminated from the text the requirement that an "impartial nominating commission" be part of the process for filling vacancies; the revised language left the filling of vacancies

[53] *Id.*, vol. 1, 259–260.

[54] *Id.*, vol. 1, 289–303, 338, 340; there are some later discussions of nonpartisan elections, but they deal with making clear which positions are subject to nonpartisan elections and working out appropriate language.

[55] *Id.*

[56] Telephone interview with Judge Dorothy Beasley, February 14, 2018.

[57] Select Committee on Constitutional Revision 1977–1981, *Transcripts of Hearings*, vol. 3, 932.

[58] *Id.*, vol. 3, 947 §VIII, ¶III.

[59] *Id.*, 820.

[60] Probably the most significant change, beyond the general restructuring and simplification of the court system, was to who had administrative authority over the courts, rather than to the system of selecting and retaining judges. At the time there was no overarching administrative structure for the Georgia judicial system. The version of Article VI drafted by the Select Committee called for "the judicial system [to] be administered by the Supreme Court" (Section XI, Paragraph I). The Overview Committee stripped out this provision and left the authority with the legislature. According to one observer, this reflected in significant part the wishes of the Speaker of the House of Representatives; telephone interview with Professor Thomas G. Walker, July 14, 2017.

entirely to the discretion of the governor who would make those appointments.[61] It is possible that the feeling in the LOC was that such a provision was not needed because the then current governor, George Busbee, had continued the practice of creating such a commission by executive order that had been started a decade earlier by his predecessor, Jimmy Carter,[62] although there is nothing in the transcripts that makes clear the reasoning behind deleting that provision.

A proposal was made to effectively leave it to the legislature to decide by law whether judicial elections would be partisan or nonpartisan. This proposal involved deleting the requirement that judicial elections be on a nonpartisan basis. After discussion, this proposal was voted down by roughly a 2 to 1 margin.[63] The discussion of partisan and nonpartisan elections clarified that the proposed requirement for nonpartisan elections did not apply to the probate courts because in many counties those courts had administrative as well as judicial responsibilities, and were covered by text in Article IX.[64] It is possible that elections for probate court judges in some counties were already on a nonpartisan basis.[65]

The proposed Article VI, Section VII considered by the full House of Representatives read:[66]

> All superior and state court judges shall be elected on a nonpartisan basis for a term of four years. All justices of the Supreme Court and the Judges of the Court of Appeals shall be elected on a nonpartisan basis for a term of six years. The terms of all judges thus elected shall begin the next January 1 after their election. All other judges shall continue to be selected in the manner and for the term they were selected on June 30, 1983, until otherwise provided by law, except that all elections for judges shall be on a nonpartisan basis.

A motion to delete "on a nonpartisan basis" and thus leave it the legislature to choose between partisan and nonpartisan elections was defeated 76 to 87.[67]

61 Select Committee on Constitutional Revision 1977–1981, Transcripts of Meetings, Legislative Overview Committee, vol. 3, 226–229.

62 Camille M. Trimble, "Awakening a Slumbering Giant: Georgia's Judicial Selection System after *White* and *Weaver*," *Mercer Law Review* 56 (2005), 1057–1058; the practice has been continued by the four men who have served as governor since 1982.

63 Legislative Overview Committee, vol. 3, 190–197. In the Legislative Overview Committee, separate votes were counted for the House and for the Senate members. In this vote, the House members voted 5 to 9 against the proposal; the Senate members voted 2 to 8 against.

64 *Id.*, 182.

65 Although the 1977 Georgia constitution provided that appellate judges would be elected in the "same manner" as was used for the General Assembly, nothing in that constitution precluded trial judges from being elected on a nonpartisan basis. Moreover, other than superior court judges, the method of election (or appointment) of trial judges could vary from jurisdiction to jurisdiction (and frequently did). By 1998, probate judges in 29 of 157 counties stood in nonpartisan elections with the rest still running in partisan elections; see Bureau of Justice Statistics, *State Court Organization 1998* (Washington, DC: U.S. Department of Justice, Office of Justice Programs, 2000), 49.

66 *Journal of the Georgia House of Representatives*, p. 149 (August 27, 1981).

67 *Journal of the Georgia House of Representatives*, p. 305 (September 2, 1981).

Interestingly, the small group of Republican representatives voted 2 to 21 against the motion, with the Democrats voting 76 to 66 in favor,[68] suggesting that the Republicans saw some advantage in moving to nonpartisan elections. However, shortly before this vote, a motion was made to delete the last phrase ("except that all elections for judges shall be on a nonpartisan basis"), which would leave elections for judges of limited jurisdiction courts other than the State Court in their current form, most – perhaps all – of which were partisan elections. This motion passed on a voice vote.[69]

In the Senate, the focus was not on the House draft of the revised constitution but on a substitute draft offered by the Senate Committee on Constitutional Revision. This substitute version retained the language concerning nonpartisan elections for judges of limited jurisdiction courts that had been deleted by the House. A motion was made to revert to the House version by deleting the phrase "on a nonpartisan basis" from the relevant paragraph of the substitute draft. That motion was defeated 18 to 26.[70] There was no apparent effort to conform the paragraph on selection to match the House version. The resulting conflict between the House and Senate was one of the issues considered in the resulting conference committee deliberations. In those deliberations, it was the House version that was adopted and then sent to the voters. The voters approved the revised constitution, which included the changes to judicial selection, with 72.9 percent voting in favor.[71] The result is that the format of elections for most judges of limited jurisdiction courts, other than the State Court, continues to be a matter decided by the legislature, with substantial variation by type of court and jurisdiction.[72]

JUDICIAL ELECTIONS SINCE 1982

Around the time of the transition from partisan to nonpartisan elections for the general jurisdiction courts was being considered, there was a major kerfuffle surrounding the retirement of a member of the Supreme Court and the choosing of a replacement. This came after Democratic governor Busbee appointed Jesse G. Bowles to the Court in April 1977;[73] Bowles ran without opposition in 1978 to

[68] This is my count based on the 17 representatives identified as Republicans in the *Georgia Official and Statistical Register* 1979–80, 60–86, which listed the members of the legislature for the 1981–82 terms.

[69] *Journal of the Georgia House of Representatives*, p. 297.

[70] *Journal of the Georgia Senate* (September 11, 1981), 355. The vote apparently was by a show of hands, and hence there is no record of who voted in favor and who voted against.

[71] See https://ballotpedia.org/Georgia_Ratification_of_the_Constitution,_Amendment_1_(1982), accessed March 21, 2019.

[72] See www.ncsc.org/sco#, accessed February 5, 2018.

[73] Much of this discussion is based on facts spelled out in Duncan v. Poythress, 515 F. Supp. 327 (N.D. Ga.1981).

complete the remaining two years of his predecessor's term but then encountered "personal problems" relating to his commute that led him to consider resigning from his position. After meeting with Governor Busbee sometime in 1979 to discuss resigning, he agreed to complete his term. As the 1980 election approached, when he would stand for a full six-year term, Bowles qualified to run in the Democratic primary. After the primary, in which he was unopposed, Bowles again began considering resigning, but after meetings with various people, including the governor, he did not resign and went on to be reelected in November, again without opposition.

After the election, Bowles decided that he would go ahead and resign. Because the judicial nominating committee was already scheduled to meet in December to discuss potential candidates for an existing opening on the Court of Appeals, Bowles decided to resign in advance of that meeting so that the committee could suggest candidates for his replacement to the governor. However, the resignation letter Bowles sent to Governor Busbee did not specify on what date the resignation would be effective. While the search for a replacement began after the receipt of the letter of resignation, there was a complication: Georgia law at the time dictated that if a judge resigns prior to his (or her) term starting, a special election had to be held. Governor Busbee announced at a press conference that he would not support a special election to fill Bowles's position because it would cost the state too much and it would result in low voter turnout. Despite his apparent resignation, Bowles took his oath of office for the new term on December 15, 1980, and began his new term on January 1, 1981. Four days later he resigned again.

After Governor Busbee appointed Hardy Gregory, a Democrat, to be Bowles's replacement, several residents from DeKalb and Fulton counties filed a Section 1983 suit in federal court,[74] challenging that appointment as violating state law and thus denying them their civil right to vote. The result was that "The district court ordered the calling of a special election to choose Justice Bowles's successor, and it enjoined Justice Gregory from running in this election as an incumbent. The court declined, however, to enjoin Justice Gregory from further service on the court";[75] the district court's decision was upheld by the U.S. Court of Appeals, but it also allowed Justice Gregory to continue to serve on the Georgia Supreme Court until the special election was held. After rehearing was denied by the Court of Appeals, Georgia filed a petition for a writ of certiorari with the U.S. Supreme Court, which was granted on February 22, 1982.[76] Oral argument, which had been scheduled for November 1, 1982, was postponed,[77] and then,

[74] Bob Ingle, "That Georgia Supreme Court Flip-Flop," *Atlanta Constitution* (May 8, 1981), 5A.
[75] Poythress v. Duncan, 657 F.2d 691, 695 (1981, 11th Cir. Ga.).
[76] Poythress v. Duncan, 455 U.S. 937 (1982).
[77] Poythress v. Duncan, 459 U.S. 941 (1982).

after Justice Gregory won the 1982 election, the petition was dismissed, presumably because the case was now moot.[78]

The plaintiffs persevered and challenged the results of the 1982 election. The federal district court ruled the election invalid because Justice Gregory was listed as an "incumbent" on the ballot, and ordered a new election.[79] That election took place on May 3, 1983. Justice Gregory won the election, which was conducted on a nonpartisan basis. His campaign manager was the executive director of the Democratic Party.[80] This was the first nonpartisan election for the Georgia Supreme Court, but it is unclear why it was conducted on a nonpartisan basis, given that the new constitution providing for nonpartisan elections did not go into force until July 1, 1983.

The first regularly scheduled judicial elections using the nonpartisan ballot format occurred in 1984. The timing of judicial elections has varied since that year. Initially they coincided with the party primaries, then for three election cycles with the general election, before reverting to taking place along with the party primaries. The elections are governed by the majority rule, which means if there are more than two candidates, there will be a runoff if no candidate receives a majority of the votes. When the election coincided with the primary, the runoff was held at the time of the general election. In the years that the judicial elections were scheduled at the time of the general election, any necessary runoffs were held at the time of runoff elections for partisan offices; it was after such a runoff was needed for the Supreme Court that judicial elections went back to being held at the time of the primary, with the runoff at the general election. Over the 17 election cycles between 1984 and 2018, 9 of the 43 elections for the Georgia Supreme Court were contested compared to only 4 contested elections over the 60 elections between 1946 and 1982. All the contested elections in the later period involved challenges to incumbents,[81] and the incumbents won all 9 elections. In only one of those elections did the incumbent receive less than 60 percent of the vote. As measured by the partisan correlation,[82] these elections were moderately partisan in the county-level voting patterns, with the correlations ranging from .324 to .762; seven of the nine partisan correlations were under .600.

In the years since the change to nonpartisan elections, through 2018, 16 of 71 (23 percent) Court of Appeals elections were contested, as were 239 of 1,445 (16 percent)

78 Poythress v. Duncan, 459 U.S.1012 (1982), "dismissed as improvidently granted." Actually, Gregory was unopposed in the general election; he had won the primary with over 60 percent of the vote; this might suggest that the Supreme Court had not realized until after the November election that the case was moot, even though the primary election was some months earlier.

79 Tracy Thompson, "Special Election Ordered for High Court," *Atlanta Constitution* (February 3, 1983), 21A.

80 Ann Woolner, "Democrats Running Gregory's Campaign for the Supreme Court," *Atlanta Constitution* (April 28, 1983), 30A.

81 There were 5 open-seat elections in the earlier period.

82 See Chapter 1 for the definition of "partisan correlation."

superior court elections. Thus, like the Georgia Supreme Court, contestation has increased for the Court of Appeals since the adoption of nonpartisan elections, having been at 11 percent prior to the switch; this increase might represent a systematic change rather than reflecting random variation.[83] However, the decrease in contestation of elections for the superior courts from the approximately 20 percent, combining both contested primaries and contested general elections, seen between 1968 and 1982 could well be nothing more than random variation.[84]

83 Two-tailed difference of proportions test, $Z = 1.711$, $p = .087$.
84 Two-tailed difference of proportions test, $Z = 1.620$, $p = .105$.

7

Mississippi

A Complex of Factors Leading to Change

In 1832, Mississippi became the first state to adopt popular elections as the means of selecting judges for all its state courts.[1] After the Civil War, judicial selection was changed to the federal model: gubernatorial appointment subject to the advice and consent of the Senate. By the late nineteenth century, there were some demands to revert to an elected judiciary, but that change did not come until the 1910s, when the voters approved two constitutional amendments, one for the major trial courts in 1910 and a second for the Supreme Court in 1914. The governor retained the power to fill judicial vacancies by appointment. Although elections were formally partisan, the one-party political structure meant that the meaningful election occurred in the Democratic primary and in any subsequent runoff. Republican challengers for judicial office were extremely rare. One could argue that judicial elections in Mississippi were effectively nonpartisan, given that the vast majority of voters registered as Democrats to be able to vote in the Democratic primaries.[2]

In 1994, Mississippi became the third Deep South state, after Florida (1972)[3] and Georgia (1984),[4] to change all judicial elections for major courts from partisan to nonpartisan. As I discuss in this chapter, the primary motivation in Mississippi does

1 David W. Case, "In Search of an Independent Judiciary: Alternatives to Judicial Elections in Mississippi," *Mississippi College Law Review* 13 (1992), 6.

2 See Bradley C. Canon, "The Impact of Formal Selection Processes on the Characteristics of Judges – Reconsidered," *Law & Society Review* 6, no. 4 (May 1972), 589, for a similar point made more generally about states with one-party political systems.

3 As discussed in Chapter 11, Florida used nonpartisan elections for its appellate courts for only a brief time before voters approved a constitutional amendment adopting a Missouri Plan system for those courts. In 1998, voters approved another constitutional amendment providing for a local option allowing circuits and counties to adopt a Missouri Plan system if voters so chose; voters in every county rejected that option in 2000, with an average of only 32 percent supporting the change, see www.judicialselection.us/judicial_selection/reform_efforts/failed_reform_efforts.cfm?state=FL, accessed September 8, 2018. See also Chapter 11.

4 See Chapter 6.

not appear to be one of partisan advantage.[5] As in Georgia, it was part of a larger effort to deal with problems facing the judicial system. Arguably, the major effect of the change to nonpartisan elections was twofold. First, it moved the effective time of judicial election from the June primary to the November general election. Second, it opened participation in judicial elections to the increasing number of Mississippians who might have preferred to vote in the Republican primary for offices such as president, members of Congress, governor, and state legislators. As I discuss at the end of this chapter, one interesting effect of the change was a decrease in the likelihood that Supreme Court elections would be contested, although there was little or no change in overall contestation in trial court elections.

BACKGROUND

Mississippi Politics

V. O. Key's account of politics in Mississippi during the first half of the twentieth century highlights two related dimensions: race and regionalism. Mississippi had the highest proportion of African Americans of any state, and in over 40 percent of the state's 82 counties a majority of residents were African American. Regionalism reflected the split between the hills and the delta, and the economic differences between those regions. The former was a region of white farmers, both tenants and owners of small farms, "rednecks" who worked land that was not particularly fertile. The delta was an area of rich farmland, owned in relatively large properties by whites, but worked largely by African American sharecroppers.[6] The delta was where the counties with a high proportion of African Americans were to be found, although race played a role in the politics of both regions.

One issue that divided the two regions was Prohibition. The primary support for Prohibition came in the hills, with much less support to be found in the delta. The division reflected that the hill–delta split went beyond race and economics to include what Key labeled "morals." Mississippi was the last state to end its statewide ban on alcohol and that did not happen until 1966, almost twenty years after Key's book was published. Key does point out one of the ironies of Prohibition in Mississippi: the state imposed and collected a tax on alcohol sold through the black market.[7] Key colorfully contrasts the two regions: "The hills are dry; the delta is wet. The hills are radical; the delta is conservative."[8] Another salient political split between the two regions was over the New Deal. The white landowners of the delta

5 The changes to judicial selection do not get even a mention in a study of Mississippi politics covering the period 1976–2008; see Jere Nash and Andy Taggart, *Mississippi Politics: The Struggle for Power, 1976–2008*, 2nd ed. (Jackson: University of Mississippi Press, 2009).

6 V.O. Key Jr., *Southern Politics in State and Nation* (New York: Alfred Knopf, 1949), 231–232.

7 *Id.*, 233.

8 *Id.*, 238.

tended toward economic conservatism and feared that some of the New Deal initiatives would threaten their economic dominance in the region. The poor white farmers from the hills were more populist in orientation and supported those New Deal programs that promised to benefit them.[9]

If one ignores presidential elections in 1948 and 1960, when Mississippi supported "Dixiecrat" candidates, the dominance of the Democratic Party was total between 1902 and 1962: there was not a single Republican in statewide office, in the congressional delegation, or in the state legislature.[10] In the four presidential elections featuring Franklin Roosevelt, less than 10 percent of voters backed the Republican candidate.[11] The Republican Party was the party of Lincoln, and into the early 1950s was seen as friendly to African Americans; the southern Democratic Party was the bulwark defending segregation and other aspects of the "southern way of life."[12]

The first cracks in the Democratic wall came in the 1960s, arguably led by the 1964 Goldwater campaign and then the 1968 Nixon campaign, both of which made strong appeals to southern whites. At the same time, Democratic presidents and the Democratic-controlled Congress were proposing and passing major civil rights laws that challenged the southern status quo well beyond the threat of court decisions such as *Brown*.[13] With the exception of Jimmy Carter, the last Democratic presidential candidate to win Mississippi was Adlai Stevenson in 1952 and 1956. The initial cracks were small, particularly in state-level politics. A Republican won a U.S. House seat in 1966, the first Republican senator came with the 1978 election, and the second seat changed to Republican hands in 1988.[14]

Republican success in winning state offices came a bit more slowly. The first Republican governor since reconstruction, Kirk Fordice, was elected in 1991, and arguably Fordice's election represented the beginning of the real shift in state-level politics in Mississippi. White Mississippians could now see that they could win statewide elections running as Republicans. Although Democrats continued to win most statewide executive offices into the middle of the first decade of the twenty-first century, only one Democrat won the governorship between 1990 and 2018. The state legislature remained heavily Democratic through the end of the twentieth century, although Republicans held a third or more of the seats in both chambers in the last years of that century. Table 7.1 shows the increasing number of seats contested by

9 Stephen D. Shaffer, "Race and Electoral Politics in Mississippi," in Dale Krane and Stephen D. Shaffer, eds., *Mississippi Government & Politics: Modernizers versus Traditionalist* (Lincoln: University of Nebraska Press, 1992), 96.

10 See https://en.wikipedia.org/wiki/Political_party_strength_in_Mississippi, accessed September 7, 2018.

11 Shaffer, "Race and Electoral Politics in Mississippi," *supra* note 9, 81.

12 Wilma Dykeman, "What Is the Southern Way of Life?" *Southwest Review* 44, no. 2 (1959) 163–166.

13 Brown v. Board of Education of Topeka, 347 U.S. 483 (1954).

14 For discussion of the emergence of the Republican Party in Mississippi over the 20 years starting in 1955, see Nash and Taggart, *Mississippi Politics*, *supra* note 5, 34–54.

TABLE 7.1 *Number of Mississippi legislative seats contested by Republicans (selected years)*

Year	House (n = 122)	Senate (n = 52)
1971	15	8
1975	15	9
1979	37	18
1983	27	11
1987	29	16
1991	46	20
1995	65	39
1999	54	26
2003	62	28
2011	81	40
2015	82	39

Republicans, starting with the 1971 election;[15] by the last election year shown in the table, in a significant number of elections, Republican legislative candidates faced no Democratic opponent.

In 1964, the character of the Democratic Party in Mississippi started to change. Two delegations from Mississippi appeared at the Democratic national convention in Atlantic City, New Jersey: a delegation representing the "regular" party and a delegation from the Mississippi Freedom Democratic Party (MFDP), which had been formed by a coalition of civil rights organizations. The MFDP challenged the credentials of the regulars. The national party proposed seating a mix of delegates from both groups, but this was rejected by both groups. However, four years later, and again four years after that, the MFDP delegation was seated rather than a delegation from the "regulars."[16] By 1980, only 40 percent of white Mississippians self-identified as Democrats, and this dropped to 32 percent in 1989.[17] Given that about three-quarters of African Americans in Mississippi identified as Democrats during the 1980s, and that African Americans comprised 35.6 percent of Mississippi's population, according to the 1990 census,[18] by around 1990, a majority of those identifying as Democrats in Mississippi would have been African

[15] I wanted to start the series shown in Table 7.1 with 1963, but the *Mississippi Official and Statistical Manual* did not list elections for the state legislature during the 1960s.

[16] Stephen D. Shaffer and Dale Krane, "The Origins and Evolution of a Traditionalistic Society," in Dale Krane and Stephen D. Shaffer, eds., *Mississippi Government & Politics: Modernizers versus Traditionalists* (Lincoln: University of Nebraska Press, 1992), 40.

[17] Shaffer, "Race and Electoral Politics in Mississippi," *supra* note 9, 91; over this same period the percentage of white Mississippians identifying with the Republican Party increased from 23 percent to 37 percent.

[18] Bureau of the Census, "1990 Census of the Population, General Population Characteristics: Mississippi" (Washington, DC: U.S. Department of Commerce, 1992), 9, www2.census.gov/library/publications/decennial/1990/cp-1/cp-1-26.pdf, accessed September 9, 2018.

American.[19] However, as late as 1988, only 20 of the 158 Democratic members of the two chambers of the Mississippi legislature were African American.[20]

Judicial Elections prior to 1994

The Mississippi Constitution of 1890 provided for a Supreme Court, circuit courts, chancery courts, and justice of the peace courts.[21] The legislature was empowered to "establish such inferior courts as may be necessary."[22] Under this constitution, judges of the circuit and chancery courts as well as justices of the Supreme Court were appointed by the governor, subject to the advice and consent of the Senate. The selection of judges of any other courts created by the legislature and the selection of justices of the peace would be determined by statute. Supreme Court justices were selected from three districts, the boundaries of which were set by the legislature. Constitutional amendments passed in 1910 and 1914 established elections as the method of selection and retention, with the governor filling midterm vacancies; Supreme Court justices continued to be selected from three districts. By 1993, the legislature had created three additional types of limited jurisdiction courts. In nineteen large counties there were now county courts to handle smaller civil cases, misdemeanors, and juvenile cases; one county had a separate family court handling adoption, paternity, and juvenile cases. There were also a large number of municipal courts handling minor misdemeanors and traffic violations; mayors, in addition to judges, were generally permitted to preside in the municipal courts, and there was no requirement that the presiding officer have a law degree.[23]

Given that the one-party character of Mississippi state politics lasted well into the 1980s, it is not surprising that contests for judicial positions, when they occurred, were to be found in the Democratic primary. Between 1946 and 1992, there were 69 elections for the Mississippi Supreme Court. Only 18 (26 percent) of those elections were contested, 16 of which occurred in the Democratic primary; not a single election was contested during the 1950s. Both elections contested at the general election were for two open seats in 1980: Republican James Arden Barnett opposed Democrat Dan Lee, and Independent Jack Tucker opposed Democrat

19 Assuming equal age distributions for whites and African Americans and ignoring the one percent of Mississippi residents from other races, I estimated that about 56 percent of Democratic self-identifiers would be African American.

20 Author's count from Table 1 in Dyron D'Andra Orey, "Black Legislative Politics in Mississippi," *Journal of Black Studies* 30 (July 2000), 797.

21 Article VI; see http://mshistorynow.mdah.state.ms.us/articles/103/index.php?s=extra&id=270, accessed September 9, 2018.

22 *Id.*, §172.

23 David Rottman and Carol Flango, *State Court Organization 1993* (Washington, DC: Department of Justice, Bureau of Justice Statistics, 1995), 372.

Armis Hawkins.[24] Three of the six elections between 1990 and 1992 were contested, two in the Democratic primary and one in the general election; Republican James Smith defeated Democrat Frank Barber in an open-seat election in 1992, winning 58.3 percent of the vote.[25] A total of 10 of the 69 elections during the period were for open seats, four of which were uncontested; incumbents lost only four of the other 59 elections.[26]

Information on the elections between 1950 and 1992 for the circuit and chancery courts has some gaps.[27] In addition, there is no ready way to determine whether an election was for an open seat or involved an incumbent seeking to retain his or her position on the bench. Judicial terms run so that there are elections for full terms only in the nonpresidential even-numbered years. I counted a total of 392 elections for the two general jurisdiction trial courts over the period 1950 to 1978,[28] only 7 of which were contested in the general elections; 5 contested general elections had Democrats opposed by Republicans and 2 had Democrats opposed by Independents. The first general election contest was in 1966, when there were 3 contests in November, 2 involving Republicans and 1 involving an Independent. Contested Democratic primaries occurred in 77 elections. Thus, overall, it appears that about one-quarter of elections between 1950 and 1978 for the two trial courts were contested.

James Alfini described the system of initial selection of trial-level judges in Mississippi circa 1970 as "bar anointment" rather than partisan election. By this, Alfini was referring to the central role played by local bar associations:[29]

> Upon the occurrence of a judicial vacancy in most Mississippi judicial districts, the local bar leaders generally get together and informally decide who among them would make the best judge ... [and then] send letters to the chosen individual encouraging him to run for office and [they would] discourage others from seeking the office.

[24] Although Jack Tucker ran as an Independent, he had long been a Democratic state senator; he entered and qualified for the election after the Democratic primary. See "Demos Win High Court Positions," *Hattiesburg American* (November 5, 1980), 9.

[25] There were primaries for both parties in this election; Smith came in first in the primary but had to go to a runoff because he got only about 41 percent of the vote.

[26] For a discussion of the factors helping to account for the advantage of incumbents in Mississippi Supreme Court elections, see Diane Wall, "Judicial Incumbency: The Case of Mississippi Supreme Court, 1932–1985), *Southeastern Political Science Review* 15, no. 1 (March 1987), 111–135.

[27] The *Mississippi Official and Statistical Register* has information for elections between 1950 and 1984 except for the 1982 primary. The volume covering 1946 and 1948 omits information on the chancery court, and the volumes covering 1986 through 1992 do not contain any information on the results of judicial elections other than for the Supreme Court.

[28] These figures omit 77 elections in 1982, for which there is no information on the Democratic primary, plus the special elections in 1982 for unexpired terms.

[29] James J. Alfini, "Mississippi Judicial Selection: Election, Appointment, and Bar Anointment," in James A. Cramer, ed., *Courts and Judges* (Beverly Hills, CA: Sage Publications, 1981), 258.

Moreover, at least some governors in making interim appointments deferred to the suggestion of the local bar association, with one governor reported as having "refused to appoint anyone until the bar had 'elected' the individual."[30] Alfini conducted interviews with lawyers and judges in Mississippi in the late 1970s, and reported general satisfaction with the initial selection system as it operated in practice. His respondents expressed skepticism that the Mississippi electorate would find a system other than partisan election acceptable. He also reported that "many expressed the belief that the local bar's involvement in the selection process tended to create a 'merit plan' for the selection of Mississippi judges in that it had the effect of putting the best local legal talent on the bench."[31]

JUDICIAL SELECTION REFORM IN MISSISSIPPI

Mississippi Was Late Coming to the Discussion

The first place one might expect to see calls to change how judges are selected, either by adopting gubernatorial appointment as part of a Missouri Plan system or shifting to nonpartisan elections, would be a publication of the state bar. The *Mississippi Lawyer* started publication in 1954, and all issues have been digitized in a searchable format. I searched for "Missouri Plan," "merit selection," "nonpartisan election," and "judicial selection." The first tangential references suggesting a change in how Mississippi should select and/or retain judges appeared in the late 1960s. One of those references is a comment on a quote from a resolution passed by the state bar at its meeting over fifty years earlier that proposed requiring potential judges to pass an examination that would evaluate their "legal learning, moral character and temperamental fitness for office to which they aspire."[32] The second was in a report on a Citizens' Conference on Mississippi State Courts that was held in September 1967; at the close of the conference, the participants adopted a "consensus statement" that called for a range of reforms to the court system, one of which was to adopt a system of selection and retention based on the Missouri Plan.[33]

Around this same time, the Mississippi legislature passed a statute creating the Mississippi Judiciary Commission (MJC). The MJC was charged with surveying the state's judicial system and preparing recommendations to improve the administration and operation of that system. Judicial selection and retention was not included in the MJC's remit. However, in its 1970 report to the legislature, the MJC provided

30 *Id.*, 259. Alfini estimated that during one 12-year period, 40 percent of new trial judges came to the bench through appointment rather than election; *id.*, 261.

31 *Id.*, 269.

32 George Van Zant, "Executive Director's Bulletin Board," *Mississippi Lawyer* 15, no. 9 (November 1968), 2.

33 "Results of Citizens' Conference," *Mississippi Lawyer* 14, no. 9 (October 1967), 4–5.

some data showing the frequency of appointments to fill interim vacancies and called for further study of the selection system, including consideration of the "'merit system" of selecting judges as recommended by the American Bar Association," noting that "many states have adopted this system" and that "in some respects it combines the better elements of both the elective and appointive systems."[34] I could find no evidence that anything came of this suggestion beyond a 1972 student note in the *Mississippi Law Journal* that drew on the report and seemed to call for the adoption of a Missouri Plan system.[35]

The first explicit calls from the bar for serious consideration of merit selection came in the mid-1970s. During the 1975 election campaign, representatives of the Judicial Selection Committee of the Young Lawyers Section of the Mississippi State Bar approached the gubernatorial candidates with the request that they consider a "bar-sponsored plan to use committees of lawyers, judges and laymen to assist the Governor in filling vacancies."[36] That same year, the outgoing president of the state bar urged members to "consider the merit selection and retention of judges"; however, he was not referring to the Missouri Plan, but to some system in which candidates for popular election were "selected on the basis of merit."[37] Exactly what such a system would look like was unclear. The state bar's annual meeting in 1976 passed a resolution calling for "a study of methods of judicial merit selection and retention."[38]

Because of the outdated nature of the Mississippi judicial system – it ranked dead last on an index of "legal professionalism"[39] – in 1977 the state legislature authorized the creation of a judicial council that would run for three years.[40] In late 1978, the Mississippi Judicial Council proposed that elections for all state judges, from justices of the peace to the justices of the Supreme Court, be nonpartisan in format. The proposal had the unanimous support of the Mississippi Conference of Judges.[41] This support is consistent with the responses from 61 Mississippi trial

[34] "Report of the Mississippi Judiciary Commission to the 1979 Regular Session of the Legislature of the State of Mississippi," 65–66.

[35] See Arlen B. Coyle, "Judicial Selection and Tenure in Mississippi," *Mississippi Law Journal* 43 (1972), 103–107.

[36] "Merit Selection of Judges Urged Upon Gubernatorial Candidates," *Mississippi Lawyer* 22, no. 1 (June–July 1975), 1.

[37] "State Bar Hails New Law Code," *Grenville Delta Democrat-Times* (June 3, 1975), 12.

[38] "Annual Report of the President," *Mississippi Lawyer* 23, no. 1 (July–August 1976), 17.

[39] Although the measure was labeled "Index of Legal Professionalism," the elements of the index dealt specifically with the court system, things such as judicial recruitment, court organization administrative support for the court system, and salary of judges; see Henry Robert Glick and Kenneth N. Vines, *State Court Systems* (Englewood Cliffs, NJ: Prentice-Hall, 1973), 11–12.

[40] Diane E. Wall, "The Antiquated Judicial System," in Dale Krane and Stephen D. Shaffer, eds., *Mississippi Government & Politics: Modernizers versus Traditionalists* (Lincoln: University of Nebraska Press, 1992), 154; the Mississippi Judicial Council was not renewed when the three years were up in 1980, *id.*, 163.

[41] "Nonpartisan Judicial Elections Proposed for Mississippi," *Hattiesburg American* (December 18, 1978), 8.

judges who participated in a national survey of judges conducted in the late 1970s. A majority of those judges expressed a preference for nonpartisan elections over partisan elections for initial selection: 32 preferred nonpartisan elections compared to 17 preferring partisan elections; another 11 preferred a system of gubernatorial appointment, either using screening by the bar or from a list provided by a nominating commission. For interim appointments, 20 preferred gubernatorial appointment with no formal screening, 24 preferred that the governor rely on bar screening, and 13 preferred that the governor appoint from a list provided by a nominating commission.[42] Although it is likely that the Council prepared draft legislation, and that the proposal was introduced in the 1979 legislative session, nothing appears to have come of the proposal.

Although no formal change came from these actions, in 1980 Democratic governor William Winter issued an executive order creating a Judicial Nominating Committee; the governor himself appointed all members, with the caveat that half of the members would be attorneys recommended by the state bar president.[43] The Judicial Nominating Committee was continued by the two governors, both Democrats, who followed Winter, but was not implemented by Republican Kirk Fordice after his election as governor in 1991.[44] Two later Republican governors, Haley Barbour (2005–2011) and Phil Bryant (2011–2019), employed a Judicial Appointments Advisory Committee to screen potential appointees.[45] In contrast to the Missouri Plan model, the governors were in no way bound to choose someone forwarded by the committees.

There was some limited action related to changing judicial selection and retention during the 1980s. I could find no mention of either nonpartisan elections or the Missouri Plan (including "merit selection"), in the *Mississippi Lawyer*, the publication of the state bar. I did find a small number of newspaper editorials over the decade expressing support for a Missouri Plan model.[46] A 1982 Citizen's Conference on the Administration of Justice recommended establishing a Missouri Plan,[47] as did a Constitutional Study Committee appointed by Governor Bill Allain in the

[42] Alfini, "Mississippi Judicial Selection: Election, Appointment, and Bar Anointment," *supra* note 29, 271–272.

[43] *Id.*, 262.

[44] Case, "In Search of an Independent Judiciary," *supra* note 1, 26; on the following pages Case describes the composition and operation of the Judicial Nominating Committee under the three governors who employed it. It may be that Winter's predecessor also employed something similar; see "Lawyers Consider Proposal for Judicial System Scrutiny," *Greenwood Commonwealth* (December 18, 1975), 9.

[45] See www.governorbryant.ms.gov/Executive%20Orders/EO%201384.pdf and http://yallpolitics.com/index.php/yp/post/33463, both accessed September 10, 2018.

[46] See "Another Good Move by Gov. William Winter," *Greenwood Commonwealth* (August 29, 1980), 6.

[47] John Emmerich, "A Better Method of Selecting State Judges," *Enterprise-Journal* (November 1, 1982), 2.

mid-1980s.[48] During this period, more attention seemed focused on redistricting court districts and circuits.

In October 1985, an African American state senator, working with a civil rights organization, brought a voting rights case asserting that the some of the judicial districts in the state were drawn in a way that discriminated against African American candidates.[49] At the time, there were only two African American judges on the state courts, one Supreme Court justice and one circuit court judge. Of particular concern was the use of at-large elections for multiple seats in some counties that the civil rights suit alleged diluted the African American vote.[50] Discussion of the need to redraw judicial districts was one of the issues considered by the short-lived Mississippi Judicial Council,[51] and it came onto the legislative agenda in 1981. In 1982, the voters approved a proposed constitutional amendment requiring judicial redistricting every ten years to adjust to population growth and shifts.[52] However, the legislature had not managed to come up with a plan for judicial redistricting by the time the civil rights complaint was filed, and about four months after the complaint was filed, the Supreme Court used a provision of the constitutional amendment passed in 1982 to take over responsibility for drawing new judicial districts.[53] A few months later, the Supreme Court put the issue on hold to await the outcome of the federal litigation concerning the judicial districts.[54]

After the federal court rejected a proposed settlement in late 1986,[55] the districting case went to trial in March 1987.[56] On April 1, the court ruled in favor of the plaintiffs, and then in early July another trial was held on how new districts should be drawn.[57] It was not until 1988, almost eighteen months after the trial, that a decision ordered that several multijudge judicial districts where candidates had run in at-large elections be divided into subdistricts, with separate elections held within

48 John Emmerich, "Bizzell Supports Court Changes," *Greenwood Commonwealth* (December 9, 1986), 1.

49 Tom Brennan, "One Objection Filed in Judicial Redistricting," *Jackson Clarion-Ledger* (November 6, 1986), 4B.

50 Cliff Treyens, "Blacks See Lawsuits as Springboards," *Jackson Clarion-Ledger* (November 7, 1985), 8A; both African American judges had been appointed to their current positions but had not yet faced the electorate although the Supreme Court justice had previously been elected to a position as a circuit judge.

51 Dennis Mamire, "Judicial Council in Trouble in the Senate," *Jackson Clarion-Ledger* (March 18, 1980), B7.

52 "All Amendments Pass," *Hattiesburg American* (November 3, 1982), 3.

53 "High Court to Take Over Judicial Redistricting," *Clarksdale Press Register* (February 12, 1986), 1.

54 James Saggus, "Court Redistricting on Back Burner," *Greenwood Commonwealth* (May 12, 1986), 4.

55 "Judicial Redistricting Junked," *Greenwood Commonwealth* (December 2, 1986), 2.

56 Beverly Pettigrew, "Redistricting Ruling to Affect 23 Other States," *Jackson Clarion-Ledger* (March 14, 1987), B1.

57 Lynn Watkins, "Judicial Redistricting Trial to Start; Court Could Decide State Election Date," *Jackson Clarion-Ledger* (July 7, 1987), B1.

the subdistricts. Some other districts were redrawn to eliminate racial discrimination. There were still some issues related to federal clearance of other districts that were to be placed under consideration by a panel of the DC Circuit of the Federal Court of Appeals.[58]

While the litigation over judicial redistricting was underway, legislation was introduced that would change judicial elections to nonpartisan ballots. There was no action in 1986, but early in 1987 the legislation changing to nonpartisan elections overwhelmingly (110–8) passed the Mississippi House, apparently without debate. The chair of the House Elections Committee told his colleagues that "it was non-controversial but had died the last year before it could be called up for debate."[59] I could find no evidence of any action being taken by the Mississippi Senate, and the proposal died with the end of that legislature in 1987. However, the passage of the bill by the Mississippi House was the start of serious consideration of changing to nonpartisan judicial elections. Arguably, three or four factors over the next several years pushed the still overwhelmingly Democratic legislature in the direction of making that change: two contested Democratic primaries for the Supreme Court, in which the incumbent was defeated; the decision of several trial judges to switch their party allegiance to Republican; and a potential concern that the increasing role of African Americans in the Democratic Party would cause an increase in the number of African American judges, particularly in districts where there was still an overall Democratic majority, but that a majority within that majority was African American. The fourth possible contributing factor was the election of Kirk Fordice in 1992 as the first Republican governor in more than 100 years.

One of the two contested primaries resulting in the defeat of an incumbent occurred in 1990, and the second in 1992. The 1990 election pitted attorney Chuck McRae against incumbent Joel Blass. Blass had been appointed in 1989 to a vacancy and was standing in his first Supreme Court election; at the time of his appointment, Blass was in private practice, having previously been on the faculty of the University of Mississippi School of Law for six years and having served in the state legislature from 1952–1960. McRae had previously served as president of the Mississippi Trial Lawyers Association and secured that organization's endorsement. He also garnered the endorsement of the Mississippi Prosecutors Association; McRae was quoted as saying, "It's the first time that the prosecutors have made such an endorsement."[60] McRae offered up criticisms of some recent criminal law decisions of the Mississippi

58 Jerry Mitchell, "Barbour Clears Way for February Judicial Elections; The Decision Ends a 2-Year Ban on Elections for Circuit and Chancery Court," *Jackson Clarion-Ledger* (September 14, 1988), A1, A10.

59 "House Bill Passes Authorizing Nonpartisan Judicial Elections," *Clarksdale Press Register* (January 22, 1986), 1.

60 "Legal Groups Back Challenger for State Supreme Court Seat," *Jackson Clarion-Ledger* (May 31, 1990), 2B.

Supreme Court.[61] Blass may have been harmed by his reputation as a racial moderate during the time he was a member of the legislature; it might not have helped when he said, "I was an outright liberal," referring to his having been a racial moderate.[62] McRae spent close to $120,000 on the election campaign, about three times what was spent by Blass. Some of the spending went into television advertising on stations in Jackson, Hattiesburg, and Biloxi, promoting McRae as "a tough judge for tough times"; other ads touted his endorsement by the prosecutors and the trial lawyers.[63] McRae handily won the primary and faced no Republican opposition in November.[64]

The second defeat of an incumbent Supreme Court justice in a Democratic primary came just two years later, in 1992.[65] In that election Justice James L. Robertson lost to former chancery judge James L. Roberts, Jr.[66] Justice Robertson was attacked by victims' rights groups and Mississippi prosecutors, based on his record in death penalty cases. Those groups charged that his decisions had virtually "done away with the death penalty."[67] The Mississippi Prosecutor's Association publicly endorsed Roberts; the one-page resolution adopted by the Association's board of directors and published in a half-dozen or more newspapers, asserted that the challenger "best represents the views of the law abiding citizens in regards to the administration of criminal justice in this state." It went on to charge that the Mississippi Supreme Court had "tied the hands of prosecutors and law officers."[68] Anonymous circulars were distributed to homes in the election district, falsely describing Justice Robertson as "believing a defendant who 'shot an unarmed pizza delivery boy in cold-blood' had not committed a crime serious enough to warrant the death penalty," when the reality was that Robertson had taken the position in a dissent that there was an error in the trial judge's instructions during the sentencing

61 Nikki Davis Maute, "Blass, McRae in Only Major Race Tuesday," *Hattiesburg American* (June 3, 1990), 1B.

62 Jack Ryan, "Blass Calls for Appeals Court," *McComb Enterprise-Journal* (June 3, 1990), 8A.

63 Andy Kanengiser, "Judge's Bench Mark: $114,913 for a Seat," *Jackson Clarion-Ledger* (June 1, 1990), 1A, 9A.

64 Andy Kanengiser, "McRae Overwhelms Justice Blass," *Jackson Clarion-Ledger* (June 6, 1990), 4A.

65 My description of this election is drawn from Case, "In Search of an Independent Judiciary," *supra* note 1, 15–19.

66 Justice Robertson had been appointed to fill a vacancy in January 1983; he subsequently ran unopposed in the 1983 election and defeated an opponent in the Democratic primary in 1984 winning about 64 percent of the votes.

67 Case, "In Search of an Independent Judiciary," *supra* note 1, 16, quoting Carole Lawes and Beverly P. Craft, "High Court Judge Coddled Criminals, Critics Say," *Jackson Clarion-Ledger* (March 13, 1992), B1.

68 "Mississippi Prosecutors' Association Endorses Judge James L. Roberts, Jr.; Resolution of the Mississippi Prosecutors' Association," *Winston County Journal* (March 4, 1992). This appears to be part of an advertising insert backing Roberts; six newspapers archived on newspapers.com carried the insert, and almost certainly there were other newspaper not archived on that site that had the insert.

phase that warranted resentencing.[69] Robertson was criticized for his vote in at least one other death penalty case.[70] Beyond the attacks on Justice Robertson's record, one might wonder whether there was at least some confusion on the part of the voters, given the similarity of the two candidates' names.[71] There is no way to know what, if anything, name confusion contributed to the outcome, but names were listed alphabetically which put Roberts before Robertson,[72] and Roberts won the election with 57 percent of the vote.

One indication that a partisan shift might have been starting in the judiciary was the decision of three circuit court judges running for reelection in 1990 from one district to switch from the Democratic to Republican Party. They had initially filed with the Democratic Party to run in its primary, but at the last minute withdrew that filing and refiled with the Republican Party. Only one other person filed to run in the Republican primary. Given that the switch was made minutes before the filing deadline, there was no way for the Democratic Party to find replacements to run for the positions. One of the three judges was quoted as saying, "I hope this will focus [attention] on the fact that judges' elections should be non-partisan. It's distasteful to me to get out and campaign, and I think it's distasteful for most judges."[73] The state Democratic Party filed a complaint with the Commission on Judicial Performance, presumably alleging that the last-minute switch was unethical. The Commission dismissed the complaint, saying that it concerned political matters rather than an issue of judicial ethics. The Commission went on to recommend that the state legislature "make future elections for judgers nonpartisan so that candidates wouldn't have to declare party loyalties."[74]

The third element in possibly motivating the legislature to change to adopt nonpartisan elections is more speculative. The federal court decision forced some adjustment to judicial districts with the goal of increasing the likelihood of African Americans winning judicial posts. Presumably, the new districts were in districts where African Americans were a majority of the voting-age population or close to a majority. White Democrats might have been concerned that in districts where African Americans were a minority of the overall voting-age population but a majority of voting-age Democrats, the nomination of African Americans in the

69 Case,"In Search of an Independent Judiciary," *supra* note 1, 18; the U.S. Supreme Court later reversed the death sentence, but on other grounds; Clemons v. Mississippi, 494 U.S. 738 (1990).

70 Case, "In Search of an Independent Judiciary," *supra* note 1, 19.

71 "Turnout Reported to Be Light," *Greenwood Commonwealth* (March 10, 1992), 1. See also, "What's in a Name? Confusion," *Jackson Clarion-Ledger* (February 17, 1992), B1; "Robertson and Roberts have been friends for a number of years, and both retell stories of being mistaken for the other."

72 See the sample ballot published in *Kosciusko Star-Herald* (March 5, 1992), 9A, and in several other newspapers archived on newspapers.com.

73 "3 Judges Switch Parties Minutes before Filing," *Hattiesburg American* (April 9, 1990), 5A.

74 Andy Kanegiser, "Panel Won't Act against Judges Who Shift Parties; Make Elections Non-partisan to Avoid Future Problems, the Panel Said," *Jackson Clarion-Ledger* (May 12, 1990), 1A.

Democratic primary would lead white Democrats to vote for the Republican candidate, and then for Republican candidates in other races. Making the judicial elections nonpartisan would avoid this possibility. I emphasize the speculative nature of this, but as is discussed later in the chapter, the eventual legislation to shift to nonpartisan elections also included elements aimed at placating African American Democrats, and those changes were the primary feature of news coverage of that legislation.

Finally, although legislation mandating a shift to nonpartisan judicial elections might have faced the threat of a veto from a Democratic governor, the election of a Republican governor in 1991 avoided that problem. At that time, Republican success in state elections was limited, and Republicans probably saw that nonpartisan elections would increase the likelihood of judicial candidates with Republican leanings winning elections. There may have been at least some perception by Democratic legislators, perhaps tied to the party switch of three incumbent judges discussed earlier, that more judges would switch and/or that having the Republican label would mean increasing risk to judicial candidates running as Democrats. Again, this is speculative.

Starting in 1990, there were increasing calls for changes to judicial selection. Both nonpartisan elections and a Missouri Plan system were raised as possibilities. Early in 1990, two state senators proposed adopting the Missouri Plan.[75] Just before the 1990 primary in which the incumbent was defeated, a number of articles and comments appeared in the press suggesting the need for change.[76] One of the articles published at this time pointed out that opposition to changing the selection system was likely to come from the African American community, which was just beginning to see some of its members winning judicial elections,[77] and that eventually did prove to be the case.[78] State judges were reported to have discussed the idea of nonpartisan elections with the governor.[79] In 1992, legislation was introduced to make judicial elections nonpartisan, but as best I could determine that legislation went nowhere.[80] The state bar devoted "special attention" to, among

75 Bill Minor, "Changes Eyed for Selecting Judges," *Laurel Leader-Call* (January 24, 1990), 4A.

76 Jack Elliott, "Some Changes Proposed in Mississippi Judicial Elections," *Laurel Leader-Call* (June 4, 1990), 3A; Jerry Mitchell and Beverly Pettigrew Kraft, "Judicial Elections: Balancing Ethics, Politics," *Jackson Clarion-Ledger* (June 3, 1990), H1; "State Supreme Court Justice Post Should Be Filled by Appointment, Not Election," *Jackson Clarion-Ledger* (June 2, 1990), 10A [reprinted editorial that originally appeared in the *McComb Enterprise-Journal*].

77 Minor, "Changes Eyed for Selection Judges," *supra* note 75; Jack Elliott, "A Better Way for Picking Judges?" *Greenwood Commonwealth* (June 4, 1990), 4.

78 Daniel Becker and Malia Reddick, "Judicial Selection Reform: Examples from Six States" (Chicago: American Judicature Society, 2003), 31, www.judicialselection.com/uploads/Documents/jsreform_1185395742450.pdf, accessed September 16, 2018.

79 Leonard A. Blackwell II, "A Modest Proposal [President's Column]," *Mississippi Lawyer* 37, no. 2 (October/November 1990), 8.

80 Ray Mosby, "Laws: Some Good, Some Bad and Some Are Just Strange," *Clarksdale Press Register* (February 15, 1992), 2A.

other aspects of the court system, judicial elections, and in his column in the *Mississippi Lawyer* mentioning this, the state bar president lamented the state of judicial elections in Mississippi.[81]

Making the Change to Nonpartisan Elections

Change was to come in 1994. It is important to note that this happened in the context of efforts to modernize the Mississippi judicial system in several ways. As of 1990, Mississippi was the largest state in terms of population lacking an intermediate appellate court. Other structural issues facing the judicial system at this time were whether to abolish the justice of the peace courts, where only a tiny fraction of justices held law degrees; whether to merge law (circuit courts) and equity (chancery courts) as had been done in almost all other states; and the ongoing issue of redistricting. Many of these issues were highlighted by the report of the Mississippi bar's Commission on the Courts in the 21st Century.[82] There were also a range of administrative issues, including staffing, salary, information technology, and the need for a state-level administrative support agency.[83] In 1993, the legislature passed a bill establishing a state-level administrative office for the courts, providing some staff support for trial judges and raising their salaries, and creating an intermediate Court of Appeals of five judges, with one judge elected from each of the state's five judicial districts.[84]

Importantly, the original version of the legislation creating the Court of Appeals called for a Missouri Plan system for selecting and retaining those judges. However, before the legislation passed it was amended, striking the Missouri Plan and applying the system of selection and retention used for the other major courts, i.e., partisan election. This change came after one legislator remarked, "If we in this house have to go around 'tending all these speakings and eat cold sweet 'taters to keep our offices, then [the Court of Appeals judges] ought to also."[85] Another summarized the argument for election: "The democratic process is nearly intolerable for us. So it must be good for judges."[86] The legislation further stipulated that the initial judges for the new court would be elected rather than being appointed by the governor as

81 Alex A. Alston Jr., "Sanctity of the Courts," *Mississippi Lawyer* 38, no. 5 (April/May 1992), 7–9.
82 Richard T. Bennett, "The Mississippi Bar: Accomplishments of Yesterday for Today," *Mississippi Lawyer* 47, no. 3 (January–February 2001), 6. The report of the commission is entitled "Laying the Groundwork for Court Reform: A Report of the Mississippi Bar's Commission on the Courts in the 21st Century" (July 1993); see also "Synopsis of the Work of the Commission on the Courts in the 21st Century," *Mississippi Lawyer* 39, no. 6 (June–July 1993), 9–10.
83 Wall, "The Antiquated Judicial System," *supra* note 40, 164–171.
84 "Legal Scholars Praise Reform to Court System," *Clarksdale Press Register* (April 6, 1993), 1; "Lawmakers Praise Session; Question Surplus Spending," *Jackson Northside Sun* (April 15, 1993), 22A.
85 Bill Minor, "Judicial Election Reform Thwarted by Cold 'Taters," *Biloxi Sun Herald* (November 8, 2001), C3.
86 Becker and Reddick, "Judicial Selection Reform," *supra* note 78, 27.

was sometimes done for new trial court judgeships. This shattered the hope of some that adopting the Missouri Plan for the judges of the new court would lead to the adoption of that system for the Supreme Court.[87]

The change to nonpartisan elections came in 1994. Arguably, the success in making a change might have been due to pressure from business interests. A group called Mississippians for a Fair Judicial System (M-FAIR) called for adopting the Missouri Plan system for selecting and retaining judges of both the Supreme Court and the new intermediate appellate court.[88] The group also called for the shortening of terms from eight to four years and a limit on campaign contributions that a lawyer could make to judges.[89] M-FAIR was probably a front group for the American Tort Reform Association,[90] and may have been motivated in part by the election of the former president of the state trial lawyers association (i.e., the plaintiffs' bar) to the Supreme Court, given that trial lawyers were major donors to judicial candidates. M-FAIR's proposals were criticized by some lawyers and at least some legislators.[91]

One challenge facing legislators in making changes in the way judges were selected was that, given Mississippi's history of voting discrimination, the 1965 Voting Rights Act (VRA) required any such changes be approved by the U.S. Department of Justice (DOJ) before taking effect. African American groups might be expected to try to get the DOJ to reject changes they saw as creating barriers to African Americans winning judicial posts, and there were concerns that nonpartisan elections would advantage Republicans, who would almost certainly not be African American.[92] Legislation (H.B. 1809) that included the adoption of nonpartisan elections passed the legislature, but the key element was increasing the number of trial judgeships and adjusting the boundaries of some districts in a way that was expected to increase the representation of African Americans on the bench.[93] It was the increase in judgeships and adjustments aimed at increasing racial diversity that was highlighted in news reporting about the legislation.[94] The bill also doubled the number of positions on the new Court of Appeals to two judges from each congressional district.

87 *Id.*, 31.
88 Bill Sumrall, "Lawmakers, Lawyers against Judicial Reform," *Greenwood Commonwealth* (January 10, 1994), 1.
89 "M-Fair Wants Court System Put in Hands of People, Not Groups," *Columbia Columbian-Progress* (January 6, 1994), 3B.
90 Stephen Herman, *America and the Law: Challenges for the 21st Century* (San Francisco, CA: Austin and Winfield, 1998), 260–261.
91 Sumrall, "Lawmakers, Lawyers against Judicial Reform," *supra* note 88.
92 See Jack Elliot, "Judiciary Outcome Awaits Justice Department Decision," *Hattiesburg American* (April 11, 1994), 5A.
93 Bill Minor, "Switch to Non-Partisan Judicial Elections Appears Certain," *Jackson Clarion-Ledger* (March 27, 1994), 3G.
94 "House Passes Plan to Add Judicial Seats; Area Would Get Fourth Circuit Judge," *Greenwood Commonwealth* (March 11, 1994), 1; "Bill Allows Blacks More Chances at Judicial Posts," *Hattiesburg American* (March 11, 1994), 4A; "Legislators Create 14 New Judgeships to Increase Minority Representation," *Jackson Clarion-Ledger* (April 2, 1984), 4B.

The votes in both chambers of the legislature were overwhelmingly in support. The House version, H.B. 1809, passed 105–16; the nay votes in the House came from 15 Democrats (at least 7 of whom were African Americans) and one Independent. An amendment to remove the provision for nonpartisan elections offered by a House Democrat failed on a vote of 31–90 with only a single Republican voting in favor.[95] The Senate version passed 34–16, with half of the nays coming from Democrats and half from Republicans. Because the two versions differed in some ways (e.g., the Senate version omitted the increase in the number of judges on the Court of Appeals), the bill went to a conference committee. The conference version passed 101–19 in the House and 41–9 in the Senate; only one Republican voted nay in the House, as did three Republicans in the Senate.[96] Thus, although there was a partisan pattern to the opposition in the House, there was no such pattern in the Senate.

The changes to judicial elections could not go into effect until approval came from DOJ. This meant that there was no way to know whether the coming November judicial elections would be conducted as partisan elections or nonpartisan elections. For this reason, the parties went ahead with judicial primaries in 1994, because no one knew whether approval of nonpartisan elections would come in time for the November election. The Mississippi NAACP and an African American bar association opposed the changes, delaying the DOJ's decision. To head off potential problems, the secretary of state's office allowed candidates to file two sets of qualifying papers, one for party primaries under the old system and a second set under the provisions for nonpartisan elections. DOJ approval came the first week of September and nonpartisan judicial elections were held in November 1994.[97]

JUDICIAL ELECTIONS SINCE 1992

The change to nonpartisan elections removed the formal role of parties in judicial elections. When party primaries were the method of nominating candidates for the general election, there were provisions for the party to select replacement candidates if the winner of the party primary withdrew before the general election. The change created a problem for the Republican Party in 1994.

In 1994 Republican Party leaders, backed by M-FAIR and other tort reform interests, had high hopes of defeating Supreme Court Justice Chuck McRae, the former plaintiffs' lawyer and strong supporter of plaintiffs in cases that came before the Court.[98] Only one candidate, state representative Mark Garriga, qualified for the

[95] A second yea vote came from one of the three independents in the House.

[96] A second nay vote in the House was cast by an independent.

[97] Beverly Pettigrew Kraft, "Justice Says New Judicial Districts OK; Approval Invalidates June 7 Primary, Setting a Non-Partisan Vote for November," *Jackson Clarion-Ledger* (September 7, 1994), 1A, 7A.

[98] Gina Holland, "Hot Race for High Court," *McComb Enterprise-Journal* (April 19, 1994), 2.

Republican primary scheduled for the June 7. Because of the uncertainty over whether the November election would be partisan or nonpartisan, both Garriga and McRae also qualified to run in a possible nonpartisan election.[99] About two weeks before the primary, the Republican governor named Garriga as his new chief of staff, necessitating his withdrawal from the Supreme Court election.[100] Garriga "resigned" his candidacy on June 15, a week after the party primaries.[101] In mid-August, the Executive Committee of the Mississippi Republican Party "certified" Natchez attorney Bob Latham as the Republican candidate for the position,[102] and Latham started campaigning for the position.[103]

On September 6, the DOJ "pre-cleared" the change to nonpartisan elections, allowing nonpartisan elections to proceed in November. Latham had not qualified to run in a nonpartisan election, and the nonpartisan election law contained no provision for replacing a candidate who withdrew after the deadline for qualifying for the nonpartisan election. Latham filed suit seeking to remain on the November ballot. After the trial court quickly made a decision dismissing Latham's suit, Latham appealed to the Mississippi Supreme Court, but that Court affirmed the trial court's decision almost instantly without hearing oral argument.[104]

Information is available on all Supreme Court and Court of Appeals elections since the change to nonpartisan ballots. Information on chancery and circuit court elections was not included in the volumes of the *Mississippi Official and Statistical Manual* for elections occurring between 1994 and 2000;[105] information is available for 2002 through 2018, either in that publication or online at the Secretary of State's website.[106] Thus, I am not able to assess what immediate impact, if any, the change to nonpartisan elections had on trial court contests.

Supreme Court Elections

Between 1994 and 2018, there were twenty-eight elections for the Mississippi Supreme Court. Elections during that period were much more likely to be contested than for the 1946–1992 period, 82 percent compared to 26 percent. The

99 See Latham v. Molpus, 642 So.2d 1340 (Miss. 1994); because there were only two candidates, there was no need for there to be a nonpartisan primary for the seat.

100 Emily Wagster, "Lawyer Is Fordice's Chief of Staff; Rep. Mark Garriga Quits Post, Supreme Court Campaign to Succeed Andy Taggart," *Jackson Clarion-Ledger* (May 25, 1994), 1B.

101 See Latham v. Molpus, *supra* note 99, 1341.

102 *Id.*

103 Beverly Pettigrew Kraft, "New Laws Put Some Out of Race; Nominee to File Suit to Stay on Judicial Ballot," *Jackson Clarion-Ledger* (September 12, 1994), 1.

104 Latham v. Molpus, 642 So.2d 1340 (Miss. 1994); the vote was 5–3, with McRae not participating for obvious reasons.

105 The Secretary of State's office does not retain information on earlier elections; in principle, the information is available in the state archive, but it is unclear what would be required to extract that information.

106 See www.sos.ms.gov/Elections-Voting/Pages/Election-Results-By-Year.aspx, accessed September 15, 2018.

percentage of open-seat elections is about the same before and after the change to nonpartisan elections, 14 percent versus 11 percent. The percentage of elections involving incumbents in which the incumbent lost roughly tripled with the adoption of nonpartisan elections, 20 percent versus 7 percent. However, that largely reflects the relative infrequency of uncontested elections since the change to nonpartisan elections; incumbents running in partisan elections between 1946 and 1992 lost 4 of the 12 elections in which they were challenged, compared to 5 of 20 in the nonpartisan elections through 2018. Almost certainly many – probably most – winning candidates since 1994 have been those who would have run as Republicans.

The first incumbent to lose in a nonpartisan election was Chief Justice Lenore Prather. Prather, who was the first woman to serve on the Court, had been appointed to a vacancy by Democratic governor William Winter. She compiled a record that one analysis described as centrist on criminal cases and liberal on economics cases.[107] However, some commentators described her as conservative,[108] and the conservative U.S. Chamber of Commerce ran ads supporting her reelection.[109] As the most senior justice, she was serving as chief justice in 2000 when she was defeated by personal injury lawyer Chuck Easley.[110] Easley criticized Prather's record in death penalty cases, asserting that "Justice Prather has voted to reverse the convictions of 100 murderers. She has voted against the death penalty more than any other member of the Supreme Court.... She has voted against the death penalty over 50 times."[111] Easley ran an ad in at least one newspaper labeling Prather as a liberal.[112] The election was close, but Easley captured 51.9 percent of the vote to defeat Prather.

Two of the other losing incumbents were brought down by attacks from business and tort reform interests. Chuck McRae, whom the Republicans had hoped to defeat in 1994 but were thwarted by the withdrawal of their candidate and their inability to have someone replace their candidate, was defeated in 2002 in an election that featured mudslinging from both sides and a lot of spending by business and tort reform groups, including on television advertising.[113] McRae was probably not helped by having been arrested earlier in the year for drunk driving.[114] He actually came in third with 23 percent in a three-candidate race; the victor in the

[107] See Diane Wall, "A Woman of Many Firsts: The Honorable Lenore Prather," *Southeastern Political Review* 38, no. 3 (September 2000), 539–540.

[108] See Sid Salter, "Is Supreme Court the Best Money Can Buy?" *Scott County Times* (October 18, 2000), 2.

[109] "Business Group Files Suit Over Canceled Mississippi Judge Advertisements," *Hattiesburg American* (October 24, 2000), 2A.

[110] "Lawyer Quits Race for Court Post," *Jackson Clarion-Ledger* (July 29, 2000), 7B.

[111] Beverly Pettigrew Kraft, "Prather, Easley on Ballot for Court Slot; Outcome Will Determine Who Chief Justice Is," *Jackson Clarion-Ledger* (October 14, 2000), 5b.

[112] "$480,000 ...," *Carrollton Conservative* (November 2, 2000), 7.

[113] "Supreme Court Race Heats Up Cool Campaign," *Greenwood Commonwealth* (November 1, 2002), 5A.

[114] Sid Slater, "Chuck McRae's Bright Red Bull's-Eye Self-Applied," *Hattiesburg American* (October 30, 2002), 11A.

election got 52 percent, avoiding the need for a runoff.[115] In 2008, Jim Smith was similarly targeted and lost his bid for reelection.[116]

Two additional incumbents lost in 2008. Oliver Diaz had been unsuccessfully targeted by business groups in his 2000 bid to keep the seat he had been appointed to in March of that year.[117] In 2003 he had been indicted on federal charges growing out of a bribery scandal; he was cleared of all charges after trials in 2005 and 2006.[118] Diaz was a former Republican legislator who had been appointed to the Mississippi Supreme Court by a Democratic governor; his opponent was a former Democratic state representative who had been appointed to a chancery court judgeship by a Republican governor. Conservative interests supported Diaz's opponent.[119] The election reported was a relatively "cordial affair,"[120] but there was at least some negative advertising directed at Diaz. The National Rifle Association–backed Law Enforcement Alliance of America attacked Diaz on decisions in several criminal justice cases.[121] Diaz lost, getting less than 42 percent of the vote.[122]

The third incumbent to lose in 2008, somewhat ironically, was Chuck Easley,[123] who had defeated incumbent Lenore Prather eight years earlier. Easley lost 2 to 1 to Appeals Court judge David Chandler. Easley accused his challenger of "being in the pocket of big business in civil matters while being soft in criminal cases,"[124] and being a "deadbeat dad."[125] Chandler had the support of medical and business interests, allowing him to substantially outspend Easley.

These defeats of incumbents reflect what has been the primary dimension of conflict in Mississippi Supreme Court elections in the years since the change to nonpartisan ballots: business vs. the plaintiffs' bar. This is part of the broader

115 Matt Volz, "Voters Respond to Personal, Professional Issues in Supreme Court Election," *Greenwood Commonwealth* (November 7, 2002), 1.

116 Jerry Mitchell, "PACs Take Charge in Campaigns; Groups Spending More Money Than Candidates on Supreme Court Race Ads," *Jackson Clarion-Ledger* (October 12, 2008), 1A, 7A.

117 Jerry Mitchell, "10 Candidates Vie for 3 Seats," *Jackson Clarion-Ledger* (May 10, 2008), 1A, 7A.

118 See Scott Horton, "Justice in Mississippi," *Harper's Magazine* (September 18, 2007), https://harpers.org/blog/2007/09/justice-in-mississippi/, accessed September 16, 2018.

119 Matt Williamson, "Diaz Not Avoiding Past in Bid to Keep Post," *McComb Enterprise-Journal* (October 13, 2008) A7.

120 Jack Elliott Jr., "Court Hopefuls: Experience the Key," *Jackson Clarion-Ledger* (October 26, 2008), 7B.

121 Jimmie E. Gates, "Million-Plus Funds Campaigns; Supreme Court Races Pulling Heavy Donations," *Jackson Clarion-Ledger* (October 29, 2008), 1B; see also Jerry Mitchell, "Group Standing by TV Ad Blasting Diaz; Panel Condemns It," *Jackson Clarion-Ledger* (November 1, 2008), 1A.

122 Jerry Mitchell, "Pierce Knocks Diaz Off Bench; Incumbent Had Been a Dissenter against Business Interests," *Jackson Clarion-Ledger* (November 5, 2008), 10A.

123 "Lawyer Quits Race for Court Post," *supra* note 110, 7B.

124 Blair Goldstein, "Chandler Leading as Final Totals Awaited in Supreme Court Bid; Easley Says He's Confident He Will Prevail Once All Votes Counted," *Jackson Clarion-Ledger* (November 5, 2008), 10A.

125 Jerry Mitchell, "AG Looks at Bogus Polling in Races; Push Polls Are Ways Groups Spread Lies, Professor Says," *Jackson Clarion-Ledger* (September 23, 2008), 4A.

movement for so-called tort reform that seeks to make it more difficult for injured parties to bring or succeed in personal injury claims and would also serve to weaken financially the plaintiffs' bar itself, which has often been a source of significant financial support for the Democratic Party. The business–plaintiffs' bar dimension was clear in one of the rare open-seat elections for the Court in 2012. That election pitted veteran plaintiffs' lawyer Richard "Flip" Phillips against a young corporate lawyer, Josiah Coleman. Coleman was endorsed by (and presumably received financial backing from) Mississippi's Business and Industrial Political Education Committee, the Mississippi Manufacturers Association, the Mississippi State Medical Association, and the Mississippi Republican Party.[126] Two outside groups, "Improve Mississippi PAC" and the "Law Enforcement Alliance of America" spent over $1 million on television advertising attacking Phillips, with Phillips's campaign spending about half that amount either responding to the attack ads or otherwise promoting Phillips. The Coleman campaign itself spent only about $125,000 promoting Coleman.[127] Coleman won the election with 58 percent of the vote.[128]

Elections for Lower Courts

There is no before–after comparison for the Court of Appeals elections because the first elections for that court came in 1994, after nonpartisan elections were adopted. In 1994, there were open-seat elections for all 10 of the new appellate judgeships, 9 of which were contested. Omitting those 10 elections, through 2018 there were 36 elections, 12 of which (33 percent), were contested – a much lower rate of contestation than for the Mississippi Supreme Court since the change to nonpartisan elections. There were only four open-seat elections, all of which were contested. Two incumbents, both standing for the first time after their vacancy appointment to the Court of Appeals, lost, one in 2000 and another in 2002. In the 2002 election, the challenger was backed by business interests and the losing incumbent by plaintiffs' lawyers.[129] There was nothing in the news coverage that suggested why the incumbent lost in 2000, and he lost handily, getting only about 42 percent of the vote.[130]

Information on those elections was not included in the *Mississippi Official and Statistical Manual* for several elections. That omission included 1994 and 1998,

[126] Jimmie E. Gates, "Who Will Be Next Judge? Coleman, Phillips in Hunt," *Jackson Clarion-Ledger* (September 14, 2012), B1.

[127] Advertising information was provided by the Brennan Center at New York University Law School; see www.brennancenter.org/analysis/buying-time-2012-mississippi and www.brennancenter.org/analysis/buying-time-state-state-spending-2012#outside, accessed January 20, 2019.

[128] See https://ballotpedia.org/Mississippi_judicial_elections,_2012, accessed January 20, 2019.

[129] Sid Salter, "Judicial Election Costs Soaring, as in the Legislature and Executive Branch Races, Special Interests Dominate, *Jackson Clarion-Ledger* (October 20, 2002), G1.

[130] Jimmie Gates, "'Novice' Wins Court of Appeals Seat; Chandler Successful in First Try for Political Office in His Second Career," *Jackson Clarion-Ledger* (November 8, 2000), 15A; Beverly Pettigrew Kraft, "2 Vie for Seat on Court of Appeals," *Jackson Clarion-Ledger* (October 28, 2000), 1B.

which means that the first information available on circuit and chancery court elections is for 2002. For the years for which information is available, about 23 percent of these elections were contested, compared to about 25 percent, counting both primary and general elections, during the years prior to the adoption of nonpartisan elections for which information is available (1946–1978). Because of the data gap, it is possible that there was some substantial difference between the three elections prior to the adoption of nonpartisan elections and the first two after.

SUMMARY AND CONCLUSION

The change from partisan to nonpartisan elections in Mississippi came as part of a larger effort to modernize the state's court system and in the context of partisan change that was happening in the state. The former appears to be the dominant factor, although arguably issues of race and party politics provided a catalyst for action. Arguably, given that most contested judicial elections prior to the 1990s occurred in the context of the Democratic primary and that the overwhelming proportion of voters participating in the party primaries voted in the Democratic primary, the shift from one party's primary to nonpartisan general elections represented a shift from one nonpartisan context to another.

The discussion in this chapter suggested how race entered the process. According to the 1990 census, 35.6 percent of the population of Mississippi was African American.[131] However, as of 1989, there were only 4 African Americans among 79 judges serving on appellate and general jurisdiction trial courts.[132] Not surprisingly, this produced a number of concerns in the African American community. A first concern was that multijudge districts with at-large elections hampered the election of African American judges. Second, there was a related concern about gerrymandering of judicial districts intended to disadvantage African American voters and African American judicial candidates. Third, the Democratic Party was shifting from majority white to majority African American; this created a concern in the African American community that shifting to nonpartisan elections would also hamper African American judicial candidates who might have won in a Democratic primary and thus would not face any Republican opponent in the general election, but now would face a white opponent who might be either Democrat or a Republican in a district that overall was majority white. Related to the latter, conservative white Democrats might have preferred nonpartisan elections because it would

[131] Bureau of the Census, "1990 Census of Population: General Population Characteristics, Mississippi" (1992), 9, www2.census.gov/library/publications/decennial/1990/cp-1/cp-1-26.pdf, accessed September 28, 2018.

[132] Wall, "Antiquated Judicial System," *supra* note 40, 157, 162. Wall notes that about 5 percent of lawyers in Mississippi were African American at this time, which meant the 4 out of 79 was consistent with African Americans' representation within the population of lawyers.

advantage a white, presumably conservative candidate over the African American, presumably liberal candidate in majority white districts.

The result was that there was notable opposition to nonpartisan elections among African American legislators. To try to win over some of the African American legislators opposing the change, the legislation included some redistricting to provide more chances that African American candidates would win elections. By 2010, 16 percent of judges in Mississippi's general jurisdiction trial courts and appellate courts were African American according to an American Bar Association report;[133] the 2010 census reported that 37.0 percent of Mississippi residents were African American.[134] A study released in 2016 reported that 25.5 percent of Mississippi's judges were persons of color, compared 42.7 percent of the state's population.[135] These are substantial increases from the roughly 5 percent circa 1990 noted previously.

Despite the political issues involved in the passage of legislation switching to nonpartisan elections, that change was largely a result of the movement to modernize the Mississippi judicial system. As noted in the body of this chapter, the legislation adopting nonpartisan elections included a range of elements aimed at that modernization: creating a statewide administrative office of the courts, providing staff support for judges, and doubling the number of judges who would serve on the Court of Appeals that had been created by the legislature the prior year. The one major element of modernization that was discussed but not done, and has still not been done as of 2019, was the merger of the circuit court and the chancery court.[136]

[133] Standing Committee on Judicial Independence, "National Database on Judicial Diversity in State Courts," https://apps.americanbar.org/abanet/jd/display/national.cfm, accessed September 28, 2018.

[134] This figure is the percent reporting a single race of black or African American; it does not include any persons who reported more than one race, one of which was black or African American. See https://factfinder.census.gov/faces/tableservices/jsf/pages/productview.xhtml?src=CF, accessed September 28, 2018.

[135] Tracey E. George and Albert H. Yoon, "The Gavel Gap: Who Sits in Judgment in State Courts?" (Report for the American Constitution Society, 2016), 24, http://gavelgap.org/pdf/gavel-gap-report.pdf, accessed September 28, 2018.

[136] Mississippi is one of only four states that as of 2018 have separate chancery courts with separately appointed or elected judges, although other states have chancery divisions within their general jurisdiction trial court. The most prominent state chancery court is in Delaware, which handles disputes involving a range of corporate matters along with a range of other traditional equity issues; see https://courts.delaware.gov/chancery/, accessed September 29, 2018. Two other states with separate chancery courts or their equivalent are Tennessee (see www.tncourts.gov/courts/circuit-criminal-chancery-courts, accessed September 29, 2018), and South Carolina; in South Carolina, equity matters are referred to Masters-in-Equity, who are a separate set of judges appointed by the governor (subject to the advice and consent of the state legislature); see www.sccourts.org/OverviewofSCJudicialSystem.cfm, accessed September 29, 2018.

8

Utah

The Two-Step[1]

In 1985, Utah voters approved an amendment to the state constitution that included an entirely new version of the judicial department article, Article VIII. As part of this constitutional change, Utah adopted a variant of the Missouri Plan. The variant was to include a provision that required Senate consent to the governor's selection from a list provided by a nominating commission. The action in 1985 made Utah the last state as of 2019 where voters approved the adoption of a Missouri Plan system. However, as will become clear in the narrative that follows, by 1985 Utah had a system in place that in practice varied only slightly from the Missouri Plan. The narrative also shows that the inclusion of provisions requiring Senate consent to judicial appointments in the final design grew out of conflict between the Republican legislature and Democratic governor Scott Matheson – the last Democrat to be elected governor as of 2019.

JUDICIAL ELECTIONS IN UTAH: HISTORICAL PERSPECTIVES

A Brief Primer on Utah Politics

Members of the Church of Jesus Christ of Latter-day Saints (LDS), Mormons, are socially and politically the dominant group in Utah. In the years prior to statehood, politics in Utah was explicitly organized around Mormons and non-Mormons, whom Mormons referred to as "gentiles." Non-Mormons organized the Liberal

[1] I owe a substantial debt to Roger Tew for his assistance in preparing this chapter. Mr. Tew served as the executive director of Utah's Constitutional Revision Commission during the time the revision of the judicial article was being developed and proposed. He granted me a long interview (May 15, 2018); that interview served to frame the research I then undertook. He subsequently responded to numerous email queries.

Party and pro-Church politicians organized the "People's Party."[2] In 1891, the People's Party disbanded and encouraged its members to divide evenly between the Democratic and Republican Parties; LDS leaders believed that if the Church's adherents were divided evenly between the two major parties, neither party "would have an incentive to demonize Mormons for electoral gain."[3] The Liberal Party dissolved two years after the People's Party had done so. These changes came in anticipation of statehood, which would be achieved in 1896.

The hope of LDS leaders that church adherents would divide between the Republican and Democratic parties faced some challenges because of historical tensions between the LDS church and the Republican Party, traceable to the role that Republican politicians had in leading anti-Mormon campaigns in the mid-1800s and to the Republican Party's founding platform, which had denounced "those twin relics of barbarism, polygamy and slavery."[4] The legislature that was elected in 1895 to take office with the start of statehood on January 1, 1896 was about 2 to 1 Republican;[5] however, only two Republicans remained in the Utah legislature as a result of the 1896 elections.[6] By 1903, Republicans had become dominant and remained dominant until the Depression, with the exception of a brief interregnum of Democratic control in the four years following the 1916 election.[7] Democrats dominated during the 1930s and 1940s, with Republicans regaining control during the 1950s. The 1960s and 1970s was a period of strong party competition, with shifts in control between the parties and periods of divided government.[8] Since the 1980s, Utah politics has been dominated by the Republican Party. Republicans have held majorities of at least 2 to 1 in the legislature most years, and except for one four-year period at the beginning of the 1990s, Democrats have not held more than one of Utah's four seats in the U.S. House of Representatives.[9] The last Democrat elected to statewide office was Attorney General Jan Graham in 1996, and as of 2019, Republicans hold both seats in the U.S. Senate, three of four seats in the U.S. House of Representatives, 23 of 29 seats in the Utah Senate, and 59 of 75 seats in the Utah House of Representatives.[10]

2 Adam R. Brown, "*Utah Politics and Government: American Democracy among a Unique Electorate* (Lincoln: University of Nebraska Press, 2018), 9; see also John Sillito, "Republican Party," *Utah History Encyclopedia*, www.uen.org/utah_history_encyclopedia/r/REPUBLICAN_PARTY.shtml, accessed May 25, 2018.

3 Brown, *Utah Politics and Government, supra* note 2, 11.

4 *Id.*, 34.

5 See Office of Legislative Research and General Counsel, A *Citizen's Guide to Utah State Government* (Salt Lake City, UT: Legislative Printing, 2005), 59.

6 *Id.*; see also Allan Kent Powell, "Elections in the State of Utah," *Utah History Encyclopedia*, www.uen.org/utah_history_encyclopedia/e/ELECTIONS.shtml, accessed January 24, 2019.

7 Office of Legislative Research and General Counsel, 59–60.

8 *Id.*

9 See https://en.wikipedia.org/wiki/Political_party_strength_in_Utah, accessed March 22, 2019.

10 *Id.*

Most important for purposes of the discussion that follows was the configuration of the Utah state government in the early 1980s, when the judicial department constitutional amendment was passed. At that time, the governor was Scott Matheson, a Democrat. He had succeeded another Democrat, Calvin Rampton. Rampton held the office for 12 years and Matheson for 8 years. Matheson, who was a Mormon, was a Stanford law graduate who had risen to the position of general counsel at the Union Pacific Railroad before running successfully for governor in 1976.[11] Matheson faced a Republican-controlled legislature in all but the first two years he served. During his entire second term, Republicans had veto-proof majorities in both chambers of the state legislature.

Judicial Selection and Judicial Elections in the Postwar Period

The Utah Constitution, adopted in 1896 as Utah became a state, provided for three levels of courts: the Supreme Court, the district court, and the justice of the peace courts. Judges of all three were to be chosen by the electors of the state at large for the Supreme Court and by the electors (i.e., qualified voters) of the relevant district for the two lower courts.[12] The governor was empowered to fill judicial vacancies occurring before the end of a judge's term.[13]

Additional trial courts could be created by the legislature,[14] and presumably the legislature could determine the method of selection and retention. As of the early 1970s, the legislature had created city courts and juvenile courts. Judges of the former were elected by the voters of the city the court served. Judges of the latter were appointed by the governor from a list of two or more candidates nominated by the Juvenile Court Commission, with reappointment following the same process at the end of a juvenile court judge's six-year term.[15] Prior to 1965, the juvenile courts were not part of the judicial branch but part of the Department of Welfare; judges were appointed by the Welfare Commission, "with the approval of the Governor."[16] In 1963, the Utah Supreme Court ruled that it was a violation of the state

[11] See Glenn Fowler, "Scott Matheson, 61, Ex-Governor of and Leading Democrat in Utah," *New York Times* (October 8, 1990), 56, www.nytimes.com/1990/10/08/obituaries/scott-matheson-61-ex-governor-and-leading-democrat-in-utah.html?pagewanted=1, accessed May 25, 2018.

[12] Utah Constitution of 1895, Article VIII, Sections 2, 5, and 8; see https://archives.utah.gov/community/exhibits/Statehood/1896text.htm, accessed May 25, 2018.

[13] *Id.*, Article VII, Section 9.

[14] The constitution did not explicitly limit the additional courts to trial courts. However, it effectively prevented the creation of an intermediate appellate court by creating a right of appeal to the Supreme Court from all "final judgements of the district courts," Article VIII, Section 9, Utah Constitution of 1896.

[15] U.S. Department of Justice, Law Enforcement Assistance Administration, *National Survey of Court Organization* (Washington, DC: U.S. Government Printing Office, 1973), 232.

[16] See Utah Family Court Task Force, "Final Report to the Utah Judicial Council, Appendix A: History of Utah Juvenile Court Studies" (December 16, 1994), www.utcourts.gov/resources/reports/FAMCTRPT/history.htm, accessed May 25, 2018.

constitution for the juvenile courts to be under the Welfare Department,[17] and the Juvenile Court Act of 1965 reconstituted them as part of the judicial branch.[18]

In 1944, Utah voters approved a constitutional amendment giving the state legislature the power to determine how judges of the Supreme Court and district courts should be selected and retained. Prior to that time, judges of both of those courts were selected and retained through partisan elections using ballots that provided for a straight-party selection. The amendment, which became effective in 1945, read:[19]

> Judges of the Supreme Court and district courts shall be selected for such terms and in such manner as shall be provided for by law, provided, however, that selection shall be based solely upon consideration of fitness for office without regard to any partisan political considerations and free from influence of any person whomsoever, and provided further that the method of electing such judges in effect when this amendment is adopted shall be followed until changed by law.

In 1949, the Utah legislature passed, on near-unanimous votes, a Missouri Plan system, but the plan was vetoed by the governor.[20] In his veto message, Republican governor J. Bracken Lee explained that the system would "remove the selection of the judiciary too far from the people."[21] Implementing legislation, described below, was not passed until 1951.

In the absence of legislation implementing the 1945 amendment, partisan elections continued, with the last partisan judicial elections occurring in 1950. There were three Supreme Court elections during the interim period: one in which the Democratic incumbent was defeated, one in which the Democratic incumbent won, and one open-seat election won by the Democratic candidate. The average partisan correlation was .654,[22] which is quite low for partisan elections. During this period, there were two contested elections for district court judgeships; the election reports did not include information on uncontested elections, and there are too few election years during the period to estimate the number of district court seats up for election during the period.

17 See *In re* Woodward, 384 P.2d 110 (Utah 1963).

18 See Jean Bickmore White, *The Utah State Constitution: A Reference Guide* (Westport, CT: Greenwood Press, 1998), 108.

19 "Joint Resolution Proposing Constitutional Amendments Relating to Supreme and District Courts and Judges," *Laws of Utah, 1943* (Salt Lake City, UT: Arrow Press, 1943), 189.

20 Francis D. Wormuth and S. Grover Rich Jr., "Politics, the Bar, and the Selection of Judges," *Utah Bar Review* 3, no. 4 (Fall 1953), 459; see also Carvel Mattson, "The President's Annual Report," *Utah Bar Bulletin*, 10 (1949), 70.

21 "Lee Vetoes Provision for Building Priority," *Salt Lake City Telegram* (March 18, 1949), 1. The legislature at the time had Democratic majorities sufficient to override the veto; however, the passage came at the very end of the legislative session and there was no provision for a special session to consider a veto override.

22 See Chapter 1 for the definition of "partisan correlation."

In 1951 the legislature passed, and the governor signed, a law implementing the 1945 constitutional amendment. The primary effect was to remove judicial elections from the partisan process by making judicial elections nonpartisan. The specific provisions included:

- Excepting justices and judges from nomination by political parties
- Providing for "direct primaries" with a separate "Judicial Nominating Ballot"
- Providing for a separate "Judicial Selection Ballot" at the general election
- Specifying how candidates will be listed on the ballot: If an incumbent is running, the incumbent is listed first on the ballot with the designation "Judge xxx, incumbent"; other candidates (or all candidates if no incumbent is running) are listed in alphabetical order
- Prohibiting candidates for judicial office from using political party designations or being active in a political party.

The law made no mention of a revised process for filling judicial vacancies. This left in place the constitutional provisions granting the governor the power to appoint persons to fill such vacancies without constraint beyond that the appointees had to have the required qualifications.

Between 1952 and 1966, there were 11 Utah Supreme Court elections, 5 of which were contested. All 11 involved an incumbent seeking to retain his seat on the Court (all were male). The incumbents won all 5 where they faced challengers, although in 2 of those elections, the incumbent received less than 55 percent of the vote. The average partisan correlation was .393. During this period there were 13 contested elections for the district court. I estimate that there would have been 48 elections for district court positions over the eight election cycles,[23] which would indicate that about 27 percent of the elections were contested.

In 1967 the legislature again exercised its power under the 1945 constitutional amendment to specify the system for judicial selection. With this legislation, the Utah system came very close to the Missouri Plan. According to the 1967 provisions, judges of Supreme and district courts were to be "selected, and a vacancy in any such office be filled, by appointment of the governor [of] one of three persons forwarded by a nominating commission."[24] Those nominating commissions

[23] I estimated the number of elections by assuming that one-third of district court positions would be up each election year, given that the term for district court judges is 6 years. I determined the number of authorized district court judgeships for each election year by consulting Utah statutes and session laws (17 positions, 1952–1956; 18 positions in 1958 and 1960; 19 positions in 1962 and 1964; and 20 positions in 1966). This does not take into account any elections that might be due to vacancies before the end of a judge's term. Thus, this approach probably underestimates the number of elections, and thus overestimates the proportion of elections that were contested.

[24] *Laws of Utah* 1967, 87.

consisted of seven members: the chief justice, one member chosen by each chamber of the state legislature, two chosen by governor, and two by the state bar association. The commissioners, other than the chief justice, served four-year terms and could not succeed themselves. The nominating commission had forty-five days to submit names to the governor; if the commission failed to meet that deadline, the governor was free to appoint any qualified person. If the governor failed to make an appointment within thirty days of receiving nominees, the chief justice was empowered to appoint one of the nominees. Later legislation eased some of these timelines.

This change to initial appointment did not spell the end of contested elections. Incumbents, either recently appointed or previously elected, had to file a declaration of candidacy in June prior to the end of their term. If an incumbent did not file a declaration of incumbency, the procedures for filling a vacancy applied, with the appointee taking office in January when the incumbent stepped down. If the incumbent did file a declaration of candidacy, persons wishing to challenge the incumbent had until the second Friday in July to file a declaration of candidacy. If one or more opponent filed a declaration of candidacy, there would be a nonpartisan election, preceded by a primary if there was more than one opponent. The incumbent was listed first on the ballot as "Judge xxx, incumbent," with the other candidates listed alphabetically after the incumbent. If no candidates filed to oppose an incumbent, there was a retention election to determine if the incumbent would continue in office. Other than the possibility of a contested nonpartisan election, the system that came into operation in the late 1960s had all the elements of the Missouri Plan.[25]

Between 1970 and 1984 there were ten Supreme Court elections. Incumbents were challenged in only two. In 1974, Justice E. R. Callister narrowly lost to Richard Maughan; the partisan correlation in that election was .203. The other contested election was in 1980. In that election, incumbent justice I. Daniel Stewart, who had been appointed in early 1979 by Democratic governor Scott Matheson, received 55.8 percent of the vote; the partisan correlation was .357. Under the 1967 statutes, unopposed incumbents stood on a retention ballot; the average yes vote in the eight Supreme Court retention elections was 86.1 percent; there was no partisan pattern in the retention elections, with the county-level correlation between the yes vote and support for the Democratic candidate for governor ranging from –.401 to +.338 (average .037), even though all justices standing in these elections were either elected as Democrats or appointed by a Democratic governor.[26]

25 The first retention elections took place in 1970. One member of the Supreme Court, who had been appointed in 1967, faced an uncontested nonpartisan election in 1968; see "A. H. Ellett: Jurist Files for High Court Seat," *Salt Lake Tribune* (June 12, 1968), 2B.

26 Only one of the justices had originally been elected, Justice J. Allen Crockett (standing for retention in 1970), elected in 1950 when elections were still partisan.

At the trial level, there were a total of 138 elections between 1970 and 1984. In 1982 and 1984, a substantial proportion of these were for the circuit courts, which replaced the city courts in 1978,[27] and were subject to the same selection system as the district courts. Only 21 (18 percent) of the trial court elections were contested. This decrease from my estimate for the prior period is likely not simply random variation.[28] Only once did an incumbent lose an election, and that was a contested election in 1984, when Ernest Baldwin, who had been on the bench since 1971,[29] was defeated by Circuit Court judge Raymond Uno.[30] In most of the retention elections, 80 percent or more of the electorate voted to retain the incumbent judge, and in no election did the incumbent receive less than 65 percent in support of retention. One of the nonpartisan elections in which the incumbent won did produce some controversy when "a highly regarded sitting judge who was forced to campaign for office."[31]

JUDICIAL SELECTION IN THE NEW JUDICIAL ARTICLE

The Constitutional Revision Commission

In 1969, the Utah legislature created the Constitutional Revision Commission (CRC). This reflected a widely held perception that the piecemeal changes that had previously been undertaken due to existing limitations in the constitution on the amendment process had hampered the significant revisions that studies by both the legislature and the executive showed to be needed. Three years earlier, in 1966, the voters had overwhelmingly (85 percent to 15 percent) rejected a proposal to hold a constitutional convention to overhaul the constitution. The CRC was charged with conducting comprehensive studies and proposing changes to the legislature which, if passed by the legislature, could be submitted to the voters for their

27 Cheryll L. May, "Utah Judicial Council History: 1973–1997" (March 1998), 13–14, www.utcourts.gov/knowcts/adm/docs/Judicial_Council_History-1973-1997.pdf, accessed May 26, 2018. The circuit courts were merged with the District courts in 1996; Utah Code, 78A-1-105, Merger of District and Court Courts.

28 Chi-square = 3.13, $p = .077$.

29 I was told on a not-for-attribution basis that "Judge Baldwin was a rather cantankerous personality who over the years had made his fair share of opponents." This is consistent with the results of a poll of the Bar Association membership, in which only 34 percent supported Baldwin; see "Results of the Judicial Poll of the Utah State Bar Association Completed October 5, 1984 [advertisement]," *Park Record* (November 1, 1984), A8; see also, "Judge Davidson Receives State Bar Support," *Vernal Express* (October 24, 1984), 3.

30 Uno, who was appointed as city judge in Salt Lake City in 1976, was the first minority member to become a judge in Utah. He was a Japanese American born in 1930 in Ogden, Utah, and was sent to a relocation camp with his family during World War II; see "Former Judge Raymond Uno Is a Giant among Citizens," *Salt Lake Tribune* (April 29, 2018), www.sltrib.com/opinion/editorial/2018/04/29/tribune-editorial-former-judge-raymond-uno-is-a-giant-among-citizens/, accessed May 30, 2018.

31 May, "Utah Judicial Council History," *supra* note 27, 15.

approval. As a first task, the CRC proposed, the legislature adopted, and in 1970 the voters approved what was referred to as the "Gateway Amendment," which made possible the comprehensive revision of individual articles in the constitution. In 1977, the legislature made the CRC a permanent body.[32]

The CRC took as its first substantive task the revision of Article VI, dealing with the legislature. Proposals were forwarded to the legislature in the early 1970s and approved by the voters in 1972.[33] The CRC then turned to Article VII, about the executive department.[34] The CRC's initial suggestions went to the voters in 1974, but less than 40 percent voted in favor of the proposed revisions. Several years of study by the CRC led to another proposed set of changes to Article VII; these went to the voters in 1980 and passed, with 56 percent voting in favor. Next on the CRC's agenda was Article VIII, about the judicial department, and it turned its attention to the judiciary in 1980.

Article VIII Revision, Round 1

There were a variety of issues regarding the judiciary in addition to the question of how judges should be selected and retained. These included the growing caseload of the Supreme Court because of a right of appeal to that Court; the judicial branch's lack of any kind of centralized structure for budgeting, administration, or rule-making;[35] and limits on the ability of the legislature to make changes to the court system to meet the needs of a population that was both changing and rapidly growing.[36]

Between 1960 and 1976 the caseload of the Utah Supreme Court had tripled. Under the Utah Constitution as it then stood, there was a right of appeal to the Supreme Court. Ending that right of appeal by creating an intermediate appellate court would require an amendment to the constitution. In the late 1970s, one

[32] White, *The Utah State Constitution*, supra *note* 18, 17. Legislation in 2011 limited the CRC's role by limiting its meetings to those called by the governor or the legislature, reflecting the view of some that it was "acting outside the authority" intended by the legislature; see Lisa Riley Roche and Dennis Romboy, "Constitutional Revision Commission Independence May End," *Deseret News* (February 7, 2011), www.deseretnews.com/article/705366164/Constitutional-Revision-Commission-independence-may-end.html, accessed May 26, 2018. Although formally still in existence, the CRC has essentially been dormant since 2011 – Roger Tew, email of May 29, 2018.

[33] White, *The Utah State Constitution, supra* note 18, 71.

[34] The CRC was also making proposals for changes to some of the substantive articles in the constitution, such as that dealing with taxation.

[35] At the behest of legislature, a report with proposals regarding the administrative issues had been prepared in the early 1970s; see "Utah Courts Tomorrow: Report and Recommendations of the Unified Court Advisory Committee" (Utah Legislative Council, September 1972). Not long after this report was published, the CRC was asked by the legislature to review the report's recommendations but decided not to recommend any changes at that time.

[36] *Id.*, 107.

member of the Utah Supreme Court, Justice Richard Maughan (briefly chief justice in 1981), assumed the role of point person in advocating for the creation of an intermediate appellate court.[37] Although the CRC was sympathetic to the Supreme Court's desire for an intermediate appellate court,[38] it wanted such a change to be part of a comprehensive revision of the judicial article.[39]

The CRC sent its proposed version of a new Article VIII, including provisions allowing the legislature to create an intermediate appellate court, to the legislature in December 1981, and it was considered in the legislature's budget session in January 1982. The proposal included a straight Missouri Plan system for judicial selection: a nominating commission, selection by the governor from a list created by the nominating commission, and retention elections. The selection/retention provisions removed the legislature's power, contained in the 1945 amendment described previously, to determine selection and retention through legislative action. One other change, unrelated to the selection issue, that proved problematic was the CRC's decision to remove any reference to the justices of the peace from the constitution itself, making it possible for the legislature to decide at some future point to abolish justice courts (as they were called).

During the January 1982 session, the Utah House of Representatives considered the proposal from the CRC as House Joint Resolution 10 (H.J.R. 10). It made two major changes, passed the revised proposal, and sent it on to the Utah Senate. The two changes were to restore the legislature's power to determine the method of judicial selection and retention, and to restore the justice courts to their constitutional standing. H.J.R. 10 stalled in the Republican-dominated Utah Senate, which was in the midst of a constitutional conflict with Democratic governor Scott Matheson.[40]

The Battle over Requiring Senate Consent for Judicial Appointments

Apparently, there was unhappiness among Republicans over some of the judicial appointments made by the Democratic governors who had been making those appointments for the prior sixteen years.[41] In 1981, the solidly Republican legislature decided that the solution to this problem was to require that the Senate consent to judicial appointees. The language of the 1945 constitutional amendment (judges "shall be selected for such terms and in such manner as shall be provided for by law")

[37] May, "Utah Judicial Council History," *supra* note 27, 16.

[38] In 1980, the CRC had supported a simple amendment that would have eliminated automatic appeals to the Supreme Court (Utah House Joint Resolution 20), but that never made it out of the legislature.

[39] Roger Tew interview, *supra* note 1.

[40] May, "Utah Judicial Council History," *supra* note 27, 18. For additional background, see also the Reports of the Constitutional Revision Commission which are available at http://utah.polarislibrary.com/search/title.aspx?ctx=20.1033.0.0.5&pos=2, accessed May 21, 2018.

[41] Roger Tew interview, *supra* note 1.

appeared to grant the legislature the power to add such a requirement. The legislation (H.B. 224) passed with little or no support from Democratic legislators. As would be expected, Democratic governor Scott Matheson vetoed the legislation, but Republicans had more than enough votes to override the veto, even with all Democrats voting to uphold the veto. Matheson then brought a constitutional challenge to the legislation, asserting that it violated the separation of powers clause of the Utah constitution.[42] He also asserted the inclusion of members of the legislature on the nominating commission violated the separation of powers clause.[43]

The Court, which consisted of four Democratic appointees and one justice who had defeated a Democratic appointee, decided 4 to 1 that the addition of a requirement that the Senate consent to judicial appointments did violate the separation of powers clause. The dissenter was one of the Democratic appointees. Four of the justices also agreed that the inclusion of the legislature in the selection of the members of the nominating commission was not a violation of separation of powers; the fifth justice argued that the issue of the nominating commission membership was moot because the governor had not objected to it when making his selections from the list provided by the commission. The language of the decision appeared to link the unconstitutionality of requiring Senate consent with the inclusion of the legislature in selecting members of the nominating commission, because the two taken together could produce a situation that the governor's "discretion and power thus [would] become curtailed to a point where his participation in the appointment process [would] become ineffective, subservient, and perfunctory, amounting to effective control by the Legislature."[44]

This ambiguity renewed the consent requirement controversy. The Court had announced its decision on January 11, 1982, which was also the day that the 1982 budget session of the Utah legislature convened. During that session, the legislature passed a revised version of the Senate consent requirement. House Bill 62 was based on the assumption that the constitutional problem was due to the combination of senatorial consent and the legislature having a role in the selection of the nominating commission. To solve this problem, the new legislation removed the legislature from any role in selecting members of the nominating commission. As with the prior bill, it passed with little or no Democratic support, it was vetoed by the governor, the veto was overridden with little or no Democratic support, and the governor sued, challenging the constitutionality of the consent requirement. Four justices again agreed that adding Senate consent violated the separation of powers

[42] See Article V, §1: "The powers of the government of the State of Utah shall be divided into three distinct departments, the Legislative, the Executive, and the Judicial; and no person charged with the exercise of powers properly belonging to one of these departments, shall exercise any functions appertaining to either of the others, except in the cases herein expressly directed or permitted."

[43] See Matheson v. Ferry, 641 P.2d 674 (Utah 1982).

[44] *Id.*, 679.

clause, but with a caveat.[45] Some of the justices drew a distinction between courts where judges stood for election and courts not involving elections. The latter category consisted of the juvenile court, whose justices were appointed and subject to reappointment. Three justices found that requiring Senate consent when no election was part of the process was not a constitutional violation.[46]

Article VIII Revision, Round 2

After the failure of its 1981 proposal, the CRC began to work again on a proposal for a new judicial article. This was slowed by the litigation over the Senate consent, which was not finally resolved until the last months of 1982, and that was too late to finalize a proposal for consideration during the regular legislative session that would convene in January 1983. The CRC ultimately decided to make only limited changes to its 1981 proposal. It would keep its decision to delete all references to justices of the peace from the constitution on the grounds that no limited-jurisdiction courts should be mentioned.

On the issue of judicial selection, the CRC decided to provide for Senate consent but to exclude the legislature from any role in the nominating commission process. The proposed selection/retention system would involve the following:

- A nominating commission would be formed, the composition of which would be established by the legislature, but which could not include legislators on the commission or the legislature's having a role in selecting members; the commission would submit at least three names to the governor.
- The governor would have to make a choice within thirty days of receiving the list; if the governor failed to do so, the chief justice would have twenty days to make the appointment from the list of nominees.
- The Senate would have thirty days to render a decision on the appointee, convening in extraordinary session if needed; the appointment would be confirmed unless rejected by a majority of all members of the Senate (i.e., an absence or abstention would effectively count as a vote in favor).
- Retention would be through retention elections, initially at the first general election after at least three years of the appointment, and thereafter at the end of the judge's term, ten years for justices of the Supreme Court and six years for judges of the Court of Appeals and the district courts.

[45] Matheson v. Ferry, 657 P.2d 240 (Utah 1982).

[46] One of the three justices upholding confirmation for unelected courts was the dissenter in the larger issue who had found that the confirmation requirement was permissible for any of the courts.

The proposed system would end the possibility of an incumbent facing an opposing candidate in a nonpartisan election. The new version of the judicial article would retain the prohibition on partisan involvement in the 1945 amendment.

The CRC's new version of the judicial article was to be considered by the legislature during the January 1984 budget session,[47] but time ran out before that could be done. Consequently, the legislature had to defer its consideration until a special session in March 1984, where it was speedily passed as Senate Joint Resolution 1 (S.J.R. 1). In the Senate, a proposal to maintain the provisions of the 1945 amendment (granting the legislature authority to set the method of judicial selection and retention) failed by a single vote.[48] The legislature did make one significant change to the selection provisions proposed by the CRC: rather than a proposed appointee being rejected only if a majority of the members *votes to reject* the appointee, an appointee is rejected unless a majority of members *votes to approve* the appointee.[49] There was one significant substantive change not related to selection and retention, giving the legislature power to amend rules of procedure and evidence adopted by the Supreme Court.[50] In addition, there were several other minor changes to parts of the proposed amendment, none of which dealt with selection and retention. The final vote on S.J.R. 1 in the Senate was 23 to 5 with one abstention; in the House, the vote was 68 to 3, with 4 members absent or not voting. All no votes came from Republicans, at least some of whom were probably dissatisfied with the elimination of the possibility of contested judicial elections.[51] The House of Representatives considered the Senate version in a committee of the whole proceeding and then passed it, 68–3, unchanged.[52] The amendment was approved by the voters the following November, with 55.9 percent voting in favor.

The passage of the new judicial article in the legislature reflected a combination of interests and factors. It had the backing of the Supreme Court because it would solve the Court's caseload problem by removing the right of appeal to the Supreme Court

[47] It was introduced during the budget session as Senate Joint Resolution 5, but the only action taken was to pass an enabling resolution that permitted its consideration during a budget session, even though it was not a budget-related matter.

[48] *Senate Journal*, Second Special Session of the Forty-Fifth Legislature (1984), 546.

[49] *Id.*, 547.

[50] *Id.*

[51] Speculation by Roger Tew, May 15, 2018, interview, *supra* note 1. One of the senators who voted no when the Senate considered the amendment campaigned against the proposed amendment as the November election in which voters would be asked to approve the change approached; see "Senator Says Proposition 3 Contains Serious Flaws" [letter to the editor from E. Verl Asay], *Orem-Geneva Times* (October 17, 1984), 2. Among other complaints made about the amendment, Senator Asay observed that the amendment "will take away the right of the people to elect judges to office, a right we have had since statehood." Asay also expressed "against" arguments, accompanied by State Representative Francis Hatch Merrill, in a series of For and Against debate-style pieces that appeared in a number of Utah newspapers; for example, *Beaver Press* (October 18, 1984), 163. The central point in the "against" arguments was the provisions concerning judicial selection and retention.

[52] *House Journal*, Second Special Session of the Forty-Fifth Legislature (1984), 525.

and effectively authorizing the legislature to create an intermediate appellate court.[53] The legislature reluctantly gave up its power to determine the judicial selection process but gained the power of the Senate to reject the governor's appointees. It had the support of the bar, which had long wanted judges selected through a Missouri Plan system.[54] Although trial court judges had resisted centralizing administrative authority under the Supreme Court, they were mollified by the authority to make administrative rules being lodged in the Judicial Council, in which trial judges were guaranteed a voice;[55] their support was probably enhanced by the prospect of no longer having to face the threat of someone mounting a challenge in a nonpartisan election. The new judicial article had the support of Governor Matheson, despite the inclusion of the Senate consent provision.[56] The governor's support is interesting, because the governor has no formal role in the constitutional amendment process. One might wonder why he expressed support for the amendment. Undoubtedly part of the reason was that he saw the need to modernize the constitutional provisions concerning the judicial department. Regarding the issue of Senate consent, by the time the amendment would come into effect, Matheson would be out of office and would not be personally affected. Although he might have been concerned that the provision would limit future Democratic governors, he might also have foreseen that, given the growing Republican dominance in Utah, the chances of a Democrat winning the gubernatorial election anytime in the foreseeable future were low. As noted previously, Republicans have won every gubernatorial election since 1984, with Democrats winning more than 40 percent of the vote only twice,[57] and often receiving less than 30 percent.

The new judicial department article did not specify the membership of the nominating commission beyond barring legislators from serving on a nominating commission and barring the legislature from having any role in selecting the members of the commissions (there would be one for appellate courts and separate commissions for each judicial district). The legislature decided that the chair of each commission should be the chief justice or an associate justice designated by the chief justice. There would be 6 additional members of each commission, 4 chosen by the governor and 2 by the Utah State Bar Association. The members chosen by the governor could not belong to the bar association,

53 Roger Tew interview, *supra* note 1.

54 The bar had been one of the major backers, perhaps the primary backer, as previously noted, of the 1949 legislation calling for a Missouri Plan, which was vetoed by the governor; see W. G. Van Cott, "Report of the Special Committee on Non-partisan Selection of the Judiciary," *Utah Bar Bulletin* 19, nos. 1–3 (January–March 1949), 31.

55 See May, "Utah Judicial Council History," *supra* note 27, 17–18.

56 See "Proposition 3 Supported," *Daily Spectrum* (October 31, 1984), 1: "Democratic Gov. Scott Matheson, Republican legislative leaders and the Utah State Bar banded together today to restate support for Proposition 3, which overhauled the state constitution's judicial article."

57 One of those elections came in 2004, when Matheson's son, Scott M. Matheson Jr., ran for governor, and garnered 41.4 percent of the vote.

and no more than two of the governor's appointees could come from one political party. The two members chosen by the Bar Association had to be of different parties. Except for the Supreme Court members, commissioners could only serve a single four-year term.[58] This structure lasted only until 1994, when the legislature abolished the existing nominating commissions and reconstituted them such that the governor appointed all 7 members and named the chairs, with the limit that no more than 4 of the members could come from a single political party; at least 2 and no more than 4 members of each commission could belong to the Utah State Bar.[59] The chief justice remained on the commissions, but as a nonvoting member.

JUDICIAL APPOINTMENTS AND ELECTIONS SINCE 1985

With the adoption of the amendment, the Utah Senate obtained the power to veto the governor's selections from the list of candidates forwarded by the nominating commission. Initially, the Senate had no clear procedure for reviewing the proposed appointees beyond taking a vote on the floor. In 2003, the Senate established a set of policies to systematize the review of appointees by its Judicial Confirmation Committee, which is charged with conducting that review and making a recommendation to the full Senate.[60] That committee has almost always given a positive recommendation and a negative recommendation does not always lead to a Senate rejection. For example, in 2012, Su Chon, a Korean American who was brought to United States by her parents as a child when they immigrated, was denied a positive recommendation. Despite the negative recommendation, the Senate did confirm her as a district court judge in a divided (17–10) vote, with all Democrats voting in favor and Republicans splitting 10–10.[61]

A positive recommendation does not guarantee Senate consent. In 2008, Governor Jon Huntsman nominated District Court judge Robert Hilder for a position on the Utah Court of Appeals. Hilder was approved on a divided vote by the Judicial Confirmation Committee,[62] but then rejected 16–12 by the Senate. There were at least two elements to the opposition that sank the nomination. The most visible

[58] *Laws of Utah* 1986, 117–118.

[59] *Laws of Utah* 1994, 1050–1052. Members of the new commissions are limited to a single, 4-year term. Two members must be selected from a list provided by the bar association, although the governor can reject the list and ask for a new list.

[60] For a detailed description of the process, see Al Mansell and Jerry Howe, "Before the Bench: The Utah Senate and Judicial Confirmation," *Utah Bar Journal* 16, no. 7 (July 2003), 26–33.

[61] Aaron Falk, "Despite Controversy, Su Chon Confirmed as Utah Judge," *Salt Lake City Tribune* (August 16, 2012), http://archive.sltrib.com/article.php?id=54702875&itype=CMSID, accessed May 29, 2018.

[62] Rebecca Palmer, "Fight Brewing over Judicial Nomination," *Deseret News* (November 13, 2008), www.deseretnews.com/article/705262539/Fight-brewing-over-judicial-nomination.html, accessed June 3, 2018.

opposition came as a campaign mounted by the Utah Shooting Sports Council; its ire was raised by Hilder's 2003 decision dealing with whether the University of Utah could ban concealed weapons on campus.[63] Additional opposition came in connection with Hilder's handling of a child custody dispute in which he had, on "the advice of a therapist, ordered a woman to stay in Utah or lose primary custody of her children. In August 2003, police shot and killed the woman after a chase and a fight with her husband."[64] The woman had shot and kidnapped her husband; she then pulled a gun on police, who shot and killed her.[65] A search of the *Journal of the Utah Senate* did not turn up any other proposed judicial appointments that the Senate refused to consent to, and one could count on a single hand the number of proposed appointments with even a single dissenting vote.[66]

As part of the retention process, Utah provided for evaluation of judges prior to their standing for retention. From 1990 through 2010, these evaluations were done by the Utah Judicial Council (UJC). Starting in 1994, the results of the UJC's evaluation for each judge were published in the state's Voter Information Pamphlets (VIPs).[67] From 1994 through 2002, the results of the evaluation as reported in the VIP stated that the judge has "been certified by the Utah Judicial Council to have met or exceeded the standard of performance for the office of judge and is qualified for retention in the yyyy general election." From 2004 through 2010, the evaluation simply stated that the judge was "certified by the Utah Judicial Council for retention in the yyyy general election." For many judges, the results of attorney surveys were included. The pamphlets also included information on the evaluation criteria. Across the hundreds of judges listed in these pamphlets, only one judge failed to be found qualified for retention (1994–2002) or failed to be certified for retention (2002–2010), but the reason was that the judge had not been in office long enough for an assessment to be done. It is possible that judges were told in sufficient time if they were to receive a negative assessment so that they could step down and avoid the embarrassment that would go with a negative assessment.[68] A study of retention

63 University of Utah v. Shurtleff, No. 03090595, slip op. at 11–12 (Utah 3d Dist. Ct. 2003).

64 Aaron Falk, "For Judge Hilder, an Exit from Controversy and on to New Legal Horizons," *Salt Lake Tribune* (August 21, 2011), http://archive.sltrib.com/article.php?id=52226486&itype=CMSID, accessed June 3, 2018.

65 Palmer, "Fight Brewing," *supra* note 62.

66 Often judicial appointments were among a long list of gubernatorial appointments consented to in a single vote. My search of the journals was less than perfect (one apparently did not OCR well), which means that there may in fact be other judicial appointees whom the Senate rejected, but it would be an extremely small number. It is also possible that some proposed appointees were withdrawn without any action by the Senate if opposition arose.

67 An archive of these pamphlets can be found at elections.utah.gov/1980-2012-voter-information-pamphlets, accessed May 29, 2018.

68 It is also conceivable that only judges with positive assessments were listed in the Voter Information Pamphlets, but that would be a rather strange practice, because there is nothing in the VIP to alert the voters to such a practice.

elections in Utah in 1996, 1998, and 2000 concluded that the evaluations had little effect on voters' decisions on whether to support a judge's retention.[69]

In 2008, the Utah legislature created the Judicial Performance Evaluations Commission (JPEC).[70] The JPEC designed a new evaluation process, and published its first results in 2012, both in the Voter Information Pamphlets and online.[71] In the JPEC system, the members of the commission vote on whether the judge should be retained, and the outcome of that vote is reported, including the vote tally, as "retain" or "not retain." Over the three election years 2012, 2014, and 2016, the JPEC published evaluations of 168 judges. Only 1 of those 168 judges received a "not retain" recommendation; that judge was Su Chon, who was standing for retention for the first time since her controversial appointment in 2012. Judge Chon was retained despite the "not retain" recommendation from the JPEC. Only 5 other judges received less-than-unanimous backing from the JPEC; 3 of those 5 garnered a single negative vote, 1 (David Marx in 2014) received three negative votes, and 1 (Darold McDade in 2016), five negative votes.

Between 1988 and 2018, there were a total of 492 retention elections in Utah for courts of record.[72] In 490 of those elections, the judge was retained. And in 487 elections, 70 percent or more of the voters approved the judge's retention. One of the judges who was retained with less than 70 percent voting in favor of retention was Judge Su Chon, who was favored for retention by only 57.6 percent of those voting on her retention. A second was Judge Homer Wilkinson, who had a 66.0 percent vote in favor of retention.[73]

The two judges who lost their retention elections were District Judge David Young in 2002 and District Judge Leslie Lewis in 2006. Young was the third judge retained by less than 70 percent; in 1996, he was barely retained by a margin of only about 2,000 votes out of 243,000 cast (50.4 percent voting in favor of retention). Young had been found by the JPC to be "qualified for retention," having met or exceeded the standards for performance; Lewis had been "certified by the Utah Judicial Council for retention." What led to the defeat of these two judges?

69 See Susan M. Olson, "Voter Mobilization in Judicial Retention Elections: Performance Evaluations and Organized Opposition," *Justice System Journal* 22, no. 3 (2001), 263–285.

70 See Rebecca D. Gill and Rafael Oganesyan, "Judicial Performance Evaluation in Utah: Preliminary Findings," a paper prepared for presentation at the 2015 Annual Meeting of the Western Political Science Association, 3, https://wpsa.research.pdx.edu/papers/docs/Utah.pdf, accessed May 29, 2018.

71 See https://elections.utah.gov/1980-2012-voter-information-pamphlets, accessed May 29, 2018.

72 There apparently were also retention elections for justices of the peace, at least there was one year's election report that included results of those elections. I have not considered them in this discussion.

73 Wilkinson had met the overall standard to receive a positive recommendation from the UJC, but received substandard scores from lawyers on several criteria; see "Two Utah Judges Don't Make the Grade," *Daily Spectrum* (September 1996), 4.

Young had been the subject of controversy dating back to 1994 or 1995. At the time of the 1996 election, one major complaint against him was that he had reduced the sentence of a man who had pleaded guilty to killing another man because the victim was gay[74] and had made a sexual advance on the defendant.[75] There were also widespread complaints about how he treated women in divorce and custody cases that came before him, and this led to a campaign in opposition to his retention.[76] By the time of the 2002 election, Young had become enmeshed in additional controversy. He had been the subject of two public reprimands from the Utah Supreme Court, one in 1999 and another in 2000, for violations of the Code of Judicial Conduct; information about the reprimands were included in the Voter Information Pamphlets for the 2002 election.[77] These pamphlets were mailed to voters, and at least some newspapers included the full text of the evaluations for judges on the local ballot. Young came under further criticism for scolding juries that returned decisions he disagreed with.[78] Not long before the 2002 election, Young attracted yet more controversy by placing on probation two men who pleaded guilty to sexual abuse of a child that involved having oral sex with a 12-year-old girl at a drinking party.[79] A group, calling itself Utahns for Judicial Reform, organized a campaign to deny Young another term.[80] Although Young had supporters,[81] only 48.8 percent of voters favored his retention.

Judge Leslie Lewis attracted wide criticism early in 2006 after a courtroom tirade directed at a pair of deer hunters accused of poaching. During that hearing, in which she indicated that she was recusing herself because of her "prejudice concerning deer hunters," she ordered that one of the spectators be handcuffed and taken to a holding cell after he stood up to leave the courtroom. About two weeks before the 2006 election, a video of the incident was posted on the internet by a

74 John Gibeaut, "Taking Aim," *ABA Journal* (November 1996), 52.

75 "Controversial Cases Need Close Look by Conduct Commission," *Park Record* (August 24, 1994), A16.

76 See Olson, "Voter Mobilization in Judicial Retention Elections," *supra* note 69, 271–275. Olson used pseudonyms for judges in her article; Young was identified as Judge Keane, who is clearly identifiable by the vote in favor of his retention in 1996 shown on page 269. A more detailed account of the 1996 retention election can be found in Susan M. Olson and Christina Batjer, "Competing Narratives in a Judicial Retention Election: Feminism versus Judicial Independence," *Law and Society Review* 33, no. 1 (1999), 123–160; in this account, Judge Young is identified as Judge Owen Bishop.

77 "Utah Voter Information Pamphlet, General Election, November 5, 2002," 76, https://elections.utah.gov/Media/Default/Historical%20VIPs/2002%20VIP.pdf, accessed May 29, 2018.

78 "Judge Scolds Jury," *Daily Spectrum* (December 6, 1999), A10.

79 "Another Move Is Launched to Oust Judge David Young," *Daily Herald* (September 28, 2002), www.heraldextra.com/news/local/another-move-is-launched-to-oust-judge-david-young/article_5298fb5e-c411-53bc-bb0f-5fa9e0e5c2a7.html, accessed May 29, 2018.

80 See Stephen Hunt, "Judge's Job Again in Jeopardy," *Salt Lake Tribune* (October 276, 2002), http://thecalkinsfamily.tripod.com/Trib/jeopardy.htm, accessed May 29, 2018.

81 Mary Ruth Hammond, "Despite His Ruling, Keep Judge Young," *Park Record* (November 2, 2002), 13.

group opposing her retention.[82] She was also facing a complaint filed by prosecutors in connection with failing to inform prosecutors of a decision to reduce from a minimum of 30 years to 20 years the sentence of a man convicted of the sexual abuse of a 7-year-old girl.[83] Finally, just a few days prior to the election, a local television station obtained a video of Judge Lewis making what many viewed as disparaging comments regarding the baptism practices of the LDS (Mormon) church.[84] The editorial board of at least one major Salt Lake City newspaper came out against her retention.[85] On election day, only 46 percent of voters supported her retention.[86]

Between 1988 and 2018, there were 48 statewide retention elections, 22 for the Supreme Court and 26 for the intermediate Court of Appeals. For these two courts, the average vote in favor of retention was 81.5 percent. In no case did less than three-quarters of the voters favor retention. Across the counties of Utah, there was some variation in the percent favoring retention, although in only a single county in a single election did less than a majority of voters favor retention. Omitting that one outlier, the lowest county-level percentage favoring retention was 60.7 percent. On average, the difference between the most favorable county and the least favorable county was 17.0 percentage points. To the extent that there was variation across the counties, that variation correlated with voting patterns in gubernatorial elections; counties more supportive of retention tended to be the counties more supportive of the Republican gubernatorial candidate. The average correlation was .351; in eight elections the correlation exceeded .6. This pattern is not surprising, given that all Court of Appeals judges and most Supreme Court justices were appointed by Republican governors.

SUMMARY

The move to a full Missouri Plan system in Utah in 1985 was the culmination of a long process that started with the 1945 constitutional amendment calling for a system of judicial selection and retention that was devoid of partisan influence. But for the governor's 1949 veto of implementing legislation, Utah would have been the first state to follow Missouri's lead in creating what had come to be called the Missouri

82 "Hunters Urged Judge's Defeat," *Daily Spectrum* (October 27, 2006). After the video was posted, Lewis received a death threat; see Paul Foy, "Utah Judge Lewis Receives Death Threat," *Daily Spectrum* (October 28, 2006), 3.

83 "Judge Cuts Sex Offender's Sentence without Telling Prosecutor" (October 31, 2006), www.ksl.com/?nid=148&sid=607579, accessed May 30, 2018.

84 "Utah Judge Accused of Religious Bias against LDS Church," Religion News Blog (November 3, 2006), www.religionnewsblog.com/16445/utah-judge-accused-of-religious-bias-against-lds-church, accessed May 28, 2018.

85 *Id.*

86 Geoffrey Fattah and Linda Thomson, "Judge Lewis Is Ousted by 54% of Voters," *Deseret Morning News* (November 8, 2006), www.deseretnews.com/article/650205386/Judge-Lewis-is-ousted-by-54-of-voters.html, accessed May 25, 2018.

Plan. The 1967 legislation moved along in that direction by having the governor appoint all judges to open seats, both for midterm vacancies and end-of-term vacancies, and instituting retention elections for incumbents who were not facing challengers in nonpartisan elections.

The charge to the Constitutional Revision Commission to undertake a thorough revision of the state constitution provided the opportunity and context to eliminate any possibility of contested nonpartisan elections. The only element of partisan politics to enter into the 1984 constitutional revision was the inclusion of the Senate's option to reject the governor's proposed appointee. This reflected the conflict between the (last) Democratic governor and the overwhelmingly Republican state legislature in the early 1980s. However, it did not produce partisan division in the final approval of the proposed judicial article. Thus, in the end, partisanship played a minimal role in Utah's gradual shift from partisan elections to a Missouri Plan system with the added element of Senate consent.

9

New Mexico

Finding Its Own Unique Approach

Efforts to alter the method of judicial selection and retention of New Mexico's state judges became an ongoing issue in the 1930s, just twenty years after statehood in 1912. Although New Mexico achieved statehood in the period when many states were changing from partisan to nonpartisan elections for judges, New Mexico, for reasons discussed in this chapter, chose partisan elections for this purpose. Efforts at reform started in the 1930s and continued with some regularity until the adoption of a constitutional amendment in 1988 providing for a unique blend of partisan elections and "merit selection."

BACKGROUND

New Mexico Politics

In 1910, the territory of New Mexico held a convention to draft what would become the constitution of the State of New Mexico. That convention was dominated by what were referred to as "Old-Guard Republicans." Republicans held 71 of the 100 seats at the convention, Democrats held 28, and the hundredth seat was held by a lonely Socialist. The dominant Republicans represented various major special-interest groups in the territory: railroads, mining, ranching, and land development. Their goal was to draft a constitution that would that would serve those interests and help the Republican Party maintain its dominance.[1]

The Republicans were less than wholly successful in their goal of maintaining dominance. The first two governors elected after statehood were Democrats, and Republicans maintained control of both chambers of the state legislature for only about a decade. For a period of four years in the 1920s, Democrats controlled the

[1] Susan A. Roberts, "A Political History of the New Mexico Supreme Court, 1912–1972," *New Mexico Law Review* 5 (1975) [Special Issue], 3–4.

House and the governor's office. Republicans briefly regained control for a period of four years, ending with the 1930 election. As was true in many places, the Depression swept in Democrats, who controlled the legislature and executive from 1933 through 1950.

Starting in 1950, Republicans periodically won the election for governor and occasionally won formal control of one chamber of the state legislature. However, beginning in the late 1970s, there were periods when one or both chambers were controlled by a conservative coalition bringing together all Republicans with a group of conservative Democrats.[2] It was the presence of this conservative coalition that facilitated the passage by the legislature of the joint resolutions that put proposals to adopt versions of "merit selection" before the voters in 1982, when it failed, and 1988, when it passed.

Judicial Selection and Elections prior to 1988

The 1910 constitution established two courts of record, a Supreme Court and a trial level district court, plus probate courts and justices of the peace. That constitution also authorized the creation of courts "inferior to the district courts" in counties or municipalities. In 1965, voters approved a constitutional amendment authorizing the creation of an intermediate Court of Appeals, and appropriate legislation was enacted the following year.[3] Legislation that took effect in 1969 replaced the justice of the peace courts with magistrates' courts.[4] Under the 1910 constitution, judges were selected and retained through elections, with the governor having unconstrained discretion to fill midterm vacancies with any person possessing the legal qualifications for the position. Starting in the early 1950s, governors voluntarily relied upon the recommendations of screening committees in making interim appointments.[5]

Whether the elections would be partisan or nonpartisan was left undefined in the 1910 constitution, presumably under the assumption that failing to specify "nonpartisan" left the elections as partisan affairs. Arguably, that "partisan elections won out over nonpartisan elections reflected the confidence of the Old-Guard Republicans who, fresh from their smashing victories in the election of convention delegates,

[2] F. Chris Garcia, Paul L. Hain, Gilbert K. St. Clair, and Kim Seckler, eds., *Governing New Mexico* (Albuquerque: University of New Mexico Press, 2006), 63–64.

[3] Thomas A. Donnelly and Pamela B. Minzner, "History of the New Mexico Court of Appeals," *New Mexico Law Review* 22 (Summer 1992), 596–598.

[4] U.S. Department of Justice, Law Enforcement Assistance Administration, *National Survey of Court Organization* (Washington, DC: U.S. Government Printing Office, 1973), 188.

[5] This practice was started by Governor Ed Mechem, who had been a strong supporter of a constitutional amendment to institute a system based on the Missouri Plan after that amendment was rejected by the voters; see Leo M. Romero, "Judicial Selection in New Mexico: A Hybrid of Commission Nomination and Partisan Election," *New Mexico Law Review* 30 (2002), 181.

felt sure they were to dominate state politics for years to come."[6] As with the legislature, Republicans succeeded in controlling the New Mexico Supreme Court for about a decade,[7] with Democrats gaining control in the 1930s,[8] as they did in the other branches of government.

Between 1946 and 1988, there were 37 elections for the New Mexico Supreme Court, 27 of which were contested by both Democrats and Republicans.[9] The proportion of uncontested elections was greater in the latter part of the period: 7 out of 16 (44 percent) between 1972 and 1988 compared to 3 out of 21 (14 percent) between 1946 and 1970. Nine elections were for open seats, and in another fifteen the incumbent was a recent appointee to the Court. Republicans won only one election, in 1980; in that election, the Republican defeated a Democrat who had been appointed to the Court fifteen months earlier.[10] Five other Republicans served on the Court between 1946 and 1988, all briefly; each had been appointed by a Republican governor to fill a vacancy and then was challenged and defeated by a Democrat in the subsequent election that occurred within eighteen months.

The initial positions on the Court of Appeals were filled by gubernatorial appointment in 1966, with the first elections occurring in 1968. Between 1966 and 1988, there were only two Republican governors; they held office for a total of six years. Only once, in 1967, did one of those Republicans have an opportunity to make an appointment to the Court of Appeals. Rather than seeking to retain his seat on the Court of Appeals in the 1988 election, that one appointee, Roberto Armijo, ran unsuccessfully for an open seat on the New Mexico Supreme Court.

Between 1966 and 1988, there were 22 elections for positions on the appellate court. Only 2 of those elections were for open seats, and those two seats were newly created to be filled by election rather than appointment; both were contested in the 1978 general election and both were won by the Democratic candidate. Democratic incumbents sought to retain their seats in the other 20 elections, 7 of which were contested unsuccessfully by Republicans. Incumbents did lose in the Democratic primary four times. The result of these elections was that only a single Republican, Roberto Armijo, served as a Court of Appeals judge between 1966 and 1990. Overall, half of the elections for the Court of Appeals between its creation in 1966 and 1988 were contested, compared to only about one-third of elections for the New Mexico Supreme Court during the same period.

6 Roberts, "A Political History of the New Mexico Supreme Court," *supra* note 1, 6.

7 *Id.*, 14–31.

8 *Id.*, 84.

9 None of the elections were contested in even one party's primary; in fact, only four involved party primaries at all.

10 It is unclear what might account for the defeat of the Democratic incumbent. One newspaper article shortly before the elections described the race as "lackluster"; see David Steinberg, "Felter, Riordan in Lackluster Race for Court Seat," *Albuquerque Journal* (October 25, 1980), B16.

Election information for the district court is not readily available. However, shortly before the vote on the 1988 constitutional amendment to change the selection system, one newspaper reported that "82 percent of the recent judicial elections in the state have involved judges running unopposed."[11] The higher likelihood of contested appellate elections suggests that something on the order of 85 percent of district court elections would have been uncontested.[12]

SELECTION REFORM

There is a long history of efforts to move away from partisan judicial elections in New Mexico. There were six serious attempts at reform over a 50-year period prior to voters approving a change in 1988.

Trying, Trying, and Trying, but No Joy: 1933–1982[13]

The earliest efforts at change came in the 1930s. In 1933, the New Mexico legislature considered two proposals. One proposal would have followed the lead of many other states that had switched from partisan to nonpartisan elections over the previous twenty-five years. The other proposal would have given the bar a unique role: there would be a primary for judicial elections, but only members of the state bar would be permitted to participate; that primary would determine who would be on the general election ballot.[14] Neither proposal received legislative approval. The next year, 1934, California adopted a system for its appellate courts that combined gubernatorial appointment with retention elections. This move by California kept interest in New Mexico alive to the possibility of changes to judicial selection, and in 1935, the New Mexico State Bar (NMSB) called a conference to discuss improvements in judicial selection. Participants at the conference came from civic, labor, and business groups as well as from the bar itself. Nothing appears to have come of that conference.

Except for an unsuccessful push for nonpartisan elections during World War II, not much happened until the late 1940s. At meetings of the NMSB in 1948, 1949, and 1950, proposals were introduced for a plan modeled on what had

[11] Coleman Cornelius, "Politics and the Courtroom: Will a Proposed Constitutional Amendment Take It Out or Put It In?" *Santa Fe Reporter* (October 19, 1988), 15.

[12] Between 1976 and 1986, 4 of 12 Supreme Court elections were contested, as were 5 of 11 Court of Appeals elections.

[13] The discussion in this section is based largely on two secondary sources: Romero, "Judicial Selection in New Mexico," *supra* note 5, 180–183; and Glenn R. Winters, "The New Mexico Judicial Selection Campaign – A Case History," *Journal of the American Judicature Society*, 35, no. 6 (April 1952), 166–176.

[14] The brief discussions in the press of this proposal do not indicate whether it would be in addition to a switch to nonpartisan elections; it is difficult to see how it would function with partisan elections.

been adopted in Missouri at the beginning of the 1940s. At the 1950 meeting, the attendees approved a draft proposal on a nearly unanimous vote, and a proposal for a constitutional amendment was introduced in the 1951 legislature. The proposed amendment specified the membership of nominating commissions. For the Supreme Court, it would consist of the Board of Bar Commissioners of the State Bar of New Mexico, with the chief justice serving as chair. For the district court, there would be two lawyers elected by the bar of the district, plus two laypersons, one appointed by the Supreme Court and one by the governor. Although the legislature was empowered to modify the membership of the nominating commission of the Supreme Court, if it did so, all commissioners had to be members of the state bar who would be elected in nonpartisan elections, and there had to be at least one commissioner from every judicial district in the state. Other than the chief justice and the Board of Bar Commissioners, commissioners could not hold public office, and no commissioner could hold an official position with a political party.

The proposal introduced into the legislature called for retention elections with the provision that if a majority voted not to retain, the incumbent could not continue in office. During legislative deliberations, this was modified so that an incumbent would be removed from office only if the vote to retain was less than 50 percent in favor, *and* the total number of votes cast in the retention election was at least 50 percent of persons voting at the election. This meant that if 100,000 persons turned out for the overall election but fewer than 50,000 voted in the retention election, the judge would be retained regardless of the percentage casting votes against retention; that is, in this hypothetical, if 49,999 voted against retention and no one voted in favor of retention, the judge would still be retained. The proposed amendment, titled Nonpartisan Selection of Judges, was submitted to the electorate, along with seven other proposed constitutional amendments, at a special election scheduled in September 1951 for the specific purpose of voting on the eight amendments.

Fewer than 37,000 voters cast ballots, and this dropped to less than 35,000 on the judicial amendment. All eight amendments were rejected, with the judicial selection amendment fairing the worst of all: only 37 percent of voters were in favor. The defeat of the proposed judicial amendment was attributed in significant part to opposition from Latino voters. Opponents argued that if the amendment were approved, Latinos "might expect no more representation on the bench."[15] Several Latino officeholders, including a US senator, a US representative, and the state attorney general, came out in opposition. Additional opposition flowed from the provision added by the legislature that if less than a majority of voters casting ballots in the overall election cast ballots in the judicial retention election, a majority voting not to retain would leave the judge in office. One newspaper columnist pointed out

[15] Winters, "The New Mexico Judicial Selection Campaign," *supra* note 13, 169–170.

that over forty years of statehood, only four "questions" asking for a yes or no (constitutional amendments, referenda, bond issues, and other special questions) on the ballot at general elections attracted votes from 50 percent or more of those casting ballots in the overall election. There were also objections that the membership of the nominating commissions gave too much power over the selection process to lawyers. It was after the defeat of the Nonpartisan Selection of Judges amendment that the sitting governor, Republican Ed Mechem, who had been a strong supporter of the amendment, instituted the practice of voluntarily using a nominating commission and selecting only from those persons nominated by the commission for his appointees; all governors who came after him over the next thirty-six years adopted this practice.

The issue of changing judicial selection/retention mechanisms arose again in the 1960s. In 1963, at the governor's request, the legislature approved the creation of a Constitutional Revision Commission (CRC) to consider "essential changes" in the constitution. About a year after its creation, the CRC recommended items for immediate attention, including calling a constitutional convention, extending the CRC for two years, and making several specific constitutional changes. It was granted the requested two-year extension.[16] In its report, the CRC recommended extensive rewriting of the state constitution. One of its specific recommendations was to adopt a Missouri Plan system for judicial selection and retention. The nominating commissions would consist of three lawyers elected by the bar; three laypersons appointed by the governor; and the chief justice, who would serve as chair. The chief justice would be empowered to make the appointment if the governor failed to do so within sixty days of receiving the list from the nominating commission. Magistrates would be appointed by the chief justice and would be subject to retention elections.[17]

In 1967, the legislature sent the question of whether to call a constitutional convention to the voters. The voters approved the convention by more than 2 to 1. The convention convened on August 5, 1969, the date set by an Enabling Act passed by the legislative earlier that year. At the convention, the judicial committee supported the adoption of an appointive system, but then divided 7 to 7 over whether such a system should be included among the proposed constitutional changes. The convention delegates then rejected the idea of making any changes to judicial selection, leaving in place the system of partisan elections.[18] However, as things worked out, it probably would not have mattered if the revised constitution had included a changed system of judicial selection and retention, because when the proposed amendments document went to the voters

[16] Garcia et al., *Governing New Mexico, supra* note 2, 32–33.

[17] *Report of the Constitutional Revision Commission*, State of New Mexico (1967), 83–86.

[18] Eric D. Dixon, "A Short History of Judicial Reform in New Mexico," *Judicature* 48, no. 1 (June–July 1989), 48.

in a special election in December 1969, it was rejected by a hairsbreadth margin,[19] 3,702 votes out of 123,072 cast.[20]

In the early 1980s, the issue of eliminating partisan judicial elections again came to the forefront. The proposal coming out of the legislature in 1981 was for a constitutional amendment adopting a system with the basic elements of the Missouri Plan. Vacancies would be filled by the governor, who was constrained to appoint someone on a list forwarded by a nominating commission. Within three years of appointment and every four years thereafter, the judge would stand in a retention election; to retain office, the judge would need to receive a majority of those casting votes in the retention election. The already existing Judicial Standards Commission (JSC) would serve as the nominating commission, and would be charged with submitting to the governor "the names of *all* [emphasis added] persons qualified for the judicial office."[21] The JSC would also have the responsibility of evaluating judges standing for retention and making recommendations that would appear on the retention ballot beside each judge's name.[22] The nine-member JSC consisted of five laypersons appointed by the governor, two lawyers appointed by the Board of Commissioners of the state bar, and two judges appointed by the Supreme Court;[23] thus, a majority of the JSC were nonlawyers. The Senate approved the amendment 31–10 and the House 48–22.[24] Only one of the 48 Republican legislators voted against the amendment. In contrast, Democrats split virtually down the middle in both chambers, 21–20 against in the House and 11–10 in favor in the Senate.[25]

The proposal came before the voters in the fall of 1982. A coalition of groups including the League of Women Voters, Common Cause, and Court Update (a local citizens' group that monitored the New Mexico court system) worked to inform the electorate that the issue would be on the ballot and supported its passage.[26] Proponents argued that the then current system was largely a system of appointment, given that 40 of the 61 state judges initially obtained their positions by

[19] Garcia et al., *Governing New Mexico*, *supra* note 2, 36. Only about one–third of the eligible voters participated in the referendum.

[20] "It's Official Now: Constitution Failed; Final Tally Shows 63,387 Opposed, 59,685 For," *Alamogordo Daily News* (December 23, 1969), 1.

[21] This was in the text of the proposed constitutional amendment passed by the legislature in 1981. It can be found in Shirley Hooper, *Laws of the State of New Mexico, passed by the First Session of the Thirty-Fifth Legislature* (Portales, NM: Bishop Printing and Litho Co., 1981), 2213.

[22] Dixon, "A Short History of Judicial Reform in New Mexico," *supra* note 18, 48.

[23] James Brooks, "Missouri Plan Holds Promise for Selection New Mexico Judges," *Santa Fe New Mexican* (August 2, 1982), A6.

[24] Bill Feather, "Judge Proposal Advocate Says New System Superior," *Santa Fe New Mexican* (October 3, 1982), A14.

[25] These figures are from the House (p. 693) and Senate (p. 425) journals for 1982; one Democratic senator was absent.

[26] *Id.*

appointment and that the current system failed to put any restraint on whom the governor could appoint; proponents also pointed to the fact that with Democrats having held the governorship for the prior twelve years, only 3 of the 61 current judges were Republicans.[27] Supporters criticized the current system in which judges financed election campaigns using contributions from the lawyers who appeared before them.[28]

Substantial opposition also arose, including from some judges. A group calling itself the Save Your Right to Vote Committee ran ads urging a vote against the amendment.[29] One critic, a former state senator and unsuccessful gubernatorial candidate, labeled the amendment "Constitutional garbage"[30] and argued that it would not "eliminate partisan politics from judicial selection."[31] Critics were also concerned about the provision requiring the JSC to forward the names of "all persons qualified" for the position, in contrast to the system used in other states where the nominating commission forwarded a short list composed of what it judged to be the best candidates.[32] Voters turned down the proposed amendment with 117,601 in favor and 139,643 against.[33] Part of the reason may have been that Democrats were less supportive, given their success in dominating the New Mexico judiciary and that the Democrats swept the state elections for statewide offices in 1982.[34]

1988: *Success at Long Last*[35]

Sometime during 1987, or perhaps 1986, two district judges began thinking about a new push for a Missouri Plan system, at least for their district. Second District judges W. John Brennan and Rebecca Sitterly drafted a plan and submitted it to the legislature. After judges from other districts objected to the plan being limited to

[27] Bill Feather, "Amendment Would Alter Judicial Selection," *Albuquerque Journal* (October 31, 1982), A9.

[28] Peter Katel, "Merit Selection Debate Centers on Money, Power; Amendment Would Change Justice System," *Albuquerque Journal* (October 17, 1982), B1.

[29] See "Vote No on Constitutional Amendment No. 1; Save Your Right to Vote," *Albuquerque Journal* (October 31, 1982), E15.

[30] Bill Feather, "Judicial Expert Blasts Proposed State Amendment," *Santa Fe New Mexican* (September 26, 1982), A8; the former senator had extensive experience with judicial reform during his tenure in the Senate.

[31] Feather, "Amendment Would Alter Judicial Selection," *supra* note 27.

[32] *Id.*

[33] New Mexico Legislative Council Service, "Piecemeal Amendment of the Constitution of New Mexico Since 1911" (December 2016), 52, www.nmlegis.gov/Publications/New_Mexico_State_Government/Piecemeal_Amendment_Dec2016.pdf, accessed August 1, 2018.

[34] "Democrats Win Impressively in Statewide Executive Offices," *Albuquerque Journal* (November 3, 1982), A3.

[35] This section draws heavily on Romero, "Judicial Selection in New Mexico," *supra* note 5, 182–184, and Sarah Elizabeth Saucedo, "Majority Rules Except in New Mexico: Constitutional and Policy Concerns Raised by New Mexico's Supermajority Requirements for Judicial Retention," *Boston University Law Review* 86 (2006), 179–186.

the one district, it was modified to include all judicial districts. The plan attracted the support of the New Mexico District Judges Association (headed by Judge Brennan), plus the major supporters of the failed 1982 effort: Common Cause, the League of Women Voters, and Court Update. The plan as drafted called for a set of bipartisan nominating commissions all chaired by the dean of the University of New Mexico Law School (who was seen as being politically neutral), gubernatorial appointments from a list forwarded by a nominating commission, and retention elections requiring a simple majority for retention.

As drafted, the plan attracted significant opposition in the legislature. Despite concerns from one of the drafters, a compromise was agreed to by the Judges' Association that added a partisan election to the system. Specifically, a judge or justice appointed to fill a vacancy would be required to seek the nomination of a political party and stand in a partisan election at the first general election after the judge's appointment, potentially facing a candidate nominated by the other party. Also, the plan was expanded to include all state judges rather than just district court judges.

The compromise that added the element of an initial partisan election resembled a system first adopted by Illinois in 1962, and then by Pennsylvania in 1968. The history of the Illinois Plan has a lot of similarities to what happened in New Mexico. In 1958, Illinois voters defeated a proposal for a Missouri Plan system, with only 36 percent of voters supporting it. Two years later, the state bar again launched an effort to get a nonpolitical system of selection and retention.[36] When a proposal for a Missouri Plan system was introduced into the Illinois legislature in 1961 as part of an extensive rewriting of the state constitution's judicial article,[37] opposition came from Chicago mayor Richard Daley and the legislators associated with the Daley political machine. To meet Daley's objections, the supporters agreed to a system in which a judicial candidate or appointee had to first win a partisan election after having secured the nomination of a political party, either through a party primary or a party convention; judges would then seek subsequent terms through retention elections, needing 60 percent of the voters in favor in order to remain in office.[38] In Pennsylvania, the second state to adopt such a system,[39] only a 50 percent favorable vote is needed for retention. Illinois voters approved the new judicial article with its selection provisions in 1962, with 65.9 percent of the voters in favor.

The proposed New Mexico plan differed from those of Illinois and Pennsylvania in an important way: In New Mexico, all vacancies would in theory initially be filled by gubernatorial appointment, even in situations involving an incumbent who chose to leave office at the end of his or her term. In the other two states, if a judge served

36 Robert Howard, "Bar Launches New Drive for Court Reform; It Backs Judicial Article Passage," *Chicago Daily Tribune* (September 24, 1960), A10.

37 See Harry G. Fins, "Analysis of Illinois Judicial Article of 1961 and Its Legislative and Judicial Implementation," *DePaul Law Review* 11 (1962), 185–255.

38 "O.K. Judicial Reform for Blue Ballot," *Chicago Daily Tribune* (July 2, 1961), 1, 2.

39 See Chapter 13.

out his or her term, there was an open-seat partisan election. In New Mexico, the governor would make an appointment whenever there was a judicial vacancy. This would occur when a judge resigned, retired, or died. In the cases of judges who were leaving office at the end of their terms, either a judge who had previously been elected or a judge who was not retained in office by the voters, their service would end on December 31, and the position would become vacant on January 1. The nominating commission would then make recommendations to the governor within the required period, and the governor would make an appointment from among those recommended.[40]

With the addition of the initial partisan election, the legislature approved submitting the plan to the voters as a constitutional amendment. In 1988, when this was happening, the New Mexico Senate was controlled by a conservative coalition of Republicans and conservative Democrats that was an on-again, off-again feature of legislative politics in New Mexico during this period; the last time around in 1981–1982, the conservative coalition had controlled the New Mexico House.[41] The vote in both chambers was strongly in favor: 33 to 7 in the Senate and 50 to 18 in the House; 20 of the 25 negative votes across the two chambers came from Democratic legislators.

There were several other important differences between the 1982 and 1988 versions. Probably the most important was that, rather than using the Judicial Standards Commission as the nominating commission, there would be a commission for the statewide appellate courts and separate commissions for each of the judicial districts.[42] The membership of the commissions would be diverse, with appointees including: justices or judges; the dean of the University of New Mexico School of Law (serving as chair and voting only to break a tie vote); four members of the state bar representing different areas of court practice (civil, criminal prosecution, and criminal defense) appointed by the president of the state bar and the judges on the commission; and three lawyers and three laypersons, with one of each designated by the governor, by the Speaker of the House of Representatives, and by the president pro tempore of the Senate. In addition, the appointments were to be made in such a way that the two largest political parties would have equal representation on each commission; the president of the state bar and the judges on a commission were empowered to make additional appointments if needed to achieve that balance.

There were five other noteworthy differences. First, the commission was not required to forward "the names of all persons qualified for the judicial office," but only "the names of persons qualified for judicial office and recommended for

[40] In practice, if a vacancy is coming up after December 31, the nominating commission may forward nominations to the governor prior to when the vacancy actually occurs, so that the vacancy can be filled immediately.

[41] See en.wikipedia.org/wiki/Political_party_strength_in_New_Mexico, accessed August 2, 2018.

[42] The language of the amendment referred to the district-level nominating bodies as "committees"; for simplicity I refer to all of the nominating bodies as "commissions."

appointment to that office by a majority of the commission." Second, the governor could, after receiving the initial list from the commission, make one request asking the commission to submit additional names. Third, if the governor failed to make an appointment within thirty days after receiving the nominations (or thirty days after receiving the additional nominations if requested), the chief justice would make the appointment; there had been no such provision in the 1982 version. Fourth, the 1982 version had included a provision that the nominating body, the Judicial Standards Board, would also evaluate each judge coming up for retention and make a recommendation regarding retention that would appear on the ballot; the 1988 proposal included nothing similar. Finally, there was no minimum or maximum number of names that had to be forwarded to the governor, meaning that the commission could, in theory, forward a single name; in the 1982 proposal, the language implied that at least two names had to be sent to the governor ("by appointing one of two or more persons nominated . . .").[43]

There were significant campaigns in support of and in opposition to the proposed amendment. A bipartisan group called People for Judicial Reform sought to frame the issue as isolating the judiciary from partisan politics and eliminating the problem that the judicial ethics restrictions resulted in uninformative election campaigns.[44] Proponents argued that the new system would replace political skills with an emphasis on competence, thereby producing more qualified judges. It would eliminate the threat to judicial impartiality created by the need to raise money and wage a campaign; it also provided an element of judicial accountability to the citizens through the retention elections.[45] The two largest newspapers in the state, the *Albuquerque Journal* and the *Santa Fe New Mexican*, endorsed the proposal.[46] Surprisingly, the New Mexico Bar Association chose to stay neutral rather than support the proposed amendment.[47]

The primary focus of the opposition was that "democracy requires selection of public officials, including judges, by the people in open elections,"[48] and the

[43] There was also a provision that did not exist in the 1982 version for what was referred to as a "grandfather clause"; under this provision, any judge already in office as of January 1 following the election adopting the amendment was deemed to have fulfilled the requirement of having to stand in a partisan election. This meant that judges who had already been elected in a partisan election and those who had been appointed too late to have stood in partisan election at the last date such elections were held would have to stand only in retention elections.

[44] Bill Feather, "Amendment Proposes Merit System," *Albuquerque Journal* (October 2, 1988), C6; see also the newspaper advertisement it ran shortly before the election, "Who's Judging the Judges," *Albuquerque Journal* (November 6, 1988), A4, and in the *Santa Fe New Mexican* (November 6, 1988), C9.

[45] Romero, "Judicial Selection in New Mexico," *supra* note 5, 183.

[46] *Id.*, 184.

[47] Coleman Cornelius, "Politics and the Courtroom." My guess is that the decision to remain neutral reflected opposition to the change from some segments of the bar, such as plaintiffs' lawyers.

[48] *Id.*

proposed system limited the public's input. This is the standard critique advanced by opponents of the Missouri Plan system when it is proposed in a state using partisan or nonpartisan elections. The opposition to the amendment came from several sectors. The most prominent opponent was Tony Scarborough, the chief justice of New Mexico. He argued that the system created what amounted to lifetime judgeships, presumably because it was so rare for an incumbent to lose a retention election. He also argued that politics would not be taken out of the process but would put it in the hands of a "private committee" rather than in a "public forum."[49] Another argument raised by opponents was that there was no empirical evidence from the experience of other states that the proposed system would produce better quality judges than the existing system.[50] Scarborough was joined in opposition by two of his four Supreme Court colleagues,[51] a retired Supreme Court justice,[52] and at least a half a dozen district court judges who signed an advertisement opposing the amendment.[53] There was also opposition from some prominent members of the criminal defense bar.[54] HALT (Help Abolish Legal Tyranny), a legal reform organization with a history of being critical of lawyers,[55] also published ads in opposition.[56]

The voters approved the amendment with 56 percent in favor. The amendment carried in 19 of New Mexico's 33 counties.[57] However, the election did not end the debate over the amendment. In an effort to stop the amendment from going into effect, an appellate judge and a trial judge who had opposed the amendment filed a petition for writ of mandamus, asserting that there were constitutional defects in the process leading to the vote on the amendment.[58] First, the state constitution did not permit lawmakers to consider constitutional amendments during sessions held in even-numbered years because, the two judges asserted, those sessions were supposed to be limited to state finance or to specific proposals from the governor. Second, the amendment was improper because it lumped several changes into a single amendment that should have been presented to the voters as separate questions.[59]

49 Feather, "Amendment Proposes Merit System," *supra* note 44.

50 Dixon, "A Short History of Judicial Reform in New Mexico," supra note 18, 49.

51 Romero, "Judicial Selection in New Mexico," *supra* note 5, 183.

52 "Vote No" [advertisement], *Santa Fe New Mexican* (November 6, 1988), E5.

53 *Id.*

54 Saucedo, "Majority Rules Except in New Mexico," *supra* note 35, 183.

55 See Doris Marie Provine, *Judging Credentials: Nonlawyer Judges and the Politics of Professionalism* (Chicago, IL: University of Chicago Press, 1986), 179; Mary Collins, "The Wrong Side of the Lawyers," *Washington Post* (January 26, 1992), www.washingtonpost.com/archive/opinions/1992/01/26/the-wrong-side-of-the-lawyers/72c32906-2f86-46fc-9578-4b6ba3e0b0a6/?utm_term=.691bdbfe645c, accessed August 3, 2018.

56 "Halt Amendment 6," *Santa Fe New Mexican* (November 6, 1988), A5.

57 Dixon, "A Short History of Judicial Reform in New Mexico," *supra* note 18, 49.

58 *Id.*, 49–50.

59 "Judges to Hear Judicial Reform Arguments Today," *Albuquerque Journal* (November 30, 1988), A5.

Because four of the justices who had taken positions on the amendment recused themselves to avoid the appearance of impropriety, the case was decided by a court composed of one Supreme Court justice and four district court judges designated to hear the case. About three weeks after hearing arguments in the case, the court rejected the petitioners' claims, allowing the amendment to take effect on January 1, 1989.[60]

JUDICIAL ELECTIONS UNDER THE NEW SYSTEM

Tinkering with the System and Efforts to Change Again

Some of those who had opposed the constitutional amendment continued to be dissatisfied with the new arrangements. One prominent concern was the difficulty in removing a judge through the retention election process. In 1994, a group of attorneys, prominently including some of the leaders of the criminal defense bar, sought to get the percentage required for retention raised.[61] Rather than 50 percent for retention, they wanted to require 65 percent.[62] Not surprisingly, judges "feverishly opposed increasing the margin to such a high threshold, fearing it would require judges to wage intense campaigns" in order to be retained.[63] One of the original backers of the 1988 change, Judge John Brennan, brokered a compromise for a 57 percent requirement. An amendment to this effect was submitted to the voters in 1994; it passed with 57 percent voting in favor.

Between 1989 and 2000, proposals to place before the voters a constitutional amendment restoring partisan judicial elections and scrapping the elements of the Missouri Plan adopted in 1988 were introduced in every legislative session. In 1997, one of those proposals was overwhelmingly passed by the New Mexico Senate, 31–3, attracting bipartisan support. Senators from both parties argued that the new system had failed to take politics out of the process. Republican senator William Davis, one of the supporters of returning to partisan elections, argued that the nominating commission process "helped give Democrats a lock on most judgeships."[64] Among the three senators voting against the proposal was the leader of the Senate Democratic majority. At the same time, there was a competing proposal backed by Republicans under consideration in the House; it would have removed constraints on whom the governor could appoint but would subject those appointments to confirmation by the Senate. That proposal cleared at least one of

60 State, *ex rel.* Chavez v. Vigil-Giron, 766P.2d 305 (N.M. 1988).

61 Saucedo, "Majority Rules Except in New Mexico," *supra* note 35, 184.

62 The only state using retention elections that requires more than a simple majority for retention is Illinois, where 60 percent is required; see www.judicialselection.us/judicial_selection/methods/selection_of_judges.cfm?state=IL, accessed August 2, 2018.

63 Saucedo, "Majority Rules Except in New Mexico," *supra* note 35, 184.

64 "Judge-Selection System May Change," *Santa Fe New Mexican* (March 9, 1997), B5.

the necessary House committees.[65] Ultimately, there was no floor action on either proposal in the House, with the House Speaker saying that such proposals could wait to be considered in 1998 because a proposal passing the legislature could not go to the voters before November 1998; however, no proposals emerged from the 1998 legislative session.

The system created in 1988, with the change to a 57 percent requirement for retention, remains in place.[66] Sometime after 2000, the introduction of legislation to change the selection tapered off. The Gavel-to-Gavel database lists only two proposals between 2008 and 2018 that called for a constitutional amendment that would change the current partisan election to a nonpartisan election format; both retained the other elements of the current system. Neither proposal introduced in 2015 and 2017 reached the floor of either chamber.

Election Patterns since 1990

A 2002 journal article provided a summary of election results during the first ten years of the operation of the new system. During that period, three governors made a total of 81 appointments across various court levels,[67] including the limited jurisdiction Bernalillo County Metropolitan Court;[68] 7 of the appointments were to the Supreme Court, 7 to the Court of Appeals, 52 to the district courts, and 15 to the metropolitan court.[69] Two Republican governors made a total of 51 appointments and the one Democratic governor during the period made 30.[70] These three governors differed substantially in the degree to which they chose appointees from their own parties. Republican governor Gary Carruthers made 14 appointments in the two years he was in office after the new system came into operation; 10 (71 percent) of his appointees were Republicans. Democratic governor Bruce King, who followed Carruthers, made 30 appointments during his four years in office, 28 (93 percent) going to Democrats. In his first four years in office, Republican governor Gary Johnson made 37 appointments, only 19 (51 percent) of which went to Republicans.

In the five general elections between 1990 and 1998, there were 80 appointees who did stand or could have stood in the partisan election that followed

65 "Judicial Races Might Resume; Amendment Would Scrap Merit System," *Albuquerque Journal* (March 9, 1997), A1.

66 See http://gaveltogavel.us/database/, accessed August 3, 2018.

67 Romero, "Judicial Selection in New Mexico," *supra* note 5, 202.

68 Bernalillo County is the most populous county in the state and includes Albuquerque. The court hears tort, contract, and landlord/tenant cases involving $10,000 or less, plus domestic violence, traffic violations including DWI/DUI, and misdemeanors; it also handles first appearances in felony cases. See https://nmcourts.gov/about-the-courts.aspx, accessed August 4, 2018.

69 Romero, "Judicial Selection in New Mexico," *supra* note 5, 202.

70 *Id.*, 203.

appointment.[71] Only 58 of the appointees remained in office after the partisan election. Of the 22 who did not continue, 19 had sought election; 9 lost in the primary, 9 lost in the general elections, and 1 was not nominated by the party committee. Three others chose not to run, either not filing a declaration of candidacy or resigning before the election.[72] Retention elections began in 1990, both for judges on the bench prior to January 1, 1989, when the new system went into effect, and for judges appointed or elected under the new system, all of whom had stood once in a partisan election. Through 1998, two judges failed to be retained, both after the percentage needed for retention had been increased to 57 percent; both had taken office under the old system. Only 31 judges who had come to office under the new system had stood in a retention election by 1998; all were retained.

I compiled information on judicial elections in New Mexico between 1990 and 2016. I summarize the patterns for the three levels of courts.

Supreme Court

Between 1990 and 2018, there were 12 partisan elections for the New Mexico Supreme Court, 10 of which were contested.[73] Under the provisions of the 1988 amendments, these elections all involved candidates who had not previously been elected to the Court. The two unopposed candidates were Democrats, and Democrats won 9 of the 10 contested elections. Republican incumbents lost 3 of the general elections, and an incumbent appointed by Republican governor Gary Johnson, but running as a Democrat, lost the Democratic primary. The one Republican appointee who won the partisan election was Judith Nakamura, and that was not until 2016.

In principle, all 12 elections should have involved an incumbent. However, due to a quirk in the system, no incumbent ran in 2 of the elections, and there was no incumbent in the general election for a third election. In 2 of those 3 elections, the incumbent was Dan McKinnon. When an appointment is made too late for the appointee to run in a party primary, the two parties' central committees name the candidates to run in November. In 1996, McKinnon was appointed by Republican governor Gary Johnson even though he was at least nominally a Democrat; he was shunned by the Democratic Party's committee, which chose District Judge Patricio Serna, who went on to win in November. Johnson appointed McKinnon to a second vacancy that arose in 1997, but McKinnon then lost the 1998 Democratic primary to Judge Petra Maes, who went on to win in November, becoming the first Hispana to serve on a state supreme court. The third situation occurred in 2002 when the appointment was not made until after the parties had named their candidates, and the appointee had not been named by either party committee.

[71] One of the 81 appointees was appointed too late to run in the 1998 election; *id.*, 207.

[72] *Id.*

[73] Given the partisan ballots in these elections, the voting patterns were highly partisan. The average partisan correlation for the nine contested elections was .91.

The first Supreme Court retention election occurred in 1994. Through 2018, there were fourteen such elections. The percent of voters supporting retention averaged 73.3 and ranged from a low of 66.1 to a high of 77.9. Given that each incumbent running in the retention elections had previously won an election as a Democrat, it's not surprising that there was often a sizeable partisan correlation,[74] ranging from .352 to .807, with an average of .581. However, although such a correlation existed, the county-to-county variation in the percent supporting retention was usually modest, and there were only a small number of examples of less than 50 percent in a county voting in favor of retention.

Court of Appeals

Between 1990 and 2018, there were twenty-two vacancies on the Court of Appeals. All but one of those vacancies were initially filled by appointment. The one exception came in 2000 when, four weeks before the November election, Governor Gary Johnson had not yet named one of the two nominated candidates to the position. At that point, the nominating commission asked the governor to hold off making the appointment and thereby allow the voters to decide. One of the persons nominated by the commission was the Democratic candidate for the position,[75] and she then won the election. Of the twenty-one persons appointed to the Court of Appeals, half were Democrats and half Republicans.

There were 22 partisan elections for the Court of Appeals between 1990 and 2018. The one open-seat election was won by the Democratic candidate. All 21 appointees ran to keep their seats. Nineteen of the elections were contested by both Democrats and Republicans, one election was contested only in the Democratic primary, and one was uncontested. All 8 incumbents running as Democrats won. In contrast, incumbents running as Republicans had mixed success, losing 9 of their 12 elections. In the 2000 elections, 3 Republican incumbents, all males, were running, but only 1 of them held onto his seat on the court; the 2 successful Democratic challengers were women. In 2018, 4 Republican incumbents were running; they all lost.

There were 21 retention elections for the Court of Appeals between 1990 and 2018. The incumbents were retained in all 21, with an average of 74.4 percent favoring retention.[76] In only two elections did that percentage fall below 70 percent: 69.1 percent in 2010 for Celia Foy Castillo and 69.4 percent in 2018 for J. Miles Hanissee.

[74] See Chapter 1 for the definition of "partisan correlation."

[75] Wren Proff, "Gov. Asked to Hold Off on Judge," *Albuquerque Journal* (October 10, 2000), C3. The governor holding off on the appointment would push into the time when the appointment would fall to the chief justice; the commission also urged the chief justice not to make an appointment if the governor decided to wait for the election.

[76] The official summary for the 1998 elections did not include information on three retention elections. The calculation in the text relies on a news report of unofficial statewide results; see "And the Winners Are . . .," *Sangre De Cristo Chronicle* (November 12, 1998), 6.

District Courts

Obtaining information on the incumbency status of the persons running in the partisan elections for district court judge presents problems because lists of the judges appointed by each governor are not readily available and incumbency status is not indicated on the election results published by the Secretary of State's office. From that published information, one can determine the number of elections, the percentage contested, and the outcome in terms of the party of the successful candidate. Between 1990 and 2016, there were 174 partisan elections for the district court, 43.1 percent of which were contested. Democrats won 57.3 percent of the contested elections. In the uncontested elections, the sole candidate was a Democrat in 71.0 percent of the elections, and a Republican in the remaining 29.0 percent. The overall result was the election of a Democrat in 65.5 percent of the partisan elections for the district court.

I located a list of 45 district court judges appointed by Republican governor Susana Martinez between 2011 and 2017.[77] Given the timing of their appointments, 40 of the appointees were eligible to stand in the partisan elections held between 2012 and 2016; one chose to resign rather than run for the position. Of the 39 who sought to retain their positions, 25 were Republicans and 14 were Democrats. All Republican incumbents secured their party's nomination; in 14 elections they had no Democratic opponent. In the 11 contested elections, the Republican incumbents won 6 and lost 5; one of the Republicans who lost his partisan election was then appointed to another open position and ran unopposed in the following partisan election. The picture was quite different for the Democrats appointed by Republican governor Martinez. Four of her fourteen Democratic appointees failed to be nominated by the party; one lost the Democratic primary, and three who had been appointed too late for the primary were not chosen by the Democratic Central Committee. Eleven Democratic appointees ran in the partisan general election following their appointment; nine were unopposed and two defeated Republican challengers. Two of those who were unopposed in the November election had previously been appointed but not selected by the Democratic Central Committee.

District court judges serve six-year terms, all of which run concurrently. This means that all district court judges who have previously stood in partisan elections stand for retention at the same time. District court retention elections took place first in 1990, then in 1996, 2002, 2008, and 2014. Between 1990 and 2016, there were 303 retention elections for district court judges. Only five failed to be retained, two in 1996, one in 2002, and two in 2014. All the nonretentions occurred after the threshold had been increased to 57 percent in 1994. All but one of the nonretained

[77] See https://ballotpedia.org/Judges_appointed_by_Susana_Martinez, accessed August 7, 2018. According to the website, this list was generated automatically using Google News; there is no guarantee that it is complete, but the number of appointments over 6 years looks about right.

judges did have a simple majority in support of retention; the one with less than a simple majority missed 50 percent by a single vote: 1,883 yes, 1,885 no. Two of the nonretained judges missed the 57 percent threshold for retention by a slim margin, 329 votes out of 18,199 cast in one case and 609 votes out of 53,620 votes cast in the other case. If the higher threshold had been in effect in 1990, three additional judges would not have been retained, one by a mere 71 votes.

In 1999, through an order of the New Mexico Supreme Court, a Judicial Performance Evaluation Commission (JPEC) was created and charged with evaluating judges and justices standing for retention. Through 2018, it had conducted a total of 198 evaluations in advance of three rounds of district court retention elections.[78] The JPEC issued positive recommendations for 180 judges, offered no recommendation for 15, and recommended that 3 not be retained.[79] Two judges with negative recommendation lost their retention bid; the third easily survived, with 67.3 percent of the voters in her district favoring retention. Sheri Raphaelson, one of the two judges who received a negative recommendation, was the judge who fell short of the 57 percent requirement by just 609 votes.

Interesting developments followed in the aftermath of two nonretentions that occurred in 2014. After the election, Raphaelson announced that she intended to remain in her position. She claimed that her retention election should not have been held in 2014 because she should have had a six-year term starting after she won the 2010 partisan election following her appointment in 2009.[80] In late November, the New Mexico attorney general's office filed a writ with the New Mexico Supreme Court, asking that Raphaelson be compelled to leave office on December 31, when her term ended.[81] The Court heard oral arguments regarding her claim in mid-December and issued a ruling at the hearing itself, rejecting Raphaelson's assertions and ordering her to vacate her position on December 31.[82]

The second nonretained judge was Albert Mitchell. Mitchell had been recommended for retention by the JPEC. He was the presiding judge in a single-judge district in eastern New Mexico.[83] A committee calling itself the Committee for Law and Order launched a campaign opposing retention, running newspaper advertisements and sending mailings to voters labeling Mitchell as too lenient on criminals

78 The evaluations are posted at www.nmjpec.org/en/, accessed August 7, 2018. A brief history of the JPEC is available at that website.

79 All JPEC evaluations for the Supreme Court and the Court of Appeals recommended retention.

80 Phaedra Haywood, "Voter-Ousted Judge Vows to Remain on Bench to 2016," *Santa Fe New Mexican* (November 7, 2014), A1.

81 Phaedra Haywood, "AGH's Office Asks High Court to Remove Judge," *Santa Fe New Mexican* (November 25, 2014), A6.

82 Milan Simonich, "State Supreme Court Rules Against Raphaelson," *Santa Fe New Mexican* (December 16, 2014), A6; State *ex rel.* King v. Raphaelson, 356 P.3d 1096 (N.M. 2015).

83 "Attorney Opposes Ousted Judge's Intent to Re-apply," *Eastern New Mexico News* (November 12, 2014), www.easternnewmexiconews.com/story/2014/11/12/publishnews/attorney-opposes-ousted-judges-intent-to-re-apply/119620.html?m=false, accessed August 7, 2018.

and slow in making decisions. The chair of that committee was the father of an individual who had been severely beaten by a man that Mitchell had released from jail.[84] As a result of that campaign, Mitchell failed to come close to the 57 percent required to be retained. After the retention election, the Judicial Nominating Commission (JNC) for the district convened to assess candidates and make recommendations to the governor.[85] Mitchell applied for what would soon be his old position. One quirk in the nominating process was that a judge of the district was required to be a member of the district JNC. As the only judge in the district, this meant that Mitchell himself would normally be on the JNC; however, he asked to be removed from the JNC.[86] Only one person in addition to Mitchell, Don Schutte, applied for the position; Schutte had been appointed to the position in 2007, but had been defeated by Mitchell in the following partisan election in 2008. The district JNC recommended both Mitchell and Schutte to the governor, and the governor selected Mitchell. Shortly after Mitchell took office in January 2015 as the now new appointee to his own former judicial position, a local attorney acting for the committee that had opposed Mitchell's retention filed an emergency petition asking the New Mexico Supreme Court to nullify the appointment. The Court ordered Judge Mitchell not to hear cases until it reached a decision.[87] After hearing arguments a few days later, the Court unanimously rejected the petition, with the chief justice noting that there is no legal bar to a nominating commission considering a candidate who is qualified for the position even if the candidate had previously failed to be retained.[88]

CONCLUSION

The most common argument against Missouri Plan type selection and retention systems raised by opponents is that it denies voters the opportunity to choose judges, handing that over to various groups of elites. In New Mexico, there were several unsuccessful efforts, including two rejections by the voters, to pass constitutional amendments creating such a system. In 1988, the New Mexico legislature put before the voters a system that enhanced the role of voters, versions of which had been

[84] Thomas J. Cole, "Bounced Judge Tries to Bound Back," *Albuquerque Journal* (December 8, 2014), 1, 4, www.abqjournal.com/507189/state-district-judge-bounced-in-election-trying-to-bounce-back.html, accessed August 7, 2018.

[85] Larry T. Aspin, "Judicial Retention Elections," in Chris W. Bonneau and Melinda Gann Hall, eds., Judicial Elections in the 21st Century, (New York: Routledge, 2017), 116.

[86] "Attorney Opposes Ousted Judge's Intent to Re-apply," *supra* note 83.

[87] "Judge Ordered to Wait for Hearing," *Eastern New Mexico News* (January 13, 2015), www.easternnewmexiconews.com/story/2015/01/13/publishnews/judge-ordered-to-wait-for-hearing/4859.html, accessed August 7, 2018.

[88] "New Mexico Court Rejects Petition over Judicial Appointment," *Albuquerque Journal* (January 19, 2015), www.abqjournal.com/528382/new-mexico-court-rejects-petition-over-judicial-appointment-2.html, accessed August 7, 2018; see also Clark v. Mitchell, 363 P.3d 1213 (N.M. 2015).

adopted in two other states, Illinois and Pennsylvania. Despite significant opposition, including from some high-ranking judges, voters approved the system. Overall, the driving force for change in New Mexico was that which I label the "legal subculture."

Nonetheless, there was a partisan element to both the 1982 and the 1988 legislative votes on the constitutional amendment. In 1982, all Republicans supported the Missouri Plan proposal while Democrats were split down the middle. In 1988, most Republicans supported the revised plan. This time a majority of Democrats did so as well; however, a significant minority of Democrats voted against the proposed amendment. The support both times from Republicans is unsurprising, given the difficulty Republican appointees often had in surviving the partisan elections after their appointment; the fact that there was a bit more Republican opposition in 1988 probably reflects a concern that retaining the initial partisan elections would serve to continue the disadvantage that Republicans faced in such elections. The opposition from some Democrats is also not surprising because of the success Democratic candidates often had in defeating Republican appointees; it is also likely that opposition from groups that typically supported Democratic legislators, such as the plaintiffs' bar, convinced some Democrats to vote against putting the 1988 amendment on the ballot, even though it did require appointees to run in a partisan election the first time they faced the voters, with subsequent elections using a retention ballot. The fact that a majority of Democrats did support the proposal probably reflects a genuine belief that the proposed system combining appointment from a nominating commission list, an initial partisan election after appointment, and retention for future terms through retention elections was likely to produce better appointments but would leave a reasonable opportunity to try to defeat appellate-level Republican appointees who were seen as problematic by Democrats.

10

Connecticut, Rhode Island, and South Carolina

Adding "Merit" to Nonelective Systems

The other chapters have focused on states that use some form of popular election to select and/or retain judges. In this chapter, I turn to three states – Connecticut, Rhode Island, and South Carolina – that do not use popular elections in either the selection or retention process but that made significant changes in their nonelectoral processes. All three states made changes that constrained the selecting authority by requiring that the selection be made from a list of candidates forwarded by a nominating commission, a process referred to by supporters as "merit selection." The systems of the three states differ from one another. In Rhode Island and South Carolina, scandals involving judges selected through the then existing system were important precipitating factors that led to the changes. In Connecticut, the change came about as part of a broader effort to modernize the state court system, although even there, the occurrence of a couple of scandals involving trial judges served to highlight the method of selection as an area needing reform.

In the sections that follow, I discuss the change in each of these three states. The discussions are much briefer than for the other states that have had major changes.

CONNECTICUT

Background

During the first half of the twentieth century, the Republican Party dominated Connecticut politics. Although there were periods of Democratic success (e.g., during the 1930s) in winning the governorship and gaining control of the Senate, Republicans were continuously in control of the Connecticut House of Representatives from 1877 until 1959, when the Democrats briefly secured a three-seat majority; Republicans regained control in 1961 and held it for another six years. The Republican dominance in the House was due to apportionment rules that provided a single representative for each municipality regardless of size. This ended in the wake of U.S. Supreme Court decisions in the 1960s mandating "one person, one vote."[1] Democrats started winning the governorship in the 1950s and became dominant in the Senate by the end of that decade.[2] Since the implementation of one person, one vote with the 1966 election, Democrats have been the dominant party, with Republicans controlling the House only for a single two-year period (1973–1974).[3]

With the ascendance of the Democratic Party, John Bailey became the dominant figure in Connecticut politics. He became chair of the Connecticut Democratic Party in 1946[4] and, along with Abraham Ribicoff, a key figure in the revival of the party. Although never elected to public office, Bailey went on to play a central role in statewide election campaigns and in the actions of the state legislature, and he effectively controlled patronage appointments including judgeships.[5] Even while serving as chair of the Democratic National Committee (1961–1968),[6] he remained the dominant force in Connecticut politics,[7] and that continued until his death in 1975.

One important feature of Connecticut government is the degree of independence of the courts specifically named in the state constitution, the "constitutional courts." In addition to controlling the appointment of staff such as clerks and messengers, the constitutional courts appointed prosecutors (state's attorneys) and public defenders, a role the courts jealously guarded.[8] The courts lost some of this power with the adoption of a state constitutional amendment in 1984 allowing the legislature to determine how the chief state's attorney would be selected and establishing a system of appointment commissions to select the state's attorney for each judicial district.[9] It is possible that the establishment of these appointment commissions for state attorneys set part of the stage for creating a judicial nominating commission.

1 See Baker v. Carr, 369 U.S. 186 (1962); Reynolds v. Sims, 377 U.S. 533 (1964).

2 Between 1959 and 2019, Republicans controlled the Senate for only 6 years; during another 2 years, the Senate was equally divided. Republicans have had more success winning the governorship, but held complete control for only 2 years between 1955 and 2019. See https://en.wikipedia.org/wiki/Political_party_strength_in_Connecticut, accessed November 29, 2018.

3 After the 1964 Supreme Court decision mandating one person, one vote for both chambers of state legislature, Connecticut canceled the 1964 legislative election, presumably because of an inability to accomplish the mandated redistricting; see Robert S. Erikson, "The Partisan Impact of State Legislative Reapportionment," *Midwest Journal of Political Science* 15, No. 1 (February 1971), 63.

4 Joseph I. Lieberman, *The Power Broker: A Biography of John M. Bailey, Modern Political Boss* (Boston, MA: Houghton Mifflin Company, 1966), 103.

5 Telephone interview with Jim Wade, November 26, 2018; see also Lieberman, *The Power Broker, supra* note 4, 217–218.

6 He obtained this position after playing a major role in the election of John Kennedy to the presidency in 1960; see *id.*, 247–259.

7 *Id.*, 260–271.

8 See Adams v. Rubinow, 251 A.2d 49, 58 n.4 (1968).

9 The members of the appointment commissions included the chief state's attorney and 6 additional members appointed by the governor subject to legislative confirmation; 2 of the 6 members had to be judges of the superior court. See Connecticut Constitution, Article XXIII.

As of 1980, judicial selection in Connecticut was governed by Article V, Section 2 as amended by Article XX, Section 2 of the state constitution:

> The judges of the supreme court, of the appellate court and of the superior court shall, upon nomination by the governor, be appointed by the general assembly in such manner as shall by law be prescribed. They shall hold their offices for the term of eight years. . .

Section 6 of the same article set age 70 as the mandatory retirement age for all judges. Sitting judges could be reappointed for additional terms. Although in the language of the constitution, the legislature appointed judges, effectively the legislature's role was to confirm the governor's nominees. By statute, a person nominated by the governor could take office as an "interim judge," pending the vote in each chamber of the legislature. Except for judges of probate, the same selection procedure applied to lower court judges, but for a term of only four years; probate court judges were elected by district, with the form of the election unspecified.

During the period between 1946 and the adoption in 1986 of a "merit selection" process that constrained whom the governor could nominate, Democrats held the governor's office for 30 years compared to only 11 years for Republicans. During this period, Democrats controlled the Senate 33 of the 41 years while Republicans controlled the House for 23 years. Although Democrats were generally stronger, having complete control (governor, Senate, and House) 16 years compared to only 6 for Republicans, the overall pattern suggests a reasonably competitive state.[10]

In the system that existed circa 1972, most persons appointed as judges had "in some way been active politically."[11] Democrats held the governorship 16 of 22 years between 1949 and 1971, but in only 11 of those 22 years did the party of the governor control both chambers of the state legislature. As of approximately January 1, 1972, those serving as judges in Connecticut included 74 Democrats, 36 Republicans, and 6 persons who were registered as Independents or for whom a party affiliation could not be determined.[12] Two Democratic governors appointed 27 of the 36 Republicans. One of those Democrats faced a Republican-controlled House of

[10] These figures are from https://en.wikipedia.org/wiki/Political_party_strength_in_Connecticut, accessed September 30, 2018. Between 1987 and 2018, Democrats have been more dominant, particularly in the legislature, where the Republicans had control of the Senate for only 2 years and shared control with Democrats a second two-year period when there were equal numbers of senators from the two parties. Republicans did not control the Connecticut House at all during that period. Even so, Democrats have had complete control, including holding the governorship, for only 10 of the 32 years, because Republicans have held the governorship for 16 years, or 20 if one includes Lowell Weicker, who was a liberal Republican for 18 years as a U.S. senator, but won the 1990 gubernatorial election running under the banner of the Connecticut Party, defeating both a Democrat and a Republican.

[11] "Final Report of the Commission to Study and Draft Legislation for the Reorganization and Unification of the Courts" (State of Connecticut, March 1, 1974), 60 [henceforth, "Connecticut Final Report"].

[12] *Id.*, 60 n. 4.

Representatives for 6 of his 10 years in office; the other Democrat had agreed to appoint a number of Republicans as judges of the new circuit court as part of the deal to replace municipal courts and justice of the peace courts with a state-supported circuit court.[13]

Reform Efforts

Constraining whom the governor could nominate required a constitutional amendment. In Connecticut amendments must be presented to the voters at even-numbered-year general elections and require the approval of the majority of those voting on the amendment. As is true in a majority of states,[14] the only way an amendment gets before the voters is by action of the legislature, and there are two different ways the legislature can send an amendment to the voters. If three-quarters of the total membership of each chamber vote in favor of an amendment, the amendment goes to the voters at the next general election. Alternatively, an amendment goes to the voters if a majority of the membership of each chamber votes in favor of the amendment in two consecutive legislatures (i.e., sessions separated by a general election).[15]

The first references I could find in Connecticut newspapers to "merit selection" as something that should be considered for adoption in the state was in 1971.[16] This report summarized an article published in 1970 in the *Connecticut Bar Journal* calling for an overhaul of Connecticut's courts and for the adoption of a system of merit selection for Connecticut judges.[17] The proposed system of merit selection would require that the governor nominate someone on a list submitted by a nonpartisan commission; the rest of the process would be unchanged, with the governor's nominee subject to "appointment" by a vote of the legislature. Unlike the Missouri Plan system, there would be no direct role for the electorate, either regarding selection or retention. Presumably, judges desiring to remain on the bench for an additional term would need to be renominated, first by the nominating commission and then by the governor, and again be "appointed" by a vote of the legislature. In May 1971, a "Citizens Conference" was held in Hartford; the conference considered "the need in Connecticut for the adoption of proposals concerning judicial selection, judicial behavior and court unification."[18] It issued a

13 "Connecticut Citizens for Judicial Modernization, First Report of the Joint Committee on Judicial Modernization" (Hartford: Connecticut Citizens for Judicial Modernization, 1972), 51.

14 See "Initiative and Referendum States," www.ncsl.org/research/elections-and-campaigns/chart-of-the-initiative-states.aspx, accessed October 25, 2018.

15 Connecticut Constitution, Article VI.

16 "Article Urges Elimination of Inferior Trial Courts," *Harford Courant* (January 18, 1971), 9. Note that my search was limited to newspapers archived by newspapers.com.

17 Peter L. Costas, "The 1970s: Will We Respond to the Need to Modernize Connecticut's Judicial System?" *Connecticut Bar Journal* 44, no. 4 (1970), 483–488.

18 "Consensus Statement of the Connecticut Citizens Conference, May 19–20, 1972, Hartford, Connecticut," *Connecticut Bar Journal* 54, no. 3 (1971), 320.

"consensus statement" with various proposals, the first of which called for merit selection of judges.[19]

The following year, a joint committee of the Connecticut Bar Association and an organization called Connecticut Citizens for Judicial Modernization published a 115-page report, the first recommendation of which was merit selection of judges.[20] In 1973, the Connecticut General Assembly created the Commission to Study and Draft Legislation for the Reorganization and Unification of the Courts. That Commission issued a report in March 1974 calling for a wide range of changes to the court system and judiciary, including some modification of the selection process as it was then operating.[21] It considered two variants of selection that involved a "merit commission." Although the Commission "approved the concept of a Merit Commission to improve the quality of judges,"[22] in the end it recommended only an enhanced role for the General Assembly's (Joint) Judiciary Committee in screening nominees after their nomination by the governor.[23]

It appears that legislative proposals for merit selection began being introduced in 1975,[24] and that year, the Connecticut Judicial Council called on the legislature to adopt a merit selection system for "nominating and appointing judges to state courts."[25] The Republican gubernatorial candidate in the 1974 election proposed a system of merit selection during the election campaign,[26] and a few days before the 1974 election, the former editor of the *Hartford Courant* published a long column advocating a selection system drawing on elements of the Missouri Plan.[27] The interest in merit selection at this time was probably prompted by a controversial judicial appointment in 1974, and this was probably the primary catalyst to get judicial selection on the legislative agenda in 1975.[28]

The controversy arose after outgoing Republican governor Thomas J. Meskill nominated J. Brian Gaffney to a position on the superior court. Gaffney was a close friend of Meskill's and a prominent political operative who had only

19 *Id.*, 321–322.

20 Kenneth Booker, "Court Reorganization Outlined; Merit Selection of Judges," *Hartford Courant* (March 7, 1972, 3; for the specific proposal, see Connecticut Citizens for Judicial Modernization, *supra* note 13, 52–71.

21 "Connecticut Final Report," *supra* note 11, 59–65.

22 *Id.*, 62.

23 *Id.*, 64–65.

24 "Gunther Urges Judges Be Nominated on Merit," *Bridgeport Post* (April 7, 1975), 21.

25 Jeffrey T. Williamson, "Judicial Council Urges Merit System for Judges," *Bridgeport Post* (February 2, 1975), 6. The Judicial Council consisted of the chief judges of the state's courts, deans of the two law schools existing at that time (Yale and University of Connecticut), and two Supreme Court justices. It is possible that the bills for merit selection were introduced in years before 1975.

26 "Steele Offers Plan on Judicial System," *Hartford Courant* (October 12, 1974), 12.

27 Herbert Brucker, "How Should Judges Be Selected," *Hartford Courant* (November 3, 1972), 16.

28 Irene Driscoll, "Gaffney Choice Boosts Talk of Judicial Reform, *Hartford Courant* (October 20, 1974), 35.

recently stepped down as chair of the state Republican Party. As allowed by Connecticut law, Gaffney was immediately sworn in as an interim judge. The appointment was made despite Meskill having been found to be unqualified for the superior court by a committee of the Connecticut Bar Association (CBA); the CBA committee did find him qualified for the lower common pleas court.[29] Gaffney's nomination expired with the end of Meskill's term. After the CBA's screening committee rejected him a second time, the new governor, Democrat Ella Grasso, informed Gaffney that she would not renominate him; Gaffney promptly resigned.[30]

In her January 1975 inaugural address, Governor Grasso announced that she would create a committee to review potential judicial selections and forward its recommendations to her.[31] Although some saw this as a positive step,[32] critics noted that the governor was not bound by the committee's recommendation.[33] A proposal to add a merit nominating commission whose recommendations would bind the governor was part of the 1975 legislative agenda.[34] The proposal received a favorable recommendation from the General Assembly's Judiciary Committee,[35] and then overwhelming support in the House, where the vote in favor was 135–9.[36] In a move that was assailed by the president of the CBA,[37] the proposal died in the Senate when it was sent back to committee on a 30–4 vote; opponents argued that the wording was too vague,[38] but one Republican leader charged that the majority Democrats were only giving "lip service" to court reform, including merit selection.[39]

In January 1976, another controversy erupted when Superior Court Judge Samuel Tedesco was arrested on charges of falsely notarizing an application for

[29] Jack Zaiman, "Meskill to Defy State Bar on Judgeship for Gaffney," *Hartford Courant* (September 26, 1974), 8.

[30] Irene Driscoll, "Gaffney Will Resign Superior Court Seat; Governor Refused to Name Him," *Hartford Courant* (January 30, 1075), 1; Irene Driscoll, "Judge Review Unit Has No Set Rules," *Hartford Courant* (January 31, 1975), 8.

[31] "Text of Gov. Ella T. Grasso's Inaugural Address," *Bridgeport Post* (January 8, 1975), 8.

[32] "Judicial Plan Has Merit," *Hartford Courant* (January 19, 1975), 10.

[33] See, for example, "One Court, Better Judges," *Hartford Courant* (March 8, 1976), 10; and "Changes in Picking Judges Draw Fire," *Hartford Courant* (April 8, 1975), 30.

[34] It appears that there may have been a recommendation for such a system by the "Commission to Study and Draft Legislation for the Reorganization and Unification of the Courts" that had been created by the legislature in 1973; see "One Court, Better Judges," *supra* note 33; and Jack Zaiman, "State Court Overhaul Given Excellent Chance," *Hartford Courant* (January 17, 1974), 1.

[35] "Judges' Selection on Merit Backed," *Hartford Courant* (April 19, 1975), 7. The committee is a joint standing committee of the two legislative chambers; there are no separate judiciary committees.

[36] "Utility Cutoff Favored," *Bridgeport Post* (May 22, 1975), 50.

[37] "Senate Move Upsets Bar Leader," *Hartford Courant* (June 1, 1975), 24.

[38] Michael Regan, "Bid to Pick Judges by Merit Shelved," *Hartford Courant* (May 31, 1975), 1.

[39] Democrats' Stand on Courts Assailed," *Hartford Courant* (June 5, 1975), 18.

renewal of a liquor license for a country club owned by members of his extended family.[40] Tedesco had served as a superior court judge for a decade, and previously had been mayor of Bridgeport and lieutenant governor of the state.[41] Six months after being charged, he was convicted in a jury trial,[42] and two months later sentenced to a small fine and disbarred.[43] Despite this new judicial controversy, legislative efforts to get a constitutional amendment on the ballot in fall 1976 were unsuccessful. Proposed legislation for court reform that included adopting a merit selection system was approved by the General Assembly Judiciary Committee,[44] and passed the Senate overwhelmingly on a 28 to 5 vote,[45] but this time the House failed to act.[46]

The 1975 and 1976 sessions marked the beginning of court reform and judicial selection reform being what some observers labeled a perennial issue before the Connecticut General Assembly.[47] Proposals for reform were introduced in many sessions until 1984, when both chambers mustered the votes to send a proposal that would constrain governors' nominations to a list of names forwarded by a nominating commission or require that the governors' nominees be approved by a commission before going to the legislature.[48] In 1978, the Assembly Judiciary Committee approved a merit selection plan,[49] and the plan passed the House, but not with quite enough votes to put it on the November 1978 ballot;[50] this time the Senate did the "dirty work" of killing the proposal by inaction.[51]

40 Richard P. Ondek and Robert H. Laska, "Judge Tedesco Is Arrested in Club Liquor License Case; Warrant Also Out for Jai Alai Figure," *Bridgeport Post* (January 9, 1976), 1; see also "Tedesco Pleads Not Guilty and Asks for a Jury Trial; Renzulli Also Arrested in Club License Renewal," *Bridgeport Telegram* (January 10, 1976).

41 "Judge Tedesco Seen Facing Second Charge," *Hartford Courant* (February 1, 1976), 8.

42 "Richard P. Ondek, "Judge Tedesco Is Found Guilty in Liquor License Fraud Case," *Bridgeport Post* (June 29, 1976), 1.

43 Richard P. Ondek, "Judge Tedesco Is Disbarred as Lawyer, Fined $250 for Felony; He Will Appeal," *Bridgeport Post* (September 9, 1976), 1.

44 "Single State Court Setup Wins Committee Approval," *Bridgeport Post* (April 1, 1976), 8.

45 Alan H. Olmstead, "Court Controversy," *Bridgeport Telegram* (May 19, 1976), 24.

46 "Assembly Gets So-So Grade," *Hartford Courant* (May 8, 1976), 18.

47 See Carol Giacomo, "Committee Votes to Consider Bill for Police Review Board," *Hartford Courant* (February 4, 1981), B2; "Committee Vote Rejects Merit Selection of Judges," *Hartford Courant* (April 3, 1981).

48 This latter form was proposed in 1977 and was strongly opposed by the CBA; see "Bar Association Raps Judge Selection Plan," *Naugatuck Daily News* (May 19, 1977), 8; the proposal died at the end of the 1977 session; see Andrew M. Nibly, "Major Legislation Withers on Vine," *Naugatuck Daily News* (June 9, 1977), 12.

49 "Major Change in Way Judges Chosen Backed," *Hartford Courant* (March 29, 1978).

50 Carol Giacomo, "House Endorses Selection of Judges Based on Merit," *Hartford Courant* (May 2, 1978), 5. The vote in the House was 109–39; to avoid the requirement of consideration by the next General Assembly, it needed 114 votes (three-quarters of the representatives) in favor.

51 Carol Giacomo, "Judicial System Unreformed, But Judges Received Raises," *Hartford Courant* (May 7, 1978), 41.

The fall 1978 elections saw at least some legislative candidates campaigning in part on the now perennial issue[52] of judicial selection reform.[53] The legislative session that followed in 1979 once again saw action by the Judiciary Committee, this time for a plan that would have a commission forward five names to the governor.[54] That legislation died in a subsequent special session when a vote in the House fell two votes short of the required majority of the membership that would have allowed a majority two years later to send the proposal to the voters;[55] the Democratic Speaker of the House favored the legislation, but the Democratic majority leader was firmly against it, with at least some of the opponents expressing concerns that the proposed system would give too much power to members of the bar.[56] Proposals were introduced in both 1980 and 1981, but died in the Judiciary Committee both years.[57] In 1982, a merit selection bill initially failed to come out of the Judiciary Committee by a single vote,[58] and an effort to reconsider that vote failed on a tie vote taken after several supportive members of the committee had left the meeting.[59] Democratic leaders generally were opposed to the change and Republicans were supportive, a split that was not surprising, given that a Democrat William O'Neill had succeeded Ella Grasso after she resigned for health reasons at the end of 1981. Democratic House Speaker Ernest Abate described O'Neill, who was running for a full term in the upcoming November 1982 election, as having "his feet firmly planted on both sides of the issue"; not coincidentally, Abate was also running for governor.[60]

Despite the defeat in the Assembly Judiciary Committee, the Senate overwhelmingly passed a compromise merit selection bill on a 29–3 vote, enough to send the measure to the voters that November if at least three-quarters of the House voted in favor. The plan called for an 11-person nominating commission, with all members of the commission appointed by the governor. When the proposal was debated in the House a few days later, some of the supporters of merit selection criticized it as a

52 See, for example, Carol Giacomo, "Merit Selection of Judges Aired," *Hartford Courant* (March 4, 1978), 2C.

53 See, for example, "Merit Selection of Judges Urged," *Hartford Courant* October 11, 1978), 41; "Curry Supports Change in Filling Legal Posts," *Hartford Courant* (October 25, 1978), 46.

54 Colin McEnroe, "Amendment to Change Way Judges Appointed Gains," *Hartford Courant* (April 19, 1979), 24.

55 Antoinette Martin, "House Turns Down Selection of Judges on Basis of Merit," *Hartford Courant* (May 22, 1979), 1.

56 *Id.*, 8.

57 Antoinette Martin, "Mandatory Jail Term Supported in Compromise on Gun Control," *Hartford Courant* (March 26, 1980), 22; Carol Giacomo, "Committee Vote Rejects Merit Selection of Judges," *Hartford Courant* (April 3, 1981), A18.

58 Tom Barnes, "Bill for Merit Selection of Judges Alive Despite Committee Vote," *Hartford Courant* (March 24, 1982), C2.

59 Tom Barnes, "Panel Votes to Broaden Police Wiretapping," *Hartford Courant* (March 26, 1982), A1.

60 Clifford Teusch, "Amid Chaos, Senate Passes Judges Bill," *Hartford Courant* (May 1, 1982), B3.

fraud because of the control that would be exercised by the governor. Nonetheless, the House did approve the measure, but with substantially less than the three-quarters required to get it on the November 1982 ballot. However, that vote was sufficient to make it possible to get the proposal on the ballot in 1984 if a majority in each chamber of the General Assembly elected in November 1982 voted in favor of the proposal.[61] Despite approval from the Assembly Judiciary Committee,[62] neither chamber voted approval in 1983, and what had been passed in 1982 was sharply criticized because of the composition of the nominating commission. One Republican legislator described the 1982 proposed constitutional amendment as "a horrendous piece of garbage, the biggest hoax I've even seen perpetrated on the state."[63]

Through this period, legislative support for some type of merit-based nominating process appears to have grown. In early 1984, O'Neill, who had been elected governor in his own right in 1982, "called for a form of merit selection of judges."[64] The governor's support for the idea did not resolve what seems to have become the major sticking point: Who would serve on the nominating commission and how would they be selected? The House initially approved a plan that would have a commission chaired by the chief justice with the 12 other members appointed by the governor;[65] because the vote was 108–38, six votes short of the three-quarters needed to get on the ballot in 1984, one of the Democratic backers of the bill brought it up again a few days later. At that time, Republicans succeeded in amending the proposal to have the legislature name 6 members and the governor 6 members; the amended version passed 110–36, still short of the 114 that would have been a three-quarters majority.[66] The second-to-last day of the legislative session, the Senate considered the proposal as passed by the House; it passed the proposal 27–9 (i.e., with three-quarters), but before doing so changed the method of selecting commission members back to all but the chief justice being appointed by the governor.[67] The House failed to act before the legislative session ended at midnight the next day, and consequently the proposal died once again.

[61] Michele Jacklin, "Selection by Merit Blocked; House Defeats Move to Change Method of Choosing Judges," *Harford Courant* (May 6, 1982), A14. The vote was 87–67; 114 votes were needed for the proposal to go to the voters without a second round of consideration by the legislature.

[62] Tom Barnes, "Gay-Rights Bill Granted Hearing in Close Vote," *Hartford Courant* (February 3, 1983), C4.

[63] Tom Barnes, "Protection for Tenants Advocated at Hearing," *Hartford Courant* (March 25, 1983), C6; I have inferred that the bill was not passed because I could find no mention of passage in the newspapers available on newspapers.com.

[64] Steve Grant, "A More Confident O'Neill Wins Respect in Legislature," *Hartford Courant* (February 7, 1984), A1.

[65] Tom Barnes, "House Approves Judge-Selection Measure," *Hartford Courant* (May 1, 1984), B3.

[66] Tom Barnes, "House Approves Change in Appointment Process," *Hartford Courant* (May 3, 1984), D4.

[67] Michele Jacklin, "Senate Approves Change in Method of Selecting Judges," *Hartford Courant* (May 9, 1984), B3.

In November 1984, Republicans won control of both chambers of the state legislature for the first time in ten years. After the legislative session started in 1985, Republicans in the Senate made clear that they wanted more control over judicial selection, complaining that qualified Republicans had not "been given the time of day"[68] regarding judicial appointments and that there had been "a systematic exclusion of Republicans."[69] Just as this issue was hitting the newspapers, a Republican state senator who was a longtime supporter of merit selection renewed his efforts for a constitutional amendment.[70] As things worked out, 1985 was the year both the Senate and House passed a proposed amendment creating a "judicial selection commission" with more than the three-quarters needed to get the measure on the ballot in November 1986. The version initially passed by the Senate, with only a single nay vote,[71] included some specification of the membership of the commission and how it would be selected. When this got to the House, the Senate's version was amended to remove any details about the commission's composition or selection, and the House passed this version 143–7, well beyond the necessary three-quarters for placement on the November 1986 ballot.[72] The Senate voted to accept the version as amended by the House, again with only a single nay vote.[73]

The contested issue of the composition of the judicial selection commission and who would select the members of the commission was resolved by a statute (Public Act No. 85-586) passed at the same time as the final votes on the proposed amendment that would take effect if the voters approved the constitutional amendment. The commission would consist of 12 members, 2 from each congressional district; not more than 6 members could belong to the same political party and none could be an elected or appointed official of the state or hold statewide office in a political party. The governor would appoint one member from each congressional district, all of whom had to be licensed attorneys. The majority and minority leaders of the two chambers of the General Assembly would appoint the other 6, all of whom had to be non-attorneys; the two leaders of the majority would each appoint 2, and the two leaders of the minority, one each. Commissioners' terms were set at six years.[74] Under the 1986 legislation, the commission dealt only with vacancies,

[68] David Find, "State GOP Battles for Bench; Senate Republicans Plan Fight to Win Court Nominations," *Hartford Courant* (February 12, 1985), B1.

[69] *Id.*, B4.

[70] Susan E. Kinsman, "State Senator Renews Push for Merit Selection," *Hartford Courant* (February 12, 1985), B4; Senator George Gunther noted that he had been introducing merit-selection legislation for 17 years.

[71] David Lesher, "Senate Supports Revision; New Amendment Would Influence Judge Selections," *Harford Courant* (May 24, 1985), C4.

[72] *Connecticut House of Representatives Journal* (June 1, 1985), 276. Note that the voting was done electronically, and the Journal does not report the votes of individual representatives.

[73] *Connecticut Senate Journal* (June 3, 1985), 24.

[74] Subsequent legislation reduced the term length of three years and forbid the immediate reappointment of a commissioner (i.e., no consecutive terms); see Connecticut Statutes §51-44a(d), accessed October 3, 2018, at www.ct.gov/jsc/lib/jsc/pdfs/sec51_44a.pdf

leaving recommendations concerning reappointment to be made by the existing "judicial review council"; later legislation transferred that responsibility to the judicial selection commission.[75]

There does not appear to have been any organized opposition to the proposed constitutional amendment when it came to the voters in November 1986, at least none was evident in my search of digitized Connecticut newspapers. An exchange of views did appear in one major state newspaper. The negative position was advanced by a Democratic state representative, who argued that the amendment was flawed by leaving the composition of the judicial selection commission to the legislature, thus creating "an open invitation to political manipulation."[76] If anything, argued the representative, the proposed amendment "makes the selection process more, not less, political."[77] Neither this position, nor any other opposition positions or materials that may have targeted voters, seems to have had much effect, because 67.4 percent of the voters supported the amendment, easily exceeding the constitutionally required majority.[78]

Judicial Selection after 1986

The system adopted in Connecticut is unique. In all other states using a nominating commission that limits the governor's choice (or, in the case of South Carolina, the legislature's choice), the commission prepares a short list of nominees when a vacancy arises; if there are multiple vacancies to be filled on a single court, the nominating commission may provide an expanded list covering the set of vacancies.[79] In Connecticut, the Judicial Selection Commission (JSC) maintains a set of standing lists from which the governor makes a selection to fill a vacancy. Persons wanting to be appointed to a particular court can apply at any time (i.e., not just when vacancies occur), and if deemed qualified, they are put on the list for that court; persons put on the list remain on it until they become ineligible for some reason (e.g., reaching the mandatory retirement age, leaving the state, or losing their license to practice).[80] An individual can be on the lists for more than one of the courts. The governor can select anyone on the list for a particular court. There are lists for the superior court, the Court of Appeals, and the Supreme Court, plus a separate list for the position of

75 Connecticut Statutes §51-44a(e).

76 Richard D. Tulisano, "No," *Hartford Courant* (October 29, 1986), B9.

77 *Id.*

78 The vote was 396,555 in favor and 192,180 against; see http://libguides.ctstatelibrary.org/ld.php?content_id=30623804, accessed October 4, 2018.

79 As discussed briefly later in this chapter, from July 1, 2007 until June 30, 2015, Rhode Island legislation allowed the governor to appoint from lists going back five years rather than limiting the choice to the list prepared for a specific vacancy.

80 Email to author from Ann Gimmartino, Manager, Connecticut Judicial Selection Commission, July 27, 2018.

Supreme Court chief justice.[81] As of January 1, 2018, 266 persons appeared on the superior court list, 62 on the Appellate Court list, 29 on the Supreme Court list, and 4 on the chief justice list.[82] In 2017, 34 persons not currently a judge applied to be on the list for one of the courts; 32 were recommended and put on a list, 1 was denied recommendation, and 1 candidate withdrew. In addition, 15 incumbent judges applied to be on a list for appointment for a different court; 14 were recommended and 1 withdrew. The JSC also reviews judges who want to be appointed to another term; in 2017 all 18 judges seeking reappointment received positive recommendations, and those recommendations were sent to the governor.

Although the system of extensive lists from which a governor can select gives the governor great leeway to make political appointments, it appears that politics has not been a major factor in judicial selection in the years that the system has operated.[83] The major exception occurred in 2018, when the governor's choice to become chief justice was rejected by the Senate, which was equally divided between Democrats and Republicans. Democratic governor Dannel Malloy selected Associate Justice Andrew McDonald who, if approved by the legislature, would have become the first openly gay state chief justice in the country.[84] Social conservatives mobilized to oppose his nomination, criticizing his support for same-sex marriage, his vote to abolish the death penalty when the matter came before the Connecticut Supreme Court, and for introducing legislation when he served in the Senate that would have empowered lay Catholics to have more say about parish financial matters.[85] Governor Malloy was not running for reelection, and some leading Republicans argued that, with echoes of the blocking of Merrick Garland's nomination to the U.S. Supreme Court, the selection should be made by the next governor.[86] The approval of the nomination was thrown into serious doubt when one Democratic state senator recused herself from the vote on the nomination because she had sought to disqualify Justice McDonald from hearing a case involving her husband.[87] With her recusal, a

81 For the position of chief justice, the governor can select someone on the chief justice list or any sitting member of the Supreme Court.

82 All of the statistics regarding the actions of the JSC are from its *Annual Report* for calendar 2017.

83 "[The] recent CJ nomination was the first serious instance of partisan gamesmanship," email from Tim Fisher, Dean, University of Connecticut School of Law, November 26, 2018 ; see also Dave Collins, "Chief Justice Nomination Enveloped by Politicking," *Seattle Times* (March 11, 2018), www.seattletimes.com/nation-world/chief-justice-nomination-enveloped-by-politicking/, accessed November 29, 2018.

84 Christine Stuart, "Malloy Will Nominate McDonald to Chief Justice," *CT News Junkie* (January 8, 2018), www.ctnewsjunkie.com/archives/entry/malloy_will_nominate_mcdonald_to_chief_justice_1_8_2018/, accessed November 29, 2018.

85 Paul Hughes, "Social Conservatives Gird to Derail Chief Justice Pick; McDonald Labeled Judicial Activist," *Waterbury Republican-American* (January 19, 2018), A1.

86 Neil Vigdor, "GOP Threatens to Derail Malloy's Chief Justice Nominee," *Connecticut Post* (February 6, 2018), www.ctpost.com/news/article/Republicans-Lame-duck-governor-12556208.php, accessed November 29, 2018.

87 Christopher Keating, "State Supreme Court; McDonald Dealt Another Blow; Democrat Withdraws from Chief Justice Nominee Vote," *Hartford Courant* (February 28, 2018), 1A.

straight party-line vote would be 18–17 against approval; if she had not recused herself and had voted in favor of the nomination, the 18–18 tie vote would have been broken by the Democratic lieutenant governor, who is the presiding officer of the Senate. The House approved the nomination by a single vote (75–74),[88] but it was defeated in the Senate on a 19–16 vote (one Democrat joined the Republicans in voting to turn down the nomination).[89] Not long after the rejection of McDonald, Governor Malloy selected Richard A. Robinson, who was overwhelmingly approved to become the state's first African American chief justice.[90]

RHODE ISLAND[91]

Background

In 1980, Rhode Island was the only state where judges were not subject to reappointment, reelection, or mandatory retirement.[92] Until 1994 justices of the Rhode Island Supreme Court could be removed by a majority vote of the state legislature declaring the justice's seat vacant.[93] Only for Supreme Court justices was tenure set by the state constitution; for judges of all other courts, tenure was left to be established by statute.[94] At that time justices of the Rhode Island Supreme Court were elected by the two chambers of the state legislature sitting as a "Grand Committee." Trial court judges, except for those serving on municipal courts or probate courts, were appointed by the governor and subject to confirmation by the state legislature.[95] In 1994, the voters approved a constitutional amendment eliminating the legislative election of Supreme Court justices and also changing the process for trial court

88 Christopher Keating, "State Supreme Court; House Narrowly Approves McDonald; 5 Democrats Join GOP Opposition," *Hartford Courant* (March 13, 2018), 1A.

89 Susan Haigh, "Vote to Confirm State Chief Justice Nominee Fails," *Bristol Press* (March 27, 2018).

90 Christopher Keating, "Supreme Court; Robinson Named Chief Justice; Historic Vote Is Unanimous in State Senate," *Hartford Courant* (May 4, 2018), 1A. One might wonder whether the Republican opposition to McDonald contributed in any way to that party's sharp losses in the 2018 legislative elections; Republicans lost 6 seats in the Senate and 12 in the House of Representatives.

91 The primary source for much of this section was the *Providence Journal* as digitized on Newsbank (www.newsbank.com) and accessed through the University of Minnesota library.

92 Massachusetts ended life tenure without a mandatory retirement age by passing a constitutional amendment in 1972 imposing mandatory retirement at age 70; see www.judicialselection.us/judicial_selection/reform_efforts/formal_changes_since_inception.cfm?state=MA, accessed October 5, 2018.

93 See *State Court Organization 1980* (Washington, DC: U.S. Department of Justice, Bureau of Justice Statistics, 1982), 409–412.

94 See Constitution of the State of Rhode Island and Providence Plantation, Annotated Edition, Done in Convention at Providence on the Fourth Day of December, A.D. 1986 (Office of Secretary of State, 1988), 30, https://helindigitalcommons.org/cgi/viewcontent.cgi?referer=https://www.google.com/&httpsredir=1&article=1026&context=lawarchive, accessed October 6, 2018.

95 *Id.*

judges. The new system was one of constrained gubernatorial appointment, requiring the governor to select from a list submitted by an "independent non-partisan judicial nominating commission," with the governor's selection subject to confirmation by each chamber of the state legislature in the case of Supreme Court justices or by just the Senate in the case of lower court judges.[96] The new system also eliminated the power of the legislature to remove a member of the Supreme Court by a majority vote declaring the member's seat vacant.

Although I found some indication of interest by the Rhode Island bar in merit selection as far back as 1957,[97] the drive to change that system came in the wake of several scandals involving the courts, including two that led to the resignation of chief justices. The change does not appear to be either part of a broader drive for court modernization or an effort to gain partisan advantage. In 1994, when the Rhode Island legislature approved sending to the voters a constitutional amendment changing judicial selection, Republicans had not controlled both chambers since 1940, and that was also the last time Republicans controlled the House of Representatives. The Senate was last controlled by Republicans in 1958, almost 40 years before the change was made.[98] In the years between 1959 and 1994, Republicans did have substantial success winning gubernatorial elections, with Republicans holding the office for 14 of those 36 years.

The first major scandal that would eventually lead to a change in judicial selection involved Chief Justice Joseph Bevilacqua. Bevilacqua was elected to the Rhode Island House in 1954 and rose to become Speaker in 1969. In 1976, while he was still Speaker of the House, the General Assembly elected him chief justice of the state's Supreme Court. Almost immediately, some questions arose regarding his links to criminals, including an allegation, later recanted, that he had harbored a robbery suspect back in the 1960s and that he had accepted payment from that suspect. Around the same time, it became public that a few years earlier, Bevilacqua had sent a letter to the state parole board vouching for the "good moral character" of an organized-crime boss being considered for parole. Shortly after becoming chief justice, Bevilacqua officiated at a wedding of the crime boss's former chauffeur, who was at the time facing an indictment for insurance fraud.[99]

96 Rhode Island Constitution, Article X, §4.

97 The March 1957 issue of the *Rhode Island Bar Journal* 5, no. 6, 1, 5–6 featured an article entitled, "Ideal Judicial Selection in a Practical World," by one of the proponents of the Missouri Plan. In 1973, the chair of the Bar Association's Special Committee on Judicial Selection Process sent a letter to the governor referencing an earlier communication that had urged him to create by executive order a "judicial nominating commission"; see "The Bar Association on Judicial Selection," *Rhode Island Bar Journal* 25, no. 3 (December 1976), 2.

98 See https://en.wikipedia.org/wiki/Political_party_strength_in_Rhode_Island, accessed October 5, 2018; as of 2018, 1940 was still the last time Republicans controlled both chambers or the House of Representatives and 1958 was the last time Republicans controlled the Senate.

99 "Joseph A. Bevilacqua Dies at 70; Rhode Island Judge Linked to Mob," *New York Times* (June 22, 1989), D3.

In 1984, the *Providence Journal* published an article reporting that the state police and some of its reporters had observed Bevilacqua "repeatedly visiting the homes of underworld figures," and the "state police alleged that [he] had also visited a . . . motel owned by men linked to gambling and drugs, for trysts with his secretary and another woman."[100] The state's Commission on Judicial Tenure and Discipline initiated an investigation with a former justice of the U.S. Supreme Court, Arthur Goldberg, serving as special counsel; as a result of that investigation, the commission censured Bevilacqua for having associated with criminals, and he took an unpaid leave of absence. The Judiciary Committee of the Connecticut House of Representatives initiated impeachment proceedings when it convened in 1986, and after two weeks of public hearings, Bevilacqua resigned.[101] After his resignation, there were reports that both federal and state prosecutors were looking into the possibility of bringing criminal charges,[102] but nothing came from those inquiries.

Reform Efforts

The year 1986 was also the occasion of a constitutional convention in Rhode Island.[103] That convention placed an amendment to judicial selection on the November 1986 ballot. The proposed system would have retained election of Supreme Court justices by the General Assembly and appointment of lower court judges by the governor, but would have constrained the selections to be from a list provided by an independent nominating commission that would also serve as a disciplinary commission with the power to discipline and remove judges; the amendment would also have established a mandatory retirement age of 72.[104] The proposed commission would be composed of 11 members with the governor appointing 4, two of whom had to be nonlawyers; the two chambers of the state legislature would elect a total of 5, two of whom would be nonlawyers; the other 2 members would be one Supreme Court justice elected by the justices of that Court and one judge from the court with the vacancy to be filled.[105] The *Providence Journal*, Rhode Island's main newspaper, editorialized against the proposal, arguing that the structure of the nominating commission would extend

[100] *Id.*

[101] *Id.*, see also "Justice in Impeachment Inquiry Quits in Rhode Island," *New York Times* (May 29, 1986), 14.

[102] "Prosecutors Eye Rhode Island Judge," *New York Times* (July 6, 1986), 42.

[103] The Rhode Island Constitution (Article XIV, §2) has a provision that the voters must be asked every ten years whether to hold a constitutional convention.

[104] John Marion, "Judging How We Pick Judges: Fifteen Years of Merit Selection in Rhode Island," *Roger Williams University Law Review* 18, no. 3 (Fall 2010), 737.

[105] John Kiffney, "Campaign '86: Independent Panel Sought to Nominate Judges," *Providence Journal* (October 14, 1986), A10.

the power of the politicians in the legislature.[106] The proposed amendment failed with 53.8 percent of voters rejecting it.[107]

Within just a few years, additional judicial scandals arose. In 1989, a family court judge was ordered off the bench and then resigned after evidence showed he had borrowed money in substantial amounts from lawyers appearing in his court.[108] In 1992, a retired superior court judge pled guilty to accepting bribes and was sentenced to six years in prison.[109] And then, the following year, Chief Justice Thomas Fay, who had served in the state legislature and as a family court judge before his election by the legislature to replace the disgraced Joseph Bevilacqua, became enmeshed in his own scandal. Even before the scandal involving Fay broke, some small changes in judicial selection were made.

In early 1992, the House of Delegates of the Rhode Island Bar Association (RIBA) endorsed a "merit selection proposal" that would have an independent commission submit a list of five candidates to the governor, who would choose a candidate on that list and submit that name to the Senate for confirmation. This plan would apply to all judicial positions not subject to popular election. It would end the practice of justices of the Supreme Court being elected by the Grand Committee, but would still allow the appointment of sitting legislators to judgeships. At the time this proposal was made, all five sitting justices of the Supreme Court were former legislators. The RIBA's proposal would also end life tenure by imposing a mandatory retirement age of 70 for judges.[110] In the summer of 1992, the governor created through an executive order an Advisory Commission on Judicial Appointments; a few weeks after the RIBA issued its proposal, the governor proposed establishing by law an advisory committee such as the one he had previously used on his own. Even though the members of the proposed statutory committee would include 3 lawyers elected by the RIBA (who would join 5 appointed by the governor, 1 appointed by the attorney general, 1 appointed by the House Speaker, and the chief judge of the court where the appointee would serve), the RIBA opposed the proposal because the recommendations of the committee would not be binding on the governor.[111] Bills for such a committee passed both chambers, but the differences were not resolved, and the bills died.[112]

106 "Vote 'No' on Question 2: Judicial Nomination," *Providence Journal* (October 24, 1986), A20.

107 Marion, "Judging How We Pick Judges," *supra* note 104, 738.

108 Karen Lee Ziner, "Judicial Commission Issues Ruling on Fayat," *Providence Journal* (February 2, 1991), A3.

109 See Tracy Breton, "Almeida's Chambers Searched; Investigators Trying to Learn If Other Lawyers Gave Judge Kickbacks," *Providence Journal* (August 9, 1991), A1; Tracy Breton, "Almeida Sentenced to Six Years; Ex-Judge Admits Bribery; Rebuked as Betrayer of Oath," *Providence Journal* (May 19, 1992), A1.

110 Tracy Breton, "Bar Association Wants Voice in Naming R.I. Judges; Too Much Politics Seen Diluting Trust in the Judiciary," *Providence Journal* (January 30, 1992), A3.

111 Scott MacKay, "Governor's Bill Proposes Advisory Panel to Screen Nominees for State Courts," *Providence Journal* (February 18, 1992), B5.

112 Judy Rakowsky, "Senate Approves Commission to Review, OK Judicial Candidates," *Providence Journal* (July 9, 1992), A6. I infer that the proposal did not pass because in February

Legislation barring elected and some senior appointed officials from being appointed to judgeships did pass in 1992; they would have to be out of office for at least twelve months before being eligible for appointment as judges. However, because justices of the Supreme Court were not "appointed" but "elected" by the legislature, it was still possible for sitting legislators and other high officials to be chosen as Supreme Court justices. This fact led to outcries that this possibility was a loophole engineered to benefit members of the legislature.[113] In early 1993, legislation was proposed, with the backing of the Democratic lieutenant governor, that would subject judges serving in courts below the Supreme Court to periodic review by a Judicial Review Panel; after the review, a judge could be denied reappointment upon recommendation of the governor and a majority vote of the Senate. Any similar change for the Supreme Court would require a constitutional amendment.[114] Just a month after this proposal became public, the scandal that would engulf Chief Justice Fay began to break.

In mid-March 1993, the *Providence Journal-Bulletin* ran a story that $2,200 had been stolen from the Supreme Court Restitution Unit in 1989, and that the theft had been covered up by the state court administrator, Matthew Smith, and his deputy. After the story was published, the Rhode Island attorney general ordered the state police to investigate the alleged theft and cover-up.[115] Smith and Chief Justice Fay were longtime associates. They had served together in the Rhode Island House of Representatives. Fay left the legislature to become a family court judge in 1978; two years later, Smith became Speaker of the House and Fay administered the oath of office on that occasion. Smith had been one of the legislative leaders initiating impeachment hearings for then Chief Justice Joseph Bevilacqua. After Bevilacqua resigned, Smith backed Fay as the new chief justice in opposition to a sitting justice who had the support of the three other justices; in the legislative election for chief justice, Fay overwhelmed the other candidate. Eighteen months later, the governor appointed Smith as Supreme Court clerk; at the same time Fay appointed Smith as

1993 the governor restructured the advisory panel he had created by executive order; see Scott MacKay, "Sundlun Sets Up Advisory Panel to Assist Him in Selecting Judges; The Governor Opts to Maintain a Strong Hand in the process by Deciding to Name All Nine Members of the Committee," *Providence Journal* (February 17, 1993), D6.

113 Judy Rakowsky, "Law May Permit Legislator to Become Judge; High Court Vacancy Prompts Debate on Apparent Loophole," *Providence Journal* (July 20, 1992), A3; William Colleran, "Waiting for Doors to (Revolve) Open," *Providence Journal* (September 20, 1992), J7.

114 Scott MacKay, "Lifetime Tenure for Judges Criticized; Weygand Seeks Review of Most on R.I. Bench," *Providence Journal* (February 9, 1993), A1. See also William M. MacKenzie, "Handcuffs and Governors," *Rhode Island Bar Journal* 41 (January 1993), 23–25.

115 John Sullivan, "State Police to Probe Theft of Court Money; Chief Justice Thomas Fay Has Instructed State Court Administrator Matthew Smith to Say Who Repaid $4,200 After It Was Stolen from the Supreme Court Restitution Unit in 1989," *Providence Journal* (March 16, 1993), A1.

state court administrator.[116] In early April 1993, Smith offered to resign as state court administrator, proclaiming that he had done nothing wrong,[117] but he did not actually resign until August.[118] Over the next month, various groups, including the RIBA, the League of Women Voters, and Operation Clean Sweep, among others, called for changes to state judicial selection.[119]

In late July, the *Providence Journal* published an article that detailed the patronage appointments to various court administrative positions made by Fay and Smith.[120] In the following weeks, a report came out about a secret fund used by Fay and Smith to pay for such things as parking tickets, repair of Smith's personal car, bus rental to the Boston Red Sox's Fenway Park, and alcohol.[121] Toward the end of August, Chief Justice Fay temporarily stepped down after he was charged on three misdemeanor counts for illegally funneling legal work as an arbitrator to a business partner.[122] Fay resigned on October 8,[123] and on April 29, 1994, pled guilty to two felony counts and three misdemeanor charges of unethical conduct; he was given a suspended sentence and disbarred.[124]

The discussion about reforming judicial selection in Rhode Island took on a new life after Fay's arrest. Various groups called for reform,[125] and about two weeks after Fay's arraignment, the Senate named a panel to study judicial reform,

[116] Dean Starkman, "Court Chief Smith Resigns; The Probe of the Cover-up of the Theft Continues; Smith Maintains That He Did Nothing Wrong," *Providence Journal* (April 9, 1993), A1.

[117] *Id.*

[118] "Smith Quits as Probe Widens; General Treasure Mayer Says Smith and Fay's Use of the Secret Fund Was 'Utterly Inappropriate,'" *Providence Journal* (August 11, 1993), A1.

[119] "Groups Score Way Justices Are Selected," *Providence Journal* (April 29, 1993), D5; Russell Garland, "Selection Process for Top R.I. Judges Unlikely to Change in This Assembly; Common Cause and the R.I. Bar Association Want an Independent Panel to Recommend Candidates for Judicial Appointments," *Providence Journal* (May 11, 1993), B5.

[120] Tracy Breton, "The Making of an Empire; Chief Judge, Top Clerk Preside Over Network of High-priced Patronage," *Providence Journal* (July 25, 1993), A1.

[121] "Smith Quits as Probe Widens," *supra* note 118; "Secret Account: How Money Was Spent," *Providence Journal* (August 14, 1993), A1.

[122] Dan Barry, Ira Chinoy, and Dean Star, "Chief Justice Fay Charged, Leaves Bench Pending Probe; Accused of Using His Position to Benefit Business Partner; Judge Had Earlier Agreed to Give Up Administrative Duties," *Providence Journal* (August 25, 1993), A1; Dan Barry, Ira Chinoy, and Mike Stanton, "Fay Leaves High Court Until Charges Are Resolved; Chief Justice to Be Arraigned Today," *Providence Journal* (August 26, 1993), A1.

[123] Dean Starkman, "Chief Justice Fay Resigns; Attorney General Says Investigation to Continue," *Providence Journal* (October 9, 1993), A1; for a day-by-day account of the events leading to Fay's resignation, see Ira Chinoy, "The Chief Justice Resigns; Chief Justice Fay's Downfall: Day by Day," *Providence Journal* (October 9, 1993), A5.

[124] Doane Hulick and Tom Mooney, "Fay Pleads Guilty to 5 Charges; The Former Chief Justice Is Given a Suspended Sentence and Loses His Right to Practice Law," *Providence Journal* (April 30, 1994), A1.

[125] "Right Now Urges Reform in Choosing Judges; Cronyism, the Group Says, Must Forever Be Removed from the Process," *Providence Journal* (August, 27, 1993), A8.

including judicial selection, in anticipation of action when the legislature convened in 1994.[126] Majorities of the members of both the House and Senate signed petitions calling for a moratorium on selecting judges until a "nonpolitical merit selection process" was put in place.[127] One indicator of the momentum for change was that the legislature decided to delay selecting a new chief justice;[128] that selection was not made until February 1995,[129] after the new system had been approved by the voters in November 1994. Throughout the fall of 1993, various proposals for the use of a merit nominating committee were raised both by political leaders and civic groups.[130]

The Rhode Island legislature convened in early January 1994, but real action on the bill did not start until March, when the Senate Judiciary Committee approved a bill that would create a system using a nominating commission from whose selections the governor would appoint judges for courts at all levels, including the Supreme Court, subject to Senate confirmation. The Senate plan would eliminate the role of the Grand Committee. The proposal raised issues of how large the nominating commission would be, and how its members would be selected.[131] A month later, the House Judiciary Committee approved a slightly different plan.

[126] "Senate Panel Named to Study Judicial Reform," *Providence Journal* (September 8, 1993), C5; Scott MacKay, "Senate Panel Tackles Judicial Selections," *Providence Journal* (September 24, 1994), A12.

[127] Scott MacKay, "Most Lawmakers Want Moratorium on Selecting Judges," *Providence Journal* (September 14, 1993), A9.

[128] Russell Garland, "Speaker Retreats on Court Election; Acting Chief Justice Joseph R. Weisberger Said He Sees No Need for the Assembly to Consider Electing Him Chief Justice Before January," *Providence Journal* (October 19, 1993), A1.

[129] Russell Garland, "Weisberger Appointed High Court's Chief Justice; Clear Sailing in the House and Senate Is Expected for Weisberger Who Has Held the Top Job on the State Supreme Court on an Acting Basis for 18 Months," *Providence Journal* (February 10, 1995), A1. The confirmation of the new chief justice did not come until mid-March; see "House, Senate Committee Confirm Weisberger," *Providence Journal* (March 10, 1995), C7; and Russell Garland, "Hail to the Chief; Justice Weisberger Confirmed; The Unanimous Senate Vote for the New Chief Justice Was the Last Step in a Selection Process Used for the First Time," *Providence Journal* (March 15, 1995), A1.

[130] Russell Garland, "Weigand Urges Merit Selection, Review of Judges; The Plan Would Establish a Nine-Member Commission to Select and Submit to the Governor Five Names for Any Court Vacancy," *Providence Journal* (October 22, 1993), B5; Russell Garland, "Judge-Nominating Panel Debated; A Common Cause Proposal Advocating a Powerful Commission Is Criticized by House Member Charles T. Knowles," *Providence Journal* (November 5, 1993), C4; Scott MacKay, "Agreement Reported Near in R. I. on New Judge-Selection Proposal; Governor Sundlun and Various Groups Are Expected to Announce Plans for a Commission to Screen and Rate Candidates for the Bench," *Providence Journal* (December 11, 1993), A6; Scott MacKay, "Sundlun Backs Panel Choosing Judge Pool; The General Assembly May Not Be Receptive to Giving Up Its Authority to Elect Supreme Court Justices, However," *Providence Journal* (December 15, 1993), C4; Russell Garland, "Right Now Offers Plan for Picking Judges; The Essence of the Coalition's Proposal Is for All Judges to Be Selected on the Basis of Merit," *Providence Journal* (December 17, 1993), B8.

[131] Russell Garland, "Judiciary Panel Oks Reform Bill; Advocates of Judicial Reform Disagree on Some Aspects of the Process," *Providence Journal* (March 9, 1994), A4.

Specifically, for Supreme Court appointees, the House's version would have them confirmed "jointly by the House and Senate."[132] Although changing the system for courts other than the Supreme Court could be done by a simple statute, the changes suggested by the Senate and by the House would require a constitutional amendment. At the end of May, the House approved, 89–5, a version of the plan proposed by its Judiciary Committee. Under this plan, appointments to the Supreme Court would require the separate approval of the House and the Senate.[133] About a week later, the Senate unanimously approved the plan, and the governor signed the legislation.[134] Part of the package was a proposed constitutional amendment that would change the selection system for the Supreme Court and embed the new system for lower courts in the constitution. The legislation called for a nine-person nominating commission, all chosen by the governor; however, five of the governor's selections had to be from names submitted by legislative leaders, one each from lists submitted by the House Speaker, the House minority leader, the Senate majority leader, and the Senate minority leader, plus one from a list submitted jointly by the House Speaker and the Senate majority leader.[135] The system as applied to courts other than the Supreme Court went into effect immediately; the new system for the Supreme Court had to await voter approval at the November 1994 general election.

Nothing in the *Providence Journal* in the months leading up to the November 1994 election suggested that there was an organized campaign to defeat the amendment changing the selection system for the Supreme Court. The little news coverage I found largely provided an analysis and/or a description of what the amendment would do and some background on why it was being proposed,[136] or a discussion of how the new process was working for the courts below the Supreme Court.[137] One exception was an op-ed piece by a African American member of the state legislature who criticized the new nominating commission for including a person who had voted against fair housing on a list of nominees and expressed a

[132] Russell Garland and Scott MacKay, "Judie-Selection Bill Is Approved; The Senate Whip, Urging Action, Says the Eyes of Rhode Island Are Upon the Legislators," *Providence Journal* (April 9, 1994), A6.

[133] Scott MacKay, "House Approves Bill to Change Judge Selection; The Measure Would Greatly Reduce the General Assembly's Role in Making Judicial Appointments," *Providence Journal* (May 27, 1994), B5.

[134] Russell Garland, "R.I. Changes the Method of Selecting Its Judges; A Panel Will Propose Candidates to the Governor, Who Will Make the Selection," *Providence Journal* (June 3, 1994), A1.

[135] *Id.*

[136] Russell Garland, "Campaign 94 Question 1: Judicial Reform; Voters to Have Say on Judicial Selection, Legislators' Pay; Scandal Prompted Merit Plan," *Providence Journal* (October 11, 1994), C5.

[137] Russell Garland, "Analysis: A New Process of Nominating Judges Tested," *Providence Journal* (September 26, 1994), A1.

concern that he and other minority members of the legislature would have less influence in the selection of Supreme Court justices.[138] The amendment itself left it to the legislature to specify the membership of the nominating commission for Supreme Court justices and the process to be used by the commission. The amendment passed on a vote of 211,394 to 91,294; i.e., 69.8 percent of voters supported the change in how Supreme Court justices would be selected.[139]

In 2007 General Assembly made one significant change to the system. Previously, the governor had to select from a candidate on the list prepared for a specific vacancy or set of vacancies. The General Assembly relaxed this requirement, allowing the governor to choose from lists of nominees going back five years. The change was proposed by the Republican governor.[140] Despite strong opposition from Common Cause, the change got strong backing from the Democratic-controlled legislature.[141] Initially the change was to sunset after one year, but it was subsequently renewed each year until 2015, when a bill (H.B. 6307) to extend for another year died in the Senate Judiciary Committee after passing the House of Representatives.[142]

As should be clear from this account, the adoption of a system constraining whom the governor could appoint as judges and ending the practice of legislative elections of Rhode Island Supreme Court justices was driven by problems that had arisen in the existing selection processes, particularly several scandals involving judges serving on Rhode Island's courts. There is little evidence of partisan or policy goals being a significant factor leading to the changes[143] or to the modification that lasted from 2007 until 2015.

[138] Harold M. Metts, "Rhode Island 'Reform' Is Racist," *Providence Journal* (October 21, 1994), A17; for a contrary view, see H. Philip West Jr., "Judicial, Legislative Reforms Do Not Hurt Minorities," *Providence Journal* (November 11, 1994), A15.

[139] See www.elections.ri.gov/elections/results/1994/referenda.php, accessed October 6, 2018.

[140] Edward Fitzpatrick, "Governor Asking for More Flexibility in Picking State Judges," *Providence Journal* (February 21, 2007), B2.

[141] Edward Fitzpatrick, "At the Assembly – Senate Approves Bill to Expand Selection for Judicial Candidates," *Providence Journal* (June 8, 2007), B1.

[142] The failure to pass the Rhode Island Senate is from the General Assembly's bill tracking system, accessed May 9, 2019, at http://status.rilin.state.ri.us/bill_history.aspx?mode=previous; additional information was provided in an email dated May 9, 2019, from John Marion, the executive director of Rhode Island Common Cause.

[143] For assessments of the system adopted in 1994, see Michael J. Yelnosky, "Rhode Island's Judicial Nominating Commission: Can Reform Become Reality," *Roger Williams University Law Review* 1, no. 1 (1996), 87–135; John Marion, "Judging How We Pick Judges: Fifteen Years of Merit Selection in Rhode Island," *Roger Williams University Law Review* 15, no. 3 (2010), 735–754; Mirya R. Holman, "Measuring Merit in Rhode Island's Natural Experiment in Judicial Selection," *Roger Williams University Law Review* 15, no. 3 (2010), 705–728; William E. Smith, "Reflections on Judicial Merit Selection, the Rhode Island Experience, and Some Modest Proposals for Reform and Improvement," *Roger Williams University Law Review* 15, no. 3 (2010), 664–700.

SOUTH CAROLINA

Background

Judicial selection for South Carolina's general jurisdiction courts, including the South Carolina Supreme Court, is the responsibility of the state legislature and has been throughout the state's history.[144] Selection of judges to serve on limited or specialized jurisdiction courts varies with some elected by the legislature, some popularly elected, and others appointed by the governor either with or without confirmation by the state legislature.[145] Until 1996, the only constraints on the legislature's choice of judges were constitutional requirements concerning the candidates' age, length of residence in South Carolina, and length of time licensed to practice law. In 1996, the electorate overwhelmingly approved a constitutional amendment constraining the legislature's selection to candidates forwarded by a nominating commission, the membership of which was left entirely to the legislature.

V. O. Key Jr. devotes one section of his chapter on South Carolina in *Southern Politics* to what he labeled "Legislative Government."[146] Not only did the legislature select judges, but it also selected persons to serve on bodies such as the highway commission, which controlled decisions to build highways, and the public service commission, which regulated public utilities. Legislators also effectively selected many local officials and controlled decision-making in the districts they represented. As one might expect, legislators jealously guarded their power and prerogatives. This is reflected in the fact that the only avenue to amend the state's constitution is through the state legislature and that requires a two-thirds vote in each chamber of the legislature, approval by a majority of the voters, and then confirmation by a majority vote in each legislative chamber.

Key subtitles his chapter on South Carolina "The Politics of Color" because, even more than in states such as Alabama, Louisiana, and Mississippi, race was a central preoccupation of politics in South Carolina, probably reflecting that until the 1930s, African Americans were a majority of the state's population.[147] As was true of other states that were part of the Confederacy, politics in South Carolina was overwhelmingly dominated by the Democratic Party. For almost 100 years, 1879 to 1974, Democrats controlled all aspects of state-level government. They controlled both chambers of the state legislature through 1994, a total of 116 years, and from 1903 through 1960, every member of the legislature was a Democrat.[148]

[144] The part of the chapter on South Carolina draws in part on a telephone interview with the John Crangle, the former executive director of Common Cause South Carolina, July 18, 2018.

[145] See *State Court Organization* 1980 (Williamsburg, VA: National Center for State Courts, 1982), 415–418.

[146] V. O. Key Jr., *Southern Politics in State and Nation* (New York: Alfred Knopf, 1949), 150–154.

[147] *Id.*, 130–131.

[148] See https://en.wikipedia.org/wiki/Political_party_strength_in_South_Carolina, accessed October 13, 2018.

One feature of judicial selection for those courts whose judges were elected by the legislature was the success of current and former legislators in winning those elections. As of 1996, the year that judicial selection reform occurred, 60 percent of the judges serving on the circuit court (the general jurisdiction trial court) were former legislators,[149] as were all five members of the South Carolina Supreme Court, including one who was a member of the legislature at the time of her election.[150] Between 1975 and 1996, 110 (47.6 percent) of the 231 open-seat elections for judicial positions had one or more current or former legislators as candidates, and a current or former legislator won 87.3 percent of those 110 elections. More than one current or former legislator ran in 26 of those 110 elections.[151] For simplicity, in the discussion that follows, I will refer to "legislators," omitting the "current or former."

The favoritism towards legislators in the judicial selection process was subject to the frequent criticism that unqualified candidates for positions were elected, and those unqualified candidates were sometimes legislators.[152] The process was also subject to criticism for early lobbying by potential candidates seeking pledges of support[153] and vote trading; the latter could involve either trading votes in judicial elections or trading votes in judicial elections for votes on other matters of interest to a particular legislator. There was one limitation that affected sitting legislators: a 1937 law forbidding legislators from being appointed to offices created during their current term.[154]

The process leading up to the election of judges by the legislature sitting in joint session included a review of candidates by a joint committee of the legislature. There were no formal guidelines governing that committee's assessment of candidates, and the committee was limited to forwarding its assessment to the full legislature; this meant that candidates the committee deemed unqualified still went forward and some such candidates were elected.[155] In May of 1974, the state bar created a commission to screen judicial candidates and report its recommendations

149 Kevin Eberle, "Judicial Selection in South Carolina: Who Gets to Judge?" *South Carolina Lawyer* 13 (May/June 2002), 24.

150 Kimberly C. Petillo, "The Untouchables: The Impact of South Carolina's New Judicial Selection System on the South Carolina Supreme Court, 1997–2003," *Albany Law Review* 67 (2004), 939.

151 I computed these figures from data collected for a report prepared for the South Carolina Senate Judiciary Committee; see James H. Ritchie, Jr., "The Judicial Merit Selection Commission: History of the JMSC and the Screening for Judges in This State," *South Carolina Lawyers* 18 (July 3006), 27–31. The data from this report are available at www.scstatehouse.gov/Archives/CitizensInterestPage/StatisticalStudyJudicialScreening/StatisticalStudyJudicialScreening.php, accessed October 13, 2018.

152 Petillo, "The Untouchables," *supra* note 150, 939.

153 "'Pledge System' Attacked," *Orangeburg Times and Democrat* (July 9, 1976), 15.

154 "New Approaches to Court Issue," *Greenville News* (January 15, 1980), 4A.

155 *Id.*, 938–939; see also "Legislators Seeking to Be Judges Said Unaware of Law," *Orangeburg Times and Democrat* (January 14, 1976), 2B.

to the legislature; the commission, which started operation about a year later, was composed of 16 members: 7 lawyers chosen by the bar and 9 nonlawyers chosen by the governor.

Reform Efforts

As early as 1961, there were calls to reform the judicial selection system by adopting the Missouri Plan, which by then had been adopted by just three states: Missouri, Kansas, and Iowa.[156] In 1972, the executive committee of the South Carolina Bar endorsed reforming judicial selection under the "concept of merit selection."[157] Newly elected Republican governor James Edwards raised the idea of merit selection for at least some judges in his 1975 State of the State Address.[158] A little over two years earlier, the electorate approved a constitutional amendment calling for a unified court system, but implementing legislation had not yet been passed;[159] there was some support for including merit selection provisions as part of that implementing legislation.[160] When finally in 1976 the legislature passed implementing legislation, the Republican governor vetoed it, citing its failure to include "an adequate method for merit selection of judges" and the lack of "a good mechanism for disciplining judges."[161] The governor later signed a judicial reform measure that did not include merit selection provisions or provisions concerning judicial discipline;[162] this came after the chief justice announced that in his opinion "the Supreme Court has the inherent authority to discipline wayward judges," a view that circuit judges later acknowledged.[163]

Despite calls for merit selection of judges from various quarters, including its inclusion in the state Republican Party's 1978 platform,[164] nothing more happened on the issue during the 1970s. This is not to say that merit selection was not a major

156 "Charleston Legislator Wants Judge Selection System Studied," *Greenwood Index-Journal* (February 1, 1961), 5. The idea of using the Missouri Plan for a limited jurisdiction court (i.e., one not necessarily subject to legislative election) had been raised in 1953 as part of a call for the creation of a domestic relations court; see Gil Rowland, "Grand Jury Recommends Domestic Relations Court," *Greenville News* (December 9, 1953), 2.

157 "Judgeship Hearings Get Bar Backing," *Aiken Standard* (January 17, 1975), 2.

158 Henry Eason, "Governor Appeals for Fiscal Restraint," *Greenville News* (January 30, 1975), 2; see also, "Gov. Edwards Says Judicial Reform Is Key Program," *Aiken Standard* (February 28, 1975), 11.

159 "Greenwood Will Host Meeting on Improving Court System," *Greenwood Index-Journal* (April 5, 1975), 9.

160 "Opportunity for Reform Praised," *Greenville News* (May 2, 1975), 20.

161 "Edwards Vetoes Judicial Bill," *Greenville News* (April 14, 1976), 1; see also "Edwards Urged to Stand By Objections to Judicial Reform," *Greenwood Index-Journal* (June 14, 1976), 15.

162 See Earl M. Middleton, "Adjournment of Legislature Comes Abruptly This Year," *Orangeburg Times and Democrat* (July 4, 1976), 10B.

163 Al Lanier, "Disciplinary Powers of Court Acknowledged," *Greenville News* (August 27, 1976), 8.

164 "S.C. GOP Party Platform Against ERA," *Orangeburg Times and Democrat* (April 10, 1978), 3B.

topic during that time. It was, but the concern was merit selection for the members of the Public Service Commission (PSC). As was noted previously, the PSC commissioners were also elected by the legislature. The debate over merit selection for the PSC produced extensive newspaper coverage during the latter half of the 1970s. Provisions for an element of merit selection were finally passed in 1979. Under those provisions, the legislature was constrained to candidates nominated by an 11-member commission, 6 of whose members were chosen by the legislature (3 each by the House and Senate) with the other 5 chosen by the governor.[165]

During the 1980s, the issue of reforming judicial selection came up with some regularity.[166] It was raised by citizens' groups,[167] the state bar,[168] and some legislators who introduced proposals for reforms.[169] Editorials calling for reform appeared with some frequency.[170] There were also several controversial selection or retention decisions made by the legislature.[171] By the end of the decade, there appeared to be some momentum for change starting to build. A statewide poll in late 1988 found that only 19 percent of the respondents favored retaining the current system; 39 percent wanted popular elections and 35 percent preferred a system that included a nominating commission.[172]

Two political events were to come together in the first half of the 1990s that arguably led to the South Carolina General Assembly passing and sending to the voters an amendment limiting the Assembly's traditional autonomy in selecting judges for the appellate and higher trial courts. Those two events were a large-scale corruption scandal involving at least one judge and the Republican Party's capture of a chamber of the legislature in the 1994 election for the first time in 116 years.

[165] Al Lanier, "PSC Bill Becomes S.C. Law," *Orangeburg Times and Democrat* (July 19, 1979), 1B.

[166] See generally, Brenda Paschal, "Filling Judges' Chairs," *Greenville News* (December 16, 1984), 1E; David Reed, "Judicial Selection Process Comes in for Criticism," *Orangeburg Times and Democrat* (January 31, 1988), 1A.

[167] "Citizens Group Endorses Merit Selection of Judges," *Greenville News* (May 19, 1980), 8B.

[168] "State Bar May Push for Merit Judges," *Greenville News* (November 15, 1981), 1B; Marilyn Rauber, "Lawyers to Tackle Ethical, Political Quandaries," *Greenville News* (June 20, 1985), 1C; Dan Hoover, "Bar to Weigh Change in Way of Selecting Judges in State," *Greenville News* (June 10, 1988), 3C.

[169] Bob Thompson, "Drummond Backs Election Changes for Judgeships," *Greenwood Index-Journal* (May 10, 1982), 18; Duncan Mansfield, "Senators Hopeful Bill Will Help in Judge Selection," *Orangeburg Times and Democrat* (January 27, 1983), 13b.

[170] See, for example, "A Better System to Retain Judges," *Greenville News* (March 4, 1982), 4A; "More Judicial Troubles," *Orangeburg Times and Democrat* (April 22, 1988), 10.

[171] Ford Fessenden, "Robinson Vote Will Test Legislature," *Greenville News* (April 11, 1982), 1D; Marilyn Rauber, "Panel's Advice Ignored; Lawmakers Pick Judge Who Is Ex-Alcoholic," *Greenville News* (June 14, 1984), 1C; Trip Dubard, "Richter Hearings Herald New Age in Judicial Selection," *Orangeburg Times and Democrat* (March 29, 1988), 10B.

[172] "Lawmakers to Review Judicial System," *Greenwood Index-Journal* (January 2, 1989), 9; see also "Judicial Selection Process in State May See Change," *Orangeburg Times and Democrat* (June 26, 1989), 1A.

The scandal arose from an FBI investigation and sting operation focused on corruption involving a range of state government officials.[173] Operation Lost Trust (OLT), as it was known, became public in July 1990. OLT had started in 1987. About three months before the scandal broke, the legislature had elected House member Tee Ferguson to a circuit court judgeship. He joined 22 other former legislators among the 31 circuit court judges. Unknown at the time of his election was that he had recently accepted a bribe to support a betting bill and had possessed cocaine on several occasions. After only four months on the bench, Ferguson took a voluntary leave of absence; a year later he was convicted on the bribery charge and later pled guilty to cocaine possession.[174] When the smoke cleared from the scandal, 27 persons had pled guilty or been convicted at trial on various charges, including 16 legislators.[175] As one might guess, OLT did not do a lot for the reputation of either the legislature or the judiciary, nor did an unrelated scandal involving claims that sex had been exchanged for court rulings.[176]

As for the partisan developments, Republican James Edwards served as governor for only four years (1975–1978), during which he faced an opposing legislature, 90 percent of whose members were Democrats. Democrat Richard Riley held the office for the next eight years (1979–1986); during his tenure, Republican strength in the legislature grew from about 10 percent to over 20 percent. Republican Carrol Campbell followed Riley. Democrats maintained control of the legislature during Campbell's eight years (1987–1994), but Republicans continued to gain strength, holding 35 percent of the Senate seats and 40 percent of the House seats during Campbell's last two years. Republican David Beasley won the 1994 gubernatorial election, and in with him came a Republican 70-to-54 majority in the South Carolina House of Representatives; Democrats continued to hold the Senate, but now with only 57 percent of the seats. It was the Republican-controlled House that first passed a constitutional amendment modifying judicial selection in 1995.

In 1990, when Democrats had strong majorities in both chambers,[177] the General Assembly passed a statute that prohibited "candidates [for judgeships] seeking pledges of support from lawmakers before being reviewed by a legislative screening committee."[178] This statute was an attempt to "create a level playing field for all

[173] For a detailed chronology of the unfolding scandal, see John V. Crangle, *Operation Lost Trust and the Ethics Reform Movement* (West Columbia, SC: Professional Printers, 2017).

[174] *Id.*, 25–26.

[175] *Id.*, 590.

[176] "Scandal Shows Reforms Are Needed," *Greenville News* [reprinted from *The (Columbia) State*] (May 8, 1994), 7.

[177] The divisions were 35–11 in the Senate and 88–36 in the House, both in favor of Democrats. See https://en.wikipedia.org/wiki/Political_party_strength_in_South_Carolina.

[178] Jeff Miller, "Ban on Lobbying by Candidates for Judgeships Advances," *The (Columbia) State* (June 7, 1970), 7A; see also www.judicialselection.us/judicial_selection/reform_efforts/formal_changes_since_inception.cfm?state=SC.

[judicial] candidates" by addressing the criticisms of South Carolina's "closed [judicial selection] process."[179] The legislation lacked penalties for violating the prohibition on pledge seeking,[180] and it is unclear how effective that prohibition actually was. The ban on pledge-seeking failed to resolve the critics' primary concerns, as evidenced several years later when the General Assembly elected two judges who had formerly served as legislators, despite a committee of the South Carolina Bar finding both to be "not qualified" for the positions.[181]

In early 1992, a proposal limiting the legislature's discretion in choosing judges to persons nominated by a screening committee was advanced jointly by the Democratic lieutenant governor, the Republican Secretary of State, and Common Cause.[182] Nothing came of this proposal, nor in connection with a proposal introduced the following year that would have had judicial candidates nominated by a seven-person panel consisting of nonlegislators.[183] As controversies surrounding the judicial selection process continued through this period,[184] so did calls for change.[185] Increasingly, lawmakers themselves were calling for reform.[186]

At the end of 1992, in response to the inaction by the legislature, the state bar decided to establish its own judicial screening panel. That panel consisted of twelve attorneys who would review the qualifications of candidates. Following the model of the American Bar Association's committee that reviewed nominees to the federal bench,[187] the state bar's committee would rate candidates as "exceptionally well qualified," "well qualified," "qualified," or "not qualified." The chief justice of South Carolina expressed the hope that the process would provide more

179 www.judicialselection.us/judicial_selection/reform_efforts/formal_changes_since_inception.cfm?state=SC.

180 See *Acts and Joint Resolutions of the General Assembly of the State of South Carolina*, 1990 Regular Session, Chapter 610, Part IV, p. 2609.

181 See https://ballotpedia.org/Judicial_selection_in_South_Carolina, accessed October 25, 2018; see also James H. Ritchie Jr., "The Judicial Merit Selection Commission: History of the JMSC and the Screening Process for Judges in This State," *South Carolina Lawyer* 26 (July 2007), 27–31.

182 "Plan Would Change Selection of Judges," www.goupstate.com/article/NC/19920114/News/605189757/SJ/, accessed October 14, 2018.

183 "Judicial Screening Panel Proposed," *Greenville News* (January 21, 1993), 3C.

184 Tom Inman, "State Bar Fiasco Reflects High Court's Influence," *Greenville News* (May 2, 1993), 2E; "James T. Hammond, "Charges Swapped Over Appeals Court Judgeship Race," *Greenville News* (May 29, 1993), 1; Tucker Lyon, "Votes on Judges Based on a Wide Array of Reasons," *Orangeburg Times and Democrat* (June 6, 1993), 8B; "Judge Bell's Election Invites Further Review," *Greenville News* (May 28, 1994), 4A.

185 Cindi Ross Scoppe, "High-Level Reformers Want to Change Way S.C. Selects Judges," *The (Columbia) State* (February 16, 1994), 5B.

186 William Fox, "Judicial Selection Process Criticized; Many Call System Demeaning, But No Consensus for Change Exists," *Greenville News* (May 29, 1994), 1F.

187 See Joel B. Grossman, *Lawyers and Judges: The ABA and the Politics of Judicial Selection* (New York: John Wiley & Sons, 1965); or Elliot E. Slotnick, "The ABA Standing Committee on the Federal Judiciary: A Contemporary Assessment," 66 *Judicature* 349–362, 385–393 (1983).

information and help insure that the best people were put on the bench.[188] The panel started rating candidates the following year and encountered controversy the first time it issued ratings. The controversy arose when the only sitting legislator, Thomas Huff, seeking one of two open positions, was rated "not qualified."[189] Huff, who was running for a position on the Court of Appeals, lost the election in the legislature.[190]

With the 1994 election, the legislative landscape changed. Republicans won 62 of the 124 House seats, with Democrats capturing 59 and Independents, 3.[191] This set off a series of party switches, with the first one in early January 1995 giving the Republicans a majority of 63 in the House of Representatives;[192] by the end of 1995, Republicans had picked up a total of 8 seats through party switches. The result was that by 1996, Democrats no longer had effective control of judicial elections. Republicans now held a majority, 88 of the 170 legislative seats, and, given that judges were elected by the two chambers sitting together, this meant that Republicans arguably had control. However, it is likely that Republicans were not confident that they would maintain control in the future, which, if true, would provide an incentive to support change. Democrats also now had an incentive to support change, because it was clear that they could no longer be confident of controlling the selection process.

Further impetus for change came in the form of several additional controversies in the courts:[193]

- Two probate judges were accused of embezzling money from estates.
- A family court judge who had been accused of demanding sexual favors in exchange for a ruling in a litigant's favor pled guilty to the resulting criminal charges.
- A magistrate judge pled guilty to fondling a woman who appeared in his courtroom.
- The South Carolina Bar evaluation of judges coming up for reelection by the legislature found that one circuit judge did not know the law.

[188] Matthew Burns, "Panel to Screen Judicial Candidates," *Greenville News* (November 25, 1992), 3C.

[189] James T. Hammond, "Bar's Judicial Ratings Process under Fire," *Greenville News* (April 30, 1993), 1A; see also James T. Hammond, "State Bar Gives Reasons for the Ratings of Judge Candidates," *Greenville News* (May 5, 1993), 2C.

[190] James T. Hammond, "Connor Defeats Huff in Close Race for Judgeship," *Greenville News* (June 3, 1993), 1A.

[191] "Wilkins Planning for Pioneering Role," *Orangeburg Times and Democrat* (November 29, 1994), 13.

[192] James T. Hammond, "Latest Switch Gives FOP House Majority; Newberry Lawmaker David Waldrop Leaves Democrats," *Greenville News* (January 4, 1995), 10.

[193] Cindi Ross Scoppe, "Push Begins for Change in How Judges Selected; Common Cause Thinks It Has Better Methods," *The (Columbia) State* (January 17, 1995), B3.

It probably helped that the Republican Party platform in 1994 called for judicial reform[194] and that the new Republican governor had campaigned in part on the need to modify the judicial selection process, in particular favoring a ban on sitting legislators being elected to judicial positions by their colleagues.[195]

Even as possible changes were under consideration by legislative committees, the election or reelection of controversial judicial candidates continued, including the reelection of the circuit court judge whom the state bar committee had found not to know the law and the election to the Supreme Court of the least qualified of the candidates for that position.[196] Those elections led the vice-chairman of the legislature's own judicial screening panel to resign from the panel; he described the process as a "grand charade" and charged that the General Assembly didn't "give a damn" about the candidates' qualifications.[197] A second member also resigned.[198] These events seemed to fuel the drive toward some type of change, and proponents of change in the legislature threatened to hold up votes on additional judge positions.[199]

In early April 1995, the Republican governor, joined by the Republican leaders of the now Republican-controlled House, advanced a proposal to have judges appointed by the governor from a list of candidates nominated by an independent commission. That commission would be appointed jointly by the governor and the legislature. Legislation to adopt the plan, which would require a constitutional amendment, was introduced by 37 House members. Unsurprisingly, the proposal was met with skepticism by the Democrats controlling the Senate.[200] A counterproposal was offered by the Legislative Black Caucus: judges should be chosen by popular election rather than by either legislative elections or gubernatorial appointment.[201] A third proposal was advanced by the Democratic leader in the House: the legislature would continue to elect judges, but the candidates would be limited to those advanced by a nine-member nominating commission whose members would be chosen by the legislature, the chief justice, the state bar

194 Telephone interview, David Wilkins, October 17, 2018.

195 "Judicial Reform Could Use Shove from New Governor," *The (Columbia) State* (January 17, 1995), A8.

196 Lisa Green and Cindi Ross Scoppe, "Burnette Rises to High Court; Deals Deliver Least Qualified to the Bench," *The (Columbia) State* (March 22, 1995), A1.

197 James T. Hammond, "Judicial Vote Leads to Resignation; Screening Panel Vice Chairman Says Lawmakers Treat Process Like 'a Joke,'" *Greenville News* (March 23,1995), 1A.

198 "2 Members Quit Judicial Committee," *Spartanburg Herald-Journal* (March 24, 1995).

199 Cindi Ross Scoppe, "Judicial Election Foes Turn Up Heat; Governor Edges Closer to Reform Camp," *The (Columbia) State* (March 31, 1995), A1; see also, "Group in House Vows to Stall Judges' Elections to Get Reform; Black Lawmakers Fear Changing Rules Now Is Aimed at Them," *Greenville News* (March 31, 1995).

200 Cindi Ross Scoppe, "Governor Wants to Select Judges," *The (Columbia) State* (April 7, 1995), A1; "GOP Says Governor Should Pick Judges," *Greenwood Index-Journal* (April 7, 1995), 1; "Competitive Move on Judicial Selection," *Greenville News* (April 12, 1995), 4.

201 Cindi Ross Scoppe, "Caucus Says Public Should Pick Judges," *The (Columbia) State* (April 13, 1995), B5; see also "Don't Elect Judges," *The (Columbia) State* (April 19, 1995), A8.

association, the trial lawyers association, and the defense lawyers association; legislators could not be nominated until they had been out of office for a year.[202] These proposals set off an effort by legislators to find a compromise.[203] By the end of April, the prospect of judicial selection reform passing the legislature in 1995 was dimming, but efforts continued on with competing plans from the two chambers.[204]

The House Judiciary Committee approved a proposal for a constitutional amendment that would have the governor appoint judges from lists forwarded by a nominating commission, but rejected a plan for a more modest change that could have been included as part of the budget bill pending in the chamber.[205] A version of that proposal, involving a nominating commission and restrictions on legislators being elected to judgeships, had been included in the Senate's version of the budget bill.[206] A couple of additional controversial judicial selections toward the end of May reignited the debate over judicial selection reform,[207] and the House unanimously passed a resolution for a constitutional amendment that would create an expanded Judicial Merit Selection Commission to review all judicial candidates and to raise the age and experience requirements for judges; it did not act on other aspects of reform, including limiting legislative consideration to those nominated by the proposed Judicial Merit Selection Commission or requiring legislators to resign from the legislature before they could become candidates for judicial positions.[208] That ended legislative action on judicial selection reform, but it did not end the controversy for the year. In mid-June, before adjourning, the legislature had another controversial judicial election when it ousted an African American female family court judge and replaced her with a white male. The incumbent had been deemed unqualified by the legislative's screening committee.[209]

Another issue that came up at the very end of the session was whether to hold a special session in October to elect judges to fill nine newly created judgeships.[210]

202 Lisa Greene and Cindi Ross Scoppe, "How to Pick Judges: Ability or Accountability; Other States' Efforts Guide for S.C. Reform," *The (Columbia) State* (April 25, 1995), A1.

203 Cindi Ross Scoppe, "Lawmakers Seek Compromise on Judicial Selection," *The (Columbia) State* (April 20, 1995), B4.

204 "Legislative Judicial Selection Reform Becoming Less Likely," *Orangeburg Times and Democrat* (April 29, 1995), 8A.

205 "House Turns Down Judicial Reform," *Greenwood Index-Journal* (May 11, 1995), 13; Cindi Ross Scoppe, "House Won't Let Judicial Reform Ride Fast Track with Budget Bill," *The (Columbia) State* (May 11, 1995), B1.

206 *Id.*; see also Cindi Ross Scoppe, "Senate Bill Would Emphasize Merit in Choosing Judges," *The (Columbia) State* (May 4, 1995), B1.

207 Cindi Ross Scoppe, "Judicial Reform Heats Up; Criticized Judge Re-Elected by 3 Votes," *The (Columbia) State* (May 26, 1995), B1.

208 Sid Gaulden, "House Leaders Agree on Judicial Reform; A Constitutional Change Would Raise Age and Experience Requirements and Create a Judicial Merit Selection Commission to Review Hopefuls," *Charleston Post and Courier* (May 31, 1995), 6A.

209 "Rogers Voted Out as Judge," *Charleston Post and Courier* (June 13, 1995), 13A.

210 Cindi Ross Scoppe, "Delay Vote on Judges, Critics Urge; October Election Date Under Fire," *The (Columbia) State* (June 11, 1995), B1.

Three legislators and two former law partners of the House Speaker were running for some of those seats. The Republican-controlled House voted in favor of the special session, but the Democratic-controlled Senate rejected the idea.[211] In July, a question arose as to whether the 1937 law barring legislators from being appointed to a state government position that had been created while they were serving in the legislature until after they had been reelected or had left the legislature applied to the nine new judgeships. Several of the seats were for the new Court of Appeals, which had been created after voter approval of a constitutional amendment in 1984; the qualifications for those positions was set by that amendment. Several additional seats were judgeships on the family court, the qualifications of which were set by statute.[212] The legislature decided to ask the Supreme Court to rule on this question,[213] and in November, the Court ruled that the law did apply to the family court positions, but not to the Court of Appeals positions, because the qualifications for that court were set by the constitution in the amendment authorizing the court. This ruling was important for the efforts to reform judicial selection, because it made clear that many of the changes being debated could not be implemented by statute but would require a constitutional amendment.[214] This was seen as a setback because a constitutional amendment required a two-thirds majority in each chamber of the legislature rather than a simple majority, and it meant that the earliest time that changes could take effect would be sometime in 1997, given that the legislature would have to confirm by majority votes in each chamber the approval of the electorate if that approval came in the November 1996 election.[215]

Things came together in 1996. Controversies surrounding judicial elections continued. The state bar came under criticism in January, when the committee that reviewed judicial candidates found four female candidates for judgeships unqualified.[216] In an election for a position on the Court of Appeals, a circuit judge endorsed by 11 past presidents of the South Carolina Bar Association[217] was defeated by ex-legislator Thomas Huff,[218] by 13 votes; as previously discussed, Huff had lost a similar election in 1993 when he was a member of the legislature, after being rated

[211] Jesse J. Holland, "Senate Rejects Special Judicial Election," *Greenville News* (June 14, 1995), 5D.

[212] Cindi Ross Scoppe, "Law Hindering Path to Judgeships; Legislators Await Decision on Their Eligibility," *The (Columbia) State* (June 19, 1995), B1.

[213] Cindi Ross Scoppe, "Court Asked to Rule on Judgeships; Lawmakers Want OK to Seek New Seats," *The (Columbia) State* (July 20, 1995), B1.

[214] Joint Legislative Committee for Judicial Screening Through McConnell v. Huff, 464 S.E.2d 324 (S.C. 1995).

[215] Cindi Ross Scoppe and Lisa Greene, "Court Backs Lawmakers' Judicial Bids; Ruling Is a Setback for Reformers," *The (Columbia) State* (November 16, 1995), A1; "Legislators Freed to Run for Some Judgeships," *Greenwood Index-Journal* (November 16, 1995), 4A.

[216] Lisa Green and Cindi Ross Scoppe, "Bar's Power over Bench Stirs Critics; Reports Can't Shake Fairness Questions," *The (Columbia) State* (January 21, 1996), B1.

[217] "Bar Presidents Weigh In," *The (Columbia) State* (February 14, 1996), A10.

[218] Huff had resigned to run for the judgeship.

"not qualified" by a bar committee.[219] In March, the Republican state attorney general proposed that the state adopt a system that included retention elections, but that proposal does not appear to have been seriously considered.[220]

Later in March, a consensus on a proposal for judicial selection reform seemed to be emerging. A Senate subcommittee approved legislation that would (1) create an independent nominating commission that would only forward qualified candidates and (2) require that legislators be out of office for a year before running for a judgeship. The House had approved a similar plan that would have required legislators to resign at the time they apply to the nominating commission.[221] Eventually, the difference regarding a waiting period for legislators had to be resolved by a conference committee.[222] The issue of the composition of the proposed nominating commission and who would name members to the commission was left to be determined in the implementing legislation. The amendment proposal and the implementing legislation were treated as a package, and it was elements of the latter that raised concerns in the House, leading to it send the proposals back to the conference committee.[223] Some of the concerns in the House included details on how long a legislator had to be out of office before seeking a judgeship and a provision providing jail time for legislators who swap votes in a judicial election.[224]

After the House did pass a version of the implementing legislation, it went back to the Senate, and the Senate balked;[225] whether the stall in the Senate reflected actual concerns about the measure or was part of an effort to get the House to go along on other legislation is unclear.[226] Two or three days later, the Senate relented and passed both the amendment and the implementing legislation.[227] The amendment

219 Sid Gaulden and John Heilprin, "Huff Defeats Howard in Appeals Court Bid," *Charleston Post and Courier* (February 15, 1996), 1A.

220 Charlie Condon, "Argument for Limited Election of Judges; State Attorney General Proposes Letting Public Keep or Reject Judges When Their Terms Expire," *Greenville News* (March 18, 1996), 8A.

221 Cindi Ross Scoppe, "Court Reform Backed; Panel: Select Judges by Merit," *The (Columbia) State* (March 22, 1996), B1; Cindi Ross Scoppe, "Senate Panel Sends Judicial Selection Bill to Floor," *The (Columbia) State* (March 27, 1996), B3.

222 "Cindi Ross Scoppe, "Committee to Settle Judgeship Tiff," *The (Columbia) State* (May 9, 1996), B4.

223 Sid Gaulden, "Judicial Reform Falters in House," *Charleston Post and Courier* (May 24, 1996), 11A.

224 Cindi Ross Scoppe, "Judicial Reform Plan Stalls in House; Backers Regroup for Tuesday Effort," *The (Columbia) State* (May 24, 1996), B3.

225 Sid Gaulden, "Judicial Reform Hung Up Again," *Charleston Post and Courier* (May 29, 1996), B5.

226 Cindi Ross Scoppe, "Game-Playing Stalls Judicial-Reform Bill," *The (Columbia) State* (May 29, 1996), B3.

227 Sid Gaulden, "Senate Accepts Reform Bill," *Charleston Post and Courier* (May 30, 1996), B1; Cindi Ross Scoppe, "Legislature Overhauls Judiciary; Third Pillar of Reforms Set," *The (Columbia) State* (May 30, 1996), A1.

and the implementing legislation had strong bipartisan support in both chambers.[228] The combination of the amendment and implementing legislation provided for the following:

- Candidates for judicial positions apply to and are screened by the Judicial Merit Selection Commission (JMSC).
- After reviewing the applicants, the JMSC forwards three (presumably the best three) candidates to the legislature.
- The legislature may reject the nominees and request a new list from the JMSC.
- Legislators wanting to be candidates for judgeships have to wait one year after leaving office or one year after the end of the filing period for reelection if they have not filed for reelection.
- Candidates may not try to lock in votes prior to being forwarded by the Selection Commission; violators are subject to a 90-day jail sentence.
- Vote swapping among legislators is forbidden and violators are subject to a 90-day jail sentence.

A companion amendment increased the age of eligibility to run for judicial office and the minimum number of years of experience as an attorney.

The two amendments went to the voters in November 1996. My search of newspapers available for the months immediately preceding that election turned up no evidence of any organized opposition. There may have been some opposition from the African American community. The chairwoman of the Legislative Black Caucus had voted against the amendment and implementing legislation, and a newspaper article about two weeks before the election reported that she was concerned that minorities would be disadvantaged in the screening process and that too much power would rest in the hands of a small group likely to be mostly, if not entirely, male and white.[229] The two amendments were overwhelmingly approved by the voters: 83.7 percent in favor of the amendment increasing age and experience requirements and 82.1 percent in favor of the amendment establishing the Judicial Merit Selection Commission and constraining the legislature's selection to candidates forwarded by that commission.[230]

One important element of the implementation legislation is the structure of the JMSC. It has 10 members, and *all* members are appointed by legislative leaders: 5 by the Speaker of the House, 3 by the chairperson of the Senate Judiciary Committee, and 2 by the president pro tempore of the Senate. Six of the ten members must be

[228] James T. Hammond, "Voters May Tighten Rules on Legislators Seeking Bench," *Greenville News* (October 27, 1996), 1A.

[229] Lisa Greene, "Voters Weigh Justice," *The (Columbia) State* (October 21, 1996), A1.

[230] Author's calculation from election results available at www.scvotes.org/data/returns.html, accessed October 14, 2018.

members of the legislature, with the other four selected from "the general Public."[231] Neither the governor nor the bar is involved in selecting the commissioners. Moreover, a public member may be removed at any time by the person who appointed that member.[232] Thus, the legislature continues to effectively control the judicial selection process: it selects members of the nominating commission, a majority of the members of the commission are legislators, the nonlegislators can be dismissed for any reason, and the legislature then elects the judges. This retention of power by the legislature is not surprising, given that the centrality of legislature in South Carolina can be traced back to the colonial period. In the words of David Wilkins, who was the Speaker of the House at the time of the change, "the legislature was not willing to give up any more power than it had to."[233]

Judicial Selection since the Change

The reforms appear to have accomplished at least one of their goals: ending the dominance of judicial candidates with backgrounds as legislators. Of the 17 circuit court judges selected in roughly the first five years after the reform, only 3 were former legislators.[234] Between 1997 and 2004, there were 64 open-seat positions considered by the JMSC and a total of 265 candidacies for those positions.[235] Only 8.7 percent of the candidates were former legislators; however, 78.3 percent of the former legislator candidates were nominated, compared to 56.6 percent of candidates without legislative experience. One or more former legislators were nominated in 19 of the 64 elections (29.7 percent), with two legislators nominated in 5 of those 19 elections; however, a former legislator won only 7 of those 19 elections. Clearly, the reforms had the dual effects of reducing the likelihood that those with legislative experience would seek a judgeship and the likelihood that those who did seek a judgeship would win the election in the legislature. However, this does not mean that the legislators compete for judicial positions on a completely level field. As of 2013, two of nine members of the South Carolina Supreme Court had previously served in the state legislature as had four of the nine members of the Court of Appeals; at the circuit level, 20 percent (10 of 49) of full-time judges had experience as members of the legislature.[236]

What has been the impact of the change in South Carolina's system of judicial selection and retention? John Crangle, who was executive director of Common

[231] South Carolina Statutes, Chapter 19, §2-19-10(B).
[232] *Id.*, §2-19-10(D).
[233] Wilkins interview, *supra* note 194.
[234] Eberle, "Judicial Selection in South Carolina," *supra* note 149, 24.
[235] I refer to "candidacies" rather than "candidates" to make clear that an individual may have been a candidate more than one time.
[236] Rick Brundrett, "Easy Road from the State House to the Court House," *The Nerve* (July 3, 2013), https://thenerve.org/easy-road-from-the-state-house-to-the-court-house/, accessed March 24, 2019.

Cause in the 1990s and one of the key participants in the drive to reform the selection process, sees the process as having produced higher quality judges:[237]

> The quality of judges in South Carolina is pretty good now in the state court system. We don't have incompetents. We don't have judges that give you home cooking, which we used to have a lot of. The judges in South Carolina [today] play it pretty straight.

A study of the South Carolina Supreme Court's decisions in criminal cases during the six years immediately after the change concludes that the change had "clearly increased the independence of the judiciary,"[238] as reflected in an increased willingness to overturn prior precedents and to defy the United States Supreme Court.

CONCLUSION

Since 1980, each of the three states in this chapter has adopted a different system of elite selection of judges that employs a nominating commission to screen potential appointees. All three describe their systems as involving "merit selection," although one might argue with that characterization with regard to the system in Connecticut.[239] In that state, the Judicial Selection Commission (JSC) is more of a screening body, determining only whether potential appointees are qualified; although the role of the JSC is described as "to evaluate, investigate and recommend qualified candidates for consideration by the Governor for nomination as judges," virtually everyone who applies is deemed qualified and goes on a standing list, from which the governor makes appointments. One could also argue that the design of the Judicial Merit Selection Commission in South Carolina is such that the politics of selection continue to be heavily partisan, because all members of the JMSC are chosen by the leaders of the majority party in the state legislature and a majority of the members must be members of the legislature.

One common element across these three states is that scandals involving judges or selection of judges played a role in prompting the changes to judicial selection, arguably a dominant role in Rhode Island and South Carolina. In those two states, it is unlikely that change would have occurred in the absence of the scandals. A second commonality across the three states is that partisanship and/or policy concerns were not a major factor in the debates surrounding the changes that did occur, although one could detect some partisan maneuvering, and in South Carolina that rise of the Republican Party had a role in the change process.[240]

[237] Crangle interview, *supra* note 144.
[238] Petillo, "The Untouchables," *supra* note 150, 943.
[239] See www.ct.gov/jsc/site/default.asp, accessed June 23, 2019.
[240] *Id.*, 960.

PART III

Unsuccessful Change Efforts

11

Florida and South Dakota

Unsuccessful Efforts to Extend the Missouri Plan

In two states, voters approved the adoption of Missouri Plan systems for the state's appellate level courts, Florida in 1976 and South Dakota in 1980, but then rejected later proposals to adopt the system for trial-level courts. This chapter examines what transpired in Florida and South Dakota.

FLORIDA

In 1953, the Florida legislature created the Judicial Council and charged it with recommending changes to the state's judicial system.[1] In April 1955, the Judicial Council recommended that the state adopt the Missouri Plan for the Florida Supreme Court, for a new set of District Courts of Appeal, and for the trial-level circuit courts.[2] However, that proposal was quickly discarded by the Florida Senate committee considering the proposal.[3] It would be more than twenty years before the plan was adopted for the state's appellate courts, although the voters of Dade County adopted a version of the Missouri Plan for local courts in the mid-1960s.[4] The Council's recommendation that an intermediate appellate court be created was adopted. However, as discussed in the following pages, voters twice rejected proposals to apply the Missouri Plan to Florida's trial courts.

1 "Judicial Council Concentrates on 5 Major Studies," *Fort Pierce News Tribune* (January 31, 1954), 3.

2 "Judiciary Changes Recommended," *Pensacola News Journal* (April 29, 1955), 5B.

3 "'Missouri' Plan of Selecting Judges Killed, 3 Appellate Courts Endorsed," *Tampa Morning Tribune* (May 20, 1985), 5A; the House committee had approved adopting a version of the Missouri Plan.

4 "Modified Missouri Plan Is Sound," *Miami News* (September 4, 1963, 6A; "Metro Amendments," *Miami News* (November 6, 1963), 1.

Background

As was true of the other southern states, Florida was essentially one-party Democratic into the 1950s. As late as 1960, there was just one Republican in the Florida Senate and only three in the Florida House. However, Florida was different from the other Deep South states. First, as early as 1940, almost half of the state's population had not been born in Florida.[5] Second, unlike most of the other southern states, there were no coherent factions in the Democratic Party;[6] Key subtitled the chapter on Florida in his seminal work on southern politics "Every Man for Himself."

The political complexion of the state started to change in the 1960s. The 1966 election of Claude Kirk as the first Republican governor since the end of Reconstruction was combined with growing Republican strength in the state legislature. The 1966 election increased the number of Republicans in the Florida Senate from 2 to 20; in the House the increase was from 10 to 39.[7] Although there would be an 18-year gap between Republican governors, and it would be the mid- to late 1990s before Republicans gained control of the legislature, politics in Florida was changed by the Republican surge in the 1960s.[8] By the mid-1990s, whites in Florida were roughly evenly split between Democrat and Republican in their party registration, and in self-identification, white Republicans outnumbered white Democrats roughly 3 to 2 (44.7 percent to 28.9 percent).[9] Starting in 1999, except for a brief period when the incumbent Republican governor declared himself an Independent, Republicans have, through 2018, maintained control of the two political branches of government.[10]

Into the 1960s, Florida had a fragmented court system, with large numbers of local courts, many of which served as revenue sources for local communities.[11] In 1965, a Constitution Revision Commission was created, in significant part to rectify apportionment problems created by the one-person, one-vote decisions of the U.S. Supreme Court.[12] The new constitution that was approved by the voters in 1968 did

5 V. O. Key Jr., *Southern Politics in State and Nation* (New York: Alfred Knopf, 1949), 87; 48.1 percent of Florida's population was born outside Florida, with the next closest of the southern states being Arkansas, at 22.3 percent. In-migration was a continuing feature of Florida's population; between 1990 and 1995, 1.2 million people moved to Florida – see Thomas R. Dye, *Politics in Florida* (Upper Saddle River, NJ: Prentice-Hall, 1998), 2.

6 *Id.*, 87–96.

7 See https://en.wikipedia.org/wiki/Political_party_strength_in_Florida, accessed January 9, 2019.

8 On the electoral fortunes of the two parties between 1968 and 1996, see Stephen C. Craig, "Elections and Partisan Change," in Robert J. Huckshorn, ed., *Government and Politics in Florida*, 2nd ed. (Gainesville: University Press of Florida), 30–65.

9 Dye, *Politics in Florida*, *supra* note 5, 14.

10 See https://en.wikipedia.org/wiki/Political_party_strength_in_Florida, accessed January 9, 2019.

11 Roger Handberg and Mark Lawhorn, "The Courts: Powerful but Obscure," in Robert J. Huckshorn, ed., *Government and Politics in Florida*, 2nd ed. (Gainesville: University Press of Florida), 151.

12 Baker v. Carr, 369 U.S. 186 (1962); Gray v. Sanders, 372 U.S. 368 (1963); Reynolds v. Sims, 377 U.S. 533 (1964).

not change the judicial article, because no agreement could be reached in the legislature on that article.[13] One change in the 1968 constitution that would be important for judicial reform was a provision that a constitution revision commission would meet in 1978 and then every twenty years with the power to submit amendments to the electorate without the approval of the legislature.[14] In late 1971, the legislature did come to an agreement on a revised judicial article, and it was approved by the voters in March 1972.[15] That amendment simplified the court system: a Supreme Court, the District Courts of Appeal, the circuit courts, and the county courts.[16] The amendment also changed judicial elections from partisan to nonpartisan.

Judicial Selection in Florida prior to 1972

Florida's Reconstruction-era constitution called for judges of both the Supreme Court and the circuit court to be appointed by the governor with the consent of the Senate. In 1885, selection of justices of the Supreme Court was changed to (partisan) elections, with the governor filling midterm vacancies. It was not until 1942 that a constitutional amendment changed the selection of circuit court judges from appointment to partisan elections, retaining the role of the governor to fill midterm vacancies.[17] The same system applied to the judges of the District Courts of Appeal that were created in 1957.

Although judges were nominally chosen through partisan elections during the middle part of the twentieth century, the effective selection system was appointive. One description of the system as it operated into the 1960s was that there existed:[18]

> a silent de facto conspiracy . . . among the judiciary, the Florida Bar, and the various governors to nullify the partisan election process. Retiring judges would resign near enough to the end of their term that time would permit no special election to be called. The governor would appoint an interim judge, who would run for reelection as an incumbent, usually supported by the state bar through local selection committees, scaring off most potential opponents.

Virtually no incumbent judges were defeated, and relatively few were even opposed because unsuccessful opponents would have to practice before the judge they had

13 "Main Portion of New Constitution Approved," *Orlando Evening Star* (July 3, 1968), 2A.

14 Robert J. Huckshorn, "Introduction," in Robert J. Huckshorn, ed., *Government and Politics in Florida*, 2nd ed. (Gainesville: University Press of Florida), 3–4.

15 See https://ballotpedia.org/Florida_Court_System,_Amendment_1_(March_1972), accessed January 9, 2019; 70.5 percent voted in favor of the amendment.

16 Handberg and Lawhorn, "The Courts," *supra* note 11, 151–152.

17 See www.judicialselection.us/judicial_selection/reform_efforts/formal_changes_since_inception.cfm?state=FL, accessed January 9, 2019.

18 Handberg and Lawhorn, "The Courts," *supra* note 11, 157.

opposed and few practicing lawyers wanted to face that possibility.[19] Even though the elections were nominally partisan, few Republicans bothered to challenge incumbent Democrats or run in the occasional open-seat election. Arguably, the contested elections that did occur were effectively nonpartisan, because they took place in the Democratic primary.

Between 1946 and 1966, there were 33 elections for the Florida Supreme Court. Only 6 of those elections were contested, all 6 in the Democratic primary. None of the 33 elections was for an open seat. At the circuit level, there were approximately 300 elections, less than a quarter of which were contested. Most of those contests were in the Democratic primary. Only 16 circuit elections over that period were contested by Republicans; Republicans won 5 of those elections and were unopposed by Democrats in another 8. Most of the Republican candidates came from the Sixth Circuit, which encompassed two counties on the Gulf Coast near Tampa. The first elections for the judges of the District Courts of Appeal were in 1958, and through 1966 there were a total of 24 elections for that court; only 2 were contested, one in the Democratic primary and one in the general election.

In 1966, Floridians elected Republican Claude Kirk governor, and he started appointing Republicans to the courts. The effect was to inject partisanship into the judicial appointment and election processes beyond the few locales where Republicans were starting to have electoral success. It also meant that Democrats leaving the bench might prefer to let voters choose their successors rather than giving that power to the Republican governor. In 1968, there were 3 elections for the Florida Supreme Court; 2 were for open seats and 1 involved an incumbent appointed in August 1968 by Governor Kirk. All three were contested in the general elections and all three also involved Democratic primaries, one requiring a runoff; one of the open-seat elections also had a Republic primary. The last partisan election for the Florida Supreme Court occurred in 1970, and it was uncontested, with an incumbent Democrat running for his fourth full six-year term.[20] That year, there were 9 seats up for the District Courts of Appeal, with no general elections but 3 contested Democratic primaries and 3 unopposed Republican incumbents.

Changing Judicial Selection

The 1972 Change to Nonpartisan Elections

Discussions of changing from partisan elections to the Missouri Plan system in Florida dated from at least the mid-1950s, when it was proposed by the Judicial Council and garnered some supported in the Florida House of Representatives, but

[19] *Id.*

[20] Information on Florida Supreme Court elections is from data collected for Herbert M. Kritzer, *Justices on the Ballot: Continuity and Change in State Supreme Court Elections* (New York: Cambridge University Press, 2015).

was then rejected by the Florida Senate. The idea of the Missouri Plan appeared with some regularity in Florida newspapers in the years before the overhaul of the Florida constitution in 1968, and the discussions of that overhaul regularly included extensive discussion of whether to adopt the Missouri Plan. This started even before the Constitution Revision Commission was created in 1965.[21] Not surprisingly, in early 1965, the Florida Bar Association came out in support of the Missouri Plan.[22] Later that year, a bill for a constitutional amendment adopting the Missouri Plan was introduced in the Senate, but there was no action on the bill.[23]

Once the Constitution Revision Commission got to work in 1966, the committee charged with rewriting the judicial article included the Missouri Plan in its draft proposal.[24] The proposal attracted opposition from a Republican leader who expressed a preference for nonpartisan elections[25] and from the state Chamber of Commerce, which expressed a preference for retaining an elected judiciary.[26] The overall Constitution Revision Commission voted 20–12 to recommend nonpartisan elections rather than the Missouri Plan,[27] although the Commission chairman continued to advocate for the Missouri Plan.[28]

The following summer, it became clear that including the Missouri Plan in a new judicial amendment faced substantial opposition in the House. A survey of House members reported a 42–6 preference against, although another 22 respondents did not indicate a preference, and a further 49 did not responded to the survey.[29] The Senate-House committee seeking to resolve the conflict over the judicial article during the fall of 1967 found something of a compromise by adopting a nominating commission system for filling midterm vacancies and changing judicial elections from partisan to nonpartisan. The latter change was probably acceptable to Democrats because some circuit judges had lost to Republicans in the 1966 election that brought in Republican Claude Kirk as governor.[30]

[21] See David Rosenbaum, "New Judicial System in Line? Missouri Plan Studied," *St. Petersburg Times* (July 28, 1964), 2B.

[22] William Purvis, "Legislation Affecting Courts to be Discussed by Judges," *Tampa Bay Times* (February 3, 1965).

[23] Maurice Harling, "'Missouri Plan' on Judges Asked," *Pensacola News Journal* (April 23, 1965), 9B.

[24] "Plan to Appoint Judges Proposed for Constitution," *Fort Myers News-Press* (September 27, 1966), 1.

[25] "'Missouri Plan' Attacked; GOP Leader Suggests Alternative," *St. Petersburg Times* (November 24, 1966), 2B.

[26] Ron Pedderson, "Constitution 'Overhauled': State C-C Groups Proposes Changes," *Tampa Bay Times* (November 22, 1966), 10B.

[27] Don Pride, "Non-Party Judge Elections Voted over Missouri Plan," *Tampa Bay Times* (December 13, 1966), B1.

[28] "Appointed Cabinet, 'Missouri Plan' Urged," *Tampa Bay Times* (January 28, 1967), B1.

[29] "2-Chamber Legislature, Annual Sessions, Elective Judges Favored in Solon Survey," *Pensacola Journal* (August 4, 1967), 8C.

[30] "A Reasonable Compromise for the Judiciary," *Miami News* (October 18, 1967), 26A.

Work in the legislature on the new constitution continued into 1968. The House-Senate conference committee tried to find a workable solution to differences on the judicial article as a self-imposed deadline approached. The differences were not over selection – it was agreed that selection would be through nonpartisan elections – but regarding the structure of the future court system. The Senate came within one vote of the required two-thirds of adopting a version that would leave most details of court structure to the legislature; that version would have added a provision for Senate confirmation of judges appointed to midterm vacancies. That Senate defeat effectively ended efforts to produce a revised article,[31] and the proposed new constitution went to the voters in November 1968 without a new judicial article.[32] The new constitution was approved by the voters, with 55.4 percent in favor.[33]

Early in 1969, the legislature resumed consideration of a new judicial article.[34] In June, the legislature passed a proposed judicial amendment to go to the voters.[35] The proposed article left it to the legislature whether judicial elections would be partisan or nonpartisan. It authorized the use of a nominating commission, but the legislature would decide whether such a commission would be used and whether the governor would be constrained by the commission.[36] The new article reflected many compromises and retained a fairly complex court structure. There was substantial opposition to the proposed amendment, including from the Judicial Council of Florida, the Board of Governors of the Florida Bar, and the Conference of Circuit Judges of Florida.[37] The voters narrowly rejected the new judicial article in November 1970, with 51.1 percent against.[38]

During the 1970 legislative session, before the new judicial article was to be voted on in November, the legislature passed a bill making judicial elections nonpartisan, which it could do because the existing judicial article said only that judges "shall be

31 "Charter 'Package' Sent to Panel for Wrapping," *Tampa Bay Times* (June 29, 1968), 1A, !oa.

32 Frank Kaperton, "Charter Ready for Voters; Legislators Adjourn Historic Meeting," *Florida Today* (July 4, 1968), 3A.

33 See https://ballotpedia.org/Florida_Constitutional_Basic_Document,_Amendment_1_(1968), accessed January 9, 2019. There were actually three votes because two sections were separated out as separate questions for the voters; see https://ballotpedia.org/Florida_1968_ballot_measures, accessed January 9, 2019. Until 2006, only a majority vote was needed to pass a constitutional amendment; in 2006 the legislature put an amendment on the ballot that would increase the needed percent to 60 percent, and that passed, somewhat ironically, with 57.8 percent in favor – see https://ballotpedia.org/Florida_Amendment_3,_Supermajority_Vote_Required_to_Approve_a_Constitutional_Amendment_(2006), accessed January 9, 2019.

34 "Committee Will Take up Revising Judicial Article," *Tampa Bay Times* (January 25, 1969), 2B; "Legislature Will Take Aim at Court System," *Tampa Tribune* (April 28, 1969), B1.

35 "Judicial Reform Finished," *Tampa Bay Times* (June 5, 1969), 3B.

36 The proposed amendment can be found at https://ballotpedia.org/Florida_Judicial_System_Restructuring,_Amendment_3_(1970), accessed January 9, 2019.

37 See advertisement published in the *Tampa Tribune* (November 3, 1970), 8A.

38 See https://ballotpedia.org/Florida_Judicial_System_Restructuring,_Amendment_3_(1970), accessed January 9, 2019.

elected." The proposal was introduced by Democratic legislators and passed in the face of substantial Republican opposition. In the House, the vote was 59–42; Democrats were 54–11 in favor and Republicans were 31–5 against.[39] In the Senate, the vote was 34–12 with all the no votes from Republicans and only two Republicans voting in favor.[40] Republican Governor Claude Kirk vetoed the bill.[41] At least part of the reasoning behind the veto was a provision that the qualifying fees paid by a judicial candidate would continue to go to the party the candidate was registered with rather than going to the state treasury. However, the conflict between the two parties over the bill almost certainly reflected a desire by Democrats to shift to nonpartisan elections as a means of protecting Democratic incumbents in areas of growing Republican strength, and Republicans' view that they would be advantaged by continuing partisan judicial elections.

Efforts to overhaul the judicial system, including changing the method of judicial selection, resumed when the legislature convened in 1971. The efforts ran on two tracks: a constitutional amendment to restructure the court system and legislation to replace partisan judicial elections with nonpartisan elections. The latter was accomplished fairly easily this time, given that the new Democratic governor, Reubin Askew, had endorsed the idea;[42] as a state senator, he had been a sponsor of the nonpartisan election bill vetoed by his predecessor.[43] A nonpartisan election bill passed the House in early April on a 91–25 vote.[44] Unlike the arrangement in the 1970 version, candidate filing fees would now go to the state, to be applied toward judicial salaries rather than going to the party the candidate was affiliated with.[45] The Senate passed a slightly different nonpartisan election bill a month later on a 30–14 vote; one significant difference in the bills was that the House version called for candidates to be listed alphabetically on the ballot, while the Senate version would have incumbents listed first with challengers, then in alphabetical order.[46] After the House balked at adopting the Senate version,[47] the Senate acceded to the House version on a 29–14 vote,[48] and the governor signed it.[49] An important provision of the bill was that all contested seats would be on the primary election ballot, and if a candidate received a majority of the primary election vote, that

39 "House Approves Non-Partisan Judicial Elections," *Tampa Bay Times* (May 1, 1970), 11B.
40 "Non-Partisan Election of Judges Is Approved," *Tampa Bay Times* (May 28, 1970), 1B, 7B.
41 "Judges' Nonpartisan Election Bill Vetoed," *Orlando Sentinel* (June 18, 1970), 3B.
42 "House Hatches Bill No. 1: No-Party Rule for Judges," *Miami News* (April 7, 1971), 10A.
43 Martin A. Dyckman, "How Florida Accepted Merit Retention: Nothing Succeeds Quite Like a Scandal," *Florida Law Review Forum*, 64, no. 5, article 11 (2012), 2, https://scholarship.law.ufl.edu/flr/vol64/iss5/11/, accessed January 3, 2020.
44 "House Hatches Bill No. 1: No-Party Rule for Judges," *supra* note 42.
45 "House Okays Open Judge Races," *Tampa Bay Times* (April 7, 1971), 1.
46 "Non-Partisan Judges Wins Senate Approval," *Tampa Tribune* (May 7, 1971), 15A.
47 "Judicial Elections Bill Trips," *Tampa Tribune* (May 12, 1971), 4A.
48 "Non-Partisan Judicial Ballots Near Certainty," *Orlando Evening Star* (May 13, 1971), 8A.
49 "Askew Signs Nonpartisan Election Bill for Judges," *Orlando Sentinel* (May 25, 1971), 11a.

candidate would be deemed elected, and the contest would not appear on the general election ballot.[50] This meant that all two-candidate contests would be decided at the primary. This system continues today.

Not long after Governor Askew signed the nonpartisan election bill, he announced that he was going to establish by executive order a set of judicial nominating commissions. The commissions would be composed of 9 members, 3 selected by the bar, 3 by the governor, and another 3 selected by the other 6. He pledged to appoint only persons recommended by a nominating commission, thus ending the use of judicial appointments as a form of political patronage.[51]

With the issue of election format resolved, legislative attention turned toward drafting another proposal to revise the judicial article. A significant part of the opposition to the 1970 version was that it left the judicial system relatively complex, with variations depending on county size. The new proposals called for a uniform structure, abolishing most or all of the limited jurisdiction courts and replacing them with either one or two such courts in all counties.[52] At a special session in December, the legislature agreed on the text of a new judicial article to submit to the voters at a special election in March 1972. The existing sixteen types of trial courts around the state would be replaced by just two courts, the general jurisdiction circuit court and a new limited-jurisdiction county court in each county.[53] The provision of importance for judicial selection was a requirement that midterm vacancies be filled by the governor from lists provided by nominating commissions. The new judicial article was approved by the voters, with 70.5 percent in favor.[54]

The new article specified that there should be a nominating commission for the Supreme Court, for each District Court of Appeal, and for each judicial circuit, with the latter making nominations for all trial-level courts within the circuit.[55] It was left to the legislature to determine the membership of the various commissions, and the legislature adopted the structure that Governor Askew had specified in his executive order: 3 lawyers selected by the Board of Governors of the Florida Bar from among practitioners in the territorial jurisdiction of the courts involved, 3 persons residing in the jurisdiction selected by the governor, and 3 nonlawyers selected by a majority vote of the other 6 members.[56]

50 *Laws of Florida* 1971, Chapter 71–49, Section 5, 150–151.

51 "Askew Will Take Judge Naming Out of Spoils System," *Tampa Bay Times* (June 1971), B1.

52 D. B. Lawrence, "Judicial Reform Coming Up Again but Chances of Success Doubtful," *Orlando Sentinel* (August 1, 1971), 19A.

53 Martin Dyckman, "Legislators Okay Judicial Reform," *Tampa Bay Times* (December 10, 1971), 1A, 4A. The final vote on the proposal was 76–33 in the House and 69–42 in the Senate; a 60 percent majority was required (see Florida Constitution, Article XI, §1).

54 See https://ballotpedia.org/Florida_Court_System,_Amendment_1_(March_1972), accessed January 10, 2019.

55 *Id.*, §10(b) of the proposed article.

56 Laws of Florida 1972, Chapter 72-404, Section 24, 1414–1415.

Adoption of the Missouri Plan for the Appellate Courts

Within a year, new proposals for judicial selection were circulating. One, put forth by the Florida Bar Board of Governors, would have had a retention election for circuit and district judges who were standing unopposed for election.[57] A proposed constitutional amendment to adopt the Missouri Plan for the selection and retention of all judges was approved in May 1973 by the House Judiciary Committee.[58] The plan attracted the support of the state bar president,[59] but the response from the bench was mixed.[60] It never progressed beyond the Judiciary Committee's approval.

The prospects for ending contested judicial elections and shifting to a full Missouri Plan changed sharply, starting in 1974. Over the course of that year and the next, scandals of various sorts engulfed 4 of the 7 justices of the Florida Supreme Court.[61] Two of the justices were forced to resign under threat of impeachment and were disbarred after being accused of criminal behavior, a third was publicly identified as suffering from alcoholism and avoided a disciplinary trial only after signing an undated letter of resignation that would go to the governor if he ever drank again,[62] and the Judicial Qualifications Commission required a fourth to submit to psychiatric treatment.[63] These scandals provided the impetus for serious consideration of the Missouri Plan.[64] The governor initially dropped his previous opposition to the Missouri Plan,[65] and then later recommended its adoption.[66] Proposals for a Missouri Plan system that applied to all judges were introduced. An alternative plan proposed to retain contested elections but require persons seeking to be on the ballot to be certified as qualified by a judicial nominating commission.[67] Both plans stalled, and then a compromise proposal that the Missouri

[57] "Retention of Judges May Be Up to Voters," *Tampa Tribune* (March 23, 1973), 18A.

[58] Virginia Eller, "Amending the Politics Out of Judgeships," *Tampa Bay Times* (May 11, 1973), 9B.

[59] David Cook, "State Bar President Pushes Merit Selection of Judges," *Tallahassee Democrat* (May 8, 1973), 5.

[60] Daniel Alarcon, "Selection Plan Splits Judges," *Tampa Times* (May 9, 1973), E1.

[61] For a history of those scandals, see Martin A. Dyckman, *A Most Disorderly Court: Scandal and Reform in the Florida Judiciary* (Gainesville: University Press of Florida, 2008).

[62] *Id.*, 19.

[63] Dye, *Politics in Florida*, *supra* note 5, 139.

[64] Jack Greene, "'Missouri Plan' Has a Chance," *Tampa Tribune* (February 3, 1975), 1; "Judicial System Overhaul Gains Legislative Muscle," *Panama City News-Herald* (February 23, 1975), 1; "Ervin Fears Probes, Selection of Judges Faces Revamping; Growing Talk among Legislators," *Fort Myers News-Press* (February 23, 1975), 8b.

[65] "Governor Favors 'Missouri Plan,'" *Fort Walton Beach Playground Daily News* (February 14, 1975), 2; see also Ormund Powers, "Governor Lauds Missouri Plan," *Orlando Sentinel* (April 30, 1975), 6B.

[66] "Legislature Session Off to Fast Start after Askew Points Way," *Orlando Sentinel* (April 9, 1975), 11A.

[67] "Two Selection Bills Are Before the Legislature; Certification or Nomination Processes," *Fort Myers News-Press* (April 27, 1975), 7A.

Plan apply only to appellate judges was suggested.[68] Efforts to find a judicial selection plan that would secure legislative approval continued through the spring, but nothing made it through by the time the legislature adjourned at the end of May. There was a floor vote in the House that attracted majority support, but not the 72 (60 percent of the membership) required for a constitutional amendment.[69]

In preparation for the 1976 legislative session, the House Judiciary Committee started looking at a Missouri Plan proposal.[70] As the start of the session approached, the Committee approved a Missouri Plan system for the appellate courts on a 7–6 vote; it rejected the inclusion of a local option that would allow the adoption of the plan for trial judges,[71] possibly reflecting the strong opposition from the leadership of several minority communities.[72] Although the plan was initially killed on the floor of the House,[73] a version of it passed the Senate in mid-May on a 28–11 vote.[74] A week later, the House voted 80–33 in favor of a slightly different version that included a requirement that there be at least one Supreme Court justice from each of the Court of Appeals districts.[75] The Senate quickly accepted the House version.[76]

About a month before the November election, an unsuccessful candidate for the Florida Supreme Court filed a federal lawsuit asking that the judicial selection amendment be removed from the ballot. He claimed that the Missouri Plan system would violate the voting rights provisions of the Fourteenth Amendment.[77] The federal judge hearing the suit declined to issue an order removing the amendment proposal from the ballot.[78] That suit was dismissed by the federal court, and the dismissal was upheld by the U.S. Court of Appeals.[79] Voters overwhelmingly approved the change to judicial selection, with 75.2 percent in favor.[80]

68 Fitz McAden, "Judge Retention Compromise Readied," *Tampa Tribune* (May 5, 1975), 2B.

69 "Judicial Reform Bill Loses Out This Session," *Pensacola News Journal* (May 30, 1975), 2B.

70 Bill Kaczor, "Panel Views Proposed Plan to Alter Judge Selection," *Pensacola News Journal* (Jan. 15, 1976), 22B.

71 "Committee Oks Judge Vote Bill, "*Fort Myers News-Press* (March 24, 1976), 5B.

72 See Drew Noble Lanier and Roger Handberg, "In the Eye of the Hurricane: Florida Courts, Judicial Independence, and Politics," *Fordham Urban Law Journal* 29 (2002), 1042; see also Dye, *Politics in Florida, supra* note 5, 6–7.

73 D. G. Lawrence, "Judicial Merit Selection Chances Slim," *Orlando Sentinel* (April 4, 1976), 25A.

74 "Judicial Reform Gets Boost; State Senate Passes Merit Plan," *Tampa Tribune* (May 19, 1976), 1, 6.

75 Sara Schwieder, "House Approves Judicial Reform Bill," *Tampa Tribune* (May 26, 1976), 1A.

76 "Voters to Get Judicial Selection," *Tampa Times* (May 28, 1976), 10A.

77 "Suit Seeks Removal of Merit Amendment; Another Amendment Is Challenged," *Tallahassee Democrat* (October 2, 1976), 13.

78 "Florida Has 5 Choices for President," *Naples Daily News* (October 13, 1976), 6B. In December, after the voters had approved the amendment, the federal judge threw out the lawsuit on the grounds that the claim was groundless; see Martha Musgrove, "Judge Denies Challenge of Merit Retention," *Palm Beach Post* (December 3, 1976), D3.

79 Holley v. Askew, 583 F.2d 728 (5th Cir. 1978).

80 See https://ballotpedia.org/Florida_Supreme_and_Appellate_Court_Judge_Elections,_Amendment_2_(1976), accessed January 10, 2019.

The nominating commissions for the Supreme Court and District Courts of Appeal were carried over from the 1972 law: 9 members with 3 lawyers selected by the bar, 3 members selected by the governor, and 3 nonlawyers selected by a majority of the other 6. In 2001, the legislature changed the nominating commissions so that now the governor names all 9 members; 4 of the appointments must be from nominees provided by the Florida Bar. The governor has almost complete discretion in naming the other 5, with the sole proviso that 2 must be members of the bar.[81] When making nominations, the bar must provide 3 names for each position, and the governor may reject all 3 and request 3 new names,[82] something Republican governor Rick Scott did repeatedly.[83] Although the governor has substantial control over the membership of the commissions, members of the bar constitute at least two-thirds of the membership of each commission, and there is no requirement that some members be nonlawyers. One restriction is that no judge or justice may serve on a nominating commission, and another is that no member of a nominating commission can be appointed to judicial office covered by the same commission while on that commission and until at least two years have passed since leaving that commission. Other persons holding public office may be selected to serve on a nominating commission.

Between 1978 and 2018, there were 46 retention elections for the Florida Supreme Court and 404 retention elections for the District Courts of Appeal. No judge or justice has failed to be retained. The average percent voting to retain Supreme Court justices was 68.6 (range: 59.0 to 76.8); the average for judges of the District Courts of Appeal was 70.1 (range: 53.1 to 81.0). As shown in Figure 11.1, the average percent voting in favor of retention has varied from election to election, although for most elections, the averages for the two levels of courts have tracked fairly closely.

The partisan correlation for statewide retention elections for Supreme Court justices has also varied over time.[84] This is shown in Figure 11.2. For the first few of those elections (1980–1986), the correlation was negative, meaning that counties that voted more heavily Republican in gubernatorial elections tended to have a higher percentage of voters favoring retention. This is interesting, given that Republican politicians had initially opposed retention elections. By the early 1990s, the sign had swung positive, indicating higher levels of support for retention in counties that tended to be more Democratic in their gubernatorial votes. The correlation was

81 See "Legal Challenge Related to the Judicial Nominating Process," Florida Senate, Issue Brief 2010-320 (September 2009), 2.

82 Florida Statutes (2018), 43.291(1)(a).

83 Linda Bond Edwards and Michael R. Band, "A Look through the Looking Glass: The JNC and Judicial Nominating Process 'Deconstructed,'" *Florida Bar Journal* (June 2018), www.floridabar.org/the-florida-bar-journal/a-look-through-the-looking-glass-the-jnc-and-judicial-nominating-process-deconstructed/, accessed January 19, 2019.

84 The partisan correlation, described in detail in Chapter 1, is the correlation between the percent voting to retain in each county with the percent voting for the Democratic candidate for governor in each county.

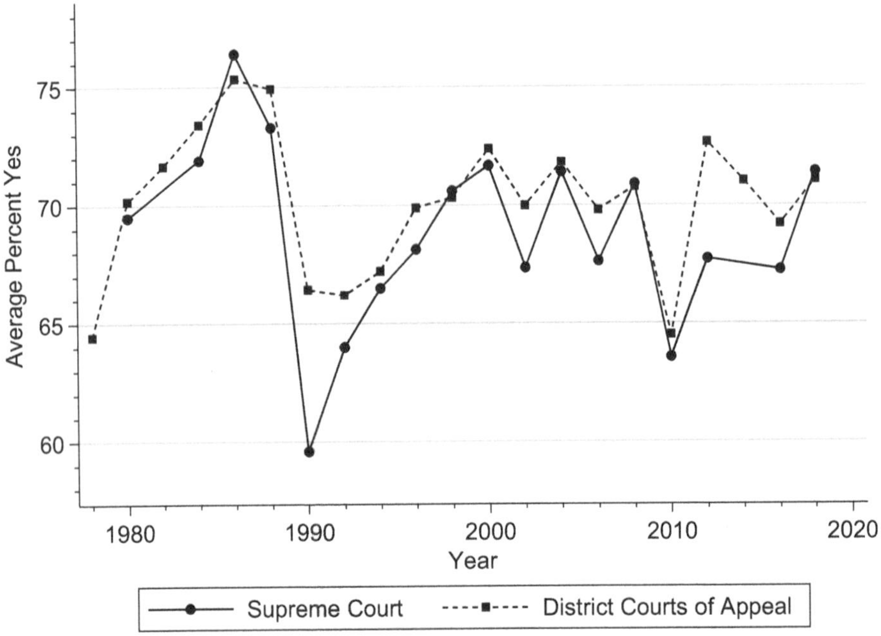

FIGURE 11.1 Average percent voting for retention in Florida retention elections, 1978–2018

particularly strong in the 2012 election, when Republicans and conservative groups mounted campaigns against the justices standing for retention, all of whom had been appointed by Democratic governor Lawton Chiles.[85] The correlation is almost as high in 2016, when the three justices running for retention were all appointed by Republican governor Charlie Crist. Perhaps this reflected that Crist had deserted the Republican Party in April 2010 and subsequently ran unsuccessfully as a Democrat for governor in 2012 and successfully for the U.S. House of Representatives in 2016.

Unsuccessful Efforts to Extend the Missouri Plan to Trial Courts

During the debates over the constitutional amendment that would have proposed legislation implementing the Missouri Plan, legislators considered applying it to all courts but backed off, given significant opposition from trial judges. They then considered including a "local option" provision in the 1976 amendment that would allow the voters of a judicial circuit to adopt the Missouri Plan for the trial courts in the circuit. In the end, the legislators decided it was best to focus on the appellate courts, where there had been some recent scandal (at the Supreme Court level).

[85] See Lizette Alvarez, "G.O.P. Aims to Remake Florida Supreme Court," *New York Times* (October 3, 2012), A20.

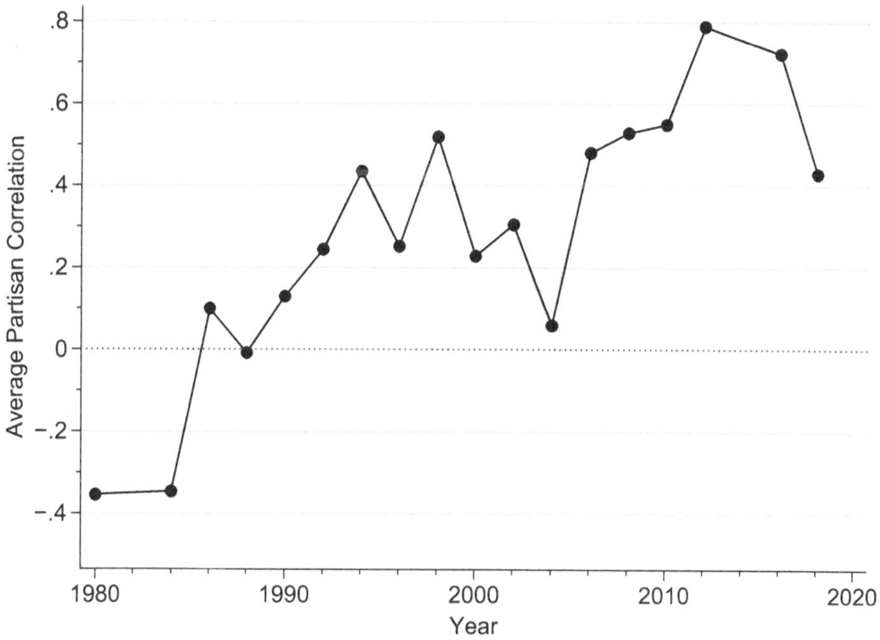

FIGURE 11.2 Variation over time in average partisan correlation in Florida Supreme Court retention elections, 1978–2018

Recall that one feature of the constitutional changes adopted in 1968 was a provision that the Constitution Revision Commission (CRC) was empowered to put proposed amendments on the ballot in 1978 and then every twenty years (i.e., 1998, 2018, etc.) thereafter. In 1978, two years after the voters overwhelmingly adopted the Missouri Plan for Florida's appellate courts, the CRC included on the ballot a proposed amendment to extend the Missouri Plan to the trial courts. The reaction to the proposal was decidedly mixed,[86] with many trial judges and many newspapers expressing opposition. The opposition of trial judges is not surprising. First, a very large proportion face no opposition and consequently do not even appear on the ballot. Second, according to one survey, between 1954 and 1974, only about 3 percent of incumbents facing an opponent lost.[87] Judges also expressed concern about having to run against their record, particularly if a case had required them to make an unpopular decision.[88] The Missouri Plan amendment

[86] One group expressing support was the Florida Chamber of Commerce; see "Chamber for Tax Changes, Opposes Other Proposals," *Fort Myers News-Press* (August 5, 1978), 5B. Another, not surprisingly, was the state bar; see Joy McIlwain, "Florida Bar Proposes to Ditch Judicial Elective System," *Tampa Times* (September 4, 1978), 8A.

[87] Ray Lynch, "Judges Oppose Judicial Revision, Merit Retention," *Orlando Sentinel* (August 24, 1978), 1, 3; the survey must have included elections involving the many limited jurisdiction courts in addition to the circuit courts.

[88] "Judges Cite Disadvantages of Merit Retention System," *Orlando Sentinel* (August 24, 1978), 3.

did better on the ballot than the other seven amendments proposed by the CRC, but was narrowly rejected by the voters with 50.9 percent against.[89]

The 1978 vote appears to have largely put the issue to rest until 1992, when there was a push in the legislature to put an amendment on the ballot that would adopt the Missouri Plan for the circuit and county courts. At least part of the impetus for this push was probably a response to a federal lawsuit challenging the system of electing trial judges at large within the circuit or county as being a violation of the federal Voting Rights Act;[90] that is, because all circuits were majority white, the system made it difficult for members of various minority groups to be elected to judgeships, and they would have more success under the Missouri Plan. During the legislature's regular 1992 session, the Senate approved the proposed constitutional amendment 27–11 (3 more votes than the required 24 that constituted 60 percent).[91] However, the House failed to act before the end of the session. When the proposal came to a vote in the Senate during the special session that quickly followed, it garnered only 22 votes, 2 short of the required 24. Several of the senators who changed their votes said they had been persuaded that the Missouri Plan would make it more difficult to increase minority representation in the trial judiciary.[92]

The CRC convened again in 1998. The CRC decided to put on the ballot an amendment that would provide a local option allowing voters in counties or circuits to adopt the Missouri Plan for their trial courts. Included in the amendment was a provision that if the amendment passed, the voters in every circuit and county would be asked to vote two years later on the question of whether to adopt the Missouri Plan for the local circuit and county courts. Where the option was rejected, the issue could be placed on the ballot by a circuit or an individual county in the future by petition, with the requirement that valid signatures be collected equal to 10 percent of the votes cast in the preceding election in which there was a presidential contest. Given that the proposal involved only creating an option, it was rather benign, and appears to have attracted little attention. Moreover, voters like to have choices, and this was something that would give them a choice. The proposal included some other changes, such as increasing the term for county judges from four to six years and allocating funding of the courts among the state, the counties, and users of the courts. The proposal passed with 56.9 percent in favor.[93]

89 See https://ballotpedia.org/Florida_Selection_and_Retention_of_Circuit_and_County_Judges,_Amendment_6_(1978), accessed January 10, 2019.

90 Susannah Lyle, "Who Should Choose the State's Trial Judges?" *Tallahassee Democrat* (January 21, 1992), 1B. The trial court refused to grant relief to the plaintiffs in the case, and that decision was upheld by the U.S. Court of Appeals; see Davis v. Chiles, 139 F.3d 1414 (11th Cir. 1998).

91 Susannah Lyle, "Senate Oks Plan for Judges," *Tallahassee Democrat* (March 11, 1992), 4B.

92 "Rule on Judges Killed in the Senate," *South Florida Sun-Sentinel* (March 26, 1992), 16A.

93 See https://ballotpedia.org/Florida_Local_Option_for_Selection_of_Judges_and_Funding_of_State_Courts,_Amendment_7_(1998), accessed January 10, 2019; 8 of the 9 amendments proposed by the CRC passed in 1998, as did all 4 amendments proposed by the legislature.

As provided by the 1998 amendment, voters were asked whether to adopt the Missouri Plan in their circuit and county at the 2000 election. There were divided views about the proposal. The Florida Bar Association supported it as did the League of Women Voters.[94] Opposition came from a range of groups, including the Christian Coalition,[95] the Cuban Bar Association, the Black Lawyers Association, and the Florida Association for Women Lawyers, who wanted to continue contested elections.[96] It is unclear what position the trial judges themselves took on the issue; however, in the prior two elections, only 10.3 percent of incumbents faced an opponent, and only 2.9 percent of incumbents lost, although this meant that one-third of those who were challenged lost.

The ballot language adopted by the legislature in 2000 was challenged in court by some proponents of the Missouri Plan. That language stated that the issue was "Shall [County Court/Circuit Court] Judges be appointed by the Governor with Retention by the Vote of the people?" In 1999, the legislature had adopted language asking voters if selection of trial judges should be through "merit selection and retention." However, in 2000 the legislature dropped that language and replaced it with what appeared on the November ballot; ostensibly, "opponents of merit retention slipped the new wording through in the last days of the legislature."[97] The Florida Supreme Court unanimously rejected the challenge to the ballot language.[98]

The change to the Missouri Plan was resoundingly defeated in every circuit and every county. The average vote in favor within the circuits was just 31.9 percent (range: 22.8 to 42.2 percent). The proposal did even worse regarding the county courts, with the average in favor of the change just 25.7 percent (range: 11.5 to 39.9 percent). There was little evidence regarding whether there was a partisan pattern within the county vote. The correlation between the county-level support for the change and the percent of voters having voted for the Democratic gubernatorial candidate in 1998 was just .253, and the correlation with the Democratic gubernatorial vote in 2002 was 0 to three places. There was a moderate correlation, .376, between the two-party Democratic percentage in the presidential election and the vote in favor of the change. (The two-party Democratic percentage is the pocentage voting Democratic, ignoring minor parties.)

94 Jim Ash, "Floridians Wrestle over Electing Judges," *Fort Myers News-Press* (November 5, 2000), 5D.

95 *Id.*

96 "Ballot Question Stirs Miami-Dade; The Miami-Dade Legal Establishment Challenges the Ballot Language on the Question of Whether Judges Should Be Elected," *Tampa Bay Times* (September 12, 2000), 6A.

97 Mary McLachlin, "Wording Change Sought on Judge Issue; Six Florida Lawyers Say Ballots May Confuse Voters About How Judges Are Chosen," *Palm Beach Post* (August 16, 2000), 16A.

98 See Kainen v. Harris, 769 So.2d 1029 (Fla. 2000); see also Jackie Hallifax, "High Court Turns Down Ballot Wording Challenge; Questions Deal with Choosing of Local Judges," *South Florida Sun Sentinel* (September 13, 2000), 6B.

There does not appear to have been a subsequent effort in Florida to push the Missouri Plan for trial court elections. In the words of one longtime observer of judicial politics in Florida, "The [2000] results were so uniformly negative that it has died."[99] However, this does not mean that there have not been efforts to change other aspects of the judicial selection/retention system in Florida.

Subsequent Developments

In 2001, the legislature made some changes to the nominating commissions. These changes probably grew out of some conflict between the Florida Supreme Court and the other two, Republican-controlled, branches of the state government, arising from a controversial decision regarding the death penalty and the Court's decisions during the 2000 presidential election vote recount.[100] The legislature passed the changes to the nominating commission on strongly partisan votes, with Republicans largely in support and Democrats largely in opposition.[101] A further proposal to require judges and justices standing for retention to obtain a two-thirds majority of the vote died in committee.[102] Under the 2001 law regarding nominating commission composition, still in effect as this was written in 2019, the governor appoints all members, although four must be selected from lists provided by the bar and two others must be lawyers (but not judges); the commissioners serve for a fixed term. A proposal was advanced in 2011 that would have allowed the governor to dismiss the current membership and appoint new members, but that proposal failed to advance.[103] An analysis of the impact of the 2001 changes over the first several years they were in effect found little change in the demographics of who was appointed to the courts, but there is some evidence that partisanship was playing a larger role, both in who served on the nominating commissions and whom the governor appointed to judicial positions.[104]

In 2014, the legislature put an amendment on the ballot that would have permitted the governor to make prospective appointments to the appellate courts. If an appellate judge does not file to stand in a retention election, or loses a retention election, the position becomes vacant in January on the same day that a new governor would be sworn in if it is also the January following a gubernatorial

99 Email from Professor Roger Handberg (University of Central Florida), September 9, 2018.

100 Lanier and Handberg, "In the Eye of the Hurricane," *supra* note 72, 1045–1049.

101 See http://ufdcimages.uflib.ufl.edu/UF/00/02/78/36/00054/00054.pdf, 331–332; and http://archive.flsenate.gov/data/Historical/Senate%20Journals/2000s/2001/s0504bv.pdf, 1506; accessed January 19, 2019.

102 Lanier and Handberg, "In the Eye of the Hurricane," *supra* note 72, 1050.

103 League of Women Voters of Florida, "Study and Action 2017–2019," 48, www.lwvfl.org/wp-content/uploads/2017/11/Study-Action-2017-2019.pdf, accessed January 11, 2019.

104 See Rebecca Mae Salokar, D. Jason Berggren, and Kathryn A. DePalo, "The New Politics of Judicial Selection in Florida: Merit Selection Redefined," *Justice System Journal* 27, no. 2 (2006), 130–138.

election. Under the proposed amendment, the governor in office in November would have been empowered to name a person to fill the position that would become vacant in January, and that would mean that an outgoing governor would be able to make the appointment rather than his or her successor, who takes office on the day the judicial position would actually become vacant.[105] Democrats opposed the amendment because they believed it was a ploy to increase the probability that three vacancies would occur in January 2019, when three justices appointed by a Democratic governor would have to leave the bench and the vacancies would be filled by a Republican governor. The then current Republican governor Rick Scott was running for reelection in 2014, and presumably Republicans believed it was highly likely he would defeat his challenger, former Republican governor Charlie Crist , who was running as a Democrat in 2014.[106] However, Scott would not be able to run again in 2018 and might be succeeded by a Democrat. Under a 2006 change to the Florida Constitution, the proposed amendment needed support from 60 percent of those voting to pass. It failed to garner even a majority, with only 47.9 percent voting in favor.[107]

Two years later, a controversy arose when three circuit court judges whose terms would expire in January 2017 but who were not planning to run for reelection submitted letters of resignation in April 2016 with effective dates in December. The clear purpose was to allow the governor to appoint the judges' successors rather than their positions being filled through election in November. A lawsuit was filed arguing that the positions should be filled by election, but the Florida Supreme Court refused to consider an appeal[108] from a divided District Court of Appeals' decision rejecting the claim.[109]

In late 2015, the Republican leadership in the legislature started discussing the idea of imposing term limits on appellate judges,[110] and legislation to this end was introduced in 2016 and 2017.[111] The Republican House Speaker described term

[105] Mary Ellen Klas, "Voters to Decide How Judges Chosen; An Amendment May Give Governors New Powers on High Court Picks," *Tampa Bay Times* (May 1, 2014), 1B, 10B.

[106] Scott did defeat Crist, but the election was close, with the two candidates separated by only about one percentage point; see https://en.wikipedia.org/wiki/2014_Florida_gubernatorial_elec tion, accessed January 11, 2019. As things worked out, the Republican candidate did win in 2018, but the election was even closer, with the candidates separated by 0.4 percent (about 33,000 votes); see https://en.wikipedia.org/wiki/2018_Florida_gubernatorial_election, accessed January 11, 2019.

[107] See https://ballotpedia.org/Florida_Prospective_Judicial_Vacancies,_Amendment_3_(2014), accessed January 11, 2019.

[108] Jim Saunders, "Supreme Court Clears Way for Scott to Appoint Judges," *Tallahassee Democrat* (June 4, 2016), A8.

[109] Trotti v. Detzner, 147 So.3d 641 (Fla.App. 1 Dist. 2014).

[110] John Kennedy, "Judicial Term Limits in Fla. Proposed for 2016 Ballot," *Palm Beach Post* (November 4, 2015), B2.

[111] Bill Cotterell, "Courts, Public Benefit from Better Communication," *Tallahassee Democrat* (January 7, 201 6), A5.

limits as a way to "curb activist appellate judges in Florida."[112] Under the proposal, appellate judges would be barred from standing for retention if they had already served twelve consecutive years in the current position.[113] The proposal attracted sharp opposition from groups ranging from the state bar to a business-aligned group that frequently disagreed with the Supreme Court's decisions. Some described the proposal as a "get-even move against the Florida Supreme Court" for its action the previous year, calling out the legislative leadership for "cheating on congressional and state Senate redistricting."[114] In 2016, the proposal passed the House 76–38,[115] but there was no action in the Senate.[116] In 2017, the proposal again passed the House, this time on a vote of 73–46, just one more vote than the 72 (60 percent) required;[117] no Democrats voted in favor and 6 of the 79 Republicans in the House voted against the proposal.[118] The proposal died again when the Senate failed to act before the end of the legislative session.[119]

In June 2017, another court battle arose regarding who would make the appointments to fill vacancies in January 2019, when three Supreme Court justices appointed by Democratic governor Lawton Chiles had to leave the bench under the state's mandatory retirement provisions for judges.[120] The League of Women Voters and Common Cause filed a petition with the Florida Supreme Court, asking it to resolve the issue of whether the outgoing governor, Rick Scott, who would be replaced the day that the justices' terms ended, could fill the positions or that would fall to the incoming governor.[121] The petitioners argued that Scott's term ended at midnight on January 8, 2019, while the justices' terms did not expire until midnight on January 9, 2019.[122] The voters had, in 2014, rejected an amendment to the state constitution that would have explicitly granted the outgoing governor the power to

[112] Richard Corcoran, "Term Limits Would Curb Activist Judges in Florida," *Orlando Sentinel* (January 14, 2017), A15.

[113] Jim Saunders, "Judicial Term Limits Get Backing in House," *Florida Today* (February 10, 2017), A8.

[114] "Full-Court Press," *Tallahassee Democrat* (February 25, 2016), A2.

[115] *Id.*

[116] "How Bills Become Law (or Not)," *Tampa Bay Times* (March 14, 2016), T10.

[117] Jim Saunders, "House Panel Oks Term Limits for Judges," *South Florida Sun Sentinel* (February 10, 2017), B3.

[118] Michael Auslen and Kristen M. Clark, "House Okays Term Limit on Judges," *Tampa Bay Times* (March 30, 2017), B8.

[119] "Session Is a Mixed Bag: Florida Got a Lot Done, Left Much Undone," *Tallahassee Democrat* (May 10, 2017), A4.

[120] At the time, the mandatory retirement provisions did not allow a judge who was 70 or older to run for another term, although when a judge turned 70, the judge could serve the balance of the current term if less than half of the term remained; see Gray Rohrer, "Top Court Hears Case to Decide Its Future," *Orlando Sentinel* (November 2, 2017), A1.

[121] Brandon Larrabee, "Groups Ask High Court to Rule on Scott Picks," *Orlando Sentinel* (June 16, 2017), B2.

[122] Brandon Larrabee, "Scott Defends Power to Name 3 New Justices on His Last Day," *Orlando Sentinel* (July 21, 2017), B2.

fill vacancies in this type of situation. The Supreme Court heard arguments at the beginning of November 2017.[123] Three weeks after the argument, Scott asked that one of the justices, a Democratic appointee who was one of the judges who would be leaving the Court, be disqualified;[124] Scott's request was rejected by the Court.[125] In mid-December, the Court dismissed the case on a 6–1 vote,[126] saying it was not "ripe" for decision because there had been no actual action by the governor regarding the possible appointments.[127]

In September 2018, Scott convened the Judicial Nominating Commission to vet potential nominees for the Florida Supreme Court. The League and Common Cause then filed suit, asking the Florida Supreme Court to block the nominating commission from preparing a list to be sent to the governor.[128] In an unsigned order issued on October 15, the Supreme Court ruled that Scott had "exceeded his authority" when he asked the nominating commission to send him a list of potential appointees by November 10, and went on to say that the winner of the upcoming gubernatorial election had "the sole authority" to make the appointments to the Supreme Court.[129] As things worked out, the Republican gubernatorial candidate, Ron DeSantis, did win the governorship in 2018 and appointed three new Supreme Court justices in January 2019.

The 2018 election was the time of the every-20-years vote on amendments proposed by the Constitution Revision Commission. There was some talk among conservatives about pushing for an amendment that would limit or end the role of nominating commissions, but that never got beyond talk.[130] There was also some consideration by the Commission of a proposal for an amendment that would specify the composition of the judicial nominating commissions, but the

[123] "Mary Ellen Klas, "High Court Weighs Who Can Appoint New Judges," *Tampa Bay Times* (November 2, 2017), B2.

[124] Dara Kam, "Scott Wants to Block Pariente from Court Appointment Case," *Palm Beach Post* (November 22, 2017), B2.

[125] Steve Bousquet, "Supreme Court Rejects Bid to Take Pariente Off Case," *Tampa Bay Times* (November 30, 2017), B3.

[126] League of Women Voters of Florida v. Scott, 232 So.3d 264 (Fla. 2017).

[127] Gray Rohrer, "Scott's Influence over Supreme Court on Hold; Ruling Keeps in Limbo Who'll Replace Justices," *South Florida Sun Sentinel* (December 15, 2017), A1.

[128] Gary Fineout, "Gov. Scott's Push to Name Justices Challenged in Court," *Tallahassee Democrat* (September 22, 2018), A3.

[129] League of Women Voters v. Scott, SC18–1573, 2018 Fla. LEXIS 2479 (Fla., 2018) (order granting petition for writ of quo warranto); see also Lloyd Dunkelberger, "Next Governor to Pick 3 Supreme Court Justices," *Tallahassee Democrat* (October 16, 2018), A2.

[130] This issue came up at a session of the 2017 Florida Bar Convention in a session on the Constitutional Revision Commission. Two of the speakers were Professor Brian Fitzpatrick (Vanderbilt Law School) and Professor Stephen Ware (University of Kansas Law School), both of whom have been critics of the role of lawyers on nominating commissions. See "2017 Annual Bar Convention: The Constitution Revision Showcase," The Florida Bar Podcast, https://legaltalknetwork.com/podcasts/florida-bar/2017/06/2017-annual-florida-bar-convention-the-constitution-revision-showcase/, accessed January 11, 2019.

Commission did not move forward with that proposal.[131] The Commission did put on the ballot an amendment that, among other things,[132] would raise the judicial retirement age to 75, and that amendment was approved by the voters.[133]

SOUTH DAKOTA

South Dakota, which has no intermediate appellate court, adopted nonpartisan judicial elections in 1921 for both its Supreme Court and the circuit-level trial court.[134] Justices of the South Dakota Supreme Court were elected by district rather than on a statewide ballot. Between 1946 and 1978, there were 32 elections for that Court, only 2 of which were contested, 1 in 1976 and 1 in 1978; the 1976 election was the first contested Supreme Court election in more than forty years.[135] One of the contested elections was for an open seat, and the other was a challenge to an incumbent who was standing for election after having been appointed about two years before; that incumbent was defeated by a 2 to 1 margin. In 1970, there was a second open-seat election, but it was uncontested.

Interest in a Missouri Plan system among members of the state bar is evident starting in the late 1960s.[136] In 1971–1972, the state convened a Constitutional Revision Commission, and the Commission produced a complete redraft of the judicial article that included adopting a Missouri Plan system for selection and retention.[137] However, the state legislature stripped out that plan and reverted to elections using "non-political" ballots. One member of the legislature, who also happened to be an associate director of the American Judicature Society (one of the major proponents of the Missouri Plan), explained that: "The legislature didn't feel

[131] Edwards and Band, "A Look through the Looking Glass," *supra* note 83. There was a legislative proposal (H.B. 477) similar to what was considered by the Commission, and another proposal (H.B. 753) that would have split the authority to appoint members of the nominating commissions between the governor and legislative leaders; neither moved beyond the proposal state.

[132] The other two judiciary-related changes included in the amendment were a section dealing with the rights of crime victims (what is known as "Marsy's Law") and a prohibition on state courts deferring to an administrative agency's interpretation of a state statute or rule in deciding a lawsuit.

[133] The amendment passed with 61.6 percent in favor; see https://ballotpedia.org/Florida_Amendment_6,_Marsy%27s_Law_Crime_Victims_Rights,_Judicial_Retirement_Age,_and_Judicial_Interpretation_of_Laws_and_Rules_Amendment_(2018), accessed January 11, 2019.

[134] "History of Reform Efforts: South Dakota; Format Changes Since Inception," www.judicialselection.us/judicial_selection/reform_efforts/formal_changes_since_inception.cfm?state=SD, accessed December 5, 2018.

[135] Terry Woster, "300,000 South Dakotans Expected at Polls," *Rapid City Journal* (November 1, 1976), 1.

[136] "Report of Court Reform Committee to the State Bar of South Dakota," *South Dakota Bar Journal* 37, no. 4 (October 1968), 39–40.

[137] "Proposed Article Revision Could Put SD in Vanguard of Judicial Reform," *Mitchell Daily Republic* (February 11, 1972), 1.

that the people would accept any selection method other than the non-political ballot."[138] The revised judicial article provided a more unified court structure and created a Judicial Qualifications Commission (JQC), charged with investigating complaints against judges and making recommendations to the Supreme Court for disciplinary actions.[139] The revised judicial article, along with the other proposals from the Constitutional Revision Commission that were sent on to the voters by the legislature, was approved at the November 1972 election with 67.1 percent voting in favor.[140]

The failure of the legislature to submit the Missouri Plan system to the voters as part of the 1972 constitutional amendments did not end the state bar's interest in seeing that change made. In 1975, the bar's Committee on Judicial Selection and Tenure and its Committee on Court Modernization jointly proposed that a constitutional amendment implementing the Missouri Plan be submitted to the voters. The committees also recommended that until such an amendment was passed, the legislature should give the recently created Judicial Qualifications Commission the task of recommending candidates for judicial appointments and that pending such legislation, the governor should issue an executive order granting the recommendation function to the JQC.[141] The next year, the state legislature did pass a bill giving the JQC the role of making recommendations of persons to fill vacancies, but the governor vetoed it.[142] A similar bill was passed and signed into law in 1978.[143] However, the law could not bind the governor, nor did the governor always follow the JQC's recommendation.[144]

In April 1978, a Republican state senator told a meeting of a county bar association that the continued election of judges in South Dakota was a "travesty and an embarrassment to our state," and announced his intention to introduce legislation for a "modified Missouri Plan."[145] Two months later, the president of the state bar told the state bar convention that the association would continue its efforts toward a Missouri Plan system.[146] When the legislature met in 1979, proposals to adopt a

[138] *Id.*

[139] See the text of the proposed amendments published in the *Deadwood Pioneer-Times* (October 4, 1972), 7.

[140] See https://ballotpedia.org/South_Dakota_Constitutional_Revision,_Amendment_E_(1972), accessed December 6, 2018.

[141] "Report of Committees on Judicial Selection and Tenure and Court Modernization," *South Dakota Bar Journal* 44, no. 3 (June 1975), 56.

[142] "Kneip Vetoes a Record Number of Bills," *Rapid City Journal* (February 29, 1976), 2.

[143] "Commission on Judicial Qualifications to Make Nominations for Judicial Vacancies," 1978 Session Laws of the State of South Dakota (1978), 205 (Chapter 149).

[144] See Mark Plenke, "Janklow Rejected Recommendations in Naming Davis," *Rapid City Journal* (February 19, 1979), 2.

[145] "Frankenfeld Calls Election of Judges a Travesty to State," *Rapid City Journal* (April 11, 1978), 8.

[146] Margaret Keeter, "Bar-Approved Plan for Pre-Paid Legal Services Aims to Improve Judicial Process," *Rapid City Journal* (June 11, 1978), 2.

version of the Missouri Plan was on the agenda.[147] The proposed system would use the previously created Judicial Qualifications Commission as the nominating body. The South Dakota Senate passed a version that included both the justices of the Supreme Court and judges of the circuit (trial) court.[148] The House retained nonpartisan elections for circuit judges,[149] but with the proviso that any midterm vacancies would be filled by the governor from a list prepared by the Judicial Qualifications Commission. The vote in the House was 50–19, with no clear partisan division.[150] In the Senate, the vote was 21–12, with a slight tendency to more opposition from the small number of Democrats in the Senate.[151]

One longtime observer of judicial selection in South Dakota recalled that the circuit judges had taken a vote on whether to support the Missouri Plan or stay with nonpartisan elections, and by a single vote, favored continuing with nonpartisan elections.[152] The proposed constitutional amendment was presented to the voters at the November 1980 election.[153] There appears to have been little opposition to the proposal.[154] The amendment passed with 54.0 percent in favor.[155]

In the summer of 1991, the South Dakota chief justice created an 11-person Judicial Election Committee to review the current judicial selection system. The chief justice explained, "The selection system has been criticized publicly and privately by lawyers, legislators, and the press."[156] Prior to the committee's creation, the South Dakota Judge's Association (SDJA) had passed a resolution calling for a system of appointment with retention elections.[157] The committee recommended

[147] "Senate Committee to Deliberate Judges Bill," *Rapid City Journal* (February 8, 1979), m6.

[148] Eric Newhouse, "Appointed Justices Bill Goes to the House," *Rapid City Journal* (March 8, 1979), 31.

[149] "Legislation; Judicial Elections," *Rapid City Journal* (April 1, 1979), 2.

[150] *South Dakota House Journal*, 1979, 1032.

[151] *Id.*, 390.

[152] Email from Thomas Barnett, September 21, 2018.

[153] The text of the amendment was printed in at least some newspapers; see, for example, *Queen City [Spearfish] Mail* (October 15, 1980), 19.

[154] I could find only one newspaper article referencing opposition; Tim Gebhart, "Crime Panel 'Strongly' Opposes Dakota Prop," *Rapid City Journal* (November 1, 1980), 2. In an article about the proposal, a state senator supporting the amendment commented that "in the last few years, we've had three incumbent justices knocked off"; see "Court Appointment Changes Proposed," *Lead Daily Call* (October 25, 1980), 1. I could find no evidence to support that; as noted earlier, a review of official reports of election results found only two contested elections between 1946 and 1978, resulting in one recently appointed incumbent being defeated. An examination of those records done by the South Dakota State Bar Association prior to the contested 1976 Supreme Court election that went back to the 1930s found no contested elections during that period; see Terry Woster, "A New Look Election; Supreme Court Contest," *Rapid City Journal* (October 31, 1977), 5.

[155] See https://ballotpedia.org/South_Dakota_Appointment_of_Judges,_Amendment_A_(1980), accessed December 7, 2018.

[156] Terry Woster, "Committee Named to Review Process of Choosing Judges," *Sioux Falls Argus-Leader* (July 30, 1991), C1.

[157] Doug Cummings, "Retention Elections Flawed, Offer Voters Little Choice on Judges," *Sioux Falls Argus-Leader* (November 8, 1991), 10A.

that the current Missouri Plan process be extended to include circuit court judges and that the Judicial Qualifications Commission make public the names of those being considered.[158]

Shortly after the report of the committee was released, a lawyer published an op-ed piece attacking the proposal, asserting that the only supporters of such a change were the judges themselves; he went on to criticize the filling of midterm vacancies by gubernatorial appointment, suggesting that such vacancies should be filled by special elections.[159] In fact, there was substantial division within the bar regarding extending the Missouri Plan to the circuit judges. At a state bar meeting, those present were asked to vote on the several recommendations of the Judicial Election Committee; there was strong support for most of the recommendations, but the group was almost evenly divided over the Missouri Plan proposal.[160] This led, in part, to a front-page newspaper article headlined, "Judicial Reform's Key Adversaries Are Lawyers."[161]

Why there was now opposition within the bar, historically among the strongest proponent of the Missouri Plan system, is unclear. One speculation is that the opposition came from lawyers who wanted to become judges but had little prospect of being nominated by the Judicial Qualifications Committee that would have a role in filling all vacancies, not just midterm vacancies, under a Missouri Plan system.[162] Those lawyers, some of whom may have had success running for other offices, most likely saw election to an open seat as their only possible route to the bench; they probably were reluctant to challenge an incumbent because if they lost, they would have to appear before the judge they had opposed. Whatever the reason, there was little or no legislative action on the committee's recommendations, and it would be over a decade before the issue of judicial selection reform again became part of the political agenda.

In 2003, the SDJA sought to have the legislature put a constitutional amendment on the ballot that would apply the Missouri Plan system to circuit judgeships.[163]

158 Terry Woster, "Panel: Judge Retention System Fair; Considered Names Should Be Public, Committee Says," *Sioux Falls Argus-Leader* (October 20, 1991), C1. It is unclear whether the disclosure referred to all persons considered, or only to "finalists"; see "Judicial Proposals Should Be Enacted," *Sioux Falls Argus-Leader* (October 28, 1991), 8A.

159 Cummings, "Retention Elections Flawed," *supra* note 157.

160 David A. Gerdes, "State Bar Committee Took Neutral Stand on Judicial Reform," *Sioux Falls Argus-Leader* (January 12, 1993), 6A.

161 Mike Trautmann, "Judicial Reform's Key Adversaries Are Lawyers," *Sioux Falls Argus-Leader* (January 4, 1993), 1A.

162 Email from Thomas Barrett, September 21, 2018.

163 An analysis of 109 circuit elections in the between 1982 (the first election after the end of nonpartisan elections for the Supreme Court) and 1998 (the last elections before the 2004 vote on ending nonpartisan elections for the circuit court) found that only 19.3 percent were contested; see Christina Fischer, "Merit Selection: A Better Method to Select South Dakota's Circuit Court Judges," *South Dakota Law Review* 49 (2004), 187. South Dakota judges run for election every eight years, and those elections happen in tandem; consequently, the elections covered occurred in 1982, 1990, and 1998.

This happened despite the fact that in the 109 circuit court elections since the adoption of the Missouri Plan for the South Dakota Supreme Court in 1980, only 17 incumbents had faced opposition and only 3 had lost.[164] The impetus for the SDJA's support for applying the Missouri Plan to circuit court judges was the previous year's U.S. Supreme Court's decision in *Republican Party of Minnesota v. White*.[165] There was concern that *White* would lead to the kind of negative advertising that had appeared in other states.[166] The Bar Commission (a part of the state bar) voted to assist the SDJA in its effort.[167] Appropriate legislation was introduced (H.J.R. 1003),[168] and the House voted unanimously to put the question to the voters as a constitutional amendment.[169] In the Senate, the vote was 27–7,[170] with all of the nays coming from Republicans.[171]

As the November 2004 vote approached, both supporters and opponents sought to sway voters. Proponents emphasized that decisions such as *White* had the potential to make the judicial elections into political campaigns. Opponents emphasized that voters would have less say on who would serve as a judge.[172] Opponents published editorials and op-ed pieces.[173] The opposition was led by members of the bar and some Republican legislators. Proponents responded with their own editorials and op-ed pieces. They also spent money, over $35,000, on advertising,[174] with one newspaper ad featuring endorsements of the amendment from several groups or persons, including the Republican governor.[175] The proponents emphasized

164 Information compiled from the South Dakota Secretary of State website and digitized newspapers; there were also eleven contested elections for open seats, but it is unclear how many, if any, open seats went uncontested.

165 Republican Party of Minnesota v. White, 536 U.S. 765 (2002).

166 Bob Hayes, "President's Page," *State Bar of South Dakota Newsletter* (February 2003), 2.

167 "Minutes of Bar Commission Meeting," *State Bar of South Dakota Newsletter* (February 2003), 4.

168 Terry Woster, "Judges Would Be Appointed under Plan; Panel Wants Voters to Decide on Constitutional Change," *Sioux Falls Argus-Leader* (February 25, 2003), 3B.

169 "Bill Update," *Sioux Falls Argus-Leader* (February 11, 2003), 3B, (reporting a 68–0 vote on "first passage in the House).

170 "Bill Update," *Sioux Falls Argus-Leader* (February 26, 2003), 3B (reporting a 27–7 vote on "first passage in the Senate).

171 See http://sdlegislature.gov/sessions/2003/HJR1003.htm, accessed December 7, 2018.

172 Terry Woster, "Voters May End Judicial Elections; Amendment on November Ballot," *Sioux City Argus-Leader* (October 2, 2004), 1B; Dennis Ross, "Judges Defend Amendment A," *Rapid City Journal* (October 20, 2004).

173 See Lance Russell, "Vote No on Amendment A," *Aberdeen American News* (October 3, 2004), 5A; "Constitutional Amendment A: The Elimination of a Constitutional Right," *Black Hills [Spearfish] Pioneer* (October 22, 2004); Lawrence M. Kostaneski, "Amendment A: Those Who Control Law, Control the Nation," *Rapid City Journal* (October 24, 2004).

174 Terry Woster,"More Than $260,000 Spent on Food-Tax Vote; State Shows Most Money Is Going to Oppose Repeal," *Sioux Falls Argus-Leader* (October 31, 2004), 5B; see also http://apps.sd.gov/st12odrs/files/0000001101.pdf, accessed December 8, 2018.

175 "Vote Yes on Amendment 'A,'" *Sioux Fall Argus-Leader* (October 31, 2004), 18A. For a second newspaper ad, see "Amendment A: What Is It?" *Sioux Falls Argus-Leader* (October 24, 2005), 7D.

choosing judges based on qualifications, insuring impartiality, and that voters retained the ability to remove judges through the retention elections.[176] Polling about two weeks before election day showed that the opposition had a strong lead: 53 percent of respondents said they would vote against the amendment, and only 30 percent were in favor.[177] On election day, the undecided voters split in roughly that same ratio as the previous poll had found, and the amendment was soundly defeated with 62.2 percent of the voters opposed.[178]

CONCLUSION

Voters in both Florida and South Dakota approved the adoption of the Missouri Plan for their state's appellate courts. They also approved constraining the governor in filling midterm vacancies on the major trial courts in their states; the governors must select from nominees provided by a judicial nominating commission. However, the voters balked when asked to end the potentially contested nonpartisan elections used for the trial courts. The opponents of adopting a full Missouri Plan system for the trial courts played on voters' desire to have a direct say regarding who served as a judge in their local communities.

In South Dakota, one might argue that there is, for most purposes, a Missouri Plan system in operation. As of January 1, 2019, 38 of 44 sitting circuit judges had been appointed to their positions. At least part of the reason for this is that South Dakota judges are "automatically retired on the first Tuesday after the first Monday of January next after the general election at which members of the Legislature are elected immediately following the attainment of age seventy."[179] Those appointed to midterm vacancies serve the balance of their predecessor's unexpired eight-year term.[180] In the two elections since the defeat of the proposals to adopt a full Missouri Plan system for the circuit court, there have been 81 circuit court elections; only 5 incumbents have been challenged and none have lost; only 7 of the 81 elections have been contests over open seats. All 6 circuit judges serving as of January 1, 2019 who had not been initially appointed to their positions had been elected to open seats.[181] As things currently stand at the end of 2019, extending gubernatorial

[176] Carson Walker, "Justice: Measure Would Keep Judges Accountable," *Aberdeen American News* (October 18, 2004), 4A; "Amendment A: Goal Is to Preserve Judicial Impartiality," *Rapid City Journal* (October 24, 2004); "Viewpoint: Judges Should Be Chosen on Qualifications," *Rapid City Journal* (October 28, 2004).

[177] Terry Woster, "Majority in S.D. Oppose Merit Selection of Judges; Amendment A Overshadowed by Larger Issues; Major Races," *Sioux Falls Argus-Leader* (October 37. 2004), 13A.

[178] See https://ballotpedia.org/South_Dakota_Merit_Selection_of_Judges,_Amendment_A_(2004), accessed December 8, 2018.

[179] South Dakota Statutes, 16-6-31.

[180] See www.judicialselection.us/judicial_selection/methods/selection_of_judges.cfm?state=SD, accessed January 18, 2019.

[181] This is based on searches conducted on January 17–18, 2019.

appointment to the few circuit court seats now won at open-seat elections and replacing the current largely uncontested nonpartisan circuit court elections with retention elections would have little practical effect on the South Dakota judiciary. In practice, the existing system differs little from the Missouri Plan.

The situation in Florida is different. Information on how many of the sitting circuit court judges were initially appointed versus how many obtained their positions through election is not readily available. Based on a listing of judges appointed during Rick Scott's eight-year tenure as governor (2011–2018),[182] plus information on candidates winning circuit court elections during the same period,[183] it appears that only a bit less than half of persons taking positions as circuit court judges in the period 2011–2018 were initially elected to their positions. Of those initially elected, about 90 percent won open seats; only about 10 percent defeated incumbents. Clearly, election continues to be an important route to obtaining a Florida circuit court judgeship, and, unlike in South Dakota, a shift to a full Missouri Plan system, something that appears highly unlikely to happen, would be a significant change.

Thus, in one of the two states where voters approved the Missouri Plan system for appellate courts but rejected it for trial courts, the initial selection system differs little from the Missouri Plan, and hence there is little reason to make a change. In the other state, a change to the Missouri Plan would be quite significant, and for that reason any proposal to make such a change would probably face substantial opposition.

[182] See https://ballotpedia.org/Judges_appointed_by_Rick_Scott, accessed January 19, 2019; the site lists 139 circuit court judges appointed by Scott.

[183] Based on information available at https://dos.elections.myflorida.com/candidates/, accessed January 19, 2019. In the 2010 through 2016 elections, nonincumbents won 117 elections; for 2012 through 2018, nonincumbents won 130 elections.

12

Nevada and Ohio

Voters Say No to the Missouri Plan

This chapter turns to two states, Nevada and Ohio, where between 1980 and 2018 proposed constitutional amendments to establish a Missouri Plan system for some or all of the state's courts were rejected by the voters. In Nevada, the legislature passed such proposals and submitted them to the voters on multiple occasions, only to have the voters reject them each time. In Ohio, the proposal got on to the ballot through the initiative procedure. In both of those states, opponents used as their primary argument that the proposed change would end the voters' power to select judges, and the proponents, arguing that the proposed change would improve the quality of the state judiciary, were not able to overcome the opponents' contentions.

NEVADA

Three times the Nevada legislature sent proposed constitutional amendments for judicial selection and retention based on the Missouri Plan to the voters, and three times the voters rejected those proposals. The voters did pass a constitutional amendment requiring the governor to fill midterm judicial vacancies from a list of candidates forwarded by a nominating commission. However, elections for open positions and for incumbents seeking to keep their positions continue to be conducted on a nonpartisan basis.

Judicial Selection Patterns

Prior to 2015, the Nevada state court systems consisted of two general jurisdiction courts, the Supreme Court and the trial-level district court, plus local municipal and justice of the peace courts handling minor matters. Until 1967, the Nevada Supreme Court had only three members; that was increased to five in 1967 and seven in 1997. After four failed attempts, the voters authorized the creation of an intermediate Court of Appeals in 2014.

Bowers and Strate provide a history of judicial selection in Nevada through the early 1990s.[1] Nevada adopted nonpartisan elections in 1915, during the period when many states were shifting away from partisan judicial elections.[2] Between 1916 (the year of the first nonpartisan judicial elections) and 1988, only 34 percent of Nevada Supreme Court elections were contested; incumbents faced no opposition in 71 percent of the elections in which they sought to stay on the bench. Over the entire history of the Nevada Supreme Court through 1988, there were 60 judicial elections in which incumbents ran for reelection; only 5 times did the incumbent lose. At the trial level, between 1916 and 1984, only 37 percent of elections were contested. Also, as is commonly true in states with elected judiciaries, a large proportion of judges initially came to their positions through appointment. Between 1916 and 1988, 57 percent of the justices of the Nevada Supreme Court initially obtained their seats by appointment; this rose to 67 percent for the period 1939–1988.[3] However, based on my data, that pattern is slightly different for the period 1950 through 2010, when only 10 of the 27 persons joining the Supreme Court were appointed. Of the other 17 judges, 14 were elected to open seats and 3 defeated previously elected incumbents.[4] At the trial level, in 2005, only 24 of 61 (39 percent) sitting district court judges came to their positions through initial appointment.[5]

Efforts to Modify Judicial Selection

Partisan politics does not appear to have played a major role in the debates over changing judicial selection in Nevada. Between 1960 and 2010, one party, the Democratic Party, had control of the governorship and control of both chambers of the legislature (the Senate and the Assembly, as the two chambers are called in Nevada) for only 10 years of the 50; there was no period of complete Republican control.[6] During this 50-year period, a Democrat served as governor for 30 years. Given the absence of party dominance, there would be little motivation to try to manipulate the selection system for political advantage.

[1] Michael W. Bowers and Larry D. Strate, "Judicial Selection in Nevada: An Historical, Empirical, and Normative Evaluation," *Nevada Historical Society Quarterly* 36, no. 4 (Winter 1993), 227–245.

[2] *Id.*, 234. Some of Nevada's judicial elections involve candidates who have well-known party affiliations; *Id.*, 236. Bowers and Strate specifically reference the 1992 election as an example; however, the partisan correlation (defined in Chapter 1) was a relatively modest .47.

[3] *Id.*, 236.

[4] During this period, 27 of 57 elections were contested, and in those contested elections the average partisan correlation (defined in Chapter 1) was .344.

[5] Vince Consul, "Thinking Boldly: 'Do We Really Elect Our Judges?,'" *Nevada Lawyers* 13, no. 9 (September 2005).

[6] Republicans did obtain complete control for 2015–2016, but that came after the most recent attempt to adopt the Missouri Plan.

The First Try

The first reference to the Missouri Plan I could find in the popular press was a brief reference in the mid-1950s, suggesting that this was something being discussed by the bar association.[7] The Missouri Plan as a possibility for Nevada first seems to appear in the late 1950s, when it was discussed in an article appearing in the *Nevada Bar Journal*.[8] There is also evidence that some elements of the state judiciary were advocating adoption of the Missouri Plan by the late 1950s.[9] The idea of adopting the Missouri Plan seems to have first gotten some political traction in the early 1960s, when a proposal to adopt the plan was seriously considered by the legislature.[10] However, the proposal failed to pass by a single vote in the legislature.[11] The following year, a Conference on the Selection of Judges was held at the University of Nevada; although there was some indication that conferees supported a plan eliminating political contests for judgeships, an effort to pass a resolution to that effect failed.[12] At least one judicial candidate that year ran advertisements expressing opposition to the Missouri Plan: "I oppose the Missouri Plan which would take away your right to vote for district judge!"[13]

Support for the Missouri Plan started to percolate a bit in 1966,[14] but did not get a solid foothold again until 1968, when a legislative subcommittee endorsed the idea.[15] A few days later, the Citizens Conference on Nevada Courts issued a range of recommendations for changing the Nevada courts, including replacing the election of judges with the Missouri Plan.[16] The following year, a proposed constitutional amendment adopting the Missouri Plan was introduced. Under the amendment provisions of the state constitution, the exact same proposal has to pass in two consecutive legislatures. A plan was approved by the legislature in late March and

7 "Nevada Politics," *Nevada State Journal (Reno)* (September 5, 1954), 24.

8 Bruce R. Thompson, "The Selection of Supreme Court Justices," *Nevada State Bar Journal* 24, no. 1 (January 1959), 13–17; see also "Report of Judicial Council, Selection and Salary Committee, Southern District," *Nevada State Bar Journal* 26, no. 4 (October 1961), 187–190.

9 "Nevada Legislative Report: Revamp Constitution," *Reno Gazette-Journal* (February 16, 1961), 13.

10 "Nevada Legislative Report; Will Reconsider Missouri Plan," *Reno Gazette-Journal* (March 3, 1961), 3.

11 "Nevada Legislative Report; Civil Rights Measure in Tatters," *Reno Gazette-Journal* (March 10, 1961), 6.

12 "Judicial Plan Aired in Reno; Formal Support Withheld at University Conference," *Reno Gazette-Journal* (December 17, 1962).

13 "Elect John Sanchez District Judge," *Reno Gazette-Journal* (November 1, 1962), 35.

14 "New Plan for Judges Supported," *Reno Gazette-Journal* (January 31, 1966), 11; "Popular Vote: 'Poor Way of Naming Judges,'" *Nevada State Journal [Reno]* (February 1, 1966), 7; Joe Midmore, "Should Nevada Judges Be Elected or Appointed?" *Reno Gazette-Journal* (April 16, 1966), 9.

15 "Committee Recommends Governor, Commission Appoint Judges," *Reno Gazette-Journal* (July 10, 1968), 26.

16 "Citizen Conference Recommendations: "'Unify Nevada Court System, End Election of Judges,'" *Reno Gazette-Journal* (July 12, 1968).

early April 1969. The legislature at the time was closely divided, with Democrats in control of the Senate (11 to 9) and Republicans in control of the Assembly (22 to 18); the proposal passed 13–6 in the Senate and 31–4 in the Assembly.[17] In February 1971, the two chambers both again passed the amendment, this time with overwhelming votes, 16 to 1 in the Senate and 31 to 4 in the Assembly.[18]

The amendment went on the November 1972 ballot. It called for a commission to nominate candidates for appointment as Supreme Court justices that would consist of 7 members: the chief justice (or an associate justice designated by the chief justice), 3 attorneys appointed by the Board of Governors of the State Bar of Nevada, and 3 non-attorneys selected by the governor. For the trial-level district court, the nominating commission would add a member of the state bar from the district (appointed by the Board of Governors of the bar) and a non-attorney appointed by the governor. The commission was designed to be politically and geographically diverse. The commission was to submit a list of three nominees, and there was no provision for the governor to reject the list and ask for another. The appointee would have to stand for retention at the next general election. Although the proposal was part of a larger overhaul of the constitutional article on the judiciary, the selection provisions ending contested judicial elections attracted strong opposition. The *Reno Gazette-Journal* urged a no vote:[19]

> A no vote should be cast with fierce spirit by Nevadans who want to maintain their rights as citizens to vote for supreme court judges. A yes vote would rob Nevadans of this right and, in effect give life tenure to those judges now in office.

The editor of the *Mason Valley News* asked, "Why is there this continual move to indicate that the electorate is just too damned dumb to choose good judges?"[20] The proposal was rejected by the voters with 61.8 percent against the amendment. However, four years later, the voters passed an amendment, with 63.7 percent in favor, that had exactly the same provisions for judicial selection *except* for the omission of retention elections;[21] that is, nonpartisan elections would continue both

[17] The nays in the Senate vote came from 3 Republicans and 3 Democrats, and in the Assembly from 3 Democrats and 1 Republican; see www.leg.state.nv.us/Division/Research/Library/LegHistory/LHs/1969/SJR23,1969_1971.pdf, 10, 24.

[18] The nays in the Assembly again came from 3 Democrats and 1 Republican; in the Senate the single nay was from a Republican; see www.leg.state.nv.us/Division/Research/Library/LegHistory/LHs/1969/SJR23,1969_1971.pdf, 23, 28.

[19] "Ballot Questions," *Reno Evening-Gazette* (November 3, 1972), 4.

[20] "Question No. 4," *Mason Valley News* (October 13, 1972), 2.

[21] See https://ballotpedia.org/Nevada_Governor_Appointment_of_State_Judges,_Question_5_(1976), accessed November 11, 2018. The proposal passed the state legislature on near unanimous votes; only 7 nays in total were cast across the four roll-call votes. Voters also passed several other amendments to the judicial article at the 1976 election, including the creation of a central administrative structure, the creation of a Commission on Judicial Discipline, and provisions allowing the legislature to increase the size of the Supreme Court; the amendment on selection had the strongest positive vote.

for open seats and for incumbents seeking to retain their positions, but appointees to fill midterm vacancies had to be filled from a list of candidates provided by a nominating commission.

The Second Try

The second attempt to shift to a Missouri Plan went to the voters in 1988. It failed, but not quite as badly as the 1972 proposal, with 55.6 percent against for the 1988 proposal. A proposal limited to the Supreme Court had been introduced in 1981;[22] it passed the Senate 11–8,[23] but there was no action in the Assembly. Calls for adopting the Missouri Plan picked up late in 1984,[24] and it passed the state legislature in 1985 and 1987 with minimal news coverage[25] but continuing editorial opposition.[26] The two votes in the Senate had small numbers of dissenters; all but one of those dissenting votes came from Democrats.[27] The vote in the Assembly in 1985 was more divided, 24–17, but there was no partisan pattern in that split (8 nays were from Democrats and 9 were from Republicans);[28] the vote in 1987 was 29–13.[29]

About two weeks before the 1988 election, the press reported on a debate between a state senator supporting the proposal and a district attorney opposing it that was held at a meeting of the Rotary Club in Reno. The proponent argued that the proposal would create an "independent and responsible judiciary" and would help Nevada "come out of the dark ages." The opponent challenged the independence argument and argued that the proposed system would actually "entrench judges deeper into the political process."[30] The two debaters had emerged as primary spokespersons for the two sides,[31] and on the Sunday before the election they

[22] Martin Griffith, "Resolution Eliminates Election of Supreme Court Justices," *Reno Gazette-Journal* (February 6, 1981), 10. See also Lee Adler, "Former Jurist Endorses a Merit System," *Reno Gazette-Journal* (February 23, 1981), 3.

[23] Lee Adler, "Senate Favors Appointed Justices," *Reno Gazette-Journal* (March 3, 1981), 12.

[24] Lee Adler, "Nevada's Way Not Only Way to Pick Judge," *Reno Gazette-Journal* (December 30, 1984), 1D.

[25] "Senate Votes to Let Judges Run Unopposed," *Reno Gazette-Journal* (April 23, 1985), C1; Laura Myers, "Bill Would Allow Nevada Judges to Be Appointed," *Reno Gazette-Journal* (April 9, 1987), 1A; "Senate Backs Plan to Appoint Nevada Judges," *Reno Gazette-Journal* (April 11, 1987), 2C; "Assembly OKs Judge Plan," *Reno Gazette Journal* (May 3, 1987), 21A.

[26] "Don't Change Election System for State Judges," *Reno Gazette-Journal* (April 25, 1985), 19A.

[27] See www.leg.state.nv.us/Session/64th1987/reports/BillVote.cfm?fldDate=1987-05-27%2000:00:00.0&BillID=1087&fldBillname=SJR17&AssemblyID=2&SessionNumber=Nelis_87R; www.leg.state.nv.us/Session/63rd1985/reports/BillVote.cfm?fldDate=1985-04-22%2000:00:00.0&BillID=1087&fldBillname=SJR17&AssemblyID=2&SessionNumber=Nelis_85R.

[28] See www.leg.state.nv.us/Session/63rd1985/reports/BillVote.cfm?fldDate=1985-05-21%2000:00:00.0&BillID=1087&fldBillname=SJR17&HouseID=1&SessionNumber=Nelis_85R.

[29] "Assembly Oks Judge Plan." Apparently, the day before voting in favor, the Assembly had voted 18–24 against; what led initially to the negative vote and then to the positive vote, is not clear.

[30] Andrea Esquer, "Lane, Raggio Debate: Sparring over Proposition 4," *Reno Gazette-Journal* (October 18, 1988), 3A.

[31] The district attorney had previously come out strongly against the proposal; see "Washoe DA Speaks of Value of Electing Judges," *Mason Valley News* (March 18, 1988), 6. The state senator had been one of the primary backers of the amendment in the legislature.

appeared on a television program, "Face the State," to present their views of the proposal,[32] described in one report as the "top ballot measure" in the upcoming election.[33] The "public notice" of the proposed constitutional amendment, printed in state newspapers, included sections "Argument for Passage" and "Argument against Passage."[34] The former argued that the proposed system "helps to ensure that judicial vacancies are filled by the most highly qualified and respected persons" and "would reduce political pressures by eliminating the need for significant contributions for election campaigns." The latter argued that the proposed retention elections might make it "difficult to assess a judge's performance without an opposing candidate's critique," and that it "would not completely remove politics from the initial selection process" but shift the emphasis "to a commission on judicial selection and the governor." The voters again rejected the proposed system.

Try Two-and-a-Half

In 1993, the Nevada Supreme Court created the Judicial Assessment Commission. The commission, which became popularly known as the Rose Commission, after Chief Justice Bob Rose who initiated it, was charged with looking at the operation of Nevada's courts and making recommendations for innovations and improvements. The results were proposals for a wide range of changes to law, judicial administration, and programming.[35] The Rose Commission also advanced what became known as the "Nevada Plan," which was similar to the system adopted a few years earlier in New Mexico.[36] The key difference was that the first election after a judge's appointment by the governor would be a nonpartisan election, rather than a partisan election that could be contested by other candidates; the governor would still be bound to make appointments from a list provided by a nominating commission, and elections after the first would use the retention format. The Rose Commission also proposed that a system of judicial evaluation be instituted. Legislation to put the Nevada Plan before the voters passed unanimously out of the Assembly Judiciary Committee but died when the Assembly voted 25 to 17 against the proposal.[37]

32 See *Reno Gazette-Journal* (October 30, 1988), 4.

33 Mike Phillis, "Judge Selection Question Tops Ballot Measures," *Reno Gazette-Journal* (October 30, 1988), 3A.

34 See *Reno Gazette-Journal* (October 26, 1988), 5, or *Mason Valley News* (October 7, 1988), sec. 2, p. 6.

35 "Simplifying the Maze: Report of the Judicial Assessment Commission of the Nevada Supreme Court" (October 2000), ii, https://nvcourts.gov/AOC/Documents/Rose_Commission_Long_Range_Strategic_Plan_for_Nevada_Court_System_1999-2000/, accessed November 11, 2018.

36 "Panel: Appoint Judges, Decriminalize Marijuana," *Elko Daily Free Press* (December 14, 1994), 1; see also "Elected Judges Subject of Judiciary Proposal," *Elko Daily Free Press* (February 2, 1995), 1.

37 "Appointed-Judges Plan Dies in Assembly Vote," *Elko Daily Free Press* (May 31, 1995), 1; the opposition came largely from Democratic members of the Assembly, but the reason for that opposition is unclear.

The Rose Commission was reconstituted in the late 1990,[38] and, in the report it issued in 2000, called again for adopting the Nevada Plan and for judicial performance evaluation.[39] One element of the selection change based on the proposals of the Commission did go to the voters in 2002. The Commission had proposed that judges not go before the voters until the first general election after they had served at least two full years in office. The voters were presented with a proposal that an appointed judge not stand until the first general election after at least one year of service, unless the term the judge had been appointed to complete ended during the first year of service.[40] Voters rejected the proposal, with 59.2 percent opposed.[41]

The Third (and Most Recent) Try

In late 2005 and early 2006, commentary and news articles about the method of selecting state judges once again began to appear. The president of the state bar published a commentary focused on the percentage of sitting judges who came to their positions by appointment rather than by election; at that time 64 of 149 (43 percent) of current judges had been appointed, most of whom were subsequently elected to those same positions.[42] The state bar announced support for a version of the Nevada Plan that had previously been put forth by the Rose Commission.[43] There was no indication of any movement on this proposal in the legislature.

The following year, a series on the Nevada courts published by the *Los Angeles Times* in early June 2006[44] became the catalyst for action by the Nevada legislature. The articles traced the cozy relationship between some Nevada judges and their friends, former clients, and former business associates. The first of the articles was titled, "In Las Vegas, They're Playing with a Stacked Judicial Deck." Another of the articles, accompanied by photos of six judges, was headlined, "Some Lawyers Say You Must Pay to Play." Much of the series focused on the role of various interests, particularly casinos and lawyers, in funding judges' election

[38] Bill Gang, "Panel to Reform Courts Resurrected," *Las Vegas Sun* (March 5, 1999).

[39] See "Simplifying the Maze," *supra* note 35, 7–9. During the mid-1990s, legislators proposed ending contested elections in the wake of some judicial elections marked by mudslinging; see Ed Vogel, "Assemblyman Wants Judges Appointed," *Las Vegas Review-Journal* (January 2, 1997).

[40] See www.judicialselection.us/judicial_selection/reform_efforts/failed_reform_efforts.cfm?state=NV, accessed November 11, 2018.

[41] See https://ballotpedia.org/Nevada_Appointed_Judges%27_Term_of_Office,_Question_6_(2002), accessed November 11, 2018.

[42] Vince Consul, "Thinking Boldly: 'Do We Really Elect Our Judges?'" *Nevada Lawyer* 13, no. 9 (September 2005), 6.

[43] "Should the Voters Pick Their Judges?" *Las Vegas Sun* (February 18, 2006); see also Vince Consul, "Thinking Boldly . . . The Nevada Plan, a Plan Whose Time Has Come," *Nevada Lawyer* 14 no. 3 (March 2006), 8.

[44] Michael J. Goodman and William C. Rempel, "Juice vs. Justice," *Los Angeles Times* (June 8–10, 2006).

campaigns.[45] In the wake of the *Times* articles, civic leaders launched an effort to reform judicial selection.[46] In November, the Nevada Supreme Court established what was known as the Article 6 Commission to review the court system,[47] with judicial selection high on the list of issues to consider.[48]

Reform of judicial selection was also on the agenda for the legislature in 2007. Three options were raised: the Missouri Plan, the Nevada plan, and a variant of the Missouri Plan that would require a 60 percent favorable vote for retention combined with a performance evaluation by a Judicial Performance Commission that would be publicly released with a recommendation regarding retention prior to the election; the latter was referred to as the "Raggio Plan" after the Senate Minority Leader, Bill Raggio, who proposed it.[49] At the end of May, both chambers of the legislature passed the Raggio Plan, with the modification of requiring 55 percent for retention.[50] The votes in the two chambers were 15–6 in the Senate[51] and 30–11 in the Assembly;[52] the support for the change was bipartisan. Two years later, the legislature again voted to put the proposed change in judicial selection on the ballot;[53] the votes were very similar to 2007, 14–7 in the Senate[54] and 29–13 in the Assembly,[55] and again support was bipartisan. Even before this approval came, critics were attacking the proposal as denying voters the power to select judges.[56]

As the November 2010 election approached, supporters of the plan created an advocacy group called "Nevada for Qualified Judges (NQJ)" to raise funds to mount

45 "Selection of Judges Might Change, *Las Vegas Sun* (June 13, 2006).

46 Scott Gold, "Nevada Leaders Move to Reform Judiciary," *Los Angeles Times* (September 3, 2006).

47 Ed Vogel, "Commission Forming to Study State Judicial System," *Las Vegas Review-Journal* (November 17, 2006), 2B.

48 The chief justice was quoted as saying that the Court had been planning to create the commission even before the *Times* series; see K. C. Howard, "Commission Begins Discussing Ways to Revamp Court System," *Las Vegas Review-Journal* (December 20, 2006), 7B.

49 Sam Skolnik, "Taking Cash Power Out of the Judiciary," *Las Vegas Sun* (March 20, 2007).

50 Sean Whaley, "Senate Vote Keeps Judicial Selection Proposal Alive for 2009," *Las Vegal Review-Journal* (May 31, 2007), 3B; see also Sam Skolnik, "Judges Win Again and Again," *Law Vegas Sun* (June 7, 2007).

51 See www.leg.state.nv.us/Session/74th2007/Reports/BillVote.cfm?VoteID=228&fldBillname=SJR2; the 6 nay votes came from 5 Republicans and 1 Democrat.

52 See www.leg.state.nv.us/Session/74th2007/Reports/BillVote.cfm?VoteID=1079&fldBillname=SJR2. The 11 nay votes came from 6 Democrats and 5 Republicans.

53 Ed Vogel, "Judicial Resolution Makes Ballot," *Las Vegas Review-Journal* (May 21, 2009), 3B.

54 See www.leg.state.nv.us/75th2009/Reports/BillVote.cfm?VoteID=90&fldReprint=0&fldDocTypeCode=SJR&fldBillNumber=2&fldBillname=SJR2*; the 7 nay votes came from 3 Republicans and 4 Democrats.

55 See www.leg.state.nv.us/75th2009/Reports/BillVote.cfm?VoteID=973&fldReprint=0&fldDocTypeCode=SJR&fldBillNumber=2&fldBillname=SJR2*; the 13 nay votes came from 8 Republicans and 5 Democrats.

56 Ed Vogel, "Judicial-Selection Plan Strips Voters' Power, Critic Says," *Las Vegas Review-Journal* (February 24, 2019), 11A; Jeff German, "Lawmakers Pave Way for Vote on Appointing Judges; Backers of Plan That Includes Retention Elections Gear Up for Referendum Next Year," *Las Vegas Sun* (June 6, 2009).

a campaign to pass the proposed constitutional amendment. The group was led by several prominent state figures, and listed retired U.S. Supreme Court Justice Sandra Day O'Connor as honorary chairwoman.[57] This effort came in the face of surveys showing voters opposed to the change by a margin of about 2 to 1.[58] In the two months before the election, the proposed change attracted strong backing from the state bar and local business groups.[59] NQJ sponsored television advertisements promoting a "yes" vote on the amendment, with some ads featuring Justice O'Connor.[60] That campaign appears to have increased support for the amendment,[61] but it was not enough to win voters' approval; only 42.3 percent of voters backed the change.[62] The thrust of the opposition was that the change would disempower voters and empower a small group of political elites.

Nevada Summary

The legislature persisted in proposing a shift away from contested elections. Given that systems using a nominating commission were adopted in other states in the wake of scandals involving the courts,[63] one might expect the 2010 exposé in the *Los Angeles Times* to have resulted in citizen support for changing judicial elections. However, even in the face of questionable behavior of judges connected to the need to raise campaign funds for reelection campaigns, the citizens of Nevada were unwilling to give up their direct role in selecting the state's judges.

OHIO

Ohio joins Nevada as a state where, since 1980, voters have been presented with a proposed constitutional amendment that would have adopted a Missouri Plan system of judicial selection and retention for one or more levels of the state court system, but they have never voted in favor of such a system or made other major changes to judicial selection or retention. Ohio differs from Nevada in that the vote on a proposed amendment came as a result of an initiative process, while in Nevada the legislature put proposals for such an amendment on the ballot. Also, unlike

57 Jane Ann Morrison, "Ignoring Polls, Big Names Get Behind Merit Selection of Judges," *Las Vegas Review-Journal* (July 24, 2010), 1B.

58 Carri Geer Thevenot, "Voters Want Final Word on Judges," *Las Vegas Review-Journal* (July 19, 2010), 1B.

59 Valerie Miller, "Rally 'Round the Ballot Measure," *Las Vegas Business Press* (September 13, 2010).

60 Ashley Powers, "Nevada to Vote on Appointment of Top Judges; Despite Some Major Embarrassments Involving Elected Judges, Many State Residents Are Cool to the Idea," *Los Angeles Times* (October 29, 2010); the ad featuring O'Connor can be accessed at https://youtu.be/aOFmdsykS4E.

61 Doug McMurdo, "Question 1," *Las Vegas Review-Journal* (October 30, 2010), 3B.

62 See https://ballotpedia.org/Nevada_Judicial_Appointment_Amendment,_Question_1_(2010)#cite_note-SunJuly-2, accessed November 30, 2018.

63 See Chapter 10.

Nevada, where voters have rejected Missouri Plan proposals on two different occasions since 1980, Ohio voters have done so only once, in 1987.[64]

Judicial Selection in Ohio

Ohio uses a unique system of judicial elections. Candidates for judicial office are nominated through party primaries, but in the general election no party affiliations are shown for judicial candidates. Only one other state, Michigan, uses a similar hybrid system of partisan nomination and nonpartisan election (only for its Supreme Court), but in Michigan, party conventions make the nominations.[65] Not surprisingly, partisanship plays a significant role in Ohio's judicial elections, particularly at the Supreme Court level.

As is true in other states, the governor makes appointments to fill judicial vacancies. In most states using elections, this means that the vast majority of judges first obtain their positions through appointment. This is not the case in Ohio, at least for the appellate courts. Between 1960 and 1980, a total of 45 judges served on the Ohio Supreme Court, but only 12 (26.7 percent) initially obtained their position by appointment. During that period, 197 judges served on the Ohio Court of Appeals, and only 26 (13.2 percent) were initially appointed. The lower percentage for the Court of Appeals reflects in part the expansion of that court during the period and a requirement that new judgeships be filled by election rather than appointment. Ohio's mandatory retirement rule, adopted in 1968, does not force judges to retire at age 70, but precludes a judge from entering office or starting a new term if age 70 is reached prior to the day the term starts. Although judges could choose to step down before the end of the term to allow the governor to appoint a replacement, that practice is not common in Ohio.[66]

Elections for appellate courts in Ohio are usually contested. Between 1960 and 1980, only 3 of 33 elections for the Supreme Court were uncontested in the general election. Noncontestation was more likely in Court of Appeals elections, with 77 of 171 (45 percent) elections uncontested in the general election.[67] Between 1950 and

[64] Ohio voters rejected a proposal for what would become known as the Missouri Plan in 1938, two years before Missouri adopted it; Kathleen L. Barber, "Judicial Politics in Ohio," in Carle Lieberman, ed., *Government and Politics in Ohio* (Lanham, MD: University Press of America, 1984), 91.

See Richard J. Ruebel, "Judicial Selection and Tenure – The Merit Plan in Ohio," *University of Cincinnati Law Review* 42 (1973) 263. The proposal was rejected by voters in every county. That same year, Michigan voters rejected a proposal to appoint state Supreme Court judges using a nominating commission; see George E. Brand, "Michigan State Bar's Work for Judicial Appointments," *Journal of the American Judicature Society* 22, no. 5 (February 1939), 197–202.

[65] Until it adopted a Missouri Plan system in 1974, Arizona had a similar system; Maryland also used a hybrid system at one time; see Barber, "Judicial Politics in Ohio," *supra* note 64, 90.

[66] *Id.*, 94.

[67] *Id.*, 103; the 3 Supreme Court elections uncontested in the general election were also uncontested in the primary.

1986 (the year before the proposed Missouri Plan was presented to voters), only 4 of 55 Supreme Court elections were uncontested,[68] 2 of which involved recently appointed incumbents. There were 9 other elections that involved recently appointed incumbents, and 8 of those appointees *lost* the election. Incumbents lost only 5 of the 33 contested elections involving incumbents who had previously won elections to the Court. Nine elections were for open seats, one of which was conducted on a write-in basis. About one-third of the elections were competitive, using the criterion of the winner receiving less than 55 percent of the two-candidate vote; in about another third, the winner received between 55 and 60 percent of the vote. Only 29 percent of the elections were won by a margin exceeding 2 to 1. Between 1950 and 1974, Republicans dominated the Supreme Court, winning more than two-thirds of the elections to the Court.[69]

Contestation and winning margins were very different in the elections for the trial level court of common pleas. In the elections occurring between 1962 and 1980, previously elected incumbents standing for reelection were challenged in 26.9 percent of elections. Incumbents lost 16.7 percent of the general elections in which they were challenged; they won 42.8 percent with margins exceeding 2 to 1.[70] Incumbents standing for election for the first time after being appointed were much more likely to be challenged in the general election: 55.6 percent faced challengers. They also did not do as well as previously elected incumbents, losing 24.8 percent of the elections in which they were challenged and winning by more than 2 to 1 in only 20.0 percent.[71]

Elections for the Ohio Supreme Court tend to be moderately partisan in their voting patterns.[72] They are more partisan in how they are conducted when the parties, and interest groups traditionally aligned with one party or the other, devote substantial resources to those elections. By the 1980s, the Court's decisions in the area of tort law had become a significant motivating force for those interest groups, as some justices were seen as aligned with tort claimants and their lawyers and others

68 These figures are from my dataset of Supreme Court elections. Between 1988 and 2018, only 3 of 39 Supreme Court elections were uncontested.

69 Lawrence Baum and Mark Kemper, "The Ohio Judiciary," in Alexander P. Lamis, ed., *Ohio Politics* (Kent, OH: Kent State University Press, 1994), 290–291.

70 Lawrence Baum, "The Electoral Fate of Incumbent Judges in the Ohio Court of Common Pleas," *Judicature* 66, no. 9 (April 1983), 424; some of the percentages reported in the text were computed based on information in Baum's tables.

71 *Id.*, 454. A small number of incumbents, about 5 percent of those previously elected and 7 percent of those running after being appointed, were challenged in the party primaries; interestingly, previously elected incumbents were more likely to lose in the primary than were judges running after having been appointed.

72 Herbert M. Kritzer, *Justices on the Ballot: Continuity and Change in State Supreme Court Elections* (New York: Cambridge University Press, 2015), 189–190; Kathleen L. Barber, "Ohio Judicial Elections – Non-Partisan Premises with Partisan Results," *Ohio State Law Journal* 32 (Fall 1971), 762–789.

as aligned with insurers and business groups.[73] More generally, elections for the Ohio Supreme Court changed in tone and intensity starting around 1980, when substantial money began to flow in, producing a level of publicity and campaign activity that contrasted to prior decades.[74]

In 1982, Democrat James Celebrezze, the brother of Frank Celebrezze, who was at the time the chief justice, defeated Republican Blanche Krupansky, who had been appointed to fill a vacancy on the court. It was a heated contest, with "roll-off" the lowest since 1942 for an associate justice election;[75] only 18 percent of those coming to the polls skipped voting in that contest. James Celebrezze had to stand for election again in 1984, because there were only two years remaining on the term to which he was elected in 1982. The 1984 election became something of a surrogate attack on Frank Celebrezze,[76] with Republican Craig Wright defeating James Celebrezze; roll-off was even less than in the election two years earlier. Then, in 1986, Frank Celebrezze himself was defeated in his bid for reelection. Celebrezze's Republican opponent, Thomas Moyer, broke the record for campaign spending in Ohio Supreme Court elections, with the total coming to $2.8 million.

The high visibility of these contests reflected two factors. First, in the late 1970s, led by Frank Celebrezze, Democrats secured a majority on the Supreme Court. That majority proceeded to hand down decisions that angered the business community. For example, although employees injured on the job receive payment through the workers' compensation system and are generally precluded from suing their employers for negligence, the Ohio Supreme Court made a set of decisions that allowed employees to obtain workers compensation payments and also to sue their employers for negligence.[77] More generally, the Court handed down a series of plaintiff-friendly decisions in tort cases.[78] Second, sharp personal conflict on the Court came into the open. Chief Justice Celebrezze openly criticized one of his Republican colleagues. Justices accused one another of "case-fixing, payoffs, lying, electronic surveillance and political orchestration."[79] Things got so bad that one

[73] See Lawrence Baum, David Klein, and Matthew J. Streb, *The Battle for the Court: Interest Groups, Judicial Elections, and Public Policy* (Charlottesville: University of Virginia Press, 2017), 19–47.

[74] The discussion that follows is based on a description of those elections by Baum and Kemper, "The Ohio Judiciary," *supra* note 69, 291–292.

[75] "Roll-off" refers to the percentage of voters who cast votes for offices toward the top of the ballot but skip the more obscure offices such as judgeships appearing further down on the ballot.

[76] "Disputes Injects Politics into Judicial Races in Ohio," *New York Times* (October 14, 1984), www.nytimes.com/1984/10/14/us/dispute-injects-politics-into-judicial-races-in-ohio.html, accessed November 8, 2018.

[77] *Id.*, 296; legislation largely overturned these decisions in 1986.

[78] Baum, Klein, and Streb, *The Battle for the Court*, *supra* note 73, 20–22.

[79] Baum and Kemper, "The Ohio Judiciary," *supra* note 69, 300.

newspaper illustrated the conflict by printing a picture from a wrestling match with the caption, "The court is now in session."[80]

The Missouri Plan in Ohio

Efforts to make substantial changes to Ohio's system of judicial selection and retention had a 50-year history by the time of the 1987 election. In November 1938, Ohio voters were presented with a proposed constitutional amendment that, had it passed, would have made Ohio the first state to adopt what became known as the Missouri Plan. Although the proposal was the result of several years of careful development and was put on the ballot through the initiative process,[81] the voters rejected it 2–1; the proposal failed to secure a majority in even one of the state's counties.[82] Support for the amendment had come from the Ohio State Bar Association (OSBA), the Ohio League of Women Voters (OLWV), a range of business groups, the Farm Bureau, and most major newspapers. Labor groups formed the core of the opposition; they were joined by the Ohio State Grange and state chapters of the National Lawyers Guild.

Between 1953 and 1977, proposals to adopt what had by then become known as the Missouri Plan, labeled "merit selection" by proponents sometime during this period, were introduced into the state legislature eight times, but failed to gain legislative approval.[83] In 1975, the Judiciary Committee of the Ohio Constitutional Revision Commission proposed that a Missouri Plan system be included as part of a revision of the judicial article of the state constitution; however, the Judiciary Committee's recommendation was not included in what was sent by the Commission to the General Assembly.[84] In 1972, Democratic governor John Gilligan issued an executive order creating a set of nominating commissions, but they were discontinued when his Republican successor, Jim Rhodes, took office in 1975.[85]

In the mid-1980s, the combination of the OSBA and the OLWV again decided to try to get a Missouri Plan proposal before the voters through the initiative process, rather than facing the frustration again of trying to get the proposal on the ballot by going through the Ohio legislature. Almost certainly, the timing reflected the shift in tone in the Supreme Court elections that had occurred over the prior several years. The initiative process required gathering signatures from

80 *Id.*, see also "Battling Supremes' Show Could Harm the Bystanders," *Dayton Daily News* (July 21, 1985), 6B.
81 Fred J. Milligan, "The Proposed Changes in the Selection and Tenure of Judges in Ohio," *Ohio State University Law Journal* 4 (1938), 159–164.
82 Howard L. Barkdull, "Analysis of Ohio Vote on Appointive Judiciary," *Journal of the American Judicature Society* 22 (1939), 197–198.
83 Owen L. Heggs, "Merit Selection of the Ohio Judiciary: An Analysis of S.J.R. 6 and a Proposal of Implementation," *Case Western Reserve Law Review* 28 (1978), 636.
84 *Id.*
85 *Id.*, 637.

enough registered voters to equal 10 percent of the most recent statewide gubernatorial vote; the signatures had to come from at least 44 counties, and a minimum of 5 percent of the registered voters in each of those counties had to sign the petition. The effort failed in 1986.[86]

OSBA and OLWV decided to try again in 1987. To get on the ballot, over 300,000 signatures from registered voters needed to be collected.[87] The supporters almost failed again. When the petitions were initially submitted, the signature count failed to meet the requirements. With the assistance of paid signature collectors, sufficient numbers of valid signatures were obtained before the final deadline to get on the ballot.[88] The specific proposal presented for the voters included the following elements:[89]

- Judges for appellate courts would be appointed by the governor from a list prepared by nonpartisan nominating commissions, one for the Supreme Court and one for each of the appellate districts.
- Half of the members of the nominating commissions would be lawyers and the other half nonlawyers.
- Members of the Supreme Court nominating commission would be appointed by the district nominating commissions; each commission would appoint one lawyer and one nonlawyer from among its members.
- Lawyer members of the district nominating commissions would be appointed by a majority vote of the Court of Appeals judges in the district; nonlawyer members would be appointed by the governor, subject to confirmation by the Senate.
- No more than half of the members could be from a single party, and persons holding elective public offices, public offices appointed by the governor, or political party offices would be ineligible to serve on a nominating commission.
- At the first general election more than two years after appointment, the judge would stand in a retention election, and subsequently stand for reelection in a retention election every six years.
- To be retained as a judge, at least 55 percent of those voting would have to favor retention.

[86] John D. Felice and John C. Kilwein, "Strike One, Strike Two. . . : The History of and Prospect for Judicial Reform in Ohio," *Judicature* 75, no. 1 (December–January 1992), 194.

[87] John D. Felice, John C. Kilwein, and Elliot E. Slotnick, "Judicial Reform in Ohio," in Anthony Champagne and Judith Haydel, eds., *Judicial Reform in the States* (Lanham, MD: University Press of America, 1993), 64.

[88] Felice and Kilwein, "Strike One, Strike Two. . .," *supra* note 86, 194.

[89] Roger K. Lowe, "Issue 3," *Columbus Dispatch* (October 4, 1987), 4D, for a summary. The full proposed amendment was published in the *Toledo Blade* (October 19, 1987), 13, https://news.google.com/newspapers?id=MkNPAAAAIBAJ&sjid=7QIEAAAAIBAJ&pg=7000%2C4343501, accessed November 7, 2018.

- Counties (or other local jurisdictions) would have the option to adopt a similar system for common pleas and municipal judges if voters in the county approved adopting that system in a separate vote.

The November 1987 election ballot consisted primarily of elections for local office plus local tax and bond questions. In addition to the judicial selection proposal, there was a ballot question concerning the distribution of lottery profits and another to authorize a $1.2 billion state bond issue.

OSBA and OLWV played the major role in promoting the Missouri Plan proposal, referred to as "Issue 3" on the ballot. Together they formed the Citizens for the Merit Selection of Judges (CMSJ) to promote Issue 3.[90] It was also endorsed by the Ohio PTA, the Ohio Farm Bureau, and the Ohio Chamber of Commerce. Most of the funding for the CMSJ, some of which was expended in the process of gathering petition signatures to get the proposal on the ballot,[91] came from the OSBA and from insurance companies;[92] according to reports filed after the election, the total expended was about $1.5 million. Some of the CMSJ's expenditures went to television ads promoting the proposal.[93] The opponents of Issue 3 included labor unions led by the AFL-CIO and both major political parties;[94] the chairpersons of both parties actually appeared together in a commercial opposing Issue 3.[95] Labor opponents organized a group they called Ohioans for the Right to Vote (ORV), which expended about $375,000, with two-thirds coming from the unions and one-third coming from the Ohio Democratic Party in the form of purchased time for television advertisements opposing the amendment.[96] Another prominent opponent was the former chief justice of the Ohio Supreme Court, Frank Celebrezze, who had come out in favor of continuing contested elections in 1985 when he was still on the Court.[97]

The campaign waged by the CMSJ, both in its advertising and in materials it distributed to voters, emphasized the problems of contested judicial elections (costs, fundraising, etc.) that might raise questions of judges' impartiality. The CMSJ argued that the proposed system would produce well-qualified judges who were

[90] One local bar association came out in opposition to the amendment, "Bar Group Opposes Change in Judicial Selection," *Columbus Dispatch* (October 4, 1987), 10B.

[91] Felice, Kilwein, and Slotnick, "Judicial Reform in Ohio," *supra* note 86, 64.

[92] Felice and Kilwein, "Strike One, Strike Two...," *supra* note 87, 196. Nationwide Insurance, which is headquartered in Columbus, Ohio, was one of the major contributors.

[93] "Ads Oppose Proposal for Appointed Judges," *Akron Beacon Journal* (October 20, 1987), B2.

[94] Felice and Kilwein, "Strike One, Strike Two...," *supra* note 87, 197; interestingly, the opposition from the Republican Party reflected a change from previous support for a Missouri Plan system.

[95] *Id.*, 198.

[96] Roger K. Lowe, "Merit Selection Backers Spent $1.5 Million in Losing Battle," *Columbus Dispatch* (December 12, 1987), 4B.

[97] Felice and Kilwein, "Strike One, Strike Two ...," *supra* note 86, 197; Felice and Kilwein incorrectly refer to Anthony Celebrezze, another pair (father and son) of prominent Ohio politicians, who were Frank's uncle and cousin.

freed from potential dependence on interest groups while at the same time providing a mechanism for removing judges who failed to live up to expected standards. The system would also bring an end to the nasty judicial election campaigns that the state had seen over the preceding few years.[98] The opponents' campaign was what has become the standard critique of the Missouri Plan: it deprives voters of the right to select judges. The fact that voters can fire judges is not the same as voters selecting judges. ORV's materials argued that the proposed system would shift power away from the people and put it in the hands of the legal profession and the governor.[99] A final criticism was the complicated nature of the proposal. The complications came from the decision of the supporters of the proposal to spell out in detail membership of the nominating commissions, selection of members, and the procedures that commissions would use. Arguably, the text of the plan, which appeared in full in at least some newspapers, was a bit disingenuous in stating in the first section that justices of the Supreme Court and judges of the Court of Appeals "shall be elected by the electors" of the state or of the relevant district. This was simply false, as was the supporters' statement, published along with the text of the proposed amendment, that "Issue 3 lets you [emphasis in the original], not political bosses, *choose* [emphasis added] our judges."[100]

The voters rejected the proposed change by almost 2 to 1. In only 8 of Ohio's 88 counties did a majority vote in favor of the change. Almost certainly, the primary reason for the proposal's defeat was the effective use by opponents of the fear that voters would no longer choose judges, that it was a threat to the "right to vote."[101] Postmortems also focused on the ineffectiveness of the CMSJ's messaging, although that was no doubt partly due to the complexity of the proposal, and the CMSJ's inability to mount an effective response to the opponent's argument about the right to vote. The CMSJ was distracted and delayed by its struggle to obtain enough signatures to get the proposal on the ballot. The opposition of organized labor and *both* political parties probably created a hurdle that was all but impossible to overcome.[102]

Subsequent Developments

The issue of changing judicial selection methods in Ohio has been all but dead in the years since the defeat of Issue 3 in 1987. In the mid-1990s, the Ohio Chief Justice

98 *Id.*, 198.

99 *Id.*

100 *Toledo Blade* (October 19, 1987), *supra* note 89, 13. The text of the proposed amendment is confusing as to what happens when judges or justices do not file for retention and serve out their terms; there is no provision for what happens in that situation. Particularly given the language at the beginning that justices and judges "shall be elected," one might read this as saying that in that situation there would be the potential of a contested election. It is left as an implication that when the term ended, there would be a vacancy that would then be filled through the nominating commission process.

101 Felice and Kilwein, "Strike One, Strike Two...," *supra* note 86, 199.

102 *Id.*, 199–200.

Thomas Moyer established the Ohio Courts Futures Commission(OCFC) to develop recommendations for improving the courts and their operation. One subcommittee of the OCFC examined the issue of judicial selection and recommended that the OCFC propose a modified form of the Missouri Plan. For its final report, the OCFC chose to do nothing more than call for further study of the issue.[103] Over the next decade, possible changes to judicial selection in Ohio came up from time to time, but there was no action.[104] In 2011, the Ohio legislature established the Ohio Constitutional Modernization Commission (OCMC). One of the committees of the OCMC focused on the judicial branch. Although the issue of judicial selection came up in that committee's deliberations, including the possibility of shifting selection to a Missouri Plan system, it ultimately made no recommendations regarding judicial selection.[105] This may have been due in part to a 2012 survey of Ohio residents that found 81 percent of the respondents opposed changing from the system of electing judges to one involving gubernatorial appointment with legislative confirmation.[106]

CONCLUSION

Despite strong support from good government groups such as the Ohio League of Women Voters, and the repeated support of the state legislature in Nevada, the voters of Ohio and Nevada have not been willing to surrender their say in who will

[103] Michael E. Solimine, "The False Promise of Judicial Elections in Ohio," *Capital University Law Review* 30 (2002), 579–580.

[104] Jacob H. Hubert, "Judicial Elections and Their Opponents in Ohio," *Federalist Society* (November 2010), 14–15, https://fedsoc-cms-public.s3.amazonaws.com/update/pdf/MoeVcJfQ6XAGSkUaEY7Rk24GewhGc1vHkom30hLm.pdf, accessed November 8, 2018. During this period there were some elections to the Ohio Supreme Court that garnered national attention; see William Glaberson, "A Spirited Campaign for Ohio Court Puts Judges on New Terrain," *New York Times* (July 7, 2000), A15, www.nytimes.com/2000/07/07/us/a-spirited-campaign-for-ohio-court-puts-judges-on-new-terrain.html, accessed November 8, 2018.

[105] Ohio Constitutional Modernization Commission, "Judicial Branch and Administration of Justice Committee Report" (July 1, 2017), www.ocmc.ohio.gov/ocmc/docs/Combo%20Report%20-%20JBAJ%20Final.pdf, accessed November 8, 2018. The OCMC was supposed to run for 10 years, but the legislature terminated it in 2017, after only 6 years; see Jackie Borchardt, "10-Year Committee to Streamline Ohio Constitution Ends Work 4 Years Early; Critics Say There's Little to Show," *Cleveland Plain Dealer* (July 21, 2017), www.cleveland.com/metro/index.ssf/2017/07/ambitious_ohio_constitution_re.html, accessed November 8, 2018.

[106] "Ohioans Want to Elect Judges, Support Tax on Oil and Gas Drilling Companies, Quinnipiac Polls Show," *Cleveland Plain Dealer* (December 12, 2012), www.cleveland.com/open/index.ssf/2012/12/ohioans_want_to_elect_judges_s.html, accessed November 8, 2018. The text of the question was: "Ohio currently elects its judges on the state Supreme Court. Some have suggested that be changed so that judges would be appointed by the governor with input from the state bar association and confirmed by the legislature. Which do you prefer: A) Keeping the current system of electing Ohio Supreme Court judges, or B) Changing to a system in which new judges would be appointed by the governor and confirmed by the legislature?" https://poll.qu.edu/search-releases/search-results/release-detail?What=&strArea=9;28;10;&strTime=28&ReleaseID=1823#Question008

serve as judges in their states. Groups opposed to the Missouri Plan have effectively used this argument in these two states, and in Florida and South Dakota where voters defeated attempts to extend the plan to trial courts. American citizens have a love affair with elections – there are actually a couple of places where the old insult, "he couldn't be elected dogcatcher" actually is meaningful because the local dog catcher, sometimes called the "animal control officer," is an elected position.[107] In practice, voters seldom pay a lot of attention to judicial races, and a very large percentage of judicial elections are uncontested. Nonetheless, as evident in Ohio, Nevada, Florida, South Dakota, and arguably New Mexico, voters are reluctant to surrender the power of the ballot box when it comes to choosing judges.

[107] Amy Kolb, "Can't Get Elected Dogcatcher? Try Running in Duxbury, Vt.," *NPR Weekend Edition Saturday* (March 24, 2018), www.npr.org/2018/03/24/595755604/cant-get-elected-dog catcher-try-running-in-duxbury-vt, accessed January 15, 2019; Doug Ireland, "Danville Animal Control Office Race Heats Up," *Danville [Virginia] Eagle Tribune* (February 3, 2013), www.eagletribune.com/news/local_news/danville-animal-control-officer-race-heatsup/article_e9430566–1bb2–56c6–84c3-f1637d86b7d6.html, accessed April 7, 2018.

13

Minnesota, Pennsylvania, Texas, and New Hampshire

Talk, Talk, Talk, but No Results

This chapter examines efforts in four states – Minnesota, Pennsylvania, Texas, and New Hampshire – to get the state legislature to put constitutional amendments on the ballot that would adopt a Missouri Plan system or, in the case of New Hampshire, to vote on a constrained appointment proposal similar to that adopted in Connecticut. In these four states, the only way for a constitutional amendment to be presented to the voters is through legislative action.[1] In one state, Texas, there were also discussions of shifting from partisan to nonpartisan elections – a change that would not require a constitutional amendment and voter approval, but there has been no action on that idea either. In Minnesota, Pennsylvania, and Texas, there has been strong support in some quarters for adoption of a Missouri Plan system, at least for the appellate courts. However, in none of those states has a proposal made it all the way through the legislature, although there has been some legislative consideration, and in three states, Pennsylvania, Texas, and New Hampshire one chamber of the legislature did approve an amendment, but it died when the other chamber failed to act.

MINNESOTA

Background

Minnesota Politics

For over 100 years, ending in the early 1970s, the Minnesota legislature was dominated by Republican and/or conservative legislators. The reference to "conservative" here reflects that when the legislature was formally nonpartisan between

[1] See www.ncsl.org/research/elections-and-campaigns/chart-of-the-initiative-states.aspx, accessed January 7, 2019.

1915 and 1972, legislators divided into conservative and liberal caucuses. There were some brief periods when the liberal caucus gained control of the Minnesota House of Representatives, but there were no such periods for the Minnesota Senate. For a period starting in the late 1920s, the traditional Democratic Party was supplanted by the Farmer-Labor Party (FL) and the FL's candidates for governor won several elections in the 1930s. In the mid-1940s, the FL merged with the Democratic Party to form the Democratic-Farmer-Labor Party (DFL), and the DFL began having some success in gubernatorial elections in the mid-1950s.

Between 1955, when the first DFL governor was sworn in, and 2018, the governorship was held by the DFL for 34 years, by the Republicans for 26 years, and by independent Jesse Ventura for 4 years. If we treat conservative control of the legislature as equivalent to Republican control and liberal control as equivalent to DFL control, the DFL held the governorship and both chambers of the legislature for a total of 14 years between 1955 and 2018, and the Republicans held them for 4 years. Between 1991 and 2018, there was just one 2-year period, 2013–2014, when a party, the DFL in this case, held full control. Thus, the best description of partisan politics between the mid-1950s and the late 2010s is that Minnesota has been highly competitive, marked largely by divided control; that was particularly true during the period when potential change to judicial selection was on the political agenda.

Judicial Election Patterns

Since 1912, judicial elections in Minnesota have been conducted on a nonpartisan basis.[2] However, at least since the mid-1970s, virtually all judges in Minnesota have been initially appointed to their positions. The latter fact arises because, since 1974, a judge must retire no later than the end of the month when he or she reaches 70 years of age;[3] replacements are appointed by the governor, with appointees then standing for election at the first general election (i.e., the even-numbered year election) occurring more than twelve months after their appointment.[4] There is also a common practice that judges who decide to leave the bench short of the mandatory retirement age resign rather than serving to the end of their term, thus allowing the governor to appoint a successor.[5] For example, in June 2019 Justice David Lillehaug, who was scheduled to stand for reelection in 2020, announced that for health reasons he would retire effective July 31, 2020, rather than serving to the end of his term and allowing for an open-seat election in November 2020; by

[2] For a brief history of Supreme Court elections in Minnesota, see Herbert M. Kritzer, *Justices on the Ballot: Continuity and Change in State Supreme Court Elections* (New York: Cambridge University Press, 2015), 21–27; a more extensive history of judicial elections in Minnesota can be found in Jesse Sater, "The History of Minnesota's Judicial Elections: A Description and Analysis of the Changes in Judicial Election Laws and Their Effect on the Competitiveness of Minnesota's Judicial Elections," *University of St. Thomas Law Journal* 10 (2012), 367–391.

[3] Minnesota Statutes, 490.125.

[4] Minnesota Constitution, Article VI, §§ 7 and 8.

[5] Email from Mark Cohen, March 14, 2019.

stepping down at the end of July 2020, he allowed the governor to appoint his successor, who would in turn serve until 2022 before standing for election as an incumbent.[6] A statutorily created Commission on Judicial Selection screens potential candidates for appointment to positions on the district (trial) courts;[7] although the governor is not bound by the commission's recommendations,[8] in practice the governor relies upon those recommendations in making appointments. Although there is no requirement to do so, since at least 1990, governors have generally created a similar commission to guide them in selecting judges of the appellate courts.[9] One important feature of the judicial elections is that, since 1950, the ballot indicates if a candidate is the incumbent.

In practice, few judicial elections in Minnesota are for open seats. Since 1950, there have been only two open-seat elections for the Minnesota Supreme Court, and there has never been an open-seat election for the Court of Appeals in the years since its creation in 1983. Between 2000 and 2018, there were 949 elections for the district court; only 13 of those elections were for open seats. Although a majority (56 percent) of Supreme Court elections between 1950 and 2018 with incumbents running were contested, only 9.0 percent of elections for the Court of Appeals (since its creation) and 8.4 percent of elections for the district court (2000–2018) were contested. No incumbent has lost an election for the either the Supreme Court or the Court of Appeals; only 4 district court incumbents out of 936 running lost between 2000 and 2018.[10]

Judicial elections in Minnesota have been, and continue to be, low visibility and with little controversy. Television advertising, either positive or negative, has been absent from elections to the Minnesota Supreme Court. If one uses the criteria of the winner receiving less than 55 percent of the vote, only 5 of 48 contested

6 Stephen Montemayor, "Lillehaug to Leave Court, Citing Illness," *Minneapolis Star Tribune* (June 15, 2019), A1, A8.

7 Minnesota Statutes, 480B.01; the Commission also screens candidates for appointment to the Workers Compensation Court of Appeals. The Commission was created by statute in 1990 (Minnesota Laws, Chap. 608, Art. 8); it replaced the Judicial Merit Advisory Commission created by executive order in 1983 (see www.leg.state.mn.us/lrl/agencies/detail?AgencyID=904, accessed November 1, 2018).

8 George W. Soule, "The Threats of Partisanship to Minnesota's Judicial Elections," *William Mitchell Law Review* 34 (2008), 706–707.

9 *Id.*, 707.

10 The discussion in the text is based on data collected for Kritzer, *Justices on the Ballot, supra* note 2. For a brief discussion of judicial elections in Minnesota during the first 25 years of nonpartisan elections, see Malcolm Moos, "Judicial Elections and Partisan Endorsements of Judicial Candidates in Minnesota," *American Political Science Review* 35 (1941), 69–75. A good journalistic discussion of judicial selection in Minnesota in the latter third of the twentieth century can be found in Pam Louwagie, "Handpicked Justice; Bypassing Voter Judgement; Despite Elections, Public Rarely Decides Who Takes Bench," *Minneapolis Star Tribune* (August 3, 2003), 1A, and Pam Louwagie, "Handpicked Justice; Who Really Chooses the State's Judges? Appoint or Elect? Debate Rages On; No Consensus on Best Way to Fill Judgeships," *Minneapolis Star Tribune* (August 4, 2003), 1A.

Supreme Court elections from 1950 through 2018 were competitive; in 30 of the 48 elections, the winner received more than 60 percent of the vote. Moreover, prior to 2010, the voting patterns in those elections seldom showed evidence of partisanship playing a role; this changed somewhat starting in 2010, when some candidates for the Supreme Court sought and received the endorsement of the state Republican Party.[11]

Hints of what might be coming appeared in 1996, when a candidate for the Supreme Court, Gregory Wersal, sought the endorsement of the Republican Party,[12] something that had not happened since the 1930s.[13] Wersal withdrew before the Party decided whether it would endorse judicial candidates. Wersal ran again in 1998, and again sought the Republican Party endorsement. The Party decided to consider such endorsements,[14] but in the end decided not to make an endorsement for the 1998 Supreme Court election.[15] In 2000, the Republican Party again considered endorsing judicial candidates, although no candidates actively sought such endorsements. There were four Supreme Court incumbents running that year, all having been appointed by Republican governor Arne Carlson; the Republican Convention delegates declined to endorse any of the incumbents, including Kathleen Blatz, who at one time had been a Republican member of the state legislature.[16] Instead, the only endorsement made for the Supreme Court was Gregory Wersal, who was challenging one of the Republican-appointed incumbents.[17] In addition, the Republican convention delegates endorsed three incumbent Court of Appeals judges; shortly after the convention ended, all three judges asked that the party "abstain from any support in any form."[18] In the end, the party did not have to

[11] See Kritzer, *Justices on the Ballot*, *supra* note 2, 24–25. In 2010, the Republican Party also endorsed a candidate for the Court of Appeals, and that candidate came close to defeating the incumbent by winning 48 percent of the statewide vote; see Douglas D. Birk, "Stuck Inside of Minnesota without Judicial Election Reform Again: A Contemporary Survey of the Political Movement to Preserve Judicial Impartiality from the Minnesota Judiciary's Point of View," *Hamline Journal of Public Law & Policy* 32 (2010), 518.

[12] Conrad deFiebre, "Supreme Court Seems Set to End Judicial Politicking; A Lawyer's Strange Case Is Just One Example of Discontent over How Judges Are Selected," *Minneapolis Star Tribune* (November 12, 1997), 1B.

[13] Moos, "Judicial Elections and Partisan Endorsements," *supra* note 10, 71–72.

[14] Conrad deFiebre, "GOP to Break New Ground, Take Up Judicial Endorsements," *Minneapolis Star Tribune* (June 20, 1998), 15A.

[15] Conrad deFiebre, "In Close Vote, Delegates Reject Endorsing Judicial Candidates," *Minneapolis Star Tribune* (June 21, 1998), 13A.

[16] Bill Salisbury, "Judge Blatz Denied GOP Nod; First-Time Judicial Endorsements Leave Party Chiefs Puzzled," *St. Paul Pioneer Press* (June 10, 2000), 1A.

[17] Robert Whereatt, "Republicans Make First Endorsement for a Supreme Court Justice; Reaction Has Been Mixed to Friday's Decision by Delegates to the State GOP Convention to Initiate a Process of Approval for State Judicial Candidates," *Minneapolis Star Tribune* (June 11, 2000), 14A.

[18] Robert Whereatt, "Decision on GOP Judicial Endorsement Likely in July; Three Judges Seeking Reelection Have Asked Party to Discontinue Support," *Minneapolis Star Tribune* (June 20, 2000), 3B.

do anything in the way of support for those candidates, because all three were unopposed.[19] In contrast to what was happening with the Republicans, the DFL "took a stand opposing such endorsements."[20]

The Republican Party, either at its convention or by its State Central Committee, continued to make endorsements over the first decade of the twenty-first century. In 2002, a challenger for a seat on the Court of Appeals was endorsed but lost the election by a margin of 2–1;[21] at least one unsuccessful candidate for district court judge was also endorsed by the Republican Party that year.[22] No endorsements were made in 2004.[23] In 2006, there were a total of eight contested judicial elections across all levels; the Republican Party endorsed one challenger for a district court position and one Court of Appeals incumbent, who was challenged but did not publicize the endorsement.[24] The endorsed district court challenger lost 56–44 and the endorsed Court of Appeals incumbent won 56–44.[25] No endorsements of judicial candidates were made by the Republican Party in 2008, and that year, Democrats reaffirmed their unwillingness to get into the judicial election endorsement game.[26]

The Unsuccessful Drive for Judicial Selection Change

Unlike neighboring Wisconsin, there was no major change in Minnesota judicial elections. In Wisconsin, by the mid-2000s Supreme Court elections had become highly partisan affairs marked by extensive television advertising, much of which was

19 Robert Whereatt, "State GOP Won't Actively Promote Appellate Candidates; The Three Judges Are Running Unopposed, so the Party Will Focus on Its Supreme Court Endorsee, Who Has a Challenger," *Minneapolis Star Tribune* (July 22, 2000), 3B.

20 Bill Salisbury, "Ventura Publicly Opposes Judicial Endorsements; Says Partisan Backing Would Compromise Courts," *St. Paul Pioneer Press* (July 7, 2000), 1B. Governor Jesse Ventura's Independence Party also opposed judicial endorsements; two small parties, the Reform Party and the Constitution Party, did vote to endorse judicial candidates.

21 Michelle Lore, "Incumbent Judges Sail through Judicial Elections," *Minnesota Lawyer Magazine* (November 11, 2002).

22 Frederick Melo, "Judicial Race Centers on One Hot-Button Decision; Sex Offender Got Custody of a Girl and Raped Her: Did the Judge Fail, or Were the Options Tragically Few?" *St. Paul Pioneer Press* (October 6, 2008), A1, www.twincities.com/2008/10/05/judicial-race-centers-on-one-hot-button-decision/, accessed January 3, 2020.

23 Barbara L. Jones, "Minnesota Republicans Don't Endorse Any Judges at Convention," *Minnesota Lawyer* (June 21, 2004)

24 Mark Cohen, "TV Campaign Ad Raises Minnesota Bar's Ire," *Minnesota Lawyer* (November 6, 2006); the one Supreme Court incumbent running in 2006 was unopposed. Another district court candidate, who came in third in the primary, obtained the endorsement of his local Republican Party; see Brad Swenson, "Campaign 2008: Tinglestad Running for Supreme Court," *Bemidji Pioneer* (August 24, 2008).

25 Barbara Jones, "Incumbents Win Seven Out of Eight Contested Races in Minnesota," *Minnesota Lawyer* (November 13, 2006).

26 Mark Cohen, "Convention: DFL Once Again Says 'No Thanks' to Endorsing Judges," *St. Paul Legal Ledger* (June 6, 2008).

negative and funded by outside groups. The developments in Wisconsin arose from some tort law decisions by the Wisconsin Supreme Court that activated conservative business interests.[27] Minnesota's Supreme Court had avoided those kinds of issues in part because of the absence of the type of legislation that led to the controversial decisions in Wisconsin,[28] and that probably resulted in the state's business community not seeing judicial elections as something deserving its attention.[29] Given the stability of judicial elections in Minnesota, one can ask what put changing the system of selection and retention of judges on the political agenda? In part, this may have reflected concerns about what was going on across the state line in Wisconsin, but the most extreme elections in Wisconsin did not occur until after the issue of changing judicial selection arose in Minnesota. Instead, the catalyst for putting change on the agenda in Minnesota was the U.S. Supreme Court's decision in *Republican Party of Minnesota v. White*.[30]

The *White* decision concerned limits on what candidates for judicial office were permitted to do. Of most concern was the "announce clause," which forbade candidates from "announcing" their views on any issue that might come before the court. The case arose in 1998 after the Republican Party, joined by Gregory Wersal, who was then running for the Supreme Court, filed suit, challenging the constitutionality of the announce clause. Wersal had been running for the Supreme Court in 1996, but had withdrawn in the wake of an ethics complaint that was filed after he distributed literature critical of some decisions by the Court;[31] his withdrawal actually came after the disciplinary body dismissed the complaint, but he feared further complaints might be filed that could lead to him losing his license to practice law. The 1998 suit that was eventually decided by the U.S. Supreme Court was a preemptory move.[32] The U.S. Supreme Court struck down the announce clause on a 5–4 vote as a violation of the First Amendment and remanded the case for reconsideration by the lower courts. The eventual August 2005 *en banc* decision by the 8th Circuit Court of Appeals[33] went beyond the announce clause to declare that "states may not prohibit judicial candidates from engaging in certain partisan activities, such as identifying themselves as members of a political party, attending political gatherings, and seeking, accepting, and using political party

27 Kritzer, *Justices on the Ballot*, *supra* note 2, 7–21.

28 *Id.*, 27–28.

29 Soule, "The Threats of Partisanship to Minnesota's Judicial Elections," *supra* note 8, 723.

30 Republican Party of Minnesota v. White, 536 U.S. 765 (2002).

31 Mary Ellen Egan, "Judging for Himself; If Greg Wersal Has His Way, Minnesota Judges Will Soon Campaign for Election Just Like Any Other Politicians," *City Pages* (June 17, 1998).

32 Kritzer, *Justices on the Ballot*, *supra* note 2, 26–27. Wersal came in third in the 1998 primary, receiving only about 8 percent of the vote; he ran again in 2000 and 2010, receiving 31 percent and 42 percent, respectively (he was endorsed by the Republican Party in 2010) in the general election.

33 Republican Party of Minnesota v. White, 416 F.3d 738 (8th Cir. 2005), cert. denied.

endorsements."[34] The *White* decision raised the specter of increased partisanship and its accompanying issues in Minnesota judicial elections.[35]

In late January 2006, immediately after the U.S. Supreme Court rejected a request to review the Court of Appeals' decision,[36] the chief justice of the Minnesota Supreme Court announced the formation of the Citizens Commission for the Preservation of an Impartial Judiciary, which was charged with making recommendations about what, if anything, should be done in response to the *White* decision. The commission was headed by former governor Al Quie and was popularly known as the Quie Commission. The Commission's final report, issued in March 2007, called for a change to a Missouri Plan system with the additional element of a "comprehensive performance evaluation of all judges to promote the self-improvement of judges and provide voters with information so that they can make informed decisions at the polls."[37] A minority report called for a system of initial gubernatorial appointment with reappointment by a judicial-evaluation commission;[38] that is, neither the legislature nor the voters would have a direct role in judicial selection or retention.

After the Quie Commission issued its report, the Minnesota Bar Association endorsed the Commission's recommendations,[39] and a new group was formed, Minnesotans for Impartial Courts (MIC), to lobby for the kinds of changes that the Commission proposed. Al Quie served as the chairperson of MIC.[40] About the same time that MIC was getting off the ground, the Minnesota District Judges Association (MDJA), a group representing judges of the district court, announced that it would lobby against changes in how judicial elections were conducted; this was a reaffirmation of a position taken by the MDJA shortly after the 2002 *White* decision, favoring the current system of nonpartisan elections over a system using retention elections.[41]

In February 2008, MIC put forward a plan based on the Quie Commission report,[42] and a short time later, several Senate committees began consideration of

34 "Judicial Selection in Minnesota: A Special Report," *Bench & Bar of Minnesota* (April 1, 2007), http://mnbenchbar.com/2007/04/judicial-selection/, accessed November 1, 2018.

35 Soule, "The Threats of Partisanship," *supra* note 8, 723–724, 727–728.

36 Dimick v. Republican Party of Minnesota, 546 U.S. 1157 (2006).

37 Governor Al Quie, Chair, "Citizens Commission for the Preservation of an Impartial Judiciary, Final Report" (March 26, 2007), www.mnbar.org/docs/default-source/judiciary-committee/citizenscommfinalreport032607.pdf?sfvrsn=0, accessed November 1, 2018.

38 *Id.*, 31.

39 Barbara L. Jones, "Minn. State Bar Assn. Approves Plan to Scrap Judicial Elections in Minnesota," *Minnesota Lawyer* (July 9, 2007).

40 Barbara L. Jones, "Nonprofit Firm Aims to Change Judicial Elections," *Minnesota Lawyer* (December 3, 2007).

41 Barbara L. Jones, "Minnesota Judges' Group Keeps Position against Changing Judicial Elections," *Minnesota Lawyer* (December 17, 2007).

42 Mark Brunswick, "Plan Takes That Long List of Judges Off Your Ballot; Proponents Hope the Idea Would Take the Acidity Out of Judicial Elections; Critics Say It Would Sever Only to Fortify Sitting Judges," *Minneapolis Star Tribune* (February 1, 2007), 1A.

the plan, including the first hearings about potential changes.[43] At one hearing, a representative of MDJA criticized the proposal as reflecting a "'problem' [that] doesn't require a solution." One reason for the MDJA's opposition was concern by district judges that they might be "blindsided by a special interest group and have no way to respond."[44] Gregory Wersal criticized the proposal as undermining accountability; he labeled the proposal "an elitist method of insulating judges from the transparency of their actions."[45] Despite the legislative hearings, no proposal for changing judicial selection reached the floor of either legislative chamber in 2008. The proposal based on the Quie Commission report was reintroduced in 2009 but failed to move forward. As one report noted, "it's hard to make a case for changing something that, so far, appears to be working well."[46]

When the proposal was introduced again in 2010, it was supported by the Democratic Speaker of the House[47] but faced opposition from antiabortion groups and the nascent Tea Party movement.[48] There was also support from the MDJA, but that support was conditional on finding some mechanism that would preclude last-minute antiretention campaigns.[49] Nothing made it through either chamber in 2010 although the proposal did get farther along in the legislative process than in prior years.[50]

In 2009–2010, the Minnesota legislature was under Democratic control. With the 2010 election, control flipped to the Republicans and prospects for action on the Quie proposals were dim at best. Although the initial proposals for a shift to a Missouri Plan system previously had some bipartisan support in the legislature, support among Republicans had faded.[51] In fact, the Minnesota Republican Party's

43 Barbara L. Jones, "Minnesota Senate Broaches Subject of Judicial Elections," *Minnesota Lawyer* (February 11, 2008).

44 *Id.* However, the position taken by the MDJA at the hearing produced some controversy among its members, with substantial numbers favoring at least some type of change; see Barbara L. Jones, "Support for Judicial Election Reform in Minn. Coalescing in Legislature," *Minnesota Lawyer* (March 10, 2008).

45 Brunswick, "Plan Takes That Long List of Judges Off Your Ballot," *supra* note 42.

46 "Act on Judicial Elections This Year; Retention Elections Discourage Special-Interest Involvement," *Minneapolis Star Tribune* (February 26, 2009), 12A.

47 Pat Doyle, "New Life for Proposal on Judicial Elections; A Plan to Let Voters Decide Whether to Retain Sittle Judges Is Decried as Elitist, Hailed as Less Partisan," *Minneapolis Star Tribune* (May 7, 2010), 2B.

48 Pat Doyle, "Judicial Retention Election Bill Is Dropped; The Bill Was Pulled by Its Sponsor Amid a Backlash from Anti-Abortion Groups and Other Interests," *Minneapolis Star Tribune* (April 27, 2010), 1B.

49 Patrick Thornton, "Power Shift Emboldens 'Retention' Advocates in Minnesota," *Minnesota Lawyer* (November 16, 2012).

50 Michelle Lore, "Judicial Election Reform Proponents in Minnesota Vow to Continue Fight," *Minnesota Lawyer* (May 29, 2010). For a discussion of the twists and turns of what happened in the legislature in 2010, see Betsy Sundquiest, "Participants Offer Discrepant Accounts of Why Judicial Retention Measure Failed in 2010," *Minnesota Lawyer* (June 16, 2010).

51 Michelle Lore, "Judicial Election Reform Proponents Move Forward: Undaunted by Incoming GOP Majority in Minnesota," *Minnesota Lawyer* (November 24, 2010).

2010 platform opposed change to the existing system of judicial elections other than removing the word "incumbent" from the ballot,[52] and the party had, for the first time since *White*, endorsed candidates for judicial office.[53] Elements of the Republican coalition, such as the antiabortion group Minnesota Citizens Concerned for Life, had opposed the Quie proposal. More generally, as noted in other chapters, the business groups that had at one time been key supporters of the Missouri Plan were backing off from that support, probably reflecting the increasing success of such groups in using advertising in other states to sway voters toward the candidates for state Supreme Court who appeared to be sympathetic to business concerns.[54] Nothing happened over the two years of Republican control. That was not surprising, given the observation by the Republican chairperson of the Senate Judiciary Committee that "any Republican lawmaker who sponsored a retention election bill was 'signing their own death warrant.'"[55]

Democrats regained control of the legislature with the 2012 election, and prospects for changes to judicial selection brightened.[56] The proposal that was introduced in 2013 produced mixed reactions from district judges.[57] Nevertheless, the proposal made it out of the House Elections Committee during that session, but there was no action by Senate committees.[58] Part of the challenge in getting significant progress on the proposal was a lack of any sense of urgency because of the absence of anything resembling what had transpired in neighboring Wisconsin, and the absence of any apparent demand for action by voters. One other explanation for inaction cited by some was "amendment fatigue" among legislators reflecting the controversy that surrounded amendments on same-sex

52 "We believe that in elections, the word "incumbent" should be removed after judicial candidates' names on the ballots and judicial vacancies should be appointed only until the next general election. Also, those voting in judicial elections must be required to be residents in the county in which the judge will preside. We continue to support the election of judges as written in the Minnesota Constitution and oppose any proposals to eliminate or limit these elections" – Republican Party of Minnesota - 2010 Standing Platform, 9, https://web.archive.org/web/20100807034901/http://www.mngop.com:80/pdfs/platform.pdf, accessed November 3, 2018.

53 Lore, "Judicial Election Reform Proponents Move Forward," *supra* note 51.

54 Bert Brandenburg, "What's the Best Way to Pack a Court? The Attack on Merit Selection for Judges," *Slate* (November 14, 2008), https://slate.com/news-and-politics/2008/11/the-attack-on-merit-selection-for-judges.html, accessed November 3, 2018; John F. Kowal, "Judicial Selection for the 21st Century," Brennan Center for Justice (2016), 16, https://slate.com/news-and-politics/2008/11/the-attack-on-merit-selection-for-judges.html, accessed November 3, 2018; Deborah O'Malley, "A Defense of the Elected Judiciary," Heritage Foundation (September 9, 2010), www.heritage.org/courts/report/defense-the-elected-judiciary, accessed November 3, 2018.

55 Patrick Thornton, "Power Shift Emboldens 'Retention' Advocates in Minnesota," *Minnesota Lawyer* (November 16, 2012).

56 *Id.*

57 Bill Salisbury, "Bill Gives Public Yea-or-Nay on Judges; Governor's Appointees Get Six Year Term Before Election," *St. Paul Pioneer Press* (March 13, 2013), A5.

58 Patrick Thornton, "Lawmakers in Minnesota Shrug; Retention Advocates Push On," *Minnesota Lawyer* (February 27, 2014).

marriage and voter ID put on the 2012 ballot by the Republican legislative majorities and then rejected by the voters.[59]

The 2014 election returned the state legislature to Republican control. However, the 2014 Supreme Court election was embarrassing for the Republican Party. The party convention had endorsed Michelle MacDonald. She was running against incumbent David Lillehaug, who had been appointed to the Court the prior year by Democratic governor Mark Dayton. At the time she was endorsed, the delegates were unaware that MacDonald had a prior arrest and conviction in connection with having been stopped on suspicion of drunk driving and had on one occasion been forcibly removed from a courtroom during her defense of a client.[60] During the campaign, MacDonald was ticketed for violating terms of driving restrictions arising from the drunk driving–related conviction. She then was escorted away from the Republican Party booth at the Minnesota State Fair,[61] and subsequently filed an election law complaint asserting that leaders of the Republican Party had tried to get her to withdraw her candidacy.[62] Although this experience, and the overall lack of success of Republican-endorsed challengers to Supreme Court incumbents, might have encouraged Republican support for a shift to retention elections,[63] that was not to be. The issue of judicial selection and retention reform dropped off the legislative agenda and had not reemerged by the end of 2018, while the Republican Party controlled both legislative chambers.

Minnesota Summary

There are several reasons that efforts to adopt a Missouri Plan system in Minnesota in the wake of the *White* decision failed. First, and foremost is the absence of support from the Republican Party. This reflects opposition from key elements of the Republican coalition, and a more general turning away from the Missouri Plan system by the conservative movement. Second, and probably just as important, is that although the drive for change that started after *White* reflected a fear that Minnesota would follow the path of Wisconsin in having highly contentious elections for the Supreme Court, that has not happened, even with the Republican Party endorsing some challengers. The result is the absence of any sense of urgency

59 Mike Mosedale, "Another Push for Retention Elections?" *Minnesota Lawyer* (November 20, 2014).

60 Cyndy Brucato, "In Aftermath of MacDonald Drama, Look for MN GOP to Change Judicial Endorsement Policy," *MinnPost* (April 4, 2015), www.minnpost.com/party-politics/2015/04/aftermath-macdonald-drama-look-mn-gop-change-judicial-endorsement-policy/, accessed November 3, 2018.

61 Doug Grow, "Michelle MacDonald and the Anatomy of a Political Train Wreck," *MinnPost* (September 9, 2014), www.minnpost.com/politics-policy/2014/09/michelle-macdonald-and-anatomy-political-train-wreck/, accessed November 3, 2018.

62 Mosedale, "Another Push for Retention Elections?" *supra* note 59.

63 *Id.*

or any feeling that changing judicial selection should be a legislative priority. Third, given that Minnesota judges below the level of Supreme Court seldom face opposition when they stand for reelection, and that almost all of them are already appointed to fill vacancies through a system employing a screening committee, a change to the system proposed by the Quie Commission has few positives and at least two potential negatives. Those negatives include the risk of a last-minute antiretention campaign arising and a performance evaluation system that would have unknown impacts. Regarding the former, under the current system, judges running for reelection know in July once the filing deadline has passed if there will be an opponent in their upcoming election; this allows time to organize a campaign, which might not be the case if an antiretention campaign arose in the last few weeks before the November election. Finally, not mentioned in the discussion above, is that there is at least some concern, perhaps unjustified, that the proposed selection and retention system would "hurt diversity on the bench and that judicial elections [are] a better way to enhance the opportunity that people of color would become judges."[64]

PENNSYLVANIA

The current system of judicial selection and retention in Pennsylvania is similar to the process in Illinois and New Mexico.[65] Judges and justices must stand in a partisan election to win an initial full term;[66] reelection for subsequent terms is by retention elections. The governor fills midterm vacancies by appointment, subject to the approval by a two-thirds vote in the Senate.[67] Prior to the adoption of the current system in 1968, all judicial elections were conducted on a partisan basis.[68] One interesting aspect of the partisan elections for the Pennsylvania Supreme Court was that starting in 1977 and ending in 2015, there was an informal norm that a person appointed to fill a vacancy on that Court would not be a candidate in the subsequent

[64] See David Schulz, "The White Cases Revisited," *Bench & Bar of Minnesota* (June 10, 2010), http://mnbenchbar.com/2010/01/the-white-cases-revisited/, accessed November 3, 2018.

[65] See Chapter 9 for information about New Mexico.

[66] One feature of the partisan judicial elections is that candidates are permitted to run in more than one party's primary, a process referred to as "cross-filing."

[67] In Illinois, the Supreme Court makes the appointments to fill midterm vacancies for the appellate courts and the general jurisdiction trial courts; see www.judicialselection.us/judicial_selection/methods/selection_of_judges.cfm?state=IL, accessed January 6, 2019. In New Mexico, the governor fills almost all vacancies, including end-of-term vacancies, by appointment from a list prepared by a nominating commission, with the appointee standing in a partisan election at the next general election; see Chapter 9.

[68] For a brief period in the early twentieth century (1913–1921), elections for the appellate courts were on a nonpartisan basis; see Sidney Schulman, *Toward Judicial Reform in Pennsylvania: A Study in Court Reorganization* (Philadelphia: Institute of Legal Research, University of Pennsylvania Law School, 1962), 44–45.

(partisan) election; appointees ran in both 2015 (losing in the Democratic primary) and 2017 (winning the general election; there were no primaries for that seat).

Early Proposals for Changing Judicial Selection and the 1968 Reform

In Pennsylvania, proposals to adopt a system of selection modeled on the Missouri Plan first appeared in the 1940s.[69] In 1947, the Pennsylvania Bar Association (PBA) endorsed a version of that plan that was labeled the Pennsylvania Plan.[70] The primary difference was that under the Pennsylvania Plan, the governor was permitted to reject the nomination list and request new ones until the list included a person the governor was willing to appoint.[71] Through the 1950s, the state bar lobbied for the plan through a Special Committee on the Pennsylvania Plan, and in 1959, the plan was endorsed by the Commission on Constitutional Revision. However, a proposed constitutional amendment to adopt the plan "failed to receive significant support in the legislature."[72] That was unsurprising, given that a 1957 survey of Pennsylvania legislators plus some judges found a preference for continuing partisan elections; in fact, the Pennsylvania Plan generally ranked third, behind both partisan and nonpartisan elections.[73]

In 1962, the Institute of Legal Research at the University of Pennsylvania published a report on judicial reform in Pennsylvania, one section of which focused on judicial selection.[74] The report surveyed local bar associations in Pennsylvania, and found that only 10 of 67 had adopted resolutions in support of the Pennsylvania Plan; the report went on to lament the absence of a systematic effort by either the PBA or local bars to mount a campaign to implement the plan, as had been done in other jurisdictions that had adopted the Missouri Plan.[75] Perhaps partly in response the Institute of Legal Research report, in 1965 the PBA published a pamphlet with the text of a proposed new judicial article that included the adoption of a Missouri Plan system for judicial selection and retention. The plan, which by then was being referred to as "merit selection,"[76] would apply to the

[69] The discussion that follows covering the period from the late 1940s through the early 1990s draws heavily on Voorhees E. Dunn Jr., "Judicial Reform in Pennsylvania," in Anthony Champagne and Judith Haydel, eds., *Judicial Reform in the States* (Lantham, MD: University Press of America, 1993), 117–138.

[70] *Id.*, 119.

[71] Schulman, *Toward Judicial Reform in Pennsylvania*, 50, *supra* note 68.

[72] Dunn, "Judicial Reform in Pennsylvania," *supra* note 69, 119.

[73] William J. Keefe, "Judges and Politics: The Pennsylvania Plan of Judicial Selection," *University of Pittsburgh Law Review* 20, no. 3 (March 1959), 624–626; judges responding to the survey were more divided, with less than half preferring partisan elections and the others equally divided between nonpartisan elections and the Pennsylvania Plan.

[74] Schulman, *Toward Judicial Reform in Pennsylvania*, *supra* note 68, 18–58.

[75] *Id.*, 57–58.

[76] See, for example, Roscoe Drummond, "Bench Reforms Need Discussed," *Kittanning Leader-Times* (September 13, 1963), 6.

Pennsylvania Supreme Court, the intermediate appellate court (called the Superior Court in Pennsylvania), and the trial-level courts in Philadelphia and Allegheny (Pittsburgh) counties; a local option was provided for the other counties to adopt the system by referendum for their trial courts.[77] The year before the PBA published this proposal, the then governor of Pennsylvania, Republican William Scranton, issued an executive order establishing a Judicial Nominating Commission, the first such commission created by executive action in the country. Scranton made a commitment to appoint only persons recommended by the Commission, but reserved the right to request additional lists.[78] This practice was continued until 1995,[79] when Republican governor Tom Ridge, who had expressed support for merit selection during his campaign for governor, issued an executive order abolishing what was then called the Appellate Court Nominating Commission.[80] Scranton also created a Governor's Commission on Constitutional Revision, which recommended that a Missouri Plan system replace partisan elections, but the state legislature failed to act on the proposal.[81]

In 1967, the state legislature placed a referendum asking whether to call a constitutional convention to consider revisions to specified parts of the state constitution, including the judicial article, on the spring ballot. The voters approved the proposal, with 61.8 percent in favor.[82] The convention convened December 1, 1967, delegates having been chosen at the November election. The convention considered a variety of proposals regarding judicial selection; debates over the proposals centered on whether judges should be elected or appointed. More than one delegate described the issue of judicial selection as the most controversial question considered at the convention.[83] The controversy focused on initial selection rather than on retention; there was substantial agreement that incumbent judges should stand in retention elections after completing their first full term on the bench; the debate was whether judges should be appointed or elected to that initial full term. A compromise was reached whereby the voters would first be asked to decide how judges should be retained, and then the following year, be given the choice of partisan election or gubernatorial appointment from a nominating commission's

[77] Pennsylvania Bar Association, "The New Judiciary Article of the Pennsylvania Constitution" (January 1965), 8–11.

[78] See Bernard G. Segal, "Nonpartisan Selection of Judges: Pennsylvania's Experiment," *American Bar Association Journal* 50, no. 9 (September 1964), 830.

[79] Dunn, "Judicial Reform in Pennsylvania," *supra* note 69, 120.

[80] Robert Zausner, "Gov. Ridge Abolished Panel That Helped to Pick Judges; A Bipartisan Board Used to Recommend Names; The Task Will Now Fall to the Governor's Lawyer," *Philadelphia Inquirer* (March 17, 1995), A1.

[81] Dunn, "Judicial Reform in Pennsylvania," *supra* note 69,120.

[82] See https://ballotpedia.org/Pennsylvania_Constitutional_Referendum_(1967), accessed December 3, 2018.

[83] See Darren M. Breslin, "Why Does Pennsylvania Have Retention Elections for Judges?" (undated), 5, http://pavotesmart.com/WhydoesPAhaveretentionelectionsforjurists.pdf, accessed December 4, 2018.

list for the first full term.[84] The amendment sent to the voters in November 1968 would create the following selection and retention process for all state judges other than justices of the peace:

- Midterm vacancies to be filled by gubernatorial appointment, subject to approval by two-thirds of the Senate (or approval by a majority for the lowest level judges, then called justices of the peace).
- If a judge chooses to leave office at the end of his or her term, or if the current incumbent had been appointed to fill a vacancy but had not yet stood for election, the position would be filled by a partisan election in which the appointee could run.
- Once a judge had won a partisan election, he or she could stand for additional terms in a retention election.

If this proposal passed, the next year voters would be asked whether all vacancies, either interim or created by a judge choosing not to stand for another term, should be filled by gubernatorial appointment from a list provided by a nominating commission with no requirement of confirmation by the Senate, i.e., voters would be asked to adopt the Missouri Plan.[85] In November 1968, the voters approved the constitutional amendment that included the first three elements, with 55.5 percent in favor.[86] The proposal to rely on gubernatorial appointment and eliminate the partisan election element was voted down the following year by a margin of less than 20,000 votes out of 1.27 million cast (49.2 percent in favor, 50.8 percent against).[87]

Later Efforts to Adopt a Missouri Plan System

The 1970s appear to have been relatively quiet regarding reforms to judicial selection.[88] At the end of the decade, voters were presented with a proposed constitutional amendment, which would extend the use of retention elections after an initial partisan election to justices of the peace (now called "district judges"). The proposal was narrowly defeated, with 49.2 percent voting in favor.

This brings us to the period that is my primary focus: the 1980s, when there were been repeated but unsuccessful efforts to get a proposal for "merit selection" before the voters. In 1980, a nonprofit organization called the Pennsylvania Joint Council on Criminal Justice appointed a Committee to Study Pennsylvania's Unified Judicial

84 *Id.*

85 Dunn, "Judicial Reform in Pennsylvania," *supra* note 69, 119.

86 See https://ballotpedia.org/Pennsylvania_Proposal_7_on_the_Judiciary_(1968), accessed December 3, 2018.

87 Breslin, "Why Does Pennsylvania Have Retention Elections for Judges?" *supra* note 83, 6.

88 I found a reference (https://ballotpedia.org/Pennsylvania_Proposal_7_on_the_Judiciary_(1968), accessed December 3, 2018) to the Pomeroy Commission which, in 1972, reportedly endorsed a Missouri Plan system, but I was unable to find anything more about it.

System, chaired by former Pennsylvania Supreme Court Justice Thomas W. Pomeroy.[89] The Committee's report, issued in 1982, called for a Missouri Plan system for the appellate courts.[90] The following year, the Pennsylvania Bar Association commissioned a survey of Pennsylvania residents that included questions about their preferred method of selection for judges of statewide courts. Only 23.4 percent preferred to elect those judges and 69.0 percent said they would accept appointment of judges as a replacement for the current system. When offered the statement, "Some people say the best way to seat judges would be to have merit selection of statewide judges by a bipartisan panel rather than the existing popular election methods. Do you, yourself, agree with this or disagree with this?" 76.5 percent agreed and only 17.8 percent disagreed.[91] Excluding local courts and focusing specifically on statewide courts may have been important for the response pattern.

In 1987, Democratic governor Robert Casey appointed a Judicial Reform Commission (JRC). The initial charge to the JRC did not include considering proposals for a Missouri Plan system that would end partisan elections, almost certainly because Casey had previously expressed support for partisan elections.[92] Despite the absence of consideration of this kind of reform from the JRC's charge, it ended up endorsing such a plan,[93] albeit with a strong dissenting report;[94] the vote in the JRC was 14–9 in favor of the change.[95] The JRC's proposal applied only to the statewide appellate courts[96] and called for a 16-person, bipartisan nominating commission, half appointed by the governor and two each appointed by various leaders in the legislature.[97] The 1988 JRC report calling for merit selection led to the formation of Pennsylvanians for Modern Courts,[98] a group that became one of the leading advocates for adopting Missouri Plan selection in Pennsylvania.

Proposals based on the JRC's recommendations came to a vote in the state legislature in 1989 and 1990. Several groups expressed strong opposition to the proposal: organized labor, the pro-life movement, and the plaintiffs' bar (i.e., the

89 Lawrence J. Haas, "Panel: Appoint Appellate Judges," *Pittsburgh Post-Gazette* (June 30, 1982), 1.

90 *Id.* See also the Committee's report, "Pennsylvania's Unified Judicial System: An Analysis with Recommendations" (1982), 77–81. A subgroup of the Committee wanted the Missouri Plan to apply to all state courts, particularly those in Philadelphia and Allegheny (Pittsburgh) counties – see 89–92.

91 "Voting in the Dark," *Pennsylvania Lawyer* 5, no. 4 (June 15, 1983), 7.

92 Dunn, "Judicial Reform in Pennsylvania," *supra* note 69, 127–128.

93 Report of the Governor's Judicial Reform Commission (January 1988), 142–201.

94 *Id.*, 202–238.

95 Dunn, "Judicial Reform in Pennsylvania," *supra* note 69, 128.

96 By this time, there were three such courts: the Supreme Court, the superior court, and the commonwealth court. The latter was created in 1970 under the terms of the judicial article amendments passed by the voters in 1968; it hears certain appeals involving state agencies and has original jurisdiction, particularly in cases involving statewide elections.

97 Dunn, "Judicial Reform in Pennsylvania," *supra* note 69, 129.

98 See www.pmconline.org/about.html, accessed December 4, 2018.

Pennsylvania Trial Lawyers Association). In a close 26–22 vote and with support from both Democrats and Republicans, the Senate approved the proposal for a constitutional amendment, with the modification of requiring confirmation of appointees by a two-thirds vote in the Senate.[99] Just a few days before this action by the Senate, the House passed legislation that would end statewide elections for the three appellate courts and have the judges and justices selected by districts.[100]

Both the proposal for district-based elections for the appellate courts and a Missouri Plan system for those courts were carried over to the following year's legislative session. In February 1990, the Senate rejected district-based elections on a 29–18 vote. Several other variations of the Missouri Plan were introduced in the House, which were considered along with the version passed the previous December by the Senate.[101] There was heavy lobbying for the Missouri Plan by supporters (the PBA, Common Cause, League of Women Voters, and Pennsylvanians for Modern Courts) and by opponents (the AFL-CIO, Pro-Life Coalition of Southeast Pennsylvania, and the Pennsylvania Trial Lawyers Association).[102] After previously turning back efforts to amend the Senate proposal,[103] the House approved an amendment, 142–48, that eliminated the merit selection provisions, thus effectively killing the proposal.[104]

Between 1990 and 2018, efforts in support of adopting the Missouri Plan in Pennsylvania continued. Most of the governors over that approximately 30-year period have supported the idea,[105] and bills to that end have been regularly

99 Russell E. Eshleman Jr., "This Time, Senate OKs Judicial Bill," *Philadelphia Inquirer* (December 13, 1989), B1. This vote came just a few days after the proposal had lost by a single vote, 25–24; see Russell E. Eshleman Jr., "Senate Defeats Bill on Judges; New Effort Set to End Elections," *Philadelphia Inquirer* (December 7, 1989), B1.

100 Russell E. Eshleman Jr., "PA. House and Senate Taking Different Roads toward Judicial Reform," *Philadelphia Inquirer* (December 6, 1989).

101 See Russell E. Eshleman Jr., "Bid to Appoint Judges in Doubt in the Legislature," *Philadelphia Inquirer* (February 27, 1990), B4; Russell E. Eshleman Jr., "Advocates of Judicial Reform Step Up Efforts," *Philadelphia Inquirer* (May 27, 1990), B1; Russell E. Eshleman Jr., "Selection of Judges Is Studied; House Ponders Altering System," *Philadelphia Inquirer* (June 4, 1990), B1.

102 Russell E. Eshleman Jr., "Foes of Merit Selection Are Jockeying for Best Shot at Bill," *Philadelphia Inquirer* (June 10, 1990), B1.

103 Russell E. Eshleman Jr., "Judicial Selection Bill Alive; Amendments Fail in House," *Philadelphia Inquirer* (June 6, 1990), B1.

104 Russell E. Eshleman Jr., "Pa. Judicial Appoints Plan Rejected," *Philadelphia Inquirer* (June 12, 1990), A1.

105 Russell E. Eshleman Jr., "Casey Proposes Plan to Appoint State Judges," *Philadelphia Inquirer* (March 5, 1991), A1; Thomas Fitzgerald, "Push to Appoint Pa. Appeals Judges Gains Ally in Ridge; He Called for a Constitutional Amendment; but Changing the Current System of Electing Judges Will Be Difficult," *Philadelphia Inquirer* (February 13, 2001), B12; Larry King, "They Can Talk Up Issues, but . . . –Judge Selection, Campaign Funding, the Right-to-Know Law – Are All Matters Viewed as Legislatively Impossible," *Philadelphia Inquirer* (May 6, 2002), B1; Marcia Gelbart, "A Renewed Push for Appointment of Phila. Judges; Two State Senators Are Trying Again to Change the Selection Process; Their Effort Failed in '05," *Philadelphia Inquirer* (September 7, 2007), B2; Amy Worden, "Rendell Calls Again for Merit Selection of Judges," *Philadelphia Inquirer* (April 22, 2010), A1.

introduced.[106] During the first half of the 1990s, several controversies rocked the Pennsylvania Supreme Court, leading to the criminal conviction and removal by impeachment of Justice Rolf Larson and the resignation of a second justice.[107] These events hyped interest in judicial selection reform, but nothing emerged from the legislature.[108] Throughout this period, the key advocates on both sides remained unchanged: the state bar, Common Cause, League of Women Voters, and Pennsylvanians for Modern Courts supporting the Missouri Plan; the trial lawyers association (now called the Pennsylvania Association for Justice[109]) and organized labor opposed.[110]

A survey done for Pennsylvanians for Modern Courts (PMC) in 2007 found that 56 percent of respondents supported merit selection of judges.[111] Then a very expensive election for the Pennsylvania Supreme Court in 2009, won by Republican Joan Orie Melvin, again spurred discussion of judicial selection reform.[112] A survey conducted several months after that election on behalf of PMC found that 63 percent of respondents supported changing the system of judicial selection and 93 percent favored a statewide vote on the issue.[113] A second 2010 survey done for Justice at Stake, a national group advocating "merit selection," found that 62 percent

[106] "Bill to End Judicial Races Offered in Pa.," *Philadelphia Inquirer* (January 28, 1992), B05; Russell E. Eshleman Jr., "Senate Panel Favors Appointing Judges; Appellate Judges Are Covered by the Measure; Voters Would Decide Whether Local Judges Should Be Elected," *Philadelphia Inquirer* (June 9, 1993), B1; Russell E. Eshleman Jr., "House Panel Oks Plan to Alter Judge Selection; Appointments Would Replace Elections," *Philadelphia Inquirer* (December 7, 1993), B3; Amy Worden and Emilie Lounsberry, "New Call for 'Merit Selection' of Judges; Two Bills Would Take the Power to Select Pa. Jurists Away from Voters," *Philadelphia Inquirer* (March 14, 2008), A1.

[107] See Emilie Lounsberry, "Charges Stir Crisis on Court," *Philadelphia Inquirer* (December 6, 1992), A1; Russell E. Eshleman Jr., "Leaders Consider Top Judges Impeachment Is a Last Resort to Resolve the Controversy; but 'Justice Has to Be Done,'" *Philadelphia Inquirer* (December 17, 1992), B1; "Justice Charged in a Drug Scheme," *New York Times* (October 29, 1993), A10; Emilie Lounsberry, "Larsen Is Convicted of Conspiracy; Justice Is Acquitted on 14 Other Charges," *Philadelphia Inquirer* (April 10, 1994), A1; Emilie Lounsberry, "Senate Convicts, Outs Larsen; Acquits Him on 6 of 7 Counts," *Philadelphia Inquirer* (October 5, 1994), A1.

[108] See Russell E. Eshleman Jr., "Picking Any Judges by Merit Is Unlikely in Pa. This Century; Disagreement Is Rife; Strong Backers Have Moved Out of the Arena," *Philadelphia Inquirer* (April 26, 1996), A16.

[109] The organization's name during much of the period was the Pennsylvania Trial Lawyers Association.

[110] Amy Worden, "House Urged to End Election of Pa. Judges; Supporters of Appointing Judges Say a Constitutional Change Is Needed," *Philadelphia Inquirer* (December I, 2009), B3.

[111] See www.judicialselection.us/judicial_selection/reform_efforts/opinion_polls_surveys.cfm?state=PA, accessed December 4, 2018.

[112] Amy Worden, "Melvin Wins Supreme Court Race," *Philadelphia Inquirer* (November 4, 2009), B1; Amy Worden, "Rendell Calls Again for Merit Selection of Judges," *Philadelphia Inquirer* (April 22, 2010), A1.

[113] Angela Coulombis, "Rendell Presses for Merit-Based Selections," *Philadelphia Inquirer* (June 10, 2010), B2.

of respondents favored replacing partisan elections of appellate judges with a Missouri Plan system.[114]

Around this time, new controversies began to swirl around the Pennsylvania Supreme Court. In April 2010, two sisters of Justice Orie Melvin were indicted on charges of violating campaign laws in connection with the justice's election in 2009. The charges against state senator Jane Orie, the third-ranking Republican in the Pennsylvania Senate, alleged that she had "illegally used her legislative office and other state resources to help her sister" in her successful campaign for the Supreme Court.[115] Janine Orie, who had served as her sister's aide in the Supreme Court justice's previous position as an appellate judge, was charged with the illegal use of state resources in the election campaign. Two years later, charges were brought against the justice herself.[116] All three Orie sisters were eventually convicted on various charges, and Justice Orie Melvin resigned from the Court.[117]

In an unrelated matter, it was reported that the Pennsylvania chief justice, Ronald D. Castille, had accepted dinners, hotel stays, plane rides, tickets to sporting events, and rounds of golf paid for by lawyers and businessmen, and that some of his benefactors had cases that could or did go before the Court. However, unlike most other states, under the ethics rules governing Pennsylvania's judges, accepting such gifts was not a violation, provided that the gifts were reported. Castille had reported the gifts.[118] No pattern of favoritism was found in a review of cases involving the benefactors.[119] Although the report may have raised concerns in some quarters, there appears to have been no clear fallout from the news report about the gifts.

Interest in reforming judicial selection was sparked somewhat by the Orie case.[120] In spring 2012, the legislature held hearings once again, on a constitutional amendment to end partisan elections for appellate judges and implement a Missouri Plan system.[121] Opposition quickly arose from organized labor, the plaintiffs' bar, and the antiabortion Pennsylvania Pro-Life Federation, and the proposal was tabled on a

[114] See www.judicialselection.us/judicial_selection/reform_efforts/opinion_polls_surveys.cfm?state=PA, accessed December 4, 2018; a survey done for Justice at Stake in 2001 found that 59 percent supported the idea of merit selection and retention of judges.

[115] Marie F. Cattabiani, "Western Pa. Scandal Touches on State High Court," *Philadelphia Inquirer* (April 10, 2010), www.philly.com/philly/news/20100410_Western_Pa__scandal_touches_on_state_high_court.html, accessed April 11, 2019.

[116] Paula Reed Ward, "Pa. Supreme Court Justice: I'll Fight Charges," *Philadelphia Inquirer* (May 18, 2012).

[117] Timothy McNulty, "Convicted, Orie Melvin Resigns from Supreme Court," *Philadelphia Inquirer* (March 25, 2013).

[118] Mark Fazlollah and Joseph Tanfani, "Castille Is Accepting of Litigants' Gifts, Trips; It's Legal, They're Disclosed; But Even If Pennsylvania's Chief Justice Shows No Favoritism, Some Question the Ethics," *Philadelphia Inquirer* (November 21, 2010), A1.

[119] *Id.*

[120] "Orie Charges May Help End Some Judicial Elections," *Philadelphia Inquirer* (May 19, 2012).

[121] Chris Bonneau, "True 'Merit' in Judicial Selections?" (April 8, 2012), www.inquirer.com/philly/opinion/inquirer/20120408_True__merit__in_judicial_selections.html, accessed June 25, 2019.

13–12 vote in the House Judiciary Committee.[122] The following year, four former governors of Pennsylvania, two Republicans and two Democrats, called for the adoption of merit selection for the judges of Pennsylvania's appellate courts.[123] During this time, bills to switch to a Missouri Plan system for appellate judges were being introduced in every legislature,[124] but there was no news coverage of action on the proposals in the state's largest newspaper,[125] although there were frequent calls to adopt merit selection in newspapers across the state.[126] Two of the bills, one in 2015 and another in 2017, were reported out of the House Judiciary Committee but were not acted on further by the House.[127] The 2017 version (H.B. 111) also included making the appellate elections district-based rather than statewide.[128] That year, former governors, now numbering five, again called for adopting a Missouri Plan system, always referred to as "merit selection."[129]

Pennsylvania Summary

The debate over merit selection in Pennsylvania has gone on for almost forty years, but the state legislature has never produced the legislation to put a constitutional

[122] Chris Mondics, "Bid to Alter How Pa. Selects Judges Fades; Pressure from Trial Lawyers, Abortion Foes, and Others Helped Sink It," *Philadelphia Inquirer* (June 15, 2012), A30.

[123] Aubrey Whelan, "Four Former Pa. Governors Call for Merit Selection," *Philadelphia Inquirer* (March 16, 2013), A1.

[124] The Gavel to Gavel database shows one or more bills to implement merit selection for appellate judges had been introduced in each of the six legislatures between 2007 and 2018; http://gaveltogavel.us/database/, accessed December 5, 2018 (search State=Pennsylvania, Type=Selection).

[125] Two exceptions regarding news coverage: Chris Palmer, "Pa. Bill Seeks to End State Court Elections," *Philadelphia Inquirer* (October 21, 2015), B5; and John Baer, "Help for Voters in Pa.'s Hapless Judicial Elections," *Philadelphia Inquirer* (November 1, 2017), B2.

[126] This statement is based on a review of Pennsylvania newspapers included in the NewsBank database.

[127] Gavel to Gavel database, *supra* note 124.

[128] The legislature was controlled by Republicans, and Democrats opposed making appellate elections district-based; see Stacy M. Brown, "GOP-Led House Resumes Attempt to Change How Judges Are Chosen," *Philadelphia Tribune* (September 17, 2018). Earlier in the year, the Senate had approved a bill that would change appellate elections to be district-based, but that did not include merit selection; see John Finnerty, "PA Senate Oks Redistricting Plan That Would Include Judicial Elections," *Harrisburg Reporter* (June 13, 2018). The passage of this bill, which was opposed by most Democrats, came after the Pennsylvania Supreme Court found that congressional districts had been gerrymandered to a degree that violated the state constitution, and redrew those districts; see Christopher Ingraham, "Pennsylvania Supreme Court Draws 'Much More Competitive' District Map to Overturn Republican Gerrymander," *Washington Post* (February 20, 2018), www.washingtonpost.com/news/wonk/wp/2018/02/19/pennsylvania-supreme-court-draws-a-much-more-competitive-district-map-to-overturn-republican-gerrymander/?utm_term=.8a3a802a237b, accessed December 5, 2018.

[129] Dick Thornburgh, Tom Ridge, Mark Schweiker, Ed Rendell, and Tom Corbet, "Former Pa. Governors: Time for Merit Selection of Judges," www2.philly.com/philly/opinion/commentary/former-pa-governors-time-for-merit-selection-of-judges-20170605.html, accessed December 5, 2018.

amendment to make such a change before the voters. Under the Pennsylvania state constitution, the only mechanism for amendment is via the legislature, and the same exact amendment must be passed by two-thirds votes in each chamber or by a majority vote in both chambers in two consecutive legislatures.[130] As of 2018, it had been over twenty years since even one chamber had passed a judicial selection amendment. Despite broad calls for change, and an organization that has been focused on accomplishing that change for over thirty years, there does not appear to be any prospect that such a change will happen in the foreseeable future.

The leaders of Pennsylvanians for Modern Courts have argued that the challenge is determining the composition of the nominating commission and who chooses them ("who picks the pickers").[131] However, the problems go beyond that question. First, various groups from multiple political perspectives have consistently opposed a system that does not include a partisan election. These include organized labor, the plaintiffs' bar, and abortion opponents. As is discussed in the concluding chapter, these longtime opponents have been joined recently by a range of conservative interests that at one time had been the primary proponents of merit selection. These new opponents view the choices made by the nominating commission as tending to be too liberal, and they have learned that they can use contested elections to defeat incumbents whose views they do not like. More generally, those who have opposed a full merit selection system do not see retention elections as a viable way of defeating judges whom they want removed from office. Moreover, opponents of the system have learned that they can effectively campaign against it on the slogan that it takes away people's right to vote for judges and puts the selection in the hands of elites.[132] This has been an effective argument and accounts in significant part for the fact that no state electorate has approved a system without the possibility of an election involving two or more candidates since Utah did so in 1984. Despite survey results suggesting support for a merit selection system relying entirely on appointment (i.e., a system without any contested elections), it is doubtful that voters presented with the option would approve it, given the negative campaign that would be mounted, arguing that voters would be surrendering *their* right to select judges.

TEXAS

A final state where efforts at judicial selection reform have been unsuccessful, with one minor exception, is Texas. I deal more briefly with Texas, because the events in

[130] Constitution of Pennsylvania, Article XI, Amendments.

[131] See Shira J. Goodman and Lynn A. Marks, "A View from the Ground: A Reform Group's Perspective on the Ongoing Effort to Achieve Merit Selection of Judges," *Fordham Urban Law Journal* 34, no. 1 (2007), 437–445.

[132] See, for example, Marina Angel, "'Merit Selection' Means Stealing My Vote," *Philadelphia Daily News* (March 24, 2008).

that state have been covered extensively by Anthony Champagne.[133] Most of what follows is drawn from his work.

Judicial Selection in Texas

Texas has two courts of last resort, the Texas Supreme Court for noncriminal matters and the Texas Court of Criminal Appeals. In addition, there is the Court of Appeals (fourteen regional courts), the trial-level district courts handling serious criminal matters and civil actions, various county-level trial courts handling misdemeanors and smaller civil actions, and various local courts (municipal and justice of the peace). Except for some judges of municipal courts who are appointed by the city's governing body, judges in Texas are elected in partisan elections, with vacancies in courts other than the local courts filled by gubernatorial appointment, subject to the approval of the Texas Senate.

As was true of other southern states, Texas was a one-party Democratic state until the last quarter of the twentieth century. Between 1875 and 1978, the only Republican to win a statewide office in Texas was John Tower, who won the 1961 special election to fill the U.S. Senate seat vacated by Lyndon Johnson after Johnson was elected vice-president;[134] several Republican presidential candidates did win the popular vote in Texas during that period. The first Republican governor since the end of the period of Reconstruction was Bill Clements, who held office for four years starting in 1979 and then for another four years starting in 1987. Between 1875 and 1980, Republicans never held more than 4 of the state's seats in the U.S. House of Representatives, never more than 4 of the 31 seats in the Texas Senate, and never more than 23 of 150 seats in the Texas House of Representatives.[135]

[133] Anthony Champagne, "Judicial Reform in Texas," *Judicature* 72 (October–November 1988), 146–153; Anthony Champagne, "Judicial Reform in Texas," in Anthony Champagne and Judith Haydel, eds., *Judicial Reform in the State* (Lanham, MD: University Press of America, 1993), 93–115; Anthony Champagne, "Judicial Selection in Texas: Democracy's Deadlock," in Anthony Champagne and Edward J. Harpham, eds., *Texas Politics: A Reader*, 2nd ed. (New York: W. W. Norton & Company, 1998), 88–104; Kyle Cheek and Anthony Champagne, "Coming to a Judicial Election Near You: The New Era in Texas Judicial Elections," *South Texas Law Review* 43, no. 1 (2001), 9–33; Anthony Champagne and Kyle Cheek, "The Cycle of Judicial Elections: Texas as a Case Study," *Fordham Urban Law Journal* 29 (2002), 907–940; Kyle Cheek and Anthony Champagne, *Judicial Politics in Texas: Partisanship, Money and Politics in State Courts* (New York: Peter Lang, 2004); and Anthony Champagne, "Judicial Reform in Texas: A Look Back after Two Decades," *Court Review* 43, no. 2 (Summer 2006), 68–79.

[134] Tower had been the Republican candidate for senator in 1960, losing that election to Johnson who, under Texas law, was allowed to be on the ballot for both his U.S. Senate seat and the vice-presidency.

[135] Until 1960, Republicans seldom held more than two seats in the House of Representatives, and in many years held no seats at all. See https://en.wikipedia.org/wiki/Political_party_strength_in_Texas, accessed November 30, 2018.

Democrats also had complete control of most of the state's courts. The first Republicans on the Texas Supreme Court were elected in 1988, two defeating incumbents and one winning an open seat. Between 1946 and 1952, there were 18 elections for the two courts of last resort, 14 of which were contested; 11 of the elections were contested in the general election by a Republican, but the largest vote share any of those Republicans received was 11.4 percent (the average was 10.1 percent). Between 1954 and 1978, there were 64 elections to the two statewide courts; only four were contested by Republicans; another 21 were contested in the Democratic primary. A sharp change started in 1980. Between 1980 and 2018, only 6 of 109 elections went uncontested, and in 90 of those elections, there were both Democrats and Republicans running.

Prior to the 1980s, business-oriented, antiplaintiff Democrats held most or all the seats on the Texas Supreme Court. Anthony Champagne attributes the break in 1980 in part to the 1976 election when an unknown candidate with a well-known name defeated the establishment candidate in the Democratic primary for an open seat.[136] That candidate, Don Yarbrough, faced no opponent in the general election, but was forced to resign within the first year when criminal charges were brought against him and he was facing removal by the legislature; voters had confused him with another Don Yarborough (note the difference in spelling), a well-known Democrat who had run unsuccessfully three times in the 1960s for the Democratic gubernatorial nomination. The following year, another unknown candidate with a well-known name, Robert Campbell, defeated a Supreme Court incumbent running for reelection; the confusion that time was probably with University of Texas football player, Earl Campbell, who had won the Heisman Trophy in 1977.[137]

These two elections served to convince the Texas plaintiffs' bar that it was possible to defeat the antiplaintiff justices and install justices who were more sympathetic to the plaintiff's side in personal injury cases.[138] The defense and plaintiffs' sides fought it out during the 1980s, culminating in the 1988 elections, when the candidates and interest groups spent over $11.4 million in connection with the six seats on the court that were at stake. Importantly, although in the past, the defense-oriented justices were all Democrats, in the 1988 election, several of the candidates supported by the defense side were Republicans, three of whom won.[139] The plaintiff-defense battle effectively ended in 1994, when the plaintiffs' bar failed in its attempt to defeat an incumbent who was a pro-defense Democrat in the Democratic primary.[140]

[136] See Champagne, "Judicial Reform in Texas," *supra* note 133, 69.

[137] Cheek and Champagne, *Judicial Politics in Texas, supra* note 133, 39–40.

[138] For a more extensive discussion of the role of the plaintiffs' bar in Texas politics, see Charles P. Elliot Jr., "The Texas Trial Lawyers Association: Interest Group under Siege," in Anthony Champagne and Edward J. Harpham, eds., *Texas Politics: A Reader*, 2nd ed. (New York: W. W. Norton & Company, 1998), 177–194.

[139] Cheek and Champagne, *Judicial Politics in Texas, supra* note 133, 41–42.

[140] *Id.*, 43.

The switch from complete Democratic control to complete Republican control of the two courts of last resort in Texas began in 1988 with the election of those three Republicans and was completed in 1998 with the defeat of the last incumbent Democrats on the two courts. No Democrat won an election to either court between 1994 and 2018. In contrast, Democrats continued to have success in courts not elected on a statewide basis. This was particularly true in some of the large cities, where the Democratic Party continued to have strength. It was enhanced by the inclusion of judges on the straight-ticket ballot option, whereby a voter could vote for all candidates of a party by marking a single box on a printed ballot or pulling a single lever on a voting machine. One result of straight-ticket voting was occasional sweeps in a county or district, in which all or most incumbents of the party disfavored in the election were voted out and candidates of the favored party were voted in.[141] This affected elections for trial judges and for Court of Appeals judges.[142]

Proposals for Judicial Selection Reform

In 1986, just before Republican candidates began having success in statewide judicial elections, the chief justice of the Texas Supreme Court, Democrat John Hill, proposed a change to a Missouri Plan system. This was not the first time the idea was raised in Texas. It had come up as early as the late 1940s, when it was proposed by the Texas Civil Justice Council and a state bar referendum favored it over partisan elections by a margin of more than 2 to 1. Support continued among these groups through the 1950s and into the 1960s; in 1962, the plan was endorsed by the then current chief justice, Democrat Robert W. Calvert. In the early 1970s, it was recommended by the Task Force for Court Improvement and was proposed for appellate judges by the Constitutional Revision Commission.[143] Like the earlier proposals and efforts, Hill's push would come to naught.

Hill create a group called the Committee of 100 to advocate for the proposal. However, he came under attack by other members of the Texas Supreme Court, who preferred to continue the existing system of partisan elections. Opponents

[141] Champagne, "Coming to a Judicial Election Near You," *supra* note 133, 12; Champagne, "Judicial Reform in Texas," *supra* note 133, 77.

[142] See Emma Platoff, "Straight-Ticket Voting Ends in 2020. For Some Down-Ballot Republicans, That Wasn't Soon Enough," *Texas Tribune* (November 16, 2018), www.texastribune.org/2018/11/16/straight-ticket-voting-cd-emmett-harris-county-texas/, accessed December 1, 2018.

[143] Cheek and Champagne, *Judicial Politics in Texas*, *supra* note 133, 83. The proposal for a Missouri Plan system for appellate judges was not included in the rewritten judicial article that was sent to the voters in 1975; see pp. 38–39 of the text of S.J.R. 11 (pp. 381–382 of the text accessed December 1, 2018, at https://lrl.texas.gov/LASDOCS/64R/SJR11/SJR11_64R.pdf#page=499). That amended article, along with seven others, was overwhelmingly rejected by the voters; see Lawrence W. Miller, "The Texas Constitution," in Anthony Champagne and Edward J. Harpham, eds., *Texas Politics: A Reader*, 2nd ed. (New York: W. W. Norton & Company, 1998), 177–194.

created a rival group, the Committee of 250, to oppose any change. About a year after making his proposal, Hill decided to resign from the Court, arguing he would be more effective in promoting the plan as a private citizen. The Republican governor appointed a district court judge from Houston, Tom Phillips, as Hill's replacement. At his swearing-in ceremony, Phillips endorsed the change Hill had proposed,[144] and then went on to back what he labeled the "Texas Plan," which was a version of the Missouri Plan that added the requirement of confirmation by the Senate.[145] The proposal attracted opposition from wide quarters. In addition to some of Phillips's colleagues on the Texas Supreme Court, the leaders of neither political party wanted to see change, and minority groups feared that a system of appointment would reduce the number of minorities serving as judges. Opponents also cited social science evidence disputing the argument that the kind of "merit selection" plan proposed would produce more meritorious judges.[146]

A 1987 broadcast on the popular television show *60 Minutes* brought some new life to the debate. "Is Justice for Sale?" raised the question of whether judges were influenced by large campaign donors.[147] One focus of the report was the large contributions by lawyers representing Pennzoil after the Texas Supreme Court refused to hear an appeal from Texaco of a Texas jury's award to Pennzoil of $10.53 billion for tortious interference of contract connected to a merger deal between Pennzoil and Getty Oil.[148] This report gave a push to stalled efforts at judicial selection reform.[149] Republican governor Bill Clements created the Joint Select Committee on the Judiciary to "study all issues relating to needed or desirable changes affecting the state's judiciary and judicial branch operations including judicial selection, campaign finance, ethics, compensation, and salary."[150] The committee made a series of recommendations including nonpartisan elections for trial courts and a version of the Texas Plan for appellate courts; it also suggested reforming campaign finance in judicial elections and removing judicial contests from the straight-ticket ballot.[151] Hill proposed a change to the previously proposed Texas Plan. First, it would apply only to the appellate courts, and second, nominees would not be confirmed by the legislature, but instead

[144] Cheek and Champagne, *Judicial Politics in Texas*, *supra* note 133, 84–85.
[145] Champagne, "Judicial Reform in Texas," *supra* note 133, 152–153.
[146] Cheek and Champagne, *Judicial Politics in Texas*, *supra* note 133, 95–96.
[147] Champagne and Cheek, "The Cycle of Judicial Elections," *supra* note 133, 931–932.
[148] Cheek and Champagne, *Judicial Politics in Texas*, *supra* note 133, 97. On the Texaco-Pennzoil case, see Tamar Lewin, "Pennzoil-Texaco Fight Raised Key Questions," *New York Times* (December 19, 1987), www.nytimes.com/1987/12/19/business/pennzoil-texaco-fight-raised-key-questions.html, accessed December 1, 2018, 44.
[149] Cheek and Champagne, *Judicial Politics in Texas*, *supra* note 133, 97.
[150] See https://lrl.texas.gov/committees/reportDisplay.cfm?subjectID=4246&subject=Judicial%20selection, accessed December 1, 2018.
[151] Cheek and Champagne, *Judicial Politics in Texas*, *supra* note 133, 97.

would run in a "confirmation election" using a retention-type yes-no ballot. These proposals went nowhere.[152]

In the mid-1990s, Democratic lieutenant governor Bob Bullock created a committee to explore possible judicial reforms. Changing the system of selection and retention would require some type of compromise among various groups. A plan was developed that shifted appellate courts to a Missouri Plan system while retaining partisan elections for trial courts; those trial court elections would be conducted in small districts, which was expected to increase minority representation on the bench. Incumbent judges and Republicans were uncomfortable with that plan. Despite opposition from both political parties and Republican Governor George Bush, Bullock was able to push a plan through the Texas Senate, but it died in the House of Representatives.[153]

In 1995, a modicum of success in reforming judicial elections was achieved with the passage of a law, the Judicial Campaign Fairness Act, placing limits on campaign contributions in judicial elections.[154] The passage of that legislation spurred renewed efforts for more extensive change. A couple of plans were proposed with various elements including appointment of appellate judges, nonpartisan election of trial judges, retention elections, retaining partisan election of some judges but eliminating straight-party voting in judicial elections, and various changes to sizes of electoral districts. The proposals failed to garner sufficient support to make it to the floor of either chamber of the state legislature.

An effort was made again in 2003. A plan was proposed for gubernatorial appointment with confirmation by the Senate and judges then running in retention elections. The proposal attracted some bipartisan support, and like one of the earlier efforts, passed the Senate, only to die in the House. By this time, Republicans had gained full control of the legislature as well as maintaining control of the governorship; despite the support of some Republicans, the dominant view in the party was against the change. Visitors to the party's website were invited to sign a petition "to protect Texans' right to elect their judges."[155] Lobbying in the House had produced enough support that the legislation to put the change on the ballot was about to be approved by the House Judicial Affairs Committee when the new Republican Speaker of the House had some staff persons tell the chairperson of the committee to pull the bill.[156]

There does not appear to have been any major drives for major changes in judicial selection after 2003. This does not mean that no legislation has been introduced for such changes. In fact, a 2017 report observed that "every recent biennial regular legislative session in Texas has featured multiple proposals to

[152] *Id.*, 97–98.
[153] *Id.*, 100–101.
[154] *Id.*, 101–102.
[155] *Id.*, 103–104.
[156] Champagne, "Judicial Reform in Texas," *supra* note 133, 77.

significantly modify the methods by which judges are selected in Texas."[157] As of 2019, none of those proposals, at least since 2009, has even made it out of committee in the legislature.[158] Moreover, in 2015, a bill calling for an "interim study regarding the method by which certain trial and appellate judges are selected" (H.B. 2088)[159] made it to the floor of the House but was voted down 90 to 51.[160] In the wake of the 2018 election, in which seventeen Republican incumbent Court of Appeals judges lost elections,[161] the chief justice of the Texas Supreme Court, Nathan Hecht, used his State of the Judiciary Address to call for ending of the partisan elections and implementing "merit selection" with retention elections.[162] Nothing is likely to come from Hecht's call.

Texas Summary

The failure of efforts to change the system of judicial selection and retention in Texas reflects in part the absence of strong interest in change from either political party. At present, Republicans are content with their electoral dominance and Democrats are probably fearful that moving to a Missouri Plan system would allow Republicans even greater dominance of the trial court bench. The defense side has learned it can succeed in electing desired candidates, so it is no longer particularly enthusiastic about the Missouri Plan. Minorities are fearful that a Missouri Plan system would decrease their representation on the bench. And, except for one factor, judges feel secure in the current system.[163] The one factor is the problem of regional or local sweeps arising from straight-ticket voting that had become very common.[164] However, in 2017, the Texas legislature voted to remove the straight-ticket option

[157] See Mark P. Jones, "The Selection of Judges in Texas: Analysis of the Current System and of the Principal Reform Options," Baker Institute for Public Policy, Rice University (January 2017), 22, www.bakerinstitute.org/media/files/files/b38e1ecc/POLI-pub-TexasJudges-011317.pdf, accessed December 1, 2018.

[158] See http://gaveltogavel.us/database/ (search "Texas" for "selection" bills), accessed December 1, 2018.

[159] *Id*; see also https://capitol.texas.gov/BillLookup/History.aspx?LegSess=84R&Bill=HB2088, accessed December 1, 2018.

[160] See https://journals.house.texas.gov/hjrnl/84r/pdf/84RDAY70FINAL.PDF#page=131, accessed December 1, 2018.

[161] One news report stated that 20 incumbents lost; see Emma Platoff and Jolie McCullough, "Texas Supreme Court Chief Justice Nathan Hecht Calls for Nonpartisan Judicial Elections, Bail Reform," *Texas Tribune* (February 6, 2019), www.texastribune.org/2019/02/06/texas-supreme-court-judicial-elections-bail-reform-nathan-hecht/, accessed June 6, 2019. However, I found only 17 when I reviewed the election returns; all of the defeats came in areas that tilt Democratic, and almost certainly resulted in part from the last hurrah of the straight-ticket ballot option (which ceases to exist starting in 2020), which included judges.

[162] See Nathan L. Hecht, "State of the Texas Judiciary" (February 6, 2019), www.txcourts.gov/media/1443500/soj2019.pdf, accessed June 6, 2019.

[163] See Cheek and Champagne, *Judicial Politics in Texas*, *supra* note 133, 105–110.

[164] See Jones, "The Selection of Judges in Texas," *supra* note 157, 2–3, 13–14.

from all ballots, effective with the 2020 election,[165] meaning that this should not be an issue in the future.

NEW HAMPSHIRE

Judges in New Hampshire are effectively appointed by the governor, subject to confirmation by an elected 5-member Executive Council, and serve without reappointment, with mandatory retirement at age 70.[166] The Executive Council is not a rubber stamp and on occasion challenges or rejects the governor's selection.[167] In 2015, the Executive Council voted 3–2 to reject a trial court nominee of Democratic governor Maggie Hassan; the opposition to the nominee, who had worked as a public defender for twenty years, was led by Republican Chris Sununu, who was joined in opposition by the two other Republicans on the Council.[168] In 2019, the Council majority shifted to the Democratic side, and that majority proceeded to reject on a 3–2 vote now governor Sununu's nomination of the attorney general, Gordon MacDonald, to be chief justice of the New Hampshire Supreme Court.[169]

In 1973, the governor created the Governor's Commission on Court System Improvement. The commission's charge was to take a broad look at the state's judicial system and make recommendations for changes. The commission's report was released in 1974 and in the realm of judicial selection called for adopting some form of "merit selection." However, the commission recognized the difficulty that might be encountered in passing the necessary constitutional

[165] Jolie McCullough, "Gov. Abbot Signs Bill to Eliminate Straight-Ticket Voting Beginning in 2020," *Texas Tribune* (June 1, 2017), www.texastribune.org/2017/06/01/texas-gov-greg-abbott-signs-bill-eliminate-straight-ticket-voting/, accessed December 1, 2018. During the preceding few years, several bills had been introduced to remove judicial races from the straight-ticket option, but none of those made much progress in the legislature; see http://gaveltogavel.us/database/ (search "Texas" for "selection" bills), accessed December 1, 2018.

[166] Formally, "All judicial officers, the attorney general, and all officers of the navy, and general and field officers of the militia, shall be nominated and appointed by the governor and council; and every such nomination shall be made at least three days prior to such appointment; and no appointment shall take place, unless a majority of the council agree thereto"; New Hampshire Constitution, Article 46.

[167] How often this occurs is unclear. I searched New Hampshire newspapers on NewsBank for the period 1970 through 2014 and found two references to rejections; see Keven Landrigan, "Judicial Picks Draws Fire at Hearing,"*Nashua Telegraph* (November 25, 2004); Tom Fahey, "Governor to Reject Delker to Superior Court," *New Hampshire Union Leader* (June 8, 2011), 3.

[168] Jonathan Cohen, "My Turn: Rejection of Nominee Was Rejection of Justice," *Concord Monitor* (November 13, 2015).

[169] John Koziol, "AG Rejected for Supreme Court; Governor Slams Executive Council Vote, Calling Democrats' Treatment of Gordon MacDonald 'Reprehensible,'" *New Hampshire Union Leader* (July 10, 2019), A1; see also, Ryan Lessard, "Future of Judicial Nominations Unclear After MacDonald Vote," New Hampshire Bar Association, www.nhbar.org/future-of-judicial-nominations-unclear-after-macdonald-vote/, accessed July 31, 2019.

amendment. In New Hampshire, constitutional amendments must be approved by three-fifths of the entire membership in each legislative chamber and then by a two-thirds majority in a general (even-year) election.[170] In the absence of a merit selection amendment, the report called for the creation of a "voluntary merit selection plan" (i.e., one that did not bind the governor) by way of an executive order and then by legislation.[171] The year following the release of the commission report, 1975, the legislature passed a bill that would have created a similar commission to make nonbinding recommendations, but it was vetoed by the governor, who had concluded that it ran "contrary to the to the clear intent of the constitution," which gave the governor and executive council that "power to nominate and appoint all judicial officers."[172] In 1977, when the Senate was considering a similar proposal, the Senate sought an advisory opinion from the state Supreme Court; the Court's opinion found that a commission could be created by executive order but not by legislation.[173] It was not until 2000 that then governor Jeanne Shaheen created by executive order a judicial nominating commission,[174] a practice followed by all governors since Shaheen. Although the governor is not formally constrained by the recommendations of the nominating commission, governors have followed those recommendations.

Between 1950 and 2006, the New Hampshire legislature was dominated by the Republican Party. There was only a single year when Democrats controlled the Senate and only five years when there were equal numbers of Republicans and Democrats in the Senate. At no time during this period did the Democrats control both chambers of the state legislature. Over that period, a Democrat held the governorship for 17 of the 57 years.[175]

In the 1990s, conflict arose between the New Hampshire Supreme Court and the Republican-controlled legislature, despite the fact that four of the five justices had been selected by Republican governors. One point of contention was a series of decisions requiring the state to develop a plan for funding schools that did not rely on local property taxes."[176] There were also issues regarding the Supreme Court's role in judicial administration and judicial discipline. In 1999, about twenty bills were introduced that would "remove judges, review them, take away some of their

[170] New Hampshire Constitution, Article 100.

[171] "Report of Governor's Commission on Court System Improvement," *New Hampshire Bar Journal* 16, no. 1 (September 1974), 69–70.

[172] Katherine M. Hanna, "New Hampshire Judicial Selection Commission: A Work in Progress," *New Hampshire Bar Journal* 42 (June 2001), 45.

[173] Opinion of the Justices, 374 A.2d 638 (1977); see also, Kevin Landrigant, "An 11-Person Panel Will Review All Gubernatorial Nominees for Judgeships under an Executive Order Gov. Jeanne Shaheen Signed Friday," *Nashua Telegraph* (July 1, 2000).

[174] See www.judicialselection.us/judicial_selection/index.cfm?state=NH, accessed July 26, 2019.

[175] See https://en.wikipedia.org/wiki/Political_party_strength_in_New_Hampshire, accessed July 26, 2019.

[176] Cynthia Gray, "Supreme Court/Legislature at Odds in New Hampshire," *Judicature* 84, no. 2 (March–April 2001), 291.

power, or limit their tenure on the bench."[177] One bill was sought to remove the chief justice, David Brock, for "usurp[ing] legislative and executive authority" and "allow[ing] the court to engage in policy-making that should be off-limits to the courts."[178] The bill did not make it to the floor of either legislative chamber. Other bills were introduced that would provide for the removal of judges, for review of judges, or would impose limits on their tenure. One proposal, supported by both the Republican Speaker of the House and Democratic governor Jeanne Shaheen, was for a constitutional amendment that would create a 7-year term for judges, who could be reappointed by the governor and Executive Council. Another proposal called for periodic performance review of judges; it was killed in the Senate on a 17–7 roll call,[179] with Republicans voting 6–5 against killing the proposal and Democrats voting 12–1 in favor of killing it.[180]

In 2000, a series of scandals involving four of the five justices broke. One justice, W. Stephen Thayer III, became the subject of an investigation by the attorney general. The report issued by the attorney general alleged that Thayer had:[181]

1. Argued an interested party's position to the Court in ... a matter in which he had disqualified himself without disclosing to the Court his financial relationship with the interested party
2. Misrepresented his practices as a recused justice in oral statements to the Judicial Conduct Committee
3. Participated in private conferences on the proposed amendments to the procedural rules of the Judicial Conduct Committee while a complaint against him was still pending before that body
4. Tried to influence the selection of judges to hear the appeal in the matter of *Thayer v. Thayer* [his own divorce case] by objecting to the selection of retired Superior Court Judge George Pappagianis.

In March 2000, Thayer entered into an agreement to resign to avoid a grand jury indictment.[182]

The investigation by the attorney general brought to light "a long-standing practice of allowing justices to comment on cases from which they were

[177] Katherine Webster, "Judges Struggle to Keep Their Independence in Face of Court Reform," *Foster's Daily Democrat* [Dover, NH], March 22, 1999.

[178] Quoted in *id.*

[179] Warren Hastings, "Plan to Review Judges Killed by NH Senate," *New Hampshire Union Leader* (March 31, 1999), C3.

[180] Unless otherwise noted, all vote tallies are my computations based on the New Hampshire legislature's website, https://gencourt.state.nh.us/nhgcrollcalls/Default.aspx, accessed July 26, 2019.

[181] New Hampshire Attorney General, "*In re*: W. Stephen Thayer, III and Related Matters" (New Hampshire Attorney General's Office, 2000), 3; quoted in Seth Forrest Gilbertson, "New Hampshire: 'Live Free or Die' But in the Meantime ...," *Albany Law Review* 69 (2006), 595–596.

[182] Gilbertson, "New Hampshire: 'Live Free or Die,'" *supra* note 181, 595.

disqualified."[183] This led the New Hampshire House of Representatives to consider impeachment proceedings against three other justices: Chief Justice David Brock, and Associate Justices Sherman Horton and John Broderick.[184] Although the attorney general's report was the legal basis for considering impeachment, the ongoing conflict between the legislature and the Supreme Court provided a motivation for the legislature to try to rein in the Court. A longtime observer of the judicial process in New Hampshire who was serving on the New Hampshire Judicial Council[185] during the time of the impeachment proceedings reported that the view of insiders was that the impeachment proceedings would not have happened but for that ongoing conflict over issues such as school finance.[186]

The House approved four articles of impeachment against the chief justice, alleging that he:[187]

1. Oversaw a practice allowing recused and disqualified justices to receive draft opinions, attend conferences on the cases, and comment on and influence rulings
2. Discussed with Thayer who would serve as substitute justices on the appeal of Thayer's divorce case
3. Telephoned a lower court judge in 1986 to check the status of a case involving a company owned by the then state senate majority leader
4. Lied under oath to the House Judiciary Committee when he denied making the call.

The votes on the impeachment articles in the House had a tinge of partisanship, with Republicans more in favor than Democrats. However, substantial numbers of Democrats voted in favor, and some number of Republicans voted against. A solid majority of Republicans voted in favor of all four articles, and on the article that had the most support, a majority of Democrats also voted in favor. Chief Justice Brock was tried before the New Hampshire Senate, but the Senate acquitted him on all charges, with not even a simple majority voting to convict.[188]

[183] Gray, "Supreme Court/Legislature at Odds," *supra* note 176, 291.

[184] Gilbertson, "New Hampshire: 'Live Free or Die,'" *supra* note 181, 596.

[185] The Judicial Council "provides assistance and information about the state's court's and justice system to all branches of state government and the [state] bar association"; see www.nh.gov/judicialcouncil/, at www.nh.gov/judicialcouncil, accessed July 26, 2019.

[186] Interview with Professor Lynn Mather, University of Buffalo (formerly, Dartmouth College, 1972–2002), July 26, 2019.

[187] Gray, "Supreme Court/Legislature at Odds," *supra* note 176, 291. The votes varied from 219–138 to 252–104; see Garry Rayno, "House Votes to Impeach Brock," *New Hampshire Union Leader* (July 13, 2000), A16.

[188] Conviction required 15 votes (two-thirds of the 22 participating senators), but no more than 8 senators voted to convict; see Gray, "Supreme Court/Legislature at Odds," *supra* note 176, 291.

No more than 8 of 22 senators voted to convict, and on the other counts only 4 or 5 voted to convict.[189]

The House considered articles of impeachment against the other two justices focusing on allegations of improper activities related to Thayer's divorce case, but those failed to pass.[190] In the remaining months of 2000, Justice Broderick was arrested for simple assault after striking his 30-year-old son at his home;[191] the charges were dropped just before the scheduled trial date after the prosecutor concluded that it was reasonable "for a father to lightly slap an adult child in the face to get his attention."[192] Also, Justice Horton decided to retire at the end of November.[193]

In the three years following the impeachment and trial of the chief justice, legislation was introduced to change judicial selection and retention. However, even as the House was considering whether to bring articles of impeachment, Governor Jeanne Shaheen issued an executive order creating a Judicial Selection Commission (JSC). Shaheen pledged to make her selections from the JSC's recommendations.[194] In 2001, the Senate passed a proposed constitutional amendment that would have a Judicial Selection Commission (JSC) prepare a list of nominees from which the governor would make an appointment. Judges would be subject to review by the JSC every ten years and could be removed by a majority vote of the JSC. The proposed amendment specified the membership of the JSC, with some selected by the governor, some by the president of the Senate, some by the Speaker of the House, and some by the chief justice. The vote on the proposed amendment was 19–5, with 4 of the 5 nays coming from Democrats; 6 Democrats and 13 Republicans voted in favor.[195] The proposal came to the floor of the House in January 2002 and was killed by a vote to table 196–162;[196] Democrats voted to table 114–16, with Republicans opposed 75–145.

[189] John Distaso and Garry Rayno, "Brock Acquitted; NH's Chief Justice Says He's Ready to Return to Work," *New Hampshire Union Leader* (October 11, 2000), A1. I could not find roll-call votes for the impeachment trial, but with the possible exception of one article, a majority of both Republicans and Democrats must have voted for acquittal, because there were 12 senators from each party in the 2000 Senate.

[190] Garry Rayno, "Broderick and Horton Narrowly Escape Impeachment by the House," *New Hampshire Union Leader* (July 13, 2000), A17; the votes rejecting impeachment were 190–135 for Horton and 177–145 for Brock.

[191] Garry Rayno, "Supreme Court Justice Broderick Arrested," *New Hampshire Union Leader* (October 30, 2000), A1.

[192] Pat Grossmith, "Assault Charge Dropped against Judge Broderick," *New Hampshire Union Leader* (December 2, 2000), A1. It was also reported that Broderick's son did not want his father prosecuted.

[193] Tom Fahey and Garry Rayno, "Supreme Court Justice Horton Retires Nov. 25," *New Hampshire Union Leader* (October 25, 2000), A1.

[194] "Would-Be Judges Now Will Go Before Committee," *New Hampshire Union Leader* (July 1, 2000), A8.

[195] Tom Fahey, "Senate OK's Amendment Plan for Review of Judges," *New Hampshire Union Leader* (May 25, 2001), A1.

[196] Kevin Landrigant, "House Rejects Judicial Reform Proposal in Post-Impeachment Change of Mood in Legislature," *Nashua Telegraph* (January 3, 2002).

The Senate tried again soon after the House rejected the Senate's 2001 version. The new proposal omitted the provision for review and removal; it also left to legislation the composition of the Judicial Selection Commission. This proposal passed the Senate unanimously;[197] it was never acted upon in the House. In 2003, the House killed two proposals. One would have established a Judicial Nominating Commission as a matter of law, but the governor would only have to "give high priority to choosing from the list of names of qualified persons submitted by the commission."[198] The second proposal was for a constitutional amendment that would have adopted a procedure modeled on the federal system: the governor would "nominate and by and with the consent of the senate, [would] appoint judges." Both proposals were rejected, the first on a voice vote to table and the second on a roll-call vote to table.[199] The latter vote was 274–102, with Republicans strongly in favor of killing the proposal 240–17, and Democrats opposed 84–25.

Between 2014 and 2019, there were no prominent efforts to change New Hampshire's system of judicial selection and retention.[200] Between 2014 and 2017, several proposals for constitutional amendments were introduced, some that would require legislative confirmation of the selections of the governor and Executive Council and some that would have replaced appointment with election.[201] All of these proposals were overwhelmingly rejected by the New Hampshire House of Representatives. One might speculate that the rejection of Chris Sununu's choice for chief justice in 2019 will lead to new proposals for changing the state's judicial selection system.

SUMMARY: FAILED REFORM EFFORTS IN FOUR STATES

The overall pattern in the first three case studies of failed reform efforts discussed in this chapter is clear. Support for the Missouri Plan system continues strong within the bar and good-government groups such as the League of Women Voters and Common Cause. Many bar leaders also support the plan, as do appellate judges. Despite that support, the legislatures of Minnesota, Pennsylvania, and Texas have been unwilling for a period of thirty-five years to put before the voters proposals to adopt that system. Opposition has long come from plaintiffs' lawyers and minority groups, the former because they want to have the possibility of defeating incumbents who are unsympathetic to plaintiffs and the latter because they fear that minority lawyers would be disadvantaged by a system lacking competitive elections. As noted

[197] Dan Touhy, "Senate Oks Court Reform Bill," *Foster's Daily Democrat* [Dover, NH] (February 2002).

[198] House Bill 130, www.gencourt.state.nh.us/legislation/2003/HB0130.html, accessed July 31, 2019.

[199] Tom Fahey, "Lawmakers Reject Changing Judicial Selection Process," *New Hampshire Union Leader* (February 7, 2003), A2.

[200] I base this on the failure of a search for "judicial selection" on NewsBank to turn up any news articles regarding proposals for such changes.

[201] See www.ncsc.org/gaveltogavel, accessed August 1, 2019.

in other chapters, in recent years, opposition to the Missouri Plan has also come from conservative and business groups, who believe that lawyer-dominated nominating panels tend to produce liberal judges and who also have found that they can use contested elections to defeat judges they do not like.

There are other state-specific elements to the failure of the legislatures to get a Missouri Plan system before the voters. In Minnesota, the problems that some thought would arise from the U.S. Supreme Court's decision in *Republican Party of Minnesota v. White* have failed to materialize as of 2019, and this cooled the effort to change the selection system. In Pennsylvania, where voters rejected a proposal to adopt a version of the Missouri Plan in the late 1960s, the state constitution makes it extremely difficult to get a constitutional amendment on the ballot: two-thirds of both chambers of the legislature must approve the exact same amendment in one legislature or a majority must do so in two consecutive legislatures (i.e., with an intervening legislative election). In Texas, proposals for a Missouri Plan system and proposals to change to nonpartisan elections have failed to gain substantial traction despite strong support from some judicial leaders. Although one might have seen the period when Texas was shifting from essentially one-party Democratic control to one-party Republican control as a significant driver for change, the shift was probably less dramatic than first meets the eye, because the dominant faction in the Democratic Party was very pro-business, which made the change in control less salient than it might have been for those interested in court staffing.

New Hampshire differs from the other three states discussed in this chapter. The efforts at change between 2001 and 2003 were precipitated by the scandals around the Supreme Court that broke in 2000. However, underlying the proposed changes was also the conflict between the Supreme Court and the legislature, particularly over the issue of school funding. None of the news reports I found suggested that reform groups such as Common Cause or the League of Women voters were active participants in the debates of over reform in those years. In the end, there was simply not enough legislative support for the changes that were proposed, perhaps because the governor had implemented a selection commission by executive order.

14

Missouri, Kansas, and Oklahoma

Unsuccessful Efforts to End "Merit" Nominating Commissions

Chapter 5 traced the history of judicial selection changes in Tennessee through 2014, when a constitutional amendment ending any constraining role for a nominating commission was adopted. Chapters 12 and 13 traced the unsuccessful efforts to institute a Missouri Plan system with a constraining nominating commission in Minnesota, Nevada, Ohio, Pennsylvania, and Texas. As discussed in Chapter 8, the last state to adopt such a system through constitutional change was Utah in 1985. In earlier chapters, I noted that the Missouri Plan has fallen out of favor with groups such as business interests, which had been historically strong supporters of the system. There is also evidence that the public is less supportive of the system as well.[1] These two factors undergird the efforts in Missouri, Kansas, and Oklahoma, all having long employed the Missouri Plan for their appellate courts (and in two of the states for some trial-level courts), to end the constraining role of judicial nominating commissions. As of 2019, there has been very limited success in those states in making such changes. The one change was in Kansas where the legislature could change selection for the Court of Appeals without the electorate having to approve a constitutional amendment.

MISSOURI

There is some irony that the Missouri Plan has come under attack in Missouri.[2] There had been previous attempts to end Missouri's Nonpartisan Court Plan (its formal name). Shortly after the Missouri Plan was adopted in 1940, an effort to repeal it was mounted, but was defeated at the polls in 1942, with only 35.8 percent

[1] Seth S. Andersen, "Examining the Decline in Support for Merit Selection in the States," *Albany Law Review* 67 (2004), 793–802.

[2] There have also been legislative proposals to limit or end the Missouri Plan in Iowa. Regarding Iowa, see Trish Mehaffey, "Study: Lawyers Have Too Much Influence on Judge Selection," *Cedar Rapids Gazette* (February 27, 2011), A1.

supporting repeal.[3] In the 1980s, the Missouri Plan again became controversial after colleagues of a Supreme Court justice accused him of "manipulating the selection process to 'hand pick' the justices who would fill three vacancies,"[4] and then the governor appointed his chief of staff to a vacancy on the Missouri Supreme Court even though the new justice was only 33 years old and had no judicial experience.[5] One result of these controversies was the introduction of bills in 1988 and 1991 to abolish the Nonpartisan Court Plan, but those bills died in the legislature.[6]

As is true in the other states where opposition to the Missouri Plan became prominent after the turn of the century, in Missouri the post-2000 attacks came from the political right. Business groups had been strong supporters of the plan when it was originally adopted but[7] are less enamored of it today. Central points of criticism are that the Missouri Plan is undemocratic,[8] and that groups tending to lean liberal, particularly lawyers, have too much influence in the nominating process.[9] In Missouri, the state constitution applies the Plan to all appellate judges plus trial (circuit) judges in the two largest counties; some additional counties have exercised a local option to adopt the plan. In 2004, the Plan came under renewed attack when a group of Republicans in the Missouri House of Representatives introduced legislation for a constitutional amendment that would subject all circuit judges to contested rather than retention elections.[10] A Supreme Court decision in 2007 favoring collective bargaining by public employees sparked speculation that Republicans would move forward with a constitutional amendment changing the selection of appellate judges to give more power to the governor and legislature.[11] However, a survey conducted late that year found that

[3] See Richard A. Watson and Rondal G. Downing, *The Politics of the Bench and Bar: Judicial Selection Under the Missouri Nonpartisan Court Plan* (New York: John Wiley & Sons, 1969), 11; for a detailed description of the effort to repeal the plan see Jack W. Peltason, "The Missouri Plan for the Selection of Judges," *University of Missouri Studies* 20, no. 2 (1945), 56–63.

[4] "History of Reform Efforts, Missouri: Unsuccessful Reform Efforts," www.judicialselection.us/judicial_selection/reform_efforts/failed_reform_efforts.cfm?state=MO, accessed May 1, 2019.

[5] *Id.*

[6] *Id.*

[7] Watson and Downing, *Politics of Bench and Bar*, *supra* note 3, 11.

[8] Stephen J. Ware, "The Missouri Plan in National Perspective," *Missouri Law Review* 74 (2009), 764–772.

[9] See "Judicial Reform," Adam Smith Foundation (undated), www.adamsmithfoundation.com/judicial-reform/, accessed December 8, 2018; Chris Bonneau, "True 'Merit' in Judicial Selections?" www.inquirer.com/philly/opinion/inquirer/20120408_True__merit__in_judicial_selections_.html.

[10] Emily Umbright, "MO Legislature Seeks to Give Voters Chance to Decide If Public or Governor Will Choose Circuit Judges," *St. Louis Countian* (April 16, 2004); the governor would continue to fill midterm vacancies under from a list submitted by a nominating commission.

[11] Jo Mannies, "Court Ruling Fuels Effort to Alter How We Pick Judges," *St. Louis Post-Dispatch* (May 31, 2007), D3; see also Kelly Wiese, "Proposal to Change Missouri Court Plan Floated," *St. Louis Countian* (November 12, 2007).

about three-quarters of the respondents did not want to change the selection and retention system.[12]

In 2008, Missouri conservatives launched a campaign to change the system of selection of Missouri's appellate judges.[13] Republicans introduced legislation for a constitutional amendment that would have changed the balance of power on the nominating commission and required Senate confirmation of appointees. A preliminary vote in the House showed strong support for the amendment (80–63),[14] but the proposal failed to gain even a majority on the final vote, which was 69–83.[15] That fall, the Republican candidate for governor, Kenny Hulshof, called for altering the composition of the nominating commission to remove the bar from playing a role and to permit the governor to reject the proposed slate of nominees and appoint his or her own candidate; appointees would have to be confirmed by the Senate.[16] This proposal fell off the political radar after the Democratic candidate, Jay Nixon, won the election.

One interesting side feature of the 2008 election was that in one county, Greene County, there was a proposal on the ballot to change the selection and retention of local circuit judges from partisan election to the Missouri Plan. As noted previously, the state constitution only required the Missouri Plan for the state's appellate courts and the two largest counties; other counties have a local option, and it had been thirty-five years since a county had changed to the Missouri Plan.[17] In a close vote, the proposal to switch to the Missouri Plan system for Greene County circuit judges narrowly passed, with 51.8 percent voting in favor.[18]

Early in 2008, conservatives organized a group, Better Courts for Missouri, with a goal of changing the judicial selection system of Missouri.[19] The following year,

[12] Bob Watson, "New Poll Claims Most Missourians Support Current Judicial Selection Plan," *Jefferson City News-Tribune* (December 16, 2007). The results of that survey can be found at www.brennancenter.org/sites/default/files/2007%20Missouri%20Public%20Opinion%20Poll%20on%20Judicial%20Selection.pdf, accessed December 12, 2018.

[13] Steve Kraske, "Missouri Conservatives Are Ready for Battle over Judge Selection," *Kansas City Star* (June 22, 2008), B3.

[14] Chris Blank, "Mo. House Approves Amendment to Change How Judges Are Picked," Associated Press News Service (April 14, 2008); 82 votes, a majority of the 163 members of the House, are required to advance a constitutional amendment.

[15] Jason Noble, "Judge Selection on Hold," *Kansas City Star* (April 18, 2008), B1.

[16] David A. Lief, "Hushof Wants Lawyers Cut Out of Court Plan," *Jefferson City News* (September 25, 2008).

[17] "Judiciary Plan Faces Ballot Test; Voters to Weigh in on Judge Selection," *Columbia Daily Tribune* (October 29, 2008).

[18] See https://greenecountymo.gov/county_clerk/election/result_output.php?id=901, accessed December 12, 2018.

[19] Scott Lauck, "Missouri's Nonpartisan Court Plan Reform Effort Gets New Name, Web Site," *Kansas City (Missouri) Daily Record* (January 31, 2008). This may be the same group reportedly organized by the local president of the conservative Federalist Society, Missourians for Open and Accountable Judicial Selection; see Donna Walter, "Court Critic Forms New Group with Possible Plans to Sue the Missouri Bar," *St. Louis Countian* (January 7, 2008).

conservatives launched a petition campaign to put a constitutional amendment on the ballot in 2010. The proposed amendment provided that the governor would continue to fill midterm vacancies from a nominating commission list, but the governor's selection would be subject to confirmation by the Senate; retention elections would be replaced by partisan elections meaning that open-seat elections would occur if a sitting judge decided to depart at the end of his or her term of office. The proposed amendment also explicitly permitted candidates for judicial office to "announce his or her views on disputed legal or political issues provided that the judge or judicial candidate [did] not make pledges or promises to render specific rulings or decisions on pending litigation"; judicial candidates would also be allowed to solicit campaign contributions.[20] The petition drive failed to obtain enough signatures by the statutory deadline despite spending over $1.5 million gathering those signatures.[21] Although the proposed amendment did not make it on to the 2010 ballot, the proponents of change made clear that they were not ready to give up and would try again, both by a petition and by persuading the Republican-dominated legislature to put the issue on the ballot.[22] If there was a renewed initiative effort in 2011, it does not appear to have gotten very far.[23]

However, in 2012, the Republican-controlled legislature voted to put a proposal on the ballot that would change the composition of the 7-member nominating commission. The commission was (and still is) composed of 3 lawyers elected by the bar from three districts, 3 nonlawyers from those same districts appointed by the governor, and the chief justice of the Missouri Supreme Court, who serves as chair.[24] Under the proposed system, the chief justice would no longer serve on the commission and the governor would appoint 4 of the 7 members; there would be no requirement that the governor's appointees be nonlawyers.[25] Part of the goal of the proponents was to reduce what some saw as too much influence in the selection process by the plaintiffs' bar.[26] Historically, the bar election of lawyers to serve on the nominating commission was a contest between the plaintiffs' bar and the defense bar,[27] and as of 2012, 8 of the previous 10 lawyers on the nominating commission had

20 See https://ballotpedia.org/Text_of_Missouri_Judicial_Selection_Amendment_(2010), accessed December 8, 2018.

21 "Initiative to Kill Non-Partisan Plan Does Not Make Ballot," *St. Louis American* (August 26, 2010).

22 Tony Messenger, "Missouri Plan for Picking Judges Draws Fire Again – Critic Aims for Direct Vote; Legislators Plan to Push for Change," *St. Louis Post-Dispatch* (November 27, 2010), A1.

23 Missouri Judicial Selection Amendment (2011), https://ballotpedia.org/Missouri_Judicial_Selection_Amendment_(2011), accessed December 8, 2018.

24 See https://www.courts.mo.gov/page.jsp?id=158, accessed December 8, 2018.

25 Virginia Young, "Judge Selection Change on Ballot; Voters Will Decide Whether Governor Will Get More Say in Filling Appeals Court Bench," *St. Louis Post-Dispatch* (May 11, 2012), A1.

26 Elizabeth Crisp, "Election Won't End Fight over Judicial Selection; Conservatives Want More Voter Input and Less Control by Governor and Trial Lawyers," *St. Louis Post-Dispatch* (October 27, 2012), A1.

27 Watson and Downing, *Politics of Bench and Bar*, *supra* note 3, 32–38.

been members of the board of the state's largest organization of plaintiffs' lawyers. Interestingly, despite the success of the plaintiffs' bar in winning seats on the nominating commission,[28] the defense bar joined the plaintiffs' bar in opposing change in judicial selection.[29]

The supporters of the amendment halted their campaign about a month before the election, after a court rejected their challenge to the ballot summary prepared by the Secretary of State's office. They objected that the summary was unfair because it stated that the amendment dropped the requirement that the governor's appointments to the nominating commission be nonlawyers and failed to state that the primary purpose was to reduce the influence of the bar by increasing the number of commissioners appointed by the governor.[30] A group organized to oppose the amendment, Missourians for Fair and Impartial Courts Committee, ran advertisements as the election approached.[31] With no active campaign in support and an active opposition campaign, less than a quarter of voters supported the amendment.[32]

The aborted effort to change the structure of the nominating commission appears to have cooled the movement to change the judicial selection system in Missouri. The Gavel-to-Gavel database of legislative proposals lists no proposals to change Missouri's judicial selection system between 2013 and 2015.[33] It does show that proposed constitutional amendments were submitted in 2016, 2017, and 2018. One proposed to end retention elections, although the judicial nominating commission would continue to provide lists from which midterm vacancies would be filled. Others would end the specific requirement that the nominating commission submit three names, with some specifying that "all qualified persons" be on the list that was sent to the governor. None of the proposed constitutional amendments made it out of committee.

KANSAS

Kansas became the second state to adopt the Missouri Plan, doing so for its Supreme Court by passing a constitutional amendment in 1958.[34] Prior to this time, judges of

[28] James Hanson, "Battle Over Constitutional Amendment 3 Continues; Missourians for Better Courts Suspend Campaign," *Springfield Community Free Press* (October 31, 2012), 13.

[29] *Id.*; see also Jason Noble, "Opposing Lawyers' Groups Stand Together for Missouri Judicial Selection Process," *Kansas City Star* (February 12, 2008).

[30] David A. Lief, "Backers of Mo. Court Changes Drop Campaign Plans," Associated Press State Wire (October 12, 2012).

[31] Scott Lauck, "First Ads Against Missouri's Amendment 3 Come in Last Days," *Missouri Lawyer's Media* (October 26, 2012).

[32] "Missouri Judicial Appointment Amendment, Amendment 3 (2012)," https://ballotpedia.org/Missouri_Judicial_Appointment_Amendment,_Amendment_3_(2012), accessed December 8, 2018.

[33] See http://gaveltogavel.us/database/, accessed December 30, 2018.

[34] See www.judicialselection.us/judicial_selection/reform_efforts/formal_changes_since_inception.cfm?state=KS, accessed December 24, 2018.

the two Kansas courts specified in the state constitution, the Supreme Court and the district (trial) courts, ran in partisan elections, with vacancies filled by the governor.[35] The adoption of the Missouri Plan for justices of the Kansas Supreme Court came after a judicial selection scandal, known as the "triple play." This occurred at the end of 1956 and the beginning of 1957 in the wake of the sitting Republican governor being denied renomination by his party in 1956, and Kansans subsequently electing a Democrat for the first time in twenty years. The chief justice, who had been a strong supporter of the Republican incumbent, was considering retirement due to illness and did not want his successor to be selected by the incoming Democratic governor, who would be sworn in on January 14, 1957. A deal was struck whereby the chief justice resigned on December 31, 1956, the incumbent governor resigned on January 3, 1957, and the lieutenant governor left his hospital bed to appoint and swear in the outgoing governor as the new chief justice.[36] Proposals to adopt the Missouri Plan had been considered in the Kansas legislature earlier in the 1950s, but had failed to get out of the legislative committees.[37] The "triple play" scandal provided the impetus for the legislature to submit a constitutional amendment to the voters, who adopted it with about 56 percent in favor.[38]

In 1972, an amendment making several changes to the judicial article was submitted to the voters. One of those changes was to provide a "local option," allowing the voters of a judicial district to adopt the Missouri Plan for the district (trial) court.[39] The amendment passed with about 63 percent voting in favor.[40] As of 2018, 17 of the 31 districts have adopted the Missouri Plan, with the remaining 14 continuing to use partisan elections.[41] In 1975, the legislature created an intermediate court of appeals and specified that selection and retention of judges for that court be through the Missouri Plan.[42] The composition and selection of the nominating commission for the Supreme Court and the Court of Appeals is

[35] There was a brief period in the early twentieth century when judges were elected in non-partisan elections, but the legislature quickly repealed the legislation; see Jeffrey D. Jackson, "The Selection of Judges in Kansas: A Comparison of Systems," *Journal of the Kansas Bar Association* 69, no. 1 (January 2000), 33.

[36] Stacie L. Sanders, "Kissing Babies, Shaking Hands, and Campaign Contributions: Is This the Proper Role for the Kansas Judiciary," *Washburn Law Journal* 34, no. 3 (Summer 1995), 577–578.

[37] Jackson, "The Selection of Judges in Kansas," *supra* note 35, 34.

[38] This is based on incomplete election results; "All Three Amendments Are Passed," *Ottawa Herald* (November 5, 1958), 1. The eventual margin of victory was 93.275 votes; "Canvass Shows Vote Margin of 102,470," *Manhattan Mercury* (November 25, 1958), 1.

[39] *Id.*

[40] This is based on 97 percent of precincts reporting; see "No Surprise in State Contests," *Council Grove Republican* (November 8, 1972), 1.

[41] See Sanford C. Gordon and Gregory A. Huber, "The Effect of Electoral Competitiveness on Incumbent Behavior," *Quarterly Journal of Political Science* 2 (2007), 111–113; Kansas's 105 counties are organized into 31 judicial districts. See also ballotpedia.org/Judicial_selection_in_Kansas, accessed December 24, 2018.

[42] Jackson, "The Selection of Judges in Kansas," *supra* note 35, 34.

specified by statute; from each congressional district, one lawyer is elected by the bar and one nonlawyer is appointed by the governor, with the chairperson elected by the bar statewide.[43] Each district court nominating commission has equal numbers of lawyers (elected by the local bar) and nonlawyers (appointed by the county commissioners of the counties within the district) plus a chair appointed by the chief justice, who is either a justice of the Supreme Court or a district court judge.[44] Under the plan, the governor fills vacancies from the list of nominees forwarded by the nominating commissions. One unique feature of the Kansas system is that by statute, lawyers, including the judge who chairs the commission, hold a majority on the nominating commissions.[45]

It appears that the Missouri Plan operated with little controversy until the early 2000s. Through this period, the Republican Party controlled the state legislature for all but two 2-year periods, when the Democrats won control of the House of Representatives. However, between 1960 and 2002, Democrats held the governorship for 20 of those 43 years. Nonetheless, Republican appointees continued to dominate the Kansas Supreme Court. One indicator of this dominance is that 36 of the 48 Supreme Court retention elections during this period involved justices who had been appointed by Republican governors; 16 of the 21 individuals in those elections were Republican appointees. Things changed after 2003, when Democrat Kathleen Sebelius became governor. During her first year in office, she appointed three new justices to the Supreme Court. They joined a Democrat who had been appointed in 1993 by the previous Democratic governor; for the first time since the adoption of the Missouri Plan, the Court had a majority of justices who had been appointed by Democrats.[46] Additional appointments in 2007 and 2009 left a single Republican appointee on the Court. Between 2003 and 2018, only 4 of the 19 retention elections involved Republican appointees; only 2 of the 10 individuals standing in those elections were appointed by Republicans.

Decisions by the Kansas Supreme Court in late 2004 and early 2005 set off efforts to modify judicial selection and retention.[47] The first decision struck down the state's death penalty on a 4 to 3 vote; one Republican appointee joined the majority

[43] *Id.*, 42; currently there are 4 congressional districts, which means that the commission has 9 members; the size changes as the state's congressional delegation contracts (or potentially enlarges).

[44] *Id.*, 35.

[45] Stephen J. Ware, "Bar Has Too Much Power in Picking State's Judges," *Wichita Eagle* (November 29, 2007), 7A.

[46] Sebelius's immediate predecessor, Republican Bill Graves, was ideologically moderate and his appointees to the Kansas Supreme Court may also have been more moderate than conservative Republicans would have preferred; see Todd A. Curry and Michael K. Romano, "Ideological Congruity on State Supreme Courts," *Justice System Journal* 39, no. 2 (2018), 139–140.

[47] Tom Bell, "Judicial Tinkering Not Wise: Anger over Supreme Court Decision Drives Effort to Add Politics to Judge Selection Process," *Salina Journal* (April 28, 2005), A5. For a good overview of what was to follow, see Erik Eckholm, "Outraged by Court in Kansas, G.O.P. Sets Out to Reshape It," *New York Times* (April 2, 2016), A1.

and one Democratic appointee was in dissent.[48] The second decision, this one unanimous and coming just two weeks after the death penalty ruling, found that the school funding was inadequate and gave the legislature about three months to come up with more money.[49] The ruling contained a threat that the courts might take over the schools if the legislature failed to act, but it seemed likely that the only way to meet the Court's demand would be a significant tax increase.

In response to the Court's decisions, Republican legislators started talking about changing the selection system. The most prominent idea was to require that those chosen by the governor be confirmed by the legislature.[50] This would require a constitutional amendment, which needs a two-thirds vote in each chamber of the state legislature.[51] However, when the proposal came up for a vote in the Senate in March 2006, it garnered only 22 votes of the 27 needed, despite Republicans holding 30 of the 40 Senate seats.[52] Although the selection system for the Court of Appeals could be changed without the need for a constitutional amendment, Republicans did not hold the two-thirds of the seats in the House that would be needed to override a near certain veto by the Democratic governor. Republican legislators continued to push for change through the remainder of Sebelius's tenure as governor.

Going into the 2010 gubernatorial elections, conservative Republicans expressed dissatisfaction with the system for selecting appellate judges, and Sam Brownback, the Republican gubernatorial candidate, was reported to have questions as to whether the existing system violated Kansans' rights.[53] This came as a group of Kansas residents filed a federal lawsuit seeking to have the current system of selecting appellate (and some trial) judges ruled unconstitutional on the grounds that the voting rights of the state's residents were violated by lawyers making up a majority of the members of the nominating commission. The suit was brought by conservative Republicans who believed that the "lawyer-dominated selection process results in liberal-leaning judges."[54] The plaintiffs were seeking a court order blocking Mark Parkinson, the outgoing Democratic governor,[55] from filling a vacancy on the Supreme Court. Presaging what would happen at the federal level

48 Tony Rizzo and David Klepper, "Kansas Death Penalty Invalid," *Kansas City Star* (December 18, 2004), A1.

49 Steven Painter, "Find More School Funds, Supreme Court Orders; Lawmakers, Facing a Court-Imposed Deadline Just Three Months Away, Are Divided on Whether New Taxes Will Be Required," *Wichita Eagle* (January 4, 2005), 1A.

50 Mike Hendricks, "Legislative Fits, Suits and Politics," *Kansas City Star* (February 23, 2005), B1.

51 Kansas Constitution, Article 14, §1.

52 David Klepper, "Plan on Senate Confirmation of Judges Fails," *Kansas City Star* (March 10, 2006), B3.

53 John Hanna, "Court Debate Hints at Tilt to the Right," *Hays Daily News* (September 7, 2010).

54 Roxana Hegeman, "Judge Refused to Bar Kans. Supreme Court Nomination," *AP News Service* (September 14, 2010).

55 Parkinson had succeeded Kathleen Sebelius when she was appointed as Secretary of Health and Human Services by Barack Obama, but he was not running for Governor in 2010.

in 2016, they hoped that the Republican gubernatorial candidate would win the coming election and then be the person to make the appointment. The federal judge hearing the case first denied the plaintiffs' request for an injunction to halt the selection process then underway and then seven weeks later dismissed the suit.[56] Despite the plaintiffs' appeal of the dismissal,[57] the outgoing governor went ahead and filled the Supreme Court vacancy.

With Brownback's victory in the 2010 gubernatorial election, Republican legislators no longer needed to be concerned about a veto of legislation that would change judicial selection. Moreover, Republicans picked up sixteen seats in the House of Representatives so that they held well over two-thirds of the seats in both chambers of the legislature, meaning they could put constitutional amendments on the ballot with no support from Democratic legislators. That did not mean that Republicans would necessarily secure the two-thirds majority needed for constitutional amendments, however. This became evident early in the 2011 legislative session, when the House voted on a proposal that would remove the nominating commission from the selection process for Court of Appeals judges and add a requirement that the Senate confirm the governor's selections; the proposal easily passed, 67–46, but that was well short of the two-thirds (84 of 125) required for a constitutional amendment to change the selection of Supreme Court justices.[58] That proposal also faced some Republican opposition in the Senate,[59] and when it came up for a vote the following year, the Senate rejected the proposal 22–17,[60] with only 17 of 32 Republicans voting in favor.[61]

Things looked to change the following year. Nine moderate Republican incumbents were defeated in the 2012 primary election by candidates pledging to back Brownback's agenda.[62] In December, a legislative retreat for continuing and incoming Republican legislators included a session featuring University of Kansas law professor Stephen Ware, who was a strong proponent of ending the use of nominating commissions that constrained the governor's choice of whom to appoint as

56 Roxana Hegeman, "Challenge to Judicial Nominations Tossed," *Wichita Eagle* (November 4, 2010), 3B. See also Dool v. Burke, No. 10-1286-MLB, 2010 U.S. Dist. LEXIS 117294 (D. Kan. Nov. 3, 2010).

57 In an unpublished decision, Dool v. Burke, 497 Fed. Appx. 782 (10th Cir. Sept. 13, 2012), the 10th Circuit upheld the dismissal on a 2–1 vote; see Roxana Hegeman, "Appeals Court Upholds Kansas Judicial Selection," *Associated Press State Wire* (September 14, 2012).

58 Fredrick Johnson, "House Would Alter Judicial Selection," *Topeka Capital-Journal* (February 24, 2011).

59 Tim Carpenter, "Jury Out on Judicial Selection Reform," *Topeka Capital-Journal* (March 18, 2011).

60 Brad Cooper, "Kansas Senators Refuse to Give Governor More Power over Judges," *Kansas City Star* (February 23, 2010).

61 One Republican abstained and 14 voted against, as did all 8 Democrats; see "Kan. Senate Roll Call on Judicial Selection Bill," *Associated Press State Wire* (February 24, 2012).

62 C. Edward Flentje, "Gov. Brownback Clears Final Hurdle to Advance Agenda," *Insight Kansas* (November 13, 2012), A4.

judges.[63] Legislators wasted little time after convening in January in getting into the issue of judicial selection. Anticipating possible change, the state bar proposed that the composition of the nominating commission be changed, with 4 members (one from each congressional district) elected by the bar, 5 appointed by the governor, and 6 selected by various legislative leaders including leaders of both the majority and the minority.[64] This was a change that the legislature could make without a constitutional amendment, both for the Supreme Court and for the Court of Appeals, because the structure of the nominating commission was determined though legislation not by the state constitution.

As legislators were starting to hold hearings on possible changes to judicial selection,[65] Justice at Stake was conducting a poll of Kansans asking their view on changing the state constitution to eliminate the role of the nominating commission.[66] The poll showed that 61 percent of the 975 respondents opposed such a change, with only 21 percent in favor. This led to the Republican chairperson of the Kansas House Judiciary Committee questioning the credibility of the poll on the grounds that it was sponsored by an organization that was backed by George Soros, who was "attempting to block judicial selection reform in Kansas."[67] Not mentioned by the critical legislator was that among self-described Republicans (48 percent of respondents compared to 28 percent self-described Democrats) only 24 percent supported the change, with 57 percent opposed.[68]

Despite the apparent opposition of the public, in January 2013 the House Judiciary Committee quickly approved a proposed constitutional amendment that would eliminate the constraint of a nominating commission and would provide for Senate confirmation of the governor's selection for justices of the Supreme Court; it specified the same system for the Court of Appeals.[69] Two days later, the

63 Brent D. Wistrom, "Lawmakers Hear Arguments for Changing State's Court Selection Process at Legislative Retreat," *Wichita Eagle* (December 8, 2012); see also Tim Carpenter, "KU Professor, Kansas GOP Urge Constitutional Amendment on Supreme Court Selection," *Topeka Capital-Journal* (February 3, 2016). Ware's view was that the dominant role of lawyers in the selection process violated the "one-person, one-vote foundation of democracy." See also Stephen J. Ware, "Selection to the Kansas Supreme Court," *Kansas Journal of Law & Public Policy* 17 (2008), 386–423; or Stephen J. Ware, "The Missouri Plan in National Perspective," *Missouri Law Review* 74 (2009), 758–766.

64 Brad Cooper, "Expect Kansas Legislature to Tackle How State Judges Are Selected," *Kansas City Star* (January 8, 2013); "Bar Association Offers to Give Up Lawyers' Majority in Choosing Supreme and Appeals Court Judges," *Wichita Eagle* (January 21, 2013).

65 John Milburn, "Legislators Open Hearing on Kan. Judicial Changes," *Associated Press State Wire* (January 17, 2013).

66 The survey was conducted January 13–14, 2012.

67 Andy Marso, "House Member: Judicial Selection Poll Not Unbiased," *Topeka Capital-Journal* (January 21, 2013).

68 See www.brennancenter.org/sites/default/files/2013_Kansas_Poll_D8D19B1CC59DC.pdf, accessed December 25, 2018.

69 "Kansas House Panel Passes Judicial Selection Change," *Garden City Telegram* (January 23, 2013).

Senate Judiciary Committee passed a similar proposed amendment.[70] Less than a week after the approval in committee, the full Senate passed the proposal on a 28–12 vote, just one more than the required two-thirds.[71] There was some question about whether the necessary two-thirds could be mustered in the House because of doubt regarding support from some or all of the 10 moderate Republicans in that chamber; Republicans could afford to lose no more than 8 of those 10, assuming that all Democrats voted against.

The legislature also moved forward with changing selection of Court of Appeals judges by simple legislation. With the expectation of the governor's signature, all that was needed was a majority in each chamber. By mid-March, both chambers had passed the needed legislation and sent it to the governor,[72] who signed the bill two weeks later.[73] The governor now had the "sole power to select nominees" for the Court of Appeals, subject to Senate confirmation.[74]

Meanwhile, the proposed constitutional amendment remained stalled in the House of Representatives.[75] An alternative amendment was suggested by the chair of the Senate Judiciary Committee; this proposal would add Senate confirmation while retaining the role of the nominating commission, but change the commission's composition so that the governor would appoint 5 of the 9 members, which would mean that lawyers would no longer hold a majority.[76] The proposal died after the state bar came out in opposition. Although the bar had previously expressed support of a plan that would diminish its role on the nominating commission, it opposed the new proposal because it gave the governor too much power;[77] the bar's proposal would have had legislative leaders from both parties appointing members of the commission along with appointments made by the governor and lawyers elected by the bar.[78] Although additional proposals were advanced after the bar's rejection of

70 John Hanna, "Kan. Senate Panel Back Judicial Selection Change," *Associated Press State Wire* (January 25, 2013).

71 Brent D. Wistrom, "Senate Oks Proposed Constitutional Amendment Changing How Judges Are Chosen," *Wichita Eagle* (January 31, 2013).

72 "Kan. Senate Approves Bill on Judicial Selection," *Associated Press Wire* (March 13, 2013); the Senate vote was 28–12, which indicates that at least 4 Republicans voted in the negative.

73 John Milburn, "Kan. Gov. Signs Court of Appeals Change Bill," *Associated Press State Wire* (March 27, 2013).

74 *Id.*

75 John Hanna, "Kansas Judicial Selection Change Being Pursued," *Associated Press Wire* (May 7, 2013).

76 John Hanna, "New Plan for Kan. Judiciary Emerges," *Associated Press State Wire* (May 14, 2013).

77 John Hanna, "Kansas Bar Opposes New Judicial Selection Bill," *Hays Daily News* (May 14, 2013).

78 "Bar Association Offers to Give Up Lawyers' Majority in Choosing Supreme and Appeals Court Judges," *Wichita Eagle* (January 21, 2013).

the Senate proposal,[79] there was no further action in 2013 beyond approval of one plan in a House committee.[80]

Over the summer of 2013, the debate over judicial selection continued, spurred in part by how the governor handled his first selection for the Court of Appeals under the new law that took effect in July. Brownback declined to reveal who was being considered for the vacant position, and then nominated, Caleb Stegall, his 41-year-old chief of staff;[81] Brownback's secrecy contrasted with the procedure of the nominating commission, which disclosed the names of the persons being considered for nomination.[82] The nominee was easily confirmed by the Republican Senate, 32–8,[83] and Stegall was sworn in on January 3, 2014. Only eight months later, his name was among three sent by the nominating commission to the governor for a position on the Kansas Supreme Court; not surprisingly, Brownback selected Stegall for the position,[84] and he was sworn in on December 5, 2014.

Despite speculation that the debate over judicial selection was far from over,[85] and prominent support for change from the state's leading antiabortion group, Kansans for Life,[86] the stalemate continued in the Kansas House of Representatives. Nothing moved forward during the 2014 legislative session. Changing judicial selection became a topic of debate in the 2014 gubernatorial election,[87] spurred in part by the Kansas Supreme Court's decision overturning the death sentences of two brothers who had been convicted of robbery, rape, and murder in connection with a

[79] John Hanna, "New Court Overhaul Plans Surface in Kansas House," *Associated Press Wire* (May 15, 2013).

[80] Tim Carpenter, "House Panel Endorses Major Judicial Overhaul," *Topeka Capital-Journal* (May 15, 2013); Brad Cooper, "In Kansas, It's Lawmakers Versus the Courts, *Kansas City Star* (May 19, 2013).

[81] Stegall had previously applied twice to the nominating commission that had now be removed from the process; both times the commission had chosen not to forward his name to the governor. See Tim Carpenter, "Senate Committee Endorses Stegall for Court of Appeals," *Topeka Capital-Journal* (September 3, 2013), www.cjonline.com/news/2013-09-03/Senate-committee-endorses-stegall-court-appeals, accessed December 26, 2018.

[82] John Hanna, "Process Stirs Angst in Kan. Court Debate," *Associated Press Wire* (September 1, 2013).

[83] Tim Carpenter, "Senate Easily Confirms Stegall to Appellate Court," *Topeka Capital-Journal* (September 4, 2013); the 32–8 vote exactly matched the Republican–Democratic split in the Senate.

[84] "Gov. Sam Brownback Names Caleb Stegall to Kansas Supreme Court," *Garner News* (September 4, 2014), https://gardnernews.com/gov-sam-brownback-names-caleb-stegall-to-kansas-supreme-court/, accessed December 26, 2018.

[85] John Hanna, "Kansas Lawmakers Aren't Done with Debate over Courts," *Dodge City Daily Globe* (September 7, 2013), 1.

[86] Celia Llopis-Jepsen, "Anti-Abortion Group Seeks Supreme Court Changes," *Topeka Capital-Journal* (January 22, 2014).

[87] Tim Carpenter, "Brownback, Davis Feud over Judge Selection, Carr Brothers," *Topeka Capital-Journal* (October 21, 2014).

crime spree that resulted in the deaths of five persons.[88] An effort was made to defeat two Kansas Supreme Court justices who had voted to overturn the death sentence. However, that effort narrowly failed; both justices barely won retention, with 52.7 percent voting in favor.[89] No previous Kansas Supreme Court justice standing for retention had received less than 60 percent. Nonetheless, Brownback was reelected in 2014, and his push for changing the selection system for the Supreme Court continued, with some arguing that the governor was linking the judicial selection to the still-unresolved issue of school finance, which had helped set off the judicial selection debate ten years earlier.[90]

When the new legislature convened in 2015, proposals for a constitutional amendment changing the selection of the justices of the Supreme Court were once again introduced. One proposal would duplicate the system that had been adopted for the Court of Appeals: abolish the nominating commission and subject the governor's nominees to Senate confirmation. A second proposal would institute popular elections for both levels of appellate courts.[91] The House Judiciary Committee approved both proposals and sent them to the full House for debate.[92] The Republican majority in the House had increased in the 2014 election, with Republicans now holding 98 seats, which meant that they could muster the needed two-thirds even if 14 of their colleagues defected. However, soon after the committee approval, another poll of Kansans was released. A majority (53 percent) favored the current system of "merit selection," and 55 percent opposed replacing the existing system with one that involved contested judicial elections;[93] 76 percent opposed switching "from the current merit selection system" to one in which "judges would be chosen by the governor without first being recommended by the panel . . . then confirmed by the state Senate . . . [and then] face periodic retention elections."[94]

88 Jeffrey Stinson, "Battle for State Court Control Intensifies," *PEW Stateline* (September 17, 2014), www.pewtrusts.org/en/research-and-analysis/blogs/stateline/2014/09/17/battle-for-state-court-control-intensifies, accessed December 25, 2018.

89 Dan Margolies, "Kansas Judges Targeted for Ouster Retain Seats," *KCUR* (November 4, 2014), www.kcur.org/post/kansas-judges-targeted-ouster-retain-seats#stream/0, accessed December 31, 2018.

90 Bryan Lowry, "Gov. Sam Brownback's Push to Change Kansas Supreme Court Seen as Linked to School Finance," *Kansas City Star* (January 24, 2015). www.kcur.org/post/kansas-judges-targeted-ouster-retain-seats#stream/0. A trial judge was also targeted for ouster for having ordered the court clerk to issue marriage licenses to same-sex couples after a federal district judge had ruled that the Kansas same-sex marriage ban was unconstitutional; that judge was also retained.

91 Tim Carpenter, "Kansas Lawmakers Tangle over Judicial Reform Amendments," *Topeka Capital-Journal* (February 11, 2015).

92 "Proposals Advance to Change How Kansas Picks Highest Court," *Associated Press Wire* (February 17, 2015).

93 "Poll Casts Doubt on Support for High Court Reform," *Wichita Eagle* (March 4, 2015).

94 See www.brennancenter.org/sites/default/files/2015%202020%20Insight%20Kansas%20Poll.pdf, accessed December 25, 2018.

Nothing further happened legislatively during 2015 regarding the constitutional amendment. Still, the conflict between the Republicans controlling the "political" branches of the state government and the courts intensified. The legislature provided funding for the state courts conditional on the Kansas Supreme Court ruling the way the legislature wanted in cases challenging a 2014 law that reduced the administrative authority of the Supreme Court.[95] The legal challenge arose because the Kansas constitution specifies that "the supreme court shall have general administrative authority over all courts in this state."[96] At the same time that the cases involving the Supreme Court's administrative power were being litigated, the Supreme Court released decisions involving abortion and the ongoing issue of school finance that the governor labeled as "politically motivated." The governor renewed his call for what he labeled a "more democratic" selection process.[97] Just before Christmas 2015, the Supreme Court unanimously (i.e., including Justice Stegall , who had been appointed by Brownback) struck down part of the law that reduced the Court's administrative authority by shifting the appointment of chief judges of the district courts from the Supreme Court to an election by the judges working in the district.[98] However, funding did not immediately cease, because an injunction kept funding flowing to the courts,[99] and the legislature repealed the defunding provision about two months later.[100]

In early February 2016, the proposed amendment, which would end the nominating commission and free governors to nominate whomever they preferred, subject to Senate confirmation, came up for a vote in the House. Some speculated that the vote was not held until 2016 so that conservatives could use votes against the proposal in campaigns to unseat Democrats and moderate Republicans.[101] The vote, 68–54, fell well short of the required 84 votes constituting two-thirds.[102] About a week after the House vote, the Supreme Court stirred the pot again by imposing a deadline of June 30 for the legislature to adopt a school finance system that met constitutional

[95] Barbara Shelly, "Gov. Sam Brownback and Kansas Legislature Mount Breathtaking Assault on Judges' Independence," *Kansas City Star* (June 18, 2015).

[96] Kansas Constitution, Article 3, §1.

[97] Luke Ranker, "Gov. Sam Brownback's Office Criticizes Court Rulings, Calls for Change in Judicial Selection," *Topeka Capital-Journal* (June 29, 2015).

[98] Edward M. Eveld, "Kansas Supreme Court Rules against Legislature in Separation-of-Powers Case," *Kansas City Star* (December 23, 2015).

[99] Jonathan Shorman, "Court Strikes Down Judicial Selection Law," *Topeka Capital-Journal* (December 24, 2015), 1A.

[100] "Impeaching Justices Next Best Thing to Defunding Courts?" *Wichita Eagle* (February 20, 2016).

[101] Edward M. Eveld, "Kansas House Debates Changing the Supreme Court Selection Process," *Kansas City Star* (February 3, 2016).

[102] Daniel Salazar, "Kansas Supreme Court Selection Change Dies in House," *Wichita Eagle* (February 4, 2016). See also John Hawks, "State Reps Defend Opposing Votes on Judicial Selection," *Ottawa Herald* (February 18, 2016); this article presents the positions of two Republicans, one who voted for the amendment and one who voted against.

standards.[103] Later, during the legislative session, a variety of bills to modify the operation, and potentially the membership, of the Supreme Court nominating commission were introduced;[104] one dealing with transparency in the nominating and selection process made it into law.[105] Earlier in the session, the Senate considered but then removed a provision that would have included "attempting to usurp the power of the legislature or executive branch" in legislation specifying grounds for impeachment of judges or justices.[106]

Over the summer of 2016, Republicans turned their attention to the 2016 Supreme Court retention elections in which four of the Democratic appointees would be standing for retention. A fifth justice, Brownback appointee Caleb Stegall, would also be on the retention ballot. As noted previously, two years earlier Brownback had come out against the retention of two of Sebelius's appointees, and they had been only narrowly retained with more than 47 percent voting to remove the two from office.[107] Brownback chose to leave the 2016 retention fight to others, but four former Kansas governors, two Democrats and two Republicans, came out in support of retaining all five justices.[108] Two former state attorney generals, one Republican and one Democrat, also came out in support of retention.[109]

Groups organized to raise funds to support or to oppose retention of the four Democratic appointees; joining the "do-not-retain" side, the antiabortion group Kansans for Life, also joined the fray.[110] A survey from the previous February found that only 21 percent of Kansans were somewhat or very dissatisfied with the Supreme

103 Jonathan Shorman, "School Funding Ruling Roils Legislature, Provoking Fury toward Justices," *Topeka Capital-Journal* (February 11, 2016).

104 Melissa Hellmann, "Kansas House Reconsiders Changing Judicial Selection Process," *Associated Press Wire* (May 1, 2016).

105 Bryan Lowry, "Brownback Signs Judicial Transparency Bill," *Wichita Eagle* (May 18, 2016); the law also required the governor to disclose the names of persons who applied for appointment to vacancies on the Court of Appeals.

106 Tim Carpenter, "Kansas Senators Dodge Fight on Judicial Impeachment Bill," *Topeka Capital Journal* (February 22, 2016).

107 Jonathan Shorman, "Former Kansas Governors Jumping into Judicial Retention Races," *Topeka Capital-Journal* (September 2, 2016).

108 *Id.* Although Brownback was not active in the campaign against retention, his PAC donated $65,000 to the antiabortion group campaigning to oust four of the justices; see Bryan Lowry, "Brownback's PAC Gives Thousands to Group Seeking to Oust Justices," *Wichita Eagle* (November 1, 2016).

109 Tim Carpenter, "Former Kansas A.G.s Bob Stephan, Steve Six Urge Retention of All Supreme Court Justices," *Topeka Capital-Journal* (October 17, 2016).

110 Jonathan Shorman, "Judicial Retention Campaigns Heat Up; Little Disclosure of Donors and Spending," *Hays Daily News* (August 15, 2016); Ryan D. Wilson, "Conservatives Aim to Oust 'Activist' Judges," *St. Joseph News-Press* (October 27, 2016). In the last days of the campaign, the Kansas State Rifle Association launched a campaign of robocalls asking voters to vote no on retention of the justices; see Jonathan Shorman, "Call Urges Ouster of 'Anti-Gun' Justices, But Group Behind Plea Admits No Recent Rulings; Kansas State Rifle Association in Robo Call Asks Voters to Non-Retain Kansas Supreme Court Justices," *Topeka Capital-Journal* (November 6, 2016).

Court with 45 percent very satisfied or somewhat satisfied; another 33 percent were neutral.[111] A survey of lawyers and judges conducted for the Kansas Judicial Evaluation Committee found that about three-quarters or more of both lawyers and judges "strongly" recommended retention of the four Democratic-appointed justices; support was weaker for Brownback's appointee to the Court, with only 39 percent of lawyers and 54 percent of judges strongly recommending that he be retained.[112] Groups opposing and supporting retention of the four Democratic appointees aired advertisements on broadcast television, each side spending about $1 million for a total of about 3,000 ad airings.[113] The ads opposing retention focused on the Supreme Court's death penalty decisions; the ads supporting retention attacked the attackers as wanting, in the words of one ad, "five Brownback clones on the Kansas Supreme Court."[114] All five justices were retained, with Brownback's appointee receiving a 71 percent positive vote and the four Democratic appointees a 55 to 56 percent favorable vote.[115] My analysis shows that there was a substantial correlation between county-level support for Brownback in the 2014 gubernatorial election and the county-level percentage voting to oust the four Democratic appointees running for retention;[116] there was no similar correlation, either for or against retention, in the vote regarding Brownback's own appointee to the Kansas Supreme Court.[117]

The retention of the justices was probably one of two factors that quieted the conservative Republicans in their legislative efforts to change the system of selecting Supreme Court justices. The second factor was the defeat of a significant number of conservative Republican legislators in 2016, either in the Republican primary by more moderate candidates or in the general election by Democrats;[118] Republicans lost 13 seats in the House of Representatives.[119] Although Republicans maintained a majority that in theory was sufficient to pass a constitutional amendment changing judicial selection, two dozen conservative Republican legislators

[111] Shorman, "Judicial Retention Campaign Heats Up," *supra* note 110.

[112] Tim Carpenter, "Legal Survey Shows 4 of 5 Supreme Court Justices Favored for Retention; Brownback's Appointee Ranked Lowest," *Topeka Capital-Journal* (August 9, 2016).

[113] These figures are based on estimates by the Campaign Media Analysis Group (CMAG) provided to the author by the Brennan Center for Justice, New York University Law School. There had been no broadcast television advertising in 2014.

[114] See www.brennancenter.org/sites/default/files/analysis/Buying_Time/STSUPCT_KS_KSFC_BROWNBACK_CLONES.pdf, accessed December 26, 2018.

[115] Jonathan Shorman, "Kansas Voters Retain All Kansas Supreme Court Justices," *Topeka Capital Journal* (November 8, 2016).

[116] This is what I have previously labeled the "partisan correlation," defined in Chapter 1.

[117] The correlation for the four Democratic appointees was .715 to .727; for Caleb Stegall, Brownback's appointee, the correlation was –.008. The correlations in the 2014 elections were .606 and .633.

[118] Tim Carpenter, "Legislative Election Postmortem Focuses on Brownback's Key Role," *Topeka Capital-Journal* (November 30, 2016).

[119] The house went from 98–27 Republican to 85–40 Republican; see https://en.wikipedia.org/wiki/Political_party_strength_in_Kansas, accessed December 26, 2018.

had decided not to run for reelection and another 14, 8 in the House and 6 in the Senate, had lost to more moderate Republicans in the primary election. As best I could determine, there were no significant efforts to change judicial selection in the 2017–2018 legislature.

The 2018 election saw conservative Republicans defeat their moderate Republican incumbents in about a half-dozen House elections. However, the partisan division was unchanged by the November election.[120] Even with more conservatives in their caucus, Republicans almost certainly lack the votes needed to push through a constitutional amendment changing judicial selection, something they might want to accomplish, given the narrow victory of the Democratic gubernatorial candidate Laura Kelly. Several weeks after the November election, Kelly announced that she would reinstitute by executive order the use of a nominating commission to screen and recommend candidates for appointment to the Court of Appeals.[121] However, unlike appointments to the Supreme Court, Kelly's selection for the Court of Appeals will still face confirmation by the Senate.

The Kansas Supreme Court's 6–1 decision in April 2019 finding that the Kansas constitution protected the right to abortion may provide renewed efforts to change the method of selection of Supreme Court justices.[122] Republicans hold enough seats in each chamber of the Kansas legislature to get a constitutional amendment on the ballot, assuming all Republican legislators backed the effort, something that has not happened in the past. The decision could lead to renewed efforts to defeat the 6 majority justices when they stand for retention; 2 will need to stand in 2020 and 4 in 2022.[123]

OKLAHOMA

Until an overhaul of the judicial article of the Oklahoma constitution that was adopted by the voters at a special election in July 1967, the Oklahoma court system was a hodgepodge of 18 different courts, and all judges were selected through partisan elections, with the governor filling vacancies on many courts through appointment.[124] Similar to Texas, Oklahoma had, and still has, a separate final court

[120] Democrats actually picked up a seat in December when one Republican representative switched parties; see https://en.wikipedia.org/wiki/Political_party_strength_in_Kansas#cite_note-25, accessed December 26, 2018.

[121] "Kelly to Change the Way Appeals Judges Are Picked," *Associated Press State Wire* (November 29, 2018).

[122] Hodes & Nauser, MDs, et al. v. Schmidt and Howe, no. 114,153, Supreme Court of Kansas (April 26, 2019), www.kscourts.org/Cases-and-Opinions/Opinions/SupCt/2019/20190426/114153.pdf). See also Sabrina Tavernise and Campbell Robertson, "Judges Find Legal Shield for Abortion in Kansas," *New York Times* (April 26, 2019), A215.

[123] None of the current justices will have to retire before his or her current term ends.

[124] James L. Sneed, "Revisiting 1967 Judicial Reform in 1998," *Tulsa World* (November 29, 1998), 6.

of appeal for criminal cases, the Court of Criminal Appeals. Until 1968, there was no intermediate court of appeals for civil matters; all civil appeals went to and were decided by the Oklahoma Supreme Court. A campaign to modernize the court system gained some momentum after the 1962 Conference on Modern Courts for Oklahoma. Among other changes, that conference called for the adoption of a system of judicial selection that produced judges who were "selected solely on the basis of their qualifications for judicial office rather than on the ability to campaign and to obtain partisan support."[125]

Efforts to reorganize the courts, including adopting "merit" selection for some or all courts, continued over the next five years. An effort to put an amendment on the ballot through an initiative process was undertaken by the League of Women Voters, and enough signatures were obtained to get the measure before the voters.[126] The effort was undoubtedly aided by a series of scandals involving justices of the Oklahoma Supreme Court: one justice was convicted of federal tax evasion, a second pled no contest on a similar charge, and a third was impeached and convicted on bribery charges.[127]

While the courts were considering the issue of whether the initiative effort had obtained sufficient signatures, the legislature in its 1967 session voted to put amendments on the ballot that did not go as far as the initiative amendment. The primary amendment was an overhaul of the structure of the court system; it included changes to selection that would make all judicial elections nonpartisan, leaving it to the legislature to specify the system for filling midterm judicial vacancies. A second amendment was also placed on the ballot, which would apply only if the reorganization amendment was adopted by the voters; that amendment would adopt the Missouri Plan for the selection and retention of appellate judges.[128] The composition of the nominating commission was specified in the amendment: one nonlawyer from each of the 6 congressional districts appointed by the governor, one member of the Oklahoma Bar Association from each of the 6 congressional districts elected by the active members of the bar in the district, and one nonlawyer at-large member selected by not less than 8 of the other commissioners, with the proviso that if 8 commissioners could not agree, the at-large member would be selected by the governor. Although organized labor announced opposition to the Missouri Plan, it was adopted at a special election held in July 1967, with 55.1 percent voting in

[125] Quoted in Jack N. Hays, "Oklahoma Moves Forward in Judicial Selection," *Tulsa Law Journal* 6, no. 2 (March 1970), 89.

[126] *Id.*, 90; the number of required signatures is based on the total votes cast for governor in the last gubernatorial election.

[127] *Id.*, 89; more detail on the scandal can be found in Phillip Simpson, "The Modernization and Reform of the Oklahoma Judiciary," *Oklahoma Politics* 3 (1994), 6–7, ojs.library.okstate.edu/osu/index.php/OKPolitics/article/download/888/799. accessed December 27, 2018.

[128] Hays, "Oklahoma Moves Forward in Judicial Selection," *supra* note 125, 91–93.

favor.[129] The legislature subsequently specified that vacancies on courts not covered by the Missouri Plan, other than justices of the peace, should be filled by gubernatorial appointment and authorized the governor to utilize the services of the judicial nominating commission if the governor so chose.[130] In 1980, legislation was passed requiring the governor to fill vacancies on the lower courts from lists provided by the judicial nominating commission.[131]

In November 1967, the Oklahoma Supreme Court verified the initiative's required signatures and thus cleared the way to put the more extensive reform that was the subject of the initiative effort on the ballot.[132] That reform would have extended the Missouri Plan to all Oklahoma judges. At a special election in September 1968, the proposal was supported by only 40.3 percent of the voters,[133] leaving the selection of lower court judges to be through nonpartisan elections. Earlier that year, the Oklahoma legislature created the Court of Appeals to reduce the burden on the Supreme Court; judges of this new court, which started operating in 1970 and which decided cases referred to it by the Oklahoma Supreme Court,[134] were chosen through nonpartisan elections until 1987, when the existing Missouri Plan for the other two appellate courts was extended to the now renamed Court of Civil Appeals.[135]

For the first twenty years (1968–1988), retention elections produced positive retention votes averaging almost 69.7 percent. The only election with a retain percentage below 62 percent was in 1968, the first year of such elections, for Court of Criminal Appeals Judge Kirksey Nix. Nix was just barely retained, with a positive vote of only 51.9 percent. Nix had won his seat ten years earlier by defeating the Democratic incumbent in the Democratic runoff election. The likely reason for Nix's poor performance was news coverage regarding his son, who was associated with what was known as the "Dixie Mafia" and was awaiting trial on murder charges in Louisiana.[136] Nix's percentage for retention is the lowest received by any judge or justice of the two courts of last resort.

During the 1990s, the average supporting retention across the three appellate courts dropped to 60.9 percent but rebounded to 65.4 percent between 2000 and 2018. The drop was precipitous; in 1988, the average vote favoring retention was 67.8 percent, but the average dropped to 57.0 percent in 1990. There does not appear to

[129] *Id.*, 94. This was the vote specifically on the Missouri Plan; the vote on the overall amendment was 52.2 percent in favor.
[130] *Oklahoma Session Laws* 1968, Chapter 49 (p. 63).
[131] *Oklahoma Session Laws* 1980, Chapter 272, §28 (p. 640).
[132] Simpson, "The Modernization and Reform of the Oklahoma Judiciary," *supra* note 127, 9–10.
[133] Hays, "Oklahoma Moves Forward in Judicial Selection," *supra* note 125, 94.
[134] *Oklahoma Statutes*, Title 20, §20-30.1.
[135] *Oklahoma Session Laws*, 1966, Chapter 97, §§1, 12–13.
[136] See Herbert M. Kritzer, *Justices on the Ballot: Continuity and Change in State Supreme Court Elections* (New York: Cambridge University Press, 2015), 223n.25; Kirksey Nix Jr. was convicted and sentenced to life in prison.

have been any specific precipitating event or set of events, and the drop came as a surprise to the judges.[137] The best explanation was a general dissatisfaction or lack of understanding of the role of the appellate courts,[138] or possibly it simply reflected the broader anti-incumbent mood of the period.[139] In 1994, there was explicit opposition to the retention of two of the Court of Criminal Appeals judges standing for retention.[140] Both of those judges, along with twelve other appellate-level judges, were retained, and the percentage supporting retention for the two judges who faced some opposition were only slightly lower compared to the others running for retention. There does not appear to have been any effort to modify the selection and retention system for appellate judges during this period.

During the 1990s, there were some calls for extending the Missouri Plan system to trial-level judges.[141] In 1999, the Oklahoma Senate passed a joint resolution calling for a vote on a constitutional amendment that would make such a change,[142] but there was no action in the House of Representatives. There were also proposals to replace the governor's role of filling trial court vacancies with special elections; in 1999, the House of Representatives passed such a bill, but it failed in the Senate,[143] and the next year, the reverse happened with the bill passing in the Senate but being defeated in the House of Representatives.[144]

Efforts to end or limit the use of the Missouri Plan for Oklahoma's appellate courts seem to have begun in the latter half of the first decade of the new century. Republicans captured control of the Oklahoma House of Representatives for the first time in the state's history in the 2004 election, and the Oklahoma Senate in 2008.[145] At this time, there was a Democratic governor, although over the 41-year period from 1968 through 2008 that the Missouri Plan had been in operation, Republicans had held the governorship for 15 years. Eight of the nine justices of the Oklahoma Supreme Court had been appointed by Democrats. In 2008, the House passed a

137 "Judges Note Negative Votes; Eight Counties Reject All State Jurists," *Tulsa World* (November 8, 1990), 5A.

138 Rob Martindale, "Unpopular Laws, System Blamed for 'No' Votes," *Tulsa World* (November 15, 1990), A1.

139 Jim East, "State Judges Expect the Worst in Retention Voting," *Tulsa World* (May 11, 1992), 6A.

140 Julie DelCour, "Appeals Judges Fret over Vote," *Tulsa World* (October 27, 1994), N15; Barbara Hoderock, "Appeals Judge Fights Critics' Ouster Efforts," *Tulsa World* (November 5, 1994), N19.

141 Laura Casaday, "State Chief Justice Urges Appointment of Judges," *Tulsa World* (November 14, 1991), 3A; Chuck Ervin, "Vote Sought to Alter System for Selecting Judges," *Tulsa World* November 12, 1998), 11.

142 John Greiner, "Senate Favors Retention Vote for State Judges," *Oklahoman* (March 11, 1999), 7.

143 See www.judicialselection.us/judicial_selection/reform_efforts/failed_reform_efforts.cfm?state=OK, accessed December 28, 2018.

144 Mick Hinton, "Status Quo Kept on Judge Selection; Defeated House Bill Called for Elections," *Oklahoman* (April 19, 2000), 4A.

145 See https://en.wikipedia.org/wiki/Political_party_strength_in_Oklahoma, accessed December 28, 2018.

measure that would lead to a requirement of confirmation by the Senate of appointments the governor made to fill appellate vacancies,[146] but it failed to pass the Senate.[147] The following year, the legislature sent a constitutional amendment to the voters that would modify the membership of the judicial nominating commission by adding two more non-attorney members, one appointed by the Speaker of the Oklahoma House of Representatives and one appointed by the president pro tempore of the Oklahoma Senate; at the November 2010 election, the change was approved by the voters, with 62.8 percent in favor.[148]

Concerted efforts to end the Missouri Plan constraints appear to have begun with the 2011 legislative session. The Republican-controlled Senate passed on a straight party-line vote a proposed constitutional amendment ending the role of the judicial nominating commission and adding a requirement of Senate confirmation; this was not something sought by Mary Fallin, the new Republican governor. The Senate also passed, again on a straight party-line vote, a proposed amendment that would have only added the requirement of Senate confirmation.[149] Both proposals died due to inaction by the House.

The assault on the judicial selection system intensified starting in 2013, at which time it was still the case that 8 of the 9 Supreme Court justices had been selected by Democratic governors. The Senate again passed a proposal that would lead to the end of the judicial nominating commission, this time on a near party-line vote (one Democrat voted in favor and two Republicans against).[150] The House failed to act during the regular legislative session. In June, after the legislature adjourned, the Supreme Court struck down legislation passed in 2009 that was ostensibly intended to "reduce the number of frivolous lawsuits and medical malpractice claims filed in Oklahoma;"[151] the Court ruled that the legislature had violated the state's "single-subject" rule by packing too many things into a single piece of legislation. This led to calls for a special legislative session to respond to the Supreme Court's decision, with some fearing that a special session would end up changing the system of judicial selection.[152] A special session was called, but it was limited to producing legislation implementing the litigation reforms in a way that would pass

146 Mick Hinton, "Judicial Selection Measure Advances," *Tulsa World* (April 25, 2008), A9.

147 See www.judicialselection.us/judicial_selection/reform_efforts/failed_reform_efforts.cfm?state=OK, accessed December 28, 2018.

148 See www.ok.gov/elections/support/10gen.html, accessed December 28, 2018.

149 Barbara Hoberock, "Two Bills on Choosing Judges Pass Senate," *Tulsa World* (March 13, 2011), A22. Note that the information on voting in the legislature is from the Oklahoma Legislature's bill tracking system, www.oklegislature.gov/AdvancedSearchForm.aspx, accessed December 28, 2018.

150 Barbara Hoberock, "Judicial Reform School Safety Measures OK'd," *Tulsa World* (March 114, 2013), A10.

151 Tim Talley, "Okla. Governor Orders Special Legislative Session," *Associated Press State Wire* (August 12, 2013).

152 Barbara Hoberock, "Special Session Focus on Judiciary Curbs Feared," *Tulsa World* (July 26, 2013), A4.

constitutional muster.[153] In a six-day special session, the legislature passed and sent to the governor twenty-five bills changing various aspects of the litigation system.[154]

Even before the special session convened, the Supreme Court's striking down of the litigation reform law produced further suggestions that changes to judicial selection might be in the offing.[155] Despite denials from the chief justice that there was tension between the Supreme Court and the other two branches of government,[156] a House committee, which had undertaken a study of judicial reform at the request of the House Speaker after the Supreme Court's June decision, was told by one speaker that the Oklahoma judges were "attacking the legislative branch of government."[157] At the same meeting, the Oklahoma Supreme Court was labeled as "antibusiness," and the idea of term limits for judges was suggested.[158] Some of the speakers criticizing the courts came from, represented, or worked with conservative national organizations, including the U.S. Chamber of Commerce, the American Legislative Exchange Council, and the Judicial Crisis Network.[159]

A week before the legislature convened on February 3, 2014, the Speaker of the Oklahoma House of Representatives filed three bills that would alter the selection and tenure of appellate judges. One would impose a mandatory retirement age of 75, one would impose a 12-year term limit, and the third would create a board, appointed by the legislature, that would evaluate state judges.[160] Two weeks into the legislative session, the Senate Rules Committee approved the proposed constitutional amendment, which would have shifted the selection of attorney members of the Judicial Nominating Commission from election by the bar to appointment by legislative leaders;[161] three weeks later, the Senate passed the proposal on a near party-line vote. However, in the House, the proposal attracted bipartisan opposition and was soundly defeated 31–65.[162]

In June 2015, the Oklahoma Supreme Court stirred the pot once again with a 7–2 ruling ordering a privately financed Ten Commandments monument removed

153 Talley, "Okla. Governor Orders Special Legislative Session," *supra* note 151.

154 Randy Krehbiel and Barbara Hoberock, "Lawsuit Reform Bills Passed," *Tulsa World* (September 10, 2013), A9.

155 Marie Price, "Change in the Wind for Judicial Selection in Oklahoma?" *Journal Record Legislative Report* (August 27, 2003).

156 Sean Murphy, "Chief Justice Disputes Tension Claims," *Tulsa World* (September 29, 2013), A24.

157 Barbara Hoberock, "Legislators Told Judges Are Attacking Legislature," *Tulsa World* (October 31, 2013).

158 Marie Price, "Oklahoma Justices Are Lightning Rod at Judicial Study Meeting," *Journal Record Legislative Report* (October 31, 2013).

159 *Id.*

160 M. Scott Carter, "Oklahoma House Speaker T. W. Shannon Files Bills to Change Judiciary," *Journal Legislative Report* (January 27, 2014).

161 Marie Price, "Bill Would Remove Oklahoma Bar Association from Selection of Judicial Nominating Commission Members," *Journal Record Legislative Report* (February 19, 2014).

162 Tim Talley, "Oklahoma House Defeats Judicial Commission Changes," *Associated Press State Wire* (April 24, 2014).

from the grounds of the state capitol.[163] The decision was based on a clause of the state constitution that forbade the use of public money or property for the support of any type of religious activity.[164] Comments from Republican legislators were blistering:[165]

> Our state Supreme Court is playing politics by issuing rulings contrary to the constitution and contrary to the will of the majority of Oklahoma voters.... This ruling is the court engaging in judicial bullying of the people of Oklahoma, pure and simple. It is time that the people chose jurists.
>
> Our country is under assault from an unelected judiciary that is continuously trying to force cultural change upon us. ... We cannot and will not stand for this.

Several legislators even called for the impeachment of the seven justices who voted to order the monument removed.[166]

Not surprisingly, legislation to remove the problematic portion of the state constitution was proposed by some legislators within days of the court's ruling.[167] At the 2016 legislative session, both chambers passed on overwhelming votes and sent to the voters a constitutional amendment that would do precisely that.[168] However, at the November 2016 election, voters rejected the amendment with 57.1 percent opposed.[169]

The Ten Commandments ruling was not the only controversial decision from the Oklahoma Supreme Court in 2015. In late October, the Court issued an order blocking a restrictive abortion law from going into effect. A lawsuit was seeking to have the law thrown out on the grounds that it violated the state constitution because it dealt with more than one subject. The Court put the law on hold and ordered that litigation over its constitutionality proceed in the trial court.[170] About a

[163] Prescott v. Oklahoma Capitol Preservation Commission, 373 P.3d 1032 (Okla. 2015); see also, Barbara Hoberock, "State Supreme Court Rules Against Ten Commandments Monument at Capitol; Ten Commandments Monument Violates Constitution, Says Court," *Tulsa World* (July 1, 2015), www.tulsaworld.com/news/capitol_report/state-supreme-court-rules-against-ten-commandments-monument-at-capitol/article_5f8354f8-e0aa-56ec-8f0b-315b4a4475e2.html, accessed December 29, 2018.

[164] Article 2, §5 of the Constitution stated, "No public money or property shall ever be appropriated, applied, donated, or used, directly or indirectly, for the use, benefit, or support of any sect, church, denomination, or system of religion, or for the use, benefit, or support of any priest, preacher, minister, or other religious teacher or dignitary, or sectarian institution as such."

[165] *Id.*

[166] Hoberock, "State Supreme Court Rules against Ten Commandments Monument at Capitol," *supra* note 163.

[167] Barbara Hoberock, "Court's Ruling Fires Up Critics," *Tulsa World* (July 12, 2015).

[168] Sean Murphy, "Oklahoma Voters to Decide on Return of Ten Commandments," *Enid News & Eagle* (April 22, 2016), www.enidnews.com/news/oklahoma-voters-to-decide-on-return-of-ten-commandments/article_cdbd3a74-08b2-11e6-bf58-878b51bfd298.html, accessed December 29, 2018.

[169] See https://ballotpedia.org/Oklahoma_Public_Money_for_Religious_Purposes,_State_Question_790_(2016), accessed December 29, 2018.

[170] Barbara Hoberock, "Oklahoma Supreme Court Puts Brakes on Abortion Law That Was to Have Gone into Effect Next Week," *Tulsa World* (October 27, 2015).

month later, a Republican state representative, upset over the Ten Commandments and abortion decisions, announced plans to introduce a constitutional amendment that would abandon the Missouri Plan and have appellate judges stand in nonpartisan elections.[171] The representative cited a survey of 500 registered Oklahoma voters reporting that 79 percent of the respondents preferred a system of judicial election with only 16 percent preferring the then current Missouri Plan system.[172] However, there was little action on the proposal during the legislative session.[173] Another measure would have effectively gutted the judicial nominating commission's role. That measure would have required the commission to forward to the governor the names of all applicants who meet the legal qualifications for the judicial position involved. The commission could, if it so chose, provide some evaluative information.[174] Different versions of this proposal passed the House and the Senate, but then died in conference committee when the legislature adjourned in May.[175] A third bill,[176] imposing a mandatory retirement age of 75 on future appointees to the appellate courts, died in committee.[177] In the end, despite much talk, no changes to judicial selection made it through the legislature in 2016.[178]

The same would be true for 2017. One representative introduced four competing measures, any one of which would have significantly changed judicial selection:[179]

- Remove the current six attorneys, selected by the bar, from the Judicial Commission, and replace them with three attorneys appointed by the Speaker of the House and three attorneys appointed by the president pro tempore of the Senate.
- Change selection of the Supreme Court and the Court of Criminal Appeals to partisan elections.

[171] "Republican Lawmaker Pushes for Election of Appellate Judges," *Associated Press Wire* (December 7, 2015).

[172] Lesa Jones, "Direct Election of State Supreme Court and Appellate Justices Proposed," *Tulsa Business & Legal News* (December 31, 2015).

[173] The proposal was H.J.R. 1037; the bill tracking system at www.oklegislature.gov/AdvancedSearchForm.aspx, accessed December 29, 2018, showed only some limited committee action.

[174] Rick M. Green, "Bill Would Let Voters Change How Some Judges Are Selected," *Oklahoman* (March 4, 2016), 6; Mick Hinton, "Oklahoma Legislature Advances Measures on Religion, Courts, Guns," *Tulsa World* (April 7, 2016).

[175] This was H.B. 3162; information on ultimate outcome is from the legislature bill tracking system, www.oklegislature.gov/AdvancedSearchForm.aspx, accessed December 29, 2018.

[176] Dale Denwalt, "Lesser of Evils: GOP Lawmaker Suggests Age Limits for Judges, Not Elections," *Oklahoma City Journal Record* (February 18, 2016).

[177] From www.oklegislature.gov/AdvancedSearchForm.aspx, accessed December 29, 2018 (H.B. 2339).

[178] See Lucia Walinchus, "Oklahoma Watch: Push Continues to Change How State Selects Top Judges," *Tulsa World* (August 14, 2016).

[179] Wayne Greene, "Legislative Assault on Judicial Independence Resumes," *Tulsa World* (January 27, 2017).

- Change the role of the Judicial Nominating Commission to that of rating nominees selected by the governor as "qualified" or "not qualified" prior to the vote on confirmation by the state Senate.
- Require the Judicial Nominating Commission to submit 5 rather than 3 names to the governor, allow the governor to request a new list of 5, and require Senate confirmation of the governor's nominee.

All four of the proposals were advanced to the Senate floor.[180] The first two were not acted upon, but the second two were approved by the Senate, with all six Democrats voting against, along with one or two Republicans.[181] The two proposals approved by the full Senate died in the House when it failed to act.[182]

Efforts to change judicial selection during the 2018 legislative session were minimal. A bill was introduced in the Senate that would have required information on the ballot about the judges standing for retention, including their age, length of service, and the name of the governor who had appointed the judge.[183] However, the bill died after being referred to the Senate Rules Committee, apparently with little if any consideration by the committee.[184]

More attempts to change the selection of Oklahoma's appellate judges may come in the wake of the 2018 election, which produced little change in the political makeup of the nonjudicial branches of Oklahoma's state government. A new Republican governor took office in January, and Republicans continue to have overwhelming majorities in both legislative chambers, having picked up one additional seat in the House while losing three in the Senate. In contrast, the Oklahoma Supreme Court continues to be heavily dominated by appointees of Democratic governors, with only 3 of the 9 justices appointed by Republicans. As long as Democrats dominate the Supreme Court, there will be tension with the other two branches of government. One of the Democratic appointees is in her eighties and another is in his mid-seventies, which could provide the opportunity for the Republican governor to swing the Court majority to a more conservative orientation

[180] Barbara Hoberock, "Senate Panel Passes Bills to Make Massive Changes to State Judiciary," *Tulsa World* (February 8, 2017).

[181] Barbara Hoberock, "Senate Passes Measures to Make Changes to the Judiciary," *Tulsa World* (March 7, 2017); information on the partisan division in the vote is from the legislature's bill tracking system, www.oklegislature.gov/AdvancedSearchForm.aspx, accessed December 30, 2018.

[182] "Most Legislation Meddling with the Judicial Selection Process Is Stymied for the Year," *Tulsa World* (May 1, 2017).

[183] Joseph P. Williams, "Judicial Reforms Aimed at Making Courts More Partisan, Less Powerful," *U.S. News & World Report* (February 13, 2018), www.usnews.com/news/politics/articles/2018-02-14/judicial-reforms-aim-at-making-courts-more-partisan-less-powerful, accessed December 30, 2018.

[184] Information from the legislature's bill tracking system, www.usnews.com/news/politics/articles/2018-02-14/judicial-reforms-aim-at-making-courts-more-partisan-less-powerful [S.B. 971], accessed December 30, 2018.

sometime in the next few years. Depending on the decisions that come out of a more conservative court, Republicans may then be content to leave the current selection and retention system in place.

SUMMARY: THREE FAILED EFFORTS TO END THE MISSOURI PLAN

In all three of the states discussed in this chapter, the push to effectively end the use of the Missouri Plan for selecting appellate judges, and possibly some trial judges, came from the conservative end of the political spectrum. Typically, the proposals were aimed at giving greater control of selection to elected officials and decreasing the organized bar's role. Some proposals sought to put constraints on the governor's choices by requiring Senate confirmation. The only significant changes that were accomplished in the three states were some modifications to the composition of nominating commissions and the removal of the Kansas Court of Appeals from the state's Missouri Plan system, which was possible through legislation, without the need for a constitutional amendment that would require voter approval.

15

Conclusion

What Do We Want in Our Judges?

The preceding chapters have discussed efforts, both successful and unsuccessful, to make significant changes in judicial selection and/or retention in almost half of the American states. The question that motivated the research reported in the book was to what degree were such efforts driven by partisan politics and/or policy concerns versus driven by concerns about professionalism and what might be labeled "good government." I had a specific expectation that partisan politics and/or policy would dominate at a time when a state was experiencing significant realignment from dominance by one political party to dominance by the other political party. I thought this would be particularly evident in the southern states using partisan elections, where one-party Democratic control was shifting to one-party Republican control. The expectation was that Democrats would want to shift away from partisan elections to prevent or at least slow Republicans taking control of the state judiciary. Although this was (and still is as I write this) clearly true in North Carolina (see Chapter 2), it was not true in Georgia (Chapter 6), Mississippi (Chapter 7), or Texas (Chapter 13).

In this concluding chapter, I review the study's findings and assess the factors that appear to be important in states making changes in judicial selection and retention over an almost 40-year period, 1980 to 2018. I also discuss two interesting patterns related to judicial selection: (1) the greater willingness of voters to accept systems reducing their role in the selection and retention of appellate judges compared to local trial judges, and (2) the increased support for more "political" modes of selection from the conservative side of the political spectrum, where historically the preference had been to reduce overt political factors that dominate in the direct election of judges. I conclude with a discussion of what Americans see as the important qualities in people who are elected or appointed as state judges.

POLITICS VERSUS PROFESSIONALISM: IMPETUS FOR CHANGE

The Increasing Role of Partisanship and Policy

I framed the partisan politics and/or policy vs. legal professionalism conflict in terms of Richardson and Vines' concepts of democratic and legal subcultures.[1] The democratic subculture emphasizes the norms of democratic representation, which implies both partisanship and policy preferences in line with the preferences of the judge's constituency; this subculture also suggests that judges' political qualifications, such as serving in other elective offices or government positions, are important considerations. The legal subculture emphasizes the norms of legalism and the legal profession, implying a commitment to "the rule of law over popular pressure."[2] In terms of judicial selection and retention, a democratic subculture places the priority on responsiveness to citizen preferences and accountability to voters. The legal subculture's priorities are legal qualifications and a commitment to the neutral application of the law, while recognizing that the application of the law is not a mechanical process and that a judge's values can play a role when the law is not clearly determinative. Tables 15.1 and 15.2 list all major successful and unsuccessful efforts to change judicial selection methods between 1980 and 2018, and include the nature of the change, the courts involved, any significant precipitating events, and my assessment of whether political partisanship played a significant role in what happened.

As noted in Chapter 1, a major goal in replacing political appointment of judges with judicial elections in the mid-nineteenth century was to make judges independent of the other branches of government. This was largely undercut by the role played by political parties and their leaders in elections, particularly regarding the selection of the candidates to run in judicial elections.[3] The two major types of changes in the twentieth century in the United States – first the adoption of nonpartisan elections and then the development of what became known as the Missouri Plan – dubbed "merit selection" by proponents – were both intended to shift the emphasis from political partisanship in judicial selection to judicial qualifications. However, the system of nonpartisan election created problems for voters, who were deprived information concerning the candidates' party affiliation, which for most voters serves as their primary voting cue. In the absence of the party cue,

1 Richard J. Richardson and Kenneth N. Vines, *The Politics of Federal Courts* (Boston: Little, Brown and Co., 1970), 7.

2 Todd A. Curry and Michael K. Romano, "Ideological Congruity on State Supreme Courts," *Justice System Journal* 39, no. 2 (2018), 141; see also G. Alan Tarr, *Without Fear or Favor: Judicial Independence and Accountability in the States* (Stanford, CA: Stanford University Press, 2012).

3 Jed Handelsman Shugerman, *The People's Courts: Pursuing Judicial Independence in America* (Cambridge, MA: Harvard University Press, 2012), 167.

TABLE 15.1 *Successful efforts to change judicial selection and/or retention method, 1980–2018*

State	Year	Courts Affected	Changed to	Motivation or Precipitating Event(s)	Indicators of Partisanship
Arkansas	2000	all	nonpartisan	Republicans: reduce Democratic Party revenue; Democrats: maintain judicial control	mixed motives
Connecticut	1986	all	constrained appointment/ constrained reappointment (court modernization)	good gov't.	some initial opposition from Democrats, but largely nonpartisan
Georgia	1983	all major	nonpartisan	good gov't./court modernization	only dissent was from Democrats
Kansas	2013	Court of Appeals	appointment/retention	Republicans unhappy with appellate court decisions	clear party split
Mississippi	1994	all	nonpartisan	good gov't., possible racial element	almost all dissent from Democrats
North Carolina	1996	superior (trial)	nonpartisan, by district (had been statewide)	part of shift to district elections related to court case	court case brought by Republicans
North Carolina	2001	district (trial)	nonpartisan	unclear; possibly to be consistent with superior court elections, but also concern by Democrats with increasing Republican success	clear party split
North Carolina	2004	all appellate	nonpartisan	partisan; Democrats feared growing Republican success	clear party split
North Carolina	2015	Court of Appeals	partisan (sort of)	partisan; Democrats. feared growing Republican success	clear party split

North Carolina	2016	Supreme Court	retention/nonpartisan (rejected by court)	partisan; protect Republican running for reelection	clear party split
North Carolina	2017	all	partisan	partisan; secure Republican control	clear party split
New Mexico	1998	all	retention/partisan	good gov't.	supported by coalition of Republicans and conservative Democrats
Rhode Island	1994	all	constrained appointment	response to scandals involving members of the judiciary	none
South Carolina	1996	all	constrained legislative election	response to appointment of unqualified legislators to judicial positions	none
South Dakota	1980	Supreme Court	nonpartisan	good gov't.	bipartisan support; opposition from some lawyers
Tennessee	1994	Supreme Court	Missouri Plan	good gov't.	none
Tennessee	2014	appellate	appointment/retention	probably political (lawyers too liberal)	strong partisan division
Utah	1985	all	Missouri Plan	good gov't.	none
West Virginia	2015	all	nonpartisan at time of primary, with no judicial primary (i.e., plurality election)	longtime goal of Republicans	moderate party split

TABLE 15.2 *Unsuccessful efforts to change judicial selection and/or retention method, 1980–2018*

State	Year(s)	Courts Affected	Nature of Change	Motivation or Precipitating Event(s)	Indicators of Partisanship
Arkansas	1980	split	nonpartisan election, broad constitution revision rejected, 63–37; given choice between Missouri Plan for appellate and nonpartisan for trial *or* nonpartisan for all, preferred nonpartisan election 56–44	probably good gov't.	none
Florida	2000	trial	local option for Missouri Plan, rejected by voters in all districts	good gov't.	initiated by Constitution Revision Commission
Kansas	2006–2014	Supreme Court	did not get out of legislature	political (Republican anger at state Supreme Court)	clear partisan division
Minnesota	2008–2014	all	did not get out of legislature	good gov't.	failed due to lack of support from Republicans, who held majority in legislature
Missouri	2012	appellate	end merit selection/modify commission	political	clear partisan division
New Hampshire	2001–2003	all	impose a nominating commission constraint	mixed (scandal and anger at Supreme Court for some decisions)	Republicans more supportive of change than Democrats

New Mexico	1992	all	Missouri Plan with 55% threshold required for retention; rejected by voters 54–46	good gov't.	Republicans unanimous in support; Democrats split down the middle
Nevada	1988	all	Missouri Plan; rejected by voters 56–44	good gov't.	none
Nevada	2010	all	Missouri Plan; rejected by voters 58–42	good gov't.	none
Ohio	1987	appellate	Missouri Plan; rejected by voters 65–35	good gov't.	brought as an initiative; opposed by both parties
Oklahoma	2008–2017	appellate	end merit selection/modify commission	political (Republican anger at state Supreme Court)	clear partisan division
Pennsylvania	1990–2018	all	Missouri Plan	good gov't.	none; lack of support from either party
Texas	1985–2003		Missouri Plan or nonpartisan elections	good gov't.	some partisan support but insufficient interest from Republicans
South Dakota	2004	trial	Missouri Plan; rejected by voters 62–38	good gov't.	none

some candidates came to rely on interest groups for the kind of backing they needed to get their names recognized by voters.[4]

In contrast to nonpartisan elections, the Missouri Plan eliminated any need for name recognition. Moreover, not having a name recognized by the public probably worked to the incumbents' advantage when they stood for retention on a yes-no ballot, because most voters would have no reason to vote no. The Missouri Plan also reduced or eliminated the role of interest groups, other than the legal profession, in the initial selection process. Given that the strongest interest groups in urban areas in the middle third of the twentieth century were labor organizations and other groups that tended to be liberal on economic issues, conservative business groups backed the adoption of the Missouri Plan. Shugerman argues that successful campaigns for the Missouri Plan came in those states that he describes as "rural-but-industrializing" where business was strong but labor and ethnic groups were relatively weak.[5]

As shown in Table 15.1, by the start of the period that is the focus of this book, the Missouri Plan had largely run its course, even though by this time organized labor was sharply declining in the private sector.[6] In the 1980s, voters in only two states approved the adoption of a Missouri Plan for some or all courts: South Dakota for its Supreme Court in 1980, the very first year of the period under consideration, and Utah for all courts in 1985. In contrast, voters in six states rejected the Missouri Plan, with voters in Nevada doing so twice. Drives to adopt the Missouri Plan in three other states failed to win the legislative support required to be presented to the voters (see Table 15.2). Moreover, two states – Tennessee, for all appellate courts, and Kansas for its Court of Appeals – terminated the element of the Missouri Plan that led to it being dubbed "merit selection": the nominating commission from whose nominees the governor was required to select judges. There were significant but unsuccessful efforts to terminate the nominating commission for all appellate courts in Oklahoma and Missouri and for the Supreme Court in Kansas.[7]

4 *Id.*, 172.

5 *Id.*, 206. For other analyses of the factors accounting for the adoption of the Missouri Plan, see Marsha Puro, Peter J. Bergerson, and Steven Puro, "An Analysis of Judicial Diffusion: Adoption of the Missouri Plan in the American States," *Publius* 15, no. 4 (1985), 85–97 (1985); and Judith Ann Haydel, "Explaining Adoption of Judicial Merit Selection in the States, 1950–1980: A Multivariate Test," unpublished Ph.D. dissertation, University of New Orleans (1987). Several studies have examined the adoption of merit selection, broadly defined; see Philip L. Dubois, "Voter Responses to Court Reform: Merit Judicial Selection on the Ballot," *Judicature* 73, no. 5 (February–March 1990), 238–247; F. Andrew Hanssen, "On the Politics of Judicial Selection: Lawyers and State Campaigns for the Merit Plan," *Public Choice* 110, no. 1–2 (2002), 79–97; or James A. Gleason, "State Judicial Selection Methods as Public Policy: The Missouri Plan," unpublished Ph.D. dissertation, Purdue University (2016).

6 See Henry S. Farber and Bruce Western, "Accounting for the Decline of Unions in the Private Sector, 1973–1998," *Journal of Labor Research* 22, no. 3 (September 2001), 459–485.

7 In 2019, the Kansas Supreme Court found a right to abortion in the Kansas Constitution, and this may lead to renewed efforts to change the method of selection for that court.

TABLE 15.3 *The role of partisanship over time in 32 change efforts*

	Largely Nonpartisan	Somewhat Partisan	Clearly Partisan
1980–1999	9	4	1
2000–2018	4	3	12

chi square = 11.87, p = .004

A careful examination of Tables 15.1 and 15.2 shows that there has been a shift over time in the role of partisanship in the efforts to change judicial selection and retention. I categorized each of the 32 efforts listed in those two tables as "largely nonpartisan," "somewhat partisan," or "clearly partisan," and then split the overall period into two subperiods: 1980–1999 and 2000–2018.[8] Table 15.3 shows that partisanship played a relatively small role in the earlier subperiod, but has become dominant in the later period.

What might explain the shift shown in Table 15.3? The most obvious explanation for the increase in partisanship is that it reflects the broader polarization that has taken place in American politics.[9] However, one must also consider that the earlier period came toward the end of a period of intense efforts for judicial reform,[10] sometimes referred to as "court modernization."[11] Moving away from the traditional political approaches to judicial selection, particularly toward "merit selection," was described as a "prerequisite of judicial modernization."[12] As the twentieth century came to an end, the court modernization movement faded, most likely because by that time many of the goals, which were heavily focused on court administration, had been accomplished.[13] Thus, it is probably the combination of a diminished focus on court modernization and increasing political polarization that explains the shift in what happened in efforts to change judicial selection and retention from 1980 to 2018.

8 The one unsuccessful campaign in Pennsylvania that extended over both subperiods is counted in the later subperiod; if it were counted in the earlier subperiod, the pattern would be even stronger.

9 Much has been written about political polarization in the United States over the last several decades. I discuss this briefly and provide citations to some of the key literature in "Polarized Justice? Changing Patterns of Decision-Making in the Federal Courts," *Kansas Journal of Law and Policy* 28, no. 1 (2019), 316–324.

10 Russell Wheeler, "Judicial Reform: Basic Issues and References," *Policy Studies Journal* 8, no. 1 (1979), 134–149.

11 See, for example, Victor E. Flango, "Court Unification and Qualify of State Courts," *Justice System Journal* 16, no. 3 (1994), 33; or Ralph N. Klep, "State Court Modernization in the 1970's: Forces for Reform in California," *Judicature* 55, no. 7 (March 1972), 292.

12 Henry R. Glick, "Innovation in State Judicial Administration: Effects on Court Management and Organization," *American Politics Quarterly* 9, no. 1 (January 1981), 52.

13 See Steven W. Hays and James A. Douglas, "Judicial Administration: Modernizing the Judicial Branch," in Jack Rabin, W. Bartley Hildreth, and Gerald J. Miller , eds., *Handbook of Public Administration*, 3rd ed. (Boca Raton, FL: CRC Press, 2007), 1008–1011.

Catalysts and Barriers

The individual chapters make clear that the specific catalyst for change efforts varies substantially. One clear catalyst is actual or expected *political realignment* or *misalignment*. This was most evident in North Carolina, but also played roles in Arkansas and West Virginia. Political misalignment was also relevant in Kansas, Missouri, and Oklahoma where one found a state Supreme Court dominated by justices selected by Democratic governors, but the state's politics had moved in a strongly Republican direction. The state Supreme Court handing down decisions that were unpopular with the dominant conservative coalition provided an additional impetus for efforts to change the selection system.

A second major catalyst is *scandal*, alleged or actual, which played roles at one time or another in Connecticut, Florida, Kansas, Nevada, Ohio, Oklahoma, Pennsylvania, Rhode Island, and South Carolina;[14] However, as shown by Nevada, scandal does not necessarily result in an actual change. In most cases, the proposed changes coming in the wake of scandal involved implementing some form of "merit" selection, either the Missouri Plan or other forms of constrained appointment. It is also true that scandal does not necessarily lead to movement for change, as is evident in the absence of significant calls for something akin to the Missouri Plan in the wake of recent (circa 2018) scandals involving justices of the West Virginia Supreme Court of Appeals.[15]

A third catalyst is *litigation*. This played a role in North Carolina and in Mississippi. In North Carolina, the litigation was brought by Republicans who challenged the use of statewide elections for the superior court, the higher level of the state's trial court. This led directly to the adoption of nonpartisan elections for the Superior Court and arguably indirectly to the adoption of nonpartisan elections for the lower-level district court. Litigation was also used successfully in North Carolina to block a shift from nonpartisan ballots to retention elections for the retention of state Supreme Court justices. In Mississippi, litigation brought under the Voter Rights Act was an element in the decision to change to nonpartisan elections, although arguably it was not the primary driver. Litigation was unsuccessful in efforts to end the Missouri Plan and force change in Tennessee and Kansas, and to block change in Florida and New Mexico.

The final major catalyst is – or, more accurately, was – *court modernization*. This played a relatively modest role in the changes that have occurred since 1980. It was a central factor in Georgia and Mississippi and a subsidiary factor in Connecticut; it was also probably a major factor in the adoption of the Missouri Plan in South

[14] In some of these states (e.g., Florida and Oklahoma), the scandals influenced changes that occurred before 1980.

[15] See Phil Kabler, "For Gov. Justice's Court, No Experience Needed," *Charleston Gazette-Mail* (September 2, 2018), 8A.

Dakota in 1980. It played an important role in pre-1980 changes in that occurred in Florida, Kansas, and Tennessee, and probably in many of the states that adopted the Missouri Plan for some or all courts in the 1950s, 1960s, and 1970s.

Some changes can be made by simple legislation while others require constitutional change. When the former is the case, political will on the part of the legislature and governor is all that is needed,[16] as was evident in North Carolina and West Virginia. When the latter is the case, the requirements for constitutional change can be a facilitator or a barrier. Facilitation occurs when the process of constitutional change does not require action by the legislature. This was evident in the unsuccessful initiative effort in Ohio for a Missouri Plan for appellate courts, and in the mixed results in Florida arising from proposals from the Constitution Revision Commission (CRC). Florida voters had approved the Missouri Plan for appellate courts in 1976 but two years later rejected the CRC's proposal to extend it to trial courts; twenty years later, voters approved the CRC's proposal for a local option for the Missouri Plan for trial courts, but then two years later defeated its actual adoption in every constituency.

More often, the requirements for constitutional amendment serve as a barrier, and constitutional change has been needed for the adoption or repeal of the Missouri Plan in most states where it has been considered. Where an initiative option exists, it can be difficult to collect the necessary signatures to get a proposal on the ballot, as happened in Missouri and nearly happened in Ohio. The difficulties of constitutional change are greater in the absence of an initiative option. In many states, the legislature must pass proposed amendments with an enhanced majority, and proposals may have to pass in identical form in two consecutive legislatures. The need for an enhanced majority has served to block efforts to end the Missouri Plan for the Kansas Supreme Court. Arguably, it was also a barrier for proposals to adopt constrained appointment in New Hampshire, where enhanced majorities of both the legislature and the electorate are needed to adopt a constitutional amendment. Finally, proponents of change may be dissatisfied with the language appearing on the ballot describing the proposed change, as happened in Missouri.

THE MISSOURI PLAN: APPELLATE VERSUS LOCAL TRIAL JUDGES

One interesting pattern highlighted in this study is the greater willingness of voters to support the Missouri Plan system for appellate courts, compared to supporting it for local trial courts. In three of the states discussed in the preceding chapters – Florida, South Dakota, and Oklahoma – voters approved the adoption of the Missouri Plan for appellate courts and then rejected it for trial courts. In Florida, the Missouri Plan was offered as a local option, but every county and district rejected it. In two states with a local option, Kansas and Missouri, many locales, an overwhelming

16 Even the governor's assent may be unnecessary if the support in the legislature is veto-proof.

majority in Missouri, have not adopted the plan.[17] In contrast, two counties in Arizona (by constitutional provision) and two in Indiana (by statute) use a Missouri Plan system for local courts.[18] As is discussed in the next section, some additional states that retained partisan or nonpartisan elections have constrained governors in filling midterm vacancies by requiring the governor to select from nominees provided by a nominating commission. Included among these states are Florida, Oklahoma, and South Dakota,[19] where voters approved constitutional amendments requiring the use of nominating commissions to fill vacancies on major trial courts.

One could make the argument that if there should be a difference in selection mechanisms for appellate versus local trial courts, that difference should be the other way around. That is, local trial courts should be selected through a Missouri Plan system or parts thereof and appellate courts should be subject to contested popular elections. The rationale for this perspective is that most of the work of trial courts is fact finding and the routine application of the law, and when there is conflict over the facts that cannot be resolved, trial courts usually rely on juries to resolve that conflict. In contrast, the work of appellate courts is focused more on determining what the law is, and in the American common law system, this often involves lawmaking, not just legal interpretation. Given the lawmaking role of appellate courts, it is those courts that voters should be more concerned about. However, it is the local courts that are, at least formally, more subject to direct popular control. I say "at least formally" because a large percentage of both partisan and nonpartisan trial court elections go uncontested.

There is evidence that the public is more concerned about professional qualifications for appellate judges than for local trial judges. This might lead voters to be more supportive of the Missouri Plan, under the label of "merit selection," for those appellate courts. There is also some evidence that the public views local connections as more important for trial judges than for appellate judges, and the use of popular elections is one way to try to ensure such connections.

Another element may be that members of racial and ethnic minorities see popular election as increasing the chances of representation on local trial courts. Empirical research on this question is mixed.[20] One study looked at the percentage of judges on state trial courts who were African American in 1986; focusing simply on the formal selection system, that study found no effect on selecting minorities, but

[17] See www.yourmissourijudges.org/missouri-plan/judicial-selection/, accessed June 7, 2019.

[18] "Judicial Merit Selection: Current Status," American Judicature Society (2011), Table 1, www.judicialselection.us/uploads/documents/Judicial_Merit_Charts_0FC20225EC6C2.pdf, accessed April 29, 2019.

[19] Constrained appointment is also used to fill midterm vacancies in several Alabama counties; see www.judicialselection.us/judicial_selection/methods/selection_of_judges.cfm?state=AL, accessed July 22, 2019.

[20] For a brief summary of research on the impact of selection system of judicial diversity without regard to level of court, see K. O. Myers, "Merit Selection and Diversity on the Bench," *Indiana Law Review* 46, no. 1 (2013), 48–50.

looking at how the judges initially came to their positions (e.g., appointment to an interim vacancy in an election state), that study found that partisan and nonpartisan elections resulted in a higher percentage of African Americans, compared to a base category of legislative selection. However, it is not clear whether there were significant differences between election and gubernatorial appointment or selection under a Missouri Plan system.[21] A more recent study suggests that there might be some effects, but that research did not consider issues such as district size or the presence of minority-majority districts.[22]

Appellate elections are typically conducted on either a statewide basis or use much larger districts than are used for trial courts. Minorities might see the likelihood of success in such elections as much more limited and might believe that minority representation would be more likely through a system of appointment, which could be a Missouri Plan system. At least for state supreme courts, there is evidence that appointive systems, with or without a nominating commission, increase the likelihood of nonwhites being appointed to positions on state supreme courts, compared to systems using partisan or nonpartisan elections.[23]

Another factor explains the barrier to adopting the Missouri Plan system for local trial courts: local political leaders want more say in choosing judges for local courts. Those leaders might believe that their influence would be limited in a system using a nominating commission composed of a combination of lawyers selected by the bar and nonlawyers appointed by elected officials such as the governor and legislative leaders. Given such a view, local elected officials would probably oppose adopting a Missouri Plan for trial courts. Unfortunately, there is no empirical research assessing if there is systematic opposition from local elected officials, or whether any such opposition accounts for the failure to adopt the Missouri Plan at the trial level in states where it is used for appellate courts, like Florida and South Dakota.[24]

[21] Barbara Luck Graham, "Do Judicial Selection Systems Matter? A Study of Black Representation on State Courts," *American Politics Quarterly* 18, no. 3 (July 1990), 328; Graham's statistical analysis controlled for African American population percentage and African American lawyer percentage.

[22] See Malia Reddick, Michael J. Nelson, and Rachel Paine Caulfield, "Racial and Gender Diversity on State Courts: An AJS Study," *Judges' Journal* 48, no. 3 (Summer 2009), 31.

[23] *Id.*; and Laila Robbins and Alicia Bannon with Malia Reddick, *State Supreme Court Diversity: Across the Country. Country Courts Fail to Reflect the Racial, Ethnic, and Gender Diversity of the Communities They Serve* (Brennan Center, New York University School of Law, July 23, 2019), 13–18, www.brennancenter.org/sites/default/files/publications/2019_07_StateSupremeCourtDiversity.pdf, accessed July 25, 2019. See also Greg Goelzhauser, *Choosing State Supreme Court Justices: Merit Selection and the Consequences of Institutional Reform* (Philadelphia, PA: Temple University Press, 2016), 103–105.

[24] As noted in Chapter 14, in Missouri and Kansas some local judges are selected using the Missouri Plan while others are subject to partisan or nonpartisan elections. Other states using the Missouri Plan for appellate courts but having contested elections for trial courts (with occasional local exceptions) are Arizona, Indiana, Maryland, and Oklahoma; see www.judicialselection.us/judicial_selection/methods/selection_of_judges.cfm?state=, accessed June 24, 2019. In addition, California and Tennessee, where no nominating commission constrains

Similar opposition might come from some local lawyers. Chapter 11 discussed the defeat of a constitutional amendment in South Dakota that would have extended the Missouri Plan to trial courts even though voters had previously adopted a constitutional amendment requiring the use of a nominating commission for filling interim vacancies on trial courts. A campaign mounted by some lawyers was part of the explanation offered for the rejection of the Missouri Plan. As noted in Chapter 11, one observer of judicial affairs in South Dakota told me that there was a group of lawyers who wanted to become trial judges but believed they would never be recommended by a nominating commission, foreclosing appointment to an interim vacancy. Continuing the then existing nonpartisan elections both for open seats and for retention of trial judges at the end of their terms offered these lawyers the opportunity to seek an open seat or to challenge an incumbent, and thereby possibly win a judgeship in one of those elections. I have no information as to whether this factor played a role in other states.

South Dakota is not alone as a state that uses the Missouri Plan for appellate courts but not trial courts, but that does require the use of a nominating commission to produce a set of candidates from which the governor must choose when filling interim trial court vacancies. This is true in Florida, Montana, Oklahoma, and Tennessee. In the case of Tennessee, the legislature created the Trial Court Vacancy Commission in 2016 as part of the legislation implementing the state constitutional amendment that freed the governor from any constraints imposed by a nominating commission in filling vacancies on the state's appellate courts.[25] There are also three states – Idaho, Kentucky, and North Dakota – that use nonpartisan elections for all major courts but require the use of a nominating commission to fill interim vacancies in all those courts. In several states (e.g., West Virginia and Minnesota), there are nominating or screening bodies, created either by statute or executive order, that assist the governor but do not constrain the governor's choice to the recommendations made by such a body.

THE GROWING CONSERVATIVE OPPOSITION TO THE MISSOURI PLAN

As noted previously, the Missouri Plan has fallen out of favor. No state has adopted it through a constitutional amendment since Utah did so in 1985.[26] The Tennessee legislature did extend its version of the Missouri Plan to the Tennessee Supreme

the governor, use retention elections for appellate courts but contested elections for trial courts; in New York, appellate judges do not stand for election, but trial judges do.

25 See Richard Locker, "Tennessee Appellate Judge Confirmation Process Approved by State Senate," *Memphis Commercial Appeal* (January 27, 2016); all 11 members of the commission are appointed by the House Speaker or the Senate Speaker, and at least 6 must be members of the bar.

26 See Chapter 8.

Court in 1994, but that legislation was subject to sunset provisions, and was then replaced in 2014 by a system that did not provide for the key nominating commission element of the Missouri Plan.[27] Since Utah voters approved the adoption of a Missouri Plan system, voters in five states have rejected proposals to adopt or extend the Missouri Plan (see Table 15.2). The last time a proposal for a Missouri Plan appeared on a state's ballot was in 2010 in Nevada, where it was rejected despite a major scandal involving state judges.[28] In two additional states, Minnesota and Pennsylvania, campaigns for adopting a Missouri Plan system have failed to make it onto the ballot.[29]

Not only has no state adopted or extended a Missouri Plan system for almost thirty-five years (as this is written in 2019), one now sees concerted efforts to undo existing Missouri Plan systems. This is not entirely new. In Chapter 14, I noted that Missouri saw unsuccessful attempts to end the use of the Nonpartisan Court Plan in the 1940s and then again in the late 1980s and early 1990s. Also, Chapter 5 discussed the Democratic-controlled Tennessee legislature's repeal of the Missouri Plan system as applied to the state's Supreme Court in 1974, just three years after adopting the plan, when it appeared that the Republican governor would have the opportunity to appoint a majority of the Court's justices. I could not find evidence of other repeal efforts prior to 2000, but since then, efforts to repeal elements of the Missouri Plan have become a prominent part of the judicial selection debate. In addition to the abandonment of the Missouri Plan for appellate courts in Tennessee, the Kansas legislature terminated the nominating commission for the Kansas Court of Appeals and repeatedly tried to pass a constitutional amendment to send to the voters that would have done the same for the Kansas Supreme Court. Vigorous campaigns to repeal elements of the Missouri Plan have also occurred in Missouri and Oklahoma.[30]

Thus, although proposals for Missouri Plan/merit selection systems continue to be introduced in state legislatures,[31] one now also sees proposals to terminate such plans, either in whole or in significant part. Aside from Kansas, Missouri, Oklahoma, and Tennessee, those proposals have made little progress through the legislative process. Between 2008 and 2018,[32] there were such proposals in Arizona (2008, 2010, 2011, 2012, 2016, 2017), Florida (2011), Indiana (2013, 2015), Iowa (2010, 2011, 2012, 2017, 2018), and Nebraska (2016); in two states, Hawaii (2013, 2016) and South Carolina (2018), where a nominating commission is used but retention is through some means other than retention elections, there have been proposals to eliminate

[27] See Chapter 5.
[28] See Chapter 11.
[29] See Chapter 13.
[30] See Chapter 14.
[31] See gaveltogavel.us/database/, accessed May 1, 2019.
[32] A list of unsuccessful reform efforts including years prior to 2008 lists only the unsuccessful efforts to end the Nonpartisan Court Plan in Missouri in the 1940s and in the late 1980s; see "History of Reform Efforts: Unsuccessful Reform Efforts," www.judicialselection.us/judicial_selection/reform_efforts/failed_reform_efforts.cfm?state=, accessed May 1, 2019.

the nominating commission. Looking only at the 14 states using a Missouri Plan system for some or all of their courts, there have been at least legislative proposals to move away from that system in eight states; the six states where there does not appear to have been such proposals are Alaska, Colorado, Maryland, South Dakota, Utah, and Wyoming.

As was clear in the chapters discussing Tennessee, Kansas, Missouri, and Oklahoma, the effort in those states to end the Missouri Plan were led by Republican legislators or conservative interest groups. Importantly, almost all the proposals to end or gut Missouri Plan systems in the other five states were introduced by Republican legislators. The only exceptions I could find were proposals to end the use of the Plan in St. Joseph County, Indiana, in 2009,[33] and in Iowa in 2011–2012.[34] Historically, business groups, quintessential supporters of the Republican Party, were principal backers of the Missouri Plan,[35] along with the organized bar and public interest groups such as the League of Women Voters and Common Cause. Organized labor, long associated with the Democratic Party, was a principal opponent of the Missouri Plan.[36] What then explains the apparent shift so that it is now the right side of the political spectrum that is opposing the adoption of the Missouri Plan or working to end it in states that use it?

I have alluded to the likely explanation in some of the preceding chapters. There are probably two major elements accounting for the increasing opposition to the Missouri Plan from Republicans and their conservative allies: (1) a perception or argument that the Missouri Plan tends to produce judges who are, in general, more toward the left than the population as a whole; and (2) business's recognition that by funding extensive advertising to support preferred candidates or to attack undesired incumbents and candidates, judges can be elected who will interpret the law and decide cases in a way that is favorable to business. I discuss each of these elements in turn.

The Leftward Skew of the Legal Profession

One group that has emerged as an opponent of the Missouri Plan is the conservative Federalist Society. In the early 2000s, the Society published a white paper entitled

[33] St. Joseph County is one of only two counties in Indiana using a Missouri Plan system for local judges; see www.judicialselection.us/judicial_selection/methods/selection_of_judges.cfm?state=IN, accessed May 1, 2019.

[34] This information is distilled from the Gavel to Gavel database, accessed May 1, 2019, at http://gaveltogavel.us/database/. In 2016 proposals to terminate Hawaii's merit selection commission and implement an electoral system of judicial selection was introduced by a Democratic legislator; however, according to the legislative website www.capitol.hawaii.gov/Archives/measure_indiv_Archives.aspx?billtype=HB&billnumber=2139&year=2016, accessed May 1, 2019, the proposal was "introduced by request of another party," which might mean it was done as a favor to a constituent.

[35] Shugerman, *The People's Courts*, *supra* note 3, 179–180, 210–211.

[36] *Id.*, 201.

"The Case for Partisan Judicial Elections."[37] The white paper criticizes the Missouri Plan for failing to produce judges who were more probusiness than had electoral systems and suggests that this may reflect lawyer self-interest in litigation, whether on the plaintiff or defense side.[38]

A leading figure in the Federalist Society's opposition to the Missouri Plan is Vanderbilt law professor Brian Fitzpatrick. As noted in Tennessee chapter, Fitzpatrick's position is that lawyers dominate nominating commissions, and because lawyers, as a whole, are more liberal (or less conservative) than the citizens of their state, the persons nominated by the commissions tend to be closer to the commissioners' ideology than to that of the state's citizens.[39] University of Kansas law professor Stephen J. Ware is a second prominent academic critic of the Missouri Plan; his argument is that the plan is elitist and undemocratic in giving such a prominent role to lawyers through their dominance on most nominating commissions,[40] and hence, the Plan lacks democratic legitimacy.[41] He is particularly critical of Kansas's system, which he described as the only state where, as of 2008, the bar selected a majority of members of the nominating commission.[42]

There is evidence to support the proposition that lawyers, taken as a whole, either nationally or in individual states, tilt left compared to the larger population to which they are compared. One approach to measuring lawyers in the aggregate relies on data based on political contributions. The key measure starts with collecting publicly available information on individuals' contributions to political

[37] The white paper was produced by a task force composed of by Michael DeBow, Diane Brey, Erick Kaardal, John Soroko, Frank Strickland, and Michael Wallace, and was reprinted in *University of Toledo Law Review* 3 (2002), 393–409. I should note that I have also argued that, if we are to elect state supreme court judges, we should do so using partisan elections, but my rationale is quite different, and I also argue that a better system would rely upon something resembling the Missouri Plan; see Herbert M. Kritzer, *Justices on the Ballot: Continuity and Change in Supreme Court Elections* (New York: Cambridge University Press, 2015), 240, 253–261.

[38] *Id.*, 401–402.

[39] See Brian T. Fitzpatrick, "The Politics of Merit Selection," *Missouri Law Review* 74, no. 3 (Summer 2009), 675–708.

[40] Stephen J. Ware, "The Missouri Plan in National Perspective," *Missouri Law Review*, 74 (2009), 758–764.

[41] *Id.*, 764–766. The charge that the Missouri Plan is undemocratic was picked up in a report of the conservative Heritage Foundation; see Deborah O'Malley, "A Defense of the Elected Judiciary," *Legal Memorandum* no. 57 (September 9, 2010), http://tht_media.s3.amazonaws.com/2010/pdf/lm0057.pdf, accessed May 2, 2019. Political scientist James Gibson has argued that judicial elections enhance the legitimacy of the courts; see *Electing Judges: The Surprising Effects of Campaigning on Judicial Legitimacy* (Chicago: University of Illinois Press, 2012), 130–132. Political scientists Chris W. Bonneau and Melinda Gann Hall argue that the key criticisms of judicial elections are not supported by empirical research; see *In Defense of Judicial Elections* (New York: Routledge, 2009), 128–138.

[42] Stephen J. Ware, "Selection to the Kansas Supreme Court," *Kansas Journal of Law & Public Policy* 17, no. 3 (2008), 391.

candidates and PACs associated with candidates and then connecting that information with other information on the ideology of contribution recipients. The result was a score ranging roughly from –2 (liberal) to +2 (conservative), which can be mapped to the ideology of known political figures. The data on individuals' contributions were then combined with lists of lawyers from Martindale-Hubbell.[43] The mean ideology score for lawyers was –.31 (median = –.52) compared to 0.05 for all donors.[44] Thus, the median lawyer was relatively close politically to Bill Clinton (–.68).[45] Other prominent figures on the left include Barack Obama at –1.35 and Elizabeth Warren at –1.57.[46]

But do judges in states using the Missouri Plan or the nominating commission aspect of the Plan tend to be more liberal than judges in states using other forms of initial selection? Fitzpatrick argues that the answer to this question is a partial yes.[47] He assembled data to classify state appellate judges serving between 1990 and 2010, including courts of last resort and intermediate appellate courts, as either Democrats or Republicans based on party registration, party primary participation, and/or political contributions to candidates of one party or the other. He then compared the percentage of judges classified as Republicans (after omitting those whom he could not classify) to the average of the percentage of voters casting ballots for Republican candidates in elections for the U.S. House of Representatives over the period and to the average in elections for the lower chamber of the state legislature.[48] Subtracting the percentage of judges labeled as Republicans from the percentage of votes cast for Republican candidates produced a measure Fitzpatrick labeled the "liberal skew," with negative numbers indicating a skew to the left (liberal) and positive numbers indicating a skew to the right (conservative). He showed results for three different classifications of formal selection,[49] acknowledging that judges in many of the states employing partisan or nonpartisan elections initially

43 Adam Bonica, Adam S. Chilton, and Maya Sen, "The Political Ideologies of American Lawyers," *Journal of Legal Analysis* 8, no. 2 (Winter 2016), 285–290. The authors note that those identified as lawyers in the database are more likely to be older, be partners, and be males, all factors that may be associated with a greater likelihood of being conservative; the result is that the database may underestimate the degree of liberalism in the entire population (p. 290 n. 8). However, younger attorneys are less likely to be elected or appointed to judgeships.

44 *Id.*, 292; the authors provide ideological estimates for lawyers by state (p. 299).

45 *Id.*, 292.

46 Adam Bonica and Maya Sen, "The Politics of Selecting the Bench from the Bar: The Legal Profession and Partisan Incentives to Introduce Ideology into Judicial Selection," *Journal of Law and Economics* 60 (November 2017), 571.

47 Brian T. Fitzpatrick, "The Ideological Consequences of Selection: A Nationwide Study of the Methods of Selecting Judges," *Vanderbilt Law Review* 70, no. 5 (2017), 1729–1754.

48 *Id.*

49 It appears that Fitzpatrick misclassified North Carolina as "nonpartisan" (p. 1753) even though, as discussed in Chapter 2, the state used partisan elections for appellate courts until 2004. He also failed to note the adoption of a nominating commission as part of the legislative selection system in South Carolina.

came to office by being appointed to fill an interim vacancy.[50] All systems of selection other than appointment without a nominating commission skewed to the left. Evidence as to whether systems employing a constraining nominating commission skewed more than other systems was mixed, depending on the classification system Fitzpatrick used.[51] Nonpartisan election systems had a level of liberal skew similar to that produced by nominating commission–based systems. In his conclusion, Fitzpatrick argued that there is a relationship between bar influence and skew, but by "bar influence," he meant whether "there were *any* [emphasis in the original] bar seats on the [nominating] commissions."[52]

An alternative perspective would be to ask whether the judiciary is ideologically representative of the bar, which would indicate that judges are not selected based on their ideology but other factors such as qualifications. Bonica and Sen used the measure of ideology based on campaign contributions to compare judges from each state to attorneys and to elected state officeholders. They compared attorneys with five or more years as members of the bar to judges (including federal judges) and found statistically significant differences between the two groups in 24 states;[53] attorneys were more liberal than judges in 21 of those states.[54] Although the authors did not report statistical tests, elected officials fell to the right of both attorneys and judges in all but 5 states. The authors also examined the relationship between judges' ideology score, attorneys' ideology score, and elected officials' ideology score, conditional on actual method of the judges' initial selection.[55] They found that partisan elections produced the judges most similar to politicians, and "merit selection" and nonpartisan elections produced judges most similar to the attorney population.[56]

Taken together, the analyses presented by Fitzpatrick and by Bonica and Sen point back to the tension between political/policy representation and professionalism as goals in judicial selection. If the goal in selecting judges is to obtain a bench that is representative of the citizenry, rather than a bench based primarily on professional qualifications, mechanisms such as partisan elections are likely to be most effective. If, on the other hand, the goal is to select judges based on professional qualifications, there is no reason to expect professional qualifications to correlate with lawyers' political ideology or political party preference; rather, in terms of

50 Fitzpatrick, "The Ideological Consequences of Selection," *supra* note 47, 1739 n.30. As discussed previously, in some of the states using partisan or nonpartisan elections, those midterm vacancies are filled through what I have called constrained appointment

51 *Id.*, 1739–1740.

52 *Id.*, 1747.

53 Bonica and Sen, "The Politics of Selecting the Bench from the Bar," *supra* note 46, 582–584.

54 Several states where there is not a statically significant difference (i.e., Idaho, Montana, North Dakota, South Dakota, and Vermont) show large gaps between attorneys and judges; the lack of statistical significance in those states probably reflects the small number of judges.

55 Bonica and Sen, "The Politics of Selecting the Bench from the Bar," *supra* note 46, 585.

56 *Id.*, 587.

ideology and partisanship, judges should have a similar profile to the legal profession as a whole within the relevant constituency. Appointive mechanisms, particularly those using a nominating commission with a significant proportion of lawyer members, are likely to come closer to achieving this result. Although there is no agreed way to assess the professional merit of persons selected to be judges, a system selecting judges who resemble the profession politically is more likely to be geared toward professional qualifications than one selecting judges who differ politically from their professional colleagues taken as a whole. This is not to suggest that a more "political" system will necessarily fail to consider the qualifications of candidates; rather, it is a question of which comes first, political concerns or professional qualifications.

Conservative Success in Winning State Supreme Court Elections

An area of law that has changed substantially over the last fifty years is the law of torts.[57] One particularly prominent subarea of change is the law of product liability, which has shifted from negligence to strict liability, at least regarding claims involving manufacturing defects.[58] Another important shift was from contributory negligence to comparative negligence; under the former, a plaintiff was denied compensation if the plaintiff's own negligence contributed in any way to the plaintiff's injury, while under the latter the plaintiff's compensation is reduced commensurate with the plaintiff's own negligence.[59] Most of the tort law changes occurred through the common law process, with various state supreme courts handing down precedential decisions that favored claimants in tort cases. One result was to mobilize business interests to oppose the reelection of state supreme court

57 See G. Alan Tarr and Mary Cornelia Aldis Porter, *State Supreme Courts in State and Nation* (New Haven, CT: Yale University Press, 1988), 34–40.

58 The seminal case starting this shift was Greenman v. Yuba Power Products, 377 P.2d 897 (Cal. 1962); the shift was later adopted by the American Law Institute when two years after *Yuba* it published a supplement to the Restatement of Torts (Second) in the form of Section 402A, which states:

> (1) One who sells any product in a defective condition unreasonably dangerous to the user or consumer or to his property is subject to liability for physical harm thereby caused to the ultimate user or consumer, or to his property, if
> (a) the seller is engaged in the business of selling such a product, and
> (b) it is expected to and does reach the user or consumer without substantial change in the condition in which it is sold.
> (2) The rule stated in Subsection (1) applies although
> (a) the seller has exercised all possible care in the preparation and sale of his product, and
> (b) the user or consumer has not bought the product from or entered into any contractual relation with the seller.

59 This is an oversimplification of "comparative negligence" in actual practice; for a brief discussion of some of the complexities, see Edward J. Kionka, *Torts in a Nutshell*, 5th ed. (St. Paul, MN: West Publishing, 2010), 137–145.

judges seen as too plaintiff-friendly and to support candidates thought to be sympathetic to business.[60]

One of the most prominent elections came in California, a state where the Supreme Court had been particularly friendly to plaintiffs. In 1986, when three justices of the California Supreme Court were standing for retention, business mounted a campaign focused on the justices' decisions in death penalty cases, but their real goal was to reshape the Court's tort-related decisions. Business interests were major funders of Crime Victims for Court Reform, an organization campaigning for the defeat of the justices.[61] Further, a key element in the defeat of the three justices in 1986 was television advertising funded by business groups.

Although interest group activity preceded the 1986 election,[62] the years immediately after the California election saw business interests successfully back candidates who opposed pro-plaintiff justices in several states, including Texas, Alabama, and Michigan.[63] A feature of many of these elections was extensive television advertising.[64] One result was the realization by business that it could effectively use advertising to influence the outcome of state supreme court elections and thus, obtain courts favorable to business.[65] Even though one of business's first successes was in the California 1986 retention election, that only served to defeat sitting justices; it did not ensure that those appointed as replacements would be business-friendly. However, as things turned out, Republican governor George Deukmejian handily defeated Los Angeles mayor Tom Bradley in the 1986 election and went on to appoint justices with the kind of perspective business preferred.[66] A better vehicle for business interests was contested elections, because they could not only oppose candidates but could also back preferred candidates. This led to what some have

[60] See Anthony Champagne, "Tort Reform and Judicial Selection," *Loyola of Los Angeles Law Review* 38 (2005), 1483–1515.

[61] See John T. Wold and John H. Culver, "The Defeat of the California Justices: The Campaign, the Electorate, and the Issue of Judicial Accountability," *Judicature* 70, no. 6 (April–May1987), 350; Shugerman, *The People's Courts, supra* note 3, 141–146. As Shugerman notes, there was an unsuccessful campaign to defeat several of the justices in 1982.

[62] See Anthony Champagne, "Interest Groups and Judicial Elections," *Loyola of Los Angeles Law Review* 34 (2001), 1391–1408.

[63] See Shugerman, *The People's Courts, supra* note 3, 247–283; also see Kyle Cheek and Anthony Champagne, *Judicial Politics in Texas: Partisanship, Money and Politics in State Courts* (New York: Peter Lang, 2004), 39–43, 119–128.

[64] Anthony Champagne, "Television Ads in Judicial Campaigns," *Indiana Law Review* 35 (2002), 669–689.

[65] On the recognition that advertising could be effective in judicial elections, see Anthony Champagne, "Judicial Reform in Texas: A Look Back after Two Decades," *Court Review* 43, no. 2 (Summer 2006), 69; Champagne links this to the impact that recognizable names had on some Texas Supreme Court elections, and the fact that name identification could be created through advertising.

[66] See "Deukmejian Names 3 To State Supreme Court," *New York Times* (February 19, 1987), A23.

labeled the "new politics of judicial elections,"[67] with the result that judicial elections have become "noisier, nastier, and costlier."[68] The bottom line is that business interests, at one time a supporter of "nonpolitical" judicial selection through systems such as the Missouri Plan, now favor contested elections into which organizations such as the U.S. Chamber of Commerce and its affiliates can pour substantial sums of money to support preferred candidates.

WHAT DO AMERICANS WANT IN THEIR STATE JUDGES?

This leads to the question of what goals citizens view as important in selecting judges. Surprisingly, this is not a question that has been extensively explored. James Gibson, in a study of the 2006 Kentucky Supreme Court election, asked respondents to rate the importance of ten characteristics they believed important for a "good Kentucky Supreme Court judge."[69] The two top characteristics were "protect people without power" and "strictly follow the law," with 72.9 percent and 71.8 percent respectively rating them as "very important." The next highest rating was for "state how [they] stand on important legal and political issues as part of their [judges'] campaigns," with 64.2 percent rating this as "very important"; notably, this was not a qualification but how respondents viewed the campaign. The two lowest-rated "characteristics" were "decide the way the majority wants" (30.1 percent rated "very important") and "base decisions on party affiliations" (18.5 percent rated "very important"). It is worth noting that judicial elections in Kentucky are conducted on a nonpartisan basis. Arguably these are less characteristics than expectations of what judges will do and are probably more relevant for decisions on whether to retain a judge than on factors to be considered in choosing a new judge. An earlier (2001) national study conducted by Justice at Stake, an organization that advocated reform of judicial selection, also focused on expectations rather than qualifications.[70]

To explore more specifically the question of qualifications, I conducted a short survey using a sample obtained with Amazon Mechanical Turk (MTurk). Respondents obtained through MTurk are self-selected rather than randomly sampled, and this means that one must be careful in interpreting results based on MTurk samples. The online nature of MTurk combined with the self-selection leads to some known biases in MTurk samples, including overrepresentation of males,

[67] See Deborah Goldberg, Craig Holman, and Samantha Sanchez, "The New Politics of Judicial Elections: How 2000 Was a Watershed Year for Big Money, Special Interest Pressure, and TV Advertising in State Supreme Court Campaigns," Brennan Center for Justice, New York University School of Law (2000); the Brennan Center has published a series of reports under this title, all of which are posted at www.brennancenter.org/analysis/new-politics-judicial-elections-all-reports, accessed May 8, 2019.

[68] Roy A. Schotland, "Elective Judges' Campaign Financing: Are State Judges' Robes the Emperor's Clothes of American Democracy?" *Journal of Law & Politics* 2 (1985), 76.

[69] Gibson, *Electing Judges*, *supra* note 41, 93–96.

[70] *Id.*, 92.

political liberals, persons with a college degree, and persons under age 45. To deal with the overrepresentation of liberals and overrepresentation of males, I did the survey in three stages.[71] The two biases I was not able to adjust for were age and education, but there was little correlation between respondents' ratings of desirable characteristics and either of those demographic characteristics.[72]

My final sample had usable responses from 669 respondents. I asked respondents to rate each of 14 characteristics (see Table 15.4) as "essential," "very important," "somewhat important," or "not important." Some of the characteristics sought to capture factors related to professionalism ("deep legal knowledge") and others aimed to capture more political factors ("strong support from the leaders of my preferred political party").[73] Each respondent was asked to rate the 14 characteristics twice, once for local trial judges and then again for state supreme court judges.[74] In addition, respondents were asked a set of standard demographic questions (gender, age, education, and the first three digits of their zip code[75]), their preferred political party, and their self-described ideology.

Table 15.4 shows two statistics for each characteristic for each court. The first column in each pair ("Mean") is the mean rating, with "essential" scored 4 and "not important" scored 1; the second column ("% Essential") is the percentage of respondents rating the characteristic as "essential." The characteristics are ordered based on the percentage of people who rated a characteristic as "essential" for state

[71] The key bias I was concerned about was that the initial sample might be biased in a liberal direction. To ameliorate this, I first did a sample of 500; I then used a feature of MTurk that allowed restricting respondents to "conservatives" to collect an additional 100 responses to balance the survey.

I was also concerned about the overrepresentation of males, because preliminary analysis showed the women on average rated all of the characteristics as more important than did men. Consequently, to balance I collected an additional sample of 65 women.

The final sample contained 329 responses from men and 336 from women including one transgender female (plus three respondents selecting "Gender Variant/Nonconforming" and one who preferred not to answer). The breakdown for ideology was 261 conservative or libertarian, 238 liberal or progressive, 165 middle of the road, and 4 other; in terms of political party identification, after collapsing Independents leaning toward one party with party's identifiers, the sample had 305 Democrats, 275 Republicans, 85 Independents, and 4 other.

[72] The strongest single correlation with age was –.176, with "experience running for and/or holding political office" for state supreme court judges; the strongest for education was –.123 with "active in community organizations" for state supreme court judges.

[73] Factor analyses (using oblique oblimin rotations) done separately for responses for the two courts show, with one minor exception, that the characteristics align with the two intended dimensions. The one minor exception was that for trial court judges, "respected by leaders of the legal community" split evenly across the two factors. One other interesting difference was that for the state supreme court, the professionalism factor was the first factor after rotation while the political factor was the first for trial courts.

[74] The introductory material alerted respondents that in New York, the highest court is called the Court of Appeals.

[75] I used the zip code to identify the respondents' states of residence. Using this information, I ran analyses to see if there were any differences based on the system of judicial selection used in a state; I found no statistically discernible differences.

TABLE 15.4 *Desirable characteristics for judges*

	State Supreme Court		Local Trial Court	
	Mean	% Essential	Mean	% Essential
Professional characteristics				
Deep legal knowledge*	3.81	88.0	3.59	66.1
Expressed commitment to protecting legal rights*	3.75	84.5	3.71	77.7
Reputation for integrity/high ethical standards*	3.75	84.0	3.70	76.1
Excelled in law school*	3.66	77.0	3.14	34.4
Substantial experience practicing law in the courtroom*	3.59	72.2	3.34	49.3
Reputation as a good listener	3.58	70.9	3.57	67.8
Respected by leaders of the legal community*	3.43	63.1	3.21	43.9
Political characteristics				
Respected by elected political officials*	2.93	40.4	2.64	24.8
Experience running for and/or holding political office*	2.47	30.3	2.13	14.3
Experience as a criminal prosecutor	2.63	30.3	2.62	25.9
Expressed willingness to be sensitive to community preferences*	2.63	23.8	3.17	48.9
Strong support from the leaders of my preferred political party*	2.33	23.5	2.13	15.5
Understands community preferences*	2.64	21.2	3.27	54.4
Active in community organizations*	2.34	15.7	2.84	31.4

* Statistically significant difference (2-tailed) between rating for trial court judges and rating for state supreme court judges.

supreme court justices. As indicated by the asterisks appearing next to all but two of the characteristics, respondents tended to differentiate between the two courts when rating the characteristics.[76]

Regarding qualifications for the state supreme court, over 80 percent of respondents rated three characteristics as "essential," all clearly reflecting what I label *professionalism*: "deep legal knowledge," "expressed commitment to protecting legal rights," and "reputation for integrity/high ethical standards." Three additional characteristics in the professionalism category – "excelled in law school," "substantial experience practicing law in the courtroom," and "reputation as a good listener" – were deemed "essential" for state supreme court justices by 70 to 77 percent of

[76] To test whether there was a difference, I used the sign test; see Sidney Siegel, *Nonparametric Statistics for the Behavioral Sciences* (New York: McGraw-Hill, 1956), 68–75. The advantage of this test is that it does not require the assumption of interval measurement or normality that is required for the matched-pairs *t*-test. I also did a matched-pairs *t*-test; interestingly, one of the comparisons, for "expressed commitment to protecting legal rights," was not statistically significant according to the *t*-test, but was statistically significant using the sign test.

respondents. The highest ranked "political" characteristic for state supreme court justices was "respected by elected political officials," but only 40.4 percent rated that characteristic as "essential." In fact, for state supreme court justices, respondents on average rated all the "professional" characteristics higher than any of the "political" characteristics.[77]

Although professional characteristics tended to be deemed the most important for local trial judges, responses regarding those judges were notably different. No characteristic was deemed "essential" for local trial judges by more than 80 percent of respondents. The top two, "expressed commitment to protecting legal rights" and "reputation for integrity/high ethical standards," were deemed "essential" by 77.7 percent and 76.1 percent of respondents, respectively. The top-ranked characteristic for state supreme court justices, "deep legal knowledge," was deemed "essential" for local trial court judges by only 66.1 percent of respondents, compared to 88.0 percent for state supreme court judges. And although 77.0 percent rated "excelled in law school" essential for state supreme court judges, only 34.4 percent thought it was "essential" for local trial court judges. Interestingly, 49.3 percent rated "substantial experience practicing law in the courtroom" as "essential" for trial court judges, compared to 72.2 percent rating it as "essential" for state supreme court justices.

Although four of the "professional" characteristics stood at the top for trial court judges, two of the "political" characteristics were rated substantially higher for trial court judges than was the case for state supreme court justices. "Understands community preferences" was deemed "essential" for trial court judges by 54.4 percent of respondents, while only 21.2 percent rated this as "essential" for state supreme court justices. Similarly, 48.9 percent rated "expressed willingness to be sensitive to community preferences" as "essential" for trial court judges compared to 23.8 percent for supreme court justices. Thus, there was measurably less emphasis on "professional" qualifications and more on "political" sensitivity for trial judges than for state supreme court justices.

Given the degree of political polarization in the United States as this was written in 2019, it is interesting that "strong support from the leaders of my preferred political party" was close to the bottom of the list for both courts. Also, one might ask whether there were systematic differences between Republicans and Democrats in preferred qualifications. The answer is largely no. Comparing Democrats and Republicans,[78] only 2 of 28 comparisons showed statistically significant differences, and those

77 Some might quibble that "experience as a criminal prosecutor" should be seen as a "professional" characteristic; however, I specifically labeled this as "experience as a criminal prosecutor" rather than "experience practicing criminal law," which I believe adds a significant political element. Moreover, when I did the factor analysis (described in a prior footnote), "experience as a criminal prosecutor" grouped with the other "political" characteristics.

78 This was done by cross-tabulating the four-category ratings with a two-category party variable that combined those who said they were independents, but leaned toward a party with those identifying with a party; "pure" independents were omitted.

differences were modest. Republicans rated "experience as a criminal prosecutor" as more important for state supreme court justices than did Democrats (33.1 percent "essential" versus 27.2 percent). Democrats rated "active in community organizations" for local trial court judges higher than did Republicans (34.1 percent "essential" versus 29.8 percent). Although both of these were statistically significant, they are of little substantive importance. The absence of partisan differences in desired qualifications is consistent with other research, which failed to find systematic differences in the preferred selection system based on respondents' party affiliation.[79]

These results help account for why voters have been more willing to adopt variants of the Missouri Plan for state supreme courts (and other appellate courts) than for trial courts. The public views the kinds of "professional" characteristics that are supposed to be emphasized by nominating commissions as more important for the state supreme court than for trial courts, and they view an understanding of and sensitivity to local "political" characteristics as more important for trial courts than for state supreme courts. However, even with these differences, "professional" characteristics tend to be deemed more important than "political" characteristics for both levels of courts, which raises the question as to why there has not been more success in recent years in adopting versions of the Missouri Plan. Essentially, there is an irony here: voters want judges with strong "professional" qualifications, but apparently tend to distrust mechanisms for judicial selection that focus on those very qualifications.

SOME FINAL WORDS

The central tension in judicial selection discussed by most commentators is between independence and accountability. In this book, I have recast that tension somewhat to: partisan politics/policy versus legal professionalism, which I link to the democratic and legal subcultures. One sees one or both of these in the various efforts, successful and unsuccessful, to modify judicial selection and retention. In some cases, one or the other is clearly the driving force; in other cases, the tension between the two is manifest.

One way to think about the tension is by asking whether we want judges to be politically reflective of citizenry or to have a set of professional qualities and qualifications such that one would expect the judges' politics to be reflective of the legal profession from which they are drawn. As argued previously, there is no reason to assume that professional qualifications vary systematically with lawyers' political preferences. As Bonica and Sen suggest, the fact that, in the aggregate, judges' ideology differs from that of their professional community is indicative of the influence of

[79] See Damon M. Cann and Jeff Yates, *These Estimable Courts: Understanding Public Perceptions of State Judicial Institutions and Legal Policy-Making* (New York: Oxford University Press, 2016), 110–111.

policy/political preferences of those selecting the judges, whether that be the voters or other elected officials. Importantly, in almost all states, elected officials on average are politically to the right of lawyers on average, and in a majority of states, judges fall somewhere between the average position of lawyers and the average position of politicians, more often closer to the former than the latter.

As shown in the previous section, when people are asked what characteristics should be important in deciding who should be elected or appointed to a judgeship, they rate characteristics associated with legal professionalism more highly than those associated with political activity and hence, with political preferences. Moreover, the "professional" characteristics are rated as more important when it comes to selecting state supreme court judges than they are rated for selecting local trial judges. This is the case even though one could argue that the decisions of the state supreme court have considerably more political importance than the kinds of routine decisions made by local trial court judges. However, it is also true that the kind of analysis required at the supreme court level is more sophisticated than at the trial court level, and hence, it is arguably correct that professional qualifications should be more important at the former. Research shows that the use of a system designed to emphasize professional qualifications over political considerations does not ignore the political;[80] given the policymaking and lawmaking role of appellate courts, some consideration of political factors should be part of the selection of judges for those courts.

The differences in desirable qualities for judges of the top-rung courts versus the trial courts do suggest that it makes sense that how judicial selection and retention works for the two levels often differs, and that it is the top-rung courts where one more often finds the use of nominating commissions charged with assessing the qualifications of potential appointees.

80 See Greg Goelzhauser, *Judicial Merit Selection: Institutional Design and Performance for State Courts* (Philadelphia, PA: Temple University Press, 2019), 54–74.

Index